TWO WORLD WARS AND HITLER

WHO WAS RESPONSIBLE?

Anglo-American Money, Foreign Agents and Geopolitics

DR JIM MACGREGOR
MBChB, DRCOG, AIAT
DR JOHN O'DOWD
PhD MBA

Two World Wars and Hitler: Who was Responsible? – Anglo-American Money, Foreign Agents and Geopolitics.
Copyright © 2024/2025 Jim Macgregor & John O'Dowd. All Rights Reserved.

Published by:
Trine Day LLC
PO Box 577
Walterville, OR 97489
1-800-556-2012
www.TrineDay.com
trineday@icloud.com

Library of Congress Control Number: 2025930611

Macgregor, Jim & O'Dowd, John. Two World Wars and Hitler—1st ed.
p. cm.

Epub (ISBN-13) 978-1-63424-504-3
Trade Paper (ISBN-13) 978-1-63424-503-6

1.World War I (1914-1918). 2. World War II (1939-1945). 3. Hitler, Adolph (1889-1945). 4. Rhodes, Cecil John (1853-1902. 5. Milner, Alfred (1854-1925). 6. Morgan, John Pierpont (1837-1913). 7. Ernst "Putzi" Franz Sedgwick Hanfstaengl (1887-1975). 8. Bank for International Settlements (1930-). I. Macgregor, Jim & O'Dowd, John. II. Title.

FIRST EDITION
10 9 8 7 6 5 4 3 2 1

This book combines both American and British English rules.

For more information: TwoWorldWarsandHitler.com

Distribution to the Trade by:
Independent Publishers Group (IPG)
814 North Franklin Street
Chicago, Illinois 60610
312.337.0747
www.ipgbook.com

Publisher's Foreword

You are an Englishman, and have consequently drawn the greatest prize in the lottery of life.

– Cecil Rhodes

We must find new lands from which we can easily obtain raw materials and at the same time exploit the cheap slave labor that is available from the natives of the colonies. The colonies would also provide a dumping ground for the surplus goods produced in our factories.

– Cecil Rhodes

Terrorism is the best political weapon, for nothing drives people harder than a fear of sudden death.

– Adolf Hitler

What luck for rulers that men do not think.

– Adolf Hitler

Claim everything. Explain nothing. Deny everything.

– Prescott Bush

If there is one thing that I have learned it is that no matter how many books one reads, there is always more to learn. I've read about war, money and geopolitics, but none expose the perifidy quite like *Two World Wars and Hitler: Who was Responsible? Anglo-American Money, Foreign Agents and Geopolitics* by Jim Macgregor and John O'Dowd.

MacGregor and O'Dowd are two Scottish scientists taking England's establishment historians to task ... for falsehoods promlugated around imperial ambitions cloaked in popular rhetoric to befuddle citizens. A scientist looks at the world much differently than "court" chroniclers. Scientists use the scientific method with controlled experiments to test hypotheses and facts, while historians rely on analysis of historical sources to *construct* narratives about past events and commentary on current affairs.

In *Two World Wars and Hitler*, MacGregor and O'Dowd take us to class with three distinguished and learned teachers:

1. Boston-born Professor Carroll Quigley taught a very influential course at Georgetown University in Washington, D.C. for over thirty years. He undertook intensive research, writing about Cecil Rhodes, his secret society and its legacy in two books, *Tragedy and Hope: A History of the World in Our Time (1966)* and released four years after his death in 1977, *The Anglo-American Establishment: From Rhodes to Cliveden (1981)*.

2. London-born Professor Antony Sutton graduated from the University of London in 1951, became an Assistant Professor of Economics at California State College, Los Angeles in 1963 and then a Research Fellow at the Hoover Institution on War, Revolution and Peace, Stanford University, where he wrote a three volume study of Soviet economic development. While there he noticed some peculiarities that led to him researching and writing many books about history, economics and secret societies.

3. Boston-born Professor Guido Preparata earned a PhD in Political Economy, MA in Economics from USC, and MPhil in Criminology from University of Cambridge. He was raised in the USA, France and Italy, has taught political economy, history, criminology, and sociology in the United States, Canada, and the Middle East. He is the author of *Conjuring Hitler: How Great Britain and America Created the Third Reich* and several more very interesting books.

The first book TrineDay published was Sutton's *America's Secret Establishment: An Introduction to the Order of Skull & Bones*. We had become friends around our research into secret societies. His publisher was retiring and the book was going out of print. I borrowed $5,000 and TrineDay was born.

After 20 some years and over 180 books, TrineDay is honored and humbled to bring this magnificent tome to fruition.

Please read, discuss, think … and act.

Onward to the Utmost of Futures,
Peace,
R.A. "Kris" Millegan
Publisher
TrineDay
February 12, 2024

This work is dedicated to the memory of Jamie Macgregor, 1984-2024.

ACKNOWLEDGEMENTS.

It gives us pleasure to thank the many writers, researchers and friends who gave so freely of their time and encouragement in this work. In particular, we are grateful to Richard K Moore, Mees Baaijen, Kris Millegan, Jan van Aken, Thomas Meyer, Andreas Bracher, Mitch Peeke and Terry Boardman. The book is attributed to two authors from Scotland but there is a third person, a German, without whom it could not have been written. In addition to much else, that close German friend spent many long months in the German archives researching and translating documents essential for the project to proceed with accuracy and veracity. He does not want to be named as co-author or identified for the straightforward reason that speaking the truth about the origins of the world wars and how Hitler came to power can see a person imprisoned in Germany. In a modern European state, it is shameful and outrageous that a good man cannot speak freely, openly and truthfully through fear – in this case not for his own safety and well-being, but for that of his family and friends. Through promotion of German Kriegsschuld - the great lie that Germany was responsible for two world wars and their attendant horrors – it has been instilled in the minds of generations of German schoolchildren and university students that they must go on bearing shame and keep their mouths shut on the matter. Since 1945, successive German governments cravenly beholden to the powerful Anglo-American forces truly responsible for the rise of Hitler and the Second World War, have ensured up to the present day in Germany that questioning Kriegsschuld or the official Anglo-American narratives of the wars is verboten. Do so and the government will make your life very uncomfortable indeed.

We hope that this book will go some way to awakening the people of Germany to the stark reality that their forebears were not responsible, and that Kriegsschuld is a gross lie intended to keep their great country a vassal state subservient to foreign powers. We pay tribute to our German friend and colleague for his generosity, courage, deep knowledge, and dedication to his country, to world peace, freedom and the truth.

CONTENTS

Photograph taken after reaching agreement for the armistice that ended World War I. This is Ferdinand Foch's own railway carriage in the Forest of Compiègne. Foch's chief of staff Maxime Weygand is second from left. Third from the left is the senior British representative, Sir Rosslyn Wemyss. Foch is second from the right. On the right is Admiral Sir George Hope.

INTRODUCTION

At 11 o'clock on the morning of 11 November 1918 the war that had begun in Europe over four years earlier ended with a tentative armistice. Some 20 million had been killed and as many wounded and maimed for life. Later known as the First World War, it officially ended in the summer of 1919 with the victorious allies, Britain, France, Italy, the United States of America and Japan placing the entire blame for the catastrophe on Germany and her allies. Article 231 of the Treaty of Versailles stated:

> The Allied and Associated Governments affirm and Germany accepts the responsibility of Germany and her allies for causing all the loss and damage to which the Allied and Associated Governments and their nationals have been subjected as a consequence of the war imposed upon them by the aggression of Germany and her allies.

This "war guilt" clause appeared proof positive that Germany had deliberately started the war. She had, after all, admitted as much by signing it. British academics fully supported the Versailles verdict, but by the 1920s American historians and researchers were demolishing it and stating unequivocally that Germany was no more to blame, indeed, less so than the other belligerents. They pointed to the injustice of the German government being denied legal representation, or the opportunity to produce evidence or witnesses on its own behalf, at the Paris peace talks held over the first six months of 1919. The German government had asked for an independent investigation into responsibility for the war but was refused. It asked for a non-partisan commission to examine the archives of countries involved but was refused. It asked to be forwarded proof of German guilt but was refused. With no German defence lawyers or representatives being allowed to present Germany's case, Versailles was a stitch-up.

The German government accepted responsibility for the war, but at the point of a metaphorical gun. Between the 11 November 1918 armistice and the Versailles Treaty that was signed in late June 1919, hundreds of thousands of German civilians were deliberately starved to death by the victorious Allies. Had Germany refused to sign the Treaty, the British naval blockade on food exports to Germany would have been intensified, with millions more dying. Half the German fishing fleet was confiscated, together with half of Germany's railway engines and wagons essential for transporting food around the country. Failure to admit guilt at Versailles would have seen Germany starved and the entire country invaded by foreign troops. It would have been divided into small, powerless entities along the lines of the old principalities that pre-dated the creation of the German Empire in 1871. Germany, as the country was known at the turn of the twentieth century, would no longer exist as anything other than a starving, third-world, rural backwater.

On 28 June 1919 in the Palace of Versailles, some 20 km west of Paris, the German representatives were given no real option but to sign the Treaty declaring Germany and her allies entirely responsible for starting the war. It was exactly five years to the day that Archduke Franz Ferdinand had been assassinated in Sarajevo – the spark that reputedly ignited the war. Many in Germany understandably railed against those who put their names to the Treaty as traitors to the nation, but such critics had little or no knowledge of the intense blackmail and dire consequences for Germany had the signatories not done so.

With the Treaty signed, sealed and delivered, blackmail gave way to extortion. Having accepted blame for the massive loss and damage to cities, towns, and villages across Europe, the "accursed" Germany was made to pay for the entire re-building. The German people were to be utterly humiliated as the belligerent outcasts in the European fold and driven into extreme poverty.

We examine historical accounts of the First World War in an attempt to reach the truth about its origins and how the Nazis arose from the disaster. As the Italian historian Guido Giacomo Preparata writes in his outstanding book, *Conjuring Hitler: How Britain and America Made the Third Reich:*

> A detailed analysis of the emergence of Nazism is generally shunned so it seems, for it might reveal too much; in truth, it might disclose that the Nazis were never a creature of chance.[1]

This book, *Two World Wars and Hitler, Who was Responsible?*, is about history rather than a history book. We are *not* historians but other professionals critiquing historians and the history they create. More specifically, we investigate the corruption of history – primarily by British academics – who have sustained a thesis of German guilt by constant repetition as opposed to reasoned proof. The American writer, historian, and deep thinker, David Hackett Fischer, discusses how "constant repetition erodes critical resistance to the most absurd suggestions." It is the technique that people in the advertising industry, public relations specialists, and propagandists thrive on.[2]

Over the past century British historians have repeated *ad nauseum* that Germany was guilty in 1914. We compare their accounts with those of historians and researchers who strongly challenge their narrative and whose work is either dismissed or studiously ignored in Britain. Were British historians deliberately spreading disinformation or was it the case that they genuinely did not understand the real origins of the war? Pulitzer Prize-winning American author, Upton Sinclair, opined: "It is difficult to get a man to understand something when his salary depends upon his not understanding it." David Hackett Fischer was more direct in his book *Historians' Fallacies*:

> There have always been many historians who were more concerned that truth should be on their side than that they should be on the side of truth. This attitude is no monopoly of any sect or generation. But wherever it appears in historical scholarship it is hateful in its substance and horrible in its results. To make historiography into a vehicle for propaganda is simply to destroy it. The problem of the utility of history is not solved but subverted, for what is produced by this method is not history at all.[3]

'Many historians' were 'destroying' history by presenting information in a misleading and biased way to promote their own agenda, according to Professor Fischer. When historians relate information accurately a different picture emerges. American scholar, John V. Denson, writes:

> When history is written truthfully, I believe that Bolingbroke gave the best definition, "History is philosophy teaching by example." If we can read history by looking at past events to determine what ideas were being followed, we can see how those ideas worked out in practice and learn lessons from the experience of others and avoid the same mistakes. The extreme importance of history and its study was cogently stated by Patrick Henry, "I have but one lamp by which my feet are guided, and that is the lamp of experience. I know of no other way of judging the future but by the past."[4]

The task of distinguishing between academic propagandists who 'subvert' history, as related by David Fischer, and those who write history

3

truthfully, such as John Denson, is not straightforward. We present the accounts of both so as to enable the reader to decide. Since paraphrasing or summarising the work of any historian or researcher can open the door to misinterpretation, we give them their own voice as much as possible.

Within weeks of the war beginning in 1914, British academics began publishing books and pamphlets blaming Germany and justifying Britain's declaration of war against her. First came *The Great War: The Standard History of the All-Europe Conflict,* edited by the Oxford University educated historian, Herbert Wrigley Wilson. It would be released in 13 large, illustrated volumes during the war years. The first pages of Volume 1 published in 1914 begin:

> The greatest war of modern times, and perhaps in the whole history of the human race, was begun by Germany using the crime of a schoolboy in Bosnia as her excuse.... Without waiting to declare war, Germany proceeded to attack France, pouring her armies through the neutral territory of Luxemburg and Belgium ...
> Thus the German people plunged humanity into the Great War.[5]

Another major series (nine vols.) *The Great World War: A History,* edited by other English academics was launched in January 1915. Volume I, page 1, states:

> We knew from the first that Great Britain embarked upon this war thrice armed through having her quarrel just; that she strove for peace to the very last risking precious hours when every minute was vital to the success of her contingent cooperation with France. But not until.... Germany's open contempt for her pledged word and all the laws of honourable warfare, could we fully realize that Great Britain had never drawn the sword in a more righteous conflict.... To anyone not blinded by prejudice, the chain of evidence issued since the outbreak of hostilities, fixes upon Germany and Austria-Hungary – and especially upon Germany – the full responsibility of shattering the peace of the world.[6]

In addition, from the very beginning of the war, and throughout, Oxford academics produced a series of small booklets titled the 'Oxford Pamphlets' that "aimed to educate the public" on the war. The first – of 87 pamphlets – was written by William Sanday, the Lady Margaret Professor of Divinity at Oxford. It stated that British theologians were in support of the government's reasoning for going to war. According to Professor Sanday, "No one could have worked for peace more sincerely" than the

British Foreign Secretary, Sir Edward Grey, and he now "had the whole nation behind him." Theologians connected to Oxford were denouncing Germany as evil, and justifying British involvement in the war. The Bishop of Oxford, Charles Gore, stated "We can wholeheartedly yield ourselves to the stream of patriotic enthusiasm which is sweeping so mightily through the nation."[7]

The Oxford University message was clear: Britain had joined the war to help save civilisation from the evil Germans, who were threatening the whole of mankind. This overt propaganda churned out by Oxford academics in the Divinity and History faculties encouraged young men from every walk of life in Britain and across the Empire to volunteer for the armed forces and kill Germans. In later pages we will see how the Oxford theologians were linked to the very people responsible for the war.

After the war, academics beyond Britain began relating a very different version of events. In 1926, American historian Harry Elmer Barnes (PhD Columbia University) challenged the Oxford school's 'Britain good, Germany evil' narrative with his book *The Genesis of the World War*. Describing the British accounts as "court history" (history written by academics beholden to those who hold the reins of power), Barnes stated that the documentary evidence relating to the conflict decisively demonstrated that the German government not only did *not* cause the war in 1914, but was distinctly opposed to its outbreak.[8] Professor Barnes wrote that he would have wasted no time on the subject if he did not believe that the truth about the causes of the war was one of the most important issues of the day. The entire matter, he said, rested upon an unfair and unjust Peace Treaty based on "the complete acceptance of the grossest forms of wartime illusions concerning war guilt."[9] Barnes added:

> There is no evidence that any responsible element in Germany in 1914 desired a world war, and the Kaiser worked harder than any other European statesman during the crisis to avert a general European conflagration.[10]

Scathing of fellow historians who continued to support the assertion that Germany was guilty in 1914, Barnes wrote:

> There is no competent and informed historian in any country who has studied the problem of the genesis of the World War in a thorough fashion who does not regard the theory of the war guilt held in Articles 227 and 231 of the Versailles Treaty to be wholly false, misleading and unjust.... If we can but understand how totally and

terribly we were "taken in" between 1914 and 1918 by the salesmen of this most holy and idealistic world conflict, we shall be better prepared to be on our guard against the seductive lies and deception which will be put forward by similar groups when urging the necessity of another world catastrophe in order to 'protect the weak nations,' 'crush militarism,' 'put an end to all further wars,' etc.[11]

If historians at Oxford and other British universities were promoting British propaganda as historical truth, where did it leave their students? Professor Barnes bluntly stated:

If we may judge by the symptoms of the last decade, students will primarily need to look for truth and guidance to themselves rather than to their professors of history and diplomacy, many of whom will probably tenaciously continue to remain devotees of the Rip Van Winkle and Pollyanna schools of historiography.[12]

It was a damning indictment of British academic historians. Students at Oxford (considered one of the world's top universities) seeking the truth about the origins of the 1914-18 war would effectively have to ignore what their professors and lecturers were teaching them and look elsewhere for it. On Germany's admission of guilt through signing Article 231 of the Peace Treaty, Barnes wrote:

Germany occupied the situation of a prisoner at the bar, where the prosecuting attorney was given full leeway as to the time and presentation of the evidence, while the defendant was denied counsel or the opportunity to produce either evidence or witnesses. Germany was confronted with the alternative of signing the confession at once or having her territory invaded and occupied, with every probability that such an admission would ultimately be extorted in any event.[13]

Barnes stated that the proceedings were completely rigged against Germany and with a metaphorical gun put to her head, a false confession of guilt for the war was extracted. News that Germany had signed and accepted the entire blame was then carried in newspapers across the world. The Allies had it in writing, so it was true. On publishing his book, Barnes was immediately attacked by the *Times* and *Observer* newspapers in London, with determined efforts to discredit him. He was, according to the British Press, a stooge being paid by Germany to absolve her of war guilt. The British Establishment closed ranks, relentlessly attacked Barnes, made him a pariah, and ensured that his book was suppressed. He wrote:

A major difficulty has been the unwillingness of booksellers to co-operate, even when it was to their pecuniary advantage to do so. Many of them have assumed to censor their customers' reading in the field of international relations as in the matter of morals. Not infrequently have booksellers even discouraged prospective customers who desired to have *The Genesis of the World War* ordered for them. Therefore, the writer has now made a second attempt to stir popular concern with this vital subject, through a method of distribution based upon private mailing lists rather than upon the usual commercial channels.[14]

Despite the widespread vilification in Britain of a well-respected American professor, Barnes' thesis received support from a campaigning British journalist, war correspondent, and author with over 30 books, Henry Wood Nevinson. In 1926, Nevinson wrote in the *Saturday Review of Literature*:

Shameful and disastrous as was the whole Treaty of Versailles, there was one clause in it that surpassed all other in shame. It was article 231 ... Other Articles in the Treaty are shameless in their bullying treatment of a gallant and vanquished enemy ... that is sure to engender future wars, but the article expresses a lie of such grossness that I wonder the hand which first wrote it did not wither. I do not wonder that the German representatives to whom it was first shown refused to sign such an atrocious perversion of the truth. Ultimately a German did consent to sign, and his consent is the most terrible evidence of the abject misery to which war, disease, and the starvation of women and children owing to the British blockade for seven months after the Armistice had reduced the German people. Whether M. Clemenceau [French prime minister] or Mr Lloyd George [British prime minister] concocted the lie, I cannot be sure, but amid all the orgy of iniquity that prevailed in Versailles in 1919, that article stands out conspicuous, and no historian will ever dare repeat it except with indignant scorn.[15]

British academic historians *did* dare repeat it, however, and their attacks on Professor Barnes grew ever more vociferous. In 1928, however, another eminent American academic, Professor Sidney Bradshaw Fay, (taught history at Harvard and Yale) published *The Origins of the World War* which indicated that Germany had unfairly been lumped with the blame. Russia and Serbia, he stated, carried considerable responsibility for the war. When assassins armed and trained in Serbia killed Archduke

Franz Ferdinand in late June, the Austrian leaders expressed the need for retribution. After years of constant anti-Austro-Hungarian provocation by Serbia, the murder of the heir to the Austro-Hungarian throne and his wife was the last straw. Austria-Hungary's long-time close ally, Germany, agreed that a reaction was now required – as did numerous other European countries. Kaiser Wilhelm II of Germany insisted, however, that it should be no more than a short, sharp, localised incursion by Austrian troops to teach the troublesome Serbs a lesson, and there must be no annexation or long-term occupation of Serbian territory.

When it became clear to Germany that Russia – the self-proclaimed protector of Serbia – was going to use the Austro-Hungarian military response against the Serbs to get involved and use it as an excuse to start a European war, the Kaiser tried to pull Austria-Hungary back from the brink. Professor Fay wrote:

> With his natural impetuosity he [Kaiser Wilhelm II] wanted Austria to take action in regard to the Serbians as quickly as possible while the whole civilized world, still under the vivid impression of the terrible assassination, sympathised with her. What this action of Austria's was to be, the Kaiser did not know definitely on July 5, and did not care to advise. But neither he nor Bethmann [German Foreign Secretary] thought it at all probable on that day that the Austro-Serbian dispute would lead to a European war. He could therefore quite safely depart on his northern cruise early next morning, as he had long planned, and Bethmann advised. This he would hardly have done if he had thought that the action which he wished Austria to take at once instead of delaying more than two weeks, would probably involve a European conflagration. It is significant that the moment he heard the kind of ultimatum Berchtold [Austrian Foreign Minister] had presented to Serbia, he started in a hurry to return to Berlin.[16]

The German kaiser, the man responsible for deliberately starting the war according to British historians, went off on his annual three-week summer cruise, making no preparations whatsoever for war.

Professor Fay added:

> One must abandon the dictum of the Versailles Treaty that Germany and her allies were solely responsible. It was a dictum extracted by victors from vanquished, under the influence of blindness, ignorance, hatred and the propagandist misconceptions to which war had given rise. It was based on evidence which was incomplete and

not always sound. It is generally recognised by the best historical scholars in all countries to be no longer tenable or defensible.[17]

The Oxford historians went on defending the Versailles Treaty, and Professor Fay clearly did not consider them to be among the "best historical scholars." Despite compelling evidence to the contrary being available by 1926, Oxford academics continued promulgating the story that Germany had deliberately started the war and was entirely responsible. Fay discussed the importance of military mobilisations as a cause of the war. It had been long recognised by all nations that the general mobilisation of the armed forces of any given country indicated its intent on war. General mobilisation of troops up to the borders of an intended enemy precluded any further chance of diplomatic negotiations to resolve issues. There was no turning back. General mobilisation meant war! In due course we shall see that Germany was the last of the Great Powers to mobilise. Serbia was the first, followed by Austria-Hungary, then Britain (its main arm the Royal Navy), then Russia, France, and finally Germany a few hours after France.

In 1929, the German-Swiss author, Emil Ludwig, published *July 1914*, a book about the Sarajevo assassination crisis and how it led to war:

> What country wanted war? Let us put a different question: What circles in every country wanted, facilitated, or began the war? ... In no country had the man at the machine, in the workshop, or at the plough any desire to break the peace, or any interest in doing so. Everywhere the lower classes feared war and fought against it till the eleventh hour. The Cabinets, on the other hand, the War Offices and interested circles that worked with them, the ministers, generals, admirals, war contractors, and journalists, were driven forward by ambition and fear, by incapacity and greed, and drove the masses forward in their turn.... While exact calculations of relative responsibility are impossible, one can say that Vienna [Austria-Hungary] and St Petersburg [Russia] stand first.[18]

Ludwig wrote of "interested circles" driven by ambition and greed being responsible for war. Did such a circle exist in Britain at the time? In his book, *The Empire of "The City," The Secret History of British Financial Power*, E. C. Knuth suggested that British foreign policy was controlled not by democratically elected politicians in the Westminster parliament, but by massively wealthy and powerful individuals in international finance in the City, London. The City comprises what is known as the "square mile"

– the financial district on the north bank of the River Thames. It has its own dedicated police force which is answerable not to the usual British police and crime commissioner, but to the City of London Corporation – a quasi-democratic form of local government with members voted in by residents and businesses within the square mile. Since only around 8,000 people live in the "square mile" (hundreds of thousands commute to work there every day in the financial sector), it is, to a considerable extent, a law unto itself with its own police force that is answerable to a private power – the bankers who control the Corporation. Knuth contends that The City is so rich and powerful that no incident occurs in any part of the world without its participation in some form or another. He writes:

> How has it been possible to erect this Internationalistic structure of misrepresentation and deception in our midst and to protect it from exposure? Why have not our professors of history, our college presidents and educators, our crusading newspapers exposed this monstrosity?[19]

Why not indeed? Describing how the Florentine statesman Niccolò Machiavelli studied the methods used by rulers to attain power, Knuth equates Machiavelli's findings to 'alleged' democratic nations such as Britain and the United States, where foreign affairs are "controlled against the will of the people":

> The findings of Machiavelli and other students of power decree that to obtain power it is essential to ignore the moral laws of man and of God; that promises must be made only with the intention to deceive and to mislead others to sacrifice their own interests, that the most brutal atrocity must be committed as a matter of mere convenience, that friends or allies must be betrayed as matter of course as soon as they have served their purpose. But it is decreed that these atrocities must be kept hidden from the common people except only where they are of use to strike terror to the hearts of the opponents; that there must be kept up a spurious aspect of benevolence and benefit for the greater number of the people, and even an aspect of humility to gain as much help as possible.
>
> It is held that the vast mass of the people are oblivious and gullible, and therefore will believe a lie which is repeated again and again, regardless of how obvious may be the fundamental facts to the contrary.... Matters should be so ordered that when men no longer believe of their own accord, they may be compelled to believe by force.... This is an application of the doctrine of power

which holds that high-minded words can be used by the powerful, the demagogue and the hypocrite, or the merely self-deluded, to arouse passion and prejudice and sentimentality for the wrong reasons in favour of disguised real aims; thus to deceive the people and to lead them by easy stages to sacrifice their own interests in the service of power.[20]

On the City's role in WWI, Knuth concludes:

The hallucination that Britain and its allies were the innocent victims of an unprovoked and unanticipated attack [by Germany] is a triumph of the propaganda machine of "The City," and its almost absolute control over world news and sources of public information.[21]

Should Knuth's work about the all-encompassing power of rich and powerful men in London be given any credence, or dismissed as conspiracy theory ranting by a mentally deranged individual? In their book *Manufacturing Consent,* American Professors Edward Herman (University of Pennsylvania) and Noam Chomsky (Massachusetts Institute of Technology) suggest that 'conspiracy theory' is a pejorative term applied to individuals in order to discourage analysis of the hidden agendas of governments and of the reality we are facing. Perennially questioning our governments, newspapers, and television news programmes – what they do and say regarding what is happening in our world – is, they say, a sign not of mental derangement but of robust mental alertness and political awareness.[22]

Another renowned American academic, Howard Zinn (Professor of political science at Boston University) similarly wrote of rich and powerful men serving their own interests, with wars arising as a consequence of them pursuing those interests. According to Zinn, there has always been a profound conflict between rich men's interests with those of the people. The ordinary man was not the enemy of the ordinary man, yet did the fighting and dying in rich men's wars. In Zinn's view, all-powerful oligarchies in the Britain and the United States remained secure in power through dominating the historical record and whitewashing their nefarious activities from it. [23]

Professors Chomsky and Zinn played important roles in helping us understand where real power in Britain and the United States of America rested, but the individual at the forefront of exposing this was another American academic, Carroll Quigley. Professor of history at the Foreign Service School of Georgetown University, Quigley spent many years studying the membership and activities of the British and US cabals and how, from the early years of the 20th century they formed the Anglo-American "special relationship" that collaborated closely in international affairs and major geopolitical events. In his books *Tragedy & Hope,* published in 1966, and *The Anglo-American Establishment,* published in 1981, Quigley named the individuals involved on both sides of the Atlantic and how they were led by Lord Alfred Milner. He revealed how they controlled politics from behind the curtain, and formed closely collaborating organisations dedicated to spreading their control across the entire world. In the *Anglo-American Establishment,* Quigley states that "no country that values its safety should allow what the Milner group accomplished." He goes on to explain in detail how they wielded immense power in politics, the press and education, and how, through their control of edu-

cation, they were able to "completely monopolize" the writing and the teaching of the history of their own period. Through that control of the historical record they have, as Professors Quigley, Zinn, and many others agree, managed to a considerable extent to airbrush their existence and activities from it.

Professor Quigley's revelations are of considerable importance to our understanding of the global catastrophe of the First World War and the subsequent rise to power of Adolf Hitler. A soldier in the lowest ranks of the German army throughout the 1914-18 war, following Germany's defeat Hitler became a minor political agitator in Munich. His powerful voice, that could readily incite large crowds to fever pitch, brought him to the attention of the victorious Allies controlling Germany in the years immediately after the war. Anglo-American banking and political elites responsible for that war, chose Hitler for a major role in post-war Germany. To that end they placed two of their senior secret intelligence agents (one English, one German-American) directly at Hitler's side in the early 1920s and funded him, groomed him for power, and helped him promote his despicable Nazi philosophy. Hitler as we shall clearly see, was selected by these Anglo-American elites not because he was a force for good in the world, for peace, but for the straightforward reason that he would prove disastrous for Germany and take her into another war which she stood no chance of winning. Having actively manoeuvred Hitler and his Nazi party into dictatorial power in Germany, those same Anglo-American elites proceeded to fund them and build their massive new military machine in preparation for another world war. Those elites planned another war, wanted another war, and would ensure that it happened.

It is virtually impossible to comprehend these matters without a grasp of the outstanding work of Professor Carroll Quigley and that of Professors Antony Sutton and Guido Preparata. The opening chapters of this book delve into Quigley's background, his research findings, and how he was aided in that research by a leading British historian, Sir Alfred Zimmern. Forearmed with that information, the reader is better placed to grasp the truth about the astonishing matters discussed in this book.

Tragedy & Hope

A History Of The World In Our Time

Carroll Quigley

CHAPTER 1

CARROLL QUIGLEY –
ORACLE OR ODDBALL?

arroll Quigley (1910-1977) – the whistleblower who revealed the existence of the Cecil Rhodes secret society – was a Boston-Irish Catholic who attended the Boston Latin School and Harvard University. He gained a B.A. in history (magna cum laude), graduated top of his class, and went on to complete master's and Ph.D. degrees at Harvard. Quigley lectured there before being head-hunted in 1941 by Father Edmund Walsh, founder and dean of the Foreign Service School at the Jesuit Georgetown University in Washington DC. Quigley would serve there as Professor of History for over 30 years. He also served on the editorial board of *Current History* and was a member of the American Association for the Advancement of Science, the American Anthropological Society, and the American Economic Association. In addition to his university teaching, Quigley lectured at the Armed Forces College, the Brookings Institution, the U.S. Naval Weapons Laboratory, the Naval College, and the Foreign Service Institute of the State Department. He was a consultant to the Smithsonian Institute and the Congressional Select Committee which set up NASA. In short, Professor Quigley was at the very pinnacle of his academic field in America.

In 1949, Quigley completed a book, *The Anglo-American Establishment, From Rhodes to Cliveden*, with compelling and thoroughgoing revelations about a secret group of rich and extremely powerful men who controlled politics, banking, the media, education and much more in Britain. According to Quigley, their aim was to preserve and expand the British Empire to all habitable parts of the world. His exposure of the secret society and its aims apparently led to Quigley fearing for his personal safety and he would not allow the book to be published during his lifetime. (It was only released in 1981 after his death in 1977.) Another book by Quigley, *Evolution of Civilizations*, was published in 1961, and his next work, *Tragedy & Hope, A History of the World in Our Time*, was released in 1966.

Quigley spent twenty years researching and writing the 1,348 page *Tragedy & Hope* which covers the history of the world between 1895 and 1965. The book is described as his magnum opus but we believe *The Anglo-American Establishment* revealing the secret society to be his prime work; indeed, it is one of the most important books ever written on twentieth century history. It is not an easy read, packed as it is with detailed information about the secret anti-democratic group that Quigley says controlled Britain in the first half of the twentieth century. He named the group the "Rhodes secret society" after its founder, the British diamond magnate, Cecil Rhodes, who made his fortune in South Africa. When Rhodes died in 1902, and his friend Alfred Milner became its undisputed leader, it became the "Milner Group." The Introduction to Quigley's *The Anglo-American Establishment* states:

> One wintry afternoon in February 1891, three men were engaged in earnest conversation in London. From that conversation were to flow consequences of the greatest importance to the British Empire and to the world as a whole. For these men were organizing a secret society that was, for more than fifty years, to be one of the most important forces in the formulation and execution of British imperial and foreign policy.
>
> The three men who were thus engaged were already well known in England. The leader was Cecil Rhodes, fabulously wealthy empire-builder and the most important person in South Africa. The second was William T. Stead, the most famous and probably also the most sensational, journalist of the day. The third was Reginald Balliol Brett, later known as Lord Esher, friend and confidant of Queen Victoria, and later to be the most influential adviser of King Edward VII and King George V.
>
> ...The creation of this secret society was not a matter of moment. As we shall see, Rhodes had been planning for this event for more than seventeen years.... Nor was the society thus founded an ephemeral thing, for, in modified form, it exists to this day [1949] ...This organization has been able to conceal its existence quite successfully, and many of its most influential members, satisfied to possess the reality rather than the appearance of power, are unknown even to close students of British history.[1]

Quigley reveals that the Rhodes secret society was devoted to the "preservation and expansion of the British Empire," and was "one of the most important historical facts of the twentieth century."[2] In *The Anglo-American Establishment* he summed up their methods as: (a) a triple-front penetration in politics, education, and journalism. (b) the recruitment of men of ability (chiefly from All Souls College, Oxford) and the linking of these men by matrimonial alliances and by gratitude for titles and positions of power. (c) the influencing of public policy by placing members … in positions of power shielded as much as possible from public attention.[3]

Quigley describes it as being made up of a small, inner circle – "The Society of the Elect" – comprising some of the most powerful men in England. In addition to the above named Rhodes, Stead and Brett, it recruited colonial administrator Alfred Milner, and banker Lord Nathaniel Rothschild, by far the richest man in the world. This inner core in turn carefully selected the membership of "The Association of Helpers" comprising inner and outer circles. Individuals in the outermost circle may not have been aware that they were under the influence of a secret society, but they knew where the real centre of power lay in Britain.

Members came from "well-to-do, upper-class, frequently titled families" whose influence was chiefly visible at the leading English private schools, Eton and Harrow, and the University of Oxford.[4] Since the leading members knew each other intimately there was no need for Masonic style secret handshakes, passwords, or oaths of secrecy (though many were Masons nevertheless). Frequent meetings were held in their grand London town houses and extensive country estates.

The secret society's outer circle, The Association of Helpers, comprised leading movers and shakers in the British Establishment, including politicians, diplomats, academics, bankers and journalists. It also had members in the United States, Canada, Australia, New Zealand and South Africa. Quigley names over 80 members of the Association of Helpers, but suggests there were others he did not name. In *Tragedy & Hope*, Quigley relates how he gained detailed information about the Rhodes-Milner Group:

> I know of the operations of this network because I have studied it for twenty years and was permitted for two years in the early 1960's to examine its papers and secret records. I have no aversion to it or to most of its aims and have, for much of my life, been close to it and to many of its instruments. I have objected, both in the past and recently, to a few of its policies … but in general my chief difference of opinion is that it wishes to remain unknown, and I

believe its role in history is significant enough to be known.... The American branch of this organization (sometimes called the "Eastern Establishment") has played a very significant role in the history of the United States in the last generation.[5]

Quigley informs us that for two years he was permitted to examine the group's papers and secret records, yet fails to elaborate on who granted him that permission or, more importantly, why. To this day, his relationship with the organisation remains a mystery. Some suggest that Quigley was chosen by the Group as its 'in-house' historian to record events for their eyes only. If so, was it a case of their trust being misplaced when he revealed their existence? Or, is it possible that they *wanted* him to do just that? As quoted above, Quigley indicates that his main objection to the Group was not its policies but the fact that it wanted to remain hidden from the public eye. Is it possible that he convinced them to emerge from behind the curtain? If that were the case however, why would he be afraid to have *The Anglo-American Establishment* published during his lifetime? It is possible that his attitude to the Group changed between writing the *Anglo-American Establishment,* and publishing *Tragedy & Hope* seventeen years later in 1966. In the Preface to *The Anglo-American Establishment* (written in 1949) Quigley states:

The Group is of such significance that evidence of its existence is not hard to find, if one knows where to look. I believe I have given the source of every fact which I mention. Some of these facts came to me from sources which I am not permitted to name, and I have mentioned them only where I can produce documentary evidence available to everyone. Nevertheless, it would have been very difficult to write this book if I had not received a certain amount of assistance of a personal nature from persons close to the Group. For obvious reasons I cannot reveal the names of such persons... In general I agree with the goals and aims of the Milner Group. I feel that the British way of life and the British Commonwealth of Nations are among the great achievements of all history. ... But agreeing with the Group on goals, I cannot agree with them on methods. To be sure, I realize that some of their methods were based on nothing but good intentions and high ideals – higher ideals than mine perhaps. But their lack of perspective in critical moments, their failure to use intelligence and common sense, their tendency to fall back on standardized social reactions and verbal cliches in a crisis, their tendency to place power and influence into hands chosen by friendship rather than merit, their oblivion [sic] to the consequences of their actions, their ignorance of the point of view of persons in other countries or of persons in other classes in their own country – these things, it seems to me, have brought many of the things which they and I hold dear close to disaster. In this Group were persons ... who must command the admiration and affection of all who know of them. On the other hand, in this Group were persons whose lives have been a disaster to our way of life. Unfortunately, in the long run, both in the Group and in the world, the influence of the latter kind has been stronger than the influence of the former.[6]

Quigley later revealed that, in addition to being given access to the Group's secret papers, he had received a great deal of information from an Oxford academic, Sir Alfred Zimmern, who had been one of its members. A leading British historian, political scientist, and Professor of International Relations at Oxford University, Zimmern was a member of the British Board of Education and the Political Intelligence Department of the Foreign Office. He was a co-founder of the Royal Institute for International Affairs (Chatham House) and drafted the blueprint for the League of Nations. Zimmern had been a member of the secret society's inner circle for ten years from 1913 to 1923, and knew all its leading members personally. Unhappy with the direction it was taking, Zimmern turned his back on the Group and on his regular visits to the United States thereafter, he revealed all to Carroll Quigley. Like Quigley in the United States, Zimmern was at the pinnacle of academia in Britain, and neither man can be dismissed with the abusive term "conspiracy theorist."

In *The Anglo-American Establishment*, Quigley gives a more detailed account of the secret society and its activities:

The Group has been the most powerful single influence in All Souls, Balliol and New College at Oxford for more than a generation: it has controlled *The Times* [leading British newspaper] for more than fifty years with the exception of three years 1919-1922; it publicized the idea of and the name "British Commonwealth of Nations" in the period 1908-1918: it was the chief influence in Lloyd George's war administration in 1917-1919 and dominated the British delegation to the Peace Conference of 1919; it had a great deal to do with the formation and management of the League of Nations and of the system of mandates. It founded the Royal Institute of International Affairs in 1919 and still controls it; was

19

one of the chief influences on British policy towards Ireland, Palestine and India in the period 1917-1945, it was a very important influence on the policy of appeasement of Germany during the years 1920-1940, and it controlled and still controls, the sources and the writing of the history of British Imperial and Foreign policy since the Boer war. It would be expected that a Group which could number among its achievements such accomplishments as these would be a familiar subject for discussion among students of history and public affairs. In this case, the expectation is not realized, partly because of the deliberate policy of secrecy which this Group has adopted, partly because the group itself is not closely integrated but rather appears as a series of overlapping circles or rings partly concealed by being hidden behind formally organized groups of no obvious political significance.... In the field of education, its influence was chiefly visible at Eton and Harrow and at All Souls College, Oxford.... The "Rhodes secret society" was a group of imperial federalists, formed in the period after 1889 and using the economic resources of South Africa to extend and perpetuate the British Empire.[7]

Just how credible are Carroll Quigley's revelations? Irish Canadian writer John P. Cafferky discussed Quigley's work and how historians responded to it:

Quigley claims he read the secret documents of this organization. His claim leaves no wriggle room: either we dismiss him as a crank, or we test his claim against the historical record ... Legitimate secret political pursuits have nothing to do with conspiracy. Our society permits the secret association of individuals and groups who wish to influence elections and government policies. Not all secret pursuits are conspiracies, but all conspiracies are by their nature secret, and they invariably clandestinely violate society's rules and laws. To reach the standard of conspiracy, the goals and the means used to achieve those goals must cross a liberally drawn line of what a modern society will tolerate. Conspiracy implies rule-breaking and more often than not it implies flagrant rule breaking. Historians object to secret organizations and theories of conspiracy because these organizations do not open their archives to scrutiny. The professional historian argues that one cannot do history without documents. The absence of documents poses a serious challenge, but ignoring a possible conspiracy neither addresses the conspiracy nor the problem of gathering the evidence. Ignoring a conspiracy does not make the problems that suggested the conspiracy disappear, and that is the fatal weakness of the academic's disdain.[8]

In 2013, the present co-author, Jim Macgregor, co-authored a book with Gerry Docherty, *Hidden History: the Secret Origins of the First World War.* Having studied Quigley's evidence about the secret society, we examined its role in the planning and conduct of the First World War and found it to be all pervasive. Quigley's work, however, is generally shunned by mainstream historians. Unlike the vast majority in that field, he was prepared to investigate conspiracies and accept that they existed. His colleagues at Georgetown University certainly did not consider him an oddball or a crank who spread outlandish conspiracy theory. When Quigley retired in 1976, the Director of the School of Foreign Services at Georgetown University, Peter F. Krogh, described him as one of the last of the great macro-historians who traced the development of civilization with an awesome capability. Professor Krogh spoke warmly of Quigley's professionalism and academic contribution:

> For over 40 years, Professor Quigley's teachings have stimulated and disciplined the thinking of students in the School of Foreign Service. His stimulating lectures on the evolution of civilization have, over four decades and for thousands of students, proverbially defined this school and its teaching. Professor Quigley's pedagogy was synonymous with discipline and polished methods of analysis and interpretation. He was justifiably known and even famous for his determination to get students to think. The result was not always fully appreciated immediately, but no teacher has been more respected by alumni, who have come to realize more and more in their professional lives the value of his education. To say that Professor Quigley has been an institution inseparable from the School of Foreign Service is to state a fact.[9]

Dr Jules Davids, Professor of Diplomatic History at Georgetown, added:

> I have known Professor Quigley for three decades as a colleague and friend at Georgetown University. His name will be indelibly linked with the School of Foreign Service, for his work has enriched the faculty history and the University. It is appropriate, therefore, that an endowed chair be created in his honor to recognize the excellence of his teaching and his many contributions to the high academic standards of Georgetown University. Maintaining the quality standard of education at Georgetown University and fos-

tering in his students a desire for education was always a foremost concern of Dr Quigley. He not only stimulated the imagination of his students, but also forced them to think independently and to challenge accepted views and traditional historical interpretations. ...The key to Carroll Quigley's success as a teacher and professor lies in his creative intellect, the depth of his insights, and the broad interdisciplinary scope of his interests, which encompass the fields of history, economics, philosophy, and the natural sciences. Dr Quigley differs from a specialized professor who moves carefully along the well-worn tracks of a narrow discipline as a person with insatiable curiosity like an iconoclast ... [10]

Bill Clinton referred to Quigley during his acceptance speech at the Democratic convention on July 16, 1992:

As a teenager I heard John Kennedy's summons to citizenship. And then, as a student at Georgetown, I heard that call clarified by a professor named Carroll Quigley, who said to us that America was the greatest country in the history of the world because our people have always believed in two things: that tomorrow can be better than today and that every one of us has a personal, moral responsibility to make it so.[11]

Kennedy and Quigley in the same breath and no mention of 'conspiracy theory'. No matter how far the Establishment's attempts have gone to blank or denigrate his work, Carroll Quigley was no conspiracy theory crank. As Professor Krogh remarked, he was a man whose work was synonymous with discipline and "polished methods of analysis and interpretation." Unlike many academic historians today, Quigley challenged accepted views and traditional historical interpretations. He was also a man who pulled no punches in revealing that it was through the power of money that the secret society was able to "monopolize so completely the writing and the teaching of history of their own period." [12] It is a sad indictment of many academic historians today, that they are all too accepting of the mainstream history narrative. We have corresponded with a number of such historians who admit to never having looked at Quigley's books. If nothing else, their lack of intellectual curiosity is quite astonishing. Dependent for their salaries, research funding, and future careers, the vast majority toe the official line. The few who deviate from the carefully prepared 'court history' script are dismissed, deemed unemployable elsewhere in academia, and their careers and livelihoods effectively ruined. In this respect, a few brave academics such as Professor Antony C. Sutton and Professor Guido Giacomo Preparata spring to mind.

Control of the writing of history was important to the secret society for many reasons, not least their ability to retain power. George Orwell wrote in *Nineteen Eighty-Four*, "Who controls the past controls the future. Who controls the present controls the past." Through their power and sway over the received history, the collective memory of the people and how they perceive reality are controlled. By whitewashing their own role from history, the individuals described by Quigley were able to *retain* power.

Before he retired from the School of Foreign Service, Quigley agreed to an interview with the *Washington Post*. It might be considered a risky decision, given that the newspaper was owned by individuals in the belly of the very beast he had been exposing. It had been bought in 1933 by Wall Street banker, Eugene Meyer, who was chairman of the Federal Reserve, and later President of the World Bank. Meyer's daughter, Katharine Meyer Graham, became de facto publisher of the paper from 1963 to 1991. She was a member of the Council on Foreign Relations (CFR) and a personal friend of many of the leading players in the U.S who Quigley had exposed. She would personally have cleared, if not indeed arranged, the Quigley interview, and one has to ask what the motive was. A *Washington Post* journalist, Rudy Maxa, was sent along to the university with his tape recorder.

The subsequent article, published in the *Washington Post* Sunday Magazine on 23 March 1975, was entitled 'The Professor Who Knew Too Much'. Its subtitle was 'Borrowing a few crucial pages from his book, the ultra-right made a scholar an unwilling hero.'

Not unexpectedly, the article was a hatchet job on Quigley, portraying him as a hero of extreme right-wing nutters and crazy conspiracy theorists. An American researcher, Kevin Cole, who reviewed the newspaper article, wrote that it did a great disservice to the historicity and veracity of the claims Quigley had made in his most famous and revelatory works.[13]

It appears that Quigley had unwittingly allowed himself to be set up. The purpose of the interview and the subsequent article was not to discuss his life's work and the truths he had revealed, but to bury them and associate his books with lunatic fringe conspiracy theorists and the mentally deranged on the extreme right:

> Though he had no way of knowing it, Quigley had just written his own ticket to a curious kind of fame. He was about to become a

reluctant hero to Americans who believe the world is neatly controlled by a clique of international bankers and their cronies. He was about to learn of the country's awesome appetite for believing a grand conspiracy causes everything from big wars to bad weather. And eventually, *Tragedy & Hope* would be pirated by zealots who would sell the book in the same brochures that advertise such doomsday products as "Minutemen Survival Tabs," concentrated vitamin tablets to help patriots survive sieges by foreign enemies.

...After the books came the letters. Brother Nelson Goodwin, a self-styled Nevada "hobo" evangelist was moved last summer to take pencil in hand and write: "Brother Carroll: I have heard somewhere that 'Snake Eyes Joe Enlai' and Mousey Dung' and 'Snake in the Grass Fidel Castro' all received their poison aesthetic doctrine in the Universities and Colleges of America. Thank God for Men like you who love our Beautiful United States, the finest nation on earth.[14]

The message was clear: This man writes conspiracy theory that attracts the lunatic fringe. English writer Sevak Gulbekian sums up how the 'conspiracy theory' smear is used to undermine and ridicule writers who expose conspiratorial action by powerful groups or governments:

In his book *Perpetual War for Perpetual Peace* Gore Vidal suggests that the American public has been conditioned to respond to the word 'conspiracy' with a smirk and a chuckle. Conspiracy, in other words, is for the nuts and the loners, and is not to be taken seriously. In this way, he argues, through the media's association of the concept of conspiracy with fringe or extreme elements, the real conspirators go unnoticed.

It is a vital point, and Vidal courageously chases and exposes genuine conspiracies by politicians, the FBI, lobbyists for the tobacco companies, and so on. But the flip-side of the conspiracy coin is the proliferation of fanciful and fantastic theories that now crisscross the globe in seconds with the help of electronic media.

The spread of the internet has democratised conspiracy theory. Millions of people now have the means to publish their own unique analysis of what is going on. A necessary consequence of this massive growth in personal digital publishing is that it is getting to be much more difficult to find the pearls among the rubbish. Someone even observed that, in the age of the internet, if you want to keep something secret you make it public... [15]

The Washington Post article fitted Gore Vidal's observation to a tee. It doubtless fulfilled its aim of having readers condescendingly smile and chuckle at the work of this 'nutty professor'. They were much too clever to be taken in by such nonsense. Best laugh it off. What sort of fools would go out and spend good money on his crazy books?

Fortunately, a copy of the actual tape-recorded interview with Quigley was discovered in a cupboard in his old office at the university some years later. It presents a different picture to that painted in the article, and provides a fascinating example of how the mainstream media grossly distorts the work of anyone who dares challenge the Establishment.

In the recorded interview, Quigley relates many astonishing facts concerning his research and conclusions yet there is no hint of this in the *Washington Post's* hatchet job. He does not, of course, discuss *The Anglo-American Establishment*, as it is in a publisher's safe awaiting his demise before being released.

Quigley informed the journalist that he had spent 20 years writing *Tragedy & Hope* and in that period had no time off at all. 'Tragedy' reflected his opinion that it was absolutely tragic that Western Civilization was heading down the drain. 'Hope' reflected the fact that when he wrote the book some ten years earlier he had hoped that Western Civilization could be saved. That had been his 'Hope,' but he was now extremely sceptical that it could be saved. "I think we are just about finished" he told Maxa.

Quigley related that he had experienced major difficulties with his New York publisher, Macmillan Inc. a division of the British Macmillan publishing house. Around the time it published *Tragedy & Hope*, Macmillan Publishing in the U.S. was bought out and merged with a company called Crowell-Collier Books. Quigley relates in the interview that Crowell-Collier was a J.P. Morgan-controlled company.

Was it purely a coincidence that the J.P. Morgan organisation had bought out the publisher with the rights to a book that was exposing J.P. Morgan as being at the very heart of a huge international conspiracy? Some writers suggest the possibility that Morgan only took over Macmillan Publishing and Quigley's work in order to keep control of it from the outset and suppress it.

Behind the scenes and unknown to Quigley, at the time *Tragedy & Hope* was published all sorts of devious games were being played. Various reports suggest that when it was released, virtually all copies of the book were removed from wholesale suppliers and retail outlets by agents of the American Establishment and burned. Quigley relates in the interview that Crowell-Collier stopped all publicity for the book after just one advertisement. He was informed by friends who attempted to buy copies from bookshops that they were being told it was out of print and no longer available. Quigley presumably thought his book had been a bestseller. He says in the interview that he repeatedly asked Macmillan/Collier why it was not being reprinted, but was always fobbed off:

> They lied to me. They told everyone it was out of print. They lied to me so many times on so many occasions. They lied and lied and lied and lied to me on everything. I learned in the summer of 1971 that they destroyed the plates of *Tragedy & Hope*.

Interviewer Rudy Maxa, was informed that this important book by one of the United States' leading academics – which had taken him 20 years to research and write – had been very deliberately sabotaged and the printing plates destroyed, yet Maxa made no mention of this in his article. (It transpired that someone had managed to obtain a copy of the book, realised its importance, and began pirate publishing it. That is how it survived and has flourished to the present day.)

In the recorded interview, Quigley seems anxious and guarded, frequently telling Rudy Maxa to switch the tape recorder off while he discusses sensitive issues: "I don't know if you want to put this on tape. You have to protect my future as well as your own." Quigley revealed how much of his information about the Milner Group came from the Oxford professor, Sir Alfred Zimmern:

> I don't think we should talk too much about this. I met Alfred Zimmern when he came here to give a speech. He was a member for ten years. He named them. He said "I resigned in 1923 because they were determined to build Germany up against France. He said, "I wouldn't stand for it so I resigned." Now I better stop talking because you see, this gets into all sorts of things.' [16]

Neither during the interview nor in his subsequent article did Rudy Maxa delve into the remarkable statement Quigley had just made: In the post Versailles years, a powerful Anglo-American group was "determined" to build up the defeated and destroyed Germany against France, the wartime ally of Britain and the United States. Quigley went on to relate that leading members of the Group were the 'godfathers' of the Council on Foreign Relations (CFR) in the United States. It was the leading American 'think tank' specialising in U.S. foreign policy and international relations – of which the *Washington Post's* publisher and owner, Katharine Meyer Graham, was a member. The Milner Group was also the founder of a similar organisation in Britain – the Royal Institute for International Affairs (Chatham House) in London. Quigley made it clear in *Tragedy & Hope* that these organisations were set up by the Rhodes-Milner Group and their allies in financial circles, crammed with their agents in various fields, and acted as fronts to exert a huge influence on the foreign policy of the U.S. and British governments. Quigley states in the interview without equivocation: "These people are for world domination."

Maxa ignored it, making no attempt to ask Quigley what he meant by it or open it up for discussion. It was a bold statement that a major conspiracy existed, yet Maxa completely blanked it in both the interview and subsequent article. From the outset, *The Washington Post* piece utterly distorted what Quigley had said. The newspaper's loud and clear message was; if you believe the world is dominated by 'a clique of international bankers and their cronies,' you are not a serious or rational person.

Maxa completely misrepresented what Quigley was saying, both in the interview and his book, *Tragedy & Hope*. Had he totally misunderstood Quigley? Had he not read *Tragedy & Hope* before going along to interview its author? Had he read it but not understood its central tenet on page 324:

> The powers of financial capitalism had a far-reaching plan, nothing less than to create a world system of financial control in private hands able to dominate the political system of each country and the economy of the world as a whole.

Quigley told Maxa that some people who spread anti-Jewish conspiracy theories were hi-jacking *Tragedy & Hope* to make it appear he supported their views. Indeed, all sorts "of nuts" were misrepresenting his work to fit their own agendas.

It is patently clear from his books and the tape recording that Quigley was *not* describing a conspiracy by "Illuminati," or Jews, or Freemasons or whatever. What he revealed was a conspiracy of rich and powerful members of the English-speaking elites in Britain and the United States who aimed "for world domination." Some of those involved were doubtless very rich Jews or very rich Christians, but Quigley never suggested at any time that religious beliefs came into it. Others, of course, have disagreed with him on that.

At the end of the taped interview Quigley makes a rather strange and rambling statement:

> I generally would think that any conspiracy theory of history is nonsense. For the simple reason that most of the conspiracies that

we know about seem to me to be the conspiracies of losers. Of people who have been defeated on the platform; let's say, the historical platform of the public happenings. The Ku Klux Klan was the, uh.… Their arguments and their … point of view had been destroyed, and defeated, in the Civil War. Well, because they're not prepared to accept that, they form a conspiracy, you see, to fight against it in an underground way. And, those people who could fight, up in the open, do so. Those who can't, go underground. It seems to me this is essentially what conspiracy [is]. The Palestinian Liberation Army is a similar thing, you see. Now I think on the whole they're pretty well a group who … has not got really very much. And so, they have to be terrorists.

Rudy Maxa interjected: "If I could play the Devil's Advocate, I think, you, talking about the 'international banking conspiracy,' they have not lost out, they simply don't want any attention. They don't want to…"

Quigley then interrupted Maxa: "Oh… I… That's…"

At that point the recording of the interview ends abruptly.

What was Quigley up to here? There is no mistaking what he wrote in his books exposing a conspiracy of rich and powerful Anglo-Americans utterly committed to world domination. He revealed how they controlled the central banks, politics, and the writing and teaching of history. In *Tragedy & Hope* he explained that in considerable detail, and during the interview he clearly stated: "These people are for world domination."

At the end of the interview (at least, the tape-recorded part of it), however, he was suggesting that any conspiracy theory of history was nonsense. Was Quigley naïve in doing this interview? Was he confused – as his ramblings about the Ku Klux Klan and Palestinian Liberation Army appear to indicate – or did he agree to the interview because he was afraid and desperately trying to protect himself? He was certainly still afraid to have *The Anglo-American Establishment* published at that stage.

If Quigley had changed his mind about the conspiracy of rich and powerful elites – as detailed by him throughout the 335 pages of *The Anglo-American Establishment* completed back in 1949 – he would surely have destroyed the manuscript to prevent it from ever being published. Anecdotal evidence suggests that Quigley told friends he had been warned by men unknown to him that he would be killed if he wrote or said anymore about the secret society and associated financial circles. Quigley wrote in considerable detail about the members of the secret society, and how they were dedicated to "the extension of British rule throughout the word."[17]

Before discussing the individuals involved in the secret society, we must look in some detail at the man who inspired them, John Ruskin, Slade Professor of Fine Art at Oxford University. All biographers of Cecil Rhodes link his ambitious plans to the teachings of Ruskin, including Saraha Gertrude Millin who writes of the huge impact Ruskin had on Rhodes at Oxford, filling him with the ideas "which came to inspire his life." According to Millin, Rhodes' "mind was buzzing with the exhortations of Ruskin and the ethics of Aristotle," and a lecture Ruskin gave in which he spoke of advancing the power of England by land and sea, "were the words that gave form to Rhodes' dream." Rhodes was "ripe for Ruskin's heroic message."[18]

Who was this man Ruskin that so attracted the hero-worship of Oxford students such as Cecil Rhodes, Alfred Milner, William T. Stead and numerous others who would go on to create the secret society, and drove them in their ambitious plan for global control?

JOHN RUSKIN (1819-1900)

Writer, gifted painter, art critic, and social reformer, John Ruskin was born in London as the only child of Scottish parents. His father, who amassed considerable wealth as a wine and sherry importer, was firmly rooted in conservatism and "utterly hated radicals"[19] John's autocratic mother, an unyielding evangelical Christian, was fiercely ambitious for her son, constantly supervising him and

never allowing toys, playthings, or other children in the house. Ruskin's sympathetic biographer, J. A. Hobson, writes:

> As we read the story of his childhood, we feel his mother's "principles" are too obtrusive to be wholly pleasing or wholly profitable. "My mother's general principles of first treatment were, to guard me with steady watchfulness from all possible pain or danger; and for the rest, to let me amuse myself as I liked, provided I was neither fretful nor troublesome." The words, "as I liked," however, require serious qualification, for "toys" were forbidden; and a sorrowful story is told of a carnally-minded aunt who gave the baby a splendid Punch and Judy, which was promptly confiscated by his mother, who said, "It was not right that I should have them, and I never saw them again."

Old-fashioned views about the place of punishment in education prevailed in the Ruskin household. "I was always summarily
whipped if I cried, did not do as I was bid, or tumbled on the stairs."
When it is added that her earliest conception of her special duty in
education took the form of forcing John to acquire long chapters
of the Bible with perfect verbal accuracy and to read the book right
through, once a year at least, from Genesis to the Apocalypse, every syllable, at a time when no skill of interpretation in the teacher
and no precocity in the pupil could have imparted a right understanding of many portions, the opinion we form of her judgment
and discretion is not too favourable.[20]

The Ruskins lived in domestic seclusion, had few friends and rarely entertained or ventured out. From his earliest days, John's parents controlled
him very tightly and schooled him at home. Believing him destined for a
high position in the church as a Bishop or Archbishop, his whole structure as a youngster was built on a biblical teaching of original sin (that
some might call brainwashing). There is no doubt that his parents loved
him, but whipped him if he fell or cried. More damagingly, perhaps, they
controlled his young mind that needed to develop, be curious, ask questions and form his own opinions.

When he was 17 and went up to Oxford University, his mother moved
with him to the town and took an apartment on High Street. She watched
over him "constantly" in Oxford to ensure his physical and moral wellbe-
ing.[21] Mother and son dined every evening together, and his father went
up every weekend. As an undergraduate, Ruskin achieved little academic
distinction apart from a prize for poetry. His few friends at university included Henry Acland who would go on to become a famous physician.

After Oxford, Ruskin enjoyed frequent nature and culture tours of Europe. Venice, which he visited a number of times with his parents, had an especially great effect on Ruskin. His father was a champion of Romanticism.
The Romantics tended to look back to the Middle Ages and its social code
of hierarchy, which they saw as 'beautiful,' like the architecture, in contrast
with the ugliness of 19th century industrialism. This looking backward to
an imagined beautiful idyllic past was a big factor in Ruskin's character, and
led naturally on to his imperialism. He began painting and writing about art,
and was twenty-three years old when he completed the first volume of his
five-volume *Modern Painters*. He was an early champion of the Pre-Raphael-
ite brotherhood, and especially praised the work of Romantic painter, William Turner, when others were severely criticising it. *Modern Painters* was

well received by the emerging and increasingly affluent middle-class in Victorian England, and Ruskin began to see his vocation as an art critic. Nowadays, Ruskin's *Modern Painters* is considered by some as mediocre at best:

> Nobody reads Ruskin these days and looking at this book one can see why. Even in its abridged form it is almost totally unreadable – a chaotic mixture of cloudy philosophy, reflections on literature and politics, a great deal of art criticism (of highly erratic quality), the whole lit up by occasional shafts of prophetic insight and descriptive passages of great rhetorical power. It is hard to understand why it was so esteemed by the Victorians in its original five-volume form.
>
> The fact has to be faced, even by his defenders (of whom I count myself one) that Ruskin was more than a little barmy. This may have had something to do with the fact that his parents were first cousins. But whatever his genetic handicaps, they were heightened by the peculiar circumstances of an upbringing which warped his nature. As an only child, he was smothered with attention by both parents. His mother was an especially baneful influence who indoctrinated him with her own repellent version of Calvinism. It was not to be wondered at that when Ruskin grew up, he found it almost impossible to form normal healthy relationships with anyone.[22]

In 1848, Ruskin married Effie Gray, the pretty 20-year-old daughter of family acquaintances from Scotland, but the marriage was a loveless disaster without physical interaction.

> The intimacies of marriage proved impossible for him, and he punished his unfortunate wife by bullying and isolation, driving her to leave an intolerable situation.[23]

Effie lived under the same roof as the emotionally damaged Ruskin for six years, before having the marriage annulled on the legal premise that it was never consummated. Ruskin refused to accept her grounds for ending the marriage, forcing her to undergo a humiliating intimate examination by two male doctors who confirmed her *virgo intacta*. Ruskin apologists would later blame Effie and her family for having 'craftily engineered' a loveless marriage with a view to 'gold-digging' the fortune Ruskin's father had amassed. The complete absence of a sexual relationship, they say, was Effie's fault, not Ruskin's.

Effie went on to have a very happy marriage with the kind and gentle artist John Everett Millais, a member of the Pre-Raphaelite-Brotherhood. Together they would have eight children. Ruskin never remarried and speculation remains rife about his sexuality and possible paedophilia. He allegedly enjoyed looking at drawings of naked pre-pubescent girls. After the annulment of his marriage to Effie, at the age of 39 Ruskin began privately tutoring nine-year-old Rose la Touche and at some stage 'fell in love' with her. When she reached the age of 18, Rose's parents refused Ruskin permission to marry her. She would die just ten years later in an institution in Dublin.

On his father's death in 1864, Ruskin inherited a substantial fortune, enabling him to fund a number of social experiments aimed at helping the poor. He encouraged independent women, and provided funding to help the social reformer, Octavia Hill, renovate low-rent tenement housing for poor working people. At the other end of the spectrum, he subsidised a girl's finishing school, Winnington Hall, in Cheshire run by Miss Margaret Bell. With Miss Bell's encouragement, Ruskin made regular visits to lecture the girls on art and nature, and occasionally stayed over in his own rooms at the school.

> Aware of the value of his patronage, she [Miss Bell] welcomed his visits, which became more frequent in the early 1860s, and encouraged him to romp with her pupils, several of whom became particular "pets" and later the chosen confidants for Ruskin's schemes of spiritual and moral renewal.[24]

'Romping' with the girls and having particular 'pets' among them, sounds alarming but it would be mistaken to deduce from it that Ruskin was indeed a paedophile. Like many adults, he innocently enjoyed being around children. Towards the end of his life Ruskin said that his inability to break free from parental control was the reason for his failure to achieve maturity.

In his middle years, Ruskin devoted ever more of his time to political considerations and formulating ideas for social reform.

> He always spoke of himself as an "old Tory," and the making of democratic machinery was always repellent to his instincts of political order. Radical philosophy formed the object of his sternest denunciations.[25]

Revolted by radicals, and the ugliness and mercenary character of modern industrialism, Ruskin was drawn to the aesthetics of the Middle Ages and to the concepts of 'nobility,' 'chivalry,' 'authenticity' and 'authority.' As a self-declared 'old Tory,' he was inclined to a conservative, paternalistic and hierarchical worldview, while abhorring radical thinkers who called for an end to the long-held, rather rigid, conservative, social order in Britain. There would always be distinct social classes, he argued, with upper class rulers whose duty was to keep order among their inferiors and raise them to a level to which they were capable. Regarding the welfare of children, Ruskin initially came close to socialist doctrine when he strongly advocated State involvement. It was, he said, the duty of the State to ensure that every child was well-housed, clothed, fed and educated.[26]

An advocate of social reform, Ruskin suggested ways in which the lives of the lower classes could be improved. He always stressed, however, the role of "authority."

> His conception of the rightful operation of "authority" in spiritual and temporal affairs, induces a complete and vehement rejection of the forms of government generally identified with democracy. It is not merely a disbelief in the efficacy of representative institutions, but a deeper distrust of the ability of the people to safeguard or advance their true interests. Even those forms of organised self-help which have won the approval of many of our most conservative minds, the co-operative movement and trade unionism, evoke in him a doubtful and imperfect sympathy. Order, reverence, authority, obedience, these words are always on his lips, these ideas always present in his mind. Radical and revolutionary doctrines and movements, as he interprets them, imply the rejection and overthrow of these principles, and are denounced accordingly. Liberty and equality he scornfully repudiates as the negation of order and government. "No liberty, but instant obedience to known law and appointed persons; no equality, but recognition of every betterness and reprobation of every worseness."[27]

Concerning the rights of women, Ruskin believed in later years that they were best placed as 'supervisors of the household'. Having earlier suggested that 'all children' – that is, girls as well as boys – should be 'well-educated' by the State, he later appears to have changed his mind. Women had no place in the sciences or medicine etc.

> In a departure from his former advice, given when he still believed redemption was possible, he counselled women to return to secluded domesticity as the only remaining haven of goodness: "the end of all right education for a woman is to make her love her home better than any other place; that she should as seldom leave it as a queen her queendom; nor ever feel entirely at rest but within its threshold."

He lost his faith in universal education, which in the current state of the world only threatened to disrupt the social order and perpetuate the harmful effects of modernity.... The "essentially right life for all womankind" was that of the peasant, which meant "scrubbing furniture, dusting walls, sweeping floors, making the beds, washing up the crockery, ditto the children and whipping them when they want it, mending their clothes, making their dinners ..."[28]

The American writer and feminist activist, Kate Millet, wrote:

Assuring us at the outset that he is no crude chauvinist, Ruskin asserts that he is steering a middle course. He seems to direct his efforts against the "left" of feminism, and his refutation is the courtly platitude that women are loved and honoured, have nothing to complain of and are even treated as royalty, so long as they stay at home.[29]

In late 1869, Ruskin was appointed Slade Professor of Fine Art at Oxford. It was rumoured that his friend from their undergraduate days, Henry Acland, helped him secure the position. Acland had become Regius Professor of Medicine at Oxford, and curator of the Bodleian Library, and certainly held considerable sway at the university.

Ruskin had some important suggestions for education and social welfare, but some of his other suggestions might not have been out of place in Nazi Germany in the 1930s:

The physical and moral education he proposes would make finer creatures of them [the lower class]; would go a long way, of itself, to "eradicate disease and stupidity and vulgarity." To do this more effectually, he proposed to regulate marriage by permitting it only to those young people who had qualified themselves by attaining a certain standard of general physical and moral culture. He would limit all incomes [of the underclasses] to some fixed maximum.... As to the church, that was to be strictly a state church, in the sense that such officers as it possessed would be salaried by the government, and their work would be in harmony with the state, not opposed to it, nor independent of it, in sects and schisms ... He said that a military despotism is the only cure for a diseased society; and while minimising occasions and opportunities for war, he felt that to effect the development of the present "Dark Age" into a more perfect civilisation, some use of force would be necessary in the administration.... Laws must be made, and laws must be administered: and to do this effectively requires a strong hand. In his state every man would be a soldier...[30]

Ruskin believed that State permission to marry would demand rigid regulations as to age and income. His suggestion that epileptics, criminals, or the victims of any serious hereditary illness should not be allowed to increase and multiply would become basic tenets of the eugenicist movement in Britain and the United States, and thereafter in Nazi Germany. In addition, Ruskin made a "stubborn and eloquent defence of war and militarism"[31] Ruskin biographer, J. A Hobson writes:

> Mr. Ruskin's curious praise of war demands separate attention. A certain tendency to worship force *qua* force, which, in spite of disclaimers, sometimes manifests itself in him, as in Carlyle, is partly responsible for his view. The romantic aspect of war which he got in childhood from Homer and from Scott never passed from him; the vivid dramatic presentation, both of the horror and the glory, evinces a certain unreality. The love of mastership, and of the self-assertion of strong men, casts a glamour over war, the most pronounced form of self-assertion. This sentiment is less a manly than a womanly quality; it is found rather in physically weak, sensitive men than in robust ones, arising from the idealisation of a quality by those who possess it not. Mr. Ruskin does not see war as it is or was; he does not see it as those few literary men who have experienced it face to face see and describe it, men like Mazzini and Tolstoy. Perhaps the pages we would most willingly delete from his works are those containing the address to young Woolwich students, reprinted in "The Crown of Wild Olive," which defend "the game of war" as that occupation in which "the full personal power of the human creature" finds effective expression, and which, "when well played, determines who is the best man."
>
> It is true that both here and elsewhere wars of sheer aggression for selfish ends of territorial or commercial aggrandisement are denounced. But few defend wars ostensibly undertaken for gain. The sanction and incitement given by Mr. Ruskin to the English nation "to undertake aggressive war, according to their force, wherever they are, assured that their authority would be helpful and protective," however laudable as a theory of national conduct, is one of the most dangerous pieces of advice that could be tendered to a people always able to persuade themselves that their interference is "helpful and protective," when it extends the influence of England over a new area of the world. It is true that the wars approved by Mr. Ruskin belong to national knight-errantry and not to selfish rapacity; but in permitting the indulgence of the war-spirit outside the limits of pure self-defence, he gives free operation to dangerous forces without providing any adequate checks.[32]

Aside from his qualified support for war, Ruskin seems to have been genuinely troubled by the miserable existence experienced by the vast majority in mid-Victorian England. It was not a fair, enlightened, democratic society he was advocating, however, it was a softer feudalism with the rich and powerful forever at the pinnacle – "a voluntary self-reformation of the governing classes."[33]

> In spite of wavering moments, this deep-rooted disbelief in democracy and a persistent disparagement of popular action stand as distinctive marks of Mr. Ruskin's teaching. The people cannot help themselves; the growing discontent with their condition, aroused by education, can never become the power for progress …The true instrument of social progress, as he conceives it, is the goodwill and intelligence of the upper classes, the landowners and "captains of industry," whose functions have been already named, "to keep order among their inferiors, and raise them always to the nearest level with themselves of which those inferiors are capable." This "raising" of "inferiors" may be safely carried on without risk of attaining any dangerous condition of equality, on account of "the wholesome indisposition of the average mind for intellectual labour."… Although he has sketched elaborate plans of political and industrial organisation, Mr. Ruskin is no true believer in public machinery, even when the working is in the hands of the illuminated "upper classes." Like most thinkers who have approached the social question from a distinctively "moral" standpoint, he finds the spring of progress in the individual will.… In a word, the Socialism, to which Mr. Ruskin looks, is to be imposed by an hereditary aristocracy, whose effective co-operation for the common good is to be derived from the voluntary action of individual landowners and employers. There must be no movement of the masses to claim economic justice; no use of Parliament to "nationalise" land or capital, or to attack any private interest… Reform must proceed from a moral appeal to the heart and the intelligence of individual members of the ruling classes…[34]

Ruskin's lectures were generally packed with students and members of the public. Indeed, the people arriving for his first lecture had to be moved at the last minute to the Sheldonian Theatre to accommodate everyone. The students at Oxford appeared to have loved him because he appealed to their youthful idealism and English patriotism. In his inaugural lecture, entitled "Imperial Duty" on 8 February 1870, he told the students:

...There is a destiny now possible to us – the highest ever set before a nation to be accepted or refused. We are still undegenerate in race; a race mingled of the best northern blood. We are not yet dissolute in temper, but still have the firmness to govern, and the grace to obey. We have been taught a religion of pure mercy, which we must either now betray, or learn to defend by fulfilling. And we are rich in an inheritance of honour, bequeathed to us through a thousand years of noble history, which it should be our daily thirst to increase with splendid avarice, so that Englishmen, if it be a sin to covet honour, should be the most offending souls alive. Within the last few years we have had the laws of natural science opened to us with a rapidity which has been blinding by its brightness; and means of transit and communication given to us, which have made but one kingdom of the habitable globe. One kingdom; but who is to be its king? Is there to be no king in it, think you, and every man to do that which is right in his own eyes? Or only kings of terror, and the obscene empires of Mammon and Belial? Or will you, youths of England, make your country again a royal throne of kings; a sceptred isle, for all the world a source of light, a centre for peace ...

And this is what [England] must either do, or perish: she must found colonies as fast and as far as she is able, formed of her most energetic and worthiest men; – seizing every piece of fruitful waste ground she can set her foot on, and there teaching these her colonists that their chief virtue is to be fidelity to their country, and that their first aim is to be to advance the power of England by land and sea ...[35]

Carroll Quigley writes:

Ruskin spoke to the Oxford undergraduates as members of the privileged ruling class. He told them that they were the possessors of a magnificent tradition of education, beauty, rule of law, freedom, decency, and self-discipline but that this tradition could not be saved, and did not deserve to be saved, unless it could be extended to the lower-classes in England itself and to the non-English masses throughout the world. If this precious tradition were not extended to these two great majorities, the minority of upper-class Englishmen would ultimately be submerged by these majorities and the tradition lost.[36]

Descending into madness, Ruskin spent his final years at Brantwood, his beautiful house on the shores of Coniston Lake in the Lake District of England. Cared for by his cousin, Joan Severn, he died from influenza on

20 January 1900. The Rhodes secret society planned to have his remains interred close to Tennyson's in Poet's Corner in Westminster Abbey, but despite much pressure from London and Oxford, Joan insisted that he must be buried in the quiet churchyard of St Andrew's at Coniston in accord with his wishes. A simultaneous service was held in Westminster Abbey.

Following Ruskin's death, an old and intimate friend (and executor of his literary estate), Charles Eliot Norton, Professor of History at Harvard, wrote to Joan, saying that all documents and correspondence that could "prove embarrassing" to Ruskin's reputation must be destroyed. Norton crossed the Atlantic and, together with Joan, burned many of Ruskin's papers in the back garden at Brantwood, including a box containing correspondence between Ruskin and Rose la Touche. When Norton returned to the U.S. he similarly burned much of the correspondence between himself and Ruskin.

Cecil Rhodes and Alfred Milner were unable to get from South Africa for the funeral of their hero, and it is unknown if any other members of the inner circle attended.

Summary: Chapter 1 – Carroll Quigley – Oracle or Oddball?

- Professor Carroll Quigley revealed that the Rhodes secret society was created in 1891

- Dedicated to the expansion of the British empire, its membership comprised rich and powerful men in England and the Commonwealth.

- The secret society was intimately linked to Oxford University, and controlled the Rhodes Scholarships there.

- The mainstream press attempted to dismiss Quigley's revelations as 'conspiracy theory'.

- On Cecil Rhodes' death, the secret society became known as the 'Milner Group'. Its leading members were inspired by the teachings of Professor John Ruskin at Oxford University.

- Ruskin, an anti-democratic reactionary and eugenicist, suggested that the empire must continue expanding by creating more colonies across the world or perish.

- Ruskin's proposed social welfare reforms advocated marked improvements in the atrocious living conditions of the masses in Victorian Britain.

- Any aspects of 'socialism' Ruskin encouraged were to be imposed under aristocratic/oligarchical rule.

CHAPTER 2

THE SOCIETY OF THE ELECT

I n the *Anglo-American Establishment,* Carroll Quigley gives a list of members of the inner circle of the secret society – "The Society of the Elect." He states that he had "documentary evidence, private information, and circumstantial evidence" for including specific individuals in the list. There were possibly others who were members, but not listed because he did not have sufficient evidence to include them.[1]

The secret society was founded in 1891 by Cecil Rhodes.

CECIL JOHN RHODES (1853-1902)

T he son of a Church of England vicar, Reverend Francis William Rhodes, and his wife Louisa Peacock Rhodes, Cecil was a sickly child suffering from asthma and possibly early tuberculosis. His eldest brother, Herbert, had gone to southern Africa to farm, and in 1870 Cecil was sent to join him in the hope that his health would improve with the dry warm climate. When their attempts to grow cotton failed, Cecil and Herbert moved to the diamond fields of Kimberley in the Northern Cape Province. In 1873 Rhodes returned to England to study at Oxford University for a single term, and was greatly influenced by  John Ruskin's vision for British imperialism. Ruskin had given his famous inaugural lecture "Imperial Duty" three years before Rhodes arrived at Oxford, but Rhodes accessed the typed notes in the library, transcribed them in their entirety in his own handwriting, and reputedly carried that document on his person for the rest of his life.

Rhodes went back to southern Africa before returning to Oxford in 1876, when he became a Freemason at the Apollo (Oxford) University Lodge. Financed initially by the financier, Alfred Beit, in 1887 Rhodes reached a crucial financial agreement with Rothschild in London which enabled him to buy out rivals in South Africa. In 1888 he formed the De Beers Consolidated Mines company, became the leading man in South Africa and extremely rich.

Rhodes never married nor had children, and decided to use his wealth to create a secret society that would promote British expansion across the world. Suffering chronic ill-health, and fearing he would die young, in 1877 Rhodes wrote a will entitled 'Confession of Faith'. In its original form – with poor grammar and punctuation – 'Confession of Faith' reads:

> It often strikes a man to inquire what is the chief good in life; to one the thought comes that it is a happy marriage, to another great wealth, and as each seizes on his idea, for that he more or less works for the rest of his existence. To myself thinking over the same question the wish came to render myself useful to my country. I then asked myself how could I and after reviewing the various methods I have felt that at the present day we are actually limiting our children and perhaps bringing into the world half the human beings we might owing to the lack of country for them to inhabit that if we had retained America there would at this moment be millions more of English living. I contend that we are the finest race in the world and that the more of the world we inhabit the better it is for the human race. Just fancy those parts that are at present inhabited by the most despicable specimens of human beings what an alteration there would be if they were brought under Anglo-Saxon influence, look again at the extra employment a new country added to our dominions gives. I contend that every acre added to our territory means in the future birth to some more of the English race who otherwise would not be brought into existence ... I look into history and I read the story of the Jesuits I see what they were able to do in a bad cause and I might say under bad leaders. At the present day I become a member of the Masonic order I see the wealth and power they possess the influence they hold and I think over their ceremonies and I wonder that a large body of men can devote themselves to what at times appear the most ridiculous and absurd rites without an object and without an end.
>
> The idea gleaming and dancing before one's eyes like a will-of-the-wisp at last frames itself into a plan. Why should we not form a secret society with but one object the furtherance of the British Empire and the bringing of the whole uncivilised world under British rule for the recovery of the United States for the making the Anglo-Saxon race but one Empire. What a dream, but yet it is probable, it is possible.... Africa is still lying ready for us it is our

duty to take it. It is our duty to seize every opportunity of acquiring more territory and we should keep this one idea steadily before our eyes that more territory simply means more of the Anglo-Saxon race more of the best the most human, most honourable race the world possesses.

　　To forward such a scheme what a splendid help a secret society would be a society not openly acknowledged but who would work in secret for such an object.... Let us form the same kind of society a Church for the extension of the British Empire. A society which should have members in every part of the British Empire working with one object and one idea we should have its members placed at our universities and our schools and should watch the English youth passing through their hands.... In every Colonial legislature the Society should attempt to have its members prepared at all times to vote or speak and advocate the closer union of England and the colonies, to crush all disloyalty and every movement for the severance of our Empire. The Society should inspire and even own portions of the press for the press rules the mind of the people.... For fear that death might cut me off before the time for attempting its development I leave all my worldly goods in trust to S. G. Shippard and the Secretary for the Colonies at the time of my death to try to form such a Society with such an object.[2]

Replacing 'despicable human beings' across Africa and elsewhere in the world with fine, upstanding Englishmen was Cecil Rhodes dream, as it had also been that of John Ruskin, who at Oxford in 1870 had advocated founding colonies everywhere as quickly as possible populated by such 'fine, upstanding Englishmen'.

When Rhodes' brother, Herbert, was killed in a shooting accident in 1879, Rhodes had vast amounts of money to devote to that dream when he later became chairman of De Beers which soon gained a virtual monopoly in the world diamond market. Rhodes took a seat in the Cape Parliament in 1881 and became prime minister nine years later. A deeply entrenched racist, he introduced legislation effectively blocking the native black Africans from voting. It was Rhodes, too, who in 1887 told the House of Assembly in Cape Town that:

> "The native is to be treated as a child and denied the franchise. We must adopt a system of despotism in our relations with the barbarians of South Africa." In less oratorical moments, he put it even more bluntly: "I prefer land to niggers."[3]

Greatly inspired by his time at Oxford, and the teachings of John Ruskin, Rhodes had been planning the secret society for more than seventeen years before introducing the concept to other British imperialists around 1889-90 and finally establishing it in London in 1891. Plagued by ill-health, Rhodes died from heart failure in 1902, aged 48, and left his wealth for the promotion of British imperialism. On his death, Alfred Milner took the reins of the secret society.

ALFRED MILNER (1854-1925)

A lfred Milner was in Egypt when the inaugural meeting of the secret society was held in February 1891, but joined it very soon thereafter. Born in Germany to middle-class English parents, Milner, a gifted scholarship student, studied Classics at Balliol College, Oxford, where he and his close friend, Arnold Toynbee, were hugely inspired by John Ruskin's imperial vision and calls for social reform. As willing students, both worked alongside Ruskin on one of his practical social experiments. Together with ten other students, including Oscar Wilde, they performed hard physical labour under Ruskin's direction to repair a road and sanitation at the  picturesque village of North Hinksey near Oxford. The road had become a rutted swamp, and posed a serious public health hazard to villagers. Milner and the others enjoyed the experience of hard physical labour and became devoted to Ruskin. The Hinksey road project, however, generated considerable cynicism and ridicule in the Press.

Milner graduated in 1877 with a first class in classics. Initially intent on a career in law, he opted instead for journalism and joined the *Pall Mall Gazette* as assistant editor. He worked under the inspirational editorship of Britain's most daring and innovative newspaperman of the age, William Thomas Stead, who was both a Radical Liberal *and* an ardent imperialist, a combination that would characterise Milner's future 'partner in crime,' Joseph Chamberlain. Milner worked under Stead as a journalist for three years (1881-1884) but never felt at ease in the profession. He stood as the Liberal candidate for Harrow in the 1885 general election for the Westminster parliament, but lost to the Conservatives, and after this defeat he turned away from party politics and espoused many of the teachings of Ruskin.

Milner was not of any political party himself and regarded party politics with disgust. ... Milner, in his distaste for party politics and for the parliamentary system, and in his emphasis on administration for social welfare, national unity, and imperial federation, was an early example of what James Burnham has called the "managerial revolution" – that is, the growth of a group of managers, behind the scenes and beyond the control of public opinion, who seek efficiently to obtain what they regard as good for the people. To a considerable extent this point of view became part of the ideology of the Milner Group ... Milner's own antipathy to democracy as practiced in the existing party and parliamentary system is obvious.[4]

In February 1884, Milner became private Secretary to the Chancellor of the Exchequer, George Goschen. In 1889, with Goschen's help he was appointed under-secretary of finance in British-occupied Egypt, remaining there for three years and gaining a reputation as a very exact and efficient financial administrator under the Consul-General, Lord Cromer (Evelyn Baring), before returning to London as chairman of the Board of Inland Revenue (1892-97). He was awarded a knighthood for his services. As a member of the Rhodes secret society, Milner was a regular weekend guest at the stately homes of Lord Rothschild, Lord Roseberry and other fellow members.

In 1897 Milner was appointed British High Commissioner for southern Africa and Governor of Cape Colony. He worked closely there with Cecil Rhodes.

The goals which Rhodes and Milner sought and the methods by which they hoped to achieve them were so similar by 1902 that the two are almost indistinguishable. Both sought to unite the world, and above all the English-speaking world, in a federal structure around Britain. Both felt that this goal could best be achieved by a secret band of men united to one another by devotion to the common cause and by personal loyalty to one another. Both felt that this band should pursue its goal by secret political and economic influence behind the scenes and by control of journalistic, educational, and propaganda agencies. Milner's intention to work for this goal, and to use Rhodes's money and influence to do it, is clearly implied in all his actions (both before and after 1902), in his correspondence with Rhodes ... [5]

Together, Milner and the Colonial Secretary Joseph Chamberlain deliberately instigated the Boer War of 1899-1902 to seize the vast wealth in the gold mines of the republics of the Transvaal and the Orange Free State. The Republics, and the numerous gold mines therein, were under the rule of Afrikaners – the white descendants of the Boers (farmers) of Dutch, French and German origin who had colonised Southern Africa from the 1650s onwards.

In the war against the Boers, 22,000 British soldiers died to bring what was then the world's richest gold-producing region under British control, and by the end of the war London had committed over 400,000 British troops in the struggle to do so. The vast wealth would be used to drive the Rhodes secret society's agenda. Some 25,000 Afrikaner farmers who took up arms against the British invasion were killed, and their farms and animals burned by the British in a scorched earth policy. Driven from their homes, the wives and children of the Boer soldiers were herded into British concentration camps as ordered by Sir Alfred Milner. An estimated 20,000 Boer women and children died from malnutrition and disease in the camps.[6] All the while, readily available food and medicines were withheld.[7] Tens of thousands of black Africans were subjected to the same fate. Rhodes and Milner ordered a 50 per cent reduction in the already meagre rations of children in the concentration camps if their fathers continued fighting against the British. The English journalist W. T. Stead (one of the first members of the Rhodes secret society, he resigned from it after falling out with Rhodes and Milner over the war in South Africa) wrote:

Source: Free State Archives Repository, VA 00000

FIGURE 1
Photograph of Lizzie van Zyl in the Bloemfontein camp, probably
a sufferer of typhoid

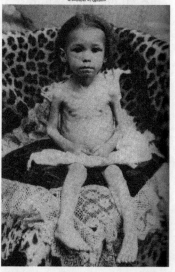

> Every one of those children who died as a result of the halving of their rations, thereby exerting pressure onto their family still on the battle-field, was purposefully murdered. The system of half-rations stands exposed, stark and unashamedly as a cold-blooded deed of state policy employed with the purpose of ensuring the surrender of men whom we were not able to defeat on the field.[8]

Presumably, the white Boer families were simply considered to be "despicable human beings" like the black Africans. Thousands of Boer children were effectively murdered, and Milner, as British High Commissioner, was morally responsible. For his part in securing the Boer gold fields for Britain, he was elevated to Viscount Milner in July 1902 by King Edward VII and sworn in as Governor of the captured Transvaal and Orange Free State. The Boers lost everything, including their gold mines. The mines had been put out of commission during the war but were now in British hands, and production could re-start. The problem however, was lack of labour. For every ten men working in the atrocious conditions in the mines one was killed, and the African labour force departed in droves. Journalist John Hamill wrote: "Human life was being sacrificed after a purgatory of toil and torture."[9] The labour problem was solved by shipping modern-day slaves from China.

> Milner and the mine owners were so desperate to augment the declining workforce that drastic measures were agreed. They looked to China, where there was a large source of surplus cheap labour. The Chinese were lured to the South African mines with false promises and outrageous lies. They were led to understand that they would be living in pleasant garden cities where, once settled, families might join them. Fit and healthy applicants were selected and kept in sheds until embarkation. Then, under armed guard, they were loaded into the holds of ships for the journey. The first ship to sail, the 3,400-ton iron-hulled SS *Ikbal*, left China on 30 June 1904 with over 2,000 men crammed in the hold like a classic eighteenth-century slave ship. It was mid-summer, with the temperature over 100 degrees Fahrenheit in the shade, as the *Ikbal* headed out on its 26-day voyage through the tropics. By the time it arrived in Durban, 51 men had died and their bodies dispatched overboard. The deaths proved no great loss to the organisers, however, for they had insured each man for $125 and netted a tidy profit from the insurance company. On arrival, the men were tagged like pieces of meat and sealed in railroad cars for the 30 hour journey to the Transvaal. The garden cities were a myth. In reality, the Chinese workers lived in hutted compounds beside the mines with 20 men in each small shack. They were unable to leave the compounds without a special permit and were fined for the slightest breach of rules. The men worked ten hours a day for a wage of twenty-five cents. In addition, they had to work at lower rates for at least six months to pay back the costs of their passage from China … Milner approved the

flogging of the Chinese workers as a necessary sanction.... It was an act of old-fashioned imperialism. Many who could not keep up with the backbreaking toil were in perpetual debt to the mines. If still alive after three years they were to be shipped back to China like spoiled returned goods. These Chinese were brought over in the prime of life to be broken on the wheel within three years for the purpose of grinding out ever greater profits for the monsters of greed who owned them.

Viscount Milner was well rewarded by his banking and industrialist friends for the tireless work he did to reinstate the mines and increase their profits. Within a year of his return to England in 1905 he was made a member of the board of the London Joint Stock Bank (later the Midland bank), a director, later chairman, of Rothschild's Rio Tinto Co., a director of the Mortgage Company of Egypt and of the Bank of British West Africa. So many lucrative posts were offered to him that he was forced to refuse, amongst others, a directorship of both *The Times* and the armaments giant, Armstrongs.[10]

From the time Alfred Milner became the undisputed leader of the secret society on Rhodes' death in 1902, Quigley re-named it "the Milner Group."

During his years in southern Africa as British High Commissioner, Milner built up a body of young assistants known in history as "Milner's Kindergarten."[11] Quigley names twenty-three members of the Kindergarten who would become members of the Association of Helpers of the secret society in the early years of the twentieth century. On their return from South Africa, they were slotted into leading roles in politics, academia, the diplomatic corps and journalism. Virtually all were graduates of Oxford University, with six becoming Fellows of All Souls College, including Geoffrey Dawson (Eton and All Souls, Oxford). As Milner's assistant, Dawson participated in the establishment of the new British administration in South Africa in the aftermath of the Boer War and became a member of Milner's Kindergarten.[12]

> As editor of *The Times* [for almost 30 years from 1912], Dawson was one of the most influential figures in England. He used that influence in the directions decided by the Group.[13]

Members of the secret society flitted about from one elite social event to another in their exclusive London clubs, Grillion's or The Club, and their great country houses and estates. Popular venues were Waldorf Astor's magnificent house and estate, Cliveden; Nathaniel Mayer ("Natty")

Rothschild's Tring Park with 3,600 acres in Hertfordshire, and Lord Robert Gascoyne Cecil's Jacobean Hatfield House, with its 40-acre garden and 2,000 acres of parkland. Each of these grand country estates was within 30 miles of central London.

All of the above-named individuals were members of the secret society, and over the years a steady flow of fresh blood was drawn from Oxford University via Balliol College and All Souls. With many of its members being Fellows of All Souls, the Milner Group was in a position to observe bright young students as potential recruits to its outer circles. Such young men would be promoted to leading positions in the civil service, the armed forces, the Church of England, newspapers and not least, politics.

Like their hero, John Ruskin, Alfred Milner and his group viewed party politics and the parliamentary system with disdain. With their men at the top in both the Conservative and Liberal Parties, they managed politics from behind the scenes and outside the arena of public opinion. Milner's antipathy to democracy as practised in the existing parliamentary system was manifest.

> To Milner and Curtis, and apparently to most members of the Group, democracy was not an unmixed good, or even a good, and far inferior to rule by the best, or, as Curtis says, by those who "have some intellectual capacity for judging the public interest."... The disdain for unrestricted democracy was quite in accordance with the ideas revealed by Milner's activities in South Africa and with the Greek ideals absorbed at Balliol or New College.[14]

Since the Milner Group had placemen in all of the major political parties, it was an illusion that the electorate was being offered a real 'choice' at general elections. The parties might vary to some degrees in their allocation of taxes, disbursement of benefits, spending on health services or the military etc., but continuity in foreign policy was sacrosanct no matter which party was in government. Quigley writes of the political situation in Britain where the Liberal Party was "merely one of two 'teams' put on the field by the same school for an intramural game."[15]

Another source of recruitment to the Milner Group was through the Rhodes Scholarships set up at Oxford and financed by money left in Cecil Rhodes' will for the purpose. Controlled by Alfred Milner between 1905 and 1925, these Scholarships were awarded to students from the United States and the British Commonwealth, with a few from Germany. According to Quigley:

The Rhodes Scholarships were merely a façade to conceal the secret society, or, more accurately, they were to be one of the instruments by which members of the secret society could carry out his [Rhodes'] purpose.'[16]

W. T. Stead (1849-1912)

A co-founder of the secret society with Rhodes and Reginal Baliol Brett (Lord Esher), William Thomas Stead (usually referred to as W.T. Stead) was a campaigning journalist – the most famous journalist of the day according to Quigley[17] – and editor of the influential London evening newspaper, the *Pall Mall Gazette*. A man of some compassion, Stead campaigned against the evils of poverty, vice, inhumanity and war. He opposed the secret society's instigation of the Boer War and would turn his back on it over its responsibility for the deaths of tens of thousands of women and children in British concentration camps. Stead drowned in 1912 on the *Titanic*.

Lord Esher (1852-1930)

Lord Esher played an extremely important role in the Milner Group's inner circle as its close linkman with the British royal family. An upper-class courtier, diplomat and politician, he was an intimate friend and *éminence grise* of Queen Victoria. In the years after the Queen's death in 1901, he remained extremely close to the new monarch, her son King Edward VII. Esher had the complete confidence of the monarchy and was its chief political adviser over a period of more than twenty-five years. He wrote almost daily letters of advice to King Edward throughout his reign from 1901 until his death in 1910.[18] Quigley does not list the king as a member of the secret society, but he most certainly knew everything about it through Esher and through the fact that virtually all of its leading members were his personal friends. As becomes clear in due course, King Edward played a hugely important role for the Rhodes-Milner Group in drawing the United States into a close friendship with Britain, and in creating the 'Ententes' (informal alliances) with erstwhile enemies, France and Russia.

LORD SALISBURY (ROBERT ARTHUR TALBOT GASCOYNE CECIL) (1830-1903)

Cecil was educated at Eton and Oxford, was a Fellow of All Souls College, Oxford, and Chancellor of Oxford University. The wider Cecil clan comprised many and varied members of the English ruling class who have held immense power. The Cecils served Queen Elizabeth I (1558-1603) and King James I (1603-1625), and would later serve Queen Victoria and King Edward VII. Indeed, they have been at the heart of the British establishment for over 400 years. Quigley writes:

> The Milner Group could never have been built up by Milner's own efforts. He had no political power or even influence. All that he had was ability and ideas. The same thing is true about many of the other members of the Milner Group, at least at the time that they joined that Group. The power that was utilized was the power of the Cecil family and its allied families.... The Milner Group was originally a major fief within the great nexus of power, influence, and privilege controlled by the Cecil family. It is not possible here to describe the ramifications of the Cecil influence. It has been all-pervasive in British life since 1886. This Cecil Bloc was built up by Robert Arthur Talbot Gascoyne-Cecil, third Marquess of Salisbury (1830-1903). The methods used by this man were merely copied by the Milner Group. These methods can be summed up under three headings: (a) a triple-front penetration in politics, education, and journalism; (b) the recruitment of men of ability (chiefly from All Souls) and the linking of these men to the Ceil Bloc by matrimonial alliances and by gratitude for titles and positions of power; and (c) the influencing of public policy by placing members of the Cecil Bloc in positions of power shielded as much as possible from public attention.[19]

Lord Salisbury had been prime minster three times over a period of fourteen years between 1885 and 1902. He also acted as Foreign Secretary and practised a policy of "splendid isolation" keeping Britain free of any alliance ties. In failing health, Salisbury resigned as prime minister in 1902 and was replaced by his sister's son, Arthur Balfour, he of the famous

"Balfour Declaration" that awarded Palestine to the Zionists in November 1917 and was addressed to Lord Walter Rothschild, head of the Zionist Federation at the time.

Quigley describes how Lord Salisbury practised shameless nepotism:

> The degree to which Lord Salisbury practiced nepotism can be seen by a look at his third government (1895-1902) or its successor, Balfour's first government (1902 -1905). The Balfour government was nothing but a continuation of Salisbury's government, since Balfour was Salisbury's nephew and chief assistant and was made premier in 1902 by his uncle. Salisbury was Prime Minister and Foreign Secretary; Balfour was first Lord of the Treasury and Party Leader in the Commons (1895 -1902); his brother, Gerald Balfour, was Chief Secretary for Ireland and President of the Board of Trade; their cousin-in-law Lord Selborne was Under Secretary for the Colonies (1895-1900) and First Lord of The Admiralty (1905-1910) ... [20]

And through intermarriage, the "Cecil Bloc" (as Quigley names it) was connected to many of the other leading players in English high society. It was intimately linked to All Souls College, a premier research college for postgraduates, which dates from 1437. Fellows of All Souls were the incumbents of professorial chairs at Oxford, including the Chairs of International Law, Modern History, Economic History, Social and Political Theory, the History of War, the Regius Chair of Civil Law, English Law, and others.[21] With their control of All Souls, and devotion to the teachings of John Ruskin, Oxford University was the spiritual home of the secret society, and could be called 'the spiritual centre' of the British Empire from the 1880s until at least the end of the Second World War.

Caroll Quigley devotes several pages to naming many high-ranking connections of Gascoyne-Cecil, including Lord Midleton, the Earl of Wemyss, Viscount Cranborne, Lord Long, Lord Curzon, the Marquess of Hartingdon, the Duke of Devonshire, Lord Lansdowne, Baron Lyttelton. "Most of these persons were related by numerous family and marital connections" which formed the background of the Milner Group.[22] Connections through marriage to the Cecils included leading British politicians, such as Herbert Henry Asquith and Sir Edward Grey. Asquith attended Balliol College, Oxford, and served as British prime minister 1908-1916. Sir Edward Grey (later Viscount Grey of Falloden) also attended Oxford. He served as the Secretary of State for Foreign Affairs 1905-1916 and later as ambassador to the United States. Later, we shall see how Asquith and Grey played major roles in taking Britain to war in 1914.

WALDORF ASTOR, (1879-1952).

A later addition to the secret society's Society of the Elect, Astor was a scion of the fabulously wealthy American Astor clan. Born in the USA, his parents moved to Britain in 1891 and took British citizenship. Waldorf was educated at Eton and Oxford, became a member of parliament, and was war-time Prime Minister Lloyd George's parliamentary secretary. In 1922 he bought the hugely influential *Times* newspaper. His American wife Nancy – Viscountess Astor – likewise became a member of the secret society's inner circle.[23] Nancy stood for parliament and became the first woman to sit as an MP in the House of Commons. When Nancy and Waldorf married in 1906, wedding presents from Astor's father included the world famous Sancy diamond and Cliveden, a grand country house and estate on the banks of the Thames in Buckinghamshire. In later chapters we see how Cliveden would become a frequent meeting place for secret society members in the inter-war years. They came to be known as "The Cliveden Set" and, as we shall see, would play a major role in appeasing Hitler and the Nazis in the 1930s.

LORD NATHANIEL ROTHSCHILD. (1840-1915)

Nathaniel (Natty) Rothschild, owner of the N. M. Rothschild bank in the City, and he and his cousin, Baron Edouard de Rothschild of de Rothschild Frères bank in Paris, were by far the richest men in the world, controlling massive swathes of global investment, and compliant monarchs, politicians and governments. The bankers held power – real power – and according to Carroll Quigley; the Rothschilds were the kings of the banking world. Rothschild financed Wellington's campaign in 1815 that led to final victory at Waterloo. The official Rothschild Archives website relates:

> Between 1793 and 1815, Britain was almost continuously at war with France, placing a huge burden on the British Exchequer. By 1813, Wellington's armies had succeeded in driving the French back to the Pyrenees, but the financial situation had become critical. Wellington desperately needed gold and silver coins, which

could be exchanged locally to pay and feed his troops and so sustain morale. J.C. Herries, the Commissary in Chief to the British government, was responsible for financing and equipping the British armies in the field. Herries sought an intermediary who could secretly obtain large amounts of gold, but without alerting the French. In January 1814, he formally engaged Nathan Mayer Rothschild. Over the previous five years, Nathan had built an extensive network of couriers, dealers, brokers and bankers to facilitate his trading activities in gold. In the process, he established a commanding position as a bullion broker in the City of London. On receiving the commission from Herries, Nathan instructed his brothers on the continent to buy gold wherever they could, secretly and in small quantities, so as not to disturb the market. Once amassed, the gold was shipped and conveyed to Wellington in southern France, enabling him to pay his troops. In 1815, following Napoleon's escape from Elba, the need for finance for Wellington's armies arose once more. Nathan was again successful in meeting the demand, raising immense sums of money in a short space of time and proposing that bullion be melted down to compensate for the shortage of coins. Drawing on finance raised by the Rothschilds, Wellington was able to pay the 209,000 English, Dutch and Prussian soldiers that had assembled in Belgium and subsequently defeated Napoleon at Waterloo.[24]

The biographers of the House of Rothschild record that men of influence and statesmen in almost every country in the world were in their pay. Some statesmen had the privilege of writing checks on the Rothschild bank at their own estimate of the value of their services ... A large part of the profligate nobility of all Europe was deeply indebted to them.[25]

Natty Rothschild was a founding member of the secret society and in its inner core, the Society of the Elect.[26] Educated at Trinity College, Cambridge, he was a good friend of fellow student, the Prince of Wales – the future King Edward VII. Natty was the great-grandson of the German-born Meyer Amschel Rothschild who famously financed the merchant banks of his five sons in Frankfurt, London, Paris, Naples, and Vienna. Operating in close collaboration, the brothers would go on to create the greatest banking dynasty in history. Carroll Quigley writes:

The merchant bankers of London ... were able to influence, if not control, governments on one side and industries on the other. The men who did this, looking backward toward the period of dynastic monarchy in which they had their own roots, aspired to establish dynasties of international bankers and were at least as successful at this as were many of the dynastic political rulers.

The greatest of these dynasties, of course, were the descendants of Meyer Amschel Rothschild (1743-1812) of Frankfort [sic], whose male descendants for at least two generations, generally married first cousins or even nieces.

...They became fully involved in domestic industry by the emergence of financial capitalism ... they were cosmopolitan and international; they were close to governments and were particularly concerned with questions of government debts.... They were almost equally devoted to secrecy and the secret use of financial influence in political life.... The influence of financial capitalism and of the international bankers who created it was exercised both on business and on governments.... Both of these were based on the assumption that politicians were too weak and too subject to temporary popular pressures to be trusted with control of the money system: accordingly, the sanctity of all values and the soundness of money must be protected in two ways: by basing the value of money on gold and by allowing bankers to control the supply of money. To do this it was necessary to conceal, or even to mislead, both governments and people about the nature of money and its methods of operation.[27]

Thus, the Rothschilds became immensely powerful across the globe. Nominally independent, their five European banks arranged many transactions together, and through frequent correspondence shared political and economic intelligence practically on a daily basis.[28]

Official Rothschild biographer, Professor Niall Ferguson, relates that Meyer Amschel Rothschild advised his five sons always to work in unity. If they could not make themselves loved they should make themselves feared. Strict intermarriage with cousins kept their wealth in the family, and with cross-border capital flows between the brothers acting together in big transactions and by pooling profits, the Rothschilds formed the biggest bank in the world – ten times the size of their nearest rivals. They became the richest people in the world; indeed, the richest family in all history. Other Jews came to regard them as a kind of Hebrew royal family: the "Kings of the Jews" as well as the "Jews of the Kings."[29] Within a few decades royal dynasties throughout Europe – including the British royal family – were beholden to them:

Lionel Rothschild [Natty's father] promoted family interests by befriending Queen Victoria's husband, Prince Albert, whose chronic shortage of money provided easy access to his patronage. The Rothschilds bought shares for Albert through an intermediary, and in 1851 Lionel 'loaned' Queen Victoria and her consort sufficient funds to purchase the lease on Balmoral castle and its 10,000 acres ... The inevitable progress of the London Rothschilds towards the pinnacle of British society was reflected in Natty's elevation to the peerage in 1885, by which time both he and his family had become an integral part of the Prince of Wales's social entourage. Encouraged by their 'generosity,' the prince lived well beyond his allowance from the Civil List, and Natty and his brothers, Alfred and Leo, maintained the family tradition of gifting loans to royalty. Indeed, from the mid-1870s onwards they covered the heir to the throne's massive gambling debts and ensured that he was accustomed to a standard of luxury well beyond his means. Their 'gift' of the £160,000 mortgage (approximately £11.8 million in 2013) for Sandringham "was discretely hushed up." Thus, both the great estates of Balmoral and Sandringham, so intimately associated with the British royal family, were facilitated, if not entirely paid for, through the largess of the House of Rothschild.[30]

Professor Ferguson writes that the Rothschilds likewise made a practice of "plying politically powerful individuals with gifts, loans, investment tips and outright bribes."[31] Politicians of every political persuasion were bankrolled, including Lord Randolph Churchill.

The father of Winston Churchill was an intimate of the Rothschild family. He formed a close association with Nathaniel [Natty], 1st Lord Rothschild, on whose behalf he reported on the development of the mining industry in South Africa. Churchill was a frequent guest at Rothschild houses. The Rothschilds made extensive loans to Churchill.[32]

When Lord Randolph Churchill died from syphilis in 1895 at the age of 45, he owed the Rothschilds £66,902.[33] It was a debt equating to around £8 million in 2023. Bankrolling Churchill's hugely extravagant lifestyle to such an extent appears an incredible act of generosity by his Rothschild friends, but there was always a quid pro quo – a favour for a favour. Through Churchill's political actions, the Rothschilds got back far more money than they gave him. In 1886, when he was the British Secretary of State for India, Churchill annexed Burma. The Rothschilds were then able to profit through a hugely successful Burma Ruby Mines share issue, and share issues in Burmese railways.[34]

In London, Natty provided the money to influence numerous leading politicians and the royal family, while in Paris, cousin Edouard provided the funds to corrupt French politics. In later chapters, we see how they ensured that politicians who favoured war against Germany attained high office in France. They controlled politicians through the power of money, showering them with "gifts, loans, investment tips and outright bribes," but they held another form of power over them; the power of knowledge. Devoted to secrecy, the Rothschilds employed hundreds of secret agents and operated the best intelligence agency in the world. Before the days of electronic communications, they used carrier pigeons and had couriers with fresh horses available. Fast boats were on constant standby at channel ports to ensure the speediest transfer of important information from continental Europe to London.

> Their uniquely fast communications networks – which relied principally on private couriers to-ing and fro-ing with copies of letters – was now also being used by the leading statesmen of the continent as an express postal service. This gave the family one form of power: knowledge. … Needless to say, the messengers could subtly alter the messages along the way; or the news could be acted upon in the stock exchanges before being passed on.[35]

Professor Rainer Liedtke of Regensburg University in Bavaria writes:

> Information – fast, and in particular, reliable information – was and is the key to decision-making in the financial world … At the time of the rapid rise of the Rothschilds from around 1820, the agents' network enlarged enormously … This was the time when the Rothschilds became a truly pan-European and, to an extent, global financial force. Agents were placed in locations which were central to certain businesses, usually ports, but also in political decision-making centres of which there were many…. When merchant houses of Western Europe developed into fully fledged private banks from the late eighteenth century onwards, they also turned towards financing states and governments, which emphasised the need for consistent and reliable political intelligence. This … was exemplified by the leading banking dynasty of the age, the Rothschilds. Two key factors helped agents in obtaining it: First, access to politicians and business people of rank. Although many agents were of rather humble origin themselves, the fact that they represented the most important bankers of their time virtually guaranteed them the attention of the highest levels of society in

their various locations. That included the relevant government officials and sometimes even the rulers themselves. Second, the Rothschilds and their agents assumed, as did everybody in business and finance at the time, that especially ministerial personnel divulged important information or favoured one with state business. Yet it came at a price, for bribes were expected and freely given. Rare exceptions to that rule were duly noted.[36]

Rothschild influence extended beyond mere individuals. The creation of Belgium and Greece as new states was underwritten by finance in the form of loans floated by the Rothschilds.[37] In 1875, they provided the advance loan that enabled Britain to acquire a substantial shareholding in the Suez Canal.[38] Globally, the dynasty had massive investments in railroads, armaments companies, and gold, diamond, nickel, and ruby mines. As we have seen, they were the financial power behind Cecil Rhodes' diamond activities in South Africa, and gold mines there. The official Rothschild Archives relate that in 1887 Rhodes visited London and secured Rothschild backing for taking control of the diamond industry in South Africa, and for De Beers. "Support for Rhodes had been encouraged by Randolph Churchill, who had been acting as consultant to Rothschilds, assessing the prospects of gold and diamond mining in South Africa."[39]

PHILIP KERR, LATER 11TH MARQUESS OF LOTHIAN (1882-1940)

Born in London, Philip Kerr, was the son of Major-General Ralph Kerr and Lady Anne Fitzalan-Howard, daughter of the Duke of Norfolk, who was the head of England's premier, non-royal, aristocratic family, which traces its line back to King Edward I in the 13th century.

Kerr studied Modern History at New College, Oxford, where because of his narcissism he was known as 'Narcissus,' before going to South Afri-

ca with the Colonial Office and becoming part of 'Milner's Kindergarten'. He joined the inner sanctum of the secret society as one of Milner's leading protégés. Kerr was appointed prime minister David Lloyd George's private secretary during the First World War and was a prominent player for the secret society at the Paris Peace Conference at Versailles. Repeatedly calling for a 'World State,' he would go on to lead the Milner Group when Milner died in 1925. Together with his close colleague Lionel Curtis, Kerr played an important role in forming Round Table groups across the world and editing the group's journal *Round Table* journal and leading the Royal Institute of International Affairs (Chatham House). In September 1939, Kerr became UK ambassador to the United States and for the last year of his life strongly urged the US to join the war on Britain's side.

Other members of the inner core of the secret society included:

Sir Abraham (Abe) Bailey, A massively wealthy South African mining magnate and financier, Bailey was a friend of Cecil Rhodes and Alfred Milner, and made substantial financial contributions to the secret society. Bailey's son, Sir John Milner Bailey, married Winston Churchill's eldest daughter, Diana.

Alfred Beit, another hugely wealthy South African gold and diamond magnate and friend and early financial backer of Rhodes.

Archibald Primrose, Earl of Rosebery. Eton and Oxford. Liberal MP, Secretary of State for Foreign Affairs 1892-94, British prime minister 1894-95.

Geoffrey Dawson, editor of *The Times* for almost 30 years, and a close friend of Milner's.

Arthur James Balfour (Lord Balfour), British Prime Minister 1902-1905, godson of the Duke of Wellington, nephew of Lord Salisbury, and as Foreign Secretary, the issuer of the 'Balfour Declaration'. The Balfour Declaration ought really to be called the Milner Declaration as it was Milner and his acolyte Leo S. Amery who drafted it. Balfour merely signed it.

Herbert A. L Fisher, Oxford educated historian, Vice-Chancellor of Sheffield University, Liberal MP and President of the Board of Education. Trustee of the Rhodes Foundation.

Lionel Curtis, read law at New College, Oxford. Fellow of All Souls. Another strong proponent of World Government. Founding member of the secret society's Royal Institute for International Affairs (Chatham House) which would drive their policies. With Philip Kerr, the co-chief architect of the British Commonwealth of Nations.

Robert Henry Brand, (1st Baron Brand) New College, Oxford and All Souls, Oxford. Worked with Milner's Civil Service in South Africa, and member of Milner's Kindergarten. Director of Lazard Brothers Bank and Lloyds Bank. Established the Imperial Munitions Board in the First World War.

The above named were but a few of the major players in the Rhodes-Milner secret organisation. Carroll Quigley names several hundred others in the Association of Helpers.

Another important organisation that would drive forward the Group's agenda was the Rhodes Scholarship scheme at Oxford University. Rhodes left money in his will to fund it and Lord Rothschild, who administered Rhodes estate, helped set it up. Quigley writes:

> The scholarships were merely a façade to conceal the secret society, or, more accurately, they were to be one of the instruments by which the members of the secret society could carry out his [Rhodes] purpose. This purpose, as expressed in his first will (1877) was: The extension of British rule throughout the world and the ultimate recovery of the United States of America as an integral part of the British Empire.[40]

Oxford, the oldest university in the English-speaking world, dates back beyond 1167 and long recognised as one of the world's leading academic institutions. The secret society's massive influence at the university is highlighted by Carroll Quigley. In *The Anglo-American Establishment*, he devotes an entire chapter to their control of Oxford, particularly All Souls College:

> All Souls, in fact, became the chief recruiting agency for the Milner Group. The inner circle of this Group, because of its close contact with Oxford and with All Souls, was in a position to notice able young undergraduates at Oxford. These were admitted to All Souls and at once given opportunities in public life and in writing or teaching to test their abilities and loyalty to the ideals of the Milner Group. If they passed both of these tests, they were gradually introduced to the Milner Groups great fiefs such as the Royal Institute for International Affairs, *The Times*, *The Round Table*, or, on the larger scene, to the ranks of the Foreign or Colonial Office.[41]

The Milner Group's influence over Oxford enabled their penetration of education, and that in turn enabled them to control the writing and teaching of history. Before the First World War, professorial chairs in modern history and the history of war were created and funded by the Milner Group. Compliant academics – usually with previous or current links to the university – were then carefully chosen to lead these new departments, and touted as the greatest historians in Britain. Woe betide any academics from lesser institutions who challenged their accounts of the First World War.

Another Oxford academic used by the Group was the geographer and explorer, Halford Mackinder. A good friend of Milner's, in 1903 he was appointed director of the London School of Economics (LSE). Mackinder delivered a lecture to the Royal Geographical Society in 1904 that would have great relevance to future Anglo-American strategic policy. In his lecture, 'The Geographical Pivot of History,' Mackinder spoke of the future importance of Eurasia in the balance of global power. He believed that as long as Russia's trans-Siberian railway remained a single and precarious line, it presented no great opportunity for development and growth. It would not be long, however, before all of Asia was criss-crossed with railways and would become the powerhouse of the world:

> The spaces within the Russian Empire and Mongolia are so vast, and their potentialities in population, wheat, cotton, fuel and metals so incalculably great, that it is inevitable that a vast economic world, more or less apart, will there develop inaccessible to ocean commerce. As we consider this rapid review of the broader currents of history, does not a certain persistence of geographical relationship become evident? Is not the pivot region of the world's politics that vast area of Euro-Asia which is inaccessible to ships, but in antiquity lay open to the horse-riding nomads, and is to-day about to be covered with a network of railways?[42]

Mackinder believed that whoever controlled the Eurasian heartland would control the world. The gateway to the heartland was Eastern Europe, and should Germany or Russia, or both working together, gain control of Eastern Europe in the foreseeable future, they would control the gateway to the Eurasian heartland and its massive resources. No matter how great the navies of Britain and America were, the heartland would be inaccessible to them, rendering their naval power useless. If Germany and or Russia came to control the Eurasian heartland, *they* would control the world, not Britain.

Some commentators believe that Mackinder's "Pivot" theory drove the Milner Group to plan a destructive war against Germany. Such a plan, however, goes back a number of years before Mackinder presented his thoughts. From its inception in 1891, the Rhodes/Milner Group was painfully aware that should Germany and Russia ever combine in a strong alliance, the prospect of global control by the English-speaking powers was doomed. For centuries, the British Empire's *modus operandi* had been divide and rule, and it was no different now. At all costs, Germany and Russia had to be kept apart.

The influence of the Milner Group in Britain, and as will be seen in due course, also in the United States of America, was massive and all-encompassing. The Group developed very close links with the U.S. in line with Cecil Rhodes' vision, and exerted enormous influence there. In the 1960s, Quigley wrote in *Tragedy & Hope*:

> The American branch of this organization (sometimes called the "Eastern Establishment") has played a very significant role in the history of the United States in the last generation.[43]

When Alfred Milner permanently returned to London from South Africa, he played a major role in forming the "special relationship" that exists between Britain and the U.S. to the present day. Through constant metamorphosis, the small group that met in London in 1891 developed into an immensely powerful Anglo-American financial and political network that, as Quigley states, became the most important factor in the twentieth century. It operated beyond democratic accountability and exerted enormous control over politics in Britain and the U.S. International bankers – based primarily in London (the City), and New York (Wall Street) – became ever more influential in the Milner Group. In the next chapter we see how, through their control of the central banks in Britain and the U.S. and through their influence on political and monetary policy, they were able to direct and harmonise British and U.S. foreign policy.

SUMMARY: CHAPTER 2 – THE SOCIETY OF THE ELECT

- Cecil Rhodes, founder of the secret society, willed his vast fortune to be used to promote its aims.

- Rhodes, his friend, Sir Alfred Milner, colonial administrator, and Colonial Minster Joseph Chamberlain, Rhodes' collaborator, bore significant responsibility for the Second Boer War of 1899-1902, and the concentration camps in which tens of thousands died.

- When Rhodes died in 1902, Alfred Milner became leader of the secret society.

- Lord Esher was a member of the society's inner-circle and kept King Edward VII fully updated on its activities.

- A significant number of the richest men in the world were members of the secret society, including Nathaniel Rothschild.

- New members were recruited through All-Souls College, Oxford, Milner's 'Kindergarten' in South Africa, and the Rhodes Scholarships at Oxford.

CHAPTER 3

THE "SPECIAL RELATIONSHIP"

Queen Victoria reigned over the vast British empire from 1837 to 1901, and relations between Britain and Germany were mostly cordial and relaxed thanks to strong family ties between the British and German royal families. Victoria was born in 1819, and her four grandparents had German ancestry embedded in their DNA. Her father, the Duke of Kent, descended from the House of Hanover, and her mother was a German Princess of Saxe-Coburg-Saalfeld. When Victoria's uncle, King William IV, died in 1837 without legitimate heirs (he had 10 illegitimate children), she became queen of the United Kingdom at the age of 18. In 1840 she married her German cousin, Prince Albert, son of Ernst, Duke of Saxe-Coburg and Gotha. Victoria had proposed marriage to him on only their second meeting when she was 20 years old.

Queen Victoria and Prince Albert had ten children. Their first, Victoria Adelaide, (born 1840 and known in the family as Vicky) married Prince Frederick of Prussia when she was 17 and in due course became the German empress and Queen of Prussia. Vicky and Frederick's eldest son (Queen Victoria's first grandchild) was the future German emperor, Wilhelm II. Born in 1859 and christened Friedrich Wilhelm Victor Albert, he was known in the family as "Willy." At the time of his birth, Willy was sixth in line of succession to the British throne. After 1871 he was second in line to rule over the newly-created Germany.

Queen Victoria spoke of Willy as "A clever, dear, good little child, the great favourite of my beloved Angel Vicky."[1] She was not so complimentary about her own first son, Albert Edward. Born in 1841 and known in the family as "Bertie," he would become King Edward VII on her death. By his late teens Bertie had upset and angered Victoria and Albert with his gambling, alcohol consumption, and trysts with married women. Prince Albert died in 1861 aged 42, just

Bertie

weeks after going up to Cambridge University to chastise Bertie about his behaviour. The distraught Queen blamed Bertie for his father's death, and said of him: "I never can or shall look at him without a shudder."[2] The Queen would later tell Bertie's sister:

> What will become of the poor country when I die? I foresee, if Bertie succeeds, nothing but misery – for he never reflects or listens for a moment and he [would] spend his life in one whirl of amusements as he does now. It makes me very sad and angry.[3]

Queen Victoria had a much better relationship with her grandson, Willy. When his father, Frederick III, died from throat cancer less than four months into his reign in 1888, Willy ascended the throne as Kaiser Wilhelm II. Uncle Bertie had little time for him. His nephew was now an Emperor with considerable power and adored by Queen Victoria, while he remained a mere prince and was disliked by her.

Wilhelm II

Kaiser Wilhelm made regular trips from Germany to visit his grandmother at Buckingham Palace or her residence on the Isle of Wight. Most summers he competed against his uncle Bertie in their racing yachts at the annual Cowes regatta. A frosty atmosphere and bad blood existed between the two, especially after 1896 when the Kaiser's yacht *Meteor II* beat Bertie's *Britannia*. Stories later emerged that after the race and being rowed ashore to the clubhouse, Bertie punched the Kaiser in the mouth when he teased him about winning. Irrespective of the veracity of the story, the future King Edward hated the Kaiser.

As Prince of Wales, Bertie spent massive amounts of money well beyond his means. He travelled far and wide across the world, including an eight-month tour of India and Nepal, (October 1875-May 1876) shooting hundreds of tigers and elephants. His Danish wife, Princess Alexandra, had long dreamed of visiting India but was left at home. She found solace in a 'platonic' relationship with equerry, Oliver Montague.

Bertie placed huge bets on horses and gambled heavily at cards. He drank copious quantities of the world's most expensive wines and champagnes virtually every day, and enjoyed seven course dinners each evening. Never having to work for a living, he had plenty of time and energy for sex with some of the most beautiful women in the world. With his charm, status, and apparent massive spending power, many females threw themselves at him. His extra-marital affairs included Winston Churchill's mother, Lady Randolph Churchill, and the famous actress, Lillie Langtry. Addicted to sex, Bertie regularly criss-crossed the English Channel to Paris where he frequented upper-class brothels.

His favourite haunt – both as Prince of Wales and King – was the high-class brothel, Le Chabanais, in Paris. It served cordon bleu meals, superb wines and champagne, and offered a wide choice of attractive women. Bertie retained his own suite at Le Chabanais and had it furnished with a massive bed, stirrups and saddles for sex games, and the now-famous *fauteuil d'amour* 'chair of love'. The bespoke contraption allowed him to indulge one of his sexual fantasies: sex with two women simultaneously.[4] For his further pleasure, the enormous bathtub in his suite was filled with champagne for bathing with women.[5]

Bertie also made regular visits to Longchamp racecourse, placing huge bets on the Prix de l'Arc de Triomphe and other big races. He was often in the casino at Monte Carlo gambling large sums on baccarat and roulette. Between sex at Chabanais and gambling at Longchamp and Monte Carlo, he was spending vast sums of money that his royal allowance came nowhere near covering. How? Professor Niall Ferguson writes:

> At Cambridge in 1861, Natty [Rothschild] was introduced to the Prince of Wales (the future Edward VII) by the Duke of St Albans. A common enthusiasm for hunting in turn led to introductions for Alfred and Leo [Rothschild] … An ardent Francophile, he was a regular Rothschild guest on the other side of the Channel too. Such contacts did not cease on his accession to the throne – rather the reverse. Members of the Rothschild family were an integral part of Edward VII's cosmopolitan social circle. … It was well known that the Prince of Wales and his brothers were inclined to live beyond their allowances provided by the Civil List. Keeping up the family tradition of lending to future rulers, Anthony [Rothschild] offered his assistance and by August 1874 the Queen was alarmed to hear of a large sum owing to de Rothschild by her eldest son. However, the Rothschilds' role between then and his accession twenty-seven long years later seems primarily to have been to keep the prince out of debt, aside from a £160,000 mortgage on Sandringham which was discreetly hushed up…. The key to the Rothschild attitude was that, as the nearest thing the Jews of Europe had to a royal family, they considered themselves the equals of royalty.[6]

On January 22, 1901, Queen Victoria breathed her last in the arms of her grandson, Kaiser Wilhelm.[7] During the last years of her reign, Anglo-German relations had soured when Germany provided the Transvaal with capital and technical expertise to counter British influence there. With German assistance, a railway was built linking Pretoria with Delagoa Bay giving the Boers independent access to the Indian Ocean. In December 1895, when the British planned to provoke an uprising of British immigrants – 'Uitlanders' as the Boers called them – in Johannesburg, Cecil Rhodes's close friend Leander Starr Jameson, military commander of the British South Africa Company, launched an armed raid to support the uprising. The British plan to seize the Boer republic failed miserably and embarrassingly when Jameson was captured by the Boers. Kaiser Wilhelm sent a telegram to Boer leader, Paul Kruger, expressing his sincere congratulations for thwarting "armed bands which invaded your country as disturbers of the peace" and "safeguarding the independence of the country against attacks from outside."[8]

British press blew up a fake crisis over the Kaiser's telegram and from that point in time, the anti-German rhetoric would be ramped up in Britian. When Edward took the throne on his mother's death in 1901, he loathed Germany generally and his nephew, Wilhelm, in particular. His Germanophobia was doubtless due in part to the sway of his wife, Princess Alexandra of Denmark.

> She developed an almost paranoid hatred of Germany after Denmark lost the disputed territories of Schleswig-Holstein to Prussia in 1864.... She loathed all Germans in general and Wilhelm in particular ... Edward's subsequent actions clearly indicated that he shared his wife's obsessive and venomous hatred of Germany.[9]

As Prince of Wales and as King, Bertie was closely linked to the Rhodes-Milner Group thanks to good friends, including Lord Esher and Lord Natty Rothschild. We have seen previously how they were important members of the society's inner circle. The Rothschilds were "an integral part of Edward VII's social circle,"[10] and from his early days as Prince of Wales, he was able to rely on them to fund his gross and beyond extravagant lifestyle.

American author, Peter Hof writes:

> After a record-setting reign of 63 years, Queen Victoria passed away on January 22, 1901, and her eldest son, Bertie, having served

the longest apprenticeship in history as Prince of Wales, was officially crowned King Edward VII on August 9, 1902. He was a womanizer, glutton, fat, balding, obsessed with uniforms and decorations, and sixty years old …. The new King let it be known early on and in no uncertain terms that he was not to be regarded as a mere figurehead and automatic rubber stamp for cabinet decisions, but intended to be a full and active participant in the nation's affairs – especially foreign affairs. Certainly, the King had opinions on domestic affairs. He was opposed to Irish home rule; opposed to women's suffrage: opposed to reform of the House of Lords; opposed to ending the Boer War; opposed to ending Kitchener's scorched earth tactics against the Boers, but it was in the realm of foreign affairs and the creation of the Triple Entente – his signature achievement – by which the King reserved top honors for himself in the annals of royal posterity.[11]

Edward VII was fluent in both French and German, and conversed in an easy, friendly, manner with leading statesmen across Europe. He was now the British monarch, but the right to make and pass legislation resided with the elected government. Constitutionally, he could undertake representational duties at home and abroad, but in no more than a symbolic role. Working closely with, if not indeed for, the men of High Finance, however, Edward pulled political strings and travelled abroad as the de facto Foreign Office Minister.

With frequent updates from his friends Lords Rothschild and Esher, the king was undoubtedly intimately acquainted with, and entirely sympathetic to, the aims of the Society of the Elect. He ruled over a large empire, and his rich and powerful friends wanted to enlarge it even further. What was there for him not to like? As an imperial and industrial competitor, Germany had to be kept apart from Russia and taken down if those two countries were to be prevented from controlling eastern Europe and the gateway to Eurasia. King Edward gave the project his full support and played a major role in preparing the ground for it. He would devote his energies – some of them – to bringing France and Russia into line with the plan to crush Germany. The first priority, however, was to promote a close relationship with the Americans, for the Milner Group "hoped to bring the United States into this organization to whatever degree was possible."[12]

The Group was painfully aware that not for much longer would Britain be able to maintain her position as *the* global superpower. World power would have to be shared, and who better to share it with than their Anglophone cousins in the United States as in Cecil Rhodes' dream? Rhodes' concept of 'English race supremacy' had only to be adjusted slightly to 'Anglo-Saxon' supremacy. Power would initially be shared but when the time came, as the English elites knew it surely would, it would be transferred across the Atlantic. Thus the strong bond that already existed between Britain and the United States was cemented in the early years of the twentieth century by none other than King Edward VII. On 6 September 1901, just eight months after Edward's accession, U.S. President William McKinley was shot in Buffalo, New York State. When he died eight days later, vice-president Theodore Roosevelt stepped into the White House. When the king approached him through trusted intermediaries, Roosevelt immediately grasped the hand of a brother freemason and fellow Germanophobe. As Prince of Wales, Edward was a stickler for correct ceremonial and an enthusiastic Freemason. He had been Grand Master of English Freemasonry throughout the world since 1874 and had only stepped down from that role because he had become king. Instead, he became "Grand Protector of the Order."[13]

As far as Roosevelt was concerned, U.S. and British interests were identical in all strategic areas of the world, and he would cooperate closely with Britain once a few contentious matters were ironed out. They included American 'right' to the Panama Canal and disputes over Newfoundland fisheries. Professor David Fromkin of Boston University writes:

> Once these and other issues were resolved, President Roosevelt would be in a position to create the entente partnership with the British Empire in world affairs that would realize what we now believe to have been his imperial vision: *dominance of the world by the English-speaking peoples.* That vision was reciprocated. "I entirely agree with you" King Edward wrote the President, "and I look forward with confidence to the co-operation of the English-speaking races becoming the most powerful civilising factor in the policy of the world." Having identical global interests, America and Britain would find themselves on the same side of practically every issue ... The two leaders were determined to establish a close friendship. Again and again the two communicated through one or another trusted intermediary. Almost as though it were a mantra, they repeated to each other that the interests of the English-speaking peoples were identical. ... An entente had been created, the special relationship between the United States and the United Kingdom ... He [Roosevelt] and King Edward were talking and acting as part-

ners and allies, even though TR knew that neither the Senate nor the American people would agree to a partnership or an alliance.[14]

As in Britain, it mattered little to those with power what "the American people" would or would not agree to. They had little say in political matters other than placing a cross on a piece of paper every four years. The vast majority were unaware that real power in the USA operated behind the Wall Street curtain.

King Edward played an important role in creating the 'special relationship' with his approach to Roosevelt in 1902, and they agreed that British and US foreign policy interests would operate in tandem. In *The Anglo-American Establishment*, Quigley presents surprisingly little detail about the American side of the relationship, but in *Tragedy & Hope* he expands on it. Together, the British and American financial circles were one of "the most powerful influences of the twentieth century" and a "very real power structure."[15] Bringing the United States into the fold was achieved with no difficulty, for those in American elite financial circles had long been staunch Anglophiles and lovers of all things English. This dated back to their English Puritan ancestors who crossed the Atlantic to New England in the 1600s. Some took the arduous two-month voyage to escape religious persecution in England, others in search of a better life or adventure. Boston became the headquarters of the Protestant revolution and the 'spiritual capital' of Christendom, with Puritan leader John Winthrop preaching that it would be "A City upon a Hill" – as in Jesus' Sermon on the Mount – and a "beacon of hope" for the world. It was reputedly the birth of so-called "American Exceptionalism," but within two generations, angry dissension began to spread among the Christian brethren over land disputes, personal feuds and political bickering.

> The spirit of brotherhood which the original settlers had counted on so heavily had lately diffused into an atmosphere of commercial competition, political contention, and personal bad feeling. Thus the political architecture which had been fashioned so carefully by the first generation and the spiritual consensus which had been defended so energetically by the second were both disappearing.[16]

Religious convictions and affiliations may have changed, and the ordinary Puritans scattered into different sects, but connections and loyalties among the wealthy, privileged and powerful families around the Boston area grew stronger down the centuries. They became part of a socially exclusive American aristocracy that maintained, indeed, deliberately accentuated their 'Englishness'. They practised intermarriage, family solidarity, and business networks to maintain and promote their power and wealth. Everyone who was anyone knew not only their family history inside out, but the intricate marital and business alliances with other famous families going back many generations. Old family bibles studiously recorded family histories, generation after generation, back to the "Great Migration" of 1620-40 from England. The October 1935 issue of *The Atlantic* wrote of the New England elites:

> Genealogy was a very popular hobby; and at every social gathering were many who could announce the precise degree of relationship between any two persons there.

The New England Puritans founded Harvard University in Cambridge, Massachusetts in 1636, and in the post-revolutionary United States a Harvard education combined with distinguished ancestry and wealth, opened doors to the highest positions of power in the land. Harvard was to the U.S. elites what Oxford was to the Milner Group. In 1861, physician, author, and dean of the Harvard Medical School, Dr Oliver Wendell Holmes, referred to these upper-class families, including his own, as "the Brahmin caste of New England." The term, which recalled the Hindu caste system, caught on and the New England elites became widely known as the "Boston Brahmin." Comprising America's oligarchical "first families," like their counterparts in the British Establishment, they considered themselves the crème de la crème of society. Like some of their elite cousins back in England, a number made their fortunes trading slaves and opium. English traditions and dress style were preserved by the Brahmin, and they were as loyal to the Crown as the most sycophantic and fawning of English royalists. On October 17, 1860, when Bertie visited Boston as Prince of Wales, he was formally welcomed by the Governor of Massachusetts as representing a country with which the American people were "united by many ties of language, law and liberty."

Most New England elites were true patriots to the American Republic's cause, but some had been deeply involved in treasonous behaviour. Back in 1808, Senator John Quincy Adams, had an urgent meeting with President Thomas Jefferson to relay evidence that certain influential individuals were plotting to withdraw the States of New England from the United States. To that end, a group of rich and powerful merchant and banking families were working in the closest collaboration with British Secret Intelligence agents operating out of Boston.

They were not turned against the cause of the American Revolution; they never adhered to that cause. These families had opposed the project of American independence, and were partners and agents of those expelled from the United States as British loyalists during the close of the war. Their principal sources of wealth and power were provided to them by the British, chiefly the British East India company, most notably profits of piracy, and of massive accumulations gained from both the African slave trade and the Far East opium traffic.[17]

Educated in a small cluster of expensive private schools and Harvard thereafter, these white Anglo-Saxon Protestants (WASPs) long believed they were set apart by destiny to rule. Most were proud Americans but also staunch Anglophiles.

> In their first century and a half, they had customarily called England 'home'; then, after having started the war for independence, they had become violently pro-English again during the War of 1812; and now again, after their horror at England's attitude during the Civil War, they had reverted to their original love. They believed, and said repeatedly, that they were of purer English stock than the English themselves. They preserved the broad *a* in their speech and the *u* in their spelling. Only the English were their social equals.[18]

By the turn of the twentieth century, the New England Brahmin had remained staunchly pro-British. They were drawn largely from the leading players in banking and business, law firms, national newspapers, Ivy League universities and major philanthropic foundations of the East Coast, hence the term "Eastern Establishment." Supporters and funders of racist eugenics, they had an almost megalomaniacal sense of their own destiny and that of the English-speaking peoples 'to civilise the world.'

> The Eastern Establishment may have its earliest roots north of Boston and in the Connecticut River Valley, but it was determined to be, not a mere regional financier faction, but the undisputed ruling elite of the United States as a whole, from Boston to Bohemian Grove and from Palm beach to the Pacific Northwest. It was thus imperative that the constant tendency towards the formation of regional factions be pre-empted by the pervasive presence of men bound by blood loyalty to the dominant cliques of Washington, New York, and the "mother country," The City of London.[19]

Professor Quigley revealed how, as in Britain, the international bankers (his term) exerted control over national politicians in the United States through bribery, blackmail, and promises of highly lucrative positions when their careers in active politics ended. The Wall Street bankers owned many if not most of the national newspapers and so controlled the avenues of information that create public opinion. The flow of money into the United States during the nineteenth century advanced banking and industrial development and helped create a new 'Money Power' of multi-millionaires such as J.P. Morgan, John D. Rockefeller, Andrew Carnegie, Cornelius Vanderbilt, and John Jacob Astor. All were associated in one way or another with top bankers in the City.

> These small groups of massively rich individuals on both sides of the Atlantic knew one another well, and the Secret Elite in London initiated the very select and secretive dining club, the Pilgrims, that brought them together on a regular basis. On 11 July 1902, an inaugural meeting was held at the Carlton Hotel attended by around 40 members of what became known as the London Chapter of the Pilgrims Society, with a select membership limited by individual scrutiny to 500. Ostensibly, the Pilgrims was created to 'promote goodwill, good friendship and everlasting peace' between Britain and the United States, but its highly secretive and exclusive membership leaves little doubt as to its real purpose. This was the pool of wealth and talent that the Secret Elite drew together to promote its agenda in the years preceding the First World War. Behind an image of the Pilgrim Fathers, the persecuted pioneers of Christian values, this elite cabal advocated the idea that Englishmen and Americans would promote international friendship through their pilgrimages to and fro across the Atlantic.[20]

The New York branch of the Pilgrims opened at the Waldorf-Astoria hotel on 13 January 1903.[21] Comprised of leading financiers, politicians and lawyers, they established a tradition of welcoming and entertaining each new British ambassador to the United States. The London branch reciprocated with every US ambassador to Britain. The ambassadorial and other leading diplomatic connections provided invaluable links between the Foreign Office in London and the Department of State in Washington. Pilgrims members in New York included leading Wall Street bankers linked to the J.P. Morgan and Rockefeller dynasties, and men in leading positions in the U.S. government.

In addition to the Pilgrims, Round Table groups (not to be confused with a charitable organization of the same name) were set up to promote the aims of the Milner Group. They were established in the United States, Britain, Canada, South Africa, Australia and New Zealand, and funded by the Astors, J.P. Morgan and the Rockefellers. They held regular 'private' meetings with "members considering themselves the intellectual standard-bearers for Secret Elite policy."[22] Most members of the New York branch of Round Table were also members of the Pilgrims. The regular private dinners and meetings of both organizations served to form close bonds between British and U.S. banking, political, diplomatic and journalistic elites. In 1910, the Group began publishing its quarterly journal, *The Round Table*, a mouthpiece of the Milner Group for internal readership. As Professor Quigley points out, long before 1914, the journal made it clear that a war with Germany was being planned.

> *The Round Table* was essentially the propaganda vehicle of a handful of people.... It was never intended to be either a popular magazine or self-supporting but rather was aimed at influencing those in positions to influence public opinion.... It is perhaps worth mentioning that the first article of the first issue called 'Anglo-German Rivalry,' was very anti-German and forms an interesting bit of evidence when taken in connection with ... what role South Africa would play in a future war with Germany. The Group, in the period before 1914, were clearly anti-German.... In view of the specific and practical purpose of *The Round Table* – to federate the Empire in order to ensure that the Dominions would join with the United Kingdom in a future war with Germany – the paper could not help being a propagandist organ...[23]

Round Table Groups played an important role in preparing both the British dominions and the United States for the coming war. Nothing was left to chance. The Empire and Commonwealth would provide a vast reserve of manpower for the British forces, with over three million soldiers and labourers fighting for Britain. The U.S. would provide another four million men and the equally important vast amounts of money needed for weaponry and ammunition.

As in Britain, Wall Street financial circles controlled politics, the press and education, and between them, the aim was to extend that control globally. Quigley wrote in *Tragedy & Hope*:

The powers of financial capitalism had a far-reaching plan, nothing less than to create a world system of financial control in private hands able to dominate the political system of each country and the economy of the world as a whole.[24]

"The powers of financial capitalism" – the bankers – planned to dominate the political system of each country and, not least, that of the United States of America. It would largely be achieved by Rothschild control of US finances via affiliated banking fronts on Wall Street that served to disguise and obscure their activities there.

Officially appointed Rothschild biographers tell us that the dynasty had little influence in the United States, but the reality, as we shall see, was very different.

August Belmont

The Rothschilds' earliest foray into American banking was in 1837, when they sent an agent, August Belmont (born Aaron Schönberg, 1813 -1890), to New York to open a front bank for the dynasty and get involved in politics. A financial genius from a very young age, Belmont was trained in banking in the Rothschild banks in Frankfurt and Naples before being sent across the Atlantic. American author Stephen Birmingham writes that he had changed his identity on arrival in America:

> But some sea change had taken place. He was no longer August Schönberg, but August Belmont. Furthermore, he was no longer a Jew but a gentile, and no longer German but, as people in New York began to say, "Some sort of Frenchman – we think."[25].

> With the United States in the grip of a financial panic in 1837, 'Belmont' organised large Rothschild loans to shore up debtor banks there: He was able, thanks to the hugeness of the Rothschild reservoir of capital, to start out in America operating his own Federal Reserve System.[26]

The National Cyclopaedia of American Biography says of Belmont:

> In 1837 he was sent to New York city to found another branch of the great Rothschild house, under the name of August Belmont &

Co. He took the first opportunity to become a citizen of the United States, and from that time was conspicuously identified with the political, diplomatic, commercial, financial, and social affairs of his adopted country. He affiliated with the Democratic party and cast his first presidential vote ... in 1844. During the same year he was appointed by the Austrian government as consul-general in the United States.... In 1853 Mr Belmont took an active part in the presidential campaign that resulted in the election of President Pierce and was appointed charge d'affaires of the U.S. legation at the Hague.... In 1856 Mr Belmont became one of Mr Lincoln's staunchest supporters and urged a vigorous prosecution of the war. He helped to raise and equip the first German regiment ... Mr Lincoln and Secretary Stewart, knowing the great influence Mr Belmont had in European financial circles, found in him a ready and willing ally in directing the minds of the financial and commercial leaders of the old world to the superior strength of the North over the South.... He wrote to the Rothschilds in London and Paris, and his letters were laid before the English and French ministers of State...[27]

Belmont organised massive Rothschild loans to the United States government – at considerable profit to his masters – and for years was Chairman of the Democratic National Committee that governed the Democratic Party. His activities gained him considerable personal wealth and a powerful voice in the Eastern Establishment. Socially, he married the daughter of Mathew C. Perry – the famous U.S. Navy Commodore whose ships forced the opening up of Japan to trade with the West in 1853 – and attended lavish house parties thrown by the Boston Brahmin elite. He gambled substantial sums on horse racing with his close friend, Leonard Jerome (who owned the famous Jerome Park racecourse and was the maternal grandfather of Winston Churchill.) On Belmont's death in 1890, his son August Jr. took over the role of Rothschild agent:

> American agent for the Rothschilds, he was not only a leading banker but played a larger civic role. He helped bail out the United States government when it was on the verge of default in 1895; he financed, built and ran New York City's first subway; and he constructed the Cape Cod Canal. He was a power broker in New York Democratic politics and his every move was chronicled in the press – the boardroom fights, his political string-pulling, his travels, his racehorses, his yachts.[28]

In the Belmonts, father and son, the Rothschilds had agents in America from 1837, funding railroads, subways, canals and a multitude of other banking and industrial ventures. The US government was in considerable debt to them and they exerted a major influence on the Democratic Party and politics in general.

Rothschild hagiographer, Professor Niall Ferguson, states that the Rothschilds made a "strategic error" in not establishing a "Rothschild house on the other side of the Atlantic."[29] Ferguson plays down Belmont's role as of no great significance and suggests:

> The reality was that the Civil War had led not only to a temporary decline in British continental influence, but to a permanent decline in the Rothschilds' transatlantic influence.'[30]

In toeing the official Rothschild line, 'court historian' Ferguson (Oxford) presents disinformation that the dynasty's influence in the United States permanently declined. He states elsewhere in his Rothschild biography that they extended their reach by using agents and affiliated banks, not only in other European markets but all over the world.[31] Yet we are expected to believe that they neglected the fastest growing market and economy in the world. The truth is very different.

From 1890 on, the leading bank on Wall Street, the J.P. Morgan bank, played a far greater role for the Rothschilds in the United States than August Belmont ever did. No bank the Rothschilds controlled in the United States had their name above the door, but through Morgan – and other banks we consider in due course – they had a massive, albeit covert, presence on Wall Street. Their modus operandi was to step in with large injections of cash to save banks and companies that were struggling and facing foreclosure, then operate them as fronts under the original company name and directors. With virtually unlimited Rothschild resources now behind these rescued banks – and there were others in the US besides J. P. Morgan – they quickly recovered and became highly profitable. In this manner, the Rothschild dynasty was able to keep its all-encompassing wealth, influence, and power in the United States hidden.

J.P. Morgan & Co

By the turn of the twentieth century Junius Pierpont Morgan was the pre-eminent banker on Wall Street. According to the unofficial Morgan biographer George Wheeler, the Morgan bank acted as a cover to conceal massive Rothschild influence in American finance:

J.P. Morgan

Part of the reality of the day was an ugly resurgence of Anti-Semitism … Someone was needed as a cover. Who better than J. Pierpont Morgan, a solid, Protestant exemplar of capitalism able to trace his family back to pre-revolutionary times?[32]

To understand how the Morgan connection with the Rothschilds came about, we must go back to events in London 175 years ago. The Morgan bank has its origins in a small American concern set up there in 1837 by George Peabody, a merchant from Massachusetts. The American bonds he sold to British investors offered higher rates of return than comparable European bonds, and business flourished. In 1854, Peabody took on a partner, Junius Spencer Morgan, who had been acting as his agent in Boston. Junius moved with his family, including eldest son John Pierpont, to London and the business was renamed, Peabody, Morgan and Company.

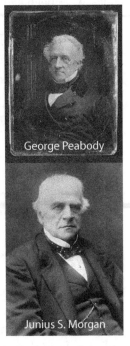

George Peabody

Junius S. Morgan

When a great financial panic swept Wall Street in 1857 and American concerns operating in Britain folded, for some reason Peabody and Morgan was saved by an injection of £800,000 from the Bank of England. It was a massive injection of cash amounting to some £120 million today. The Bank of England was a private shareholders' bank in which the Rothschilds were the leading players. We have seen how Wellington's army at Waterloo was saved in 1815 by Rothschild gold, and just ten years later the Bank of England itself had been saved from collapse thanks to the Rothschilds who backed it with a large amount of gold. The Rothschild Archive relates:

> By 1825, Britain was running a trade deficit, leading to substantial outflows of gold from the country and a sharp monetary contraction. This, in turn, triggered a collapse in asset prices and the failure of a number of commercial banks. By mid-December, "an indescribable gloom was diffused through the City," according to *The Times*. The Bank of England's gold reserves were almost completely exhausted and the suspension of cash payments was imminent, threatening widespread financial turmoil. The rescue of the Bank was a remarkable achievement which owed everything to the international nature of the Rothschilds' operations.[33]

The Bank of England was massively indebted to the Rothschilds and was to all intents and purposes now controlled by them. In 1857 it provided the loan to save Peabody, Morgan and Co., at a very reasonable interest, with further large amounts promised if and when required. It would never have been sanctioned without the Rothschilds say so. Appeals for help from all other banks with American connections in Britain were declined.[34] Thanks to the Rothschilds, Peabody, Morgan & Co became *the* American bank in London and was now in a position to make a killing on the American markets.

George Peabody was feted by both the British and American elites, and was the first American to be awarded the Freedom of the City of London. He retired in 1864, devoted his time to 'philanthropy,' and was awarded a Congressional Gold Medal for donating to charities for the poor in London. Queen Victoria personally praised him for his "princely munificence" and presented him with a miniature portrait of herself wearing the world-famous Koh-I-Noor diamond.[35] Peabody was publicly portrayed as a great humanitarian, but in private some considered him one of the meanest men that ever walked, having allegedly fathered numerous illegitimate children and left them totally unprovided for. When Peabody was dying in 1869, Bertie (the Prince of Wales) unveiled a magnificent statue of him alongside the Royal Exchange in The City. A permanent internment was earmarked for him in Westminster Abbey, but Peabody's will stipulated that he should be buried in his birthplace, Danvers, Massachusetts. When he died on 4 November 1869, his funeral ceremony and temporary burial took place in Westminster Abbey.

Since he wished to be buried in the United States, one month after the Westminster Abbey funeral, Queen Victoria ordered Peabody's remains disinterred and taken across the Atlantic on the newly built HMS *Monarch*, the biggest and grandest warship in the Royal Navy. A maudlin funeral chapel was created on *Monarch* with tall candles burning above a black-draped coffin. In America, the ship and its escort of cruisers were met by US warships. John Pierpont Morgan, in charge of funeral arrangements, devised a tribute of "martial splendor," with British and American soldiers marching together behind the financier's coffin.[36]

The 'Freedom of London' award; a statue in the City; a funeral in Westminster Abbey; his body transported across the Atlantic on the world's greatest warship – all this indicated just how close Peabody was to the British Establishment. With him gone, Junius Morgan was now the leading player in coordinating high finance between the City and Wall Street.

He renamed the bank J. S. Morgan & Co. and continued working closely with/for the Rothschilds in issuing US bonds in London. Huge sums were involved in today's money and, of course, large profits.

> Altogether, N.M. Rothschild was involved in issuing no less than £267 million in U.S. bonds ... between 1873 and 1877. These loans were designed not only to stabilise American finances but also to enable the U.S. to adopt the gold standard in the foreseeable future.[37]

Junius's son, John Pierpont Morgan (1837-1913), had been brought into the London business before Peabody died. Formerly a student at the English High School in Boston, much of his education took place in England and he became immersed in English culture and tradition. Pierpont, as he liked to be known, trained with his father and Peabody before moving to New York in 1858 to join Duncan, Sherman & Co. During the Civil War he made a huge profit buying 5,000 obsolete smooth-bore carbines for $3.50 each from the government armoury. He had them rifled at very little cost, then sold them back to the Union army for $22 apiece.[38]

Pierpont Morgan never fought in the Civil War, but made considerable profits from it. Official Morgan biographer, Ron Chernow, commented:

> The unarguable point is that he saw the Civil War as an occasion for profit, not service.... Like other well-to-do young men, Pierpont paid a stand-in $300 to take his place when he was drafted after Gettysburg.[39]

J.P. Morgan made over $26,000 in a few weeks from his rifle deal when soldiers fighting and dying for the Union cause were paid $16 per month. In 1860, he joined Anthony Drexel, a banker originating from Philadelphia, and together they opened a bank on Wall Street, Drexel, Morgan & Co. His father in London pumped $5 million into the bank which then acted as agent for himself and the Rothschilds. When Anthony Drexel died in 1893, Pierpont became the sole owner and the famous J.P. Morgan & Company was born. By the turn of the century, Morgan was considered the richest and most powerful man on Wall Street. The economic crises of the late 1890s had revealed that the Morgan Bank held more money and gold than the Treasury Department.[40]

None of this was possible without the immense wealth of Rothschild behind him. Morgan biographer, George Wheeler relates that Pierpont was "a mere bond salesman for his father's London firm"[41] yet by the

1890s he apparently had more money and gold than the U.S Treasury. When his father, Junius, was killed in a carriage accident in Monte Carlo in 1890, Pierpont had all letters between them over a thirty-year period burned, thus "destroying perhaps the most important chronicle of Anglo-American finance in the late nineteenth century."[42]

J.P. Morgan and August Belmont Jr., played a major role during the great financial meltdown in the United States in 1893. In one of the worst collapses in U.S. banking history, many state and even national banks failed. More than 8,000 businesses and industries went under, 15,000 commercial enterprises were declared bankrupt, 156 railroads went into receivership, and the great Union Pacific railroad declared itself insolvent. "Wage earners and heads of families were transformed into little more than beggars – and their dependents to something less. Many lost their homes to the banks and Federal troops were called out to quell civil unrest."[43] Belmont and Pierpont Morgan – read Rothschild – stepped in to 'save' what was left of Treasury Reserves, and made a killing through it.

Two years later (February 1895) President Grover Cleveland struck a deal with J.P. Morgan to save the country's collapsing gold reserves. A syndicate, including Rothschild, was formed to supply the Treasury with $62,000,000 worth of gold in exchange for government bonds. The amount is the equivalent in purchasing power today of around $2,266,144,000. The business proved hugely profitable to Morgan/Rothschild when they resold the bonds almost immediately at a marked-up price.

With money in short supply, honest politicians in the US were calling for the reintroduction of government-issued dollars (popularly called Greenbacks) that President Lincoln had issued during the Civil War to foil the bankers usurious interest rates. The Greenbacks came to an end after Lincoln's assassination, and since then the bankers had kept a tight grip on the money supply. They lied to the public that allowing the government to issue money would lead to dangerous levels of inflation. At the Democratic convention in 1896, the populist Democratic Party presidential candidate, William Jennings Bryan, gave his stirring "Cross of Gold" speech about the dire necessity for reform of the US monetary system. Bryan insisted that the government had to take the control of money away from the bankers, who were responsible for the economic depression and its disastrous consequences for the people.

Outgoing President Grover Cleveland was also a Democrat, but he was an agent of J.P. Morgan and the Wall Street banking interests. Cleveland favoured money that was issued by the banks and he backed the bankers' gold standard. Bryan was opposed to both, and argued in his winning nomination speech:

> We say in our platform that we believe that the right to coin money and issue money is a function of government.... Those who are opposed to this proposition tell us that the issue of paper money is a function of the bank and that the government ought to go out of the banking business. I stand with Jefferson ... and tell them, as he did, that the issue of money is a function of government and that the banks should go out of the governing business.... When we have restored the money of the Constitution, all other necessary reforms will be possible ... until that is done there is no reform that can be accomplished.... You shall not press down upon the brow of labor this crown of thorns; you shall not crucify mankind upon a cross of gold.[44]

William Jennings Bryan was a caustic critic of bankers and the phenomenal expansion of banking power. He was not the first. Thomas Jefferson had argued that the Republic and the Constitution were in constant danger from the so-called "Money Power" – the banking monopoly that manipulated the political power of the state and gained control over money issue:

> The issuing power of money should be taken from the banks and restored to Congress and the people to whom it belongs. I sincerely believe the banking institutions are more dangerous to liberty than standing armies.[45]

Abraham Lincoln had proposed that instead of the Federal Government borrowing money from the bankers, the bankers should borrow from the Treasury. It would mean that bankers would be unable to create fictional wealth through a central bank. Professor Antony C. Sutton wrote: "It was particularly important to the international bankers that they succeed with Lincoln. If Lincoln implemented public control of finance in the United States, then other nations would pluck up courage to strip financial power from their bankers."[46]

Lincoln was shot dead, and William Jennings Bryan would have known the risk he was taking, but throughout the presidential election campaign of 1896 he railed against Wall Street bankers making astronomical profits while impoverishing the country and the working man. The U.S. government should not be a perpetual borrower from the banks at interest when there was no need whatsoever for it, said Bryan. Corrupted politicians had effectively handed a few mega-rich bankers on Wall Street a private money monopoly which charged the government interest for borrowing it. The straightforward answer, Bryan told the electorate, was for the government to keep money issue in the public realm where it belonged.

Bryan was starved of electioneering funds and ridiculed in the controlled mainstream press as economically illiterate. Republican presidential candidate, William McKinley, was heavily promoted by the Wall Street bankers, given a campaign treasure chest and copious positive coverage in the newspapers that were owned and controlled by the bankers. It was, as Carroll Quigley later explained, simply part and parcel of the Money Power control of politics. They understood that nothing was more dangerous to their power than the public discovering and understanding how corrupt and unnecessary it was for control of the nation's money supply to be in private hands. McKinley won 51 per cent of the popular vote to Bryan's 46 per cent and carried 23 States to Bryan's 22. Once again, Wall Street bankers had their man in the White House.

It may seem irrelevant to spend so much time discussing Money Power control of politics and much else in the United States at that point in time, but the reason for doing so becomes clear as the narrative unfolds. This would be the very power that financed the Milner Group's war on Germany 1914-18, and the rise of Hitler and the Nazis in the 1930s. Crucially, these financial circles controlled the writing of history and were thus able to whitewash their activities from it. Carroll Quigley revealed how they achieved this through the organization of tax-exempt fortunes into educational foundations in the United States. It was through those foundations in leading universities that they managed the manipulation of the writing of history.

> This group, which in the United States was completely dominated by J.P. Morgan and Company from the 1880s to the 1930s was cosmopolitan, Anglophile, Internationalist, Ivy League, eastern seaboard high Episcopalian, and European-culture conscious.. Their connection with the Ivy League colleges rested on the fact that the large endowments of these institutions required constant consultation with the financiers of Wall Street.... As a consequence of these influences as late as the 1930s, J.P. Morgan and his associates were the most significant figures in policy making at Harvard, Columbia, and to a lesser extent at Yale.... The chief officials of these universities were beholden to these financial powers and usually owed their jobs to them.[47]

Wall Street bankers were controlling politics, leading universities, and the writing of history, but it has to be clearly understood that "behind the Wall Street bankers were powerful British financiers."[48] J.P. Morgan was the most powerful banker on Wall Street, but behind him was the hidden power of the Rothchilds.

During his regular visits to England, Morgan mixed in both business and social circles with men closely linked to the Rhodes-Milner secret society, including the Rothschilds and especially King Edward VII. He was, indeed, one of them.

> In 1906 Pierpont vouchsafed a private tour of his art collection at 13 Princes Gate, the [London] townhouse he inherited from his father, to King Edward VII. He had given the king financial advice, and the two often met at European watering holes ... As a coronation gift, Pierpont had given the king a $500,000 tapestry, which set off a long-lasting relationship between the House of Morgan and British royalty.[49]

The tapestry may only have been a loan for Edward's coronation, but it was symbolic of the close relationship between the two. Morgan was as close to the Rothchilds as King Edward, and with the dynasty's resources behind him, he played a major role in creating massive industrial trusts, including US Steel in 1901. He controlled at least one-fifth of all corporations trading on the New York Stock Exchange,[50] and had huge investments in American railroads. Morgan didn't build, he bought. Monopoly, not competition, was the name of the game, with competitors simply being bought out. Pierpont and his partners now held 72 directorships in 112 corporations, with major American insurance companies coming under his control. He also created a fleet of over 120 merchant ships, "dwarfing even the French merchant marine,"[51] and owned the White Star shipping line, which included the *Titanic*. On the banking side, a wave of mergers created a "Money Trust" that saw Wall Street "snowballing into one big Morgan-dominated institution."[52]

> Within the financial sector, Morgan acted as a welder, craftily merging the greatest banks, trusts and insurance companies into a single construct, "a solid pyramid at whose apex he sat." Through stock ownership and interlocking directorates, Morgan spread his control across the First National Bank, National City Bank, the Hanover Bank, the Liberty Bank and Trust, Chase National Bank, and the nation's major insurance companies.[53]

J.P. Morgan now 'sat at the apex' of American banking, industry, railroads, shipping, and insurance, but the Morgan enterprise was simply an extension of Rothschild in the City, London.

While Morgan and his cronies on Wall Street were building these huge monopolistic trusts that negated the 'competition' principle of capitalism, Theodore Roosevelt (TR) entered the White House after President McKinley was shot. He projected himself as an opponent of big business, a politician who 'would take on the bankers and their gigantic trusts.' But Roosevelt was a banker's man, and it was no more than stuff and bluster for public consumption. Ron Chernow writes:

> Although the Roosevelt-Morgan relationship is sometimes caricatured as that of trust-buster versus trust king, it was far more complex than that. The public wrangling obscured deeper ideological affinities ... Roosevelt saw trusts as natural, organic outgrowths of economic development. ... Both T.R. and Morgan disliked the rugged individualistic economy of the nineteenth century and favoured big business ... In the sparring between Roosevelt and Morgan there was always a certain amount of shadow play, a pretense of greater animosity than actually existed ... Roosevelt and Morgan *were secret blood brothers*.[54]

Morgan apparently owned a massive banking, insurance and industrial empire worth billions, yet when he died in 1913 his estate was valued at only $68 million. It is a mind-boggling sum to ordinary mortals, yet paltry when compared to the fortunes of the Vanderbilts, Astors, Rockefellers and other U.S. tycoons who were well below Pierpont in the financial pecking order. Why was this?

> The possibilities are obvious that a major portion of the wealth and power of the Morgan firm was, and always had been, merely the wealth and power of the Rothschilds who had raised it up in the beginning and who sustained it through its existence ... Regardless of one's interpretation of the nature of the relationship between the House of Morgan and Rothschild, the fact remains that it was close, it was ongoing, and it was profitable to both.[55]

This is borne out by the fact that while other banks went under in the bank panics of 1873, 1884, 1893, and 1907, Morgan's bank always had more than sufficient funds to survive.[56] In December 1912 Morgan appeared before the Congressional Pujo Committee investigating unconstitutional activities of bankers. When asked about the vast power he wielded, Morgan replied that he wielded no such power. The Committee's counsel, Samuel Untermyer, asked him:

> "Your firm is run by you, is it not?"
> "No Sir."
> "You are the final authority, are you not?"
> "No Sir."
> "You never have been?"
> "Never have."[57]

Was Morgan lying or was it a very rare and frank admission that he was not the real power behind the massive organisation that virtually owned the United States? Whatever the truth, Untermyer failed to probe any deeper into Morgan's astonishing response.

Pierpont Morgan and a number of other Wall Street bankers swapped shares and seats on each other's boards, and with so many overlapping directorships it became almost impossible for any outsider or concerned politician to discern who actually owned what. A later investigation by the Pujo Committee would reveal Morgan and associates held:

> One hundred and eighteen directorships in 34 banks and trust companies having total resources of $2,679,000,000 and total deposits of $1,983,000,000.
>
> Thirty directorships in 10 insurance companies having total assets of $2,293,000,000.
>
> One hundred and five directorships in 32 transportation systems having a total capitalization of $11,784,000,000 and a total mileage (excluding express companies and steamship lines) of 150,200.
>
> Sixty- three directorships in 24 producing and trading corporations having a total capitalization of $3,330,000,000.
>
> Twenty-five directorships in 12 public-utility corporations having a total capitalization of $2,150,000,000.
>
> In all, 341 directorships in 112 corporations having aggregate resources or capitalization of $22,245,000,000."
>
> Twenty- two billion dollars is a large sum – so large that we have difficulty in grasping its significance.[58]

Through the corrupt Money Trust, industries, insurance companies, railroads, transportation, and public utilities across the United States were gobbled up leaving virtually the entire nation in the hands of a few men on Wall Street. Those few men were themselves in the hands of a much greater power across the Atlantic in London.

Economics researcher, lawyer, and author Ellen Hodgson Brown states bluntly: "J.P. Morgan was an agent of powerful British banking interests."[59] And so too was his son, Jack, who took over the company in 1913.

J.P. MORGAN JR.

Pierpont Morgan's son, John Pierpont Morgan Jr. (1867-1943), known to all as Jack, was a Harvard graduate sent to manage the Morgan bank in London. He stayed there for eight years and, like his father and grandfather before him, became a devoted Anglophile. Jack returned to New York in 1905 and took control of the Morgan empire when his father died in 1913. Jack delegated authority to trusted lieutenants and spent much of his time in the England he loved. Although he kept a looser grip on the bank than his father, Jack insisted that all associates held true to one of Pierpont's central values, "loyalty to Britain."[60] Jack and his wife Jessie spent half their lives in Britain, not as exiled Americans but as naturalized English.[61] Each August they went to the extensive Gannochy estate they leased in Scotland for the grouse shooting season with invited guests including King Edward VII and his son (who later became King George V). Like his late father before him, Jack was an integral part of the Anglo-American Establishment. Ron Chernow writes:

> Where other partners at 23 Wall Street harboured some secret envy or suspicion of their British brethren, Jack Morgan had no such reservations. He regularly spent up to six months a year in England and was fully bicultural. For him, the war [the First World War] was a holy cause as well as a business opportunity ... he inhabited a black-and white world in which loyalty to England found its equal and opposite emotion in hatred of the Germans ... Jack told friends that the shooting had made him more fervently anti-German and more eager to see the United States enter the war on the Allied side. He reviled the Germans as "Huns" and "Teuton savages" – he relished colourful epithets – and exhibited a latent bias against Germany that he had inherited from his father ... Pierpont always accused the Germans of double-crossing him.... So, there was an edict put down that "we would never do business with the Germans."[62]

Jack Morgan, like his father and grandfather before him, was unstinting in serving England. His reward came when the Morgan bank was chosen by the British government as sole purchasing agent for war materiel from the

United States throughout the First World War. J.P. Morgan & Co was by far the biggest war profiteer in the United States, but much of its astronomical profit made its way back to the N.M. Rothschild bank in the City, London.

Another Wall Street bank linked to the Rothschilds that profited from the First World War was Kuhn, Loeb & Co.

KUHN, LOEB & CO.

Opened in New York City in the 1860's by two merchants, Abraham Kuhn and Solomon Loeb, as a clothes manufacturing business, it profited from the Civil War by selling military uniforms. In 1873, a young German banker, Jacob Schiff, (1847-1920) moved to New York and bought into Kuhn, Loeb & Co with financial backing from the Rothschilds.[63] Schiff created a banking arm of the business which, within a couple of decades, became a hugely important bank on Wall Street. It is only possible to understand the incredibly rapid rise of this bank from nothing to major player in American finance when one realises that Jacob Schiff was very closely linked to the Rothschilds and sent to the US as one of their covert agents. In its December 1912 issue, *Truth* magazine in the

Jacob Schiff

United States informed its readers that Jacob Schiff was head of the great private banking house of Kuhn, Loeb & Co *'which represents the Rothschild interests on this side of the Atlantic.'*[64] Jacob Schiff's father, Moses Schiff, was a Rothschild broker in Frankfurt am Main.[65]

> For many years the early Schiff's shared ownership of a two-family house with the Rothschilds. Located in the old Jewish quarter, the house was marked on the Schiff side by a ship and on the Rothschild side by a red shield, symbols from which the surnames of the two families had originally derived.[66]

On moving to Kuhn, Loeb, Jacob married Solomon Loeb's daughter, Therese, and by the early 1880s was in charge of the bank. Like the Rothschilds other Wall Street front, J.P. Morgan and Co., it was soon controlling great swathes of American industry, insurance and railroads. Schiff worked closely with the Rockefeller bank and managed many syndicates with J.P. Morgan.[67]

Pierpont Morgan had created a gigantic Money Trust on Wall Street, and Jacob Schiff and Kuhn, Loeb and Co., were part of it. With Kuhn, Loeb business skyrocketing, two other young German bankers linked to the Rothschilds, Felix and Paul Warburg, were sent across the Atlantic to assist Schiff. Like him, they became naturalised Americans. Felix married Schiff's daughter, Frieda, and Paul married Solomon Loeb's daughter, Nina.

The Warburg brothers came from the M.M. Warburg Bank in Hamburg that started in 1798 as a pawnbroker and moneylender business. The Warburg family were in close contact with the Rothschilds around the time the French army abandoned Hamburg in 1814, and they acted as agents for the dynasty when the Rothschilds replenished the city's silver stocks. The small Warburg outfit ticked along until the end of the Crimean War, when a deep deflation in 1857 left it floundering. The bank was saved by an Austrian bank, Credit-Anstalt, when it put "a vast amount of money at the Warburgs disposal."[68] Carroll Quigley reveals that Credit-Anstalt was "a Rothschild institution."[69] Just as they rescued the Bank of England and the Peabody and Morgan Bank, the Rothschilds stepped in with "a vast amount of money" and saved the Warburg bank from closure. It was not an act of charity or simply helping out old friends in trouble. As ever, it was a hard-nosed expansion of Rothschild power.

The Warburg bank was now beholden to the dynasty, but continued under the original Warburg name with the eldest of five brothers, Max, in charge. He had previously been trained in banking with the Rothschilds in London.[70] With Rothschild money, M. M. Warburg now grew from a tiny firm with only a handful of employees that was on the brink of collapse, to one of the biggest banks in Germany by the time of the First World War. Max remained in Germany and became deeply involved in German secret intelligence during the war, while brother Paul would play a key role for the Money Power in creating the United States central bank – the Federal Reserve System. The enormous significance of this is discussed below.

By the turn of the century, the Kuhn, Loeb bank was seen on Wall Street as the principal rival to J.P. Morgan & Company and publicly touted as the Jewish bank versus the Protestant Morgan bank. The Rothschilds succeeded in concealing the fact that they controlled both of them. In his 1998 Rothschild biography, Niall Ferguson, perpetuates the myth that the dynasty failed to establish a strong foothold in the United States. That, says Ferguson, was "the single biggest strategic mistake in their history."[71] The reality was very different.

J. D. Rockefeller

Rockefeller controlled around 90 percent of America's oil refining, and worked in close association with both Jacob Schiff and J.P. Morgan. The Rothschilds provided Rockefeller with financial backing to buy Chase Bank on Wall Street, with the money being funnelled through Jacob Schiff at Kuhn, Loeb.[72] Rather than have Rockefeller outside their tent pissing in, they brought him in and he worked with them in monopolistic collusion. He operated closely with Jacob Schiff and J.P. Morgan in buying up railroads and a multitude of industries – including the United States steel industry – so that by the early twentieth century this Wall Street syndicate dominated a hundred corporations with more than $22 billion in assets. The Rockefeller-Morgan syndicate had a virtual stranglehold on the energy business in the United States, and in later chapters we see how they owned the oil wells and refineries in Romania that supplied Germany throughout the 1914-18 war.

Creating the Federal Reserve System and Controlling U.S. politics

By the early twentieth century, in addition to controlling the finances of Europe, the Rothschilds had massive, albeit hidden, influence in the United States. One major task remained there before war could be instigated against Germany: the creation of a central bank through which they could control the United States money supply and politics. Carroll Quigley explained how central banks were at the core of the financial cabal's control:

> The powers of financial capitalism had another far-reaching goal, nothing less than to create a world system of financial control in private hands *able to dominate the political system of each country* and the world as a whole. This system was to be controlled in a feudalist fashion by the *central banks* of the world acting in concert, by secret agreements arrived at in frequent private meetings and conferences. The apex of the system was to be the Bank for International Settlements in Basle, Switzerland, a private bank owned and controlled by the world's central banks *which were themselves private corporations* ... Each bank sought to dominate its government by its ability to control Treasury loans, to manipulate foreign exchang-

es, to influence the level of economic activity in the country, and to influence cooperative politicians by subsequent economic rewards in the business world.[73]

Wall Street bankers had long been corrupting individual American politicians and influencing presidential elections, but the United States had no central bank and Wall Street would have to create one if it was to dominate the government outright. Such domination was imperative not merely for ensuring that the United States would join the war against Germany when the time was right, but for providing the vast bulk of the money that would fund the Allies war efforts.

Honest politicians in Washington – and there were some – were alert to the dangers of a privately owned central bank, so its creation would have to be achieved clandestinely. Moreover, Wall Street had to devise a strategy to convince Congress and the American people that the bank was not a private cartel (which it was) but an agency of the United States government.

At New Jersey station on 20 November 1910, a group of seven men dressed as a duck shooting party boarded a private rail carriage owned by Senator Nelson Aldrich of Rhode Island. Aldrich was an associate of J.P. Morgan with extensive holdings in banking, manufacturing, and public utilities, and considered to be the political spokesman for big business.

Blinds on Aldrich's railway car were drawn and it was hooked up to a locomotive which left the station around midnight heading south. The seven men were going to Jekyll Island, a luxury holiday retreat owned by America's wealthy elite off the coast of Georgia. Regular staff at the exclusive complex – who would know the men from previous visits – had been sent home for nine days and replaced by strangers as temporary cover. Never a duck was shot, for the men were there in utter secrecy to thrash out plans for a central bank and the utter corruption of American finance.

The seven 'duck shooters' were representative of the international bankers:

> Nelson Aldrich, the Republican "whip" in the Senate, Chairman of the National Monetary Commission, business associate of J.P. Morgan and father-in-law of John D. Rockefeller, Jr.

> Abraham Piatt Andrew, a Harvard economist and Assistant Secretary of the U.S Treasury.

> Frank A. Vanderlip, president of the National City Bank of New Jersey, the most powerful of the banks at that time representing Rockefeller.

Henry P. Davidson, senior partner of the J.P. Morgan Company.

Charles D. Norton, president of J.P. Morgan's First National Bank of New York.

Benjamin Strong, head of J.P. Morgan's Banker's Trust Company.

Paul M. Warburg, of Kuhn, Loeb & Co.[74]

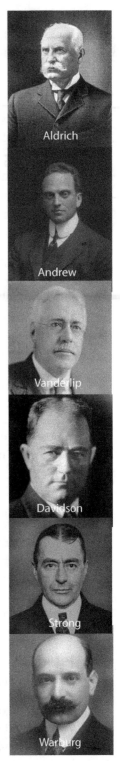

Aldrich

Andrew

Vanderlip

Davidson

Strong

Warburg

The title "Central Bank" had to be avoided in order to deceive the American people, so the Jekyll Island plotters decided to name it the "Federal Reserve System" implying that it was a government institution.

> What emerged was a cartel agreement with five objectives: stop the growing competition from the nation's newer banks; obtain a franchise to create money out of nothing for the purpose of lending; get control of the reserves of all banks so that the more reckless ones would not be exposed to currency drains and bank runs; get the taxpayer to pick up the cartel's inevitable losses; and convince Congress that the purpose was to protect the public.[75]

The legislation for the central bank was known as the "Aldrich Plan" after Nelson Aldrich, but Paul Warburg is widely recognised as the master theoretician who led the others in the great banking scam that creates money from thin air. Over the three years after the Jekyll Island conspiracy, Warburg wrote many newspaper articles and toured the country lecturing about the virtues of a central bank and softening up the public for its introduction. Everyone was assured that the Federal Reserve would decentralize banking power *away* from Wall Street.

> Most of Warburg's writing and lecturing on this topic was eyewash for the public. To cover the fact that a central bank is merely a cartel which has been legalized, its proponents had to lay down a thick smoke screen of technical jargon focussing always on how it would supposedly benefit commerce, the

public, and the nation; how it would lower interest rates, provide funding for needed industrial projects, and prevent panics in the economy. There was not the slightest glimmer that, underneath it all, was a master plan which was designed from top to bottom to serve private interests at the expense of the public.[76]

The 'Federal' Reserve System was to be owned entirely by a handful of men from the American banking dynasties on Wall Street, including Morgan, Warburg, Schiff and Rockefeller who, as we have seen, were all linked to Rothschild in one way or another. The money supply would not be government issue, but private money issued by private banks. It would create money, issue it at interest, dictate how much interest would be charged, and control the volume of money in circulation.

> The Federal Reserve System constructed on Jekyll Island had powers that King Midas could never have contemplated. The objective was to establish a franchise to create money out of nothing for the purpose of lending, get the taxpayer to pick up any losses and convince Congress that the aim was to protect the public. When the proposals took shape in Congress ... President Taft refused to support the bill on the grounds that it would not impose sufficient government control over the banks. The Money Power decided that Taft had to go.[77]

The bankers needed a man in the White House who would sign the legislation for the new central bank, and selected a little-known university administrator, Woodrow Wilson, as their puppet. With substantial financial backing the bankers ensured he won the Democratic party nomination. Professor Antony C. Sutton wrote:

> Wilson's acceptance speech was written on board the *Corona*, [Wall Street banker Cleveland H. Dodge's yacht] while they planned the strategy for the coming campaign. In brief, Woodrow Wilson was in the hands of the Money Trust, had lied to the American public about his true position on the trusts and Wall Street and betrayed the Jeffersonian-Jacksonian tradition of the Democratic Party.[78]

In 1912, President Taft was clear favourite with the American public for a second term in office, but the election was rigged to ensure his defeat.

> The election of 1912 was a textbook example of power politics and voter deception. The Republican President, William Howard Taft, was up for re-election. Like most Republicans of that era, his politi-

cal power was based upon the support of big-business and banking interests in the industrial regions. He had been elected to his first term in the expectation that he would continue the protectionist policies of his predecessor, Teddy Roosevelt. ... Once in office, however, he grew more restrained in these measures and earned the animosity of many powerful Republicans. The ultimate breach occurred when Taft refused to support the Aldrich Plan [for the creation of a central bank.] He objected, not because it would create a central bank which would impose government control over the economy, but because it would not offer enough government control. He recognized that the Jekyll Island formula would place the bankers into the driver's seat with only nominal participation by the government ... From that moment forward, Taft was marked for political extinction.[79]

For the 1912 presidential election, a new political entity, the Progressive Party – popularly known as the "Bull Moose" Party – was created from scratch with substantial backing from the bankers. The plan was to divide the Republican vote and enable their chosen man, Woodrow Wilson, to sail through the middle. King Edward's old friend, Theodore Roosevelt, was drafted back into politics to head the new Bull Moose party. Roosevelt's expenses were met by Wall Street, which also provided two-thirds of Woodrow Wilson's campaign funds.[80] President Taft got no backing from the bankers.

Woodrow Wilson wrote academic briefs for the banking Trusts while publicly campaigning against them. It was a re-run of Theodore Roosevelt's anti-Trust bluster and lies eight years earlier. Starved of electioneering funds and hammered in the controlled press, Taft gained only 23% of the votes cast while Roosevelt took 27%. Woodrow Wilson went to the White House on 42% and could now repay the bankers by signing off the Federal Reserve Act.

> Wilson was elected President. And the ballots had hardly been counted when Wall Street bustled about to arrange "currency reform." By early December 1912, Colonel House [Wilson's Wall Street minder] had already talked with key members of Congress to get them behind Wilson, and when Paul Warburg telephoned House on December 12, 1912, the Colonel told him that the plan was ready.[81]

The new president began softening the American people to the view that a central bank was essential for stabilising the economy and preventing recurrences of financial crises and bank failures such as the country had experienced in 1907. He stated that the bank would be outside the control or influence of bankers because monetary policy was too important to be left in the hands of private interests. Like many, if not most, politicians before and since, Wilson was a convincing liar.

In December 1913, the majority of members of Congress would be conned into voting for the Federal Reserve Act. Professor Sutton describes it:

> Congressional passage of the Federal Reserve Act in December 1913 must count as one of the more disgraceful unconstitutional perversions of political power in American history. Certainly it is hard to think of any act that has had greater effect and illegally transferred more monopoly power to a conspiratorial clique. ... The act transferred control of the monetary supply of the United States from Congress to a private elite. Paper fiat currency replaced gold and silver. Wall Street financiers were able now to tap an unlimited supply of fiat money at no cost ... In 1913 the democratic party leadership came under strong pressure from Woodrow Wilson and New York banking lobbyists to ensure that opposition did not water down the currency bill ... Most Congressmen had no idea what the bill was about.[82]

Monday, 22 December 1913, was a black day in American history. While many members of the House had already gone home for Christmas, the Federal Reserve Act was rushed through without time for proper debate or investigation. Professor Sutton described the unseemly haste:

> During this brief 23 hours the major differences were reconciled, worded, printed, distributed, read by every member of the House [who was still present], discussed, pondered, weighed, deliberated, debated and voted upon. This miracle of speediness, never equalled before or after in the U.S. Congress, is ominously comparable to the rubber stamp lawmaking of the banana republics.[83]

At 11 P.M. the document was delivered to Woodrow Wilson who was waiting, pen in hand, to sign the Act into law. For public consumption, it was presented as a regional banking system and given an innocuous name; The Federal Reserve System. It disguised the fact that it was not, as people assumed, a branch of Government, but owned and controlled by a handful of astronomically wealthy bankers. "The original Federal Reserve board represented those very interests that Woodrow Wilson assured the American

Sutton

public would *not* be represented in the Federal Reserve System." Chairman of the Board was William G. McAdoo, "a prominent Wall Street figure."[84] A banker's man, McAdoo had served on Wilson's election campaign, and the new president appointed him secretary of the Treasury. McAdoo's wife (and mother of his seven children) died in 1912 and he married Woodrow Wilson's daughter, Eleanor. Paul Warburg of the Kuhn, Loeb bank – the leading schemer at Jekyll Island – was another key appointment to the Board. Professor Sutton commented:

> The Federal Reserve is a private monopoly of money credit created by Congress under highly questionable circumstances which is beholden to the Chairman of the Board and whose decisions cannot be changed by government or anyone else. A free society under the rule of law? The United States has quietly become a hostage to a handful of international bankers. And just dare any Congressman challenge Fed authority![85]

The individuals who owned and controlled the new central bank were the leading American members of the Anglo-American secret cabal, as detailed by Professor Carroll Quigley. They had successfully manipulated the political power of the state to gain a money machine monopoly that could create money from thin air, and Thomas Jefferson's stark warning was consigned to the garbage bin: "The issuing power [of money] should be taken from the banks and restored to Congress and the people to whom it belongs. I sincerely believe the banking institutions are more dangerous to liberty than standing armies."[86] The secret cabal of Anglo-American elites controlled the European central banks and had now successfully created the one they had long coveted; a central bank of the United States. The bill was legally in place as an act of Congress before the morning newspapers hit the streets. "By clever sleight-of-hand political manoeuvring, it was precisely the opposite of what the public had been promised."[87] Professor Sutton:

> The Republican leader did not know what was in the Act nor was he given the opportunity to find out what was in the Act.... Both Finance Committee Chairmen, Congressman Glass and Senator Owen, had conflict of interest with personal banking interests and stood to gain from the bill. Meetings to discuss the bill were held

without knowledge of committee members.... Major sections of the bill were settled without consultation and railroaded into final form. There is indisputable evidence of outside banking influence upon Congress.... Most of Congress had no idea of the contents of the final bill and certainly none had the opportunity to reflect and consult with the broader base of the electorate.... As Congressman Lindbergh stated on December 23, 1913:

"This Act established the most gigantic trust on earth. When the president signs this bill, the invisible government of the Money power will be legalized. The people may not know it immediately, but the day of reckoning is only a few years removed."[88]

And so the Anglo-American financial elite got the final crucial piece of the jigsaw in place before commencing their war against Germany. Carefully selected individuals were now at the head of the new central bank in the United States, and at all of the old and well-established central banks in Europe. Carroll Quigley revealed that the men so positioned were utterly beholden to the financial cabal:

It must not be felt that these heads of the world's chief central banks were themselves substantive powers in world finance. Rather, they were the technicians and agents of the dominant investment bankers of their own countries, who had raised them up and were perfectly capable of throwing them down. The substantive financial powers of the world were in the hands of these investment bankers who remained largely behind the scenes in their own unincorporated private banks. These formed a system of international cooperation and national dominance which was more private, more powerful, and more secret than that of the agents in their central banks.[89]

International financiers were now able to dominate the political system of the United States as well as Britain. Professor Guido G. Preparata writes that so-called 'democracy' was a sham, the ballot "a travesty."[90] With the president in the White House now in their pocket, and the US central bank set up and ready to open its doors in 1914, the stage was well and truly set for the cabal's war. As always, it was a war that would prove enormously profitable to them. Should any losses occur, they would become a burden initially on the US taxpayer, and finally on the German people through the payment of massive reparations. And quite apart from endless money to fund their war, the British ruling elite now knew for certain that they could count on the United States to answer the call to war whenever they issued it.

Summary: Chapter 3 – The 'Special Relationship'

- Edward VII had strong blood ties to German royalty, yet hated all things German and his nephew, Kaiser Willhelm, in particular.

- When VII ("Bertie") was Prince of Wales, his mother Queen Victoria detested his gambling, whoring and drinking, and the fact that he was massively in debt to the Rothschilds.

- King Edward is not named as a member of the Rhodes/Milner secret society, but Carroll Quigley confirms that he was intimately involved with it through his close links to Lord Rothschild, Lord Esher, and other members of its inner circle.

- Foreign affairs was not officially within King Edward's constitutional remit, but he acted as de facto Foreign Secretary and promoted a strong bond of Anglo-American friendship with President Theodore Roosevelt.

- Staunchly pro-British, the 'Eastern Establishment' believed in the destiny of the English-speaking peoples to 'civilise' the world.

- Milner Group organisations such as Round Table and Pilgrims promoted intimate ties between the oligarchical powers of Britain and the USA in order to advance their globalist aims.

- Leading Wall Street organisations, J.P. Morgan & Co, and Kuhn, Loeb & Co, had monopolistic control over American banking, the steel and shipbuilding industries, railroads, insurance, newspapers and, not least, politics.

- The Rothschilds covertly controlled those Wall Street organisations, and profited massively from them.

- A central bank – the Federal Reserve System – was clandestinely created by Morgan and Kuhn, Loeb bankers who were ultimately beholden to the Rothschilds. Their political placeman, Woodrow Wilson, signed the legislation to bring the central bank into existence. Creating money from thin air, the Federal Reserve would fund the First World War on a mountain of debt.

CHAPTER 4

WAR BY ROYAL WARRANT

I n early nineteenth century, Britain had a very narrow franchise with the vote restricted to a small group of wealthy land and property owners aptly named the 'English ruling class.' The Parliamentary Reform Act of 1867 gave the franchise to a million more male voters, but that still left five million of the seven million men in Britain – most of the British working class – with no vote or voice in parliament. Members of parliament were unpaid (until 1911) meaning those standing for election to Westminster had to be men of independent means. British governments alternated between two principal political factions, the Conservatives and the Liberals. The typically aristocratic and wealthy Conservatives believed in small government and preserving the status quo of elite rule. Liberals came more from the middle classes and were often merchants or business-owning bourgeoisie.

When Rhodes, Milner, Rothschild, and others formed their secret society in 1891, the party in power was Conservative, with Robert Gascoyne-Cecil, third Marquess of Salisbury as prime minister. Gascoyne-Cecil and his extended family were major players in both the English ruling class and the secret society. As previously described, Gascoyne-Cecil (Lord Salisbury) was educated at Eton and Oxford University, and a Fellow of All Souls College at Oxford. Carroll Quigley relates that the secret society held massive clout at Oxford and was the "most powerful single influence in All Souls."[1] Indeed, "the Milner Group merged with All Souls."[2]

In 1892, Gascoyne-Cecil was replaced as prime minister by the Liberal, William Ewart Gladstone. The son of a wealthy merchant and slave owner, Gladstone was likewise educated at Eton and Oxford, and a Fellow of All Souls. He was not, however, a member of the Rhodes-Milner Group. Gladstone served as prime minister until replaced by the Conservative Earl of Rosebery in 1894. Lord Rosebery (Archibald Philip Primrose) was educated at Eton and Oxford and he too was a Fellow of All Souls. He served as prime minister 1894-1895. Professor Quigley places him in the secret society's inner circle.[3] When Rosebery left 10 Downing Street in

1895, Gascoyne-Cecil returned as prime minister. He served again until 1902, before handing power to his nephew Arthur Balfour, who was educated at Eton and Cambridge. Balfour was yet another important member of the secret society's inner core of the "Society of the Elect."[4]

Thus parliamentary power was shared among these English elites and close friends. As Carroll Quigley expressed it, they were in fact two football teams put on the field by the same elite private school. Leading members of the Conservatives and Liberals were friends from childhood at the elite schools – usually Eton or Harrow – and leading universities – Oxford or Cambridge. They wined and dined together in the same expensive private members clubs in London and flitted from one great country house and spectacular social event to another.[5]

It may seem a distraction to be discussing the intricacies of British politics in the late nineteenth and early twentieth century, but this was the crucial period during which the 'hidden hand' of the Milner Group formulated its plan to destroy Germany. They knew Britain on her own could never defeat Germany, and that the great armies of France and Russia would be needed to do much of the fighting and dying. American historian and Rhodes Scholar at Oxford, Robert K. Massie, writes:

> Great Britain had decided not to tolerate German hegemony on the Continent. From this vague but powerful instinct flowed the Entente with France, the rebuilding of the Royal Navy, and the Entente with Russia.[6]

KING EDWARD AND THE *ENTENTE CORDIALE*

Fresh from his 'special relationship' success with Roosevelt and the Americans, King Edward now devoted time to healing old wounds between Britain and France. Lord Salisbury had been actively involved in softening Anglo-French relations, and Edward VII now stepped in to play a major role in wooing the French. On a visit to Paris in the spring of 1903, Edward VII addressed President Émile Loubet and the French Cabinet:

> It is scarcely necessary to tell you with what sincere pleasure I find myself once more in Paris, to which, as you know, I have paid very frequent visits with ever increasing pleasure, and for which I feel an attachment fortified by so many happy and ineffable memories. The days of hostility between the two countries are, I am certain, happily at an end. There may have been misunderstandings and causes of dissension in the past, but that is all happily over and for-

gotten. The friendship of the two countries is my constant preoccupation, and I count on you all who enjoy French hospitality in their magnificent city to aid me to reach this goal.[7]

King Edward constantly wooed the French – England's traditional enemies – and the end result was the 1904 Entente Cordiale between Britain and France. Its true aim, together with the later agreement with Russia, was the isolation and encirclement of Germany, but pro-establishment historians attempt to dismiss it as no more than a loose Anglo-French agreement to settle "some continuing colonial disputes."[8] Historian Gordon Martel perpetuated the myth:

> The Anglo-French 'entente' was not an alliance. No enemy was singled out. No contingencies were provided for. No coordinated activities were planned. The entente was simply a settlement of colonial disputes that had been simmering for the last quarter-century.[9]

Historian John F.V. Keiger dismisses such nonsense, correctly relating that with the signing of the Entente Cordiale, Franco-British military cooperation began in preparation for war.

> Franco-British relations had been consolidated to a certain extent by the commencement in December 1905 of secret conversations between the British and French General Staffs [military] on possible joint action in a conflict in which both countries might become involved. Perhaps intended only as a temporary measure … they became a permanent part of the Entente. Though Britain maintained her previous position of refusing to commit herself to France in the event of war, the French, and in particular Paul Cambon, came to view such help as virtually certain.[10]

Lord Lansdowne, the Secretary of State for Foreign Affairs (November 1900 – December 1905), was not a member of the Rhodes-Milner Group. He had no wish to become embroiled with Germany, but accepted that antagonizing her was part of the price to be paid for an entente with France, and quietly accepted King Edward acting as de facto Foreign Secretary. Professor E.W. McCullough writes:

> The apprehension that the entente might lead to complications which would be unpalatable to some sections of the British public required another elaborate game of make-believe. It was necessary to pretend that the entente was merely a settling of differences between England and France, aimed at ending An-

glo-French antagonism but having no political significance. It was even suggested that it might be a prelude to a similar agreement with Germany. ... The acceptance of this myth by some historians rests largely on the belief that the colonial agreements of April 1904, constitute the entente. In fact, these agreements were made possible by the Entente Cordiale, which came into existence slowly and was established in the summer of 1903 by Edward VII's visit to Paris in May and President Loubet's visit to London in July ... Loubet said that the king's visit would be the seal of the rapidly strengthening cordiality, and would be universally recognized as such. When Eugène Étienne [French politician] visited London in July he told Lansdowne he believed that "the most serious menace to the peace of Europe lay in Germany" and that an Anglo-French understanding "was the only means of holding German designs in check." France would also be able to influence Russia and relieve England of many of her troubles with that country. Lord Cromer [Diplomat and banker] expressed to Lansdowne the opinion that one of the main attractions of the rapprochement with France was the hope that it would lead to an Anglo-Russian arrangement and thus isolate Germany.[11]

France had been in a stable alliance with Russia following agreements of 1891-94, and Cromer continued to impress on the less than enthusiastic British Foreign Secretary that the Entente Cordiale with France would greatly encourage the creation of a Triple Entente, an alliance of sorts, between Britain, France and Russia. "Nothing could be plainer."[12]

Edward VII played a significant role in bringing about the much-needed realignments with erstwhile foes France and Russia, ending years of Britain's 'splendid isolation'. France and Russia were needed in a new capacity: as Britain's friends and allies. This was agreed in secret by the Milner Group without the knowledge or consent of most members of the Cabinet, and the vast majority of MP's.

The alliances would have been unacceptable to most Members of Parliament and the general public but were enacted for one single purpose; to throttle Germany. There was no real opposition to be voiced because the real opposition did not know it was happening.[13]

King Edward's trips to France were reported by the British press as being purely for pleasure and had little to do with any diplomatic agreements with France. American historian, Sidney B. Fay, sees it differently;

Who were the originators of the Entente Cordiale and what were their motives? M. Tardieu, who stood close to Delcassé and had good information, says, "The English King was the initiator of the *rapprochement*. He it was who both conceived and facilitated it while many still believed that the moment was premature." Lord Cromer spoke of it as the "work of that very eminent diplomatist, His Majesty the King, and Lord Lansdowne." That the main impulse to it came from the side of England and not France grew to be a very general opinion both in England and on the Continent, and it was certainly greeted with more general enthusiasm in England than in France.[14]

Interestingly, in her address to a State Banquet held in Paris on 5 April 2004 to celebrate the centenary of the Entente Cordiale, Queen Eliabeth II stated:

I am proud of the part my great grandfather, King Edward VII, played in this historic agreement. It *was his initiative*, and that of your President Loubert, to insist on reciprocal State Visits in 1903 which did so much to create the popular atmosphere for the successful political negotiations to settle our colonial disagreements the following year.[15]

So much for establishment historians denying the king's major role in creating the Entente Cordiale. It set the European stage and with an Anglo-French agreement there would be no difficulty to make war with Germany when the time was considered right. Many in France remained bitter at her defeat in the Franco-Prussian war of 1870, with the loss of the provinces of Alsace-Lorraine to the new unified Germany. They blamed Germany for the Franco-Prussian war but various historians, including the Briton, Michael Howard, suggest otherwise:

There can be no doubt that France was the immediate aggressor, and none that the immediate provocation to her aggression was contrived by Bismarck, but the explanation that the conflict was planned by Bismarck ... is one which does not today command general assent.[16]

Irrespective of where the blame lay in 1870, a deep revanchism now pervaded certain conservative and nationalist circles French politics – a burning desire to make war on Germany in order to regain the 'Lost provinces'. King Edward encouraged this revanchism, making frequent trips across the English Channel to sweet-talk the *revanchistes* and assure them that Britain would do all in its power to help them take Alsace and Lorraine from Germany. He also agreed that the French, together with the Spanish, could have a free hand in Morocco without British interference, in return for British control in Egypt.

The Entente Cordiale of 1904 was no mean feat, for it ended a century and more of serious antagonism between France and England. Come the day and the hour, France and Britain would form the western component of the ring of steel surrounding Germany, while Russia, and later Italy, would complete the ring to the east. War was being carefully planned by Britain and her new ally, France, but the truth would forever be perverted by British pro-Establishment historians. Regarding the British propaganda view of history: Professor Edward E. McCullough of Concordia University, Montreal, wrote:

> The Great War provides by far the best example of the falsification of history for propaganda purposes. The history of the last ten years before the war is a classic example of the kind of manipulation used to produce the beliefs which support militarism. It gives strong support to the view that war is unrelated to any failure in political organization, but exists only because evil nations oppose good nations. The currently popular history of Europe between 1870 and 1914 is pure mythology. The picture of Germany as an aggressive, expansionist disturber of the peace is completely unrelated to the actual events of the period. Until after the turn of the twentieth century it was almost universally recognized that the German Empire was a conservative, stabilizing force whose policy upheld the status quo.... The propaganda view of history is particularly important for England because the disastrous results of the policy it followed make it imperative for her advocates to insist that there was no alternative. They do this by perpetuating the idea that German policy left England no choice other than to support France and Russia against a German attempt to destroy the British Empire and dominate the world.[17]

The 1904 Anglo-French Entente cemented by King Edward VII was a highly significant event in determining the future of the twentieth-century. With France having been allied to Russia since 1891, the king would soon turn his attention to converting it to a Triple Entente with Britain.

> King Edward had managed to smooth over the relationship between two traditional enemies who had been at war – or close to it

– for centuries. … Even before the ink was dry on the 1904 Entente Cordiale, King Edward planned a similar arrangement with Russia, but he was obliged to wait for the end of Russia's catastrophic confrontation with Japan.[18]

Edward's role in drawing the Russians into a triple pact against Germany in 1907 is discussed in due course, but we must consider how a potential major hurdle to the Milner Group's plan for war had first to be overcome.

We have seen how controlling both major political parties in Britain was straightforward, but the Milner Group faced a potential problem in 1905. The Conservative government was unpopular after the Boer War and had suffered a series of by-election defeats to the Liberals. The last general election had been held in 1900 and, as the time for another loomed, it looked very likely that the Liberal Party would gain a substantial majority. The problem came in the shape of Liberal Party leader, Sir Henry Campbell-Bannerman. He was not a member of the Milner Group, had no idea that such a group existed, and was detested by Milner and his acolytes for being a pacifist. As prime minister, Campbell-Bannerman would never countenance Britain planning a war against Germany. There were, however, three senior figures in the Liberal party who knew what the 'hidden hand' was up to and would lend their full support to war: Sir Edward Grey, Henry Herbert Asquith, and Richard Haldane.

Grey and Asquith had been students at Balliol College, Oxford (Alfred Milner's college) and were selected and nurtured there by the ruling elite as future political leaders. Richard Haldane, who had gone to Edinburgh University, was a high earning lawyer in London. Carroll Quigley relates that the three were "close to the Milner Group politically, intellectually, and socially."[19] They would ensure that preparations for war with Germany ran smoothly, but how were they to deal with their pacifist party leader, Campbell-Bannerman?

Known to all as "CB," Campbell-Bannerman had been the member of parliament for the constituency of Stirling in Scotland since 1868 and rose quickly through the ministerial ranks under Gladstone. He had been leader of the opposition Liberal Party since 1900. The son of a draper from Glasgow, he attended Glasgow University then Trinity College, Cambridge. Campbell-Bannerman spoke French, German and Italian fluently, and visited the continent over several months each summer with his beloved wife Sarah. An internationalist, he was against the pursuit of narrow

British interests as pursued by 'little Englanders'. The Liberal Party in the House of Commons was split between right-wing Imperialists like Grey, Asquith, and Haldane, as opposed to those such as Campbell-Bannerman who steered a middle course and preferred Britain to co-exist in a family of friendly nations. He eschewed laissez-faire and social coercion in favour of a democratic type of liberal socialism with shorter working hours for working men, and equitable internationalism. Campbell-Bannerman supported Irish Home Rule, Free Trade, and improved living conditions for the masses. He had privately spoken against Milner for causing the Boer War and the horrors of the British concentration camps wherein thousands of women and children perished. Consequently, Grey, like Milner, detested him. Liberal Party historian, Iain Sharpe writes:

> Campbell-Bannerman ultimately blamed the British government for the Boer War and believed it an unnecessary blunder, while Asquith regarded Britain as more sinned against than sinning. ... Asquith and Grey supported the diplomacy of Sir Alfred Milner, the British High Commissioner for Southern Africa and Governor of Cape Colony, with whom they had close personal ties. C-B, on the other hand, was privately critical of Milner's belligerent approach and struggled to resist expressing these views in public.... Despite C-B's attempts to preserve unity, Grey and Haldane, along with other Liberal Imperialists, believed that Campbell-Bannerman's leadership was resulting in an unsustainable fudge over the war and hoped for Rosebery to return to the leadership with Asquith leading the party in the House of Commons.... C-B's notorious 'methods of barbarism' speech in June 1901, in which he denounced the conditions in which Boer prisoners were being held in concentration camps in South Africa, plunged Asquith into open confrontation with his leader.... While C-B was sincere in his comments on the suffering in the concentration camps, Asquith joined with Liberal Imperialists in seeing it as a sign that the party leadership had been captured by the pro-Boers.[20]

The Times, and other British newspapers owned or controlled by members of the Milner Group, supported such nonsense, and ran a campaign vilifying Campbell-Bannerman in the eyes of the public. He reflected, however, the feeling of the majority of Liberals in the shadow cabinet and the party as a whole with his "New Liberalism" and had their support. The Milner Group was painfully aware that Campbell-Bannerman was a pacifist anti-imperialist and would have to be dumped if their plan for war was to progress. They could not risk having a man of such views in 10 Downing Street. The subterfuge and duplicity employed by Milner and his close ally, King Edward, to sideline the decent and honourable Campbell-Bannerman is amply revealed in a 1973 biography by British historian and diplomat, John McMoran Wilson: *CB: A Life of Sir Henry Campbell-Bannerman.* For anyone who believes that conspiracies do not happen in British politics, the book is essential reading.

In July 1905, Richard Haldane went to Buckingham Palace for dinner with King Edward and his personal private secretary, Lord Knollys, to discuss the Campbell-Bannerman situation and get their guidance.[21] Eight weeks later, Haldane, Grey and Asquith travelled to Grey's remote fishing lodge near Relugas in the north of Scotland to plot how best to get rid of Campbell-Bannerman. If the Liberal party won the next election as expected, they would exert pressure on him to take a peerage and shuffle off to the House of Lords. He would be politically neutered, and Asquith would lead the Liberals in the House of Commons. Grey would be Foreign Secretary and Haldane Secretary of State for War. If "CB" refused to go to the House of Lords, all three would refuse to serve in the Cabinet. The Relugas conspirators returned to London, and Haldane wrote to Lord Knollys:

> When I had some confidential conversations with you in the end of July you asked me to let you know if any new development took place in the situation of the opposition.... I have just returned from a private conversation with Asquith and Grey. We had, as you know, formed the view strongly that Sir H. C.B. might go to the upper house leaving Asquith to lead the Commons with Grey by his side. But we have within the last few days been made aware that this course will not be acceptable to a certain section of the party. Pressure will doubtless be put on Sir H. C.B. to retain his lead in the Commons ... Asquith, Grey, and I feel that were this to happen we could offer no real service ... and we have decided, in such case, that it would be best for us to intimate to Sir H.CB. that we should stand aside.[22]

Lord Knollys replied that the King strongly opposed them resigning, and insisted they must serve in the Cabinet no matter what happened. It would prove disastrous for the continuity of foreign policy (as decreed by the Milner Group) if Campbell-Bannerman remained in power and they declined to serve as senior members of his new government. A different solution would have to be found.

In early October 1905, the King summoned Haldane, and the Conservative prime minister Lord Balfour, together with Lord Esher to the palace to discuss the Committee of Imperial Defence (CID) that Balfour had created in 1902. The CID was hugely important for it was by that secretive committee that military plans for the coming war against Germany would be coordinated. Haldane advised the king that Campbell-Bannerman opposed the CID, while he, Grey and Asquith fully supported it. The King had his eminence grise, Lord Esher, placed permanently (and unconstitutionally) on the committee as a permanent member. Through Esher, Edward VII would have a powerful voice in all discussions.

Following the Buckingham Palace meeting, Haldane reported back to Asquith and Grey that their Relugas plot had been approved by the King. He would ask CB to Sandringham in November, suggest a peerage, and tell him a younger man was needed to run the government. Haldane added that everyone was "fully alive to the importance of secrecy and reticence. If tongues are held we have secured very cordial and powerful assistance."[23] King Edward and the leader of the Conservative Party, Arthur Balfour, were effectively deciding how an incoming Liberal government should be composed, and the three Liberal Imperialists were complicit.

Irish-Canadian historian, John Cafferky writes:

> The evidence shows that Balfour, the King, Knollys, and Esher (a leader in the secret society) colluded in shaping the incoming Liberal Government, a collusion that at best was constitutionally suspect, and at worst outright conspiracy.[24]

As a leading player in the secret society, Lord Balfour knew his Conservative government's days were numbered. That posed no problem provided other Milner Group men were at the top in the incoming Liberal government and the pacifist Campbell-Bannerman was rendered impotent. Accordingly, Balfour resigned as Prime Minister on December 4, 1905. Instead of the King then dissolving Parliament as would have been the norm, he invited Campbell-Bannerman to Buckingham Palace the following day. Campbell-Bannerman had little or no idea that he was being stitched up and had fully expected the King to invite him to form the next government. Instead, at the Palace on December 5, he was shocked, "sore and wounded" when the King asked him to take a peerage and leave the House of Commons. As the saying goes, he was to be 'kicked upstairs.' The Relugas trio also encouraged him to go, but having taken advice from his wife and many supporters in the party, "CB" resolved to remain in the House of Commons as prime minister.

On 5 November *The Times* – the secret society's leading newspaper – carried their propaganda that having Edward Grey in the Cabinet would be the chief guarantee against the "rashness" of Campbell-Bannerman. *The Times* claimed that due continuity would be maintained in foreign affairs with Grey in charge of foreign policy. The following day, 6 November, *The Times* suggested Campbell-Bannerman should go to the House of Lords. Then again on the following day it kept up the pressure:

> The opinion gains ground that Sir Henry Campbell-Bannerman will eventually waive his objections ... to his elevation to the upper house... It is becoming plain that he cannot otherwise secure the inclusion in his cabinet of the men upon whom he must depend.[25]

Despite the intense pressure he was now under to accept a peerage and depart the House of Commons, Campbell-Bannerman refused to budge. It was a brave stance, but he made a serious error in appointing Asquith as Chancellor of the Exchequer, and Grey as Foreign Secretary. He offered Haldane the Home Office but Haldane insisted on becoming the Minister of War. The Relugas trio was now in a strong position to influence and control government policy if they could circumvent the prime minster. We should emphasise that neither Campbell-Bannerman nor others in the Cabinet had any idea whatsoever that Grey, Asquith and Haldane were closely linked to a powerful secret society that was plotting a war on Germany.

Having substantial support elsewhere in the Party and the country generally, Campbell-Bannerman immediately called a general election and fought the campaign on "Peace, Retrenchment and Reform." He told the country that his party would reduce spending on armaments and divert the money to education and social welfare reform. It was music to the ears of the electorate, and the Liberals won a landslide victory in the general election held in early 1906. The warmongering secret society's man, Arthur Balfour, lost his constituency to the Liberal candidate and left the House of Commons. He would, however, quickly be found a safe Tory seat, and returned through a by-election.

Could the new pacifist prime minister have stopped war planning in its tracks? He appeared to have the upper hand over the Relugas conspirators, but he had made the mistake of giving them senior Cabinet posts, and they were able to undermine him. Campbell-Bannerman's 73-year-old wife, Charlotte, was in poor health and her weight had ballooned. While Campbell-Bannerman devotedly cared for her in 10 Downing Street, Asquith – who was sixteen years younger – offered his 'sincere' support and 'kindly' deputised for him in his prime ministerial duties. Eight months after his election victory, Campbell-Bannerman's beloved wife and inseparable companion for 46 years died. He then suffered a series of heart attacks and spent much of his time depressed and alone in his apartment in Downing Street. The Irish MP Thomas O'Connor wrote of "CB":

> The Prime Minister, in 10 Downing Street was less happy than the cottager that tramps home to his cabin ... He was visibly perishing, looked terribly old, and some days almost seemed to be dying himself; and there was little doubt in the mind of anybody who watched him that if the double strain were prolonged, he would either die or resign.[26]

Campbell-Bannerman was a broken man, and power was effectively in the hands of Asquith, Grey and Haldane. The Liberal Party's peace, retrenchment, and social welfare manifesto that had won them the overwhelming support of the British people was kicked into the long grass and abandoned. Campbell-Bannerman would resign and die just weeks later. The Milner Group now held all the aces and their secret planning for war progressed without hindrance, with massive spending on the army and Royal Navy.

Now head of the Foreign Office, Edward Grey, just like Lansdowne before him, would defer to the King and Lord Esher on the crucial issue of alliances and much else. Grey had only been abroad on one short occasion and spoke no foreign languages. He happily agreed to the King making foreign trips to conduct alliance negotiations though this was unconstitutional. Diplomat Sir Roger Casement wrote:

> Sir Edward Grey was by constitution, temperament and lack of training, no less than the absence of the special qualities needed, unfit for the post the exigencies of political party life placed him in charge of, on the return of the Liberals to office, after ten years of exclusion from power in December 1905.... He knew little of foreign countries, or the life of other peoples. He was not a student of history, a profound thinker, a well-read man or one even who moved much among his own countrymen. His tastes were those of a stay-at-home country gentleman, a Whig rather than a Liberal in political outlook, and one who preferred to be left alone with a

fishing-rod on the banks of a quiet stream.... When, in December 1905, the Liberals returned to office, with Sir Edward Grey at the Foreign Office, they did not return to power in matters of foreign policy. The system was already well established.... No Minister, however strong, could have broken the power of the ring of irresponsibles around the King who drove the coach of state surely and relentlessly to a well-planned war with Germany. A strong and far-seeing man, a statesman, might have resisted, fought and resigned. Sir Edward Grey was none of these things. At heart a peace-loving, a domestic, a quiet man, he had been raised to an office he was wholly unfitted for and chiefly just for that reason. The powers that drove the car of state did not want a wiser man.[27]

According to Professor Quigley, the power and influence of the secret society in British imperial affairs and foreign policy since 1889, "although not widely recognized, can hardly be exaggerated."[28] With Grey as Foreign Secretary, top positions in the Foreign Office were now filled with other members of the Milner Group. Charles Hardinge, close friend of King Edward, and Ambassador to Russia, was a member of the secret society. [29] In 1906 he was moved to the Foreign Office in London in the very important post of Permanent Under-Secretary for Foreign Affairs. Hardinge, whose brother Arthur was a Fellow of All Souls, advised Grey and the ministerial team on international policy, and was head of the Diplomatic Service, which included all British ambassadors. He became King Edward's right-hand man in foreign affairs. Quigley writes:

> Charles Hardinge, although almost unknown to many people, is one of the most significant figures in the formation of British foreign policy in the twentieth century. He was the close personal friend and most important adviser on foreign policy of King Edward VII and accompanied the King on all his foreign diplomatic tours ... He was probably the most important single person in the formation of the Entente Cordiale in 1904 and was very influential in the formation of the understanding with Russia in 1907.[30]

Hardinge would later be promoted to Viceroy and Governor-General of India and was replaced at the Foreign Office by Sir Arthur Nicolson (Oxford university). As British Ambassador to Russia (1906-1910), Nicolson too would play an important role with King Edward and Charles Hardinge in the Anglo-Russian agreement of 1907. His son, Harold Nicolson, (Balliol, Oxford) would similarly go on to do significant work in the Foreign Office for the Milner Group. Hardinge and Nicolson Sr. were an immense help to King Edward and the secret society in creating the alliances against Germany. Sir Edward Grey may have been the elected representative at the Foreign Office, but King Edward, Charles Hardinge, and Arthur Nicolson guided the policy behind the scenes while Grey brushed off any potentially difficult questions in parliament.

On taking power, Asquith, Grey and Haldane immediately bolstered the Committee of Imperial Defence. The British army had struggled to defeat the determined Boer farmers in South Africa, and a radical and rapid shake up of the military was urgently needed.

> The reshaping of the armed forces had to be led by a trusted man. It fell to Esher to ensure that the chosen incumbent in the War Office was such a trusted agent. He proceeded to influence the future development and organisation of Britain's military policy and appointments for the remaining years of King Edward's reign. His position was entirely unconstitutional, but his role continued unchallenged, protected by his membership of the Secret Elite and the king's patronage.
>
> One of the most important features of the Secret Elite plan for war was to keep an iron grip on foreign policy. The long-term drive to war had to be imprinted on the departmental mindset at the War Office, the Admiralty and, in particular, the Foreign Office. Governments might rise and fall, but the ultimate objective had to be sustained, no matter the politics of the day.[31]

The CID was a secretive and very exclusive group. Lord Esher and King Edward knew that its work preparing British forces for a European war had to remain hidden from parliament and the people. Of the new Cabinet formed in 1906, only Asquith, Grey and Haldane were aware of its real purpose. Campbell-Bannerman certainly knew *of* the CID, but was effectively kept in the dark regarding its true role. Richard Haldane was the committee's political link. It was packed with other members of the Milner Group, including Lord Roberts, commander-in-chief of the armed forces and a longstanding friend of Milner's from the South Africa campaign. Robert's protegé, Sir John French, served on the committee and in 1907 was appointed Inspector-General of the Army. King Edward was able to voice his opinion at the regular CID meetings through Lord Esher. Esher's man, Sir George Clarke, was positioned as permanent secretary to the CID, and colluded with Edward Grey in deceiving Campbell-Bannerman.

The pacifist British prime minister was kept in the dark about the secret Anglo-French military negotiations taking place in preparation for war.[32]

It is important to understand that the Committee of Imperial Defence was, from 1906, planning and meticulously preparing for a war against Germany without the slightest knowledge of the people, parliament, or the majority of members of the British Cabinet. The true purposes of the informal alliances created with France and Russia were also kept hidden despite the best efforts of men such as the journalist and pacifist, E.D. Morel, and politician, John Morley. As we shall see, the most tightly guarded secret of all was the close military arrangements between Britain and Belgium.

In making Britain's small standing army ready for the task ahead, War Minister Richard Haldane immediately set to work. He would later (1920) publish a book, *Before the War*, to explain away the policy pursued toward Germany by Great Britain through the eight years immediately preceding 1914. According to his whitewash, Britain was a peace-loving nation with no intent whatsoever on war against Germany. It needed, however, a well-trained, disciplined army as an "insurance policy" against possible German aggression. He indicated that Campbell-Bannerman was fully aware of this. As always, the big lies are the best lies. Haldane wrote:

> Could we then, reconsider our military organization, so that we might be able rapidly to dispatch, if we ever thought it necessary in our own interests, say, 100,000 men in a well-formed army, not to invade Belgium, which no one thought of doing, but to guard the French frontier of Belgium in case the German Army should seek to enter France in that way. Sir Edward Grey consulted the Prime Minister, Sir Henry Campbell-Bannerman, the Chancellor of the Exchequer, Mr. Asquith, and myself as War Minister, and I was instructed, in January 1906, a month after assuming office, to take the examination of the question in hand. This occurred in the middle of the General Election which was then in progress. I went at once to London and summoned the heads of the British General Staff and saw the French military attaché, Colonel Huguet, a man of sense and ability. I became aware at once that there was a new army problem. It was, how to mobilize and concentrate at a place of assembly to be opposite the Belgian frontier...[33]

THE BELGIAN CONNECTION.

In the midst of a general election campaign in 'peace loving' Britain in 1906, with the Liberal Party standing on a platform of "Peace, Retrenchment and Reform," some of its leaders were busy in London examining the fastest way to get the British army to the Belgian frontier to fight Germany.

Ties between Britain and Belgium were close thanks to intimate, long-standing links between the British and Belgian royal families. Leopold, the youngest son of the Duke of Saxe-Coburg-Saalfeld, married Princess Charlotte of Wales, daughter of King George IV, took British citizenship and was made Field Marshal in the British army. In 1831 he was crowned the first king of Belgium. Leopold's nephew, Prince Albert, married Queen Victoria, and was the father of King Edward VII. Queen Victoria was close to Leopold, considering him her favourite uncle and father figure. When Leopold I died in 1865, his son took the throne as King Leopold II – Queen Victoria's first cousin. Leopold II ran the Congo in central Africa as his own personal possession, and Belgian soldiers there became infamous for the brutality meted out to African labourers. Tens of thousands had one or both hands chopped off if they did not collect a stipulated quota of rubber or ivory, and upwards of ten million Africans reportedly perished under the rule of Leopold II.[34]

Leopold II amassed huge personal wealth from the suffering of the Africans, and as the horrors became widely known, pressure was applied on the Belgian government to take control and alleviate the atrocities. Leopold agreed, but before the hand-over he sold the profitable rubber businesses and other wealth generators in the Congo to Nelson Aldrich and wealthy banking and industrial interests in the United States.[35] The financial elite in the U.S. retained half the profits, with Leopold retaining the other half. Nelson Aldrich as we have seen, was an integral member of the Anglo-American Establishment in setting up the corrupt Federal Reserve System. The African state was annexed in 1908, to become the 'Belgian Congo'. Belgian taxpayers now incurred the huge cost of running it as a Belgian colony, while the substantial profits from it were shared by King Leopold and the American elites.

A treaty between major European Powers had been signed back in 1839 wherein all agreed to recognise and uphold the neutrality and independence of the newly-formed state of Belgium. By 1913, however, Britain and France were breaking that treaty through their secret military arrangements with Belgium. For almost ten years prior to the outbreak of war against Germany, senior military personnel in Belgium, Britain and France had been working in the closest cooperation to prepare for that war.

From 1905 onwards, Britain's military link with Belgium was one of the most tightly guarded secrets, even within privileged circles ... At the Committee of Imperial Defence meeting on 26 July 1905, they agreed to treat the special sub-committee that would take forward joint planning with the French and Belgian military personnel as so secret that minutes would not be printed or circulated without special permission from the prime minister.... A British force of 105,000 would be sent to Belgium.... A fully elaborated plan detailed the landings and transportation of the British forces, which were actually called "allied armies," and at a series of meetings they discussed the allocation of Belgian officers and interpreters to the British Army and crucial details on the care and "accommodation of the wounded allied armies.".... Confidentiality was stressed repeatedly, and, and above all, the necessity of keeping the conversations secret from the Press was explicitly spelled out.[36]

In 1906, British General, Sir Henry Wilson, spent the entire summer reconnoitring the Franco-Belgian border making detailed notes on the topography. Thereafter, he made repeated visits to Belgium to check out the anticipated battlefields. Wilson worked closely with leading figures in the Belgian army, and top-secret agreements on military cooperation between Britain and Belgium were being put in place years before the outbreak of war.

With British and French bank loans, Belgium now spent huge sums of money on a military build-up. In 1912 the Belgian army was enormously expanded to 150,000 men in the field, 60,000 in auxiliary services, and 130,000 in defensive garrisons. 340,000 men in all.[37] It was a gigantic force for a supposedly neutral nation of only 7.5 million people. In 1913 compulsory military service was also introduced in Belgium.

> Nothing was being left to chance. Top secret guidebooks for the British military dated 1912 contained highly detailed maps of Belgian towns, villages, and rural areas, including railway stations, and church steeples suitable for observation posts, and oil depots, roads, canals and bridges. British-Belgian military tactics had been worked out in fine detail, including the role of intermediary officers, interpreters, English translations of Belgian regulations, hospital accommodation for the British wounded and more ... Lieutenant-Colonel Bridges confirmed to the Belgians that Britain had an army composed of six divisions of infantry and eight brigades of cavalry – 160,000 men in all – and that "everything was ready" to go.[38]

Belgian neutrality was a myth. Anglo-Belgian joint military planning was "ready to go" against Germany in 1912. A German diplomat, Alexander Fuehr, working in the German embassy in New York, published a book in 1915, *The Neutrality of Belgium.* Fuehr wrote:

> It created considerable astonishment in Europe when, in 1907, it was announced that Great Britain had finally consented to the absorption of the Congo State by Belgium, a step which was entirely against British interests; and it was generally rumoured that doubtless the unexpected settlement of this affair *was a bargain between the two merchant-kings on European thrones – Edward VII and Leopold II –* a bargain likely to be profitable to both sides. There is hardly any doubt now that at that time Belgium, through her king, bargained away her status as a perpetually neutral country by entering into a military compact with England. It was England, therefore, which caused Belgium to embark upon a course of very costly army reorganization, crowned by the law of 28 May 1914, by which that country practically adopted universal compulsory service and raised the war strength of her army to nearly half a million men, the necessary funds for this undertaking being provided by a loan in London. And it was England which forced "neutral" Belgium to become her secret ally, in the event of a European conflagration.[39]

Predictably, Fuehr's book was dismissed by British historians as German propaganda and fabrication. We now know that it most certainly was not.

Thanks in large part to King Edward, the United States, France and Belgium had been successfully roped into the Milner Group's war plans. Several pieces of the alliance jigsaw had still to be put in place, however, Russia in particular.

KING EDWARD AND THE RUSSIANS

The Milner Group plan for a Triple Entente of Britain, France and Russia almost came unstuck in July 1905 when Czar Nicholas II and his cousin, Kaiser Wilhelm II, sailed in their royal yachts to rendezvous at the Swedish island of Björkö for confidential talks. Russia, at the time was at war with Japan, a war whose origins had much to do with British connivance. Britain had entered a treaty with Japan in 1902 aimed at Russia,[40] and the Czar was resentful and angry at

115

Britain for encouraging the Japanese. His ire was justified, for Britain had built a modern fleet of warships for the Imperial Japanese Navy which she then encouraged to attack the Russian fleet. British banking houses, the Rothschilds in particular, raised over £5 billion at today's value to assist Japan, and almost half her war debt was financed through bonds sold mostly in London and New York.[41] In a surprise Japanese naval attack on the night of 8-9 February 1904, with no declaration of war, Japanese destroyers raced into Port Arthur, the Russian naval base in Manchuria, and torpedoed the Russian fleet. Some warships were sunk, others managed to escape to the open seas. The following year, in the naval battle of Tsushima, the Japanese navy all but destroyed Russia's only remaining fleet, which had sailed halfway round the world only to be routed.

At Björkö (24 July 1905), with the Tsushima disaster (27-28 May) fresh on his mind, Czar Nicholas agreed a mutual defence treaty with Kaiser Wilhelm wherein they would come to each other's aid if either country was attacked. The czar indicated that he would attempt to bring France into the agreement if Germany would let France have Alsace-Lorraine. Germany and Russia in alliance was the Milner Group's greatest geopolitical nightmare, and within days of the Björkö meeting, King Edward was desperately trying to find out exactly what had been agreed. On the kaiser's return to Germany, he wrote to Czar Nicholas that Britain only wanted to make France her 'cat's paw' (tool) against Germany, as she had used Japan against Russia. It was an entirely accurate assessment. Wilhelm advised Nicholas that King Edward, "the arch intriguer and mischief-maker in Europe," was now hard at work trying to discover precisely what had transpired at Björkö. The king had asked Count Alexander von Benckendorff, the Russian ambassador at London, to go immediately to Denmark to find out what had been agreed. Benckendorff met there with the Dowager Empress of Russia, and the Russian ambassador

Izvolsky

to Copenhagen, Alexander Izvolsky, and reported back to King Edward.

> How they managed to kill the Björkö Treaty is further testament to the power the Secret Elite extended across Europe.... This dangerous treaty had to be quashed ... Russia was already in desperate financial Straits after Tsushima and in need of fresh loans. The Paris Bourse had deeper, more reliable pockets than the Berlin banks and had traditionally been the main source of financial backing for Russia. The Secret Elite threatened to pull the financial plug unless

the Czar came to his senses. Much to the disappointment of Kaiser Wilhelm, the opportunity to realign Europe towards a greater peace fell before it reached the first hurdle. Czar Nicholas backtracked, and the treaty never was, though as Wilhelm bitterly reminded him: "We joined hands and signed before God who heard our vows." His desperate appeal fell on deaf ears ... Russia became the victim of British trickery, manipulated into a different treaty that was designed not to protect her or the peace of Europe but to enable the Secret Elite to destroy Germany.[42]

The Russian diplomat who cooperated most closely with King Edward in his intrigues to secure an Anglo-Russian agreement, was Alexander Izvolsky. He had served in various positions abroad, including Japan, before ending up in a relatively unimportant posting to Copenhagen in 1904. King Edward, married as he was to the sister of the Danish wife of Czar Alexander III, held considerable sway in the Danish Royal Court and got positive feed-back about Izvolsky's Anglophilia and dislike of Germany and Austria.

> A courtier and a snob, Izvolsky had an almost morbid ambition to court the high born at home and abroad. He regarded himself as called to make a rapprochement with England.[43]

When Izvolsky received an unexpected visit from the mighty King Edward in person at the Russian consulate in Copenhagen back in April 1904, it was the outstanding event of his life. Sycophantic and ingratiating in the royal presence, he eagerly agreed with the king when he expressed his great satisfaction over the cordial agreement with France and hoped for a similar entente with Russia. King Edward judged that Izvolsky could be a useful tool in the future, and wrote to his nephew, the Czar, expressing his "great pleasure" at meeting him:

> In him you have a man of remarkable intelligence and who is, I am sure, one of your ablest and most devoted servants.... My earnest desire, which I am convinced you will share, is that at the conclusion of the war our two countries may come to a satisfactory settlement regarding many difficult matters between us, and that a lasting agreement may be arrived at, similar to the one we have lately concluded with France.[44]

The king's glowing reference about Izvolsky to the czar would, as was intended, lead to Izvolsky gaining a far greater position than the backwater post in Copenhagen. Carroll Quigley relates that the Milner Group bought and controlled politicians everywhere, and Alexander Izvolsky appears to have been a prime example. According to historian G. P. Gooch:

> He [Izvolsky] suffered a terror of losing caste through any failure in his clothes, his carriages, his furniture, his acquaintances, and his relatives. His desire to shine led him, a man of very modest means, to hunger for the opportunity to gratify his extravagant tastes. His selfish materialism was as undeniable as his ability. ... His vanity and affectations so deliciously described by Harold Nicolson, suggest that a fine intellect was mated with a rather shoddy soul.[45]

Izvolsky was widely read and hardworking, but the fact that his modest salary was insufficient to support his extravagant tastes made him susceptible to bribes. King Edward visited him again in 1905, then in 1906 the now expensively attired little Russian visited London for three weeks. He was completely in tune with King Edward's wishes and it was very apparent that he would do his bidding. Before leaving London, Izvolsky stated that the foreign policy of Russia must rest on the immutable foundation of the alliance with France, but must be fortified and enlarged by an agreement with England. On his return to Copenhagen from London, Isvolsky was summoned by the Czar to St Petersburg and appointed Russian Foreign Secretary. It was a stunning promotion. King Edward's intrigues were entirely successful. The British elites now had a man at the top of the political tree in Russia who was entirely in tune with their aim of crushing Germany. Genuine British friendship for Russia was not involved. This was business, and as Kaiser Wilhelm had stated, Britain would use Russia as a cat's paw. With Izvolsky in charge of foreign affairs, Russia could now be readily manipulated into a treaty that, in due time, would help the Milner Group and its allied financial cabal crush Germany. King Edward made frequent visits to Paris to seal the Entente Cordiale in 1904. He would now woo the Russians, but had to stay well clear of the *Russian* capital.

> The most frightful things were being done in Russia at the time: lynchings, tortures, burnings alive. And so prevalent was the terror that it was not deemed safe to invite the King to St Petersburg.[46]

The diabolical events in the Russian capital and elsewhere in the country, however, did not stop Edward courting Russia. The next move came in March 1907 when an Imperial Russian naval squadron, including the

Battleship *Tsesarevich,* was invited to pay a courtesy visit to the naval base at Portsmouth on the south coast. King Edward ordered the Admiralty to provide a special train to bring some Russian officers and ratings to visit London.

> On March 27, in accordance with the King's command to the Commander-in-Chief at Portsmouth, a party of the officers and men of the Russian squadron visiting Portsmouth went as His Majesty's guests to London. The party consisted of eighteen Russian officers and one hundred Russian seamen, and it was entertained at luncheon and dinner at the Grand Hotel, Charing Cross. After luncheon the men, accompanied by some of the officers, went to the Hippodrome to witness the afternoon performance; and they were afterwards driven through the city. In the evening the Alhambra was visited, and the officers were accompanied by the Russian Ambassador, Lord Tweedmouth, Sir Edward Grey, and Admiral Sir John Fisher. A telegram was sent to King Edward in the course of the evening: "The Russian officers and seamen visiting London from the squadron at Portsmouth, having drunk Your Majesty's health, most respectfully wish you all happiness and desire to express their gratitude for their visit to your capital." A hearty welcome by the public was extended to the party as it drove through the streets of the metropolis. Though but a little thing in itself, it is such actions as these that go to build up an understanding between nations and strengthen the entente cordiale between friendly powers.[47]

The Times talked of rapprochement with Russia as a natural and inevitable follow-on to the Entente Cordiale with France. The red carpet was laid out for the Russian sailors, with the Foreign Secretary, Edward Grey, and Admiral Fisher in attendance.

> While the British public was softened up in anticipation of an alliance with Russia, the Bear was being enticed into a honeytrap.[48]

King Edward had no need to travel to strife-torn Russia to implement an Anglo-Russian agreement. His loyal servant, Arthur Nicolson, had been sent to the key post of British ambassador in St Petersburg in 1906, and was on good terms with the new Foreign Minister, and King Edward's 'friend,' Isvolsky. It was Nicolson who "carried forward the negotiations which culminated in the Anglo-Russian Convention of August 1907."[49]

The Convention ironed out differences between Britain and Russia over their spheres of influence in Persia, Afghanistan and Tibet. None of these countries belonged to Britain, yet without the permission of Persia (now Iran) it was divided into three zones, with Britain controlling the south and Russia the north. A small middle 'neutral zone' separated them and was graciously left to the Persians. It was seen as a gross insult to the whole of Islam, with the British government lying to critics that Persia's ancient independence would be respected. In a British Parliamentary debate on 6 February 1908, Lord Curzon stated:

> I am astounded at the coolness, I might even say the effrontery, with which the British Government is in the habit of parcelling out the territory of powers whose independence and integrity it assures them, at the same time, it has no other intentions than to preserve.[50]

King Edward arranged to pay the czar a visit in June 1908, but St. Petersburg remained a dangerous city. Instead, he sailed in the royal yacht with an impressive escort of British warships to meet Nicholas at the Bay of Reval (now Tallin) in Estonia. Protests erupted in the British parliament over the visit and what was happening in Russia. Around 100 members of the Russian parliament – the Duma – had been sent to Siberia or held in local prisons, and almost 2,000 protestors had been executed. Sir Edward Grey calmed the British members of Parliament, assuring them it was purely a family visit and that no convention or treaty with Russia would be discussed. (They had no knowledge of the Anglo-Russian agreement of 1907.) For the 'family visit,' King Edward took along his constant companion on foreign trips, secret society member and leading string puller in the foreign office, Sir Charles Hardinge. Admiral Sir John Fisher, head of the Royal Navy, and Sir John French, Inspector General of the army, joined them for good measure with a team of private secretaries. On the Russian side with the czar was Russian prime minister, Pyotr Stolypin, foreign secretary Alexander Izvolsky, and a group of diplomats. King Edward's meeting with Czar Nicholas at Reval was arranged not with a family gathering in mind, but for the very serious business of adding Russia to the now well-established Anglo-French Entente. It proved an overwhelming success when the King "sealed the Triple Entente."[51]

If the Milner Group was to be successful in encouraging Russia into war against Germany, it would require profound changes to the long-entrenched British foreign policy of resisting Russian expansion towards the Black Sea Straits. Control of the Straits – the narrow passage from the Black Sea to the Aegean Sea – would afford Russian ships access to the

Mediterranean and beyond from their home ports on the Black Sea. It had been Russia's holy grail for centuries. Edward Grey instructed ambassador Nicolson to inform the Russians that Britain would no longer oppose this. "The old policy of closing the Straits against her, and throwing our weight against her at conference of the Powers" would be "abandoned."[52]

Britain had long thwarted Russian control of the Straits[53] yet that is what the czar was offered. Just as old enemy France was enticed into an alliance with the assurance of regaining the 'Lost Provinces' of Alsace-Lorraine, Russia was now lured to Britain's side with the golden carrot of Constantinople and the Straits. The Ottoman Turks barred Russian ships access to the Straits, so Russia's massive grain harvest, and much more, were consequently unable to be exported throughout winter because her ports in the north were frozen solid. Once Germany and her Ottoman allies were defeated, Russia would be given year-round access to the world's oceans for her merchant fleet and warships from the Black Sea. It was an astonishing promise that the British elites had no intention whatsoever of keeping.

In 1909, the czar and Alexander Izvolsky reciprocated King Edward's trip to Reval, and sailed to England in order to consolidate the agreement. Off Spithead near the Isle of Wight, in a mighty show of British naval strength, one hundred and fifty-three British warships were arranged in three parallel rows for inspection by the czar on his royal yacht.

The Anglo-Russian Convention was signed on 31 August 1907. Years of machiavellian scheming by the secret society and King Edward paid substantial dividends. Germany was now surrounded by the proverbial 'ring of steel'.

Kaiser Wilhelm was well aware that the Triple Entente was a loaded pistol pointed at Germany. His friend, Count Otto Zedlitz-Trützschler, related a discussion they had on the matter:

> The Kaiser began to talk freely about the policy of England and grew rather excited. He complained bitterly of the intrigues that his uncle, the King of England, was carrying on about him. He said he knew all about them from private letters from France, and King Edward was equally hard at work in every other country.... "He is a Satan; you can hardly believe what a Satan he is."[54]

King Edward was indeed 'hard at work' plotting in other countries including Spain and Italy. Two significant tasks remained for him: Ensuring that Spain did not ally with Germany, and detaching Italy from the Triple Alliance with Germany and Austria-Hungary.

KING EDWARD AND THE SPANISH

On 8 April 1907, with the usual impressive escort of British warships, King Edward sailed on the royal yacht *Victoria and Albert* to Cartagena in south-east Spain for talks with King Alfonso XIII. Alfonso was married to Edward's niece, Princess Victoria Eugenie. Her mother, Beatrice, was Queen Victoria and Albert's fifth daughter. Alfonso toasted King Edward's health, and Edward returned the toast:

> We reciprocate the desire that the ties between our two houses and our countries, which are founded not only on historical tradition, but also on a community of interests and a real sympathy, may be strengthened and drawn closer by these happy events.[55]

On 12 April, the Belgian Chargé d'affaires in London, E. Cartier, wrote to the Belgian Foreign Ministry about Edward's trip to Spain:

> The English are getting more and more into the habit of regarding international problems as being almost exclusively within the power of King Edward. ... The proof of this attitude of mind is the total absence of discord between the two great historic parties [Conservative and Liberal] in all matters relating to England's political destinies.. It is this fact which makes it possible for Sir Edward Grey to carry on Lord Lansdowne's work without hesitation and without incident. ... King Edward's visit to his royal nephew at Carthagena was no doubt specifically inspired by the desire to strengthen the ties that unite Spain to Great Britain, and as much as possible to weaken German influence in Madrid.[56]

The astute Belgian diplomat could see that British foreign policy now being pursued by the Liberal government was exactly the same as that of the Conservatives, and that King Edward, not Sir Edward Grey, was the power behind it. On 18 April 1907, another Belgian diplomat – the Belgian Minister in Berlin – wrote to his Foreign Minister in Brussels:

> Like the Treaty of Alliance with Japan, the entente cordiale with France and the negotiations pending with Russia, the King of England's visit to the King of Spain is one of the moves in the campaign to isolate Germany that is being personally directed with as much perseverance as success by his Majesty King Edward VII. ... England has promised to assist in reconstructing the Spanish fleet and fortifying the Iberian coast ... There is some right to regard with suspicion this eagerness to unite, for a so-called defensive object, Powers who are menaced by nobody.[57]

The sharp-witted Belgian ministers recognised that King Edward's diplomacy was aimed at forming alliances and firm understandings with just about every country other than Germany. Like all but a very select few, they had no knowledge whatsoever that their own 'neutral' little country had likewise been drawn in by British subterfuge.

KING EDWARD AND THE ITALIANS

Immediately following the highly successful visit to Spain, the royal yacht and its escort set course for Italy, a country that had been in the 'Triple Alliance' with Austria-Hungary and Germany since 1882. King Edward had just played a major role in securing a friendly understanding with Spain, and his job now was to detach Italy from the Triple Alliance. He had earlier attempted to detach Austria-Hungary from Germany, with no success.[58]

On 18 April 1907, the royal yacht steamed into Gaeta harbour south of Rome with an escort of no fewer than eight battleships, four cruisers, and four destroyers. The grand spectacle left no doubt as to the importance of the occasion. King Victor Emmanuel III, who had arrived the previous evening in his personal yacht, the *Trinacria,* was there to greet the British monarch with his own escort of twelve Italian warships and their accompanying torpedo boats. Edward was reportedly the first English sovereign to set foot in Italy since Richard the Lionheart on his way to the crusades six centuries earlier.

> The monarchs interchanged visits, and lunch was served in the saloon of the Italian royal yacht *Trinacria,* after which King Edward and Queen Alexandra returned on board the *Victoria and Albert,* which sailed for Naples. After the meeting of the two Kings, a semi-official note was issued at Rome. "The private manner in which the King of England is meeting the King of Italy at Gaeta is a fresh proof of the personal sentiment and affection uniting the two Sovereigns," so it ran. "The meeting was not actuated by political aims, yet it will produce the best effect on the intimately cordial relations of Great Britain and Italy. The interview between the two Sovereigns, whose pacific sentiments are known, is a promise and guarantee of peace to the whole world."[59]

Thus, Edward's visit to the King of Italy at Gaeta was explained away with the usual lie that it was 'a purely social occasion with no politics involved.'

The entire point of journey to Gaeta was to disrupt the alliance between Italy and Germany. The Belgian Minister in London, Count Charles de Lalaing, wrote to the Belgian Foreign Minister:

It is plain that official England is pursuing a policy that is covertly hostile, and tending to result in the isolation of Germany, and that King Edward has not been above putting his personal inflßuence at the service of this cause.[60]

In that same communication of 24 May 1907, the Belgian Minister in London described how the British "yellow press" had been conducting a vile anti-German propaganda campaign. He specifically named the *Daily Mail, Daily Mirror, Daily Express*, the *Evening News* and the *Weekly Dispatch*. The British Press Baron, Lord Northcliffe, had exclaimed in an interview: "Yes, we detest the Germans, and with all our hearts ... I would not allow the least thing to be printed in my paper [*The Times*] which might offend France; but I should be very sorry to publish anything whatever that might please Germany."[61]

On May 30, the Belgian Ambassador in Berlin, Baron Jules Greindl, wrote to Brussels in a similar vein to Count de Lallaing's communication. Greindl was recognised as a highly intelligent and fair man and a keen observer of the international scene with no axe to grind. His communication is worth quoting at length:

> England is jealous of the gigantic strides made by Germany in industry and commerce, and in her mercantile fleet. She is so used to being without a rival that any competition seems to her to be an act of trespass in her own domain.
>
> England feigns fear in view of the growth of Germany's navy. Their sincerity seems to me to be more than doubtful. She must know that, even in the very far future, it will be practically impossible for Germany to attack her. On the contrary, it is Germany who has every reason to be afraid. For centuries past England has set herself to destroy every foreign naval force as soon as it reached a certain standard of strength. First Holland, and then France met with this fate. Next came the turn of Denmark. Whose vessels were destroyed without the ghost of an excuse by Admiral Nelson, who had entered Copenhagen as a friend.. It was the feeling of apprehension in Germany which aroused popular support for the development of the German Navy, until it should at least be strong enough to play a defensive part. The majority of the nation would not hear of this development so long as any possibility seemed to remain of being able to rely on England's friendship. Or, at least, on her neutrality.
>
> This mistrust is further fostered by the personal zeal shown by the king of England in making ententes with the whole world, excepting Germany, and yet he has no grievances against her that can be stat-

ed. The Press makes it worse by presenting each success won by England in the field of foreign politics as contributing to the isolation of Germany as its final object. And who will say that the Press is wrong in this respect? Far from provoking the tension in her relations with England, Germany is the sufferer by it. This is shown by the repeated attempts at a rapprochement, which invariably originate in Berlin.[62]

Jules Greindl summed the situation up almost perfectly. He had, of course, no knowledge of the fact that the entire situation was being driven by a small faction in England bent on world domination. Entirely on their behalf, King Edward VII took control of foreign policy from Edward Grey and set out to create alliances and 'friendships' that suited and enabled their intention to crush Germany. Had Machiavelli been alive at the time, it is entirely likely that the British monarch could have taught him a few lessons.

Detaching Italy from the Triple Alliance was finalised in October 1909 when Czar Nicholas II arranged a meeting with the Italian king at Racconigi, south of Turin. "From this meeting emerged the very important and very secret Russo-Italian Agreement signed by Isvolsky and the Italian foreign Minister, Tommaso Tittoni."[63] Italy double-crossed its German and Austrian allies while Britain, France and Russia now knew with some certainty that once war began, Italy would initially remain neutral before joining them against Germany, which she did in May 1915.

EDWARD TAKES HIS LEAVE

In March 1910, Edward VII was on holiday at Biarritz on France's Atlantic coast when he suffered a severe episode of bronchitis. He returned to Buckingham Palace at the end of April and died on 6 May. He had left no stone unturned in his efforts to isolate Germany, yet his prime role in setting the international stage for the horrors of the First World War is whitewashed from the accounts of pro-Establishment British 'court historians'. If Edward is mentioned, it is with the usual Orwellian doublespeak as 'a great man' and 'Edward the peacemaker.'

SUMMARY: CHAPTER 4 – WAR BY ROYAL WARRANT

- From 1906 and the lead up to the First World War, democracy in Britain was a sham.

- The Germanophobe King Edward VII acted as Minister for Foreign Affairs and set about building the alliances necessary for war against Germany

- King Edward and his 'unofficial foreign office' subordinates played the major role in creating the 1904 Entente Cordiale with France.

- Campbell-Bannerman, the anti-war Liberal leader who became prime minister in late 1905, was sidelined by the Liberal Imperialists within his party,

- The Committee of Imperial Defence began preparing the British forces for war against Germany. Their activities were unknown to the British people, parliament, and the majority within the Liberal Cabinet.

- Through 1906 – 07, and in utter secrecy Britain and Belgium co-operated closely in joint military planning for war against Germany. Belgium's supposed 'neutrality' was a sham.

- King Edward was instrumental in securing a leading position in Russian politics for his puppet, Alexander Izvolsky, and together in 1907 they drew Russia into the Triple Entente with Britain and France.

- King Edward visited Spain and was successful in ensuring that they would not side with Germany. He immediately went on to Italy where his wooing would reap rich rewards when war came.

Chapter 5

Britain – "Invaluable
to the Cause of Human Liberty"

K ing Edward's second son, Prince George Frederick Ernest Albert (his first son died in 1892) was crowned in Westminster Abbey on 22 June 1911 as King George V. He had served in the Royal Navy for fifteen years, joining as a 12-year-old cadet in 1877 and leaving as a commander. King George abolished all German titles held by the royal family and later changed the official family name from Saxe-Coburg-Gotha to Windsor.

George V

Like his father before him, George V's closest adviser was Lord Esher, the man who wielded considerable power in England and acted as the monarch's

Lord Esher

voice and ears in the Milner Group, and the Milner Group's voice in the monarch's ears! George did not have the same impactful role as his father in preparing for the planned war on Germany, but did everything the Milner Group asked of him. King George was also a close associate of Richard Haldane, who was busy reshaping and modernising the army in preparation for war, and of Admiral Sir John (Jacky) Fisher

who was undertaking a "Ruthless, Relentless, and Remorseless" reorganisation of the navy. Fisher ordered around 160 warships scrapped and had them replaced with fast, modern vessels fit "for instant war."[1] The excuse fed to the British people for the vast expenditure on new Dreadnought battleships was that Germany had started a "naval race" with Britain and would rule the waves if Britain did not stay ahead. The people who had voted overwhelmingly at the last election for peace, and armaments spending to be transferred instead to social welfare programmes, swallowed the lie.

One of Admiral Fisher's greatest contributions to British naval power came with the decision to install oil-fired boilers on all new warships rather than coal. The ships would be able to raise steam significantly faster, be more manoeuvrable, and have a greater range without the need to refuel. The potential problem was that Britain had massive coal deposits, but no oil. The answer lay in Persia. Britain and Russia had just partitioned the country into spheres of influence, allowing Russia to take control of the north with most of its commerce and cities, including the capital Tehran, while Britain took the apparently worthless desert in the south. It appeared a very generous gesture to Russia, but a British geologist, George Reynolds, had just struck oil there in 1908 – a lot of it. An oil refinery was being built by the British owned Anglo-Persian Oil Company close to the Persian Gulf at Abadan and would be operational by 1912. For the next 50 years the Abadan refinery would be one of the largest producers in the world, and ensure oil supplies for the Royal Navy's new warships. In a highly unusual occurrence that puzzled many in Britain, the British government bought a majority share in the Abadan complex. Few if any outside the Milner circle knew war was coming, and that everything was carefully being put in place for it.

> A number of interlocking steps were being taken secretly in Britain so that war would not catch the nation unprepared ... Winston Churchill, backed strongly by his ministerial colleague, Sir Edward Grey, steered the government's Anglo-Persian Oil Company bill through parliament.... It was a calculated move. Oil supplies were guaranteed for the navy.[2]

Taking control of South Persia also enabled British forces to protect the Persian Gulf and the Persian border with that part of India which is now Pakistan. Most generously, the British allowed the Persians to retain control of a central portion of their own country. In the usual British imperialist manner, the carve-up was conducted with little or no discussion with the Persian authorities or people. Britain and Russia took exclusive commercial rights and seized tax revenues. A book, *The Strangling of Persia*, by William Morgan Shuster makes for grim reading about the crimes carried out against the Persian people at that time.[3]

The Persians would pay a heavy price for the Milner Group's intrigues. In late 1911, when Russian forces executed more than a thousand Persian nationalists in the northern city of Tabriz, the British government made no protest. Newspapers abroad reported Persian women being violated in front of their children, and women and children being butchered in cold blood. Russian artillery "mowed down every living creature in the streets."[4]

Possession of northern Persia and advance into Afghanistan was part of Russia's reward for aligning with Britain, but the big carrot was always the promise of Constantinople and the Straits once Russia had played its part in crushing Germany.

Italy's reward for leaving the Triple Alliance with Austria-Hungary and Germany was a licence to invade Cyrenaica and Tripoli in north Africa – then part of the Ottoman Empire. Numerous approaches by the Ottoman government to ally with Britain, France and Russia were rejected. The Turks were very deliberately pushed towards Germany and Austria-Hungary as part of the Milner Group's strategic planning. It would be well-nigh impossible to carve up the Ottoman Empire – and for Russia to be promised Constantinople – if the Turks were allied with Britain in the war, so they had to be directed to the side of the enemy and defeated. As already discussed, Russia was drawn in with that empty promise that would never be fulfilled. The oil-rich Turkish controlled lands of the Middle East and, of course, Palestine, were always destined for British hands. One cannot help feeling a grudging admiration for the complex planning by the Milner Group in the decade before 1914 to get all the players aligned for the planned war.

In 1911, Italian troops invading Libya with British approval were captured at Mechiya Oasis by Turkish forces, and shot. The Italian army responded by massacring a large number of the local population, including several hundred women and children seeking shelter in a mosque. They were burned alive when it was deliberately set alight with them trapped inside.[5] The atrocities in Persia and Libya were met with cynical British government indifference, and went virtually unreported in the British press. It was critical that Russia and Italy were not alienated. Sir Edward Grey insisted that London and St Petersburg were working in tandem and he fully endorsed Russian policy.[6] The Russians carried out terrible atrocities in Persia, but anyone who imagines that Britain was a benign presence there should read Dr Mohammad Gholi Majd's book, *The Great Famine and Genocide in Persia, 1917-1919*. Using sources from American diplomatic dispatches, the reports of American missionaries, contemporary newspapers, eye-witness accounts, and the memoirs of British military officers who served there, Majd presents stomach-churning accounts of how Britain intentionally created famine conditions in Persia that led to the genocide of millions of innocent civilians. It was successfully covered up thanks to financial circles' control of the Press and of the writing of history. Compare the silence, if not indeed approval, of the British authorities on Russian and Italian atrocities, with their faux outrage over the following events in Morocco that same year.

Morocco Crisis 1911

French and Spanish troops had been occupying Morocco in defiance of the Algeciras Act of 1906 in which all of the Powers had agreed to uphold Morocco's integrity and independence. In 1911, France sent an additional large number of troops to occupy the northern inland city of Fez on the pretext that French nationals there were in danger. In reality, it was part of a move to turn Morocco into a French protectorate with British approval. Baron Greindl, the perceptive Belgian ambassador in Berlin, telegraphed his foreign minister in Brussels:

> Since the Act of Algeciras ... little by little the French have got possession of everything, taking advantage of incidents which have arisen automatically, and creating other openings when they were needed. Can the expedition [of French troops to Fez] now be regarded as anything other than an act of the same farce? Sultan Mulai Hafid has already lost his precarious hold over his subjects because he has to submit to become a mere tool in the hands of France.[7]

French troops now occupied much of Morocco, and were treating German commercial interests there with contempt. When they directly interfered with the mining rights of a German company, the German secretary of foreign affairs, Alfred von Kiderlen-Wächter, considered a protest and symbolic gesture were warranted. A small German gunboat with a crew of 125, which was en route home from Africa, was ordered to anchor off the coast of Morocco in the bay of Agadir. Built for colonial service, the *Panther* was an old tub past her scrapping date. Despite the crew never going ashore, nor firing guns, nor making menacing moves of any kind, all hell broke loose in the controlled British and French Press with their ridiculous exaggeration.

Sir Edward Grey erupted with indignation and moral outrage. The Germans, he said, knew no law outside force. How dare Germany anchor a "warship" off the coast of a "neutral" country whose independence was "guaranteed" by Britain? British and French newspapers informed the public that in ordering *Panther* there, Germany was demonstrating her determination for world hegemony. She was "trying to break" the Entente Cordiale between France and Britain and "instigate a European war."[8] The hypocrisy was breath-taking. France had torn up the Treaty of Algeciras that had guaranteed Morocco its independence: French troops had invaded the country, but that was glossed over as of no concern. Assuring its reader that the French had no intention of staying in Morocco, *The Times* congratulated France for:

> Laying her plans so frankly before the world, confident in their honesty and without fear that they can give rise to any rational misgivings of her purposes. Readers were assured that French troops would stay only as long as was "absolutely necessary."[9]

Agadir was then a small, isolated, coastal village situated on a large sandy bay with no pier or jetty, yet the British press suggested the *Panther* visit signalled Germany's intention to build a naval base there that would challenge the Royal Navy. British Foreign Secretary, Edward Grey, encouraged the ridiculous hysteria.

> Edward Grey urged the French prime minister to adopt a belligerent attitude that would probably have led to war had he yielded to the advice. In a moment of supreme irony, Sir Arthur Nicolson, permanent under-secretary at the Foreign Office since 1910, complained to the German ambassador in London that by anchoring the *Panther* off Agadir, Germany was violating the Act of Algeciras. He made no mention of the fact that France and Spain already had 100,000 troops occupying the country. *The Times* warned menacingly that Germany was claiming 'absolute European predominance,' and Grey personally blamed Germany for creating a 'new situation'.… Sir Hew Strachan, emeritus professor of the history of war at Oxford University, and Fellow of All Souls, wrote in 2003: "What had been a Franco-German dispute about colonial ambitions, designed to be resolved by diplomacy, now became an issue of vital national interest to Britain. Germany had deployed sea power beyond the purlieus of its immediate geographical waters; this was a direct threat to the premier navy in the world."[10]

How utterly absurd. Just days before *Panther* dropped anchor off Agadir, the British home fleet had assembled at Spithead to mark the coronation of King George V. Comprising 165 warships, the fleet (it was merely the Home Fleet) included 32 battleships, 24 armoured cruisers,

12 cruisers, 67 destroyers, 12 torpedo boats and 8 submarines. Crewed by 60,000 officers and men, the fleet at anchor covered 18 square miles off the English coast. Britain's royal yacht, *Victoria and Albert,* carrying the newly-crowned king on his inspection of the fleet that day, had a crew of 336 and was four times the size of the *Panther.* The statement by one of Britain's leading 'court historians' that the small gunboat bobbing at anchor off Agadir almost 2,000 miles away was a "direct threat" to the mighty Royal Navy was as ridiculous as his accounts blaming Germany for the First World War. The *Panther* at Agadir was purely a token gesture of Germany's well-warranted annoyance at France's trampling of the Algeciras Act into the sand.

> That Germany did not intend a permanent occupation of Agadir is clear. That she did not seek political position in Morocco is also clear. She intended to say that the situation there was undergoing change to her disadvantage, and that the time for new negotiations had arrived.[11]

British hypocrisy reached still greater heights when the Chancellor of the Exchequer, David Lloyd George, in a speech in London in July 1911, delivered a stern warning against "German expansion":

> Personally I am a sincere advocate of all means which would lead to the settlement of international disputes by methods such as those which civilization has so successfully set up for the adjustment of differences between individuals, and I rejoice in my heart at the prospect of a happy issue to Sir Edward Grey's negotiations with the United States of America for the settlement of disputes which may occur in future between ourselves and our kinsmen across the Atlantic by some more merciful, more rational, and by a more just arbitrament than that of the sword. But I am also bound to say this -- that I believe it is essential in the highest interests, not merely of this country, but of the world, that Britain should at all hazards maintain her place and her prestige amongst the Great Powers of the world. Her potent influence has many a time been in the past, and may yet be in the future, invaluable to the cause of human liberty. It has more than once in the past redeemed Continental nations, who are sometimes too apt to forget that service, from overwhelming disaster and even from national extinction. I would make great sacrifices to preserve peace. I conceive that nothing would justify a disturbance of international goodwill except questions of the greatest national moment. But if a situation were to be forced upon

us in which peace could only be preserved by the surrender of the great and beneficent position Britain has won by centuries of heroism and achievement, by allowing Britain to be treated where her interests were vitally affected as if she were of no account in the Cabinet of nations, then I say emphatically that peace at that price would be a humiliation intolerable for a great country like ours to endure. National honour is no party question. The security of our great international trade is no party question; the peace of the world is much more likely to be secured if all nations realize fairly what the conditions of peace must be.[12]

The speech was a threat directly aimed at Germany, and everyone knew it. 'Great, beneficent, heroic Britain,' was a potent influence "invaluable to the cause of human liberty." The deceit, arrogance, and hypocrisy of the British political puppets and their financial masters knew no bounds. It was Britain that ruled the waves, so how dare Germany anchor a small "warship" off the coast of Morocco? Historian Joachim Remak stated, "It was imperialism at its bluntest as well as its most hypocritical."[13] Millions of innocents in Persia were slaughtered, and children roasted alive in a mosque in Libya as a consequence of Britain's geopolitical intrigues with not one word of protest or denunciation uttered by 'great and beneficent Britain'. Yet according to the British government, by anchoring *Panther* at Agadir, the Kaiser and Germany threatened the peace of the world and would be in serious trouble should they attempt to humiliate mighty Britain. The conceit and hypocrisy of the British government here was matched only by its arrogance.

The German government protested to Sir Edward Grey about Lloyd George's speech and his 'hallucination' that Germany was considering establishing a naval base at Agadir. It was ridiculous to suggest that Germany was treating Britain as of no account in the cabinet of nations. It was crass warmongering language to suggest that Britain would go to war with Germany if she did not mend her manners. If the British government had intended to complicate and upset the international situation, it could not have chosen a better means than the Chancellor of the Exchequer's speech.[14]

Lloyd George, Edward Grey, and fellow political puppets did not, of course, believe a word of what they were saying about Germany. It was all for public consumption, to turn public opinion steadily against Germany. The majority in Britain had voted against militarism in 1906, and their opinion had to be changed. English historian Geoffrey Barraclough wrote:

It casts a bright, and not very flattering light on the moral standards of the age, and in particular on those of the ruling class. Prevarication, half-truth, double talk, and double standards of morality, were other characteristics of the imperialism of the times.[15]

The *Panther* incident and the Morocco crisis were blown out of all proportion to make Germany the enemy. Lloyd George's infamous Mansion House speech was a threat designed to increase international tension. Winston Churchill admitted that it was playing with fire, but the Kaiser refused to play along with their warmongering and poured cold water on it. Professor Sidney B. Fay writes:

> It might indeed easily have led to war, had not the Kaiser and [German Chancellor] Bethmann been determined not to allow the Moroccan affair to cause a European conflict.[16]

Britain might well have further manipulated the Morocco affair, but Russia was not fully prepared militarily for war at the time. The crisis passed, but it served to focus the minds of the Milner Group. If Russia was not yet properly prepared for war, was *Britain*? On 23 August 1911, a special meeting of the Committee of Imperial Defence was called to discuss the matter. It was essentially a war briefing with Germany as the projected foe.[17] Esher, Asquith, Grey, Haldane, Churchill and Lloyd George attended, together with the top brass of the Army and Navy.

> The meeting lasted all day. Great maps were produced and the details of the German Schlieffen Plan were demonstrated with great accuracy. General Wilson (later Field Marshal Sir Henry Wilson) was a dedicated and far-sighted soldier. He had been working since 1906 on one project: to support the French army in a war against Germany. He knew the French general staff and their army dispositions. Secret information was regularly relayed to him from the continent, and his own office was plastered with a gigantic map of Belgium on which every road, milepost, railway junction, river and canal had been identified following his reconnaissance trips through the Belgian countryside. So it would start in Belgium then. Three full years before the event, the Committee of Imperial Defence was taken through a meticulously accurate explanation of how war was to begin in 1914.[18]

If one looks behind the curtain it becomes patently clear that over a considerable number of years before 1914, British elites were planning war against Germany. A glimpse behind that curtain is provided by *My Diaries, A Personal Narrative of Events, 1888-1914* by English diplomat Wilfrid Scawen Blunt. An upper-class Englishman, Blunt spent years travelling in the Middle East and living in Egypt. He met and befriended Lord Randolph Churchill, and following Churchill's death in 1895, he helped his son Winston write a book about his father and they became close friends.

In *My Diaries,* Blunt describes many meetings over the years with Winston Churchill, who by 1912 was a member of the Asquith Cabinet and First Lord of the Admiralty – the political head of the Royal Navy. The diary entry for 19 October 1912, describes a social weekend at Blunt's country estate with Winston and Clementine Churchill, and other close friends, George Wyndham and his wife, Lady Grosvenor. Wyndham, (Eton and Sandhurst) was intimately linked to the secret society. He had been a good friend of Cecil Rhodes, and private secretary to Arthur Balfour. Blunt relates:

> Among other things discussed was that of *the coming European war* and the chances of a German invasion. This, Winston declared, could be easily effected on the east coast.... He said the idea of the Fleet being a sufficient safeguard was entirely out of date, and without a strong army there was no safety. He also believed in the coming of a war in which we shall be involved to prevent France being overpowered by Germany ... Winston is also a strong eugenist. He told us he had himself drafted the Bill which is to give power of shutting up [imprisoning] people of weak intellect and so prevent their breeding. He thought it might be arranged to sterilise them. It was possible by the use of Rontgen rays, both for men and women, though for some women operations might be necessary. He thought that if shut up with no prospect of release without it, many would ask to be sterilised as a condition of having their liberty restored.[19]

Churchill's tongue loosened with alcohol, but he was by no means drunk according to Blunt. Here was a senior member of the British Cabinet and close associate of Asquith, Grey, and the secret society openly discussing the coming war with Germany almost two years before it began in 1914. British mainstream academic historians *never* refer to this, preferring the fantasy that Britain was as shocked as everyone else in August 1914 at the turn of events. Blunt's book is in the public domain and freely available on the internet for all.[20]

135

Should Blunt be dismissed as a fantasist? Historian Warren Dockter relates that Blunt's extensive diary of his political and social affairs are widely regarded as valuable and reliable sources. He was considered "a shrewd observer of men and reliable recorder of their opinions."[21]

Can 'court historians' be excused for omitting such evidence from Blunt's diary on the premise that they are simply unaware of it? Perhaps they are also ignorant of the debate in the British parliament decades later when Blunt's work was discussed. Lord Bedford:

> There were influential people in Britain long before 1914 animated by trade rivalry and jealousy of what they believed to be Germany's challenge to British sea power, and for a long time the *Daily Mail* was conducting a venomous hatred campaign against Germany. Mr. Wilfred Scawen Blunt, in his book *My Diaries*, relates how the present Prime Minister [Winston Churchill], when speaking to him in 1910, referred to "the coming war with Germany." He relates how the late Lord Fisher [Admiral and First Sea Lord] made vain efforts to ensure the "Copenhagening" of the German Fleet. I am open to correction, but I understand that term to mean the annihilation of the German Fleet by a sudden attack before there had been a formal declaration of war. If I am correct in this interpretation, I cannot help wondering whether the Japanese have studied the methods of strategy recommended by the late Lord Fisher. [He is referring to the Japanese navy's sudden, unannounced, attack on the Russian fleet in Port Arthur on 8-9 February 1904 without a declaration of war.] When Lord Fisher failed to get approval for this idea, he complied with the request of Mr. Churchill to help him to proceed with the great task which he, Lord Fisher, *had been engaged in for six years*, as First Sea Lord – namely, *preparation for a German war*. Mr. Blunt, who had been entertaining the present Prime Minister, further records that the First Lord of the Admiralty had become most truculent about international affairs, being *engrossed in preparation for war with Germany*.... And I have no hesitation in saying that if one country more than another was responsible for the outbreak of war in 1914, it was Tsarist Russia, the first country to mobilize; for Russia mobilized before Germany. Russia was determined to get Constantinople and the control of the Straits, and foresaw that this might be secured during the European war.[22]

Wilfrid Scawen Blunt's revelations, together with Lord Bedford's later statement in Parliament are, of course, not in themselves definitive proof that Britain was preparing for war against Germany years in advance of the

Sergei Sazonov

event. When taken in conjunction with much other evidence, however, the case becomes compelling. For at least eight years Britain had been planning and preparing for war against Germany. No-one questioned Lord Bedford's assertions in parliament, and no British historian has written about them. Such awkward truths are best ignored and swept under the carpet.

Another important event whitewashed by British historians took place in late September 1912 when King George V invited the new Russian Foreign Secretary, Sergei Sazonov, to join him at Balmoral Castle. Sazonov writes in his memoirs:

I arrived in London at the end of September, and in a day or two proceeded, in company with our Ambassador to England, Count Benckendorff, to Scotland, where King George was then staying with his family. I spent six days at Balmoral castle as the guest of the King, and preserve the pleasantest recollection of the friendly spirit of hospitality which the Royal family displayed towards me. I feel that I owed this to the intimate relations which had so long existed between the late Tsar and his English relatives. Sir Edward Grey, the British Minister for Foreign Affairs, who had come to Balmoral to meet me at the invitation of King, arrived on the same day as myself; and Mr Bonar Law, the leader of the Conservative Party – then in opposition – who subsequently became Prime Minister of Great Britain, arrived next day. By a wise custom established in England by an ancient parliamentary tradition, foreign policy is excluded from the political questions on which the Government and the Opposition adopt irreconcilable attitudes. Thanks to this custom the foreign policy of Great Britain during the last two centuries has maintained a continuity and steadfastness which other and younger parliamentary governments rarely succeed in establishing. Our mornings at Balmoral were devoted to official discussion of political questions … in the course of my conversations with the King and Sir Edward Grey, I touched upon one question which, ever since 1909 – that is from the moment when the probability of war with Germany emerged from the misty distance into the realm of political possibilities – had begun to attract the attention of our Admiralty.[23]

Sazonov goes on to describe how the Russian Naval General Staff had worked out a detailed plan for the naval defence of its Baltic Ports and

St Petersburg against the German navy. He astutely observed that British foreign policy remained constant no matter the political party in power at Westminster. The role of the opposition is to question and scrutinise the work of the government, but in foreign policy they were always in cahoots. It was 'ancient tradition' in the debating chamber that foreign policy was sacrosanct and accepted without protest. The democratic process was further undermined by the fact that leading politicians in both major parties were acting in concert in doing the bidding of the Milner Group/the City. This was exemplified by the Balmoral meeting where Bonar Law was present throughout. Transparency in British politics was non-existent. In later chapters we see how, in 1914, the vast majority of MPs in the House of Commons and most members of the actual Cabinet, had no inkling whatsoever of the alliance commitments the British government had made to France and Russia or the planning for war at meetings such as that at Balmoral Castle in September 1912. Make no mistake: planning for war is what it was. Sazonov related:

> As a favourable opportunity occurred I felt it useful, in one of my conversations with Grey, to seek information as to what we might expect from Great Britain in the event of a conflict with Germany … Grey declared unhesitatingly that should the anticipated conditions arise Great Britain would make every effort to strike a crippling blow at German naval power…. On his own initiative Grey then gave me a confirmation of what I already knew through Poincaré – an agreement exists between France and Great Britain, under which in the event of war with Germany, Great Britain has accepted the obligation of bringing assistance to France not only on sea but on land, by landing troops on the continent…. The King touched on the same question in one of his conversations with me, and expressed himself even more strongly than his Minister…. His Majesty cried that any conflict would have disastrous results not only for the German navy, but for Germany's overseas trade, for, he said, "We shall sink every single German merchant ship we shall get hold of." These words appeared to me to give expression not only to His Majesty's personal feelings but also to the public feeling predominant in Great Britain as regards to Germany.[24]

British pro-Establishment historians tell us that Britain harboured no notion of war against Germany, and never planned such an event. 'Devious warmongering Germany,' they say, was responsible. The Germans used Vienna's reaction to the assassination of the heir to the Austro-Hungarian throne, Archduke Franz Ferdinand, in Sarajevo in June 1914 as an excuse to spring a European war on totally unsuspecting nations.

The Archduke's official visit to Bosnia-Herzegovina and Sarajevo in 1914 was always going to be problematic. Formerly part of the Ottoman Empire, Bosnia and Herzegovina had broken free from Ottoman rule in 1875-6, only to be handed over to Austria-Hungary by the Great Powers at the Congress of Berlin in 1878 while still remaining 'officially' under nominal Ottoman control for thirty years. In 1908 Austria-Hungary had then formally annexed the two provinces. A large Austro-Hungarian force of over 200,000 soldiers had been needed to quell dissent in the two provinces.[25] On a positive note for the people, widespread banditry was stamped out, 200 primary schools were built together with 2,000 kilometres of road and 1,000 kilometres of railways.[26]

Despite the annexation by Austria-Hungary, in Serbian eyes Bosnia-Herzegovina remained firmly as an extension to their pan-Slavist ambition for a greater Serbian kingdom of Yugo-Slavia. St. Petersburg backed the pan-Slavist ambitions and had Russia been in a position to back them in 1908, Serbia would most likely have gone to war with Austria-Hungary over the annexation. Canadian lawyer, geopolitical analyst and author, John S. Ewart, conducted a forensic analysis of the Balkan events prior to the First World War, and published a major work, *The Roots and Causes of the Wars (1914-1918)*. He wrote:

> Russia wished to retain the friendship of Serbia, for Serbia was the geographical bar to her rivals; France needed the friendship of Russia; and the United Kingdom needed the friendship of both, for her impending struggle with Germany. Had Russia been as well prepared for hostilities as she was in July 1914, the world war would have commenced in 1908.[27]

In 1908 Russia was militarily and financially weak after her war against Japan and was in no position to force the issue. Financial powers stepped in to rectify this. Having financed Japan's war against Russia in 1905-06, the London and Paris banks now poured large loans into Russia to rebuild her army and navy. The bankers would make significant profits in interest from those loans, and it should be understood that all wars are massively profitable for bankers.

Despite her crippling military and financial losses in its war against Japan, Russia promised continued support to Serbia and pan-Slavist ambitions. Britain gave Russia the green light to do so knowing full well that trouble between the Slav nationalists and Austria-Hungary could provide the spark for war. That, indeed, was Britain's object, but in 1908 Russia was in no position other than to accept the Austro-Hungarian annexation of Bosnia and Herzegovina. In London, the Milner Group was well aware that the annexation would stoke serious Slav anger and resentment, and that anger could be manipulated to antagonise and provoke Austria-Hungary into a reaction. British historian Niall Ferguson writes:

> Grey sanctioned the Russian sponsorship of Balkan Slav nationalism with his eyes open, as he made clear in a letter to his ambassador in Berlin, Sir William Goschen, in November 1908:
> "A strong Slav feeling has arisen in Russia. Although this feeling appears to be well in hand at present, bloodshed between Austria and Servia would certainly *raise the feeling to a dangerous height* in Russia; and the thought that peace depends upon Servia restraining herself is not comfortable."[28]

"Raise the feeling to a dangerous height"! Ferguson offers no opinion as to who or what was behind all of this. Could he really have had no idea? We have to bear in mind that Ferguson was a product of Oxford University and a fully paid-up – and well-paid – member of the British establishment whose strong support for the British Empire, Margaret Thatcher, and the Iraq War are well documented. The strong possibility of bloodshed between Serbia and Austria-Hungary arose thanks to the London and Paris financial circles' backing of Russian and Serbian military expansion and the carte blanche they gave to stoke trouble in the region.

Serbia, a Balkan country with a history of regicide, had long been viewed condescendingly by the Great Powers as a primitive backwater, a land with few if any valuable natural resources other than pigs. Funding Serbia was not an act of benevolence by the bankers and investors of the West.

> Serbia was perfectly placed as the epicentre for a seismic explosion that would blow away the old order. With her many nationalist Pan-Slav and fiercely anti-Austrian secret societies, Serbia provided the perfect location from which the Secret Elite could activate the European war. Austria's annexation of Bosnia-Herzegovina in 1908 generated a deep, bitter and lasting resentment amongst the Serbs, not least because it defied their ambition to bring all Serb peoples into a unified state called Yugoslavia. Serbia's long-standing hatred of Austrian rule grew exponentially from the first day of the annexation in 1908 until it culminated in war. The Serbs could never have

waged a successful war against the might of Austria on their own but were assured of Russian support by Isvolsky who actively encouraged Serbia to wrest Bosnia-Herzegovina from Austria as their rightful entitlement. Serbia's finance minister, Milorad Draskovic, confidently claimed: 'Our people have faith in Russia. It is said of us that we are merely Russia's armed camp. We do not take that as an insult.' It was not by accident that Alexander Isvolsky played a significant role in creating the perilous conditions in the Balkans. The Secret Elite used him and their diplomatic and commercial agents in Serbia and Bulgaria to identify prominent individuals and organisations that they could influence. Far from being passive observers, the Secret Elite in London made certain that their agents influenced events at every opportunity.[29]

The Milner Group held considerable sway in Russia through consecutive Foreign Secretaries, Alexander Izvolsky and Sergei Sazonov. Izvolsky was transferred from that post to Paris in 1910 as Russian Ambassador. His crucial role there was to coordinate Russian and French war preparations. His chosen replacement at the Foreign Office, Serge Sazonov, was, as we have seen, similarly drawn into the elite circle of British royalty and high finance with his six-day visit to Balmoral to ensure his unwavering cooperation.

In France, the Milner Group's leading player was Raymond Poincaré. Born in 1860 into a wealthy family in Lorraine, as a child he witnessed the Franco-Prussian War (1870-71) and the German annexation of Alsace-Lorraine. A lawyer, Poincaré joined the French parliament as a deputy at age twenty-seven in 1887. He became a minister in 1893, prime minister in 1912, and president of France in 1913. Historian Sean McMeekin relates the widespread opinion that Poincaré won the presidency in 1913 thanks to corrupt French jour-

Raymond Poincaré

nalists being bribed to the tune of two million francs per year. Isvolsky boasted of his role in getting Poincaré the presidency in 1913, reporting triumphantly to Sazonov in St Petersburg: 'We are therefore, for the period of his seven-year term of office, perfectly safe from the appearance of such persons as Caillaux ... at the head of the French Government.'[30]

Until early 1912 the plans in London and Paris for war against Germany faced a formidable obstacle in French prime minister Joseph Caillaux who favoured a French alliance with Germany.[31] Caillaux's concessions to Germany and friendly overtures to her during the Moroccan crisis of 1911, greatly alarmed the Anglo-American cabal and their French allies and sealed his political fate. Professor Edward McCullough writes:

> Caillaux's crime was that he preferred conciliation of Germany to war. There were many in both France and England who agreed with him, but unfortunately, they were unable to make their view prevail.[32]

Caillaux's removal from power and replacement with the German-hating Raymond Poincaré provides a classic example of the financial elite's control of politicians and politics.

Manipulating key placemen into positions of political power in any country is a complex challenge but one in which the elite cabal of the West was well practised. The radical French prime minister Joseph Caillaux, who had instigated diplomatic negotiations with Germany and resolved the crisis over Agadir, had to be replaced. His belief that "our true policy is an alliance with Germany"[33] was incompatible with the plans of the anti-German elites in western capitals. Caillaux had many enemies but none more deadly than Alexander Izvolsky, the principal foreign agent of those elites. Though he had given up his post as Russian foreign secretary in 1910 and had moved from St Petersburg to Paris as the Russian ambassador, Izvolsky had not been demoted or reduced in rank. His principal roles were the coordination of war preparation between Russia and France, and helping to corrupt French politics.

Izvolsky was provided with substantial funds to bribe the French press into turning public opinion against Caillaux and like-minded politicians. A right-wing revanchist lawyer, Raymond Poincaré, was selected as the man to replace Caillaux and lead France to war. Born in Lorraine, Poincaré was consumed by hatred of Germany and harboured a fierce determination to regain the provinces for France. He later conceded: "I could discover no other reason why my generation should go on living except for the hope of recovering our lost provinces."[34]

> Be clear about this: from the outset, Poincaré knew that he was funded and supported by outside agencies to turn France against Germany. He was fully aware that he owed his political success to hidden forces that sponsored his rise to power in France. He sold his soul to the Secret Elite in order to regain Alsace-Lorraine. Poincaré was personally involved in the bribing of the French Press, advising Isvolsky "on the most suitable plan of distribution of the subsidies."[35] Subsidies indeed. This was outright corruption in its

most blatant form. French newspaper editors were paid large sums to subject Caillaux to a torrent of abuse. ... Under immense personal and political pressure, Caillaux resigned in January 1912. Poincaré was elected prime minister and foreign minister, and, for the first time, France was committed to the revanchist cause. It was a pivotal moment in European history.[36]

Poincaré worked closely with Isvolsky in Paris to prepare the ground for war. Large sums of money were used by Isvolsky not only to bribe the French press into denouncing Caillaux and praising Poincaré, but to write violently anti-German and anti-Austro-Hungarian articles. Every month, large sums flowed into the coffers of French newspapers, including: *Le Radical, La Lanterne, Le Figaro, Le Temps, La Libre Parole, L'Aurore,* and *La Liberté.*[37] The money originated in massive French bank loans to Russia, some of which made its way back to France via Isvolsky. The French investment banks were dominated by the Rothschilds' Banque De Paris et de Pay Bas (Paribas) which was part of the Londo-Paris financial axis.

> Like Lord 'Natty' Rothschild in London [whom Quigley revealed was an inner core member of the secret society], Baron Edouard de Rothschild in Paris controlled massive swathes of global investment banking. The London and Paris cousins worked in tandem so that the funds that flowed to Russia were strictly directed to the war aims of the Milner Group and its allies The large amount of money Isvolsky used to corrupt French politics and the Press appeared to come from Russia. It did, but only via a circuitous route. The slush fund was siphoned off from the huge loans that were transferred there from Paris. This indirect funding structure meant that the money was borrowed in Paris, at a cost to the Russian taxpayer, and redirected back to France to provide Isvolsky's slush fund. It was a clever system whereby all of the loan debt and the interest accrued on it was ultimately repaid by the Russian people.
>
> ...The sums involved were enormous. Isvolsky requested three million francs alone to buy off the *Radical*, a paper owned by one of Poincaré's most outspoken opponents in the Senate. The money was passed directly by Isvolsky to an intermediary and on to the French minister of finance, Louis-Lucien Klotz, who shamelessly disbursed it to the politicians who would effectively vote for Poincaré.[38] The general public did not at that time vote for their president. Electors were limited to senators and deputies, which made bribery and corruption relatively straightforward. The financial elites went to great lengths to ensure that the money could not be

traced back to Russia or, worse still, to Paris and London. Poincaré's opponents were bribed to vote for him, and opposition was silenced. Nothing was left to chance.[39]

Poincaré weeded out opponents and critics within the government, replacing them with yes-men so that foreign policy decisions taken by the Cabinet were nearly always unanimous. "Poincaré set out to make French foreign policy a one-man affair and was completely successful."[40] He controlled French foreign policy with an iron fist, brooking no interference from other politicians, apart, that is, from Sir Edward Grey in England. According to Professor Fay, Poincaré always consulted Grey and as far as possible ensured that French foreign policy conformed to that of Britain.

Grey

There was in fact more harmony and mutual confidence between France and England, though they were only "friends," than between France and Russia who were allies. It was a striking example of the fact that a well-established friendship is better than an alliance. Many writers, however, … have argued that there was a complete unity also between Paris and St Petersburg; that Poincaré and Izvolsky worked harmoniously hand in hand, though they are not agreed as to whether the Frenchman was the tool of the Russian, or vice versa. Their arguments rest largely on the Isvolski correspondence and their conviction that Isvolski and Poincaré were both working for war, the one to get Constantinople and the Straits, the other to recover Alsace-Lorraine…. In 1912, under the Premiership of M. Poincaré, the character of the alliance began to be changed. France began to support more actively Russia's aggressive policies in the Balkans, and assured her that France would give her armed support if they involved Russia in war with Austria and Germany.[41]

By 1912, Russia was assured of armed support from France and France was assured of armed support from Britain. Dominic Lieven, Senior Research fellow at Trinity College, Cambridge writes:

Russian diplomats and soldiers quickly registered the shift in France's mood. The military attaché in Paris, Count Grigorii Nostitz, reported in January 1912 the view of a senior French general that "never since 1870 has France been in so favourable a strategic position. Its army is in very good condition … its finances could not be better, and as the events of last year [the Morocco crisis] showed, one can count fully on its people's patriotism. France has two powerful allies, whereas … the Triple Alliance is coming apart at the seams. Paris now was convinced that in the event of war a British expeditionary force would arrive and the Allied armies would outnumber Germany even on the western front.[42]

Poincaré was correct to be convinced of British support. It had been long planned. Come the time, the British army would arrive within days to support France and Belgium against Germany. We have seen how French and British military strategists – in close but top-secret collusion with their Belgian counterparts – had been deeply involved in planning war against Germany for several years. On the western front, French, British and Belgian forces would outnumber the entire Germany army, which would also be forced to defend Germany against massive Russian forces in the east. As provided for in the secret Franco-Russian Military Convention of August 1892, France and Russia would carefully coordinate the general mobilisation of their armies to ensure that Germany had to defend two fronts, east and west, at the same time. On Franco-Russian relations around 1912, American historian, Professor Laurence Lafore writes:

> In 1908, the French had expressed great hesitation in supporting the Russians in their policy of hostility toward Austria. In 1912, they were actually egging the Russians on. The principle [sic] reason for change was a new administration in France, along with some domestic political disputes and a new diplomatic calculation. Raymond Poincaré became Prime Minister and Foreign Minister in 1912, after having occupied other posts in the cabinet. He was a conservative and vigorous nationalist, a man of provincial rather than cosmopolitan outlook, a native son of Lorraine, the province partly lost to Germany in 1871. In contrast to most recent leaders, he was inclined to revive the dream of *revanche*, of a successful war against Germany to be followed by the recovery of Alsace and Lorraine. While French foreign policy in the past decade had been both spirited and highly successful, it looked toward security rather than revenge. But now a perceptibly different tone entered French diplomacy.[43]

As prime minister then president, Raymond Poincaré devoted himself to preparing France and Russia for the coming war, but there remained a fly in the ointment: the French ambassador at St Petersburg, Georges Louis. The anti-war Louis recognised the dangerous warmongering collusion between Poincaré, Sazonov and Isvolsky. Like Caillaux before him, Louis therefore had to go. After "a good deal of trouble," George Louis was uprooted "on Poincaré's orders"[44] Professor Barnes writes:

> On February 17, 1913, M. Louis was dismissed and replaced by M. Théophile Delcassé, a man who was scarcely second to Poincaré in his desire to avenge 1870. In fact, Delcassé had been the most tireless of all French diplomats in the generation preceding 1912 in working toward the diplomatic isolation of Germany, and the organization of an effective coalition against her.... When Delcassé had completed his mission he returned to Paris to collaborate with Poincaré and Isvolski at home. He was succeeded by Maurice Paleologue, one of the most ardent members of the Poincaré clique.[45]

Before departing Paris for the Russian capital in early 1913, Delcassé told his revanchist co-conspirator, Maurice Paléologue, that his "sole aim" was to ensure that the Russian armies would be prepared to make any necessary offensive in fifteen days. "As for the diplomatic twaddle and old nonsense about the European equilibrium," he told Paleologue, "I shall bother with it as little as possible: it is no longer anything but verbiage."[46]

There is no question that France, Russia and Britain were being prepared for a war pre-ordained by the financial elites. British historians throughout the last 100 years have attempted to set in stone the fallacy that in July 1914, Germany persuaded Austria-Hungary to make war on Serbia and presented her with a 'blank cheque' to do so. An Austro-Hungarian conflict with Serbia was, they suggest, then used as the excuse by Germany to start a European war in a bid for global conquest. Such fantasist historians never discuss the reality that France was egging Russia on to war and sending vast amounts of money to prepare her for it. By July 1914, eighty per cent of direct Russian government debt was held in Paris[47] After Poincaré was bought into power with bribes and corruption of the French Press in 1912 and Delcassé was installed in St. Peterburg in early 1913, French money poured into Russia with strict conditions attached: (1) The number of troops in the Russian army had to be quickly and substantially increased. (2) Strategic railroads for the rapid transport of the Russian army up to Germany's borders must begin immediately in agreement with the French General Staff.[48] With vast amounts of foreign money now being made available to Russia, the Russian parliament passed a law extending the term of military service from 3 to three 3.5 years, thus increasing the army by almost 500,000 men. To further expand the Russian army, French loans financed a significant increase in the annual contingent of Russian army recruits. The Imperial Russian Navy, which had been decimated in the war against Japan in 1904, also underwent a rapid expansion.

Poincaré's determined activities preparing for war were also evident on the home front. In August 1913, his Three-Year Service Law was approved by the French senate, whereby all fit males aged twenty and over were now required to undertake full-time military service for three year, not two years before. Within a year the French standing army grew to a peacetime strength of some 827,000 men, and virtually matched the strength of the standing army of Germany despite the fact that France had a population some 20 million less than that of Germany. In addition, all men who had previously served time as conscripts in the French army were now held as reservists, and by the outbreak of war France would be able to mobilize around 4 million men. Moreover, the combined armies of Russia, France and Britain would be joined by a Serbian force. In February 1914 the Serbian prime minister, Nikola Pašić, went to St Petersburg for a meeting with the Czar and told him that Serbia could field half a million men. The Czar said that would be sufficient, and agreed to Pašić's request for Russia to provide 120,000 rifles, munitions and howitzers. The meeting ended with Czar Nicholas declaring "for Serbia we shall do everything."[49]

The spring and summer of 1914 may have been marked in Europe by "an absence of international tension" and "a period of exceptional calm,"[50] but behind the scenes French money was paying for the mobilization of Russian army reserves across the entire Empire.[51] It was also paying for the arms Russia was now giving to Serbia. By late July 1914, Russia had a standing army of 1.5 million men with another 3 million reserves, and a brand-new railroad system to convey them to Germany's eastern borders. France had a total of 4 million regulars and reserves to attack Germany from the west. Britain had a small standing army of 250,000 but through a vast propaganda exercise, another half million volunteers would be enlisted within weeks. Millions of men from Canada, New Zealand, Australia and elsewhere across the British empire would also enlist. The Belgian army had approximately 250,000 men. Serbia had 500,000 men.

The German army of 4.5 million men, together with half-a-million Austro-Hungarian and 150,000 Turks, was heavily outnumbered in 1914. Italy would remain neutral until May 1915 when she declared war

147

on Austria-Hungary. Her original standing army of some 350,000 grew during the war to around 5 million. Establishment historians present Germany in 1914 as a super-militarised state, but the facts speak differently. Professor L. C. F. Turner, (Australia) writes:

> Contrary to popular belief, Imperial Germany was not a super-militarized state. For many years she had been conscripting barely fifty per cent of her manpower of military age, while France was conscripting over eighty percent and also drawing heavily on North African manpower. In spite of their great superiority in population – sixty-eight millions against forty millions – the Germans could only count on slight numerical superiority over the French Army and had to reckon with Russia as well.[52]

From Paris, Isvolsky wrote to inform Sazonov that the French War Ministry was energetically preparing for military operations in the very near future and that Poincaré's major concern was "to prevent a German movement for peace."[53] One single sentence summed up the true situation. Poincaré and his financier masters were not concerned that Germany *would go* to war with them, but that she would *not*. Contrary to the utter falsehood presented by British 'court historians,' Germany had no desire whatsoever to go to war. As we will see in the following chapters, the Allies carefully created the circumstances in which Germany would be left with a stark choice in 1914: Either fight to defend herself against the advance of millions of Russian, French, British, and Serbian troops, or allow them to overrun the entire country and destroy Germany as a national entity.

Summary: Chapter 5 Britain – "Invaluable to the Cause of Human Liberty"

- In the pre-war years, Britain rapidly expanded its navy with massive new, oil-fired "Dreadnought" class battleships and assorted other vessels.

- A reliable source of oil to power those ships was discovered by British geologists in southern Persia.

- Britain partitioned Persia, taking the oil-rich south and allowing Russia to take the north as an additional sweetener for joining the conspiracy against Germany in 1907.

- With Britain's blessing, Italy invaded Libya and carried out atrocities against the Libyan people.

- Germany objected to French troops invading neutral Morocco and anchored a small gunboat off the coast there as a token gesture. British pro-Establishment historians stated the gunboat presented a threat to the mighty Royal Navy.

- A close friend of Winston Churchill's revealed that in 1912, Churchill was 'engrossed' in preparing Britain for war against Germany.

- Later in 1912, King George V invited the Russian Minister for Foreign Affairs, Serge Sazonov to Balmoral for six days to butter him up.

- To create a spark that would ignite that war, British elites sponsored Russian and Serbian intrigues in the Balkans against Austria-Hungary.

- In France, leading newspapers and members of parliament were heavily bribed to destroy the reputation of the pacifist prime minister, Joseph Caillaux, and bring the warmonger and financier's puppet, Raymond Poincaré to power.

- The Milner Group/High Finance now had the political leaders in Britain, France and Russia in their pocket, and preparations for war on Germany moved on apace.

Aged Austrian Emperor Loses His Nephew at an Assassin's Ha

The Daily Mirro

LATEST CERTIFIED CIRCULATION MORE THAN **960,000** COPIES PER DA

No. 3,332. Registered at the G.P.O. as a Newspaper. MONDAY, JUNE 29, 1914. One Halfpen

HEIR TO THE AUSTRIAN THRONE AND HIS WIFE SHOT DEAD IN STREET SERAJEVO AFTER BOMB HAD FAILED.

The Duchess of Hohenberg.

The Archduke Francis Ferdinand.

The Archduke, his wife and their family.

Another assassination in the history of the unhappy House of Hapsburg occurred yesterday, when the Archduke Francis Ferdinand, heir to the throne of Austria, and his wife, the Duchess of Hohenberg, were shot dead as they were leaving the railway station at Serajevo, the capital of Bosnia. The fatal shots were fired by an eighteen-year Servian student who had been banished from Bosnia. Before firing the revolver anot assassin had flung a bomb into the carriage, but it failed to explode.

CHAPTER 6

AN AVENUE OF ASSASSINS

War did not break out over Morocco in 1911 for a number of reasons. Primarily: (1) Germany refused to take the bait and had no intention of getting involved in a European war. (2) The Russian army was not yet strong enough to attack Germany, and the railways for mobilising it were still being built.

By the early months of 1914, Russia's army was up to full strength, and the railway networks essential for rapidly transporting her forces up close to Germany's borders had almost been completed. Britain, France and Belgium, having liaised constantly with joint military planning since 1906, were similarly well prepared. Despite the lies of the British Press, academics, and jingoists to the contrary, Germany, had prepared her army for defence with no desire or intention to start a war. Newspaper stories about a naval race between Germany and Britain, and British spy novels about Germany preparing to launch a major war and invading Britain lies and propaganda carefully concocted by the agents of the Milner Group. The problem facing the Milner Group was not that Germany might *start* a war, but might *refuse* to enter one. With the Triple Entente forces fully equipped and ready to go, the problem that now concentrated minds in London, Paris and St Petersburg was how to ensure Germany would rise to the bait, get the war started, and then blame Germany for starting it. It did not take a genius to figure out that the answer lay in the troubled Balkans – the mountainous region in south-eastern Europe which included Bosnia-Herzegovina, Serbia, Romania, Bulgaria. Montenegro and Albania.

As detailed in the previous chapter, Austria-Hungary had annexed Bosnia-Herzegovina in 1908, incurring the wrath of Serbian nationalists who planned to incorporate Bosnia-Herzegovina into a Greater Serbia. There were other South Slav nationalists who did not want a Greater Serbia but a genuine Yugoslavia in which all the component peoples would be 'equal'. Thirdly, there were those Bosnian nationalists who wanted neither of these two options but simply a Bosnia independent of both Austria-Hungary and Serbia.

Russia saw herself as the self-proclaimed protector of her South Slav cousins in Serbia and, with British encouragement, actively backed their intrigues against Austria-Hungary. Serbia was constantly irritating, provoking, and goading Austria-Hungary, and the carefully orchestrated slaying of the Austrian Archduke and his wife by a group of young Bosnian students trained and armed in Serbia would be the final straw that elicited a military response by Austria's exasperated leaders. Germany's alliance (since 1879) with Austria-Hungary would prove to be her Achilles heel. When Austria-Hungary reacted against Serbia after the Archduke's assassination, Russia would step in to support Serbia and the alliance systems would come into play with France and Britain joining Russia. The question remained, would Germany go to war in support of Austria-Hungary?

Archduke Franz Ferdinand (1863-1914) was Emperor Franz Joseph's nephew but the relationship was cold, with Ferdinand virtually frozen out at court. Ironically, for the man who would be shot dead in Sarajevo, his position as heir to the Austro-Hungarian throne arose thanks to a bullet. When Franz Joseph's only son, Crown Prince Rudolf, shot himself in a suicide pact with his mistress in 1889, Franz Ferdinand was next in line for the Habsburg throne. The Emperor's memory of his gifted and brooding son doubtless overshadowed his relationship with "the abrasive and temperamental" Ferdinand.[1] It was not until five years after his son's suicide that Franz Joseph reluctantly agreed to appoint Franz Ferdinand his presumptive heir.

Ferdinand greatly upset the Emperor and the royal court in 1900 by marrying a woman with no royal blood. He had been romantically linked to an Austrian Archduchess, Marie Christine, but fell in love with her lady-in-waiting, Sophie Chotek. Having declared his intent to marry Sophie against the wishes of the Emperor and the Habsburg imperial family, he was isolated at court.

> Franz Ferdinand had to wage a long campaign, enlisting the support of archbishops and ministers and ultimately of Kaiser Wilhelm II of Germany and of Pope Leo XIII, in order to secure permission for the union. Franz Joseph eventually gave in, but remained unreconciled to the marriage until the couple's violent death in 1914. His heir was obliged to swear an oath excluding the as yet unborn children of his marriage from the line of succession to the Habsburg throne ... Sophie, forbidden ever to carry the title archduchess ... was not permitted to join her husband in the royal box at the opera, sit near him at gala dinners, or accompany him in the splendid royal carriage...[2]

Franz Ferdinand wasn't 'banished,' but the situation at court became socially very difficult for him as his fiancée and then wife was not accepted there. Apart from their good friend Kaiser Wilhelm II, other royals slighted the kind and decent woman at every turn. In 1914, an opportunity arose for the couple to temporarily escape the demeaning strictures of the Austro-Hungarian court and be seen together in an official capacity. In January that year, the Archduke, as Inspector-in-Chief of the Austro-Hungarian Army, announced plans to visit Bosnia-Herzegovina in late June to observe manoeuvres of the 15th and 16th Austrian Army Corps stationed there. He indicated that Sophie would be joining him on the trip. The manoeuvres, to be held on difficult terrain near Sarajevo, were part of the army's routine training and not, as British 'court' historians have suggested, in preparation to "invade Serbia."[3] The itinerary included a two-day inspection of the military exercises, followed on 28 June by a visit to the city of Sarajevo to officially open the new national museum. Their three children would remain at home at Artstetten castle in lower Austria.

The Archduke's visit to Bosnia was announced by the Austrian government in March 1914, and in the *Neue Freie Press* in Bosnia. It inadvertently gave those intent on assassinating him ample time to plan and prepare. 28 June was an unfortunate date for the Sarajevo visit owing to its historical importance to the Serbs as a day of commemoration. It was the 525th anniversary of medieval Serbia's epic resistance against, but terrible defeat by the Turks at the battle of Kosovo in 1389, which ended Serbian independence for nearly 500 years. It is unknown if the date was chosen deliberately in order to be provocative, or whether the Austro-Hungarian authorities chose it unaware of its historical connections.

From the time Franz Ferdinand's trip to Sarajevo was made public, the plan to assassinate him began to take shape. From the earliest stages, the Russian government knew of the plan and approved it. Under instructions from two leading Russian politicians closely linked to elite groups in the West, Alexander Isvolsky and Sergei Sazonov, Russian diplomatic and military personnel serving in Serbia gave the green light to the Serbian authorities. This would be no spur of the moment killing by a crazed lone gunman, but one that was carefully planned and orchestrated by a team of young Bosnian assassins. Serbian army officers, with the tacit blessing of the Serbian authorities, funded, armed, and trained the assassins in the hope and expectation that Austria-Hungary would react to the murder with military action against Serbia. A blank cheque promise of Russian military support for Serbia was issued, if and when an Austro-Hungarian attack came.

Prior to 1914, the population of Bosnia-Herzegovina comprised 43 per cent Bosnian Serbs, 32 per cent Muslims, and 23 per cent Croats.[4] Franz Ferdinand was well informed of the dissatisfaction felt by Serbs and Croats within the Austro-Hungarian Dual Monarchy, and aware of the dangers to it if something was not done to satisfy the ethnic groups. He strongly disapproved of the oppressive policy of the ruling Magyar magnates in Hungary, and although criticised for favouring the small na- tionalities, it was, according to Professor Fay, "a reproach which did honor to his wisdom and sense of justice."[5] Professor Fay adds:

> A further indication of Franz Ferdinand's intention of making con-
> stitutional reforms in the direction of curbing the power of the
> Hungarian magnates and extending political rights to the minor
> nationalities is seen in various draft proposals which have been
> published from his papers. One of the most recent of these is the
> draft Manifesto One he had prepared for publication in case the
> old Emperor's periodical bronchial trouble should sometime sud-
> denly cause his death and open the way for a new regime. Though
> expressed in somewhat vague and general terms, it indicates that
> the heir to the throne was a true friend to the Croats and Bosnian
> Serbs and that he intended important constitutional reforms in the
> interests of all the minor nationalities before taking the oath to the
> Hungarian Constitution.[6]

In attempting to prevent the Austro-Hungarian empire being ripped apart by Slavic dissent, and the prospect of a Balkan Federation linked to Russia, Archduke Ferdinand favoured what he considered a more liberal political solution for the empire's Slavic peoples. It would be in the shape of trialism, a reorganised tripartite monarchy that would give Slavs more say, as opposed to the present dual monarchy. Ferdinand was unpopular with Serbian rulers and the pan-Slavist movement, not because he aimed to repress Slavs but because he wanted to give Slavs in the empire greater freedom. "There was nothing which adherents to the Greater Serbia idea more feared than a change of Austrian policy which would make Serbians contented with Austrian rule and reluctant to fight for independence."[7]

Young Bosnians would throw the bombs and fire the bullets, but the plot to kill Franz Ferdinand went far deeper than a group of young rad- icals aiming to further Pan-Slavist ambitions. Unbeknown to them, the assassination was being encouraged and facilitated by a covert power working to a far different agenda. Conflict between Austria and Serbia was only of interest to them if it drew Germany into war. With Russia now ready, and all the cards carefully stacked in favour of the Triple Entente, the assassination was seen as an opportunity for doing just that. As we shall see, the aftermath required careful manipulation to ensure Germany was drawn in no matter how reluctant. Prior to 1914, Serbian agents had constantly been provoking Austria-Hungary, but thanks to German influence, Austria-Hungary had always pulled back from military retaliation.

> The Secret Elite failed to find their spark for the international conflagration in the Balkans because Germany, in the person of the Kaiser, restrained Austria-Hungary from overreacting to Serbia's deliberate provocation … yet it was clear that Austria-Hungary could only absorb so much pressure before the integrity of the state was destroyed. The war-makers required an incident so violent, threatening or dangerous, that Austria-Hungary would be pushed over the brink. Austria-Hungary was aware of the dangers that lay across the Serbian border. Their military intelligence had intercepted and deciphered a large number of diplomatic telegrams that detailed Russian involvement with several Serbian activist groups. They knew that Isvolsky's placeman in Belgrade, Nicholas Hartwig, was manipulating the Serbian government to destabilise the region. … They knew of his links back to Sazonov in St Petersburg, and to Isvolsky and Poincaré in Paris, but they were not aware of the real power centred in London. No-one was. The links in the chain of command from London went further and deeper and was more sinister when extended from Hartwig into the Serbian military, their intelligence service and the quasi-independent nationalist society, Black Hand. And deeper yet into the young Bosnian political activists who were willing to pull the trigger in Sarajevo – students whose ideas on socialism and reform were influenced by revolutionaries like Trotsky.[8]

Baron Nicholas Hartwig, Russian ambassador at Belgrade from 1909, had helped create a system of alliances in the Balkans that lead to turmoil and wars. A pan-Slavist violently opposed to Austria following its annexation of Bosnia-Herzegovina in 1908, he was a key player in the chain of command involved in the plot to kill the Archduke. The assassins were armed and trained in Serbia by members of the Serbian army under the command of Colonel Dragutin Dimitrijević, a man dedicated to the

Le colonel Dragontine Dimitriévitch. (Apis.)

destruction of Austria-Hungary. Dimitrijević, head of Serbian military intelligence, worked closely with both Nicholas Hartwig and Viktor Artamanov, the Russian Military attaché in Serbia. Hartwig held immense sway in Belgrade. Indeed he was so powerful that no leading politicians in Serbia made any major decisions on foreign policy without first consulting him.[9] Hartwig, in turn, did nothing without consulting Sergei Sazonov, the Russian foreign minister.

We saw in a previous chapter how Sazonov had been drawn into the British elite's plan for war against Germany during his stay with King George V and Edward Grey at Balmoral Castle in Scotland in September 1912. Understanding the links between the British elites and Sazonov, between Sazonov and Hartwig, and between Hartwig and Colonel Dimitrijević, of Serbian intelligence, is the key to understanding Archduke Ferdinand's assassination and the proximate origins of the First World War.

Sazonov was in constant touch with ambassador Hartwig in Belgrade. Hartwig was no shrinking violet, and was perfectly placed for the deeds that lay ahead.

> Hartwig, who handled the relations between the Russian and Serbian governments in 1914, was one of the most notorious and corrupt characters among the unscrupulous Russian diplomats of the pre-war period.[10]

The English traveller, writer, and Balkans expert, Edith Durham, wrote of Hartwig's enormous sway in Serbia, and direct influence there on the royal family and the prime minister, Nikola Pashitch (Pašić).

> De Schelking, secretary to the Russian Legation in Berlin, gives a picture of Hartwig's immense influence: "Shortly after his arrival in Belgrade, Hartwig created a most exceptional position for himself. The King, Prince Alexander, Pashitch, none of these made any decisions without consulting him first. ... Every morning his study was besieged by Serbian statesmen who came to ask advice."[11]

Hartwig was closely linked to the man who would arrange the training and arming of the Sarajevo assassination squad, Dragutin Dimitrijević. A huge bull of a man with enormous strength and energy, he became known to all as Apis, a reference to the sacred and revered bull of ancient Egypt. Dimitrijević's ambition in life was the establishment of a Greater Serbia, a South Slavic State to be called Yugoslavia, which included Bosnia and Herzegovina. The most influential military officer in Serbia, he was also chief of Serbian Military Intelligence and, crucially, the founder and leading figure in "Black Hand" (the nickname of a secret society whose Serbian name *Ujedinjenje ili Smrt* meant "Unification or Death"). Deeply implicated in regicides and political murders in Serbia, in 1903 Apis and the Black Hand played a leading role in the gruesome murders of the Serbian King, Alexander Obrenović, and his wife, Queen Draga. The royal couple were slashed and stabbed to death in their palace bedroom, their bodies chopped into pieces, and thrown onto a manure heap in the palace grounds. Apis was badly wounded by royal bodyguards that night, being shot in the chest, hip, arm and leg, but survived due to his immense strength.

Hailed thereafter in the Serbian parliament as "the saviour of the fatherland"[12] for freeing the country from the yoke and corruption of the Obrenović dynasty, it was Apis and his Black Hand organisation that colluded with Russia in the Sarajevo assassination plot.

> In 1913-1914 the Serbian plotting against Austria for the emancipation of Bosnia and Herzegovina and the independence and unification of Jugo-Slavia exceeded all previous developments, and among these intrigues was the "Black Hand" plot which actually brought on the World War. The background to the plot to assassinate the Archduke Franz Ferdinand, heir apparent to the Austrian throne, must be found in the general plotting of the "Black Hand," the most aggressive and active of the various groups which were busy organizing intrigues in Serbia against the Austrian government. Among the membership of about one hundred thousand were many important officials in the Serbian army and administrative force. They were encouraged in their activity by Russian funds, the instigation of secret Russian agents, and the definite understanding between the Serbian and Russian governments that Russia would intervene to protect Serbia against any just punishment by the Austro-Hungarian Dual Monarchy ... Even before January 1914, the "Black Hand" had decided that their great stroke should be the assassination of Franz Ferdinand, and they awaited an appropriate and suitable time for the execution of the plot.[13]

Edith Durham wrote of Black Hand as a 'mafia-type society' that had infiltrated the Serbian government, civil service, army and police. The Serbian prime minister, Nikola Pašić (Pashitch) was an integral part of the plotting against Austria-Hungary:

> To assert that Pashitch, who, with his set, had worked to make Great Serbia ever since they had removed the Obrenovitch from its path

in 1903, was innocent of plotting against Austria in 1909-10, is to ask for too much credulity. Had not Russia already said the road to Constantinople lay through Vienna? England had previously been uneasy about the regicides, [of King Alexander and Queen Draga in 1903] and had demanded their [the army officers] dismissal from the Serb army, but now ceased to trouble about them. They were probably needed to teach in the bandit school of the Narodna Odbrana. And henceforth they held important posts. The original gang of some fifty murderers, officers and civilians, developed into a formidable society called the Tsrna Ruka (Black Hand), which became a government within a government. The Black Hand was responsible to none. Many members of the Government were reported to belong to it, a convenient Jekyll and Hyde arrangement, by means of which crimes of all kind could be committed, for which the Government took no responsibility, and of which it denied all knowledge. King Peter having been put on the throne by this gang, had naturally no power over them, and [his son] Prince Alexander was reported to have joined the society...

Members of the Tsrna Ruka joined the police force, and so secured their plans against police interference. By means of a paper called *Pijemont* they preached violent chauvinism, and advocated savage methods.... Efforts on the part of politicians, who disapproved of its methods, to break up the society failed. Unexplained deaths took place. The Black Hand brooked no interference.[14]

Black Hand's newspaper, *Pijemont,* was part-financed by King Peter, the man who gained the throne in 1903 thanks to Apis and the gruesome murders of King Alexander and his wife.

King Peter did not hide the fact that he owed the crown to Apis and the conspirators. A thin petite man in his 70's, he was practically a stranger in his own land having left Belgrade in 1858 as a fourteen-year-old boy. He returned forty-five years later on appointment as king, but stayed out of politics, knowing that his survival was solely dependent on the goodwill of Apis and the army.[15]

King Peter's son, Prince Alexander, was close to Apis and Black Hand. He became heir apparent when his older brother, Prince Djordje, was forced to stand aside after kicking his butler in the abdomen so severely that the poor man died shortly thereafter.[16]

Edith Durham reported that "corruption in all branches of the Administration" was the essence of Serbian rule.[17] Leading politicians, the royal family, army, and police force existed in an atmosphere of corruption, violence and intrigue under the heavy influence of Black Hand and its leader, Dimitrijević. The man who led the 1903 regicide now planned to have another member of European royalty dispatched. He would excuse the deed with the lie that Franz Ferdinand was planning war on Serbia.

> The head of the Intelligence department of the Serbian General Staff, Colonel Dimitrijević, arranged the whole thing. At a meeting of the "Black Hand" on the 15th of June, he announced, that in his opinion, the impending Austrian manoeuvres in Bosnia were only the prelude to war against Serbia; the Archduke Francis Ferdinand was the soul of this enterprise. Consequently he (Dimitrijević) had made all the necessary arrangements to dispose of the Heir to the Throne and so prevent the war. As all but two of those present expressed themselves against the plan, the Colonel promised not to carry out his project, but in reality he left the preparations already made to take their course.[18]

Apis publicly stated that the military manoeuvres Franz Ferdinand was scheduled to oversee in Bosnia in June 1914 were not a routine training exercise as announced but preparation for an imminent war on Serbia. Many observers, including historian Sidney B. Fay have dismissed that as utter nonsense. Fay relates that the Archduke's fatal trip to Bosnia was first arranged in September 1913, and writes:

> The Bosnian maneuvres of 1914 are commonly represented by Austrophobe writers as "planned as a kind of rehearsal for military operations against Serbia." ... There is no truth in these assertions.[19]

Historian Harry Elmer Barnes says it was Serbia, not Austria-Hungary, that was making ready for war. Serbia "had been preparing for the conflict actively for more than a year, and for several months had been receiving shipments of arms from Russia in anticipation of the ultimate struggle with Austria."[20] In making those preparations, Apis was acting in the full knowledge of the Russians. "Russian encouragement of the general plotting is fully established.... Dimitrijevic worked in collusion with Artamanov, the Russian military attaché in Belgrade."[21] The plot received Russian approval, with a promise to protect Serbia from Austria. The complicity of Hartwig and Artamanov was fully and independently confirmed.[22]

The Assassins.

The young assassins who gathered in the Serbia capital, Belgrade, in the spring of 1914 belonged to a group known as Mlada Bosna (Young Bosnia). It was the collective name for a number of secret societies in Bosnia with a shared hatred of Austria. Professor Fay writes:

> Mlada Bosna was impatient with the politicians, the bourgeoisie, and all legal forms of opposition. It repudiated all notions of "trialism" as a solution of Serbo-Croat national aspirations. [the concept suggested by Franz Ferdinand] It was recruited from the youth of the "small and insignificant classes" – peasants, journeymen, schoolteachers, and the sons of priests and young students. Its members were impatient and "desperate." They had begun to feed upon Russian revolutionary and anarchistic literature, especially the writings of Herzen and Kropotkin. They were fired with the success of the Russian revolution of 1905. They developed the "cult of the individual deed," that is, they believed that terrorist acts of assassination were the best means of putting a speedy end to the temporizing methods of Bosnian politicians and throwing off all Austrian control to prepare the way for a new "Jugoslav" nationalism. Deeds of revolutionary terrorism served two great purposes: they created panic among the ruling authorities: and they uplifted the national spirit of the masses.[23]

The guiding spirit of the Young Bosnia movement, Vladimir Gacinović (aged 24 in 1914), was a revolutionary from Herzegovina who, during his studies abroad, had formed a friendship with Leon Trotsky and other Russian revolutionaries.[24] In early 1914, Gacinović plotted to assassinate the Austrian governor of Bosnia-Herzegovina, Oskar Potiorek, but for various reasons did not proceed with the attempt. Thereafter, Franz Ferdinand became the target.

Dr. James Lyon, a Balkans expert, relates that Gacinović was a key player in recruiting the assassins. He had moved to Belgrade in September 1911, joined Black Hand, and became a member of the Central Committee representing Bosnia-Herzegovina. He subsequently formed Black Hand cells in several cities, including Sarajevo, and recruited the main Sarajevo conspirator Danilo Ilić. "The only other conspirator who appears to have been fully inducted as a Black Hand member was Gavrilo Princip."[25]

Gavrilo Princip (1894-1918), the man destined to kill Franz Ferdinand and his wife, was born in Grahovo in rural Western Bosnia to a Serbian peasant family. Like other members of Mlada Bosna he migrated back and forth between his home and Serbia 'to study'. They were well received in Belgrade and enjoyed the "freer and more congenial air" there.

> Princip, with the personal approval of M. Ljuba Jovanović, the Serbian Minister of Education, passed off three years' work in less than two years, in spite of the fact that he was spending much of his time in political discussions and in travelling back and forth.[26]

Professor Fay discusses the role played by Ljuba Jovanović in the Serbian government in the summer of 1914, and the fact that he was an active member of Narodna Odbrana.[27] Yet another Serbian nationalist group founded in 1908 at the time of the Austro-Hungarian annexation of Bosnia-Herzegovina, Narodna Odbrana [National Defence] promoted anti-Austro-Hungarian propaganda and trained paramilitary forces for war against her. John S. Ewart writes:

> Serbia was still in the throes of reconstitution, and her military preparations were far from complete. Several patriots decided to supplement this deficiency by private enterprise. Committees were founded all over the country to enrol and train volunteers for the defence of the country. Within a very short time a considerable army of volunteers was created.[28]

In 1909, Narodna Odbrana was supposedly transformed into an organisation solely for promoting Serbian and South Slave culture, but continued its military activities clandestinely. In 1911, the supposed 'cultural society' issued a provocative anti-Austro-Hungarian statement:

> The Narodna Odbrana proclaims to the people that Austria is our first and greatest enemy. Just as once the Turks attacked us from the south, so Austria attacks us today from the north. If Narodna Odbrana preaches the necessity of fighting Austria, she preaches a sacred truth.[29]

Professor Fay writes that Ljuba Jovanović, professor of history at the University of Belgrade, and founder and active member of Narodna Odbrana, was 'personally acquainted' with Gavrilo Princip in Belgrade.[30] The link between the assassin Princip and Jovanović is important given that in addition to being a professor of history, Jovanović was a member of the Serbian government as Minister of Education and Minister of Internal Affairs. As we have seen, he facilitated Princip's studies in Belgrade. Fay adds:

161

Princip quickly came into touch with the "Black Hand" *comitadjis* in the Belgrade coffee houses, and, according to his own declaration, was taken into the Narodna Odbrana by its secretary, Major Vasitch. When the Balkan war broke out, he (Princip) went to the Turkish frontier to receive military training with *comitadjis* under Major Tankositch, another leading "Black Hand" terrorist and agitator. But being only sixteen years old, with a small weak body, he was sent home by Tankositch.[31]

According to Professor Fay and Dr. Lyon, in addition to being a member of Mlada Bosna (Young Bosnia) the Archduke's assassin, Gavro Princip, was also a member of Narodna Odbrana *and* Black Hand. That, and his connection to a Serbian government minister, are facts that no British 'court historian' ever mention. The fake history has to be perpetuated that Princip and others in the assassination squad were independent operators acting on their own volition without the knowledge of the Serbian or Russian authorities. Sir Hew Strachan (formerly Chichele Professor of the History of War at All Souls College, Oxford) dismisses the assassination squad as "amateurish and incompetent" students and apprentices.[32] R.W. Seton-Watson – who trained under secret society inner-core member Prof. H A. L. Fisher at Oxford – writes of Princip and the others:

> Their heads were already full of terrorist ideas, and that the barest promoting from their friends at home was needed to set them in motion. It also proves, incidentally, that the initiative came from Bosnia, not from Serbia.... The initiative lay, not with the those who so recklessly provided arms to the three of them in Belgrade, but with Ilić and Pusara in Sarajevo, and above all with Gacinovic in Lausanne.[33]

Thus, the deep involvement of the Serbian government, Black Hand and Apis, together with the Russian's Hartwig and Artamanov, in the Sarajevo crime have been whitewashed by British court historians. They put the assassination down to a few immature leftist students egged on by their friends in Bosnia.

Gavro Princip passed the winter of 1913/14 in Hadžići, a small town to the southwest of Sarajevo, but moved back to Belgrade in February. He shared a cheap room with his cousin and other Young Bosnia members, Trifko Grabez (age 18) and Nedeljko Čabrinović (age 19). Gavro's old childhood friend, Danilo Ilić, a young journalist in Belgrade and deeply involved with Black Hand, brought them to the attention of Milan

Ciganović, a trusted Black Hand associate of Colonel Apis. These young men formed the core of the assassination team that would be trained by Serbians and financed with Russian money. Balkans specialist Dr James Lyon (PhD in History from the University of California) writes:

> Whatever the level of Artamanov's involvement, Russian money clearly financed Princip, Grabez, and Cabrinovic's living and travel expenses.[34]

After discussing their ability and determination to carry out the task, Apis gave his consent, and they were provided with weapons and shooting practice in forests around Belgrade. It is unknown if Princip and the others were ever in Apis's presence. They were expendable pawns, and had no inkling whatsoever of the multiple links above them in a chain of command that stretched from Apis and Artamanov into Russia and beyond. They were proud to have been chosen for the special mission, would carry it out to the best of their ability, and prepared to die for the Pan-Slav cause.

Crucially, Apis's Black Hand friend involved with the assassination plot, the above-mentioned Milan Ciganović, was also a trusted associate of Serbia's prime minister, Nikola Pašić:

> Pashitch knew that it had been hatched in Belgrade and that it was Serbian officers, leaders of the Black Hand, who held all the threads of it, provided the perpetrators with weapons, bombs and funds and helped them to cross the frontier into Bosnia. The go-between who had kept these officers in touch with the conspirators was, as we have seen, that railway employee Ciganovic, who, while a member of the Black Hand, was probably also Pashitch's informer about what went on in that society, on which the Serbian government had every reason to keep a watchful eye. Hence the opening of proceedings against the accomplices in the outrage would have caused a most terrific scandal, which would have done immense harm to Serbia and served as a justification for extreme demands on the part of Austria. And where would the scandal have stopped seeing that Black Hand had contact with the highest in the land? And what would be the consequences if it were discovered that Pashitch had been notified of the plot?[35]

Confirmation that the Serbian prime minister, Nikola Pašić, *was* fully aware of the plot being hatched in Belgrade also came from Ljuba Jovanivić who was Minister of Education in the Pašić, cabinet in 1914 and, as we have seen, knew Gavro Princip personally. Jovanivić wrote in 1924:

> I do not remember if it was at the end of May or the beginning of June [1914], when one day Mr Pashitch said to us that certain persons were making ready to go to Sarajevo to murder Franz Ferdinand who was to go there to be solemnly received on St Vitus day.[36]

Some historical accounts relate that Nikola Pašić issued instructions for the assassins to be stopped and arrested at the border, but that his order came too late as they had already crossed into Bosnia. Irrespective of the veracity of that claim, Professor Fay relates that the Serbian prime minister should immediately have informed the Austrian authorities of the plot, and given them the names and details of the plotters to aid their arrest in Bosnia.

> But Mr Pashitch and his cabinet did nothing of the kind. Furthermore, after the crime had been committed, they should have made a searching enquiry into the incriminated secret organizations in Serbia, and arrested all the accomplices who had helped hatch or carry out the plot. Instead, they sought to conceal every trace of it, and denied all knowledge of it, in the hope that Austria would be unable to discover their complicity.[37]

Had the Austrian authorities been informed by Pašić, it is not entirely certain that they would have been successful in finding and arresting the entire assassination squad before 28 June. It is certain, however, that Franz Ferdinand's visit to Sarajevo would have been cancelled. Had that been the case it is tempting, but mistaken to think there would have been no subsequent war, for the power elite would assuredly have had a plan B in place.

When confident that the young Bosnians were ready for their mission, Black Hand arranged their safe passage across the border with weapons and bombs. Each was given a small vial of cyanide to swallow immediately Franz Ferdinand had been killed. Their suicide would ensure the trail could not be traced back to Serbia. Princip and some of the others arrived in Bosnia in late May and stashed the guns and grenades in safe houses in various towns and villages before making their way to Sarajevo. The weapons would be collected as the fateful day drew close. Meantime, they went about their usual daily routines, hoping not to attract the attention of the police.

On Thursday 25 June, a guard of honour and band greeted the royal couple when they arrived at Ilidza station, some ten miles to the west of central Sarajevo. The Hotel Bosna in Ilidza had been taken over, expensively refurbished, and would be their base for the duration of the visit. Franz Ferdinand spent most of the following two days observing army manoeuvres to the west of Ilidza, while Sophie visited schools, an orphan home, and various cathedrals and mosques in Sarajevo. Crowds warmly greeted her everywhere.

GUNS AND BOMBS

The morning of 28 June was clear and sunny over Sarajevo when the royal party took the short train journey from Ilidza into the city. The visit was planned virtually to the minute. On arrival at Sarajevo rail station, a fleet of cars would convey them to Sarajevo army barracks for an inspection of troops. They would then go on to the town hall for a short reception before going to officially open the new Sarajevo museum. Sarajevo's 120 police officers, and a few additional men drafted in from rural areas, were sparsely spaced out along the route facing the crowds. One senior police officer later remarked: "Security measures on 28 June were in the hands of Providence."[38] Much has been made of the lack of security for the Archduke's visit, with suggestions that Governor Potiorek was in on the assassination plot. No evidence exists to substantiate that. Professor Fay indicates that the low security measures were dictated by the Archduke himself. "He did not wish to be protected by heavy guards of soldiers and secret police, but preferred to ride about freely in an open automobile."[39]

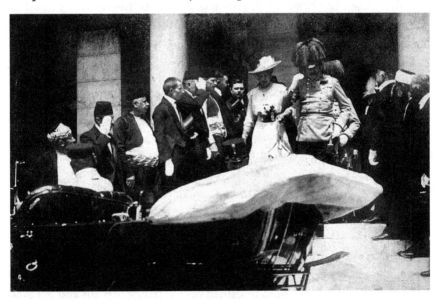

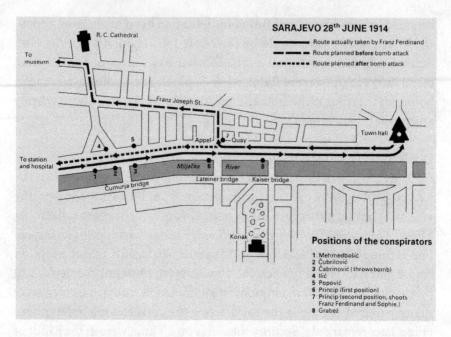

Seven Young Bosnia assassins were spread out at intervals along Appel Quay on the route to the town hall. The Archbishop of Sarajevo later described it as "a regular avenue of assassins." Nedeljko Čabrinović was first to act, breaking the cap fuse on his old-style hand grenade bomb and lobbing it at the Archduke's car. The driver apparently saw it coming, accelerated hard, and the bomb bounced off the folded canvas roof immediately behind the heads of the royal couple onto the road. It exploded, injuring several spectators and occupants of the car behind. Čabrinović immediately swallowed the cyanide, jumped over an adjacent rail, and fell into the Miljacka River below. The poison failed to kill him, however, and vomiting profusely he was dragged out onto the grassy bank opposite by police officers and members of the public. The Archduke immediately told his driver to stop and issued an order to check on the wounded. They were now sitting ducks, but nothing further untoward happened and the car raced off to the town hall.

After a tense 20-minute meeting, rather than proceeding directly to the museum as planned, Franz Ferdinand insisted on being taken to the hospital to visit the wounded. At 10:45 A.M. the motorcade departed the town hall, heading back along Appel Quay with the Archduke's car now second in the convoy with Governor Potiorek and another official aboard. What happened next has been the subject of much debate over the past century. The driver, allegedly, had not been informed of the change of plans and believed they were still heading on the pre-arranged route to the new museum rather than the hospital. When he turned right off Appel Quay into Franz Josef Street. General Potiorek ordered the driver to stop and reverse back to Appel Quay. Standing just six feet from the precise spot the car stopped before reversing was Gavrilo Princip. He stepped forward, shot both the Archduke and Sophie, and immediately swallowed the cyanide. It almost appears as if his victims had been served up on a plate.

Like Nedeljko Čabrinović, the cyanide failed to kill Princip. He was grabbed by police officers, beaten, and dragged away to the police cells vomiting profusely.

Bizarrely, rather than proceeding immediately to the hospital for urgent medical help, Potiorek ordered the driver to take the two victims to the Governor's palace. Unconscious, if not already dead, both were carried to rooms in the palace. The deaths of both victims were confirmed at 11:30 A.M. The earlier celebratory booming of cannons echoing out over Sarajevo gave way to the tolling of church bells. Most of the assassins were rounded up with suspicious ease and taken into custody.

The bodies of Franz Ferdinand and Sophie were conveyed to Trieste by an Austro-Hungarian warship, then on to Vienna by train. The imperial guard was conspicuous by its absence on 3 July as the coffins were taken by horse-drawn hearse for a brief and simple funeral in the Hofburg chapel in Vienna. Word had gone out that a dozen Slav assassins had made their way to the city, leading to most of Europe's royalty and leading politicians apologising in advance for their absence.

> The service itself began at four that afternoon and was over by four-fifteen. Some of the family members there complained it had been a 'third-class funeral' and showed their respect for the couple by walking behind their hearses as the bodies were taken to the railway station for the journey to Artstetten.… It was a difficult journey back, especially the night crossing of the Danube on a raft-like ferry during a violent storm on the choppy river. The horses almost bolted at a fissure of lightning and were only narrowly restrained from racing the coffins into the river.… At Artstetten there was one more service before the internment in front of hundreds of guests. Many who were expected did not come.[40]

Meanwhile, in Belgrade Serbian officials were assured of Russian protection if and when Austria-Hungary responded to the murders with military action. Professor Barnes writes of the Russian complicity:

Russian encouragement of the general plotting is fully established. The Russian minister in Belgrade, Hartwig, was informed of the plot long before its execution.... Dimitrijevic worked in collusion with Artamanov, the Russian military attaché in Belgrade He received Russian approval, a Russian subsidy and the promise of Russia to intervene to protect Serbia from Austria. The complicity of Hartwig and Artamanov in the Sarajevo Plot was fully and independently confirmed to the writer by informed Serbians in the summer of 1926.[41]

At the time of the assassination and thereafter, the lie was carefully concocted that Serbia had played no part in it. Professor Fay writes:

In the expectation that Vienna would be unsuccessful in establishing any connection between official Serbia and the deed on the Miljacka, it was decided to conceal everything, to pose as unconcerned and innocent, to make a demonstration of sorrow, and to try to get off as cheaply as possible in giving satisfaction to the country whose royal couple had been murdered.[42]

Professor Fay describes an admission made by the Serbian education minister, Jovanović, in the 1920s:

As is well known, the Government did not fail to do all it could to show their friends and the rest of the world how far removed we were from the Sarajevo conspirators. Thus, on the very same evening upon which it was known what Princip had done, Stojan gave orders that the Belgrade police should forbid all music, singing, and merry-making in public places; everything was suspended, and something like official mourning began. Mr Pashitch expressed to the Vienna Government our regret at the loss which a great neighbouring Power had suffered and his execration at the deed itself. At the Requiem in the Catholic Church of the Legation on July 3, on the day when the funeral of the murdered Heir to the Throne and his wife took place in Vienna, the Government was represented by several Ministers. I, too was among them. I wished to show that even I, who more than any of the others might have been thought to have approved of Princip's deed, was on the contrary entirely in agreement with what our Cabinet were doing. Nevertheless, this occasion and the short stay in the church were unpleasant to me, I felt myself among enemies, who did not desire peace with us."[43]

In response to Jovanović's statement, Professor Fay wrote:

What a study in the psychology of a guilty conscience! Knowing of the plot a month beforehand, doing nothing effective to forestall it, terrified at first that Serbia will be isolated and attacked, then hopeful that the truth could be concealed, the Minister of Education goes to church in pretend mourning for the murdered victim for the sake of the good impression it will make. No wonder he felt "unpleasant."... To persons not blinded by prejudice or propaganda, it will not come as such a total surprise that the serious historian can no longer maintain the theory that the war-guilt was all on the side of Austria, and that Serbia was an innocent victim.[44]

The Serbian government undertook no investigation into the Archduke's assassination. In Belgrade, leading Serbian politicians attended Requiem mass in pretend mourning, and to pray for the eternal rest of the souls of the man and woman whose murders they had plotted. The sham sorrow and condolence had to be tempered, however, with the need to inflame and provoke the Austro-Hungarians sufficiently to make them react. Consequently, the Serbian Press praised the assassination as a "patriotic act and a glorious national achievement."[45]

The Serbian press, in the days following the murders, widely transgressed the limits not only of minimal decorum but of elementary prudence. The murders were openly applauded, the Habsburg Monarchy vituperatively denounced.[46]

In the days following the assassination, "the whole world expected that Austria-Hungary would deal severely with Serbia."[47] Messages of support poured into Vienna, but it was a faux sorrow and condolences that were extended to the old emperor by top politicians in Britain, France and Russia – the very countries secretly planning the destruction of his empire. Franz Joseph and his Ministers were encouraged to believe that all Europe was in sympathy with Austria-Hungary and understood their need to take strong action. That, indeed, was exactly what they hoped he would do. President Poincare in Paris offered 'sincere condolences,' while in Britain Sir Edward Grey assured the Austrian government that he fully understood how Austria-Hungary had been wronged by Serbia and "conceded the fact that the Serbians would have to be humiliated."[48] In his address to parliament in London two days after the murders, the British prime minister, Herbert Henry Asquith, spoke of his abhorrence of the crime and offered his profound sympathy to Emperor Franz Joseph and the Austrian people who have "always been our friends."[49] Professor Douglas Newton writes:

...the British Foreign Office expected some kind of 'punitive expedition' against Serbia. Grey seemed resigned to it. Every imperial power indulged in this kind of chastisement. When on Monday 6 July the German ambassador, Prince Karl Max Lichnowsky, gave broad hints that Austria-Hungary contemplated 'military action,' Grey sought only an assurance that no annexation would follow. Lichnowsky gave it readily. In the words of Lichnowsky, Grey 'seemed to understand' that Austria-Hungary must take 'energetic measures'.[50]

Edward Grey informed the German ambassador that Britain would understand a military response against Serbia provided there was no annexation of Serbian territory. Grey was fully aware that this message would be relayed to the Austrian government. Indeed, he directly informed the Austro-Hungarian ambassador in London, Count Mensdorf, that he recognised their claim about Serbian complicity in the Archduke's murder, and that Austria-Hungary's requirements for retribution and satisfaction were justified. Grey added that the British Government had to take account of public opinion which was currently favourable to Austria, but that would change if Austria 'proved stubborn.'[51] Grey did not clarify what he meant by "stubborn," and the ambassador did not ask him to clarify, but the gist of the British Minister for Foreign Affairs message to the Austrian government was that they were now entirely 'justified' in dealing harshly with Serbia and should get on with it. In Vienna, the British Ambassador, Sir Maurice de Bunsen, visited Austro-Hungarian Foreign Minister, Leopold Berchtold, to discuss the matter. Thereafter, Berchtold reported:

> The British Government has followed the course of the crisis with the greatest interest: it sympathises with our way of seeing things and perfectly understands our grievances against Servia. It did not mind saying that it had no love to spare for Servia, and knows very well that Servia has committed a number of misdeeds in the past.[52]

Austria-Hungary was getting feedback from Britain through multiple sources with one clear message: 'We support you taking strong action against Serbia.'

Grey, Poincaré, and Sazonov did nothing to reduce the tension. The Secret Elite agenda required them to play a deadly game of charades that left Berchtold convinced that Europe understood his dilemma. Austria-Hungary had to stop the Serbian-inspired rot.

Grey played his cards perfectly. He may never have read Sun Tzu's *Art of War*, but the first rule of war is deception, and deception was an art at which Sir Edward Grey and his Foreign Office associates were absolute masters.

Reassured by support from across Europe, Berchtold came to the logical conclusion that he was expected to punish Serbia for the crime of Sarajevo. Other governments, even the entente governments, appeared to approve the need for retribution.[53]

This sympathy for the Austro-Hungarian cause against Serbia was a deception of the first order. The Austro-Hungarian government had to believe it had the moral backing of the world's superpower, Britain, for taking military action. Many honest historians have stated that Austria-Hungary would likely have refrained from a major confrontation with Serbia had Britain discouraged rather than encouraged her. It has to be understood that at that point in time neither Austria-Hungary nor Germany had the slightest knowledge or suspicion that Britain was actually orchestrating the great deception with France and Russia. If they could get Austria-Hungary to take the bait, Germany could be reeled in with her.

In Paris, the Minister of Foreign Affairs, M. Bienvenu-Martin, played France's part in the duplicity. He discussed the French government's attitude with the Austro-Hungarian Ambassador who immediately reported his comments back to Vienna:

> He would not discuss the text but admitted freely that the events of recent times and the attitude of the Servian government had made energetic action on our part a matter that could be understood.... The minister visibly avoided to defend or condone the attitude of Servia in any way whatever.[54]

In St Petersburg, Sergei Sazonov was likewise joining the orchestrated deception, informing the Austro-Hungarian Ambassador that he "had no heart for the Balkan Slavs." They were "a heavy burden for Russia," and Austria had "no conception" of what Russia had already suffered through them.[55]

The message came loud and clear from all quarters; those damned Serbs needed to be taught a harsh lesson. The last thing the financial elite's agents in Britain, France and Russia wanted was for Austria-Hungary to show restraint. Following the outpouring of sympathy and understanding, the Austro-Hungarian leaders were undoubtedly left with the impression that they would be considered weak and ineffective if they *did not* punish Serbia. In Britain, the controlled press was playing its part in that charade by expressing condolences to Austria and roundly denouncing Serbia. Professor Sidney B. Fay called it a "newspaper incitement to war":

> On July 16 the London *Times* [then owned and controlled by members of the secret society] denounced "the reckless and provocative language which a good many Serbian newspapers are alleged to have used, both before and after the crime that has shocked Europe."... Next day the influential *Westminster Gazette* [owned by Lord Astor, inner-circle member of the secret society] justified Austria's desire to clarify her relations with Serbia, after a crime believed to have its origins in Belgrade and to be part of a deliberate attempt to tear away the Serb provinces of the Dual Monarchy. Austria "cannot be expected to remain inactive."... This attitude on the part of the powerful English papers gave great encouragement to Austrian hopes that England would remain inactive towards a 'localized' Austro-Serbian conflict.[56]

The British weekly magazine, *John Bull* – with a circulation of three-quarters of a million and reputedly the largest circulation of any weekly journal in the world – was similarly adamant that Austria-Hungary's position was entirely just. In the aftermath of events in Sarajevo, it described Serbia as "a hotbed of cold-bloodied conspiracy and subterfuge" that should be wiped from the map of Europe. The *Manchester Guardian* declared that Serbia's record of cruelty, greed, hypocrisy and ill-faith was unmatched. "If it were physically possible for Serbia to be towed out to sea and sunk there, the air of Europe would at once seem clearer."[57]

The Austro-Hungarian authorities were considering responding to the assassination with a strong ultimatum to Serbia, but in the first instance considered it prudent to seek the views of Britain. The response, yet again, was part of the great deception that was encouraging Austria-Hungary into a harsh response.

> Before the ultimatum was finally shaped, the Austrians sent out two "feelers" to Great Britain implying that Austria was contemplating severe actions against Serbia. The English responses were such that led even the Russians to regard them as a distinct encouragement to Austria to go ahead with her plans. Like Germany, Austria then counted upon British neutrality and believed, probably correctly, that Russia and France would not wage war without assurances of British support.[58]

Following the Sarajevo killings, Austria and its German alliance partner were tricked into believing that just about every 'decent European' supported Austria-Hungary against 'nasty' Serbia. Reassured with this support from across Europe, the Austro-Hungarian government logically concluded that it was expected to punish Serbia for the crime of Sarajevo.

Summary: Chapter 6 – An Avenue of Assassins

- Serbia, backed by Russia, had for years been provoking Austria-Hungary.

- Planning the assassination of Archduke Franz Ferdinand began in March 1914 when his visit to Sarajevo in June 1914 was publicly announced.

- The young Bosnian student assassins received weapons training in Serbia, with weapons and bombs provided by the Serbian army.

- Nikolai Hartwig, the Russian ambassador to Serbia, and Viktor Artamanov, Russian military attaché, encouraged the assassination and promised full Russian support for Serbia if/when Austria-Hungary reacted.

- The Russian ambassador was giving Russian support on the instructions of his superior in St Petersburg, Serge Sazonov, the Russian Minister for Foreign Affairs who was deeply implicated with the English elites and their longstanding plans for war on Germany.

- Following the assassination, British newspapers owned or controlled by the members of the Milner Group expressed their disgust and their view that Austria would be fully justified in taking action against Serbia.

- Most countries expressed their deep condolences to Emperor Franz Joseph, especially Britain, which created the strong impression that they were encouraging Austria-Hungry to act against Serbia.

CHAPTER 7

THE JULY CRISIS

F ranz Ferdinand was disliked in Austrian court circles because of his morganatic marriage, but was a popular figure with the Austrian army and it wanted blood. Field Marshal Conrad von Hötzendorf was eager to mobilise the army immediately for war against Serbia, but Foreign Minister, Count Leopold von Berchtold, said evidence of Serbian complicity would first need to be provided and public opinion prepared for strong measures. Not least, their German allies would need to be consulted. On 5 July, an emissary from the Austrian government, Count Alexander von Hoyos (*chef de cabinet* to von Berchtold), went to Potsdam Palace (35 km west of Berlin) with a letter to Kaiser Wilhelm from Emperor Franz Joseph and a memorandum from the Austrian government to Chancellor Bethmann-Hollweg.

Franz Joseph's letter advised the Kaiser that the assassination was not the act of an individual, but a "well-organised conspiracy," the threads of which extended to Serbia. The Austrian emperor proposed, first and foremost, the formation of a new Balkan League that was friendly to the Central Powers. His letter concluded:

> You too will be convinced after the recent terrible events in Bosnia that there can be no further question of bridging by conciliation the difference that separates Serbia from us, and that the policy pursued by all European monarchs of preserving the peace will be at risk for as long as this hotbed of criminal agitation in Belgrade remains unpunished.[1]

The Austro-Hungarian government believed it was necessary to strike firmly at the root of the plot but, according to Professor Christopher Clark, they presented the Kaiser with no clear plan as to how they were going to do this.

> What strikes the present-day reader about these communications is their panicky lack of focus ... There is no explicit request for German assistance; there are no policy proposals, no list of options, just a grim, unfocused panorama of threat and foreboding.[2]

The Kaiser's meeting at Potsdam on 5 July is of crucial importance to our understanding of the true origins of the First World War and we must consider it in some detail. The significance of the meeting rests in the fact that absurd lies and fake history were related about the meeting at the peace talks in 1919 to blame the kaiser for the war

We will see in due course in chapter 13 how a great lie was spun that Wilhelm, together with Germany's top military chiefs and leading bankers, met at his Potsdam residence on 5 July 1914 and agreed to use the Archduke's assassination as an excuse to plunge the world into a war that would enable Germany to seize control of Europe and the world. While some British pro-Establishment historians perpetuate that lie to the present day, honest and genuine academics elsewhere, including Professor Sidney B. Fay, dismiss it as the nonsense it is.

> While the German Kaiser had hitherto generally inclined to protect Serbia from dangerously excessive demands by Austria and hoped for a peaceful settlement of their difficulties, now, after the murder of one of his best friends, whom he had just been visiting, by assassins who had admittedly come from Belgrade, his indignation against the Serbians was thoroughly roused. His marginal notes [written on the Austrian memorandum delivered to him on 5 July] excoriate them as "murderers," "regicides," and "bandits." He sincerely felt that the monarchical principle was in danger; that the spirit that led them to murder their own king and queen in 1903 still dominated the country; that all monarchs, Czar Nicholas II most of all, ought to support, instead of opposing, any action on Austria's part which aimed at the suppression of the unscrupulous agitation which had been going on for years among Serbians and which, as he was now informed by Berchtold, threatened the very existence of his Austrian ally, and had made his own personal friend its victim. ... With his natural impetuosity he wanted Austria to take action in regard to the Serbians as quickly as possible, while the whole civilized world, still under the impression of the terrible assassination, sympathised with her. What this action of Austria's was to be, the Kaiser did not know definitely on July 5, and did not care to advise. But neither he nor Bethmann thought it at all probable on that day that the Austro-Serbian dispute would lead to a European war.[3]

Another American historian, Professor David E. Kaiser, believes that the Austro-Hungarians had in fact decided to go to war with Serbia before Count Hoyos's meeting on 5 July with the Kaiser, and that neither the

Kaiser nor his government were in any way responsible for pushing them into that decision:

> The crisis of July 1914 was not unleashed by the German government ... most of the Austro-Hungarian leadership had already decided upon drastic action against Serbia *before* Count Hoyos went on his mission ... The chronic paralysis over questions of war and peace within the German government makes it unlikely that Berlin ever would have provoked war out of the blue: To a certain extent the Germans had to be pushed into war by exogenous impulses.[4]

The "exogenous impulses" that pushed Germany into war will be examined later. Kaiser Wilhelm advised Count Hoyos that he and the German government were not blind to the troubles being caused by Russian and Serbian Pan-Slavists and agreed that they constituted a considerable danger to Austria-Hungary.

> The only remark made about Serbia was that the Kaiser naturally could not take part in any question pending between that country and Austria-Hungary, as they were not within his competence. But the Emperor Francis Joseph could rest assured that His Majesty would be true to their old friendship, and stand by Austria-Hungary within the obligations imposed on him by the alliance.[5]

Kaiser Wilhelm had long opposed action by Vienna against Serbia but now believed that Austria-Hungary was so seriously menaced by the Pan-Slavs that "further inactivity was inconsistent with the duty of self-preservation."[6] Berlin would back Vienna if it decided on military action, but Wilhelm advised Vienna that it should move at once in order to keep such action localised to an Austria vs. Serbia conflict, and that there must be no annexation of Serbian territory. In other words, it should be limited to a show of strength with a short, sharp, incursion of troops across the border into Belgrade and then withdrawal. To this day, the Kaiser's response on 5 July has been wilfully misrepresented by most British court historians as Germany giving Austria a 'blank cheque' to attack Serbia in order to deliberately start a pan-European war. The reality was that the 'blank cheque' for war was issued not by Germany, but by Russia with her promise in the weeks and months before the assassination to support Serbia militarily whenever and however Austria-Hungary reacted.

No responsible German military or naval authorities were recalled from leave after the Kaiser's meeting with Count Hoyos. Historian A.J.P.

Taylor states that no warning was issued that war might be imminent. No troops were moved. No military preparations were made for war, and "during the whole month of July German military intelligence recorded no special activities."[7]

Kaiser Wilhelm departed the following day for his long arranged three-week summer cruise. Professor Sean McMeekin writes that as the kaiser prepared to leave on the Monday morning [6 July], he summoned Germany's active-duty army and navy officers who were covering for Moltke and Tirpitz on vacation. Wilhelm advised General Hermann von Bertrab from the General Staff and Admiral Eduard von Capelle of Austria-Hungary's plans to take action against Serbia, and emphasised that he did not think Russia would intervene. The Kaiser believed that his cousin, the czar, was hardly likely to intervene given that the root cause was a regicide. Consequently, it would remain a purely Balkan concern.

> It was surprising that a man of the emperor William's character should overestimate the feeling of monarchical solidarity, but the same view was taken in other quarters.... Added to this there was the mistaken belief that Russia was not by any means prepared for war, a belief for which there was no justification.... Finally, the optimistic view taken of the situation was based largely on the fact that there had recently been a steadily increasing improvement in the relations between England and Germany.
>
> ...If England adopted an attitude friendly to Austria and Germany in a possible diplomatic conflict, the chances were that France would not make up her mind to fight, and Russia would not start hostilities without French armed support. Three mistakes – overestimation of the Tsar's feeling of solidarity, underestimation of France and Russia's preparations and will for war, and a false estimate of the attitude England would be likely to adopt – were responsible for Germany having underestimated the magnitude of the risk Austria's action against Serbia must involve.[8]

If Kaiser Wilhelm underestimated the magnitude of the risk, and made mistakes in early July 1914, they were honest mistakes based on the information available to him. He had no knowledge of the top-secret military collaboration between England, France, and Russia, and, indeed, Belgium, that had been ongoing for years, or their intricate and well-developed plans for a destructive war against Germany. Whether one wishes to label it blissful ignorance or astonishing naivety, the kaiser concluded that no preparatory military measures for war needed to be undertaken.

He left at 9.15 A.M. on 6 July for his Baltic cruise, and Chancellor Beth-mann-Hollweg returned to his family home at Hohenfinow. Both, according to Professor McMeekin, were satisfied with their declaration of support for Austria-Hungary and content to let Vienna's policy take its course.[9]

Wilhelm had advised the Austro-Hungarians that Germany would support them, but how could they be certain? Over the preceding three years of Balkan conflict, Germany had constantly restrained Austria-Hungary from any aggressive action in the region which might involve Germany in conflict,[10] and Vienna could not necessarily now count on German support. American historian, Professor Samuel R. Williamson writes:

> The Balkans Wars [1912 – 1913] had shaken Vienna's confidence about German support if a crisis arose. On three occasions the Habsburgs had nearly gone to war; in each instance the Germans had counselled caution and prudence.[11]

It can be argued that German constraint of Austria-Hungary should have continued following the events in Sarajevo, but this was different because the assassination was very personal for the Kaiser. His good friends, Franz Ferdinand and Sophie, had been brutally murdered, and there was news that a dozen Serbian assassins were on their way to Austria to kill *him* if he attended the funerals. He was depressed when leaving for his summer vacation two days after the funerals but was most certainly not planning to start a European war over it. Professor McMeekin writes:

> There have always been serious problems with the full-on thesis about Germany's deliberate launching of a world war. As even its supporters realize, the botched execution of the Austro-German plot to isolate and punish Serbia hardly suggests brilliant "cold-blooded" design, The original plan conceived by Bethmann -Hollweg during the Count Hoyos visit in early July was to forge a fait accompli, a chastisement of Serbia by Austrian arms to be completed before the great powers could react. Bethmann-Hollweg was clear from the start about the objective of localizing the conflict. While Moltke, [German Chief of the General Staff] a notorious pessimist, was less sanguine about the prospects for limiting the war's scope, he too chimed in from Carlsbad [where he was on holiday] with the hope that "Austria must beat the Serbs then make peace quickly." It was Austria's own prevarication in July that undermined the German strategy.[12]

Official letters, despatches and reports passing between German diplomats and high German officials in government over those critical July days were collected in the post-war years by the Czech-Austrian philosopher, Karl Kautsky. Edited by Count Max Montgelas in *The German Documents relating to the Outbreak of War*, they were published by Oxford University Press. Known as the "Kautsky Documents," they show that after the meeting with Count Hoyos and Bethmann-Hollweg at the palace on 5 July, the Kaiser sent for General Erich von Falkenhayn to discuss the matter. Thereafter, although not instructed to do so, Falkenhayn went to see Field Marshal von Moltke, commander-in-chief of the German army, who was on holiday at Karlsbad. When von Moltke read copies of Emperor Francis Joseph's letter, and the Austrian government's memoir, it appeared to him that Austria-Hungary would march on Serbia "if necessary," but the Vienna Cabinet had not by that stage made any definite decision. Falkenhayn likewise felt that nothing was likely to be decided within the next few weeks, so there was no need for the Field Marshal to curtail his holiday.

The impression Wilhelm had of a steadily increasing improvement in the relations between England and Germany indicates that the English charade in that direction had proved successful. Just four days before the assassination, major battleships and cruisers of the Royal Navy had paid a courtesy visit to Kiel harbour in Germany, and the officers and men of both navies fraternised in a friendly fashion. Then, later in July, when the Kaiser's brother, Prince Henry, was sailing at the Cowes regatta, King George invited him for dinner. The king assured Prince Henry, (who was grand admiral of the German fleet) that Britain bore no ill-will towards Germany.[13] King George V was well aware of the anti-German conspiracy, and in inviting the Kaiser's brother for dinner he was playing his part in the British deception.

> This was no chance meeting but one primed by the Secret Elite to deceive the kaiser. Over a private dinner the king promised that "we shall try to keep out of this, and shall remain neutral." The reassuring news was telegraphed that same evening to Berlin. ... Though the kaiser and Prince Henry were his cousins, King George had no hesitation in maintaining the deception. Naturally, the kaiser laid great store in the promise. Here was something infinitely more worthy than the huckstering of politicians. He had the word of a king.[14]

Via his brother, Kaiser Wilhelm was effectively informed by King George that Britain would remain neutral. It was hoped that the ruse would make him more confident about spurring Austria-Hungary on to action. The very last thing the British elites wanted was Wilhelm restraining Vienna as he had done on previous occasions. Of course he wanted some sort of justice for his murdered friends, but the British elite-controlled history that says he used their deaths as an excuse to start a major European war is nonsense. John S. Ewart writes:

> There still remains for treatment the frequently repeated statement that Germany, having made diligent preparation for war, launched it at the moment that best suited her purpose – at "the selected moment," or, as Sir Edward Grey phrased it … "the chosen moment." The charge is easily answered. Publication of the Foreign Office records of Germany and Austria-Hungary make perfectly clear not only that Germany did not select 1914 for a European war, but that she was strongly opposed to its outbreak. Unquestionably, she agreed to the Austro-Hungarian pressure upon Serbia, and urged expedition of its prosecution; for, in her view, punishment of Serbia was necessary for the maintenance, unimpaired, of the integrity of the Dual Monarchy, and, consequently, for Germany's own military security.… But it is equally unquestionable that when it became apparent that local war would immediately take on European proportions, Germany endeavoured to effect accommodation of this difficulty.[15]

When considering the Sarajevo crime and its aftermath, it is essential to keep in mind that warmongers in Britain were feigning friendship towards Germany while carefully manipulating events across Europe to ensure her destruction. It was not a deeply 'unfortunate' event in which countries unwittingly slid or 'sleepwalked' into war as some have suggested. American author Peter Hof writes:

> It is often alleged that in the summer of 1914, European statesmen in a haze of confusion and miscalculation stumbled blindly, unwitting and unwillingly into war. Nothing could be further from the truth. In fact, during the month after the Sarajevo murders, events played out with such uncanny predictability that it seemed as if they had been pre-ordained.[16]

Pre-ordained, indeed. A great deal of planning and effort had gone into the Sarajevo killings as a means to provoke a reaction from Austria-Hungary. Canadian historian Edward E McCullough:

The assassination of the heir to the Austrian throne on June 28, 1914, was not an isolated incident but the culmination of a long campaign aimed at the destruction of the Austro-Hungarian Empire, of which Russia was the instigator and Serbia the enthusiastic tool.... Seen in its proper perspective, the murder was the real and sufficient cause for Austria to attempt to put an end to the Serbian threat to her existence.[17]

Cambridge political scientist and philosopher, G. Lowes Dickinson, agreed that Austria had just cause to take military action against Serbia, and posed the crucial question as to why it was not allowed to remain a localised conflict.

For years the little state of Serbia had been undermining the Austrian Empire. What was the Empire to do in self-defence? ... I do not believe that there was a State in existence that would not, under similar circumstances, have determined as Austria did, to finish the menace once and for all by war.... The pertinent question is, therefore, why was the war not localised as Austria and Germany intended and desired?[18]

Despite overwhelming evidence that Germany neither desired nor planned a European war, some historians cling doggedly to the "war guilt" clause of Article 231 in the Versailles Treaty. Anika Mombauer, lecturer in European History at the Open University in England, writes:

In Berlin, the possibility of a Balkan crisis was greeted favourably, for such a crisis would ensure that Austria would definitely become involved in a resulting conflict. Most historians would today agree that Berlin's decision makers put substantial pressure on Vienna to demand retribution from Serbia and that they were happy to take the risk that an Austro-Serbian conflict might escalate into a European war.[19]

It is alarming that history students at the Open University are being taught such outright falsehood. It is definitely not true that "most historians" today agree that German leaders put substantial pressure on Austria-Hungary to demand retribution and were happy to take the risk of a European war. Had Mombauer written "most pro-Establishment historians" (such as herself) agreed, she would be on a much more accurate track. Was the support Germany offered Austria-Hungary following the assassination substantially different from that offered by Britain? As we saw in chapter 5, the British Foreign Secretary, Sir Edward Grey, offered his condolences and assured the Austrians that Britain fully understood that Serbia "would have to be humiliated."[20] At the same time, in the British parliament, the prime minister spoke of his abhorrence of the assassination, how Austria-Hungary had always been Britain's friend, and offered his profound sympathy.[21] Pro-Establishment historians illogically claim that Kaiser Wilhelm's sympathy and support for Austria-Hungary to act against Serbia was warmongering while almost exactly the same response by Sir Edward Grey was aimed at keeping the peace. Professor Douglas Newton, by no means 'compliant' historian, writes:

> The British Foreign Office expected some kind of 'punitive expedition' against Serbia. Grey seemed resigned to it. Every imperial power indulged in this kind of chastisement. When on Monday 6 July the German ambassador, Prince Karl Max Lichnowsky, gave broad hints that Austria-Hungary contemplated 'military action,' Grey sought only an assurance that no annexation would follow. Lichnowsky gave it readily. In the words of Lichnowsky, Grey "seemed to understand" that Austria-Hungary must take "energetic measures."[22]

Historian Laurence Lafore – who worked for a time for the U.S. State Department and Office of War Information in Washington and London – suggests without proof that the German leaders all being on holiday at the time was a deception to lull France and Russia into a false sense of security and conceal Germany's real intent:

> After the Hoyos Mission, the conduct of the German leaders was strikingly, indeed suspiciously, relaxed. Moltke remained at Carlsbad with his mineral waters. The Navy Minister, Tirpitz, was at another spa, similarly sipping. Jagow, the Secretary of State for Foreign Affairs, was still away. And now the Chancellor left for his vacation and the Emperor went away for a cruise on his yacht ... There is evidence that this wholesale holiday-making was a ruse to conceal the approaching crisis...[23]

Lafore states, "there is evidence" that all of Germany's leaders going on holiday at that critical period "was a ruse" but he fails to present one single piece of such evidence. Researching this critical period over many years, we have certainly never found any.

Professor Sean McMeekin, currently one of the leading historians of the First World War, writes that the relatively relaxed atmosphere in Berlin in early July was not some dastardly deception. Neither Kaiser Wilhelm nor Chancellor Bethmann-Hollweg knew for sure what Austria-Hungary intended but offered their support. It differed from the support offered by Britain only in that it was genuine, and if any ruse existed in early July 1914, it was on the part of Britain and Russia. McMeekin reveals "Russian cryptographers had broken the Austrian diplomatic codes," and it was likely that Russia was actually better informed of Austria-Hungarian intentions than Germany at that stage.[24] What *were* those intentions?

AUSTRO-HUNGARIAN MINISTERIAL COUNCIL, 7 JULY

Having first sounded out their ally on 5 July at Potsdam, when the Austro-Hungarian ministerial council met in Vienna on 7 July, Foreign Minister, Leopold von Berchtold, and other Austrian ministers agreed they should conduct a sudden, surprise attack on Serbia. Hungarian Premier, Count Tisza, however, argued against precipitate action. Professor Barnes writes:

> He [Count Tisza] insisted that the first move should be adequate diplomatic demands upon Serbia. If these were refused, he would approve a war on Serbia provided the Austrian ministers agreed in advance not to annex any part of it. Tisza expressed himself as believing that territorial aggrandizement at the expense of Serbia would surely bring in Russia and provoke a European war. Berchtold and his group sharply maintained the opposite position, and contended that even the most thorough-going diplomatic victory over Serbia would be useless, as Serbia could not be trusted to fulfil her promises. War was necessary and the quicker the better. The longer it was postponed the more dangerous would become the Serbian nuisance, the more overwhelming the military strength of France and Russia and the larger the probability that they would interfere in any local punitive war of Austria upon Serbia. Tisza, nevertheless, refused to yield, and the council came to the following decision: (1) All present wish for a speedy decision of the controversy with Servia, whether it be decided in a warlike or a peaceful manner. (2) The council of ministers is prepared to adopt the view of the Royal Hungarian premier according to which the mobilization [of the army] is not to take place until after concrete demands have been addressed to Servia and after being refused, an ultimatum has been sent. (3) All present except the Royal Hungarian premier hold the belief that a purely diplomatic success, even if it ended with a glaring humiliation of Servia, would be worthless

and that therefore such stringent demands must be addressed to Servia, that will make a refusal almost certain, so that the road to a radical solution by means of a military action should be opened.[25]

J.S. Ewart writes that "rightly or wrongly," the Austrians believed that reducing Serbia's military strength through war was necessary if they were to maintain the territorial integrity of their country. "A mere diplomatic success would in their opinion have availed nothing."[26] Count Tisza would not agree to immediate action. And another factor militating against a swift response was that many Austro-Hungarian troops were on harvest leave. Christopher Clark explains:

> In rural areas of the Habsburg lands, military service in summertime created serious disruption by keeping young men away from their homes and fields at the time when most crops were harvested. In order to alleviate the problem, the Austrian General Staff had devised a system of harvest leaves that allowed men on active service to return to their family farms to help with the crops and then rejoin their units in time for the summer manoeuvres. On 6 July, the day before the meeting, Conrad had ascertained that troops serving in the units at Agram (Zagreb), Graz, Pressburg (Bratislava), Cracow, Temesvar (Timisoara), Innsbruck and Budapest were currently on harvest leave and would not be returning to service until 25 July.
>
> So Conrad had little choice: he could issue an order to cancel new leaves (and he did), but he could not recall the many thousands of men already on summer leave without seriously disrupting the harvest, disaffecting peasant subjects in many national minority areas, overcrowding the railway system and awakening suspicion across Europe that Austria was planning an imminent military strike.[27]

The immediate military strike was not going to happen. On 8 July, U.S. President Wilson's special envoy and eminence grise, Edward Mandell House, sent a note to Kaiser Wilhelm on the royal yacht. House had met with the kaiser just days before at Potsdam, and was now in London. He wrote:

> Sir,
> Your Imperial Majesty will doubtless recall our conversation at Potsdam, and that with the president's consent and approval I came to Europe for the purpose of ascertaining whether or not it was

possible to bring about a better understanding between the Great Powers, to the end that there might be a continuation of peace, and later a beneficent economic readjustment which a lessening of armaments would insure. Because of the commanding position your Majesty occupies, and because of your well-known desire to maintain peace, I came, as your Majesty knows, directly to Berlin. I can never forget the gracious acceptance of the general purpose of my mission, the masterly exposition of the worldwide political conditions as they exist today and the prophetic forecast as to the future which your Majesty then made. I received every reasonable assurance of your Majesty's cordial approval of the President's purpose, and I left Germany happy in the belief that your Majesty's great influence would be thrown in behalf of peace and the broadening of the world's commerce...

I have the honor to be, Sir, with the greatest respect, your Majesty's very obedient Servant,
Edward M. House.[28]

No indication there of *German* warmongering, and it is worth noting that in an earlier letter (29 May 1914) House wrote to President Wilson that: "Whenever *England* consents, France and Russia will close in on Germany and Austria."[29] Four weeks *before* the Sarajevo assassination, the US president was being informed that a European war would commence whenever England agreed to it. It was all the more telling because House operated at the heart of the Anglo-American Establishment

SERBIA'S DENIALS

In the aftermath of the assassination, the Serbian authorities repeatedly lied and denied they had any part in it. Cognizant of Tisza's admonition that proof was needed of Serbian involvement, Vienna set up a judicial enquiry. On July 11, Dr, Friedrich von Wiesner, the Austrian Foreign Ministry's top legal adviser, was sent to Sarajevo to investigate. On 13 July, he issued an interim report with three major points:

1) The Greater Serbia movement aimed to sever the southern Slav region from Austria-Hungary by revolutionary violence.

2) The Serbian officials, Tankosić and Ciganović had trained the assassins, supplied the weapons, and got them safely across the border into Bosnia.

3) He [von Wiesner] had, as yet, found nothing to show or even lead one to conjecture the complicity of the Serbian government,

or that it directed or prepared the crime or supplied the weapons. Nevertheless the plot had originated in Serbia. It had been carried out by secret societies whose activity had been tolerated by the Serbia government. From the statements of those charged with the crime, it had been ascertained that the crime was resolved upon in Belgrade and that it was prepared with the assistance of a Serbian state official named Ciganovic and of Major Tankosic. These two men provided the bombs, ammunition and cyanide.

Dr von Wiesner's interim report stated there was, as yet, no evidence that the government of Serbia provided the bombs and murder weapon, but it had been proved beyond all doubt that they came from the Serbian army magazine at Kragujevac. "Judging by the statements made by the accused," von Wiesner added, "we can scarcely doubt that Princip, Čabrinović and Grabez were secretly smuggled across the frontier into Bosnia with bombs and arms by Serbian organs at the instigation of Ciganović."

Von Wiesner, who had only been in Sarajevo for 48 hours, stated that much of the evidence had yet to be examined and "investigations are being made with all speed."[30] Within days of sending his interim report, von Wiesner had unearthed evidence that the Serbian government was indeed privy to the conspiracy. He confirmed much of what Vienna already knew through de-coded Serbian intelligence reports.

Despite the rock-solid evidence of Serbian and Russian involvement that came to light, British historians would continue denying it. In 1919, Sir Charles Oman wrote that the evidence Austria had against Serbia was falsified and that no confidence could be placed in any word of it.[31] Oman was an Oxford graduate, Chichele Professor of Modern History at Oxford, and a Member of Parliament. Crucially, he was a Fellow of All Souls College, the secret society's enclave at Oxford from which, according to Professor Quigley, they controlled the writing and teaching of history. Oman certainly played a role in concocting a false history of Sarajevo and of the First Word War, but the master of historical whitewash was Professor R.W. Seton-Watson. He wrote that "by deliberate action" Vienna and Berlin had created a situation "from which nothing short of a miracle could have saved Europe," and "the main responsibility for the outbreak of war must therefore rest upon their shoulders."[32]

Seton-Watson was yet another Oxford historian purveying fake history on behalf of the Milner Group. He ludicrously stated that Austria-Hungary was largely responsible for the Archduke's assassination, and that Germany had then used it as a pretext for starting a European war. The

Germans, he says, were intent on such a war before Austria had even responded with an ultimatum to Serbia on 23 July. In Seton-Watson's view, the Russians, Nicholas Hartwig and Victor Artamanov – who, as we have seen, were pulling the strings in Belgrade – had nothing whatsoever to do with the assassination:

> A few wild pamphleteers have even gone so far as to suggest official Russian complicity in the Archduke's murder – a charge altogether too frivolous to require refutation.[33]

Seton-Watson studied history at Oxford University under the tutelage of H.A.L. Fisher and the pair became friends. That friendship was of considerable significance, for Quigley places Fisher at the very core of the secret society – the 'Society of the Elect.'[34] As we recall, Professor Quigley revealed that the Milner Group completely monopolised "the writing and teaching of the history of their own period," and Robert Seton-Watson's book, *Sarajevo*, is a classic example of the Group's creation of fake history. Professor Sidney B. Fay (American) was evidently so disgusted by Seton-Watson's accounts that throughout his own book, *The Origins of the World War*, he systematically destroyed Seton-Watson's work with rational argument, historical facts, logic and solid evidence. Sadly, it is not only in older books that we find Establishment whitewash. Essentially, most British historians created – and continue to create – a false historical narrative of the First World War to absolve the Anglo-American Establishment of guilt and falsely blame Germany. It has taken many years for honest historians and independent researchers across the world to unpick the myriad lies, falsehoods, and fake history created about the origins of the war in 1914.

In Vienna in early July 1914, it was finally agreed that a tough ultimatum would be sent to the Serbian government. If it failed to agree to all points in the ultimatum within 48 hours, Austria-Hungary would make war on her. The Austro-Hungarian authorities decided not to deliver the ultimatum until after the scheduled visit of French President Raymond Poincaré and Prime Minister René Viviani to Russia. They naively judged that if they waited until Poincaré and Viviani had departed St Petersburg before presenting the ultimatum to Serbia, it would lessen the chance of French and Russian collusion and involvement in the crisis.

FRENCH LEADERS GO TO RUSSIA

During the July crisis, René Viviani, the socialist recently voted in as French Prime Minister and Foreign Minister, and Raymond Poincaré, the President of France, made what proved to be an important trip to St Petersburg. Unlike the warmongering Poincaré, Viviani was a "radical of distinct pacifist inclinations."[35] Niall Ferguson writes:

> Overtly anti-militarist socialist parties were in the electoral ascendent in most of the future combatant countries. In France the April 1914 election returned a left-wing majority and Poincaré had to let the socialist René Viviani form a government.... Nowhere was the anti-militarist Left stronger than in Germany, which had one of the most democratic of all European franchises.... The evidence is unequivocal: Europeans were not marching to war, but turning their backs on militarism.[36]

British Establishment journalist and author, Sir Max Hastings, absurdly writes that Poincaré professed to welcome the trip to Russia as a holiday and was sailing "under the illusion of peace." [37] The revanchist Poincaré was known to be a bad influence on Russia and was going there to bolster the conciliatory and wavering czar's resolve and ensure that Russia stuck to the long-agreed plan for war on Germany. Another British pro-Establishment historian, Professor John F. V. Keiger, makes the equally ridiculous suggestion that Poincaré showed little interest in foreign affairs, and his policy towards Germany and Austria-Hungary would be 'one of peaceful coexistence.'[38]

René Viviani represented the majority anti-war view in France, and his trip to St Petersburg with the warmongering Poincaré would prove very interesting. The French Cabinet questioned if it was desirable for both the president and prime minister to leave France for such a long period when the international situation was so tense.

> Jean Jaurès, the veteran French Socialist and historian, distrusting the policies of Isvolsky and Poincaré, refused to vote credits for the trip, declaring that it was dangerous for France to become increasingly entangled in adventurous Near East questions, and in treaty arrangements of which the French public neither knew the text nor the consequences. But the French President and his Prime Minister embarked from Dunkirk on the cruiser, France, on July 15 and were welcomed five days later off Peterhof by Sazonov, Paléologue [French ambassador to Russia], and Isvolski, and the Tsar. Poincaré and Paléologue in their memoirs have left elaborate and picturesque accounts of all the ceremonial occasions with which the following three days were filled, but they say very little of private conversations which were exchanged.[39]

Of course 'little was said' about their private discussions. Indeed, most of the documents relating to the trip would be destroyed. Official accounts had to make it appear that this was no more than an innocent, relaxing cruise on the Baltic, with a courtesy call on the friendly and equally 'peace-loving' czar. As the Russian party stood on the royal yacht, *Alexandria*, awaiting Poincaré's arrival on July 20, Czar Nicholas stated within earshot of the French ambassador that he did not believe Kaiser Wilhelm wanted war: "Unless Germany has gone out of her mind altogether she will never attack Russia, France and England combined."[40] Docherty and Macgregor write:

> They boarded the warship *La France* at Dunkirk on 15 July. After five days at sea, Sazonov, Isvolsky and Paléologue – the French ambassador at St Petersburg – warmly welcomed them to Russia. This was no innocent state visit. Nor was its timing a matter of chance.
>
> Poincaré's very presence in St Petersburg was ominous. If he had sought a peaceful resolution to the Austro-Serbian crisis, a letter to the czar would have been sufficient. Had Poincaré warned the Russians that France would *not* go to war over Serbia, that would have been the end of the matter. Nicholas II would never have had the confidence to act alone. Poincaré stiffened his resolve. Every action taken by Poincaré resonated with the Secret Elite agenda. On his arrival, he boarded the Czar's yacht, *Alexandria*, and immediately went into deep and private conversation with him.[41]

Czar Nicholas was fully aware that England would be joining Russia and France in the coming war. His foreign minister Sazonov, as we have seen, had spent a week at Balmoral Castle in Scotland being wooed and drawn into the fold of the cabal by its British political agents and King George V. On those lovely peaceful summer days at Peterhof Palace in July 1914, everyone of importance – apart from Viviani – understood the reality. Europe was to be plunged into a cataclysmic war. That war was planned not by Austria-Hungary or Germany, but by the psychopaths manipulating it that way on the orders of their elite masters in London.

The Austro-Hungarian ambassador at St Petersburg, Count Frigyes Szapáry, spoke with Poincaré and thereafter reported to Vienna that the French president had a belligerent attitude and was exercising anything but a calming influence on Russia. It appeared to Szapáry that France and Russia "were making ready for war." His assessment was 100 per cent accurate. Professor McMeekin:

Clearly, both Poincaré and Sazonov were willing to risk war by refusing to countenance Austria's demand on Serbia – and they came to this decision *before*, not after, reading the actual text of the ultimatum.[42]

British academics Sir Hew Strachan and J.V.F Keiger fundamentally disagree with McMeekin's assessment. Professor Strachan, a leading British Establishment historian at Oxford, states that Poincaré "firmly believed that the solidarity of the alliance system in Europe helped create a balance which *prevented* war."[43] Strachan paints Poincaré as a peacemaker, counselling the czar on Russian restraint, and on Russian encouragement of Serbian restraint. Professor Keiger writes:

> Assessments of Poincaré's role in the so-called July crisis have become a good deal more muted since the polemical days of the 1920s and 1930s. Far from believing any more that France played a crucial role in the events which led to war, recent scholarship suggests that she was the most passive of the great powers, following events rather than creating them.[44]

John F.V. Keiger, Ph.D., University of Cambridge, was Professor of International History at Salford University and former Director of Research in the Department of Politics and International Studies, Cambridge University. He was an adviser to the British Foreign Office, the House of Commons Defence Select Committee, and a British Establishment 'court historian'. Keiger said that France being the most passive of the great powers and playing little or no part in the instigation of the First World War was backed by "recent scholarship." On checking the sources that he gives as "recent scholarship," we find his own book of whitewash, *France and the Origins of the First World War* and yet another, *Russia and the Origins of the War,* by D. C. B. Lieven.

Keiger suggests that the decision to go to Russia in the middle of July and leave France without its senior political and foreign policy decision makers for two weeks was "an indication that the French were unaware of serious trouble on the international scene,"[45] and that Poincaré was merely a holidaymaker in Russia.

A *serious* scholarly contribution to our understanding of Poincaré's visit comes from the American academic Marc Trachtenberg, Professor of Political Science at UCLA. He writes:

> For years there was a certain tendency in the historical literature to play down the role that France had played during the crisis, and

especially to minimize the importance of the St. Petersburg talks. France was often portrayed as caught up in events she was scarcely able to control. "Russian decision-making," says Hew Strachan in the first "was remarkably little influenced by France." The result was that "almost regardless of what it did, France would be dragged into an unwanted war."[46]

It is an almost perfect illustration of the manner in which the Establishment historians follow and stick to a false narrative no matter how absurd or copious the evidence to the contrary. Marc Trachtenberg compares and contrasts the British whitewash accounts of the July crisis with those of honest scholars. In considering the work of Professor Stefan Schmidt – *Frankreichs Aussenpolitik in der Julikrise 1914: Ein Beitrag zur Geschichte des Ausbruchs des Ersten Weltkrieges* – Trachtenberg writes:

> He [Schmidt] begins by arguing that the French government – and above all, Raymond Poincaré, President of the Republic, and the key French policy maker at the time – took a hard line during the crisis, and in particular in the important meetings held with the Russian leadership in St. Petersburg from July 20 to July 23.
>
> French policy, in his view, was by no means passive or irrelevant. Very important choices were made. Above all, the French government – and that meant essentially Poincaré – made it clear to the Russians that France would support Russia if an armed conflict broke out over the Serbian question. The policy could have been different. France could have tried to restrain Russia, but Poincaré especially chose not to. ... The French decision to support Russia unconditionally was of profound importance. Schmidt argues – and here again he follows in Albertini's footsteps, but with a somewhat stronger argument – that Russia would scarcely have pursued the policy she did if the French had taken a more moderate line.

Trachtenberg then lays out his own views:

> The evidence that Schmidt gives to support that interpretation, which he found in all sorts of places, is in fact really quite extraordinary, and it's marshalled very effectively in the book. The two sections developing that argument about French policy during this key phase of the crisis (pp. 65-104) are in fact a model, to my mind, of what historical analysis should be. ... And what had Poincaré said in his talks with the Russian leaders? It seems quite clear, from the evidence Schmidt presents, that Poincaré used very firm language in a meeting he had with the Tsar just before leaving St.

Petersburg. It is hard to avoid the conclusion, reading this section, that Poincaré had given the Russian monarch the assurance that France would support his country unconditionally, not just diplomatically, but militarily as well.

Schmidt's basic arguments struck Professor Trachtenberg as "very solid":

> The French government – and that meant essentially Poincaré personally – did take a hard line in the crisis: Russia, in fact, had effectively been given a blank check. But how is that policy to be understood? ... The real problem has to do with the question of motivation. Why, exactly, did the French pursue the policy they did? ... On July 30, 1914, on the very eve of the war, a prominent French general wrote his son that "a better occasion would never be found" – a view echoed at the time by both Doulcet [French minister plenipotentiary] in St. Petersburg and the French military attaché in Berlin. And Poincaré himself wrote in his diary on August 6, just after the fighting had begun, that an early negotiated peace would be just about the worst thing that could happen, because it would deprive his country of the fruits of a victorious war.[47]

On Poincaré's trip to Russia, Professor Sean McMeekin writes:

> Not a single scrap from this summit has ever surfaced, despite extensive research by both Soviet scholars and the editors of the official French documentary collection on the outbreak of war. In similar vein, there are conspicuous gaps in the dispatches of Maurice Paléologue, France's ambassador at St Petersburg, lasting an entire week following the archduke's assassination. Paléologue did not report on Sazonov's reaction to the news from Sarajevo until 6 July 1914, and he omitted the entire period of the presidential summit from the 20th to the 23rd. The second gap is particularly suspicious, considering that planning for the July presidential summit had been underway for six months.[48]

McMeekin adds that Ambassador Paléologue, himself a son of Lorraine, was a close friend of Poincaré's who was expressly appointed to St Petersburg "in order to press Sazonov into a harder anti-German line."[49] Poincaré told Paléologue, "Sazonov must be firm and we must back him up." Poincaré's visit "allowed Russia to act in full confidence of France's support, but without the slightest restraining counsel from France's president."[50] It must constantly be borne in mind that both Sazonov and Poincaré were essentially political yes-men of Anglo-American financial elites.

Academic historians insist on the use of documents to build a thesis but like dead men, destroyed documents tell no tales. Regarding the gaps in the documents relating to Poincaré's visit to Russia, Professor Douglas Newton of the University of Western Sydney writes:

> Caches of documents have vanished – most obviously documents on the French state visit to Russia in mid-July 1914. Crucial figures such as Maurice Paléologue, the French ambassador in St Petersburg, and Raymond Poincaré, the French President, sanitised their archives after the war.[51]

If Poincaré and Paléologue were, as Strachan, Lieven and Keiger suggest, acting in good faith as honest peace brokers on the Russian visit, why 'sanitise' their archives thereafter? The reality was, Austria-Hungary's decision to withhold its ultimatum to Serbia until Poincaré had departed Russia was a complete waste of valuable time, for he had been planning this war for years before the events in Sarajevo. This is borne out by U.S. Senator and war researcher, Robert L. Owen, who spent several years in the 1920s researching dispatches between the Russian, French, and British Foreign Offices that survived the cull. In his book published in 1927, *The Russian Imperial Conspiracy 1892-1914*, he lays bare the overwhelming influence of Sazonov, Poincaré and Grey in planning war. On Poincaré, Owen writes:

> When Raymond Poincaré became President (with treaty-making powers) he immediately and repeatedly assured the Russian statesmen that they could rely with confidence upon the diplomatic support of Russian policy in the Balkans, and upon French support in case of a general war flowing therefrom. The week before the Russian mobilization Poincaré was in St Petersburg strengthening the Russian will to war. When the general war grew more intensely threatening he refused to try to exercise any moderating influence with Russia.... He did not because he willed war ... the Czar mobilized under Poincaré's encouragement.[52]

Senator Owen had no inkling of the overwhelming role of the Anglo-American financial elites in the genesis of the 1914-18 war – very few did before Carroll Quigley's research– but his book is a significant contribution to our understanding of the war's origins. He writes that crucial documents were either destroyed or crammed with lies and propaganda and utterly compromised:

Neither the Russian nor French governments really believed that the German government intended aggressive war on them but the military preparedness of Germany and the bombast of some of its chauvinists laid a convenient but false foundation for the French and British propaganda that the German leaders had plotted the brutal military conquest of the world…. The truth itself was completely hidden from sight, first because the archives were so profoundly secret, then further obscured by wilful falsehood and by a flood of propaganda against the German Government.[53]

Owen concluded that the thousands of dispatches he researched proved that it was completely wrong to suggest, as many British historians of the time did (and still do) that the Entente Allies were fighting a war to defend themselves and the United States from the criminal design of Kaiser Wilhelm II to dominate the world by military force.[54]

Russia's strategy, says Owen, "was to put the moral odium on Germany." The Austro-Hungarian response to Serbia was indeed a pretext for war. Not by Germany, however, but by Russia and France.[55]

Professor Sidney B. Fay agrees. Poincaré's visit "greatly strengthened the militarist group in Russia, headed by the Grand Duke [Nikolai] who wanted Sazonov to take a more aggressive attitude and who were continually trying to exert pressure on the peace-loving Tsar."[56]

The 'war spirit champagne mood' that Kaiser Wilhelm feared would be encouraged in St Petersburg by Poincaré, was evident at a banquet given by Grand Duke Nicholas in Poincaré's honour on the evening of 22 July. In his memoirs of that evening, French Ambassador, Maurice Paléologue recounts that Princess Anastasia and Princess Militza were "talking excitedly" to him about the "forthcoming war" before the Austrian ultimatum to Serbia was even delivered:

The ambassador adds:

> During the meal I sat next the Grand Duchess Anastasia and the dithyrambics continued, mixed with prophecies: "War is going to break out. Nothing will be left of Austria. You will get Alsace-Lorraine back. Our armies will meet in Berlin. Germany will be annihilated." Then suddenly – "I must control myself; the Tsar is looking at me."[57]

The bellicose utterances and joy of women tipsy on champagne could be dismissed as of little relevance had they not been married to men who knew exactly what was being planned. Anastasia's husband, Grand Duke Nickolai Nikolaevich, was the czar's cousin and Commander-in-Chief of the Imperial Russian Army. For years he had been "the brain and the fist of the Russian war party against Germany."[58] Grand Duke Nikolai and Duchess Anastasia were Francophiles who spent much time in Paris together and had crossed the border into Germany to collect 'hallowed' Lorraine soil. He had recently been on joint Franco-Russian military manoeuvres and training with the French army – a fact kept closely guarded by the Entente. Barbara Tuchman writes that on several occasions before the war, the Grand Duke was in France on manoeuvres with Divisional Commander, General Foch, and was "extravagantly feted" for his known dislike of Germany.[59] Tuchman adds:

> With delight the French repeated the remarks of Prince Kotze-
> bue, the Grand Duke's aide, who said his master believed that
> only if Germany were crushed once and for all and divided up
> again into little states each happy with its own court, could the
> world expect to live in peace. No less ardent a friend of France
> was the Grand Duke's wife Anastasia and her sister Militza who
> was married to the Grand Duke's brother, Peter. As daughters
> of King Nikita of Montenegro, their fondness for France was in
> direct proportion to their hatred of Austria.[60]

The coming war was not purely about defeating the German army in battle, but 'crushing Germany once and for all' and dividing it up into "little states." An inveterate teutophobe, Grand Duke Nikolai certainly knew that war was about to be forced upon Germany, and clearly so too did his wife, Anastasia. Princess Militza, Anastasia's sister, was married to another of the czar's cousins, Grand Duke Peter Nikolaevich, who was Adjutant General in the Imperial Russian Army. Like his older brother, he knew exactly what was in the offing. The princesses' father, the king of Montenegro, was a staunch supporter of Serbia and its pan-Slavist ambitions. His telegram to Anastasia on 22 July clearly indicates that he too knew that a European war was about to be unleashed in which Germany would be crushed. Like the French ambassador, Poincaré was well aware of the anti-German sabre rattling and jingoism at the czar's banquet, but what about Viviani? Why was the anti-war French prime minister not strenuously objecting?

Silencing Viviani – Prime Minister of the French Republic

Viviani

Troy Paddock, Professor of Modern European History at Southern Connecticut State University (USA), writes that the anti-war socialist René Viviani "preferred a negotiated settlement to the crisis," whereas Poincaré "supported an aggressive Russian position, even if it meant war."[61] German historian, Stefan Schmidt, supports the view that Viviani was very much against the idea of France going to war for the sake of Serbia.[62]

Viviani had the dual role of the prime minister of France and the supremo of French foreign affairs as Foreign Minister. He held a powerful position as head of government and leader of the Council of Ministers with control of the French budget. It is reasonable to assume that he would have played a significant role in opposing the dogs of war on the visit to Russia in July 1914. Without rock solid promises of French military support, Czar Nicholas would never have intervened in the Austria vs. Serbia affair. Russia had a bigger army than Germany, but on its own would be wiped out by the better trained German soldiers determined to fight to the death in defence of their homeland. Why then did the anti-war Viviani not press his opinions on Czar Nicholas and do all in his formidable power to discourage Russia from mobilizing for war against Austria and Germany? Professor Douglas Newton writes that on the trip to Russia Viviani was slow to resist Poincaré's dominance, and every key decision was taken by Poincaré.[63]

Viviani was no shrinking violet, but Poincaré had somehow been able to silence him. Politically, the post of prime minister was the most powerful position in France, with the presidency a somewhat empty ceremonial role. However, when Poincaré gained the presidency in 1913 thanks to Isvolsky arranging in financial circles huge bribes of the French Press and Deputies, he went about sidelining consecutive prime ministers and making the presidency a position of power. That, however, does not explain how prime minister Viviani was unable to take an anti-war stance on the trip to Russia. The trip was supposedly no more than a ceremonial presidential visit, and it has to be asked why Poincaré took Viviani with him in the first place. With Viviani's substantial victory at the recent

May election, it was clear that the majority in France supported his so-cialist and pacifist view. Had Poincaré not taken him to Russia during the July crisis, the French electorate, radical Republicans, and others in the Chamber and Council of Ministers would have rallied round Viviani's anti-war stance. Had the prime minister remained in Paris and declared against French support for Russia in 'defence of Serbia,' Poincaré would have been isolated. It was then entirely possible that without a cast-iron promise of French support, Russia would never have intervened in the Austria-Hungary vs. Serbia crisis and it would have remained a localised conflict as desired by Germany. Viviani, however, was absent from Paris for two crucial weeks.

Viviani and Poincaré sailed from France on 15 July 15 and would not return until 29 July. The timing was critical. Viviani was no friend of Poin-caré's, and certainly not part of his exclusive Establishment circle. He had no inkling that Poincaré had secretly been liaising with British, Russian and Belgian elites in planning war on Germany for at least two years. Like the majority in the British Cabinet, who had been kept in ignorance of the unfolding war plans, so too had the French Cabinet of Ministers been uninformed.

During those two utterly crucial weeks for the future of Europe and the world, Viviani had to be taken away from France yet muted in Russia. How did Poincaré and his closest team members actually achieve that? Poincaré's diaries highlight that Viviani suffered a "serious and embarrass-ing" attack of "neurasthenia" during the visit to Russia which meant Poin-caré had to conduct all discussions throughout.[64]

Neurasthenia is an old-fashioned, ill-defined, medical term for symp-toms and signs of mental and emotional disturbance, confusion, irrita-bility, headache, general muscle weakness and lethargy. Poincaré later wrote that Viviani became nervous and agitated, and repeatedly uttered "imprudent" words or sentences which demonstrated "a complete igno-rance of foreign affairs." He added dismissively that Viviani only relaxed when talking about socialism, Jean Jaurès and Edouard Vaillant.[65] Jaurès and Vaillant were socialists in the Chamber of Deputies who would sup-port a general strike in an attempt to circumvent French participation in war. (Jaurès's voice against war would be silenced on 31 July 1914, when he was shot dead.)

Viviani was a fit and healthy 51-year-old, yet something very dramatic and disturbing happened to him on the trip to Russia. It was *not* due to sea-sickness. William Jannen (Ph.D. Modern European history, Columbia University), writes:

> Viviani, prime minister and foreign minister of France, suffered what appeared to be a nervous breakdown. He had been distracted all through the visit, often talking to himself, sometimes swearing loudly, ignoring his hosts, and finally becoming so uncontrollable that Paléologue had to order a doctor from the French hospital to take Viviani away.[66]

René Viviani was sincere in his commitment to peace and finding a diplomatic solution to the crisis but due to the sudden onset of 'illness' during the trip, he was unable to counterbalance the influence – the warmongering – of Poincaré and his close ally, Maurice Paléologue, the French Ambassador. The behaviour of Viviani was utterly bizarre for a peaceable, intelligent, and well-natured man and it has to asked: was he maliciously drugged – with ergot perhaps – in order to incapacitate him and make it appear he had lost his marbles?

Whatever the cause of the "neurasthenia," Viviani had no influence whatsoever on the Russian visit other than being labelled a nutcase. On returning to Paris and being informed of his disgraceful behaviour in the czar's presence, he was acutely embarrassed, kept a low profile, and did whatever Poincaré told him. Had Poincaré made the French Press aware of the goings on in Russia, Viviani's career as prime minister would have been over before it really got started. He suddenly abandoned his pacifist principles, performed a *volte-face,* and supported the three-year military service law despite his own party and the Radical-Socialist party having pledged to repeal it. On 4 August, he would read out a war propaganda address written by Poincaré: "In the coming war France will be heroically defended by all its sons, whose sacred union will not break in the face of the enemy."[67]

Austria-Hungary acted as soon as Poincaré's visit to Russia ended.

When the French party boarded the warship *La France* and departed for home via Stockholm on 23 July, the Austro-Hungarian ambassador in Belgrade handed an ultimatum to Serbia's prime minister, Nikola Pašić. Serbia was given 48 hours to respond positively to all ten points of the ultimatum. Refusal would mean war. As we have seen, the Austro-Hungarian authorities believed that delaying delivery of the ultimatum until Poincaré had departed Russia would lessen the risk of Russia coming to Serbia's aid. Professor Sean McMeekin believes the delay had the opposite effect. Austria-Hungary holding back the ultimatum was in fact "the worst scenario of all" because following Poincaré's visit and assurances of French military intervention, "it allowed Russia to act in full confidence of France's support."[68]

Professor Barnes also concluded that Poincaré's visit provided "a solemn affirmation" of obligations imposed by the Franco-Russian alliance, and France effectively issued a blank cheque ("we will support you whatever you do") to Russia. If Russia moved against Austria-Hungary or Germany, France would do likewise. Poincaré would later boast that he felt safe in taking this belligerent stand on his trip to Russia "because he had in his pocket a letter from King George V promising British support in the impending crisis."[69]

The Austro-Hungarian ultimatum would be presented to the world by complicit historians as being so harsh and demeaning that Serbia could never have accepted it. It was, they say, deliberately made unacceptable in order to ensure war. Perhaps it was, but only a localised war against Serbia. The real war, the pan-European war, had been decided upon and planned for in London, Paris, and St Petersburg not days, weeks or months before, but years.

On 24 July, the British Ambassador at St Petersburg, Sir George Buchanan, sent a telegram to Sir Edward Grey in the Foreign Office:

> The French ambassador gave me to understand that France would not only give Russia strong diplomatic support, but would, if necessary, fulfil all obligations imposed on her by the alliance.[70]

The message was loud and clear, when Russia went to war, France would be joining her. Despite the overwhelming evidence, British historians continue to suggest otherwise. David Stevenson, an Establishment man and Professor of International History at the London School of Economics, writes:

> It is likely that before Poincaré and Viviani left St Petersburg the French and Russians had an inkling of what was coming, but they discussed only a diplomatic response to it.[71]

Niall Ferguson, another pro-Establishment British historian who yet likes to make out that he's something of a renegade, writes that Poincaré *did* make it clear that if Russia went to war, France would also. But the fact was, according to Ferguson, Russia did not want war.[72] Sir Max Hastings,

(Oxford) journalist, writer, Fellow of the Royal Historical Society, and arch-purveyor of British Establishment-line history, writes:

> Some historians believe that in St Petersburg Poincaré stiffened the resolve for war of Sazonov. … But it remains hard to see why the St Petersburg summit should be condemned as a malign conspiratorial affair, and some seek to do so even in the absence of evidence to that effect.[73]

Can Stevenson, Ferguson, and Hastings really be completely unaware of the evidence presented as early as 1926 by Professor Sidney B. Fay that the Russians began taking "progressive steps towards secret military measures preparatory to mobilization and to a general European War" *after* the French ambassador at St Petersburg repeatedly assured them of French support?[74] Of course they were aware of the evidence. Most British historian of the First World War are not in the business of relating truth, but of protecting the British Establishment. They spin the facts and tell whatever lies are necessary to that end.

The ultimatum handed to Serbia's prime minister, Pasic, on July 23 insisted that:

1. The Serbian government must suppress any publications or organisations which incited hatred of Austria-Hungary.

2. Narodna Odbrana must be dissolved.

3. Army officers guilty of propaganda against the Austro-Hungarian monarchy should be dismissed.

4. Judicial proceedings should be taken against accessories to the Archduke's assassination.

5. Major Tankosić and Milan Ciganović should be arrested.

6. The movement of weapons across the frontier into Austria-Hungary must be prevented.

7. Representatives of the Austro-Hungarian Government must be allowed to collaborate in Serbia with the authorities there in suppressing subversive movement directed against the territorial integrity of Austria-Hungary.

8. Delegates of the Austro-Hungarian government must be allowed to take part in investigations in Serbia relating to the assassination.

9. The Serbian government must notify the Austro-Hungarian government without delay that all measures had been carried out.

10. A response was expected by 5 o'clock on Saturday evening 25 July Failure to comply with all points on the ultimatum or the time deadline would mean war.

A flurry of telegraphs passed between Belgrade, St Petersburg, Paris and London, and it was agreed among them that all demands in the ultimatum should be accepted apart from two. It was imperative that Austria did not get satisfaction on all points or the excuse for war would evaporate. To appease world opinion, it had to appear that Serbia was being entirely reasonable in her response.

Sazonov advised the Serbs to be extremely moderate in their reply. If they felt helpless in the face of an Austro-Hungarian invasion, they should offer no resistance, retire without fighting, and appeal to the Powers for protection.[75] The world was not to be made aware of the secret military agreements and arrangements that had long been in place between Serbia and Russia, and Serbia was to be presented as a neutral and innocent little nation being attacked by a merciless bully.

At 9:30 P.M. on the evening of 24 July, the British Foreign Secretary, Sir Edward Grey, telegraphed Belgrade with his input. Like Sazonov, he advised the Serbians to express concern and regret, give a favourable reply on as many points as possible, and not present Austria with a blank negative.[76] Philippe Berthelot, at the French Foreign Office, advised the Serbs they should "try to gain time" by offering satisfaction on all points except allowing Austro-Hungarian officials to take part in a Serbian investigation, as it would be "inconsistent with her sovereignty." She should "attempt to escape from the direct grip of Austria by declaring herself ready to submit to the arbitration of Europe."[77] That would appeal to peace lovers everywhere, and it would appear that little Serbia had nothing to hide and was happy to go before the international court at The Hague. Professor Barnes:

> If France and Russia were to precipitate a European war in the guise of protectors of Serbia, it was necessary to do everything possible to make such intervention attractive before European and world opinion. Serbia must be made to appear a "brave and innocent little country" who had gone to extreme limits in surrendering to the Austrian demands – but had not quite acquiesced.… To carry out this program of putting the "soft pedal" on Serbia, the Russian Ministerial Council of July 24, 1914, decided to advise Serbia to avoid above everything else declaring war on Austria,

and to make a response conciliatory in tone and content alike ... Philippe Berthelot, deputy political director of the French Foreign Office, and an influential person with Poincaré, once boasted [he] had drafted in outline the Serbian reply to Austria. The reply was formulated in very conciliatory language, feigned great friendliness for and humility toward Austria, and seemed to consent to everything of significance in the Austrian ultimatum while actually rejecting the only really important item in it. In this way, Serbia, as well as France and Russia later, were put in a good light before world opinion and Austria in an equally disadvantageous position when she proceeded to carry out the secret plans of the Austrian ministers and attack Serbia. In the diplomatic ruses of the Entente before the War there was no more clever bit of subterfuge than the planning of the Serbian response to Austria ... it even completely deceived the Kaiser.[78]

On 25 July at 3 P.M. – two hours before the deadline given by Austria for a response – Serbia formally mobilised its armed forces.

Frantic military preparations got under way. State archives, the treasury and the civil service decamped from Belgrade to the interior city of Nish. Before they handed over their Reply, and in the knowledge that it failed to meet the Austrian demands, the Serbians declared their intent. Serbia was getting ready for war.... Pasic personally delivered the formal Reply a few minutes before 6 P.M. on 25 July, and the Austrian ambassador and his entire legation were on their way home on the 6.30 P.M. express from Belgrade.[79]

The Reply was exactly as London, Paris and St Petersburg had dictated. The Serbian government would comply with most of the Austrian points, but could not be held responsible for articles in the Press or the "peaceable work of societies." The Serbian government was "pained and surprised" at the accusations that members of the Kingdom of Serbia were involved in the preparations of the assassination. There was no proof that Narodna Odbrana or other societies in Serbia had committed any criminal actions, but they would dissolve any society that acted against Austria-Hungary. It was a breath-taking lie, for the Black Hand was active throughout Serbia and deeply involved in the Archduke's assassination. Vienna responded:

The propaganda of the Narodna Odbrana and affiliated societies hostile to the monarchy fills the entire public life of Servia; it is therefore an entirely inacceptable reserve [sic] if the Servian Government asserts that it knows nothing about it.[80]

The Serbian Reply stated that an investigation would begin into all who had participated in the outrage, but the Serbian government would not accept the cooperation of Austro-Hungarian officials as this would be a violation of the constitution. Regarding Germany's response to all of this, British pro-Establishment historian Professor Norman Stone writes:

> Injured innocence was paraded as the plot went ahead – the Kaiser off on his yacht, the foreign minister on his honeymoon, the chief of the general staff taking the water. ... War was to be provoked, and the murder of the Archduke provided a perfect occasion. The Austrians were told that they should use it to attack Serbia, Russia's client, and the means chosen was an ultimatum, containing demands that could not be accepted without the loss of Serbia independence.[81]

Stone, as we have seen, was Professor of Modern History at Oxford University for thirteen years in the 1980's and 90's. According to the Oxford school, dear old England and her fair-minded allies were completely innocent of wrongdoing while the devious, dastardly Germans used the assassination to provoke a major European war. And while they were deliberately starting that war, every leading player in Germany went off on holiday as part of their deceitful scheming. Such nonsense is the norm among British Establishment historians who lie about virtually everything regarding the First World War, and the biggest lies are the best lies. Historical truth about the First World War has been completely inverted. For example, David Stevenson, Professor of International History at the London School of Economics, writes:

> It is ultimately in Berlin that we must seek the keys to the destruction of peace ... Germany willed a local war between Austria-Hungary and Serbia, deliberately risked a continental war against France and Russia, and finally started one.[82]

As we have seen, the facts are clear that in early July 1914 Kaiser Wilhelm did *not* dictate in any shape or form to the Austro-Hungarians how they should react to the assassination. *If* they did decide to attack Serbia in retribution – and it was their decision – he supported it and suggested they should do so at once while world opinion was sympathetic to their cause. In Wilhelm's mind, it was to be no more than "a chastisement of Serbia" as professor McMeekin properly termed it.[83]

Leading politicians and diplomats in Britain, France and Russia gave Vienna the impression that they too were sympathetic to the Austro-Hungarian cause. Neither Emperor Franz Joseph nor Kaiser Wilhelm had any inkling at that point in time that such encouragement was only part of a great deception. Later in July, when it did become clear to him that they would intervene, the Kaiser would do all in his power to pull it back from the brink and prevent war. He was the *only* European leader to do so. The claim by British Establishment history that suggests otherwise is a lie and a disgrace to academic and scholarly integrity.

Would Serbia's acceptance of the Austrian ultimatum really have destroyed her 'independence? Vienna wanted cross border police 'collaboration' in suppressing subversive movements directed against Austria-Hungary, and in investigating the crime of 28 June. They were not demanding to be allowed to participate in Serbian court procedures, only in the police investigations. With Serbia's refusal, the government in Vienna responded that neither international law nor criminal law had anything to do with it. It was purely a matter of the two states liaising and cooperating and could be readily solved by way of special agreement:

> If the Servian government misunderstands us here, this is done deliberately, for it must be familiar with the difference between 'enquête judiciaire' [judicial enquiry] and simple police researches.... Precedents for such police intervention exist in great numbers.... It tries to justify its refusal by showing up our demands as impossible.[84]

By the beginning of the twentieth century there were indeed many precedents for international police cooperation, and it is, of course, the norm nowadays. After all, this was no mere robbery or international fraud case; the heir to the throne of Austria-Hungary and his wife had been killed! An extremely serious matter! Had the Serbians nothing to hide in 1914 they could readily have agreed to it without the slightest danger to Serbia's independence. Moreover, they appeared to have no qualms whatsoever concerning their 'independence' when Russia's man, Hartwig, was effectively running the show in Belgrade. The Serbian Reply stated it had not been possible to arrest anyone in connection with the assassination, and proof of guilt was required from Vienna. If Austria-Hungary was not satisfied, the matter could be referred to the International Tribunal of the Hague, or to the 'Great Powers'.

> The demands made by Austria were neither unexpected nor unfair. The responses from the entente group were disproportion-

ately overexcited. Berchtold's [Austria's foreign minister] delay gifted them a three-week window in which to manufacture their considered reaction. The Serbian reply was a diplomatic triumph designed by the Secret Elite to appear conciliatory but trigger the Austrian military threat and all that would ensue. Germany had become concerned at the slow pace of the Austrian demands on Serbia, and the Kaiser for one was delighted that the Serbian reply seemed to remove any likelihood of war.[85]

With tension escalating, Kaiser Wilhelm broke off his summer cruise and returned home. On first reading the Serbian response, he declared it a diplomatic triumph, and with it *'every cause for war* falls to the ground.' It was not the response of a man allegedly orchestrating events towards a European war. Indeed, from the outset the Kaiser was dead set against letting a local war grow into a European war which would bring in Russia, France and Britain against Germany. He urged Vienna *against* all-out war against Serbia, and simply to occupy Belgrade temporarily until such times as the Serb promises were carried out.[86]

Wilhelm may have been delighted with Serbia's response, but it was not as conciliatory as it first seemed:

> To the unwitting, it appeared as though all points bar two had been accepted and that 'poor little Serbia' had yielded to the immense and unfair pressure from her neighbours ... Wilhelm jotted on it: 'A brilliant performance for a time-limit of only 48 hours. This is more than one could have expected!' he was convinced that the Austrians would be satisfied, and that the few reservations Serbia had made on particular points could be cleared up by negotiations. Kaiser Wilhelm's immediate and spontaneous response clearly indicated his belief, indeed his joy, that all risk of war had been removed ... Wilhelm's analysis was sadly naïve. He accepted the Serbian concessions at face value, but the Austrians did not. The Reply included carefully constructed conditions and reservations that were not immediately apparent. First impressions can often be misleading. While the Serbian response appeared to consent to virtually every Austrian demand, it was so hedged with qualifications that the Austrians were bound to take umbrage. Only two of Austria's demands (numbers 8 and 10) were accepted in their entirety, while the answers to others were evasive. Reservations and lies had been carefully disguised by skilful dissembling.[87]

In framing the Reply, the Serbs had heeded British, French, and Russian instructions. It had "not been possible" to arrest anyone in Serbia connected to the crime – Ciganović in particular. That implied that they had *tried* to arrest him, but it proved impossible and he 'must have fled the country.' As we have seen, Ciganović was a trusted confidant of the Serbian prime minister, Nikola Pašić, and was protected by him from the fall-out after Sarajevo. He had been ordered into hiding with the full knowledge of the prime minister and the Serbian chief of police.

> The Serbian government spirited Ciganović out of Belgrade three days after the murder and sent him to Albania, not to return to Belgrade until a month after the war began. The military commandant of an important railway station arranged his escape, and instructed the railway service to remove his name from its personnel books. The Austrians were told that he was unknown in Belgrade, where he was in fact a well-known figure. The Serbs informed them that a warrant had been issued for his arrest, but that he could not be found.[88]

The Serbian rejection of the Ultimatum, and the departure of the Austro-Hungarian ambassador from Belgrade on the evening of 25 July brought diplomatic relations to an end. The Serbian government had mobilised its army against Austria-Hungary at 3 P.M. that day, and Austria-Hungary followed suit with a partial mobilisation at 9:30 that evening. Conrad von Hötzendorf, Chief of the Austro-Hungarian General Staff, informed for Hötzendorf, informed foreign minister Count von Berchtold that the Austrian army would not be ready for military operations against Serbia until approximately 12 August. He advised against any declaration of war until then, but von Berchtold told him "the diplomatic solution will not hold so long," and declared war on Serbia on 28 July.[89]

Summary: Chapter 7 – The July Crisis

- Before deciding on how to respond to the Archduke's assassination, Austria-Hungary sent an emissary to discuss the situation with her German ally.

- Wilhelm strongly cautioned that if Austria-Hungary contemplated military action against Serbia, it should do it immediately in order to prevent it escalating.

- Germany's military and naval leaders were on holiday. The kaiser, believing the situation would remain local between Austria and

Serbia, did not recall them from their vacations and went off on his own annual three-week summer cruise.

• Leaders of the other major Powers sent Emperor Franz Joseph messages of deepest condolence and gave the false impression that they expected Austria to take action against Serbia.

• When the Austro-Hungarian leaders met on 7 July, the Hungarian premier would not sanction immediate military action. Evidence of Serbian involvement first had to be established.

• At the height of the crisis, French president Poincaré and prime minister Vivani sailed to Russia for talks with Czar Nicholas. The anti-war Viviani suffered a strange mental melt-down during the trip. Almost immediately they departed for home on 23 July, Russia began mobilising her forces for war on Germany.

• Austria-Hungary presented a ten-point ultimatum to Serbia, with a 48 hour deadline to agree to all points. When Serbia failed to do so, Austria-Hungary declared war on Serbia on 28 July 1914, exactly one month after the assassination in Sarajevo.

CHAPTER 8

MOBILISATION,
"THE MOST DECISIVE ACT OF WAR"

Within hours of Poincaré and the stricken Viviani boarding *La France* for home on 23 July, General Dobrorolski, head of the Mobilisation Department of the Russian General Staff, was ordered to have everything prepared for the proclamation of mobilisation. At 3 P.M. on 24 July – more than 24 hours before the deadline for the Serbian reply to the Austrian ultimatum – the Russian Council of Ministers ordered the mobilisation of 1,100,000 troops, together with the Baltic and Black Sea fleets.[1] In addition, the czar agreed that preparation should be made for the mobilisation of thirteen army corps whenever Sazonov deemed it appropriate. The Russian minister of war, Vladimir Sukhomlinov, was directed to proceed immediately to make ready the stores of war materiel for transport to *the German* frontiers. The Minister of finance, Pyotr Bark, was ordered to call in all Russian money in Germany and Austria.[2]

After the hastily convened meeting of the Council of Ministers on 24 July, Foreign Minister Sazonov lunched with the British ambassador Buchanan and the French ambassador Paléologue at the French Embassy. These two were the western elites' diplomatic enforcers, who ensured that London and Paris were kept fully updated. Sazonov confirmed that the czar had approved both the mobilisation of over 1 million men and the Russian navy and said that the imperial order (*ukase*) was not to be made public until he, Sazonov, considered that the moment had arrived to enforce it, but all the necessary preliminary preparations for the mobilisation had already begun.

> Sazonov confirmed that Russia was prepared to "face all the risks" and Paléologue reiterated Poincaré's 'blank cheque,' placing France unreservedly on Russia's side. Poincaré had explicitly instructed Paleologue to reassure Sazonov by prompt and persistent promises of French support.[3] ... Sazonov was thus constantly reassured that

France would stand shoulder to shoulder with Russia, but what about Britain? Sir Edward Grey and King George V had assured Sazonov of British support at Balmoral in 1912, but he was confused by the overtures of friendship voiced by Britain to Germany since then. Sazonov was not sufficiently astute to realise that such mind games were designed to mislead and were an intrinsic part of the deception. Germany had to be led to believe until the very last minute that Britain would remain neutral. An official treaty between Britain and Russia, which Sazonov so keenly desired, would have destroyed that cover. Grey was determined to hold to the official line that 'England' could be more effective if she posed as a mediator at all costs. His charade had to be maintained. Germany had to be kept guessing. The following morning, 25 July, the Russian Council of Ministers rubber-stamped the military plans and confirmed their readiness for war.[4]

All military divisions in Russia were instructed to return immediately from summer camps to their regular quarters. Cadets undergoing training at military academies were promoted to officer rank, and new cadets were enrolled. All troops were equipped and made ready for transportation to the frontiers. A state of war was proclaimed in towns facing Germany and Austria, and a secret order given for the 'Period Preparatory to War.'[5] The order enabled Russia to begin mobilising her armies against Germany without formally declaring war on her. All the while, British, French and Russian officials made conciliatory statements intended to keep Germany quiescent. In London:

> Sir Edward Grey stubbornly insisted … that the Austro-Serbian dispute did not concern him. This lie went unchallenged. He chose to distance himself and the Foreign Office from what transpired in Vienna and Belgrade, and its impact on St. Petersburg. By making no parliamentary reference to events in that part of the world, he hid the Secret Elite's diplomatic incitement to war behind a screen of apparent lack of interest in the Austro-Serbian conflict. He consulted daily with Sir Arthur Nicolson [Permanent Under Secretary for Foreign Affairs], and had a powerful anti-German ally in Sir Eyre Crowe [Assistant Under Secretary for Foreign Affairs]. These two almost outbid each other in their distaste for Germany and their indulgence of Russia.… In sharp contrast, the foreign secretary's public stance was of mute disinterest in the events that they expected to lead to war. Theirs was an ignominious deception, for they knew that this was a dispute from which a general war would

ensue, and far from being disinterested, they were intimately complicit.[6]

Britain's attitude was crucial. Sir Edward Grey had only to inform France and Russia in one unequivocal sentence that Britain would under no circumstances get involved in war, and they would have pulled the plug on the entire venture. Knowing Russia was mobilising for war against Germany, Edward Grey expressed no protest for the straightforward reason that all was going almost exactly to plan. As we have seen, Edward House's memo to President Wilson in May 1914 stated that "Whenever England consents, France and Russia will close in on Germany and Austria." Sir Edward Grey's apparent silence and lack of protest to Russia and France was the 'consent' from England that House spoke of: *Qui tacet consentire videtur* [he who is silent is assumed to agree]. In other words, Grey's silence implied consent. Grey did not want to stop Russia attacking Germany, his aim was to ensure it happened. but he had to be seen in the eyes of the British public as an honest broker. By 25 July 1914, the European war was effectively underway. That day, the French Ambassador at St. Petersburg, Maurice Paleologue, saw Isvolsky off at the railway terminus. He wrote in his diary:

> At seven o'clock this evening I went to the Warsaw station [in St Petersburg] to say goodbye to Isvolsky who is returning to his post [in Paris] in hot haste. There was a great bustle on the platforms. The trains were packed with officers and men. This looked like mobilization. We rapidly exchanged impressions and came to the same conclusion: 'It's war this time.'[7]

On 25 July both the French and Russian ambassadors knew that Russia's mobilisation meant war. Professor Sean McMeekin presents compelling evidence that the Russian mobilisation – which began as soon as Poincaré left Russia – was the factor that actually triggered the First World War. Some eighty years before McMeekin, another leading American war historian, Sidney B. Fay, had also placed great emphasis on the Russian mobilisation:

> At the Council of Ministers, held at Krasnoe Selo on the afternoon of July 25 the Tsar's ministers had decided on a number of preparatory military measures. They included the wide-reaching preparations of the "Period Preparatory to War" which were intended to facilitate a Russian general mobilisation *against Germany* as well as

against Austria; they had been ordered before dawn on July 26, had been going on actively ever since, and had caused increasing alarm at Berlin in spite of the beguiling assurances of Sazonov and Sukhomlinov [Russian Minister of War] that no mobilization measures against Germany were intended.[8]

The Russians were playing the same game of deception, manipulation and misrepresentation as the British and French, constantly assuring the German government that they bore Germany no ill will. All the while they were mobilising their armies to crush her. On the night of 25-26 July, the entire area of Russian Poland that bordered Germany was placed under martial law and all six military districts were placed in a state of war. Sean McMeekin explains:

> Harbors were mined, horses and wagons were assembled for army baggage trains, depots were prepared for the reception of reservists, and all steps were taken to facilitate the impending mobilization …There is also certain evidence to suggest that the *Russians began to mobilize considerably earlier than they made out.*… Manfried Rauchensteiner, a leading Austrian historian of the eastern front, went still further than this, arguing that the unexpected speed of Russia's mobilization against Austrian Galicia in August 1914 suggests that "the Russians began mobilizing *towards the beginning of July* and systematically prepared for war." An early, secret mobilization of this kind was entirely consistent with the understanding of the Period Preparatory to War by members of Russia's General Staff – and by Tsar Nicholas II. "It will be advantageous," a secret military commission had reported to Sukhomlinov on 21 November 1912 … "to complete concentration without beginning hostilities, in order to deprive the enemy irrevocably of the hope that war can still be avoided. *Our measures for this must be masked by clever diplomatic negotiations,* in order to lull to sleep as much as possible the enemy's fears."[9]

The Archduke's assassination having been used to engineer the confrontation between Austria and Serbia, it would now be employed as the excuse to draw Germany into war. The target was never Austria-Hungary but Germany. Massing the Russian and French armies on German borders for invasion would force Germany to react in her own defence.

All Russian army leave was cancelled. Regular army units, conscripts and reserves were brought to pre-arranged assembly points, and together with their heavy weapons, ammunition, and food supplies, were made ready for war. With the preliminary preparations in place, as soon as the order for general mobilisation was issued all troops and equipment would be deployed by rail as rapidly as possible to execute the invasion of Germany. Speed was of the essence. It was akin to drawing a gun with the first to do so gaining a huge strategic advantage. We saw in earlier chapters how, to that end, western financial elites had been pouring vast loans into Russia since 1912 to fund the construction of new railroads that ran up close to Germany's eastern borders. It was not some generous gesture to help Russia develop transport infrastructure in her rural south-west. The purpose was to facilitate the rapid mobilisation of her armies against Germany.

Russia, France and Britain began mobilising their armies and navies as secretively as possible after the Sarajevo assassination, and all the while Germany had made no threatening moves whatsoever in the direction of war. Kaiser Wilhelm was working to preserve the peace, while the fleets and armies of his opponents were busily being prepared for war.[10]

On 27 July, two days before Poincaré and Viviani arrived back in France, General Joffre, commander-in-chief of the French army, reassured the Russians they would get France's full support. Both he and Adolphe Messimy, the French war minister, were urging Russia to speed up its mobilisation and deploy as fast as possible against Germany.[11] On the streets of Paris meantime, thousands of anti-war protestors were being baton charged and arrested by the gendarmerie. The leader of the French anti-war movement, Jean Jaurès, had but four days to live before his assassination.

In Britain, the Royal Navy was mobilised. The entire home fleet had conveniently been brought together at Spithead on the south coast of England two weeks earlier for a 'royal review,' and was anchored in lines that stretched for forty miles.[12] Rather than being dispersed to their territorial

waters thereafter as was customary, the entire fleet remained 'concentrated' at Spithead from July 15 to make ready for war. Then, on 28 July:

> Secret orders were sent at 5 P.M. on the Tuesday evening for the rapid movement of the First Fleet to Scapa Flow [Orkney islands] beginning under cover of darkness and passing through the Straits of Dover early next morning without lights. Only officers were to be told the destination.... The decision to move the ships to their war stations was made at the Admiralty on the morning of Tuesday 28 July. And the orders were issued at 5 P.M. This was before news reached London, at 7:20 P.M., of the Austrian declaration of war against Serbia.... Therefore, Britain's mighty navy was almost wholly mobilised, and the fleet ordered to war stations before it was clear that war would explode, even in the Balkans, and before diplomacy to avoid it was exhausted.... On Thursday 30 July the newspapers reported departure of the fleet. The Liberal newspapers loyally insisted there was no 'sinister inference' to be drawn. It was all precautionary, to meet 'all emergencies.'... The incitement to the Entente could not have been more dramatically signalled.[13]

Thus, the Royal Navy – the core of Britain's military power – was fully mobilized by Winston Churchill on 28 July and ready for action.[14]

> Churchill was exhilarated. Six months later, after the first battle of Ypres. With tens of thousands of British soldiers in their graves. He would say ... "I think a curse should rest on me because I am so happy. I know this war is smashing and shattering the lives of thousands every moment and yet – I cannot help it – I enjoy every second."[15]

Already surrounded by the Triple Entente Powers since 1907, Germany now, step by inexorable step, was being pushed by them towards the precipice of a European war.. Bethmann-Hollweg, German foreign minister, was alarmed and angry at Vienna's failure to communicate with Berlin. On 28 July he sent a telegram to Austrian foreign minister Leopold von Berchtold which began: "The Austro-Hungarian Government, in spite of repeated questions as to its purposes, has left us in the dark." Bethmann insisted that if the Austro-Hungarian government adopted a "wholly uncompromising attitude," a "gradual revulsion of public opinion against it in all Europe would have to reckoned with..." He added that the Austrians must make clear to St Petersburg that they had no intention to annexe any Serbian territory, and that their military measures were aimed solely at a temporary occupation of Belgrade in order to secure a guarantee of future good behaviour on Serbia's part towards Austria-Hungary.[16] That same day in Berlin, 28 July, the head of the German army (Chief of the General Staff), Helmuth von Moltke, wrote an impressive appraisal of the dire political situation:

> There is no doubt that no European state would show anything other than human interest in the conflicts between Austria and Serbia, if it were not for the danger latent in it of a general political debacle that today already threatens to unleash a world war. For five years already Serbia has been the cause of tension in Europe, which by now is exerting pressure on the political and economic life of the nations concerned that is becoming intolerable. Austria has until now endured, with a forbearance bordering on weakness, the constant provocations and agitations directed at the undermining of its statehood by a people who have gone from regicide in their own country to the murder of an Archduke in a neighbouring country. It was only after the latest horrific crime that extreme measures were taken to cauterize, with red hot iron, the abscess that was threatening to poison the body of Europe. One would think that Europe would feel obliged to show gratitude for this. The whole of Europe would have breathed a sigh of relief if its mischief-maker had been appropriately chastised, and peace and order had been re-established in the Balkans. But Russia took sides with the offending country. It was this that turned the Austro-Serbian issue into a thundercloud that threatens any moment to burst over Europe.... Austria has only mobilized part of its forces (the Eighth Army Corps) against Serbia. Just sufficient to carry out its punitive expedition. In response to this, Russia is making preparations to mobilize, in the shortest possible time, the army corps of the Kiev, Odessa and Moscow military districts, a total of twelve army corps, and is taking comparable preparatory measures in the North as well, on the borders of Germany and the Baltic.... The longer our neighbours continue with their preparations, the quicker they will be able to complete their mobilization. Thus the military situation is becoming more unfavourable for us daily, and if our opponents are allowed to continue their preparations undisturbed, this could have dire consequences for us."[17]

The following day, 29 July, von Moltke wrote to his wife saying he found it "heart-breaking" to see how unaware Kaiser Wilhelm was of the seriousness of the situation.[18] His assessment was unfair, for at that very moment in time both Wilhelm and Bethmann-Hollweg were desperately trying to resolve the crisis through diplomacy. Unaware that hidden forces in Britain, France and Russia were deliberately steering the crisis to all-out war, Bethmann-Hollweg informed St Petersburg and London that he was doing his best to get discussions underway between Vienna and St Petersburg, and that Germany would do its utmost to preserve the peace as "war between the Great Powers must be avoided."[19]

Bethmann-Hollweg reiterated his desire to cooperate with England, and on the night of 29 July he spoke to the British ambassador in Berlin, Sir Edward Goschen. He reaffirmed Germany's will for peace and his and the kaiser's attempts to keep the trouble localised.

That same day, 29 July, the leader of the French Socialist Party, Jean Jaurès, wrote to the leader of the Belgian Labour Party, Emile Vandervelde, that the French government had the power to stop Russia from mobilising for war against Germany. It was "a war that had been long sought and deliberately fomented by nefarious forces in France and England to fulfil morbid ambitions."[20] Jaurès's desperate appeals to the international socialist movement to prevent war were in vain. Forty-eight hours after his note to Vandervelde he was shot dead; Vandervelde and the Belgian Labour Party would go on to support the war.

No evidence whatsoever of Germany's desperate attempts to prevent war in 1914 would be permitted at the Paris peace talks five years later. In conjunction with Bethmann-Hollweg's diplomatic efforts, the kaiser was pleading with the czar to calm the situation, stop the Russian mobilisation, and avoid war. The order for general mobilisation by any given Power was recognised by all countries as signalling the first act of war; there was no going back from such an order.

> In the first decades of the twentieth century, the general mobilisation of the armed forces of a major power signalled its intent on war. Plans for bringing together regular army units, conscripts and reserves, equipping these troops and transporting them to border assembly points had been worked out with great precision. Modern railway systems were the key. The entire process had to be conducted by rail and the general staffs had worked for years to perfect the timetables. From the moment the command to mobilise was given, everything had to move at fixed times, in precise order, down to the number of train axles that would pass over a given bridge within a given time. Each action in the mobilisation process led logically to the next, in lockstep precision, combining in a practically irreversible escalation to war. In terms of strategic

planning, the assumption was that the advantage lay always with the offence, and that speed was of the essence. European leaders believed that a one-to three-day lead in mobilisation was militarily significant for the course of the war, leaving vulnerable anyone who delayed.[21]

Apart from pro-Establishment British historians (usually from Oxford) and their misrepresentation, historians in other countries over the past century have made it clear that Russia's general mobilisation was responsible for the world war that started in July 1914. Professor Barnes (USA) wrote that the Franco-Russian military convention was very specific in stating that the first country to mobilise must be held the aggressor. The order for general mobilisation "is war," and Russia, France and Britain acted on that premise. Russia was the first Great Power to order general mobilisation in July 1914 and that "blocked every possible road to peace."... "Only an implacable determination upon war can explain the Russian action."[22]

George F. Kennan, formerly Professor of History at the Institute for Advanced Study at Princeton University, wrote of Russian General Nikolai Obruchev's views on mobilisation at the time of the Franco-Russian military pact in the 1890s. (Obruchev was Russia's leading military statistician and planner):

> Obruchev's first point was that in view of the fact that the process of mobilization by the leading European powers was now normally measured "not in weeks but in days and hours," mobilization by the French and the Russians, "in the light of the inevitable approach of war," must take place simultaneously. Mobilization, Obruchev wrote, "can no longer be considered as a peaceful act: on the contrary, it represents the most decisive act of war." This meant that at the moment of mobilization, "no further diplomatic hesitation is permissible. All diplomatic decisions must be taken in advance..."[23]

Kennan added that both general staffs – Russian and French – "not only viewed mobilization as an outright act of war but insisted that all normal operational decisions be based on that assumption."[24] Article II of the Franco-Russian convention meant that even a partial mobilisation by Austria acting alone would be sufficient to trigger a general mobilisation on the Franco-Russian side and thus assure the inauguration of hostilities against Germany.[25]

This particular point ... was of great potential importance; for it would not have been difficult for the Russians to provoke a partial Austrian mobilization whenever it might suit them to do so.[26]

Russia provoking Austria-Hungary into a partial mobilisation is exactly what was achieved thanks to Franz Ferdinand's assassination and Serbia's refusal to fully comply with the subsequent Austro-Hungarian ultimatum. Austria-Hungary's partial mobilisation was against Serbia, not Russia, but despite having no alliance agreements of any sort with Serbia, Russia got involved. It was no spur of the moment decision, but one that had been long-planned and dictated by financial circles in the City of London via their Russian political puppets, Sazonov and Isvolsky.

The Franco-Russian military convention dictated that if either France or Russia became involved in a military conflict with another country, *both* would respond immediately with all disposable forces. They would begin mobilisation "immediately and simultaneously," and pursue it without interruption from the very first hours. The aim was to make it impossible for the enemy – i.e. Germany – to gain a decisive advantage over either of them in the first days of the war. The plan envisaged Germany having 1,550,000 men in frontline positions by the 14th day of mobilisation. France would likewise have 1,550,000 in place by day 14, and Russia would have 1,600,000. The main body of the Russian army with at least 800,000 Russian troops, would be focussed on the German border:

These men should be concentrated as fast as possible on the German frontier "in such a way as to facilitate an advance that would permit them to make contact as quickly as possible with the German concentrations in order to deprive them from the outset of all possibility of shuttling their forces between east and west."[27]

A sizeable Russian force would attack Austria-Hungary, but the bulk of both the Russian and French forces would be concentrated against Germany's borders, forcing Germany into a reaction. This war against Germany was long in the planning. Twenty-two years before the outbreak of war in 1914, when the Franco-Russian convention was being drawn up, Russian foreign minister Nikolai Giers took the plan to Czar Alexander III for his opinion. He was highly enthusiastic:

"We must be prepared to attack the Germans at once, in order not to give them time to defeat France first and then to turn upon us ... We must correct the mistakes of the past and destroy Germany at the first possible moment." With Germany broken up, he argued, Austria would not dare move. Giers put the question: "But what would we gain by helping the French to destroy Germany?" "Why, what indeed?" replied the Tsar. "What we would gain would be that Germany, as such, would disappear. It would break up into a number of small, weak states, the way it used to be."[28]

Apart from pro-Establishment historians and a few blinkered others, it is recognised that the Russian order for general mobilization started the European war in 1914. Professor Fay wrote:

> The fact is that in St Petersburg and Paris, as well as in Berlin, the maxim had long been accepted by military men, and by the highest political authorities that "mobilization means war."… In the plans of the General Staffs everywhere on the Continent, mobilization was bound up with the "plan of campaign," which provided not only for the march to the frontier but in most cases the crossing of the frontier to get the advantage of the offensive and the waging of war in the enemy's country.[29]

Douglas Newton, former Professor of History at the University of Western Sydney writes:

> The Russian decision to order general mobilisation had been made between 7 P.M. and 9 P.M. on Wednesday 29 July. The decision came at a meeting attended by Sazonov, the Foreign Minister, Sukhomlinov, the Minister of War, and General Yanushkevich, the Chief of Staff. It was endorsed immediately by the Tsar over the telephone and 'received with enthusiasm' by the Russian military planners in St Petersburg. As one expert has argued, it was this decision that 'effectively shattered any prospect of averting a great European war.'[30]

When Austria-Hungary declared war on Serbia on 28 July, Russia used it as the *casus belli* and officially moved from partial to general mobilisation. As long planned, it was not purely against Austria-Hungary but against Germany which had done nothing whatsoever to antagonise Russia – or anyone else for that matter. With Russia now charging down the road to war, Kaiser Wilhelm telegraphed the czar:

> Remembering the hearty friendship which for long had bound us two securely together, I am throwing my whole influence into the scale to induce Austria-Hungary to seek for an open and satisfac-

tory understanding with Russia. I confidently hope for your assistance in my endeavours to put aside all difficulties that may arise.[31]

The czar responded on 29 July, imploring his cousin to restrain Austria-Hungary from "going too far." That is exactly what Wilhelm had been doing when advising Vienna that it must make its point in Belgrade then get out without annexing any Serbian territory. Germany made no move to general mobilisation,

In Russia that same evening the czar issued the order (*ukase*) for general mobilization. Dobrorolski had the appropriate ministers sign the document and just after 9 P.M. made his way to St Petersburg's central telegraph office. The order was just about to be sent out to all principal centres in the Russian empire when the czar changed his mind and ordered it not to be sent. The kaiser telegraphed the czar again the following morning, 30 July:

> My ambassador is instructed to draw the attention of your Government to the dangers and serious consequences of a mobilization. I said the same to you in my last telegram. Austria-Hungary has only mobilised against Servia, and only a part of its army. If, as appears from your communication and that of your government, Russia is mobilising against Austria-Hungary, the role of mediator which you intrusted to me in friendly wise, and which I accepted at your express request, is jeopardised, if not rendered impossible. The whole burden of decision now rests upon your shoulders, the responsibility for war or peace.[32]

In London that same day, the German ambassador, Karl Max Lichnowsky, begged the foreign secretary, Sir Edward Grey, to do all he could to prevent Russian forces mobilising on Germany's borders. Germany would have little choice other than to react, and the consequences would be "beyond conception." Grey promised to keep Sazonov as "cool-headed as possible."[33] Grey dictated four telegrams over that 24-hour period that purported to show he had done everything to maintain the peace. Later, however, it transpired that the telegrams had never been sent. "It was part of a cosmetic charade to imply that Britain had made every effort to prevent war."[34]

Grey was not alone in his criminal manipulation of the official documents to conceal the truth. The Australian historian, Christopher Clark writes:

The Russian general mobilization was one of the most momentous decisions of the July Crisis. This was the first of the general mobilizations. It came at a moment when the German government had not yet even declared the State of Impending war, the German counterpart to the Russian period Preparatory to War which had been in force since 26 July. Austria-Hungary, for its part, was still locked into a partial mobilization focussed on defeating Serbia. There would later be some discomfort among French and Russian politicians about this sequence of events. In the Orange Book produced after the outbreak of war by the Russian government to justify its actions during the crisis, *the editors backdated by three days the Austrian order of general mobilization so as to make the Russian measure appear a mere reaction to developments elsewhere.* A telegram dated 29 July from [Russian] Ambassador Shebeko in Vienna stating that an order of general mobilization was 'anticipated' for the following day was backdated to 28 July and re-worded to say 'The Order for General Mobilization has been signed' – in fact, the order for Austrian mobilization would not be issued until 31 July, to go into effect the following day. The French yellow Book played even more adventurously with the documentary record, by inserting a fictional communiqué from Paleologue dated 31 July stating that the Russian order had been issued 'as a result of the general mobilization taken secretly, but continuously, by Germany for the past six days …' In reality, the Germans had remained, in military terms, an island of relative calm throughout the crisis.[35]

British pro-Establishment historians fail to mention, let alone discuss, this disgraceful interference with the official documents by the British, French and Russian authorities who maliciously altered dates and times for the major events that led directly to war in order to provide a false chronology indicating that Germany and Austria-Hungary were instigating events, not reacting to them. In the real world, Bethmann-Hollweg and Kaiser Wilhelm genuinely tried to apply the brakes and gain some control of the deteriorating situation. They held to the fading hope that British diplomatists were men of honour and placed great store on the reassurances that King George V had given to the kaiser's brother just days earlier. Wolfgang Effenberger writes of Wilhelm:

One can only assume that his positive family ties to the English royal family had blinded him to the sophisticated geostrategic policies of the English administration – he simply could not imagine it. In addition, he was obviously not versed enough in larger military-strategic contexts – he preferred to occupy himself meticulously with the designs of his war fleet, which was ineffective from the outset – to counter the impending danger for Germany.[36]

In St Petersburg on 30 July, the czar, in response to the kaiser's pleas for peace, said that the military measures now coming into operation in Russia had been decided upon five days earlier. That is, Russian mobilisation began on 25 July. That fits with the diary entry of Maurice Paleologue for 25 July which records that when he saw Isvolsky off that evening, the St Petersburg station was packed with soldiers, and that both concluded: "It's war this time."

The czar stated that the Russian mobilisation was "in defence against Austria's preparations," but Austria-Hungary had made no preparations by 25 July. Nicholas II was either lying or completely out of touch with the mobilisation against Germany that was being firmly dictated by Sazonov. Whatever his view, he was seriously wavering, having first issued the general mobilization *ukase* and then withdrawn it. In response to Wilhelm's despairing telegram, the czar advised that he was sending General Tatishchev to Berlin with "instructions." Docherty and Macgregor write:

> His cousin's appeal to reason struck a chord. Deep in those early morning hours, his mind uncluttered by the baying of warmongers, Nicholas made a bold decision to stop the madness. He telegraphed the kaiser that he would send his personal emissary, General Tatishchev, to Berlin with explanations and instructions that would broker a peace. Tatishchev was the czar's own representative at the emperor's court and as such was outside the control or influence of politicians or the military. Czar Nicholas's message held great promise, but Tatishchev never made it to Berlin. Unbeknown to the czar, Sazonov had him arrested and detained that night just as he was about to enter his compartment on the St Petersburg – Berlin train. It was an act of treason. Sazonov secretly defied the czar's express command and thwarted the highest level of personal diplomacy between the two heads of state. By hauling Tatishchev off the train, he removed what would have become an awkward complication: one that could have stopped the war. Sazonov, urged on by senior members of the Russian military in St Petersburg, begged the czar to ignore the German pleas. The telegrams from Kaiser Wilhelm had clearly influenced him, but Sazonov insisted they were a ruse, that the Germans were lying and trying to buy time to split the Russian and French alliance and so leave Russia

vulnerable to a devastating attack, Czar Nicholas relented under sustained pressure and on the afternoon of 30 July again ordered general mobilisation. This time, nothing would be permitted to stop it. Sazonov instructed General Janushkevich to issue the order then 'smash the telephone' and keep out of sight for the rest of the day in order to frustrate any further attempt by the czar to countermand the mobilisation. It was a conspiracy inside the conspiracy.[37]

According to the German writer, Hermann Lutz, Sir Edward Grey "actually encouraged Russia to mobilise."[38] We concur. Grey encouraged the mobilisation with his consent of silence and calm acceptance of its 'inevitability.' On 30 July, the *Manchester Guardian* ran an editorial:

> Not only are we neutral now, but we could and ought to remain neutral throughout the whole course of the war. We have not seen a shred of reason for thinking that the triumph of Germany in a European war in which we had been neutral would injure a single British interest, however small, whereas the triumph of Russia would create a situation for us really formidable. If Russia makes a general war out of a local war it will be a crime against Europe. If we, who might remain neutral, rush into war or let our attitude remain doubtful, it will be both a crime and an act of supreme and gratuitous folly.[39]

The following morning, 1 August, the lead editorial in the London *Daily News* agreed. It spoke of Europe facing the greatest calamity in history due to the actions not of Kaiser Wilhelm or Germany, but of Czar Nicholas and Russia. Britain had a crucial role in preserving the peace and must play it.

> The peace of every land, the happiness of every home in Europe, the very bread by which we live, hang at this moment upon the will of one man, the Czar of Russia. It is he who has his hand on the avalanche. It is he who with one stroke of the pen, one word of the mouth, one motion of the head can plunge Europe into a sea of blood and bury all the achievements of our civilization in anarchy. And at St. Petersburg, there sits the man who has every one of these lives and millions more at his mercy, and who can at one word let hell loose upon the face of Europe. Is he a man we can trust with this momentous power? Is he the man for whom we are going to shed our blood and our treasure? ...The question is for us! For though the Czar has his hand on the avalanche, it is we who have our hand on him. It is we who in the last analysis must say whether

Europe is to deluged with blood. We see the Czar with his hand on the avalanche looking towards England for the one assurance that he needs. Let England say "No, you touch it at your own risk and peril," and his hand will drop. Let England falter, temporize, equivocate, and he will plunge us into ruin with the rest. … It is our neutrality which is the only protection that Europe has against the hideous ruin and combustion on the brink of which it trembles. Let us announce that neutrality to the world! It is the one hope. There is no other. We can save Europe from war even at the last moment. But we can only save it by telling the Czar that he must fight his own battles and take the consequences of his own action. If the British government does this, it will do the greatest service to humanity in history. If it does not do it, it will have brought the greatest curse to humanity in history. The youngest of us will not live to see the end of its crime.[40]

Sir Edward Grey, who had the fate of Europe resting in his hand, failed to act. He presented himself as an honest broker for peace, but knew exactly what had been agreed during Poincaré's visit to Russia, and that Russia had started mobilisation on 25 July. He made no attempt to dissuade St Petersburg for the simple fact that it had been long planned. With the mobilisation of Russia's massive armies on Germany's eastern borders, and the French armies in the west, the encirclement that Germany long feared would be accomplished. Would she either meekly accept the entire country being overrun by those forces – which vastly outnumbered her own – or would she implement the Schlieffen Plan and come out fighting in self-defence?

As the crisis deepened in late July, various proposals and counter proposals for negotiations emanated from London, Berlin St Petersburg and Vienna. Professor Fay wrote that when Edward Grey proposed mediation, Germany was more than willing to cooperate with England on mediation between Austria-Hungary and Russia:

In view of the sweeping statements often made that Germany blocked all Sir Edward Grey's peace proposals, it is interesting to note the attitude of Germany, and compare it with that of Russia and France. *Germany at once expressed approval.* On Saturday morning, July 25, when the British Chargé at Berlin presented it, the German Foreign Office was still optimistic that the conflict could be localized. It had been informed that Berchtold [Austrian foreign minister] had told the Russian Ambassador in Vienna that "Austria-Hungary had no intention of seizing Serbian territory." It thought that this assurance might exercise a calming effect at St Petersburg, but if not – if relations between Austria and Russia became threatening – then Germany "was quite ready to fall in with Grey's suggestion as to the four powers working in favour of moderation at Vienna and St Petersburg."... The German Foreign Office immediately reaffirmed its approval of mediation between Austria and Russia, should "localization" become impossible.

...France also, like Russia, took a negative attitude toward Sir Edward Grey's proposal for mediation between Austria and Russia ...Thus it was not so much Germany, as Russia and France, who failed to give approval to Sir Edward's Grey's proposal for mediation by the four Powers if Austria and Russia mobilized.[41]

Docherty and Macgregor write that Grey, who was close to the Milner Group, was treated with reverence by the British Establishment, and untouchable.

His strategy from 25 July onwards was to make it appear that he sought answers to intractable problems by offering possible solutions, and to urge the Germans in particular to cling to the hope that peace was still possible. Grey knew precisely what had been arranged by and through the Poincaré visit. Sazonov and the Russian military had begun mobilisation. His prime objective was to gain time for the Russians by delaying Germany's defensive response. He achieved this by presenting Britain as an 'honest broker' for peace ... British neutrality sat at the epicentre of this charade like a prize exhibit at an auction.... The Germans repeatedly sought clarification about England's intentions, but Grey held to the official line. Britain was not bound by any obligation to enter into war. He had told this lie so often he might even have started to believe it.[42]

Sir Edward Grey had *to appear* to be working for peace when proposing mediation, but he knew full well that Poincaré in France, and Sazonov in Russia, were well aware that it was a smokescreen and would reject it. Grey's proposals to maintain peace were never sincere, but the German government's positive response demonstrates conclusively that Berlin genuinely desired peace, not war. Germany would later be charged with not only offering no plans for peace in July 1914, but with firmly rejecting all plans offered by other states. As Professor Barnes states "exactly the reverse was the case."[43]

In an editorial on 30 July, the Milner Group's leading mouthpiece in the Press, *The Times,* spoke up for war:

> We can no more afford to see France crushed by Germany, or the balance of power upset against France, than Germany can afford to see Austria-Hungary crushed by Russia and that balance upset against Austrian and Hungarian interests.[44]

It was yet more obfuscation, for Germany would only attempt to crush France if France, in conjunction with Russia, attempted to invade Germany, and that is exactly what was imminently in prospect.

That same day, 30 July, the German ambassador at St Petersburg, Count Pourtalès, informed the kaiser by telegram that Sazonov had openly stated that cancelling the order for mobilisation was no longer possible.[45] Wilhelm immediately replied to Pourtalès:

> ... Frivolity and weakness are to plunge the world into the most frightful war, which eventually aims at the destruction of Germany. For I have no doubt left about it: England, Russia and France have agreed among themselves – after laying the foundation of the *casus foederis* for us through Austria – to take the Austro-Serbian conflict for an excuse for waging a war of extermination against us ... Either we are to shamefully betray our allies, sacrifice them to Russia ... or we are to be attacked in common by the Triple Entente for our fidelity to our allies and punished, whereby they will satisfy their jealousy by joining in totally ruining us. That is the real naked situation *in nuce*, which has slowly and cleverly set going, certainly by Edward VII, has been carried on, and systematically built up ... and finally brought to a conclusion by George V. And thereby the stupidity and ineptitude of our ally is turned into a snare for us.... The net has been suddenly thrown over our head, and England sneeringly reaps the most brilliant success of her persistently prosecuted purely anti-German world policy against which we have proved ourselves helpless, while she twists the noose of our political and economic destruction out of our fidelity to Austria, as we squirm in the net. A great achievement which has aroused the admiration even of him who is to be destroyed as its result! Edward VII is stronger after his death than am I who am still alive. And there have been people who believed that England could be won over or pacified, by this or that puny measure!!! Unremittingly, relentlessly she has pursued her object ... until this point was reached. And we walked into the net...[46]

It was an impressive summation. The scales had fallen from Wilhelm's eyes. Any tendency to bravado, posturing, and, above all, naivety, evaporated when he suddenly recognised at this late stage that England was at the root of it. In reality, all of his telegrams and attempts to maintain the peace over the past days had been pointless. The decision for war had been taken four days earlier with the Russian order for the "Period Preparatory to War" on 26 July. Cambridge historian, J.M.K. Vyvyan, wrote:

> There is little doubt that most senior members of the Russian General Staff regarded the introduction of 'The period preparatory to war' as the first step towards general mobilization, and from this point on viewed with equanimity the outbreak of a general European war. Dobrorolski says: "The war was already a settled matter, and the whole flood of telegrams between the Governments of Russia and Germany represented merely the stage setting of a historical drama."[47]

INTO THE ABYSS

On the morning of 30 July, Kaiser Wilhelm and Chancellor Bethmann-Hollweg sent telegrams to the Austro-Hungarian foreign minister, Leopold von Berchtold, with pleas to accept mediation. When von Berchtold failed to respond, a very angry Bethmann-Hollweg sent another urgent message saying that Austria-Hungary had a right to seek retribution against Serbia, but that Austro-Hungarian intransigence and failure to heed advice was placing Germany in an untenable situation; she was being drawn into a world conflagration against her wishes.[48] Bethmann-Hollweg still looked for a glimmer of hope, but Russia's official general mobilisation order that same day, July 30, 1914, meant there was no turning back. It would plunge Europe into the abyss.

> The Russian general mobilization was the decisive calamity ...
> There was no question in 1914 but that general mobilization by a great power must be followed by hostilities.... It must be stressed that for Russia to bring diplomatic pressure to bear on Austria, it was unnecessary for her to mobilize; all that was required was that she should threaten to do so.[49]

The Russian general mobilisation was the mechanism by which the First World War was started, and by the following day reports were pouring into Berlin that Russian forces were beginning to mass on Germany's eastern borders and were readying for invasion. Bethmann-Hollweg telegraphed London to say that this was a mortal danger to Germany at the very moment he was mediating for a peaceful solution. Germany made a categorical demand that the French government declare whether it would remain neutral in a German-Russian war, with an answer expected within eighteen hours. If France was going to join Russia in the war against Germany, Germany would have to initiate the defensive Schlieffen Plan and move against both of them.

Germany's military leaders were imploring the kaiser to respond in kind to the Russian general mobilisation but Kaiser Wilhelm refused to issue the order, clinging vainly to the hope that it could still be averted if the czar came to his senses. At 1:00 P.M. on 31 July, however, a "Threatening Danger of War" was proclaimed in Germany, and a number of measures were taken. Bethmann-Hollweg telegraphed Vienna to inform the government there that it was likely Germany would be forced to order mobilisation within forty-eight hours. He implored Austria to divert her main military effort against Russia, not Serbia.[50]

On 1 August, Kaiser Wilhelm sent his final telegram to the czar:

> ... Immediate affirmative clear and unmistakeable answer from your government is the only way to avoid endless misery. Until I have received this answer alas, I am unable to discuss the subject of your telegram. As a matter of fact I must request you to immediately order your troops on no account to commit the slightest act of trespassing over our frontiers.[51]

Russia had already ordered general mobilisation, however, and that meant her armies were definitely going to invade both Germany and Austria-Hungary. There was no chance that once mobilised the Russian forces would simply 'stand on the frontier' as militarily ignorant British apologists have claimed might have been possible. War was definitely about to break out from the Russian side, even though Germany had not yet ordered general mobilisation; diplomacy had in effect ended and Russia had committed itself. That same day, Saturday 1 August, Alexander Isvolsky in Paris telegraphed Sazonov in St Petersburg:

> The French Minister of War [Joffre] has declared to me in a tone of hearty enthusiasm the firm decision of the French Government for War, and begged me to confirm the hope of the French General Staff that all efforts will be directed against *Germany*, and that Austria will be treated as a *quantité négligeable*.[52]

Germany, not Austria-Hungary, was and always had been the target. The planning and organisation of this war to crush Germany had been ongoing for more than a decade, and the conspirators in London, Paris, and St. Petersburg were heartily enthusiastic to see it coming to fruition. Isvolsky's telegram to Sazonov confirmed that France had firmly decided on war before Germany had even mobilised against Russia. Straining at the leash in Paris, Joffre informed Poincaré that he could no longer assume the responsibility of command if the President did not order a French general mobilisation. At 3:45 P.M. on 1 August, the French order was issued. Germany responded in kind at 5:00 P.M. and was "the last of the Great Powers to take this final and supreme military measure."[53]

On August 1, Foreign Minister Bethmann-Hollweg telegraphed a note to Pourtalès, his ambassador in St Petersburg, to present to Sazonov. It was a declaration of war. There had been no need for him to do so since Russia had already started the war without such a declaration. Pourtalès asked Sazonov three times to call off the Russian mobilisation. Three times he received a negative answer. Pourtalès therefore handed him the declaration of war, went across to the window, and wept. Professor Fay wrote:

> Falkenhayn and, and, and especially Tirpitz, were opposed to such a declaration of war against Russia. They thought it an unnecessary, foolish and clumsy mistake in diplomatic technique, which would make an unfortunate impression on public opinion and brand Germany before the world as the aggressor. Pourtalès also was of this opinion. The course of events showed that he was right. But, at the moment, Bethmann and Jagow seemed to have believed that a violation of Belgian neutrality prior to Germany's being formally at war with Russia would affect world opinion more adversely than a German initiative in declaring war.[54]

Germany's declaration of war was understandable but a tactical mistake as it would be used by Britain, France and Russia to brand Germany the aggressor. The Russians had more savvy than the Germans who were playing by the old-fashioned 19th century legal book in declaring war. The German military and the German Foreign Ministry believed it was the honourable thing to do to declare war before fighting. Rather like a duel. The Entente Powers were in the new 20th century world; The German military and legal mind, was not.

Russia had been mobilising with the definite intent of attacking Germany, but Sazonov had been instructed that he *should not* make an actual declaration of war. The vital message oft repeated by Grey to Poincaré and Sazonov was that France and Russia must, as far as possible, conceal their military preparations and intention for war until Germany had swallowed the bait. The British people would never support the aggressor in a European war, and it was imperative that Germany should be made to appear the aggressor. It was akin to bullies goading, threatening and ganging up on a single boy in the school playground, but the moment he had the audacity to defend himself, he was to blame. What else could Germany have done? She was provoked into a struggle for life or death. It was a stark choice: await certain destruction or strike out to defend herself. Kaiser Wilhelm had exposed his country to grave danger and almost lost the one precious advantage Germany had by delaying countermeasures to the Russian mobilisation in the forlorn hope of peace. The German army depended entirely upon lightning success at the very start of a war on two fronts. Germany's only effective defence was through offence.[55]

Germany declared war on France on 3 August, and again, that declaration would later be misrepresented by most British historians as proof positive that Germany was responsible. She had, after all, declared war on Russia and France, not the other way round. The vast majority of the British accounts of what happened that fatal weekend have to this day been pure sophistry and a complete misrepresentation of the true situation. Bethmann-Hollweg had stuck to the internationally accepted protocol of declaring war prior to commencing it. The reality was that Germany was the *only* major Power in Europe that had genuinely tried to prevent war, was the last to mobilise, and was not responsible for the outbreak of the war in any shape or form.

In the last week of an epoch that was rushing towards oblivion, the warmongers in London, Paris and St Petersburg forced the pace with unrelenting determination. Localised Austrian retribution on Serbia had deliberately been transformed by the Secret Elite into an altogether greater cause for carnage. Diplomacy had been made to fail. Dishonest men could now throw up their hands in horror and cry 'inevitable' war. Democracy was contemptuously abused by hidden forces that had the political and financial power to manipulate public opinion. Propaganda misrepresented motive, moulding fear into hysteria and empowering the madness that swept reason

229

aside. The great plan for war against Germany that would establish the primacy of the British Empire was almost complete. The last requirement was the 'just cause' to win over and inspire the British people.[56]

The Milner Group had long known that British troops fighting in defence of 'gallant little Belgium' would provide the 'just cause' to shift British public opinion in favour of war. The myth of Belgian 'neutrality' had to be preserved at all costs, and it was the reason why a deep veil of secrecy was employed to conceal Anglo-Belgian military cooperation and planning over the eight years before 1914. The great cover-up succeeded. Belgium remained a 'violated,' 'neutral' country in the eyes of the British public, and hundreds of thousands of young British men would be duped into giving their lives trying to protect her 'neutrality' against the invading 'Hun'.

PERFIDIOUS ALBION MAKES HER MOVE

Any semblance of democratic discussion or decision-making by the British parliament on whether or not Britain should go to war was cast aside. Professor Douglas Newton explains:

> The standard history of Britain's choice for war [in 1914] is far from the truth.... The decision to go to war was rushed, in the face of vehement opposition, in the Cabinet and Parliament, in the Liberal and labour press, and in the streets. There was no democratic decision for war. The history of this opposition has been largely erased from the record, yet it was crucial to what actually happened in August 1914. Two days before the [British] declaration of war four members of the Cabinet resigned in protest at the war party's manipulation of the crisis. The government almost disintegrated. Meanwhile large crowds gathered in Trafalgar Square to hear the case for neutrality and peace. Yet this cry was ignored by the government. Meanwhile, elements of the press, the Foreign Office, and the Tory Opposition sought to browbeat the government into a quick decision. Belgium had little to do with it. The key decision to enter the war was made before Belgium was invaded.[57]

The majority of the British Cabinet opposed intervention in the European crisis, arguing that no vital British interests were involved.

> On 1 August the Cabinet decided against any immediate despatch of the British Expeditionary Force to the Continent, and forbade Churchill to proceed to the full mobilisation of the Navy.[58]

This demonstrates the stark truth that the majority of Cabinet members had been kept in the dark about the true state of affairs. They 'forbade' First Lord of the Admiralty, Winston Churchill, from mobilising the Royal Navy, completely unaware that he had already done so days earlier. Many of the Cabinet members were likewise kept in ignorance of an eleventh-hour development that might have prevented a pan-European war. On Saturday 1 August, Sir Edward Grey sent a telegram to a close associate, George Goschen, a member of the Cecil Bloc in the secret society and whose father was a close friend of Alfred Milner's. The telegram gave a summary of a conversation Grey had just had with Prince Lichnowsky, the German ambassador in London. Professor Newton describes the telegram:

> It recorded the German ambassador asking whether "if Germany gave a promise not to violate Belgian neutrality we would engage to remain neutral." Grey declined. "I replied that I could not say that; our hands were still free, and we were considering what our attitude should be." Lichnowsky then asked whether Grey could not "formulate conditions" under which Britain might "engage to remain neutral." Lichnowsky had "even suggested that the integrity of France and her colonies might be guaranteed." The exchange revealed Germany's willingness to increase her offer to achieve safety in the west. At the very least, it was an invitation to negotiate. And Grey had replied that he "felt obliged to refuse definitely any promise to remain neutral on similar terms, and I could only say that we must keep our hands free."... Grey would not offer British neutrality to Germany on any conditions – even when Germany offered to respect Belgian neutrality. Grey's critics were appalled at his failure to pursue the German offer. He should have sought its authorisation at the very least... Germany was prepared to offer not only the neutrality of Belgium but the integrity of both France and her colonies.[59]

Grey's agenda is exposed; Britain would join France and Russia against Germany, *irrespective* of Belgium. Grey informed his close friend, Viscount Goschen, about Germany's offer but never informed the Cabinet of this at its two meetings on Sunday 1 August nor the House of Commons the following day.

At 7:00 P.M. on 1 August, before Germany had declared war on Russia, Kaiser Wilhelm sent a telegram to King George V confirming that Lichnowsky's discussion with Sir Edward Grey had official approval.

Germany would respect Belgian neutrality and would not attack France if Britain guaranteed France's neutrality. Essentially, Britain, France and Belgium would be spared the horrors of war, while Germany and Russia would have to slug it out between them. With no intention whatsoever of responding positively to the kaiser's earnest peace proposals, King George summoned Grey to Buckingham Palace to help frame a response. They were swatted aside in one dismissive sentence: "I think there must be some misunderstanding of a suggestion that passed in friendly conversation between Prince Lichnowsky and Sir Edward Grey."[60]

Thus, the curt, almost contemptuous response of Grey and the king cost millions of lives. Had they agreed not to get involved, France would most likely have stood down. It is beyond doubt that a terrified czar would then have immediately contacted the kaiser with peace terms. For Germany would have annihilated Russia fighting on her own.

In reality, however, George V was never going to accept the kaiser's olive branch. Like his father before him, he was fully aware and supportive of the plans of Milner and his allies. Like Lichnowsky's offer to Grey, the kaiser's telegram to King George reiterating the peace offer was concealed from the British Cabinet, Parliament, and people.

Grey batted away Germany's peace proposals, but his position was weak. Asquith assessed that seventy-five per cent of the Liberal members of parliament favoured absolute non-intervention,[61] and thus it appeared very likely that war would be rejected in a parliamentary vote. It depended to a large extent on how Conservative members of parliament voted, but that uncertainty was quickly resolved. During the morning Cabinet meeting on Sunday 2 August,

> ...the Liberal prime minister, Asquith, received a note from Bonar Law and Lord Lansdowne in which the Conservative leaders offered their 'unhesitating support' to the Government in any measures it might consider necessary for the object of supporting France and Russia.[62]

With the British Establishment closing ranks, it was now entirely possible that anti-war Liberal and Labour members of parliament would lose *if* it was put to a vote.

On Sunday 2 August, the despairing German ambassador, Prince Lichnowsky, went to 10 Downing Street at breakfast time to plead with Asquith for British neutrality. If Britain remained neutral, she could mediate and avert a war of annihilation for the civilization of Europe. Seemingly blind to the fact of British deception, Lichnowsky reported to Berlin that the British leaders were "holding back and still friendly." Later that morning (at 11:00 A.M.), the British Cabinet met to discuss the situation. Attended by nineteen ministers, the meeting lasted for three hours. Grey spoke of 'premeditated German aggression' in declaring war on Russia, and said that he was "outraged" by the way in which Germany and Austria had put aside all attempts at accommodation while marching steadily to war.[63] Thanks to the barefaced lies of Grey and Asquith, the majority of the Cabinet were completely unaware that the German authorities had in fact made every attempt to maintain the peace. It was Grey, not Germany, that "had put aside all attempts at accommodation while marching steadily to war." Lying came easily to Sir Edward Grey. On numerous occasions over recent years, he stood at the dispatch box in the House of Commons and solemnly assured parliament that Britain had no secret obligations to any other country of any kind whatsoever.

> Ministers denied point blank in Parliament that the country was in any sense committed. They denied it on the public platform. They insisted that our relations with Germany were satisfactory and improving.[64]

There are some who say that the mark of a successful politician is the ability to lie convincingly. If so, Sir Edward Grey was successful. He ramped up the anti-German rhetoric and threatened to resign if the Cabinet did not agree to British naval support for France. Asquith said he would join him, and read the letter he had just received from Bonar Law, leader of the Conservative party, stating that the Tories stood firm for intervention. It would be "fatal to the honour and security of the UK to hesitate."[65]

After much passionate debate and moral blackmail, with some ministers protesting that it would embroil Britain in war, the Cabinet was bounced into agreeing that Britain should pledge naval support for France. British warships would defend French ports and shipping if attacked by the German navy. Immediately the meeting ended at 2 P.M., Grey hurried to the Foreign Office and relayed the news to the French ambassador, Paul Cambon: If the German fleet came into the Channel or through the North Sea to undertake hostile operations against French coasts or shipping, the British fleet would give all the protection in its power.

Meanwhile in nearby Trafalgar Square, a crowd of some 20,000 was gathering for a peace rally.

At 6:30 P.M. that same day, 2 August, a second Cabinet meeting (lasting 90 minutes) was held at 10 Downing Street. Some regarded the pledge of naval protection to France as tantamount to a declaration of war, and symbolised a form of alliance with France about which most of them were completely unaware. Grey deftly shifted the debate to Belgium and stated forcefully that Britain's standing as a Great Power would be damaged forever if they did nothing while neutral Belgium was "crushed" by invading German forces. He cited the 1839 Treaty of London wherein all European Powers recognised the independence of Belgium. The Treaty required Belgium to remain neutral in perpetuity, and the signing Powers would guarantee that. The majority in the Cabinet that evening were totally unaware of the top secret military arrangements and joint planning between Britain and Belgium that had been ongoing since 1906 and had utterly negated the 1839 treaty and Belgium's neutrality. Grey, of course, did not enlighten them, and once more threatened to resign if Britain did not support France:

> I believe war will come and it is due to France they shall have our support.... We have led France to rely upon us, and unless we support her in her agony, I cannot continue at the Foreign Office
> ...We cannot take half-measures – either we must declare ourselves neutral, or in it. If we are to be neutral I will go.[66]

John Burns, President of the Board of Trade protested that Grey and Asquith were behaving as though handcuffed to France, and resigned from the Cabinet. Three other Cabinet members would follow him out the door over the next 24 hours: John Morley, John Simon, and Lord Beaumont. A junior minister, Charles Trevelyan, also resigned.

Professor Newton writes:

> Their resignations were protests against an act of partisanship, which they believed had destroyed Britain's chance to mediate during the crisis. In addition these resignations were protests against the 'bouncing' of the Cabinet. The Radicals accused the men of the inner circle of making crucial decisions that had pre-empted the decisions of the Cabinet as a whole. They had used their key positions to hurry the nation toward war. The charge could be heard in Morley's recollection ... that the Cabinet's leaders were 'artfully' nudging the neutralist ministers, one step at a time, to accept a war of Entente solidarity. Similarly, Morley had explained to Burns too that his protest was against the persistent manipulation of the Cab-

inet. The charge could be as well in Beauchamp's complaint that the Cabinet had been 'jockeyed' into war. ... In every case, Cabinet had been faced with a *fait accompli.* ... The pattern is unmistakable. Asquith and his satellites, a small knot of interventionist ministers, had exploited their Cabinet positions to drive the Cabinet ineluctably toward war. It was a triumph of the inner Executive over both Cabinet and parliament.[67]

Lord Haldane, Lord Chancellor 1912-1915 and a member of that 'inner circle,' would later proudly relate:

> At eleven o'clock on Monday morning, August 3, 1914, we mobilised without a hitch the whole Expeditionary Force, amounting to six divisions and nearly two cavalry divisions, [160,000 men] and began its transport over the Channel, when war was declared thirty-six hours later. We also at the same time successfully mobilized the Territorial Force [trained part-time soldiers] and other units amounting to over half a million men. The Navy was already at its war stations, and there was no delay at all in putting what we had prepared into action ...[68]

Britain's army and navy were mobilised for war before the matter was even discussed in parliament, and 36 hours before Britain declared war on Germany. According to many British pro-Establishment historians, Britain mobilised 160,000 men in August 1914, yet here was Richard Haldane, a senior member of the Cabinet, stating it was over half a million men.

Later that day (2:45 P.M. 3 August) after some routine parliamentary questions – Sir Edward Grey made a speech before a packed House of Commons. He began

> Last week I stated that we were working for peace not only for this country, but to preserve the peace of Europe. To-day events move so rapidly that it is exceedingly difficult to state with technical accuracy the actual state of affairs, but it is clear that the peace of Europe cannot be preserved. Russia and Germany, at any rate, have declared war upon each other. ... First of all let me say, very shortly, that we have consistently worked with a single mind, with all the earnestness in our power, to preserve peace. The House may be satisfied on that point. We have always done it.[69]

Grey began with a profound lie that he had worked to preserve the peace, and continued with other lies:

I come first, now, to the question of British obligations. I have assured the House – and the Prime Minister has assured the House more than once – that if any crisis such as this arose, we should come before the House of Commons and be able to say to the House *that it was free to decide* what the British attitude should be, that we would have no secret engagement which we should spring upon the House, and tell the House that, because we had entered into that engagement, there was an obligation of honour upon the country.... The most awful responsibility is resting upon the Government in deciding what to advise the House of Commons to do. We have disclosed our mind to the House of Commons. We have disclosed the issue, the information which we have, and made clear to the House, I trust, that we are prepared to face that situation, and that should it develop, as probably it may develop, we will face it. We worked for peace up to the last moment, and beyond the last moment. How hard, how persistently, and how earnestly we strove for peace last week, the House will see from the Papers that will be before it. [70]

Grey lied that he had disclosed to parliament the information he had, but he failed to inform members of parliament of the kaiser's offers regarding Belgian neutrality and a peaceful accommodation with France. He painted a picture of Europe in a state of collapse and that it was all owing to German aggression. If Belgium fell to the Germans, he said, Holland would follow then Denmark. If Britain remained neutral it would sacrifice its respect, good name, and reputation before the world. He ended his speech:

The situation has developed so rapidly that technically, as regards the condition of the war, it is most difficult to describe what has actually happened. I wanted to bring out the underlying issues which would affect our own conduct, and our own policy, and to put them clearly. I have put the vital facts before the House, and if, as seems not improbable, we are forced, and rapidly forced, to take our stand upon those issues, then I believe, when the country realises what is at stake, what the real issues are, the magnitude of the impending dangers in the West of Europe, which I have endeavoured to describe to the House, we shall be supported throughout, not only by the House of Commons, but by the determination, the resolution, the courage, and the endurance of the whole country.[71]

The leader of the Conservative opposition, Bonar Law, spoke in response:

> The right hon. Gentleman has made an appeal for support, and it is necessary I should say a word or two. They shall be very few. I wish to say, in the first place, that I do not believe there is a single Member of this House who doubts that, not only the right hon. Gentleman himself, but the Government which he represents, have done everything in their power up to the last moment to preserve peace, and I think we may be sure that, if any other course is taken, it is because it is forced upon them, and that they have absolutely no alternative.... Everything he has said I am sure is true.... The Government already know, but I give them now the assurance on behalf of the party of which I am Leader in this House, that in whatever steps they think it necessary to take for the honour and security of this country, they can rely on the unhesitating support of the Opposition.[72]

When the Speaker announced that he was now going to end the session, a backbench Liberal member of parliament and pacifist, Edmund Morrell, asked if members were to be given an opportunity to debate the proposed intervention of the country in war. Prime Minister Asquith replied that it would have an early opportunity, *but not today*. The Speaker had to calm angry Liberal and Labour members of parliament by announcing that he would return to the chair at 7 P.M. and give them an opportunity to debate the issue. At that evening session in the House of Commons, Sir Edward Grey was first to speak. It was a bizarre situation where members of the opposing party cheered his speech wildly, while his own Liberal party members sat in glum silence:

> I want to give the House some information which I have received, and which was not in my possession when I made my statement this afternoon. It is information I have received from the Belgian Legation in London, and is to the following effect: – Germany sent yesterday evening at seven o'clock a Note proposing to Belgium friendly neutrality, covering free passage on Belgian territory, and promising maintenance of independence of the kingdom and possession at the conclusion of peace, and threatening, in case of refusal, to treat Belgium as an enemy. A time limit of twelve hours was fixed for the reply. The Belgians have answered that an attack on their neutrality would

be a flagrant violation of the rights of nations, and that to accept the German proposal would be to sacrifice the honour of a nation. Conscious of its duty, Belgium is firmly resolved to repel aggression by all possible means.

Of course, I can only say that the Government are prepared to take into grave consideration the information which it has received. I make no further comment upon it.[73]

Britain's Minister for Foreign Affairs, Edward Grey, then departed the House of Commons (together with prime minister Asquith) without waiting to hear what members of parliament had to say about the matter or give them an opportunity to vote on it. Over the following two-and-a-half hours, numerous Liberal party members of parliament spoke passionately against Britain's involvement in the war. The following extracts from the Hansard record 'War in Europe' House of Commons Debate 03 August 1914 vol 65 cc1848-84' are representative of the opinions expressed by members of parliament that evening after Grey and Asquith had scurried off:

Josiah Wedgewood:

I represent, in this House, some 70,000 people in the Potteries, and I think it is about time we here considered what those people are going to endure during the coming months. The right hon. Gentleman on the Front Bench told us in his wonderful Jingo speech – can anybody deny that it was a Jingo speech – that the Army and Navy were ready, to the last trouser button, to do their duty. …I think hon. Members must realise that this is not going to be one of the dear old-fashioned wars of the eighteenth century over again…

Edmund Morrell:

… In my opinion it is perfectly possible for the Governmentto arrange an honourable neutrality with Germany, a neutrality which would be perfectly honourable to this country. I regret very much the policy we are pursuing. I regret it still more because I think the country is being rushed into war without its knowledge…

Percy Molteno:

As a supporter of the Government that came into power as a Government of peace, and with a sense of my responsibility to my Constituents, I do not feel that I can keep quite silent on this stupendous occasion, when we are asked practically to assent to a course which may involve us in this terrible war. No part of this country has been invaded at present; no vital interest in this country has been attacked. Yet we are asked to assent to war with all its terrible consequences. The Government have no right to plunge this country into this war for anything short of our own vital interests.

...They have brought us to the brink of disaster without our knowing, and without our being warned. I say that, at the last moment, they should give the people of this country a chance to decide. This is a continuation of that old and disastrous system where a few men in charge of the State, wielding the whole force of the State, make secret engagements and secret arrangements, carefully veiled from the knowledge of the people, who are as dumb driven cattle without a voice on the question. And nobody can tell the country what are the important considerations that ought to weigh with us in taking part in this tremendous struggle.

Arnold Rowntree:

I want to take this opportunity of raising my voice against England going into this war. The Foreign Secretary said that this House would have an opportunity of saying Yea or Nay to any proposition made, but I regret to think that already he has very largely pledged the House by the answer he gave to the French Ambassador on Sunday, and I, as a very humble Member want, at any rate, to take this opportunity of saying that I for one will having nothing to do with this war.

Sir John Jardine:

As a Liberal sent here two or three times by my Constituents to carry out peace, retrenchment, and reform, I feel with the deepest seriousness any approach of war, because I know that war contradicts all those three topics.

Sir William Byles:

We heard the shouts of exultation which came from the other side [Conservatives]. It is not more than a dozen men in Europe that have brought this thing about, yet tens of hundreds of thousands of people in these four or five nations will be reduced to terrible want and misery. That is what men shout about with glee!

Llewellyn Williams

...If you asked any man in this country, whatever his politics might be, whether he would calmly contemplate the entrance of this country into this quarrel, he would have said, "No." He would have begged and implored the Government to stay their hand. Even to-day this country does not want war. But I know perfectly well what will happen. The incitement in the Press, with which we are too familiar, will inflame public passion.... Now is the only time to speak, before the war fever has come to its height. I beg and implore the Government, especially some on the Treasury Bench, [He meant David Lloyd George] who know what war fever means, to use every effort in their power to avert this terrible calamity, not only to our prosperity, but to the civilisation of the world.

One after another, Liberal members of parliament condemned the Liberal government's action in dragging the country into a cataclysmic war. Conservative member of parliament and former prime minister Sir Arthur Balfour rose to shut down the debate. It should be recalled that Balfour was an inner-circle member of the Rhodes/Milner secret society, the very organisation that had been planning the war for over a decade.

Arthur Balfour:

We know-perfectly well this is not a Debate upon the tremendous national issue brought before us earlier in the day. Nominally we are discussing the same subject, whereas the House of Commons, in its strength, was called together this afternoon to hear an exposition of policy upon an occasion to which there has been no parallel in our lifetime, and may be no parallel in the lifetime of those of the next generation, What we have been having to-night are the very dregs and lees of the Debate, in no sense representing the various views of Members of this House ... I would, therefore, earnestly ask and appeal to them, and, still more, do I appeal to the rest of the House to allow us to finish our proceedings to-night without dragging on this relatively impotent and evil Debate.

The anti-war exhortations of elected representatives of the people in the so-called 'mother of parliaments,' the 'beacon of democracy,' were the 'dregs' of an 'impotent and evil debate' and dismissed as inconsequential. Thus ended the one and only opportunity that the British people – the "dumb-driven cattle" as member of parliament Percy Molteno had ironically termed the electorate – to debate the forthcoming war through their representatives.

The dumb-driven cattle were being herded towards the global abattoir for reasons they would never properly know. A few men wielding the whole force of the state, with secret arrangements and secret agreements, had unleashed the demon war and sanctioned the slaughter. Molteno pointed an accusatory finger at the politicians who had fronted the decision, but it was the Secret Elite who hid their all-powerful influence behind the carefully veiled parliamentary screen,[74]

There was to be no formal parliamentary debate or vote on the matter as promised several times by the lying, hypocritical, Sir Edward Grey. He and other warmongers railroaded their plans through parliament just as they had railroaded them through the Cabinet. It is entirely likely that Arthur Balfour, inner-circle member of the Rhodes-Milner secret society, close personal friend of Alfred Milner, creator and chairman of the Committee of Imperial Defence (CID), was specifically sent to the Commons that night to shut the debate down. Less than a year later, Balfour would serve in a coalition government as First Lord of the Admiralty.

On 4 August, prime minister Asquith informed the House of Commons that the king of Belgium had asked Britain for protection. The British government had consequently warned the German authorities to remove troops from Belgium and respect her neutrality. Britain expected a positive response to that effect from the German authorities by midnight German time. (11 P.M. British time). Professor Newton writes:

> "There is a Cabinet meeting at midnight to consider the German reply to our ultimatum, and it is morally certain that we shall declare war," Hankey [Secretary of the Committee of Imperial Defence] proudly told his wife that night. Not so, There was no Cabinet meeting at midnight. Characteristically for the Asquith government, the ultimate step was taken not by Cabinet, but rather by a small clique bunkered down in the Cabinet room. A mere coffee-table's worth of the Cabinet gathered there on the night of Tuesday 4 August: Asquith, Grey and Haldane, [allies of the Milner Group] joined later by Lloyd George and McKenna. This little assembly made the final choice for war. In this sense, as Keith Wilson argues, 'the Cabinet, as such, never did make a decision for war.[75]

When no satisfactory response came from Germany, King George V held a Privy Council (with only three Privy Councillors present) at Buckingham Palace at 10:35 P.M. and signed a declaration of war. Thereafter, British government issued the following statement:

Owing to the summary rejection by the German Government of the request made by his Majesty's Government for assurances that the neutrality of Belgium will be respected, his Majesty's Ambassador to Berlin has received his passports, and his Majesty's Government declared to the German Government that a state of war exists between Great Britain and Germany as from 11 P.M. on August 4, 1914.[76]

SUMMARY: CHAPTER 8 – MOBILIZATION, "THE MOST DECISIVE ACT OF WAR

- Before President Poincaré left St. Petersburg for home on 23 July, he reassured Russia of France's participation in the coming war. Russia immediately began its preparations for military mobilisation.

- Russia proclaimed a 'State of War' in towns facing Germany and Austria.

- An 'exhilarated' Winston Churchill mobilised the entire Royal Navy fleet for war on 28 July, and the cheerful General Joffre, French C-in-C, began mobilising the French army.

- While Russia, Britain and France were mobilising, they sent sham reassuring telegrams to Berlin encouraging the kaiser's attempts with Austria to preserve the peace.

- The prime objective of Sir Edward Grey in London was to gain time for the Russian mobilisation by delaying Germany's defensive response.

- General mobilisation by any country meant war, and Kaiser Wilhelm pleaded with the czar to halt the Russian mobilisation.

- Kaiser Wilhelm offered to respect Belgium's neutrality and avoid war with France. His peace efforts were rejected in London.

- Of the European Powers, Russia and France mobilised first, Germany last.

- Sir Edward Grey and other schemers in the British government repeatedly lied to parliament and withheld crucial information.

- Members of parliament were promised a deciding vote on Britain's stance regarding war, but they were not given one. Britain declared war on Germany on 4 August 1914.

CHAPTER 9

THE 'SCHLIEFFEN PLAN'

To this day most British historians promote the discredited narrative that Germany was responsible for the outbreak of the world war in August 1914. They claim that in the decade prior to the war, Germany spent enormous amounts of money creating massive military and naval forces that would enable them to conquer Europe. The facts relate a different story:

The 1912 and 1913 bills increased the peacetime strength of the German army to 748,000. But the forces of Russia and France had grown more rapidly in the preceding years. The Russian and French armies had a total peacetime strength in 1913-14 of 2,170,000. Compared with a combined German and Austrian strength of 1,242,000: a discrepancy of 928,000. In 1912 that gap had been only 794,665: while in 1904 it had been just 260,982. This meant that at its full war-time strength, the German army totalled around 2.15 million men, to which could be added 1.3 million Habsburg troops; whereas on a war footing the combined forces of Serbia, Russia, Belgium and France numbered 5.6 million.[1]

Over the previous decade, France and Russia had grown their armies at a faster rate than the allegedly 'militaristic' Germany. The figures quoted above from Professor Niall Ferguson do not include the 500,000 British troops that were, according to British War Minister, Richard Haldane, rapidly shipped across to France and Belgium in August and September 1914 to face the German army. Additionally, some 2.3 million colonial troops from Canada, Australia, New Zealand, India, South Africa, and other colonies joined Britain. Italy, Germany's erstwhile ally, would also enter the war against her, bringing 300,000 troops in the first instance. The U.S. would likewise join the Allies against Germany in 1917 with some 2 million troops.

Far from thinking of starting a European war of conquest, the heavily outnumbered Germany's major concern was how she could possibly defend herself against a two-front attack by France and Russia. On 2 August 2 1870, France – determined to assert its dominant position in continental Europe – invaded Germany but was defeated and consequently lost Alsace-Lorraine. Now allied with Russia, revanchists in France were determined on another war with Germany to regain the 'lost provinces'. The German quandary was how to defend against a simultaneous attack by France from the west and Russia from the east, when their combined forces heavily outnumbered Germany's.

Before retiring in 1905, German army chief, Field Marshal Alfred von Schlieffen, prepared a *Denkschrift*, a memorandum, that considered Germany's defence capabilities. He calculated that a French attack would require a German army of 96 divisions, but Germany had only 72 divisions. The odds of success against France alone were not great, and if Russia should join France – in accordance with their military alliance ratified in 1894 – the outlook was bleak. Following his retirement, Schlieffen set out his thoughts in an unofficial memo in early 1906 that considered a co-ordinated attack on Germany by France *and* Russia. He believed that 10 Divisions might initially hold back a Russian invasion in the east since Russia would be slow to mobilise, and the bulk of the army could defend against France.

Since assuming command in 1891, Schlieffen had always believed that attack was the best form of defence. The French had constructed heavy fortification lines close to the Franco-German border, however, and he considered it best to bypass them rather than attack head-on. His strategy was to deploy a number of divisions there to defend the border, while a strong right wing would rapidly transit Belgium and Luxemburg then bypass the heavily fortified Paris either to the west or the east depending on the situation. Those forces would then envelop the French army from the rear in a large pincer movement up against German troops on the Franco-German border. If a rapid victory over the French could be accomplished, the majority of German troops would then rapidly be transferred east to bolster the 10 Gertman divisions sent to hold back the Russians. Schlieffen considered it possible if France could be defeated quickly, Russia would give up the fight.

The offensive through Belgium was not, as British historians have suggested for a hundred years, proof that Germany initiated a war of European conquest. In reality, it was a defensive move by going on the offensive. It presented the best, indeed, probably the only chance of success in destroying the enemy's ability to attack Germany, but it depended on the German right wing getting beyond Paris and defeating the French army within 6 weeks. It was a very tall order.

Militarily it had long been considered that the best form of defence was attack, with a pre-emptive strike against the enemy. The military general of China in ancient times, Sun Tzu, had declared; "Attack is the secret of defence; defence is the planning of an attack."[2] Across many centuries thereafter, military strategists – including General George Washington – had employed such a strategy.

It is important to recognise that French Intelligence was in possession of Schlieffen's memorandum by 1906. At that time a letter signed "*Le Vengeur*" (The Avenger) was sent to the French Chief of Staff with an offer to hand over the German mobilisation plan for war with France in return for 60,000 francs. The offer was accepted.[3] The information indicating that Germany would mount an offensive defence against France through Belgium was, of course, passed to British Intelligence. General Sir Henry Wilson's detailed analysis of the Belgian topography and top secret joint planning with the Belgian army from 1906 onwards came about in response to that information. Eight years before the war commenced, the French, British, and Belgian authorities knew that Germany's only chance lay in attacking France through Belgium, and that it was exactly what Germany would do when faced with a simultaneous French and Russian attack. Professor E McCullough (Canada) writes:

> The Germans made many mistakes, but they were not stupid enough to rely on French neutrality in a Russo-German war. Believing, quite correctly, that they would be forced to fight on two fronts against superior forces, they chose the plan that would give them a chance of knocking out France before the slower Russians could get underway.[4]

It has been suggested that Germany would have stood a better chance of victory if she had defended on both fronts, or if she had defended against France in the west and concentrated on an offensive in the east against Russia. Such counter-factual scenarios make for interesting discussion and attempting to imagine how events might have turned out had different strategies been adopted. It would, we believe, be mistaken to consider that the German military authorities had been so wedded to the 'Schlieffen Plan' that they failed to consider all other options for fighting a defensive war on two separate fronts, East and West. Rightly or wrongly, they chose to launch a major offensive in the West against France and defence in the east against Russia. As it transpired, the 'defence' against Russia was surprisingly so successful in the initial stages that the German army attacked there too with considerable success.

The erroneously termed 'Schlieffen Plan' (it was actually an unofficial memo Schlieffen wrote *after* he retired) would be wilfully misrepresented at Versailles in 1919 as a purely offensive military strategy against France, and evidence that Germany had 'long-planned' a war' of aggression. Schlieffen, however, was never at any time planning such a war. He clearly understood that the German army was significantly smaller than that of France and barely capable of coping against her alone. The charge that he planned for a war of aggression against the overwhelming combined forces of France and Russia is absurd. The 1905 *Denkschrift* – Schlieffen's last official memorandum before retiring – informed his political masters that the size of the German army was insufficient to defend against France, and was a plea to the government to provide more defence funding. It is worth considering the comments of Professor L.C.F. Turner (Australia) regarding the state of affairs in 1914:

> Contrary to popular belief Imperial Germany was not a super-militarized state. For many years she had been conscripting barely fifty per cent of her manpower of military age, while France was conscripting over eighty per cent and also drawing heavily on North African manpower. In spite of their great superiority in population – sixty-eight millions against forty millions – the Germans could only count on a slight numerical superiority over the French army and had to reckon with Russia as well. It was in vain that Schlieffen had urged General von Einem, the very conservative Prussian Minister of War between 1903 and 1909, to consent to army increase essential to the successful application of his plan.[5]

Had Kaiser Wilhelm and the German government long been intent on a European war of aggression – as charged by the victors at Versailles in 1919 – Schlieffen's plea in 1905 for an increase in the army would *not* have fallen on deaf ears. As we have seen, Professor Niall Ferguson writes that it was not the German army that rapidly increased in size in the decade before the 1914-18 war, but the French and Russian armies. The major problem with Schlieffen's suggested strategy was the insufficiency of troops to carry out the envisaged pincer movement as planned.

When Schlieffen retired in late December 1905, Kaiser Wilhelm replaced him with Helmuth von Moltke (1848-1916) as chief of the German General Staff. Moltke would serve from January 1906 until replaced in September 1914. In his early thoughts on defence against a simultaneous attack by France and Russia, Moltke, like Schlieffen, considered that a frontal attack on the French forts around Verdun would offer little chance of success, and a rapid traversing of Belgium would present the only chance of victory. He was aware, however, that Belgium, with 5 divisions of infantry, was likely to resist.

With the forces actually available to him, Moltke envisaged 62 divisions in the west, with 54 of them forming the right wing that would traverse Belgium. The other 8 divisions would defend the France-Germany border to the south and be ready to trap the French armies in a pincer movement. A decisive victory would have to be achieved over the French within six weeks of mobilisation to enable the rapid transfer of sufficient troops east to defend against the Russian invasion. With only 62 divisions facing France rather than the 96 as determined necessary by Schlieffen, however, it was a virtually impossible task.

In 1913 a new finance bill in Germany enabled Moltke to increase the standing army by 136,000 men to 890,000 officers and men, but increases in the French and Russian armies had quickly offset that. France introduced the three-year law, which immediately expanded her army. Russia also spent larger sums on her forces, with much of it from loans provided by French banks. Christopher Clark writes:

> In March 1913, massive sums were approved by the Tsar for artillery and other armaments in a vastly ambitious scheme.... As a consequence, the peacetime strength of the Russian army in 1914 was *double* that of the German, at around one and a half million men, and 300,000 more than the combined strengths of the German and Austro-Hungarian armies.... These measures were complemented by the French-financed Russian strategic railway programme.... Since 1905, Germany's answer to the predicament had been the Schlieffen Plan, which aimed to resolve the problem of a war on two fronts by first mounting a massive strike against France, accompanied by a holding operation in the east. Only when the situation on the western front had been resolved would Germany swing eastwards against Russia. But what if the balance of forces between the two alliance blocs shifted to the point where the Schlieffen Plan no longer made sense?[6]

What indeed? The stark question is: did the so-called Schlieffen Plan *ever* at any time make sense? Schlieffen was playing with numbers that did not exist in 1905, and would not exist even by 1914.

For their great plan to succeed, the powerbrokers in London, Paris and New York knew that France and Russia always had to be ahead of the

Germans in the arms race. No matter how Germany attempted to try and redress the balance, she could never be allowed to succeed. Christopher Clark writes: "In 1904, the combined strength of the Franco-Russian military had exceeded the Austro-German by 260,982. By 1914 the gap was estimated at around 1 million and it was widening fast."[7] It was the same regarding British naval supremacy. Throughout the decade before war, if the Germans built a new battleship, Britain would build at least two to retain the advantage.

France and Russia were well ahead in the size of their combined armed forces and, as we have seen, ensured they were also ahead in mobilisation in 1914. When the Russian general mobilisation led to war, the German army comprised 85.5 divisions. It was still 10.5 divisions short of the number Schlieffen considered necessary for defeating France alone, never mind the massive Russian army in the east which itself was double the size of the entire German army.

On German mobilisation in August 1914, Moltke ordered 9 divisions to East Prussia to try and stem the Russian invasion, and the remaining 76.5 divisions west to face France. Of this force in the west, 16 divisions defended the France-Germany border, while 54 divisions comprised the right-wing that would march on France via supposedly neutral Belgium. Moltke held 6.5 *ersatz* (replacement) divisions in reserve. No matter how he deployed those 76.5 divisions in the west, they were still 20 divisions short of the necessary number as dictated by Schlieffen ten years earlier. To this can be added the difficulty that the French army had grown massively since Schlieffen's assessment, and it was now likely that far more than 96 divisions would have been necessary for Germany to stand any realistic chance.

In August 1914 the German army's advance through Belgium was, in many instances, poorly organised. Moltke hoped for, and seems to have accepted as likely, that traversing Belgium would be relatively straightforward using its road and rail infrastructure. He appears not to have considered the likelihood that Belgian troops would destroy roads, bridges, railway junctions, and other key transport infrastructure as they retreated before the Germans. Tens of thousands of young men on all sides would die before German troops approached within 30 miles of Paris. They had successfully pushed British and French forces back, and after taking the French town of Maubeuge near the Belgian border in early September, the now overconfident Moltke ordered 2 corps (4 divisions) east to bolster the 9 divisions facing the Russians. He later stated: "I recognise that this was a mistake, and one that we would pay for at the Marne."[8]

The retreating French and British forces quickly regrouped and counterattacked successfully at the Battle of the Marne, 5-12 September. The German advance was halted, and the subsequent retreat marked the end of Moltke's modified "Schlieffen Plan." A broken man, Moltke informed the kaiser that the war was lost. On 14 September, he was dismissed from his post as Chief of Staff. In an assessment of the "Schlieffen Plan," historian J.M. Winter (USA) writes:

> Whether or not the Schlieffen Plan could have worked is one of the most debated topics in military history. Critics of Moltke's tactics usually concentrate on the fact that his right wing (initially on the northern side) was not eight times stronger than his left wing, as stipulated by Schlieffen, but only three times stronger. They also question the wisdom of the decision to move north and east of Paris rather than south and west in an enveloping assault on the city, and point to the creation of a 48 km (30 mile) gap between the German First and Second Armies as a fatal mistake, leading to defeat at the Marne.
>
> But these might-have-beens ignore three fundamental problems which doomed the Schlieffen Plan from the start. The first concerns human endurance; the second, logistical difficulties; the third, communications problems. The plan failed to take account of the limitations of the individual soldier and of the systems which supplied and directed him.
>
> First, the men of the German First Army had to cover 30-40km (20-25 miles) per day. Is it a surprise that by early September many units were simply exhausted, and that others had been reduced to 50 percent of their original strength? Secondly, their lines of supply were so extended that, even had they won the Battle of the Marne, they almost certainly could have gone no further. Thirdly, the speed of the operation outpaced the communications system between the Front and high command situated in Luxembourg, 240km (150 miles) away. Thus, Moltke could not obtain enough information to direct the campaign. In fact, the crucial decision of 9 September to withdraw the German right flank from its original route to the River Aisne was taken not by Moltke but by First and Second Army staff officers and Lt-Col. Hentsch, sent by his commander to find out what was going on. The fog of war had simply obscured the battlefield from the people at the top who needed to know. More than just human error was involved in the collapse of the Germans' grand design of winning the war in its first months and repeating their spectacular successes of 1870-71. The German army had tried the impossible.[9]

"Tried the impossible," indeed, but that was evident from day one given what they were facing – the combined military might they faced of France and Russia, as well as Britain with her massive empire. The Milner Group and the London banking elites associated with it had drawn Germany into a trap from which there was no escape. To an extent the Germans had been snared through a combination of their own errors and naivety, but it is to their credit that they attempted to break out of the trap and fought valiantly for freedom as opposed to rolling over like a cringing dog being beaten by its master.

Conventional British court historiography relates that Germany built a massive, well-oiled, military machine with the direct intent of seizing European and global power in 1914. Regrettably these lies are disseminated to this day by supposedly upstanding, honest, academics at Oxford University and other British institutions. Such academics adhere to the fake narrative and simply ignore or dismiss the evidence presented by many learned academic historians across the world that it was not Germany that started the war of 1914-18, but Russia with her general mobilisation.

One British propagandist, George Thomson, stated in his book, *The 12 Days*, published in 1964:

> Beckoned by the ghost of Count Schlieffen, the grey flood of the German army poured into Belgium. At Verviers, obeying orders, they shouted '*Vive la Belgique!*' as they marched over the frontier line. The Belgians were not impressed with the friendly demonstration. The Plan, on which Schlieffen had spent so many years, was the ultimate expression of the Prussian genius in degeneracy. The German army was a superb machine; the Schlieffen Plan was the working instructions that came with it.... It involved breaking Germany's word and made it almost certain that Britain, bound in honour and interest to defend neutral Belgium, would join the battle in the West at the side of France. But the more British soldiers on the Continent the better, said Moltke. The gendarmes would arrest them.[10]

Here we have the old chestnuts, the lies, that are now accepted by many in Britain thanks to constant repetition by British 'court' historians: The Schlieffen plan represented Prussian degeneracy; The German army was a 'superb machine'; Germany 'broke her word'; Britain went to war to defend 'neutral Belgium.' To this day, the British Establishment's academic lie factory continues to churn out this bilge.

In his book, *War by Timetable*, published in 1969, A.J.P. Taylor writes:

When cut down to essentials, the sole cause for the outbreak of war in 1914 was the Schlieffen Plan – product of the belief in speed and the offensive.[11]

A later historian, Annika Mombauer, a German working for the British Establishment, writes that it was the "Schlieffen Plan" that drew an 'unwilling' France into war:

France did not have the luxury of deciding for or against the war, as Germany's Schlieffen Plan would automatically embroil France in the fighting.[12]

Another such German-born purveyor of the conventional Anglo-American line, Holger Herwig, was Professor of History at the University of Calgary, and Research Professor at the Canadian Centre for Military, Security and Strategic Studies which is linked to the Department of National Defence. An Establishment man through and through, Herwig writes:

... The Schlieffen Plan has become synonymous with militarism run amok, with operational considerations trumping statecraft, and with rote mechanics of war replacing the art of war.[13]

No doubts there then. The Schlieffen Plan was unbridled German militarism and with it, Germany let loose the dogs of war. In the diabolical slaughterfest of 1914-18, what Herwig means by the "art of war" is unfathomable.

Yet another British pro-Establishment historian, Gary Sheffield, writes that the "Schlieffen Plan" was a key element in Germany's lust for power. Had France failed to honour its pledge to Russia and remained neutral in July 1914, Sheffield states that it "would probably have been invaded anyway, courtesy of the Schlieffen Plan."[14] Such is the nonsense that passes as academic history in Britain. Gary Sheffield, who was Warfare Historian at the British Army Staff College, adds:

Aided and abetted by Austria-Hungary, Germany's behaviour in July 1914 was the most important single factor in bringing about the First World War. The German leadership wanted hegemony in Europe and was prepared to go to war to achieve it. Article 231 of the Treaty of Versailles, the 'war guilt clause,' which declared that the Great War was "imposed upon" the Allies "by the aggression of Germany and her allies" was, therefore, fundamentally correct.[15]

Such utterly fake British claims about various aspects of the First World War, including the Schlieffen Plan, held sway for some years, but in 1999, historian and former US infantry officer, Terence Zuber, put the cat among the pigeons by stating that the Schlieffen Plan, supposedly one of the pillars of 20th century military history, had *never* actually been the German war plan. He was scathing about historians who contended that it was the proximate cause of the Great War, was emblematic of German militarism, and that it proved German war guilt.[16]

Zuber explains that the so-called "Schlieffen plan" that outlined Germany's future response to a two-front war had no authority whatsoever. It was written after Schlieffen had retired and was no longer in a position to make decisions. Terence Zuber's work generated heated debate, and among the British pro-establishment historians who challenged his thesis was Annika Mombauer, the previously mentioned academic at the Open University. In a response to Mombauer's attack on his thesis, Zuber wrote:

> Annika Mombauer contends that the Schlieffen plan was an offensive war plan, which proves German guilt for starting the Great War. She does not find it necessary to prove this assertion by referring to the actual war planning documents or the official military histories. Instead, Mombauer relies on "common knowledge" and "truthiness" (if it sounds true, it must be true).
>
> In fact, the French and Russians attacked the Germans, and the first battles of the war were fought in East Prussia, Alsace and Lorraine – on German territory. Of the four great land powers, the Germans were the last to begin major offensive operations.
>
> Since Mombauer says that offensive war plans equals war guilt, she must maintain that in the first battles of the war the Russians and French were not attacking, and the Germans were not on the defensive. Mombauer thinks that it is "generally accepted" that the Great War began "with a German attack on France and Belgium." "Common knowledge" notwithstanding, it is clear that in the first major battles, the French and Russians were attacking and the Germans were on the defensive. On 14 August the Russians began their advance into East Prussia with the 1st and 2nd Armies, including 20 infantry and 8 cavalry divisions, roughly 500,000 men, while the French 1st and 2nd Armies attacked into German Alsace and Lorraine. The first major battles of the war, at Stallupönen and Tannenberg in East Prussia and in Alsace and Lorraine, were fought on German territory. In fact, of the four great land powers in 1914, the German army was the last to conduct major offensive

operations. The right wing of the German army in the west did not begin its forward movement until 18 August, four days after the French attack into Lorraine, and did not make serious contact with the French, who were also attacking into Belgium, until 22 August.

Mombauer says "…. we know what actually happened in August 1914. German troops invaded Luxemburg and Belgium and were headed for France, while French troops were initially ordered to halt within ten kilometres of Germany…" Once again, this is completely wrong. Poincaré, the President of France, had ordered the deployment of the covering force (five corps of a 25 corps-strong French army) to the Franco-German border on 30 July with the stipulation that it remain 10 kilometres from the border. This stipulation was rescinded on 2 August, the day that the French and Germans began mobilization, and the entire French army was granted complete freedom of movement ("Le gouvernement rend donc au general commandant en chef *liberté absolue* du movement"). Joffre made full use of this freedom of movement: the French VII Corps attacked into Alsace on 7 August. The French 1st and 2nd Armies began their offensive into Lorraine on 14 August. The German army did not begin to advance until 18 August.

… Mombauer also says, "Of course France also had an offensive war plan … but the difference is that France did not attack Germany in 1914 (false news of such attacks was spread in Germany to justify the German attack!), but rather Joffre ordered the French troops to remain behind the front until he was certain of Germany's approach."

If the French had an offensive war plan, but weren't going to attack the Germans, who were they going to attack?[17]

Terence Zuber's response to Mombauer, utilising now readily available irrefutable evidence, is a masterly exposition and meticulous demolition of the lazy propaganda that passes for scholarship in British academic war-history departments. His articles – which are published on the internet[18] are essential reading for any student wishing a proper understanding of the true origins of the 1914-18 war. The description of his book, *Inventing the Schlieffen Plan, German War Planning 1871-1914,* published in 2014 reads:

The existence of the Schlieffen plan has been one of the basic assumptions of twentieth-century military history. It was the perfect example of the evils of German militarism: aggressive, mechanical, disdainful of politics and of public morality. The Great War began in

August 1914 allegedly because the Schlieffen plan forced the German government to transform a Balkan quarrel into a World War by attacking France. And, in the end, the Schlieffen plan failed at the battle of the Marne. Yet it has always been recognized that the Schlieffen plan included inconsistencies which have never been satisfactorily explained. On the basis of newly discovered documents from German archives, Terence Zuber presents a radically different picture of German war planning between 1871 and 1914, and concludes that, in fact, there never really was a "Schlieffen plan."[19]

Troy R.E Paddock, professor of European history at Southern Connecticut State University, discusses the Zuber debate in his book, *Contesting the Origins of the First World, An Historiographical Argument,* published in 2020. Paddock writes:

> While Zuber's critics have tried to dismiss his work as an "interesting footnote," its impact is far more significant than his detractors are willing to concede. If the "Schlieffen Plan" was how Gerhard Ritter described it, then Zuber has "won" the debate. There was no such thing as the Schlieffen Plan. Even Terence Holmes, Zuber's most persistent critic, conceded that the plan was not for a two-front war in 1914. If it was any kind of war plan at all – and he and Zuber still disagree – it was for a one-front war against France in 1906. Zuber's critics have tried to minimize what Zuber has done ... by stating that he is not saying anything new.... Zuber has done exactly what Mombauer has called for. He has used very precise language to try "to put the history of German war planning back on a firm professional military and historical foundation" For Mombauer this does not appear to be important ... Zuber's contention is that Schlieffen's strategic thinking focussed on counterattacks (yes, through Belgium), not on offensives. It is this point that causes most consternation. Schlieffen was concerned about force numbers and made decisions on the basis of numerical superiority or inferiority. Gross recognizes this when he writes, "The examples mentioned clearly demonstrate that Schlieffen planned counter-attacks only in the case of numerical inferiority when an offensive was not possible." The difficulty here for Gross (and others) is that after the Franco-Russian agreements of 1892-1894, Germany was always going to be the numerically inferior party. This fact suggests that counterattack played a key role in German military planning in a world that its political and military leaders considered increasingly unfriendly.... The question of whether German war planning

was more aggressive or reactive is why the significance of Zuber's work goes beyond the realm of German war planning.... Mombauer notes, "Nor was Germany attacked by France in 1914 – whatever their agreement with Russia might have held in store." Nowhere does Mombauer mention that France's agreement with Russia included the promise to join Russia in war against Germany if Germany mobilized its forces. Mombauer also neglects to mention that France did not even wait for German mobilization and ordered its own forces to mobilize 30 minutes before Germany did.[20]

The first German troops crossed the Belgian frontier on 4 August and met with some resistance. Villages were destroyed and towns badly damaged, including the library and other national treasures at Louvain University. When Belgian civilians were killed, the German authorities insisted that many of them had actually been *franc-tireurs* – civilian snipers – or had obstructed their troops in some way. The heated debate over the deaths continues to this day.

THE "RAPE" OF BELGIUM

As the German army made its way across Belgium to France, reports began to emerge that they had raped and pillaged and killed upwards of six thousand innocent Belgian civilians. In 2003, Thomas Fleming, author, historian and president of the Society of American Historians, attempted to shed some light on the matter:

> In 1912, at King Albert's behest, the Belgian parliament increased the army to 340,000 men, a large force for a country of 7 million. Many of these soldiers were untrained "civic guards," who did not wear uniforms, beyond shoulder ribbons or an insignia pinned on their shirts. When these units joined the uniformed regulars in resisting Germany's invasion with gunfire, they ignited an old grievance in the minds of the advancing Germans. In the Franco-Prussian War of 1870-1871, after the Germans smashed the French army and the government surrendered, there was an attempt to arouse a levee en masse [mass uprising]. This idea of citizen resistance originated in the wars of the French Revolution, in which the entire population was summoned to resist invaders. Thousands of *franc-tireurs* took up the fight, inflicting many casualties on the Germans.
>
> In Belgium, the Germans decided the civic guards were *franc-tireurs*, symptoms of a *levée en masse*.... Time was of the essence, and Belgian resistance was fatally delaying the German goal of a quick victory against the French. Also in this explosive mix was

the inexperience of the German army's rank and file ...; Spooked by rumours of franc-tireurs everywhere, the Germans frequently opened fire on each other in the darkness, inflicting numerous casualties and deepening their rage against the recalcitrant Belgians and their obvious spurious neutrality. Retaliation was virtually inevitable – and bloody. Civilians were seized and many were executed. Towns and villages, including Louvain's world-famous medieval library, went up in flames. Wellington House [British propaganda headquarters] soon had a new propaganda theme: atrocities.[21]

Soldiers killing civilians is morally repugnant and utterly abhorrent in any war. There can be no excuses. The fundamental atrocity here was the war itself and in the final reckoning we must blame those responsible for that war. To an estimated 6,000 civilian deaths in Belgium must be added an estimated 6 to 10 million civilians killed worldwide by war's end. Thereafter, around 1 million civilians were starved to death in Germany in 1919 when the food blockade was needlessly continued.

Is it possible that some of the damage to towns and villages in Belgium in those early weeks of the war was caused by the Belgians themselves? The first British propaganda history of the war, *The Great War, The Standard History of the All-Europe Conflict,* published in late 1914, (editor H. W. Wilson, Oxford) gives an account of the early events, and praising the efforts of the Belgians:

> The Belgians, retiring on Liege, destroyed everything before them – bridges, tunnels, railway rolling stock. Village after village was fired in order that it might not give shelter to the invaders. Thus the village of Boncelles was dressed with tar, which was poured on all the woodwork. The soldiers [Belgian] then set fire to the church, the presbytery and two large villas. When the Belgians came to a tunnel they pulled up the rails for some distance inside and then ran an engine in ... In places the roads were ruined, explosives being planted underneath, connected by electric wires, and detonated as German troops advanced. Traps were set everywhere. At each corner a sharpshooter waited ready to die provided he had killed some of the enemy first.[22]

Sharpshooters (*franc-tireurs*) were waiting at each corner to kill German soldiers, and it is unreasonable to suggest that the soldiers should not return fire because those trying to kill them were in civilian garb. Wellington House, the British government's official war propaganda headquarters in London, was quickly up and running with reports posted in British, American, Canadian, Australian, and New Zealand newspapers about German atrocities in Belgium.

A flood of stories portrayed the Germans as monsters capable of appalling sadism. Eyewitnesses described infantrymen spearing Belgian babies on their bayonets as they marched along, singing war songs. Accounts of boys with amputated hands (supposedly to prevent them from using guns) abounded, without even a hint of a blush for the way the Belgians had done the real thing in the Congo. Tales of women with amputated breasts multiplied even faster. At the top of the atrocity hit parade were rape stories. One eyewitness claimed that the Germans dragged twenty young women out of their houses in a captured Belgian town and stretched them on tables in the village square, where each was violated by at least twelve "Huns" while the rest of the division watched and cheered. At British expense, a group of Belgians toured the United States telling these stories. Woodrow Wilson solemnly received them in the White House.[23]

American historian, Thomas Fleming, relates that the German authorities had permitted eight American news reporters to accompany the German army through Belgium. Those reporters sent a telegram to the Associated Press stating that they were united in declaring the German atrocity stories groundless. After accompanying the German troops across hundreds of miles through Belgium they were unable to report a single incident of unprovoked reprisal. The discipline of the German soldiers "was excellent" and there was no truth to the atrocity stories.[24]

The Milner Group in London and their allies had long planned and deliberately started this war, but managed to convince the world that it was Germany with her dastardly Schlieffen plan. Having got the war underway, Milner's men directed the propaganda narrative in order to influence international public opinion – especially American – and convince the world that Germany and German society were intrinsically evil. Liberal member of parliament, Charles Masterman, was placed in charge of the War Propaganda Bureau (Wellington House) Masterman was close to the Liberal Imperialists (e.g. Grey, Asquith, Haldane, Churchill) who had played such a significant role in deliberately bringing about the war. He was 'one of them'.

Masterman recruited many writers and academics sympathetic to the Milner Group if not indeed members of it. They included; James Headlam-Morley, a historian who was a member of the secret society;[25] John Buchan (Oxford), one of the best fiction writers in Britain, had been Milner's Private Secretary in South Africa, and was a member of the secret society.[26]

Newspaper editors – including Geoffrey Dawson, member of the inner circle of the Milner Group – were called to a meeting at Wellington House to facilitate and coordinate British newspaper propaganda. John Buchan was employed to write and publish a monthly magazine, *Nelson's History of The War*, promoting British fake war history throughout 1914-18. Buchan, who was later placed in charge at Wellington House, had served in Milner's Kindergarten in South Africa. He was Milner's secretary and became a member of the 'Association of Helpers' of the secret society.

Everyone involved in the Wellington House lie factory was sworn to the utmost secrecy, and very few, even in parliament, knew of its existence until long after the war. As the Wellington House tales about German atrocities in Belgium became more and more lurid and bizarre, however, people began to question their authenticity. Where did these stories come from? Who were the 'witnesses'? Could such evil deeds really have been perpetrated in the twentieth century by Europeans? The Milner Group had to act fast to head off growing cynicism and 'substantiate' the stories. In the now time-honoured British tradition, they formed an official Committee to whitewash the matter.

Few would fail to be impressed by the official announcement that a committee of investigation had been appointed by "His Britannic Majesty's Government." On 15 December 1914, the Right Honourable Viscount Bryce, formerly British ambassador at Washington, was appointed to chair the committee which would examine:

GERMAN BREACHES OF RULES AND USAGES OF WAR AND ACTS OF INHUMANITY IN INVADED TERRITORIES TREATMENT OF THE CIVIL POPULATION

(a) KILLING OF NON-COMBATANTS

(b) TREATMENT OF WOMEN AND CHILDREN

(c) THE USE OF CIVILIANS AS SCREENS

(d) THE LOOTING, BURNING, AND DESTRUCTION OF PROPERTY

2. OFFENCES AGAINST COMBATANTS

(a) KILLING THE WOUNDED OR PRISONERS

(b) FIRING ON HOSPITALS

(c) ABUSE OF RED CROSS AND WHITE FLAG

Viscount Bryce (1838-1922) was a widely travelled and a highly regarded academic – especially in the United States. He attended Oxford University, was a Fellow of Oriel College, Oxford, and had been Regius Professor of Civil Law at Oxford. Bryce was also a Liberal member of Parliament until February 1907 when he was appointed Britain's ambassador to the United States, where he would remain in post until 1913. He was also an important member of the 'transatlanticist' Pilgrims Society (founded 1902) which shared similar aims with the Milnerites. Bryce befriended Presidents Theodore Roosevelt and Woodrow Wilson, and greatly strengthened the Anglo-American 'special relationship'. In short, Bryce was an Establishment man through and through and was very close to the individuals in England who had deliberately brought about the war.

Prime Minister Asquith appointed others to the committee who would serve under Viscount Bryce's chairmanship:

Sir Fredeick Pollock (Eton and Cambridge), a leading barrister in England and K.C. (King's Counsel). Sir Alfred Hopkinson, K.C., another leading barrister and former Liberal MP. H.A.L Fisher, (New College, Oxford) historian, Vice-chancellor of the University of Sheffield, and leading player in the Milner Group. Carroll Quigley places Fisher at the heart of the Rhodes-Milner secret society's Society of the Elect.[27] He was a member of All Souls and one of the "chief instruments by which the Milner Group recruited new blood into All Souls."[28] Apart from Milner himself, Fisher was one of the chief recruiters for Milner's 'Kindergarten' and gave the Milner Group a powerful hold over All Souls at Oxford.[29] Through that control over Oxford University, we have seen how the Milner Group controlled the writing of the fake history of the war.

Prime Minister Asquith also appointed two barristers (and safe pairs of hands for the establishment) to be Joint Secretaries to the Committee: Mr E. Grimwood-Mears (Oxford). (He would also serve as secretary to the Royal Commission whitewash on the Easter Rising in Dublin in 1916), and Mr W.J.H. Brodrick (Oxford.)

Of all the men appointed by Asquith to the German 'atrocity' investigating committee, only one, Harold Cox, could perhaps be considered an Establishment 'outsider.' The Royal Commission headed by Bryce examined witness statements and diaries over the early months of 1915, and issued a 61-page report on 12 May 12, 1915.

THE REPORT

To the Right Honourable H. H. Asquith, First Lord of H.M. Treasury.

... For some three or four months before the appointment of the Committee, the Home Office had been collecting a large body of evidence. [Taken from Belgian witnesses, some soldiers, but most of them civilians from those towns and villages through which the German Army passed, and from British officers and soldiers.] More than 1,200 depositions made by these witnesses have been submitted to and considered by the Committee. Nearly all of these were obtained under the supervision of Sir Charles Mathews, the Director of Public Prosecutions, and of Mr. E. Grimwood Mears, barrister of the Inner Temple, whilst in addition Professor J. H. Morgan has collected a number of statements mainly from British soldiers which have also been submitted to the Committee.

The labour involved in securing, in a comparatively short time, so large a number of statements from witnesses scattered all over the United Kingdom, made it necessary to employ a good many examiners. The depositions were in all cases taken down in this country by gentlemen of legal knowledge and experience, though, of course, they had no authority to administer an oath. They were instructed not to "lead" the witnesses, or make any suggestions to them, and also to impress upon them the necessity for care and precision in giving their evidence.

They were also directed to treat the evidence critically, and as far as possible satisfy themselves, by putting questions which arose out of the evidence, that the witnesses were speaking the truth. They were, in fact, to examine them, so far as the testimony given provided materials for cross-examination.

The Report details many alleged German atrocities against the civilian population, and concludes:

> From the foregoing pages it will be seen that the Committee have come to a definite conclusion upon each of the heads under which the evidence has been classified.
>
> It is proved:
>
> (i) That there were in many parts of Belgium deliberate and systematically organised massacres of the civil population, accompanied by many isolated murders and other outrages.
>
> (ii) That in the conduct of the war generally innocent civilians, both men and women, were murdered in large numbers, women violated, and children murdered.
>
> (iii) That looting, house burning, and the wanton destruction of property were ordered and countenanced by the officers of the German Army, that elaborate provisions had been made for systematic incendiarism at the very outbreak of the war, and that the burnings and destruction were frequent where no military necessity could be alleged, being indeed part of a system of general terrorisation.
>
> (iv) That the rules and usages of war were frequently broken, particularly by the using of civilians, including women and children, as a shield for advancing forces exposed to fire, to a less degree by killing the wounded and prisoners, and in the frequent abuse of the Red Cross and the White Flag.
>
> Sensible as they are of the gravity of these conclusions, the Committee conceive that they would be doing less than their duty if they failed to record them as fully established by the evidence. Murder, lust, and pillage prevailed over many parts of Belgium on a scale unparalleled in any war between civilised nations during the last three centuries.
>
> Our function is ended when we have stated what the evidence establishes, but we may be permitted to express our belief that these disclosures will not have been made in vain if they touch and rouse the conscience of mankind, and we venture to hope that as soon as the present war is over, the nations of the world in council will consider what means can be provided and sanctions devised to prevent the recurrence of such horrors as our generation is now witnessing.
>
> Bryce Report[30]

Professor Trevor Wilson writes:

> By the time that Bryce began compiling his report, much of the British case against Germany had come to depend on his ability to function as any journalist on a Sunday paper: to tell a tale that would make his readers' flesh creep.[31]

Bryce released his 'flesh-creeping' report on 13 May 1915. Historian Tom Fleming relates that Wellington House had it translated into 30 different languages for global readership and ensured that it went to every newspaper in the United States.

After the war, historians who sought to examine the documentation for Bryce's stories were told that the files had mysteriously disappeared.[32] [Thomas Fleming, *The Illusion of Victory, America in World War I*, p. 53-54.] Niall Ferguson appears to be one of many historians who consider the atrocity stories to have been fabricated. He writes:

> Pre-war photographs of Russian pogroms were reprinted to 'illustrate' stories of German behaviour in Belgium. The *Sunday Chronicle* was one of many British papers which alleged that the Germans had cut off the hands of Belgian children, while the former scaremonger William Le Queux related with ill-disguised relish "the wild orgies of blood and debauchery" in which the Germans allegedly indulged, including "the ruthless violation and killing of defenceless women, girls and children of tender age." Other writers had great fun imagining sixteen-year-old girls being "forced to drink" and then "violated successively" on the lawn before having their breasts "pierced with bayonets." The bayoneted baby was another favoured image. J.H. Morgan even threw in a charge of "sodomy ... of little children." At least eleven pamphlets on this subject were published in Britain between 1914 and 1918, including Lord Bryce's official Report on Alleged German Atrocities, and Wellington House under Masterman ensured that a high proportion of them were translated and sent abroad. Atrocities exported well. Several American Liberty Loan posters used images of scantily clad Belgian nymphs at the mercy of simian Huns to entice prurient savers to buy war bonds.[33]

Current co-author Jim Macgregor, together with Gerry Docherty wrote:

> The Bryce Report was a propaganda coup of the highest order. It was translated into 30 languages and dispersed across the

globe by every British propaganda service. In the United States, the *New York Times* of 13 May 1915 ran Bryce's verdict on three full pages with pictures and unequivocal headlines ... "German atrocities are Proved" and "Premeditated Slaughter in Belgium, "Young and Old Mutilated, "Children Brutally Slain, Arson and Pillage Systematic," "Countenanced by Officers," "Civilians Used as Shields." The *New York Times* could hardly have bettered itself in supporting the Allied cause. However, the American Irvin Cobb, in Belgium in 1914 as a correspondent for the *Saturday Evening Post*, wrote: "I had been able to find in Belgium no direct proof of mutilations, the torturing and other barbarities which were charged against the Germans by Belgians ... fully a dozen seasoned journalists, both English and American, have agreed with me, saying that their experiences in this regard have been the same as mine."[34]

Professor Harry Elmer Barnes wrote:

Next to the contention that Germany wilfully launched the World War, the leading myth in Entente propaganda was the assertion that Germany introduced into her conduct of the war the most frightful and savage practices. These were explained by some as being due to the fact that the German race was utterly uncivilized; indeed, was quite incapable of being civilized. Such atrocious conduct was deemed but natural for a nation of "Huns." ... Among the forms of atrocious conduct with which the Germans were charged, we may mention the crucifixion of French and Belgian soldiers, cutting the hands of numerous Belgian children, the rape of innumerable Belgian women and girls, cutting the breasts of Belgian and Polish women, robbing not only private homes but churches and hospitals ... Great Britain was the most systematic and efficient in *inventing* and publishing these tales and she made a great stroke in getting James Bryce to affix his signature to a singularly complete and varied collection of stories of German savagery and rapine in Belgium. This so-called "Bryce Report" was released in the United States shortly after the sinking of the *Lusitania,* and had a great effect in estranging American opinion from Germany on account of the confidence which the American citizens reposed in Mr. Bryce. The Atrocities Myth was the chief instrument utilized by the British propagandists and the American financial interests in "educating" American opinion up to the point where we were willing to enter the War.[35]

By no means was the propaganda concerning German 'atrocities' manufactured by Britain alone. The French authorities were busy in their own lie factory. Professor Joseph Ward Swain (American) wrote in the 1930s:

> The Bryce Report of 60 pages was followed by nearly 300 pages of blood-curdling testimony. It was so successful that it was followed by many others. According to revelations made since the war, the French government early established the *Maison de la Presse* in Paris, where atrocity stories were manufactured to suit morbid taste. "Its principal work consisted in making photographs and cuts of wooden figures with hands cut off, tongues torn out, eyes gouged out, skulls crushed in, and brains laid bare. These pictures were sent as unassailable evidence of German atrocities to all parts of the globe. In the same room fictitious photographs were made of bombarded French and Belgian churches, violated graves and monuments, scenes of ruin and desolation. The staging and painting of these scenes was done by the best scene painters of the Paris Opera." Such imposture was not confined to this one establishment, however, and a British general claims the dubious honor of having invented the most gruesome lie of the entire war – the story of a "corpse factory" in which the Germans boiled down the bodies of dead soldiers into fertilizer and soap.[36]

A crucial question remains: Did Belgian refugees in Britain in 1914-15 relate atrocity stories to the British authorities, or was it the British authorities who actually invented them? Historian Niall Ferguson (Britain) relates that the official British propaganda headquarters in London – Wellington House – was deeply involved in promoting anti-German lies. Genuine photographs of Russian pogroms and atrocities taken long before August 1914 were falsely used to represent stories of reprehensible German behaviour in Belgium. Charles Masterman, chief of Wellington House, ensured that the stories were widely translated and sent abroad.[37]

In the 1970s Professor Trevor Wilson, military historian at the university of Adelaide, researched the origins of the Bryce Report and described its publication as "a particularly powerful stimulant to hate." Wilson relates that a review of the Press in the United States following release of the Report was compiled by Wellington House in May 1915. It stated that even in papers hostile to the Allies there was not the slightest attempt to impugn the correctness of facts alleged because Lord Bryce's prestige in America put scepticism out of the question.[38] Masterman wrote to Bryce on 7 June: "Your report has swept America. As you probably know even the most sceptical declare themselves converted, just because it is signed by you."

Professor Wilson questions if such confidence in Bryce and his report was warranted. He considers Bryce to have been an open-minded man initially, but it was difficult to avoid the conclusion that once committed to the task, he "took pains to avoid any course of action" which might oblige him to disbelieve the main body of the atrocity tales. That, adds Wilson, "appears to have been true of all but one of the members of his committee," Harold Cox, who was prepared to probe the evidence thoroughly.

The principal material for investigation by the Bryce committee consisted of 1,200 depositions recounting acts of atrocity by German troops in Belgium. Most of the depositions had been made by Belgian civilians living as refugees in Britain (there were 180,000 such refugees in April 1915); the rest by British and Belgian soldiers stationed either in Britain or France. The large majority of the depositions had been taken by a team of English barristers appointed for the purpose, but not under oath. The only other material before the Bryce committee consisted of diaries taken from German soldiers who had been killed or taken prisoner. These diaries freely recounted the execution of civilians allegedly for shooting at German soldiers or aiding the forces of the Allies.[39]

Before the Bryce committee was even formed in December 1914, the witness depositions and diary entries had already been sifted 'by lawyers' working for the British government. Those considered relevant had been transcribed into official, typed documents. Some members of the committee considered it necessary to conduct interviews with the Belgians who had made the statements in order to assess their veracity and make them swear to the truth under oath. Professor Wilson:

> If this collection of depositions and diaries was to substantiate the heavy charges being laid against the German authorities, it would require thorough probing. Yet from the outset Bryce was under pressure to forego any such investigation. This is plain from the terms in which, in a letter of 4 December 1914, he was asked to head the committee by the Liberal Attorney-General, Sir John Simon. … Simon stressed that the "value of this investigation entirely depends upon the known impartiality and authority of those who compose the Committee." But he was also at pains to indicate that much of the groundwork of the inquiry had already been done. Some "trained staff investigators at Scotland Yard," in cooperation with the Public Prosecutors department, had begun collecting evi-

265

dence. Certain members of the Bar, who had volunteered their assistance, had then "used their special training to sift the stories thus selected, rejecting mere rumour, and exposing what remained to the severe scrutiny which is traditional in British legal procedure." Thus a "limited number of stories of outrage" had been subjected "to a very precise test."[40]

Essentially, the government had already completed the work on the evidence. Lord Bryce, Professor Fisher and several leading legal players who would give it credibility in the eyes of the public were simply to rubber-stamp it. The man who coordinated this deceit, Sir John Simon, was Attorney-General (chief legal adviser to the Crown), but he was much more than that. An Oxford University graduate, Simon had been a President of the Oxford Union and became a Fellow of All Souls in 1897. He was close to the Milner secret society; indeed, Carroll Quigley lists him as a member of the "Outer Circle" of the Society's "Association of Helpers."[41] We have seen how the leading academic historian on the Bryce Committee, H.A.L. Fisher was also a Fellow of All Souls – the Milner Group's enclave at Oxford – and a member of the inner core of the secret society. Together with Lord Bryce, member of the Milner Group-aligned Pilgrims, the entire investigation into supposed German atrocities was put together by the very people who had planned and started the war. What would be presented as a "careful and scrupulous investigation into alleged German crimes in Belgium," was a stich-up from the beginning.

The lone dissenting voice on the committee, Harold Cox, demanded that all statements alleging German atrocities must be examined thoroughly, but his dissent was crushed by Bryce and Professor Fisher. Interestingly, the section of the Report dealing specifically with the allegations of German atrocities against women and children was conducted by the one member who just happened to be right at the heart of the Milner Group: H.A.L. Fisher.

Some of the 'corroborating' evidence allegedly came directly from diaries taken from dead German soldiers. Diary entries supposedly freely recounted the execution of civilians and looting and plundering by the German army. The Bryce Report stated that the diaries were in one respect "the most weighty part of the evidence." How convenient then that the diaries mysteriously disappeared and all that remained were the official typed accounts of what was alleged to have been in them.

We believe that the official typed accounts of supposed German diaries by "trained investigators at Scotland Yard," were actually the product of the vivid imagination of the propaganda department at Wellington House.

Carroll Quigley writes about Wellington House in *Tragedy & Hope*:

> This agency was able to control almost all information going to the American press and by 1916 was acting as an international news service itself, distributing European news to about 35 American papers which had no foreign reporters of their own. ... The German violation of Belgium was constantly bewailed, while nothing was said of the Entente violation of Greek neutrality. A great deal was made of the Austrian ultimatum to Serbia, while the Russian mobilization which had precipitated the war was hardly mentioned. In general, manufacture of outright lies by propaganda agencies was infrequent, and the desired picture of the enemy was built up by a process of selection and distortion of evidence until, by 1918, many in the West regarded the Germans as bloodthirsty and sadistic militarists, while the Germans regarded Russians as subhuman monsters. A great deal was made, especially by the British, of "atrocity" propaganda; stories of German mutilation of bodies, violation of women, cutting off of children's hands, desecration of churches and shrines, and crucifixions of Belgians were widely believed in the West by 1916. Lord Bryce headed a committee which produced a volume of such stories in 1915, and it is quite evident that this well-educated man, "the greatest English authority on the United States," was completely taken in by his own stories. ... There were several reasons for the use of such atrocity stories: (a) to build up the fighting spirit of the mass army; (b) to stiffen the civilian morale; (c) to encourage enlistment, especially in England, where volunteers were used for one and a half years; (d) to increase subscriptions for war bonds; (e) to justify one's own breaches of international law or the customs of war; (f) to destroy the chances of negotiating peace; (g) to win the support of neutrals... [42]

We consider that the vast majority, if not all, of the German atrocity stories were manufactured by Wellington House. The supposed original atrocity depositions by over a thousand Belgian refugees in Britain, and the so-called war diaries of dead German soldiers, didn't simply disappear as the official records would have us believe; they never existed in the first place.

We may appear to have spent an inordinate amount of time on this topic but it was of huge importance, not merely in recruiting fresh cannon fodder to the British army, and swinging American public opinion in favour of the war but, as Quigley relates, "destroying the chances of negotiating peace." We have seen how a quick victory over the German army and a peace settlement was the last thing the Milner cabal wanted. They had spent the previous decade and more carefully and determinedly planning how to start a war that would not simply defeat Germany militarily, but crush her commercially, economically and industrially. It was well understood in London that that would only be achieved by a long, grinding war of attrition. The will for war among the British and American people could best be generated if they were made to live in fear. To that end, Germany had to be portrayed as an evil monster that constantly threatened their families and the entire world.

To maintain popular enthusiasm and support for the ever bloodier conflict, British, French and (later) American propaganda tirelessly depicted their German adversaries as vicious, criminal "Huns," and portrayed the German emperor, Kaiser Wilhelm II, as a rapacious lunatic monster in human form. The London *Financial Times* told readers in June 1915 that the Kaiser had personally ordered the torturing of three-year-old Belgian children, even specifying the tortures to be inflicted. Rudyard Kipling wrote in the London *Morning Post*: "There are only two divisions in the world today, human beings and Germans."[43]

Professor Trevor Wilson added:

> The first half of 1915 was a special time of hate in Britain: for in this phase of the Great War atrocity mongering reached its peak. Tales of outrages committed by Germans replenished the queues at the recruiting offices and triggered off indiscriminate violence in Britain against residents of German origin or (supposed) German sympathies. But more importantly, they reinforced the conviction that – although the end of the struggle might be much farther off than had initially been expected – no resolution of the conflict was acceptable short of total victory.[44]

In Britain, the public had to be softened up to the fact that this was going to be a long war, and the notion that all the eager volunteers of the first weeks and months would be home by Christmas was quickly dispelled. To keep recruitment numbers up sufficiently to replace the appalling number of young men being killed, the propaganda and fear of a German victory had to be constantly cranked up by the daily newspapers and leaders of the Anglican Church. The *Daily Mail*, for example, published correspondence from the artist Sir William Blake Richmond, a protégé of John Ruskin at Oxford:

> Neither England nor civilized Europe and Asia is going to be set trembling by lunatic William, even though by his order Rheims Cathedral has been destroyed. This last act of the barbarian chief will only draw us all closer together to be rid of a scourge the like of which the civilized world has never seen before. The madman is piling up the logs of his own pyre. We can have no terror of the monster; we shall clench our teeth in determination that if we die to the last man the modern Judas and his hell-begotten brood shall be wiped out. To achieve this righteous purpose we must be patient and plodding as well as energetic. Our great England will shed its blood willingly to help rid civilization of a criminal monarch and a criminal court which have succeeded in creating out of docile people a herd of savages.[45]

"We must be patient and plodding" was the message from this Ruskinite as he encouraged the men of England to "shed their blood willingly" and be prepared to "die to the last man." Like most others who were calling on young men to make the 'ultimate sacrifice.' Sir William Blake Richmond would die peacefully in his bed as an old man.

The Anglican church proved one of the biggest recruiters with its unflinching support for the war.

> Though *The Church Times* recognised the need for "shame at the sin of war," it threw its weight unreservedly behind the British Government, as it had in the Boer War. Hostilities had been "forced upon us against our will," despite the "persistence of the Cabinet" and the "wholehearted endeavours of the King." The German nation had "become the tool of the Junker Party and of that spirit of aggressive militarism which has gained an increasing ascendancy of late years." The war was entirely just.... The battle is one for our national existence. The actions of Germany were "a menace to Christianity" and thus "recourse to arms is a matter beyond our choice."... Prayers for victory were called for, the war was frequently equated with a Christian crusade, and the pacifists received a tough time from Anglican critics. The overtly patriotic Bishop of London, at an open-air service outside St. Mary church in Cannon Street, said: "Some funny things are done in answer to conscience. I am one of those who think that conscientious objectors are all wrong. It is more truly obeying conscience to throw yourself

into battle." Similarly, the Dean of Manchester Cathedral preached against pacifism in the week war was declared. He made it clear that "the no war at any price party" would find no sympathy with him. A pacifist letter to *The Church Times* came in for heavy criticism.[46]

In October 1914, The Archbishop of York, Cosmo Lang, insisted "there could be no peace until the German spirit had been crushed." As a Christian leader, he appealed for "friends of peace" to support the war.[47] An active recruiter, Archbishop Lang had studied at Balliol College, Oxford, was president of the Oxford Union in 1883, and, according to Professor Quigley, was a Fellow of All Souls for 40 years.[48] In the 1930s, he would strongly support the appeasement of Nazi Germany.

Randall Davidson, the Archbishop of Canterbury – leading clergyman in the church of England – addressed the Anglican bishops in February 1915. "Britain could not, without sacrificing principles of honour and justice more dear than life itself, have stood aside and looked idly on the world conflict."[49]

The greatest of all the warmongers in the Church of England was Arthur Winnington-Ingram, Bishop of London. At Westminster Church in February 1915, he advised a meeting of clergymen that they must foster and increase the fortitude of the nation, and inculcate *a happier and brighter view of death* among those in their parishes who had lost a son, brother, or husband in the war. Winnington-Ingram wrote:

> ...To save the freedom of the world, to save Liberty's own self, to save the honour of women and the innocence of children, everything that is noblest in Europe, everyone that loves freedom and honour, everyone that puts principle above ease, and life itself beyond mere living, are banded in a great crusade – we cannot deny it – to kill Germans: to kill them, not for the sake of killing, but to save the world; to kill the good as well as the bad, to kill the young men as well as the old, to kill those who have shown kindness to our wounded ... to kill them lest the civilisation of the world should itself be killed.[50]

The good Bishop, who helped recruit tens of thousands of young men who would die in the mud and gore of the trenches 'for God and England,' collapsed playing golf at the age of 88 and died peacefully two days later.

The great British lie factory, Wellington House, working in tandem with the controlled mainstream press and leading members of the Anglican church, proved a huge success at keeping recruitment up for the 'long war' with 2.5 million men volunteering in Britain between August 1914 and December 1915.

SUMMARY: CHAPTER 9 – THE 'SCHLIEFFEN PLAN'

- It was alleged that by 1914 Germany had purposefully built a massive army to conquer Europe.. The facts reveal that the combined French and Russian forces greatly outnumbered those of Germany.

- Facing a threat on two separate fronts from those French and Russian armies, in 1906 the recently retired Field Marshal, Alfred von Schlieffen, suggested that a small military force should be sent east to hold back a Russian invasion, while a much larger force attempted a quick knock-out of France.

- The German force facing the French in the west would comprise a left wing defending the German border with France, while a larger right wing traversed Belgium and attempted to defeat the French army in a pincer movement to the south-east of Paris. It was recognised that victory over the French would need to be achieved within 6 weeks in order that troops could be transferred eats against Russia

- The German military action against France through Belgium was a defensive plan based on the well-recognised premise that attack is the best form of defence. It was wilfully misrepresented by Entente propaganda as unbridled German militarism.

- The German right wing got to within 30 miles of Paris before being forced to retreat by combined French and British forces. Stalemated trench warfare was the result for the next three-and-a-half years.

- German troops were accused of committing horrendous atrocities against Belgian civilians on their advance through Belgium, and an official British enquiry confirmed the accusations. They were later proven to be lies created by British propaganda agents and newspapers.

- The British newspapers and the leading clergymen of the Church of England produced a barrage of anti-German propaganda and vile lies about Kaiser Wilhelm in order to promote enlistment in the British army.

CHAPTER 10

SOME DISTURBING TRUTHS

By early 1915 the conflict in the west had settled into the bloody stalemate of trench warfare. On the German army's retreat from the Marne in September, Erich von Falkenhayn had replaced the dejected and rejected von Moltke as Chief of Staff and ordered the troops to adopt defensive positions and 'dig in'. The British and French armies did likewise, and within months a network of opposing trenches wove its way in parallel lines for almost 500 miles from Belgium's North Sea coast down through France to the Swiss Alps. At some points the trenches were in such close proximity that on a still night with lulls in artillery fire, the men in the opposing lines could hear each other talking.

Straight ahead was the only way for either side, and many major battles – such the Somme and Verdun – would be fought in vain attempts to break through the lines. Billions of shells and bullets would be fired with each and every one racking up a tidy profit for the armaments manufacturers. All armies would incur astronomical losses, with additional millions badly wounded and maimed for life. In attempting to gain a few kilometres here and there, tens of thousands of men would be slaughtered every day, but the Western Front would remain virtually static for the next four years.

> Despite the millions of soldiers killed and wounded, nowhere along its entire length of nearly 500 miles had the front line moved in either direction by more than a few hours' walk. Military history had not seen the likes of this before ... [1]

Men lived in rat-infested trenches with their skin constantly irritated by blood-sucking lice, trench foot, infection, and mustard gas attacks choking and temporarily blinding them. The nauseating stench of death, and remnants of rotting flesh that was once their comrades, forever filled the air. One soldier wrote;

> Death lies about in all its forms. A limbless body here, the tunic fitting the swollen body like a glove. A body without a head like a rum

jar without a label. A form fast turning green, lying in a pool of grey-green gas vomit. Death in a thousand different masks. A youngster not much older than myself is bringing his insides up. Poor blighter. It's a pity. Heaven knows when our next rations will arrive.[2]

American historian Adam Hochschild writes that the social class divide between rich and poor in England continued amidst the carnage and horror in the British trenches.

In addition to the stink of decomposing bodies, which grew worse with the spring thaw, another smell came to be indelibly associated with the trenches: that of human waste. Many soldiers simply relieved themselves in the nearest shell hole. There were also pit latrines in small, specially built, dead-end trenches, but if a shell struck one, it blasted the contents in all directions, leaving the men covered with faeces. Behind the lines, some officers pursued foxes and hare with hunting dogs they had brought to France. "This afternoon we went off to the hunt," one officer wrote to the *Times*, "half a dozen couples of beagles and a good field went off after bunny at a fine pace, but, fortunately for bunny, there were plenty of wide ditches in this flat country, and she and all the rest got away Scot free."[3]

On the Eastern Front, the German army fared better, driving the Russian invaders back and inflicting massive losses. At the Battle of Tannenberg in late August 1914, the Russian Second Army was annihilated by the German Eighth Army under the command of Field Marshall Paul von Hindenburg. Over 90,000 Russian troops were taken prisoner, and more than 30,000 were killed or missing. With only 10,000 of his 150,000 men left, Russian commander Aleksander Samsonov ordered a retreat, headed into a forest, and shot himself. After such losses, the thought of facing the czar was too much for him. The Russian army also suffered heavy losses of around 250,000 men against Austro-Hungarian forces in the Battle of Galicia in late August-early September. The Austrians suffered some 400,000 losses. The scale of the suffering on all sides in this needless war was almost unimaginable.

The Eastern Front was much longer and more fluid than in the west, with trench warfare never fully developed. After four years of war in the East, Russian losses were staggering with almost 2.5 million men killed, 4 million badly wounded, and 3 million taken prisoner.

The Ottoman Empire entered the war on the side of Germany in October 1914. Italy, supposedly Germany's ally, joined Britain, France and Russia in May 1915. The United States initially stayed out of the war but supposedly neutral Americans were selling bonds and purchasing weapons, ammunition, and much more for Britain. Mind-boggling profits were to be made, and the Anglo-American financial circles ensured they were the ones who made it. In 1915 an Anglo-French delegation arrived in New York to negotiate a loan which was eventually settled at $500,000,000, an astronomical sum then. John Moody, American investor and expert financial analyst, wrote:

> From now on [following the loan agreement] all purchases of the British and French were paid for in this way. After this credit was exhausted, these Governments continued to borrow in Wall Street, usually pledging American securities. Not only did England and France pay for their supplies with money furnished by Wall Street, but they made their purchase through the same medium. The House of Morgan had always maintained close and confidential relations with the British government and the British public. The necessity of buying war materiel by the billions in the United States soon produced a state of chaos in London. Contract hunters and contract jobbers pounced upon the British War Office.... Unless some disaster was to result, it was evidently necessary to select some trustworthy agency in this country [U.S.] which could be depended upon to mobilize American industry, place the European orders in the right quarters, and attend to all the details. Inevitably the House of Morgan was selected for this important task. Thus the war had given Wall Street an entirely new role. Hitherto it had been exclusively the headquarters of finance; now it became the greatest industrial mart the world had ever known.... Wall Street began to deal in shells, cannon, submarines, blankets, clothing, shoes, canned meats, wheat, and the thousands of other articles needed for the prosecution of a great war.[4]

J.P. Morgan had been selected as Britain's sole purchasing agent for war supplies from the United States, and as exclusive financial agent for all British borrowing on Wall Street. From the very start, Morgan men assigned to the task were purchasing supplies at the rate of $10,000,000 a day. (Worth around $300 million per day in 2023.) They extended existing munitions factories and constructed hundreds of new plants. The entire production of the massive Bethlehem Steel Company in Pennsylvania – which was now controlled by Morgan's Steel Trust – was handed over to weapons production.[5] The anti-war Secretary of State, William Jennings Bryan, advised President Wilson not to allow the Rothschild-backed

Morgan and Co., to raise loans and credits for Britain, but pro-war Robert Lansing at the State Department insisted that an embargo on arms sales by private companies – as opposed to the US government – would be unconstitutional.[6] Effectively silenced, and sickened by the whole sordid affair, the principled William Jennings Bryan handed his resignation letter to President Wilson.

Geopolitical and economic analyst William Engdahl commented on the situation:

> The British Empire and Britain herself were virtually bankrupt at the outbreak of war in 1914. But British financial officials were confident of the backing of the United States and the Anglophile circles of New York banking ... Morgan, with its franchise as sole purchasing agent for the entire Entente group, became virtual arbiter over the future of the U.S. industrial and agricultural export economy. Morgan decided who would, or would not, be favored with very sizeable and highly profitable exports for the European war effort against Germany. ... The position of this private banking house was all the more remarkable since Woodrow Wilson's White House at this time was professing strict neutrality. But that neutrality became a thinly veiled fraud, as billions of dollars of vital war supplies and credits flowed to the British side over the next years. As purchasing agent alone, Morgan took a 2 per cent commission on the net price of all goods shipped. ... All of this activity was in strict violation of international law regarding a neutral, which forbade allowing belligerents to build supply bases in neutral countries. ... By 1917, the British War Office had placed purchase orders totalling more than $20,000,000,000 through the house of Morgan.[7]

None of this happened ad hoc. It had long been planned by the financial cartel allied to the Milner Group. As noted in an earlier chapter, the head of the Morgan empire, J.P. Morgan Jr. (Jack) spent six months each year in Britain and considered himself more English than American. Charles M. Schwab, Morgan's man in charge of Bethlehem Steel, had a direct cable communication with the Admiralty in London, with the messages coded and decoded by the chief Naval Censor. It was an arrangement that continued throughout the war.[8] Bethlehem Steel sent much of the ammunition and heavy and light weaponry it produced to Britain via Canada, but it also shipped significant quantities through New York to England on passenger liners which criss-crossed the north Atlantic. One such vessel was the *Lusitania*.

THE LUSITANIA DISASTER

On 7 May 1915, the British ocean liner, *RMS Lusitania*, en route from New York to Liverpool, was torpedoed and sunk by the German submarine, U-20, some 12 miles off the south coast of Ireland. 1,198 passengers and crew were lost, including 128 Americans. Their deaths greatly inflamed anti-German feelings in the U.S., and when the Bryce Report on supposed German atrocities in Belgium was added to the mix five days later, Germany's name was mud in America. The *Lusitania* sinking, like the 'Belgian atrocities.' had a significant impact on turning public opinion in the United States against Germany, and its eventual entry into the war.

The German government claimed the liner was a legitimate target because it operated under the orders of the Royal Navy and was carrying munitions to England through a declared war zone. In August 1914 Britain announced a naval blockade on food and military material reaching Germany, and in November declared the North Sea a war zone. Germany retaliated by applying a similar blockade on Britain, and declaring the seas around Britain a war zone. Ironically, having applied a much larger blockade on Germany, the British authorities questioned the legality of the German blockade. In their book, *Freedom of the Seas,* former Royal Navy commander and member of parliament Joseph Kenworthy, and co-author Sir George Young, write:

This first submarine campaign was logical and legal. Logical because if the British were entitled and enabled to starve German women and children the Germans had the right to do the same if they could to the British. Legal because the right of submarines to sink at sight under international law could be sustained without stretching any more points than had been strained by the British in making rubber and food contraband.[9]

Kenworthy considered the German blockade a legal, but a futile and foolish move. Futile because British ships had only to disguise themselves as neutral. Foolish because it would turn public opinion, especially in America, against Germany. British merchant ships not only attempted to disguise themselves as neutral, but on occasions flew the U.S. Stars and Stripes in order to trick U-boat commanders. When President Wilson's close adviser, Edward Mandell House, sailed to England in early 1915 on board the *Lusitania,* she raised the United States flag on nearing the British coast. Rules for naval blockades went back centuries and were internationally agreed in an attempt to preserve life at sea.

It was correct practice to halt an *unarmed* ship with a shot across the bows, search it and, if it was from a neutral country, let it go. If it was a merchant vessel belonging to an enemy, then the crew and passengers became hostages, and the cargo and ship were taken as prizes. In the event of a shortage of prize crews, or being too far from a friendly port, then the ship and cargo could be destroyed. These principles, known as the Cruiser Rules, had been accepted with minor modifications by all the maritime powers. They applied however to *unarmed* merchantmen. Churchill's action in arming British merchant ships immediately stripped them of their right to expect such treatment. In the lower echelons of the Admiralty it was realized that no submarine would ever dare undertake the dangerous practice of surfacing and ordering a heavily armed ship to halt and submit to search. Even if it did so successfully and its orders were obeyed, what was a submarine to do with the crew, passengers, and prize? The submarine... had no alternative but to give those on board the opportunity to take to the boats and then sink its prize.[10]

In the earliest stages of the war U-boats observed the Cruiser Rules. Ships were stopped and their crews ordered to take to the boats before their vessel was sunk. That all changed in early 1915, however, when British naval authorities under Winston Churchill developed the so-called

Q-ships. Cargo vessels – some upwards of 5,000 tons – they were taken over by the Royal Navy and manned by navy sailors and teams of armed Marines. 4.1 inch guns were fitted on the upper deck but cleverly concealed so that U-boat commanders were unaware of them. If a U-boat surfaced and stopped the ship for inspection, the Q-ship crew immediately removed the camouflage and opened fire with the heavy guns and machine guns. Numerous German submarines had been caught in the trap and destroyed. The Marines seldom took prisoners, with German sailors swimming towards the Q-ships for rescue being shot in the water. In addition to these camouflaged gunships, captains of British merchant ships were encouraged to take every opportunity to ram and sink U-boats if they surfaced. Britain had effectively abandoned the humanitarian Cruiser Rules and U-boat captains reciprocated. Rather than surfacing, giving crews the time to abandon their vessels, and running the risk of being fired on by camouflaged ships or rammed, they now began firing their torpedoes from periscope depth without warning.

Was there any truth in German claims that the *Lusitania* was carrying munitions from the United States to Britain when she was torpedoed on 7 May 1915? Is it conceivable that the British and American authorities would place civilians on oceangoing passenger liners in danger by using them as human shields to safeguard the transit of significant quantities of munitions through Germany's declared blockade?

In 1903, the British shipping line Cunard was struggling financially. Over the previous decades it had profited by carrying emigrants to the U.S. and Canada, but by the turn of the century Cunard was fast losing passengers on the north Atlantic routes to other shipping lines, including J.P. Morgan's White Star Line, and Germany's HAPAG (Hamburg-America) Line. Both had been constantly modernising their fleets, and in order to compete, Cunard desperately needed new superliners that were bigger, faster and more comfortable than those of White Star and Hamburg-America. The British government agreed to finance the construction of two new passenger ships with a 20-year loan at low interest. The *Lusitania* and her sister, *Mauretania*, would become the biggest and fastest passenger ships in the world and win back the coveted Blue Riband award for the fastest Atlantic crossing. *Lusitania* was built in John Brown's shipyard on the river Clyde near Glasgow. Her keel was laid in August 1904 and at the time of her launch on 6 June 1906, she was the biggest ship ever built at 785 feet in length and with a displacement of 41,440 tons. She had nine decks – including the hold – and could carry 3,100 passengers and crew. Driven by six state-of-the-art Parsons turbine engines, *Lusitania* could achieve a top speed of 25 knots (28.7 mph or 46 km/h.)

The British government's financing of the ships came with strings attached.

> The subsidy allowed the government to participate in the design of the ships, which included a secret compartment where weapons and ammunition could be stored aboard the ship. This subsidy further allowed the British government to take full control of the ships during wartime.[11]

Deck mountings for guns were fitted so that *Lusitania* and *Mauretania* could be readily converted to armed merchant cruisers. At the advent of war, *Lusitania* was requisitioned by the British Admiralty, and listed as an auxiliary naval cruiser in *Jane's Fighting Ships* – the internationally recognised reference book of all the world's warships that was published annually. She was likewise listed as an armed merchant cruiser in Brassey's *Naval Annual* of 1914, and the British *Naval Pocket Book*.[12] The German authorities, of course, had access to these publications and were fully aware of the status of *Lusitania* as an armed merchant cruiser.

On 3 October 1914, the chairman of Cunard, Alfred Booth, met senior naval officials in London to discuss the Admiralty use of the *Lusitania*. Passenger numbers were down due to the war, and the ships were losing money. Cunard wanted to lay them up until the war was over, but Sir William Greene, Permanent Secretary to the Admiralty, and one of the founders of Naval Intelligence, insisted *Lusitania* must continue her transatlantic voyages. The government would continue the maintenance subsidy, pay for cargo space, and cover the ship's insurance. Booth wrote thereafter to his cousin: "In essence, Sir William ordered me to be a high grade contrabandist in the National Interest."[13] Eugene Windchy, U.S. Information Agency Science Adviser, wrote:

> In American Law it was not legal to carry passengers and explosives on the same ship, but during the war British liners routinely carried both together. They hid the munitions and filed false manifests. It was all done with the connivance of two American officials. They were Lansing at the State Department and Dudley F. Malone, the collector of customs in New York City. Also involved was a Boston blue blood, Charles P. Sumner, who was Cunard's manager in New York. When Sumner learned of this illegal activity, he was shocked and refused to allow munitions aboard *Lusitania*... Cunard doubled Sumner's salary, and he offered no more protests. A British

naval attaché was moved to Cunard's New York office to keep an eye on things.[14]

When torpedoed by U-20 on 7 May 1915, there is no doubt whatsoever that *Lusitania* was an auxiliary cruiser of the Royal Navy, but was there any truth in the German allegations that she was carrying significant quantities of munitions? The British and U.S. governments admitted that she had over 4,000 cases of .303 cartridges on board, but no explosives. In 1999, an English researcher, Mitch Peeke, approached various records offices in Britain and America in an attempt to uncover official documents that might clarify the situation. Peeke writes:

> The Public Records Office [London] have a huge collection of files, all of which one assumes would be diligently filed and cross-referenced. Ha! Semi-organised chaos is a better description of what I found there, particularly with such a controversial subject as munitions being shipped aboard the transatlantic passenger liners ... I gained little of any real value Then it struck me. If you want to hide a stolen Christmas tree, what better place to hide it than in a forest of Christmas trees![15]

Having exhausted all official British records offices, Peeke turned to the U.S.:

> I found America a far more accessible place! Nobody pulled the shutters down. In fact, they went the extra mile for me. Having gone through U.S. Customs Archives, The Museum of the City of New York, The Library of Congress, and the *New York Times* Archives, I was finally rewarded with a suggestion that I try the personal archive of President Franklin D. Roosevelt. When I asked why, I was told that FDR was a man who'd actually wanted to know what skeletons were in the U.S. closet. In 1940, he'd demanded the full copy of the *Lusitania*'s manifest. He got it. Having read it, he kept it under lock and key. Having spoken to the staff at the FDR Archives and explained my quest for this particular Holy Grail, I was permitted to pay for the manifest to be digitally photographed page by page, plus the memo to FDR from the then Collector of Customs in New York. After a little more negotiation, I was given the necessary permission to make my copy public via our website. All this, whilst still holding down a full-time job, changing my career mid-term and being a father.[16]

The supplementary *Lusitania* manifest for the fateful voyage discovered by Mitch Peeke in the FDR files indicates that the *Lusitania* had indeed been carrying far greater quantities of munitions than had been admitted. To be exact: three million .303 rifle bullets, 5,000 three-inch shrapnel shells in 1,250 crates. And 18 cases of fuses. Peeke believes the U-20's torpedo ignited some 120 tons of munitions, causing the ship to sink within 18 minutes.

It has to be asked why a doggedly determined 'amateur' investigator who worked full-time as a driving instructor was able to uncover such important historical documents when professional, full-time, well-paid, academic historians were apparently unable to do so. Thanks to his research there is now no doubt that *Lusitania was* carrying munitions in significant amounts and that her passengers were effectively being used as human shields.

Adding further intrigue to the *Lusitania* saga, Richard B. Spence, Professor of History at the University of Idaho, found evidence that a British secret intelligence agent, Aleister Crowley, operating in New York in early 1915 was linked to the *Lusitania* sinking.

British Naval Intelligence in London had sent Crowley to New York in late 1914. Coincidentally, he had sailed there on the *Lusitania*. Born in Warwickshire, England, Crowley had gained a coveted place at Cambridge University to study philosophy thanks to the patronage of his mother's friend, Robert Gascoyne Cecil, the Marquess of Salisbury.[17] Cecil, as we have seen, was British Prime Minister on three occasions between 1885 and 1902 and head of the 'Cecil Bloc' that was allied to the Rhodes-Milner secret society.[18] The date and means by which Crowley – an occult-

Crowley

ist and practitioner of black magic – was inducted into British Intelligence is unknown. What *is* known is that he was sent to the U.S. in 1914 posing as an Irish nationalist who hated England. A British academic and expert on Crowley, Tobias Churton, writes:

> Crowley arrived in America in 1914, according to the *Lusitania* passenger manifest, as "Irish" from England. After an initial uneasy period he allowed himself to be identified as one in favour of revolution for a free Ireland against British rule and a sympathiser with Germany's cause.[19]

Crowley worked closely in New York with Wall Street banker Otto Kahn of the Kuhn, Loeb & Co Bank. (See Chapter 3) Kahn, who was

281

close to both British Intelligence and J.P. Morgan Jr., was whole-heartedly pro-British, and his name crops up regularly in Crowley's wartime and postwar writings as a friend.[20] Crowley joined a team of agents in New York working for the closely collaborating U.S and British intelligence services. Among them was Belle da Costa Greene, J.P. Morgan's ravishing librarian and alleged lover, and Ernst 'Putzi' Hanfstaengl, a Harvard graduate who features prominently in later chapters of this book alongside Adolf Hitler. British intelligence operating in New York was headed at the time by the British Naval Attaché, Captain Guy Gaunt. He was directly answerable to Naval Intelligence in the old Admiralty building in London, wherein the top secret 'Room 40' is of special interest to us in the *Lusitania* story.

Created on the outbreak of war in 1914 by Rear-Admiral H. F. Oliver and other naval officers, including Captain Reginald 'Blinker' Hall, Room 40 was the code-breaking section of Naval Intelligence that intercepted and deciphered secret German naval codes. In the first weeks of the war Britain had dredged up and cut Germany's subsea telegraph cables which ran from Emden in Germany down the English Channel to Spain, Africa and the Americas. Unable to communicate with these countries by cablegram, German had to rely on postal mail or wireless telegraphy.

The German navy communicated using three principal secret wireless codes and ciphers but, unknown to them, within months of the war starting Room 40 was in possession of all three of them. British naval intelligence was thus able to decode the German Navy's wireless messages from radio transmitter stations to all warships and U-boats on the high seas. Indeed, Room 40 was frequently decoding German Admiralty messages before the recipients in German surface ships or U-boats had managed to do so.

> Political and military instructions and information had to be sent by wireless and Britannia ruled the wireless waves. Their interception proved of the utmost importance when Germany proceeded to use the upper air much as she used the under waters for ruthless warfare.... German wireless messages to the official and unofficial agents abroad were soon being read in Whitehall more quickly and correctly than in the Wilhelmstrasse. More than once the scratch staff of British amateurs followed with amusement the wireless wranglings of the German cypher experts trying to disentangle the knots in which some urgent message had got tied by their complicated devices – knots which the English had at once cut by the technical methods and machines they had invented à l'improviste.[21]

Through close monitoring and de-coding of the German wireless messages, Room 40 could tell with considerable accuracy where U-boats were operating in the seas around Britain, as large liners such as *Lusitania* were entering those seas from the Atlantic. At the time of the *Lusitania* sinking in May 1915, Room 40 and Captain 'Blinker' Hall operated under the overall command of Admiral Jacky Fisher (First Sea Lord), and the political head of the navy, Winston Churchill (First Lord of the Admiralty). Aleister Crowley was but one of their many secret agents.

Posing as an anti-English Irish Republican, Crowley successfully infiltrated a German intelligence and propaganda cell operating in New York that was dedicated to countering British propaganda and keeping America out of the war. Well aware that *Lusitania* was circumventing the U-boat blockade by carrying American munitions on every return voyage to Liverpool, Crowley's task was not to try and conceal that fact from the German intelligence unit in New York, but to reveal it. Professor Spence asks how likely it is that British Naval Intelligence was instigating the destruction of the *Lusitania* with the aim of outraging Americans and bringing the U.S. into the war:

> The charge is not as outlandish as it may first sound. Whether or not the *Lusitania* was specifically targeted as the sacrificial victim, elements in the Admiralty's intelligence section were endeavoring to provoke the Germans into inflammatory actions, and they had placed agents in enemy camps for just that purpose. One such operative who had insinuated himself into the confidence of German agents and diplomats in the United States, was Aleister Crowley. He later claimed not only to have helped convince his German friends that the *Lusitania* was a man-of-war, but also to have encouraged them to disdain and provoke the Americans.[22]

Crowley passed himself off so successfully he was able to associate not only with German intelligence agents but with men at the top of the German diplomatic service in America.

> He rubbed elbows with the German ambassador to the U.S., Count Johann von Bernstorff; Military Attaché, Franz von Papen, (who would later become Vice-Chancellor of Germany under Hitler); and Karl Boy-Ed, German Naval Attaché and secret intelligence agent.[23]

In other words, British intelligence had infiltrated the leading German diplomatic and secret service agencies in the United States of America. Professor Spence adds:

Thus he [Crowley] became more than a mere propagandist. Lange-laan [British writer] recounts that the Germans came to place great faith in his "intuition" and saw him as an indispensable guide to the mentality of the Americans and the British. He especially impressed them with his ability to predict the actions and reactions of the British. It was almost as though he could see into the inner sanctums of Whitehall. The possibility that he was a British double agent plying them with disinformation apparently eluded them.[24]

While conducting research for his Crowley biography (published 2008) Professor Spence – like Mitch Peeke in his searches for the *Lusitania*'s manifest – discovered that many files had been weeded leaving "a meagre or misleading residue of the unredacted version." Spence knew that British Intelligence had extensive files on Crowley, yet was unable to find a single file in the official British records. He noted: "An imaginative person might suspect a concerted effort to erase Aleister Crowley from the official record."[25]

In his book, *Aleister Crowley in America*, Tobias Churton expands on Professor Spence's accounts of the astonishing influence the British agent was able to exert on the German leaders in the U.S. We must bear in mind that Crowley studied psychology at Cambridge, which was/is recognised as one of the world's leading universities:

> Crowley ... claimed to have subjected German propagandists to his "reading of American psychology," which indicated that *Americans would be cowed by ruthless strength determinedly and pitilessly expressed*. The Germans apparently respected Crowley's intellect where the mind's inner workings were concerned. He had a way with crisp rationalizations that appeared logical and superior, and which gave his advice trajectory and accuracy ... Crowley claimed that he got his point about "American psychology" over to von Bernstorff [ambassador], Munsterberg [leading German-American psychologist], von Papen. [Military attaché], Boy-Ed [Naval attaché], and other parties to the point of influencing a recommendation to Berlin concerning the validity of an act or acts of unequivocal force to shake Wilson into strict neutrality with public quiescence.[26]

The act of "unequivocal force" encouraged by Crowley was to be a U-Boat torpedoing the *Lusitania*. The German embassy in the U.S. believed it would 'cover' itself by adequately warning passengers not to sail on her. On the day *Lusitania* was scheduled to depart New York, 1 May

1915, some fifty American morning newspapers published an advertisement prepared and paid for by the Imperial German Embassy in Washington. It warned Americans of the risk of crossing the Atlantic on British ships:

> NOTICE. Travellers intending to embark on Atlantic voyages are reminded that a state of war exists between Germany and her Allies and Great Britain and her Allies; that the zone of war includes the waters adjacent to the British Isles; that in accordance with formal notice given by the Imperial German Government vessels flying the flag of Great Britain or of any of her Allies are liable to destruction in those waters; and that travellers sailing in the war zone in ships of Great Britain or her Allies do so at their own risk. [27]

That same morning the *Washington Times* carried a front-page article with the headline: "*Lusitania* Passengers Warned of Ship's Doom." It reported that warnings had been issued that the ship would be sunk on her trip to Liverpool. The newspaper added that Cunard officials in New York laughed at passengers' fears, saying "*Lusitania* could show her heels to any submarine." The article concluded: "Extreme precautions were taken by Cunard officials in the inspection of baggage."[28]

The Cunard officials may well have been cautiously inspecting passengers baggage as they boarded the ship, but apparently missed the 1,250 crates of three-inch shells and 18 cases of fuses that had been loaded into the hold in the full knowledge of the U.S, Collector of Customs, Dudley Malone. A lawyer and a friend of Woodrow Wilson's, Malone had helped organise Wilson's campaign in the rigged presidential election of 1912. Wilson rewarded Malone by appointing him Assistant Secretary of State, and to the post of Collector of the Port of New York. This well-paid position was considered the 'prize plum' of Federal patronage. Malone was thus closely linked to the American side of the Anglo-American power structure and, like his boss Woodrow Wilson, was therefore at least complicit in sending munitions to Britain on passenger ships. Mitch Peeke writes:

> In order to get the vital munitions aboard the chosen passenger ships, it became standard practice to file a false manifest with the US Collector of Customs in New York, D.F. Malone, who knew exactly what was taking place, but who had been instructed to turn a blind eye. Malone would issue the sailing clearance certificate on the basis of a loading manifest showing only a general cargo. De-

spite his declaration of strict neutrality, President Woodrow Wilson clearly knew what was taking place, as did his new secretary of State, Robert Lansing.[29]

In yet another twist to the tale, around the very time *Lusitania* was being nudged by tugs from Cunard Pier 54 out into the Hudson, the U.S. ambassador to Britain, Walter Hines Page, wrote to his son, Arthur, forecasting the blowing up of a liner with American passengers. That same day Page wrote: "If a British liner full of American passengers be blown up, what will Uncle Sam do? *That's what's going to happen*."[30] Page, as we have seen, was very close to the Milner Group and a member of the Pilgrims society.

On a visit to London that same week, Edward Mandell House – President Wilson's eminence grise – was asked exactly that same question by Foreign Secretary Sir Edward Grey.[31]

As he carefully steered *Lusitania* down the Hudson past the Statue of Liberty that Saturday afternoon, 58-year-old Captain William Turner was well aware of the press speculation about the risk to his ship. He would later confide that he had expected the sailing to be either delayed or cancelled. A quiet, reserved man, Turner had no formal education, having gone to sea as a boy. He had worked his way to the top, was vastly experienced, and considered a fine master mariner. He had captained *Lusitania* and other big ships on this route many times. Earlier in 1915, he was in command of the liner *Transylvania* bound for Liverpool when he received an Admiralty order to divert to Queenstown (close to Cork in southern Ireland) because three British ships had been sunk by German submarines in the area the previous day.[32]

Turner's command of the *Transylvania* on that particular New-York Liverpool run is worth considering. A large passenger liner, it was diverted into Queenstown because of a U-boat threat off southern Ireland. Another British vessel, *SS Ausonia* had likewise been diverted. Eugene Windchy writes:

> ... Two Cunard passenger steamers "having valuable cargo" had been ordered to the Irish port of Queenstown, (now Cobh) to be kept safe from submarine attack, Admiral Oliver wrote on the wireless page, 'Deflected into Queenstown on account of 2 seventy-ton guns on board for R.N. [Royal Navy]' The huge 14-inch diameter gun barrels, made by Bethlehem Steel, were not mentioned on the ship's manifests, but passengers saw them lying on the open decks. Four American passengers complained to the State Department

about being held incommunicado at Queenstown for two days and also about the presence of the gun barrels. One would think that the observation of seventy-ton gun barrels ought to have settled any question of whether British passenger ships carried munitions. It did not. Robert Lansing received the complaint and initialled it, but he evidently did not pass it on to Secretary Bryan or the neutrality officials in New York. Possibly Lansing did his duty by informing the President since the two shared the secret effort to help Great Britain as much as possible. Note that the liners had to be protected because of their 'Valuable cargo.' not because innocent passengers were on board.[33]

The *Lusitania's* usual passage was to the south of Ireland before entering the St George's Channel between Ireland and Wales, then heading into Liverpool on a high tide. On this fateful voyage, despite Room 40 knowing for certain that a U-boat was sinking ships directly on the course *Lusitania* would take along the south coast of Ireland, the Admiralty in London did not divert Captain Turner on this occasion. They could readily have warned him in plenty of time to steer a course via the *north* of Ireland into Liverpool since they were aware that no U-boats were operating there at the time.

Lusitania had an official top speed of 25 knots or 29 miles per hour, and at full power could complete the Atlantic crossing in five days. To conserve coal and reduce costs, however, Cunard had ordered six of her twenty-four boilers to be shut down. Maximum speed was consequently reduced by 4 knots. Her funnels had been painted black, and her name and port of registry painted out in accordance with Admiralty instructions. She flew no flags on this trip, British or American. The weather was fine and the sea smooth as she covered 3,000 nautical miles of the Atlantic ocean at a steady 21 knots.

> After the tension and uncertainty that accompanied the *Lusitania's* New York departure, the normal shipboard routine quickly re-established itself. Deck games were played, people could be seen taking the air as they strolled around the promenade areas, and mealtimes were eagerly anticipated. The war seemed to be a million miles away to the *Lusitania's* passengers.[34]

Late on the Tuesday afternoon (4 May) the Admiralty transmitter at Valentia in Ireland sent a general all-ships warning: 'Submarines Active Off South Coast of Ireland'.

On 6 May, as *Lusitania* was approaching southern Ireland, Captain Turner took all necessary precautions. He ordered bulk-head doors and portholes shut, and lifeboats swung out on their davits. Blinds on all portholes were to be drawn during the hours of darkness. All bright lights were to be switched off, and passengers were advised not to smoke or show any lights on the promenade deck. Lookouts were doubled, including two men sent to the crow's nest. At 00.05 on 7 May 7 another Admiralty message was sent.

> To All British Ships 0005: Take Liverpool Pilot at Bar [the sand bar at Liverpool Bay] and Avoid Headlands. Pass Harbours at Full Speed, Steer Mid-Channel course. Submarines off Fastnet.[35]

Fastnet was an uninhabited rock some 4 miles off the south-west tip of Ireland. In peacetime its lighthouse guided ships in from the Atlantic but in these dangerous days of submarine attacks, transatlantic ships generally stayed well off Fastnet as they headed on either to Southampton on the south coast of England or through St George's Channel to Liverpool on the west coast.

Other messages passed between the Admiralty and *Lusitania* between 5 May and 7 May, but no record of them survives. A former British Naval Intelligence officer, Patrick Beesly, writes:

> Nothing, *absolutely nothing*, was done to ensure the liner's safe arrival. The mysterious signals that passed between the Admiralty and the *Lusitania* between 5 and 7 May may well hold the answer. The file seems to have been in the possession of the Admiralty as recently as 1972. *Now it has vanished again.* ...I am reluctantly driven to the conclusion that there *was* a conspiracy deliberately to put the *Lusitania* at risk in the hope that even an abortive attack on her would bring the United States into the war. Such a conspiracy could not have been put into effect without Winston Churchill's express permission and approval.[36]

Once again, we learn that British documents relating to important events in the war simply 'vanished.' Beesly states that while there was still time for *Lusitania* to change course for Liverpool by the northern route around Ireland, Captain Turner telegraphed the Admiralty and actually asked for permission to divert to that route which was currently free of U-Boats, but was refused.[37] Beesly adds:

> By far the most difficult question to answer is just why no effective steps were taken to protect the *Lusitania*. Why, in stark contrast

to the information sent to the naval authorities on previous occasions when U-boats were operating in the Irish Sea ... was nothing passed to Queenstown and Liverpool? Why was this ship with its cargo vital to the war effort and the hundreds of human beings on board, not diverted? Why were no destroyers sent to Queenstown or even to the St George's Channel? ... Can one really accept a foul-up as the complete explanation?

But if it was no foul-up, then it must have been a conspiracy, and a great deal that is otherwise inexplicable would fall into place.... One still has to answer the question *why* precautions to ensure *Lusitania's* safety, which had been taken on previous occasions and which could and should have been taken on her last voyage, were conspicuous by their absence. As Schwieger [captain of U-20 which sank the *Lusitania*] wrote in his log:

"It is remarkable that today [7 May] there should have been so much traffic despite the fact that two large steamers were sunk south of the St George's Channel yesterday. It is also inexplicable that the *Lusitania* was not routed via the North Channel."[38]

Even the master of the German submarine found it incomprehensible that the *Lusitania* had not been re-routed north of Ireland when he was sinking numerous ships to the south directly in her path.

Schwieger's U-20 was built at Danzig and launched in 1912. It had a complement of 4 officers and 31 men, weighed 650 tons, had a 10.5 cm deck gun and carried 6 torpedoes. The submarine had a top surface speed of 15.4 knots, and 9.5 knots when submerged. Room 40 knew for certain that U-20 was active off southern Ireland at the Old Head of Kinsale on 5 May – the very place it would torpedo *Lusitania* 48 hours later. Schwieger stopped a three masted wooden ship, the *Earl of Lathom*, carrying a cargo of potatoes and bacon from Limerick to Liverpool. When it was clear to him that the old vessel had no armaments and was incapable of ramming, he surfaced and ordered the *Lathom's* crew to take to the boats. He then had his men sink her by lobbing hand grenades onto her deck. The *Lathom's* crew rowed ashore and reported immediately to the Naval authorities.

Later that day Schwieger encountered a much larger British ship, the *Cayo Romano*, further east off Queenstown. He pursued her and fired a torpedo but missed. The *Cayo* reached Queenstown safely, reported the incident, and the information was immediately passed to the Admiralty in London.

Schwieger then took U-20 east into St George's Channel. On 6 May he fired a torpedo into the 5,800 ton British steamer, *SS Candidate*. It failed to sink the vessel, however, and Schwieger allowed her crew to escape. A U-20 boarding party discovered the *Candidate* had concealed deck guns, and Schwieger fired shells from his own deck gun into her waterline until she went down. Later that same day, he intercepted *SS Centurion*, sister ship to the *Candidate*. It was 5,495 registered tons with a crew of 44. She too was armed and Schwieger took no chances. His torpedo hit the *Centurion* under the foremast and as she began to sink the crew abandoned ship. An hour later when she was still afloat, Schwieger surfaced and finished her off with his deck gun. Again, the ship's crew immediately informed the Admiralty.

That same day U-20 pursued the White Star liner, *Arabic*, out of Liverpool. With a registered capacity of 1,400 passengers, it was lucky to escape and continue the outward-bound journey to America. (*Arabic's* luck would run out 3 months later when she was sunk by a U-boat off Kinsale.) U-20 had three torpedoes left and, like all U-boats, was under strict orders to keep two for the homeward journey lest they come across a major British warship.

By the early hours of the morning, 7 May, as *Lusitania* approached the Irish coast, the Admiralty was fully aware of three British ships being sunk, and two having very close escapes.[39] They knew the location of U-20 thanks to verbal reports from rescued crews, reports of visual sightings, and through intercepted wireless messages. U-20 was wreaking havoc and devastation in the waters *Lusitania* was about to sail through.

A huge map in the Admiralty was updated round the clock with different brightly colour coded pins and markers – each representing a ship or submarine. Staff could tell at a glance the area in which U-Boats were operating, and their proximity to Allied ships.

> Ever since she'd left her base, U-20's messages were being intercepted and deciphered immediately by the Room 40 intelligence team. In fact, U-20 had her own ledger at Room 40. That ledger is now in the National Archives at Kew, London ... Page 4 of U-20's ledger from those files clearly shows that the British Admiralty had intercepted and decoded EVERY message and sinking report from U-20, right up to the sinking of the *Lusitania*. Page 5 follows U-20's voyage home afterwards via her intercepted messages. It clearly proves that those in charge of the Admiralty were fully informed of U-20's activities throughout her patrol.[40]

On the morning of 7 May, as *Lusitania* closed on the Irish coast 25 miles south of Fastnet, a thick fog rolled in. Captain Turner reduced speed to 15 knots as he guided her east towards St George's channel for Liverpool. No naval escort was sent to protect the *Lusitania*, despite the fact that naval vessels were available to do so. Further along the coast at Milford Haven, a flotilla of four destroyers and two Q ships were tied up in harbour. Their duty was to counter U-boats and escort and safeguard valuable cargo. *HMS Legion, Lucifer, Linnet* and *Laverock* were all modern warships having been launched within the past two years. They were capable of 29 knots (33 mph) and would have been at *Lusitania's* side had they been despatched the previous evening to rendezvous with her before she passed Fastnet.

The Admiralty, under whose orders *Lusitania* sailed, had at least three options for protecting her: The safest was a diversion to the north. While *Lusitania* was still 200 miles out in the Atlantic in the early hours of 7 May, (when the Admiralty was telegraphing all ships warnings of U-boats off Fastnet), Turner could have been ordered to divert and take *Lusitania* into Liverpool via the northern channel. Going round the north of Ireland was a well-used route for ships approaching Liverpool from the Atlantic. It had recently been declared free from mines, and Room 40 knew that no U-Boats were currently operating there. Did the telegraphic messages between *Lusitania* and the Admiralty up to 7 May 'vanish' because they clearly demonstrated that the Admiralty had refused Captain Turner's request for permission to divert to the north? It is impossible to understand why the Admiralty refused if it had truly wanted to protect her.

The second option for the Admiralty was to have sent two or more of the fast destroyers sitting idle at Milford Haven to protect her.

> Hitherto, escorts had been rushed from Milford Haven to Fastnet to protect cargoes of mules and the diversion of the *Transylvania* and *Ausonia* to Queenstown at the first hint of the presence of a U-boat … whenever a threat materialized in these waters.[41]

Cargo vessels with mules and passenger ships were given the destroyer escort, but not *Lusitania* with almost 2,000 passengers and crew despite all the publicity and threats that she would be sunk. It is unlikely indeed that the cautious Schwieger would have run the risk of going anywhere near the *Lusitania* and being rammed by the fast destroyers. U-boats in those early days of the war were slower to submerge than later versions, and a number had indeed been rammed and sunk with the loss of their entire crews.

The third Admiralty option, with or without destroyer protection, was to order *Lusitania* into Queenstown harbour as per the *Transylvania* and *Ausonia* weeks earlier. The Admiralty in London failed to issue that order, but some researchers state categorically that Vice-Admiral Coke – who was in charge of the Royal Navy station at Queenstown – was becoming so concerned at London's lack of action that he took it upon himself to send a telegraph to *Lusitaniu* ordering her to divert into the safety of Queenstown.

On 7 May, around 11 A.M. as *Lusitania* broke through fog into hazy sunshine, Captain Turner increased speed to 18 knots. He had his bearings set on the northern side of St George's channel some 120 miles ahead. He had kept well clear of land as ordered, and the Irish coast was but a smudge on his port side. A messenger from the Marconi room brought Turner a telegraph sent from Vice-Admiral Coke at Queenstown via the Valentia wireless station at 11.02 A.M. That message has been the subject of considerable controversy ever since. Admiral Coke had been forbidden to initiate any instructions to ships not under his command without permission from the Admiralty in London. Additionally, he was not allowed to send any specific information to ships by radio. Researcher Colin Simpson suggests that the *Lusitania's* situation appeared so grave to Coke that he felt he had to do something about it. Simpson adds:

> Perhaps Coke asked the Admiralty for permission to divert the *Lusitania* into Queenstown. Any positive explanation is impossible and conjecture is the only answer, as the pages of both the Admiralty signal register and Coke's signal log are 'missing' (for the only period during the entire duration of the war) – according to the head of the Admiralty Archives. The Admiralty however categorically denies and has done so before four courts of law – and over fifty-seven years – that any message, coded or otherwise was sent to *Lusitania* at 11:02 A.M. on the morning of 7 May. Fortunately a certified copy of the transmission log of the naval station at Valentia (on the Irish west coast) has survived and this clearly shows that the *Lusitania* received a twelve-word message in naval code addressed to MFA [*Lusitania's* call sign] at 11:02 G.M.T. [Greenwich Mean Time] which was promptly acknowledged by the *Lusitania* with the code word of the day 'Westrona'. The message was taken to Captain Turner who took some time to decode it, as it was the first he had ever received in that code. To the end of his life he was adamant that it instructed him to divert into Queenstown ...[42]

Mitch Peeke writes:

> He [Coke] had tried all morning to obtain a firm decision from the
> Admiralty in London. In the end he had been so worried that he
> had taken it upon himself to divert the *Lusitania* into Queenstown.
> Turner immediately altered the ship's course 20 degrees to port.
> The turn to port was so sudden that many passengers momentar-
> ily lost their balance. The *Lusitania* was now closing to the land at
> 18 knots on a course North 67 East. The clock on the bridge said
> 12.15 GMT.[43]

Mitch Peeke times the sudden turn to port at 12:15 P.M. Another
book, *The Lusitania Disaster*, by Thomas A. Bailey (Stanford) and Captain
Paul Ryan (U.S. Navy) has a map showing *Lusitania* some 20 miles off the
coast and heading towards the St George's Channel. The map indicates
the sudden turn to port at 12:40 with *Lusitania* now heading for land directly towards Queenstown.

Captain Schwieger surfaced at 12:45. With the fog having cleared, vis-
ibility was now good. At 13:20 he spotted the four tall funnels of *Lusitania* about 13 miles distant to the west. The klaxon squawked, U-20 submerged, and ran at her top submerged speed of 9 knots on a course that
converged with *Lusitania* some 12 miles south of the Old Head of Kinsale.

A torpedo was loaded into a forward tube and at 14.10 Schwieger fired it
at a distance of some 550 metres with a 3-metre depth setting. Through his
periscope, around 60 seconds later he watched as the torpedo hit *Lusitania*'s starboard side. A waterspout rose just below the bridge and forward
of the front funnel. He fired only one torpedo but its strike was, according
to Schwieger, followed by a second larger explosion. He noted in his log:

> An unusually heavy detonation takes place with a very strong ex-
> plosion cloud (far beyond the front funnel). The explosion of the
> torpedo must have been followed by a second one (boiler or coal
> or powder?). The superstructure above the point of impact and the
> bridge are torn asunder…[44]

A lookout on the *Lusitania* had spotted the stream of bubbles from the
torpedo heading straight towards them and shouted a warning, but Turner had no time to take evasive action. He was standing at his usual spot
on the port side of the bridge when the torpedo struck, and was running
across the bridge when the massive second explosion rocked the entire
ship and she immediately began listing to starboard.

Turner looked at the Pearson's Fire and Flood indicator board. It was going absolutely mad, showing fire and extensive flooding in the whole of the forward section ahead of boiler room No 1. The tall column of water and debris now cascaded down and wrecked one of the forward starboard lifeboats. A glance at the commutator revealed that *Lusitania* was already listing five degrees to starboard and was also down by the head.... Watching through his periscope, Schwieger could not believe that so much havoc could have been wrought by just one torpedo.[45]

The *Lusitania* was doomed. The torpedo had struck the bow end of the ship forward of the front funnel where the munitions were stored. The secondary internal explosion blew out a huge section of her hull and the sea rapidly poured in.

All the evidence supports the view that this explosion was among the munitions on the orlop deck.[46]

At 14.11 hours the Marconi room began sending repeat SOS signals. 'COME AT ONCE. BIG LIST, 10 MILES SOUTH OLD KINSALE.

Lusitania was still underway as the bow went down, and she ploughed ever deeper under the water. Turner rang the engine room to order 'full astern'. He had to slow the ships momentum to get the lifeboats launched safely, but as *Lusitania* listed further over to starboard and went down at the bow, lowering the boats became extremely hazardous. Some were successfully let down into the sea while others snagged, toppling the occupants into the cold water. Only six lifeboats out of forty-eight were afloat, and carrying survivors. Within 18 minutes the *Lusitania* had disappeared below the waves. 1,201 of the 1,962 passengers and crew were lost, including 94 children. A married couple, the Cromptons, and all six of their young children drowned. Of 159 Americans on board, 128 perished. Three German stowaways locked in the cell also drowned. Captain Turner stayed on the bridge prepared to go down with his ship, but was swept off as she went under. Like hundreds of others, he treaded water until rescue vessels arrived from Queenstown some two hours later.

On receiving the *Lusitania's* SOS, the shocked Admiral Coke at Queenstown immediately ordered a multitude of small vessels to go to the rescue. He instructed the cruiser HMS *Juno* to make full speed to the scene, then signalled the Admiralty in London with the news. Admiral Fisher ordered Coke to order *Juno* to return immediately to harbour because he 'did not want her to suffer the same fate'. With the fast *Juno* withdrawn from the rescue mission, it would be two hours and more before much smaller vessels arrived. Some survivors were being taken to nearby Kinsale, but the Admiralty intervened and ordered them taken instead to Queenstown. 761 people survived. Almost 300 bodies were recovered from the sea and buried in local cemeteries. The remains of 885 victims were never found.

Schwieger on U-20 observed the carnage for some minutes before lowering his periscope and setting a course for home with two torpedoes remaining. He headed out past Fastnet and up the west coast of Ireland then Scotland.

Patrick Beesly writes:

> Room 40's post-war verdict was that, 'There has never been any direct evidence to prove that submarine officers were ordered to sink the *Lusitania*, but from prisoners' statements it is clear that in German naval circles a view prevailed that Schwieger had definitely been ordered to lie in wait with a view to torpedoing her... The repeated broadcasts from Norddeich [the Radio station in north Germany that transmitted messages to U-boats] concerning her scheduled arrivals and departures from Liverpool show quite definitely that she, in common with other large liners also mentioned in the broadcasts, was considered by the Admiralstab as a prime and legitimate target for U-Boats from the moment that unrestricted warfare was announced.[47]

With Norddeich transmitting details about *Lusitania's* scheduled arrival to U-20 and other submarines, Room 40 in the Admiralty would have known instantly through their interception and decoding that the big liner was a target. That alone makes the fact that they did nothing whatsoever to protect her all the more disturbing. The Admiralty's cover-up operation began almost immediately. They had taken no measures at all to protect *Lusitania* when a much safer route was available, and escort destroyers were sitting idle at Milford Haven. The ship had gone down in a very short space of time due to the explosion of munitions which the Admiralty's Trade Division had loaded aboard her in New York. There would be an official inquiry, but it would have to be very carefully managed to ensure the truth would never see the light of day. A problem with the cover-up arose almost immediately. Five bodies and numerous survivors had been taken to Kinsale before the Admiralty stepped in to insist that all must be taken to Queenstown. In accordance with law, the Kinsale coroner, John Horgan, insisted upon an inquest. A known Irish republican sympathiser and no lover of England, Horgan was likely to start asking a lot of awkward questions, as survivors were talking about a second massive explosion on the ship. Horgan hurriedly set a date for his inquest the day after the sinking with a jury comprising 12 local traders and fishermen. Captain Turner told them of the second, internal explosion immediately following that of the torpedo, and how it tore the hull to pieces on the starboard side beneath the bridge and well forward of the funnels. Turner said he *had* received instructions from the Admiralty, but refused to disclose what they were. An honourable man, he felt bound by Admiralty oath to secrecy and was thus unable to discuss crucial telegraphs to and from his ship. That, of course, included Admiral Coke's 11.02 A.M. telegraph ordering him to divert immediately to Queenstown. Turner broke down in tears and Coroner Horgan excused him from further testimony.

On behalf of the Admiralty, leading barrister, F. E. Smith, (Oxford graduate) contacted the Crown Solicitor for Cork and ordered him to stop Horgan's inquest immediately. An official Board of Trade enquiry chaired by Lord Mersey was to be held in London in four weeks' time, therefore any discussion on *Lusitania* was now *sub judice*.

To conceal the truth a scapegoat for the disaster had to be found, and it would be Captain Turner. Leading players at the Admiralty were going to blame him for the loss of his ship. He would be accused of having taken the *Lusitania* close to land despite his Admiralty orders to steer a course well off the coast in 'mid-channel so as to avoid submarines. He would be accused of failing  to follow an order to zig-zag when he had never received such an order. He would be accused of unnecessarily reducing his speed to 18 knots when he had been ordered to proceed at maximum speed.

Admiral Oliver and Captain Webb at Room 40 in London cooked up an 'official' report on the *Lusitania* sinking that blame Turner. The only thing that could save him was the signal sent by Vice-Admiral Coke which ordered him to divert into Queenstown. That was the only reason he had been approaching close to land, but Coke's message was going to vanish into thin air like much else in this sordid tale. Mitch Peeke writes:

It should be noted that the page on which that signal [ordering Turner to divert into Queenstown] was recorded is the only page missing from the Admiralty signals log for the whole of the First World War. Before Lord Mersey's enquiry was convened, Captain Turner had to attend an interview with the Board of Trade solicitors. Also present at the interview was a representative of the Admiralty. The details of Captain Webb's report were set out for Turner and he was told that at no time had he been ordered to divert into Queenstown. The Admiralty list of signals drawn up by Admiral Oliver was shown to him and he could see for himself that the vital signal, the one sent to him in naval code, wasn't there. As all of his papers, including the *Lusitania's* log and her signals register, had gone down with the ship, there was nothing in Turner's possession with which to counter Webb's allegations. ... He could hardly stand up in court and accuse such an august body as the British Admiralty of lying, without having overwhelming evidence to support him. Now Turner should have known exactly where he stood. They were going to blame him for the loss of his ship; the ship they had failed to protect. But he seems to have been unable to grasp this situation fully, as was later evidenced by his manner at the enquiry.[48]

The plan to destroy Captain Turner's reputation as a decent, honest, and fine master mariner, went into overdrive. Quite incredibly, Captain Webb at the Admiralty in London inferred that Turner was in the pay of the Germans, and that a German spy in the Cunard office in New York had passed instructions to him before sailing. The implication was that Turner had deliberately guided *Lusitania* into the path of U-20 at a low speed without zigzagging. In stitching Turner up, Captain Webb's report was passed to Admiral Fisher, he underlined Webb's suggestion that Turner was in the pay of Germany, and wrote in the margin: "Fully concur. As the Cunard Company would not have employed an incompetent man – the certainty is absolute that Captain Turner is not a fool but a knave." Fisher added: "I hope Captain Turner will be arrested immediately after the Inquiry, *whatever* the verdict or finding may be."[49]

Admiral Fisher sent notes to Sir William Greene, Secretary of the Admiralty and Winston Churchill, First Lord of the Admiralty: "I feel *absolutely* certain that Captain Turner of the *Lusitania* is a scoundrel and has been bribed. No seaman in his senses would have acted as he did. Ought not Lord Mersey to get a hint?" (Lord Mersey would head the Inquiry.) On reading Webb's and Fisher's notes the following day, Churchill wrote:

"Fully concur. I consider the Admiralty case against the Captain should be pressed before Lord Mersey by a skilful counsel, and that Captain Webb should attend as a witness, if not employed as an assessor: *We shall pursue the Captain without check.*"[50]

Desperate words from desperate, guilty, men, including the disgraceful Churchill. Had the truth of the *Lusitania*'s sinking emerged – the truth about who was truly responsible for the death of 1,198 innocents and the destruction of urgently needed munitions – justice would have been served by having Churchill, Fisher, and the rest of this scheming, privileged cabal of English elitists face a firing squad. Ordinary British soldiers suffering severe shell shock in the trenches were being taken out and shot at dawn for far less.

Under no circumstance could the truth be allowed out. The entire sordid affair would have to be whitewashed, and that whitewash was liberally applied at the official inquiry held in London the following month.

THE MERSEY INQUIRY

Under the Merchant Shipping Acts, a formal investigation into the loss of the *Lusitania* was held at the Central Hall, Westminster, from 15-18 June 1915. It re-convened on 1 July at the Westminster Palace Hotel, and on 17 July at the Caxton Hall, Westminster. The investigation was led by Lord Mersey, Wreck Commissioner, assisted by Admiral Sir F. S. Inglefield and several senior Royal Navy and Merchant Navy captains.

> Sir Frederick Inglefield, who had hauled down his flag as the Admiral Commanding the Auxiliary Coastal Patrol Forces, was sent to sit in judgement on the fate of the ship which his own patrols had failed to protect. Shortly after the case he retired from the service at his own request, From the start Sir Frederick either believed, or had been told to believe, that Captain Turner was guilty. He had studied Captain Webb's memorandum before the case started, and was aware of Churchill's and Fisher's comments. It is probable that in any ordinary court of law he would have been debarred from taking part. Churchill's and Fisher's strictures could have left little room for independent thought.[51]

Four of the Inquiry's sittings were held in public, and two in camera (in private with the press and public excluded.) That is, part of the Inquiry was to be conducted in secret, allegedly 'in the public interest.' The sitting at the hotel, which supposedly *was* in the public interest, was not announced to the public or press until *after* the meeting had been held. The Admiralty's case was presented by two of the most eminent lawyers of the day and dyed-in-the-wool Establishment men – Sir Edward Carson, the Attorney General, and F. E. Smith (Oxford), the Solicitor General. Smith was the best friend of Winston Churchill who had overseen this particular conspiracy.

Britain has long been notorious for whitewash public inquiries and heavy bias in favour of the ruling Establishment and big business in such inquiries, but the Mersey Inquiry must rank amongst the most corrupt of all time. It made a mockery of truth and justice, focussing on Webb's lies about Captain Turner's handling of the *Lusitania,* with no question whatsoever asked about the Admiralty's failure to protect her. Witnesses were carefully selected to suit the official lie that the massive explosion on the *Lusitania* was due to the ship being hit almost simultaneously by two torpedoes. All questions to be asked at the Inquiry were carefully prese-lected. Every surviving member of the crew had given statements to the Board of Trade, but only 13 of those 289 depositions survived the official cull. Each of the 13 begins with the identical opening sentence stating that two torpedoes were involved, and that they struck the ship much fur-ther back towards the stern than actually occurred.

Passengers were invited to submit evidence, and 135 did so. Almost one hundred survivors who had previously given statements that they heard the second massive explosion which sank the ship were never called to give evidence, while six individuals who had *not* heard the explosion *were* selected to appear. Not one passenger or crew member accurately re-

ferring to the explosion being well forward of the front funnel was called to give evidence.

To cover the Admiralty's back, Captain Turner was to be thrown to the wolves and blamed for the loss of *Lusitania*. He had, the Admiralty suggested, been kept informed at all times of enemy submarines and been given definite instructions but deliberately disobeyed them, thus placing his ship in grave danger. He had been ordered to zigzag but failed to comply. In truth, the Admiralty's zigzag order to merchant vessels had been approved on 25 April 1915, but its distribution had not even started until 13 May, so it could not possibly have been in Turner's possession when he took the *Lusitania* across the Atlantic on the fateful voyage. He had been ordered to proceed at full speed, they said, but had only been doing 18 knots which was short of the ship's maximum.

With regard to the *Lusitania* diverting to Queenstown, it was flatly denied that any such instruction had been sent. The Marconi wireless room operator who took the coded telegraph from the naval transmitter at Valentia at 11.02, and responded to it eight minutes later was not called to give evidence. Neither was Admiral Coke, the man who sent it. Coke's signal had to be airbrushed from existence because it demonstrated incompetence and worse at the Admiralty in London. Coke tried urgently to divert the liner to safety; why hadn't *the Admiralty*? The official line was that Captain Turner had been instructed to stay well out to sea and disobeyed that instruction by heading closer to shore. He had in fact been heading for Queenstown as ordered, but Admiral Coke's message at 11.02 on 7 May was never allowed to surface at Inquiry.

The top legal brains in Britain had the decent, honourable Turner tied in knots. The poor man was still shell-shocked just weeks after losing his ship, his best friend, and so many passengers in such a horrendous manner. '

> Turner, that simple seaman, did not stand much of a chance in the witness box against the array of legal talent mobilised to prove him guilty.[52]

Mitch Peeke writes:

> Captain Turner was quite alone and for him it was all a nightmare. Alfred Booth, Cunard's chairman, observed, "Poor Will appears thoroughly bemused by the whole affair. He consistently clings to Aspinall (Cunard's senior counsel) for support." Initially, Aspi-

nall was having an exasperating time trying to get Captain Turner to give answers of more than one word. Turner just could not, it seems, understand fully what the Admiralty were doing to him or why they were doing it. He was constantly confused about the evidence and gave his answers reluctantly. This, of course, only served to further the nature of the Admiralty's case against him.[53]

A false manifest presented at the Inquiry disclosed that cases of cartridges had been present in the lower deck near the bow, but they were not involved in any explosion because, according to the Admiralty lawyers, "two torpedoes struck the ship much further astern than where the cartridges were stowed." It was suggested that even had the cartridges been subjected to fire, they would not have exploded. No mention whatsoever was made of the 1250 cases of shells, or 18 cases of fuses, that were loaded in the same hold space as the cartridges. Like the 'divert to Queenstown' message and much else, it was completely airbrushed from existence. Patrick Beesly writes:

> The fuses consisted of fulminate of mercury, a highly sensitive substance.... But to admit all this would have been to concede the German claim that the liner sank so quickly, and with such appalling loss of life, only because her cargo, contraband in German eyes, exploded. Filled shells, even unfused might conceivably have been caused to explode by one torpedo; if the fulminate of mercury fuses were also in the same area, an enormous explosion would have been inevitable. Such facts would not only have blunted the revulsion of the world against German brutality, it would have raised questions about the British policy of shipping dangerous munitions in passenger vessels.... It had somehow to be shown that the second explosion testified to by one and all, had nothing to do with Lusitania's cargo. The only way to do this was to produce 'evidence' that it occurred much further aft than in fact was the case. ... The 'first' torpedo had struck not forward of the first funnel and below the bridge, as in fact it did, but between the second and third funnel – i.e. well away from the munitions. A second torpedo (according to the Admiralty) had almost certainly struck the ship even further aft. A 'third' torpedo had missed the ship and this had been fired from the port side indicating that more than one U-boat had been involved.[54]

So outrageous were the lies that they might as well have added that a German Zeppelin flew over and dropped bombs on the Lusitania. As

Patrick Beesly and many others have pointed out, dives on the wreck of the *Lusitania* clearly show that her bottom, forward of the forward funnel, had been blown *outwards*, not inwards, and her bows 'nearly severed from the rest of the hull.

Concerning munitions, the official Mersey Report concluded:

> The cargo was a general cargo of the ordinary kind, but part of it consisted of a number of cases of cartridges (about 5,000). This ammunition was entered in the manifest. It was stowed well forward in the ship on the orlop and lower decks and *about 50 yards away from where the torpedoes struck the ship. There was no other explosive on board.*[55]

Regarding the U-boat strike, the Inquiry stated:

> At 2 P.M. the passengers were finishing their mid-day meal. At. 2.15 P.M., when ten to fifteen miles off the Old Head of Kinsale, the water being then clear and the sea smooth, the Captain, who was on the port side of the lower bridge, heard the call, "There is a torpedo coming, sir," given by the second officer. He looked to starboard and then saw a streak of foam in the wake of a torpedo travelling towards his ship. Immediately afterwards the *Lusitania* was struck on the starboard side *somewhere between the third and fourth funnels.* The blow broke number 5 life-boat into splinters. *A second torpedo was fired immediately afterwards,* which also struck the ship on the starboard side. *The two torpedoes struck the ship almost simultaneously.* Both these torpedoes were discharged by a German submarine from a distance variously estimated at from two to five hundred yards. No warning of any kind was given. It is also in evidence that shortly afterwards a torpedo from another submarine was fired on the port side of the *Lusitania.* This torpedo did not strike the ship: and the circumstance is only mentioned for the purpose of showing that perhaps more than one submarine as taking part in the attack. The *Lusitania* on being struck took a heavy list to starboard and in less than twenty minutes she sank in deep water. Eleven hundred and ninety-eight men, women, and children were drowned.[56]

Regarding the claim of Captain Turner's "incompetence," so eagerly pursued by Churchill and the Admiralty, Lord Mersey saw it differently and with some compassion:

> After the disaster occurred Captain Turner, as was unanimously admitted, bore himself according to the best traditions of the Brit-

ish Mercantile Marine. He was on the bridge when the vessel was struck, and he remained there to the last, going down with his vessel. His first order was to lower all the boats to the rail a command obeyed as far as possible and he then ordered "Women and children first." He also had the ship's head turned towards the land, but the vessel had become unmanageable owing to the damage to the engine-room. It was not until he had been in the water for three hours that Captain Turner was rescued.

The conclusion at which I have arrived is that blame ought not to be imputed to the captain. The advice given to him, although meant for his most serious and careful consideration, was not intended to deprive him of the right to exercise his skilled judgment in the difficult questions that might arise from time to time in the navigation of his ship. His omission to follow the advice in all respects cannot fairly be attributed either to negligence or to incompetence. He exercised his judgment for the best. It was the judgment of a skilled and experienced man, and although others might have acted differently and perhaps more successfully, he ought not, in my opinion, to be blamed. The whole blame for the cruel destruction of life in this catastrophe must rest solely with those who plotted and with those who committed the crime.

Concerning the conduct of the Admiralty, Lord Mersey applied liberal coats of whitewash:

At the request of the Attorney-General part of the evidence in the Enquiry was taken in camera. *This course was adopted in the public interest.* The evidence in question dealt, firstly, with certain advice given by the Admiralty to navigators generally with reference to precautions to be taken for the purpose of avoiding submarine attacks; and secondly, with information furnished by the Admiralty to Captain Turner individually of submarine dangers likely to be encountered by him in the voyage of the *Lusitania*. It would defeat the object which the Attorney-General had in view if I were to discuss these matters in detail in my report; and I do not propose to do so. But *it made abundantly plain to me that the Admiralty had devoted the most anxious care and thought to the questions arising out of the submarine peril, and that they had diligently collected all available information likely to affect the voyage of the "Lusitania" in this* connection. I do not know who the officials were to whom these duties were entrusted, but *they deserve the highest praise for the way in which they did their work.*[57]

Lord Mersey, like Lord Bryce with the Belgian atrocity report, was fully prepared to lie through his teeth. Protecting the British Establishment was his number one concern, not uncovering the truth and exposing the guilty men at the Admiralty and Room 40. No, they 'deserved the highest praise.'

The British Establishment knows how to look after such loyal servants willing to perjure themselves for the cause. Following the travesty of the truth that was the Mersey Inquiry, Mersey himself was rewarded with a Viscountcy – a high ranking position in the British peerage system.

Captain Richard Webb, Director of the Admiralty Trade Division and the man who created the litany of lies about Captain Turner's handling of the *Lusitania*, returned to sea. He was promoted to Rear-Admiral and later to Admiral. He was appointed Knight Commander of the Order of St Michael and St George, a British order of chivalry.

F.E. Smith was knighted in 1915, appointed Lord Chancellor (a high-ranking position in the British Cabinet) and was invested as the Earl of Birkenhead. Throughout, he remained Winston Churchill's closest friend.

Edward Carson was appointed First Lord of the Admiralty in 1916, elevated as a Minister in the War Cabinet of Lloyd George, and created a life peer as Baron Carson.

Winston Churchill was removed from the Admiralty following the disaster in Gallipoli but would soon be brought back into the Cabinet as Minister of Munitions. In his book, *The World Crisis, 1915,* published in 1923, Churchill was still spouting lies about the *Lusitania* disaster, Turner's command, and the torpedo strike. Concerning the charge that Captain Turner had failed to maintain top speed and zigzag as instructed. Churchill wrote in 1923:

> In spite of these warnings and instructions, for which the Admiralty Trade Division [Captain Webb] deserve credit, the *Lusitania* was proceeding along the usual trade route without zigzagging at little more than three-quarter speed when … she was torpedoed eight miles off the Old Head of Kinsale by Commander Schwieger in the German submarine U 20. Two torpedoes were fired, the first striking her amidships with a tremendous explosion and the second a few minutes later striking her aft.[58]

Churchill's account was, of course, a blatant lie like much else he wrote about the war. He shared responsibility for the deaths of some 1,200 innocent men, women and children, and the Admiralty cover-up thereafter, but had the gall to condemn others:

> On two supreme occasions the German Imperial Government, quenching compunction, outfacing conscience, deliberately, with calculation, with sinister resolve, severed the underlying bonds which sustained civilization of the world and united even in their quarrels the human family.[59]

Excrementum vincit cerebrum: the excrement of fake and corrupt information (aka bullshit) baffles brains. Churchill, the silver-tongued liar whose mouth and pen copiously spewed 'excrementum.' would become Prime Minister of Britain and voted the greatest Briton of all time. On the other hand, the decent, brave and honest Captain Turner retired and went to live in an isolated cottage in Devon. "Often depressed and convinced that people avoided him because he didn't go down with his ship, he lived the life of a recluse. He never forgave Churchill for blaming him for the loss of the *Lusitania*."[60]

Summary: Chapter 10 – Some Disturbing Truths

- The United States of America remained 'neutral' in 1915 in that it did not send troops to the British and French allies, but it sent just about everything else.

- Astronomical sums of money were involved and the Anglo-American High Finance who shared responsibility for the war made vast profits from it. One of their own, J.P. Morgan, was appointed as sole purchasing agent in the USA.

- The American people were against the U.S. getting involved in the war, and public opinion had to be hardened against Germany with shocking lies about German 'atrocities' in Belgium and the sinking of the *Lusitania*.

- Passenger liners, including *Lusitania*, were illegally carrying weapons and munitions from New York to Britain. The passengers were effectively being used as human shields.

- Naval Intelligence in London had cracked German naval codes and were fully aware that the *Lusitania* was a target for U-boats operating off the south of Ireland. The U-boat, U-20, was sinking

British ships in the waters into which the *Lusitania* was directly heading on her way to Liverpool.

• The Admiralty in London could readily have diverted the *Lusitania* north around Ireland on a safer route to Liverpool, but did nothing. They could have diverted her into the safety of Queenstown harbour but did nothing. They could have sent readily available British warships to escort her safely to Liverpool, but did nothing.

• The Vice-Admiral at Queenstown disobeyed the Admiralty and sent a telegraph to *Lusitania* to divert immediately to Queenstown, but she was torpedoed on her way there. A second massive explosion of the munitions she was illegally carrying tore her hull apart and sent her to the bottom within 20 minutes with a huge loss of life, including many U.S citizens.

• An official whitewash Inquiry in London covered up the Admiralty's complicity in the sinking, including that of Winston Churchill and Admiral Sir John Fisher, and blamed the completely innocent captain of the *Lusitania* captain, Willian Turner, for dereliction of duty.

• With the publication of the falsified Bryce Report the same week in 1915 as the *Lusitania* disaster – and the loss of American lives in the disaster life being blamed on 'sub-human.' 'evil' Germany – the great lie of the sinking of the *Lusitania* succeeded in turning the American people in favour of war.

CHAPTER 11

WAR IS A RACKET

Under pressure from the United States after the sinking of *Lusitania* and another passenger liner, SS *Arabic,* with loss of American lives, Germany ended unrestricted submarine warfare in September 1915. It would recommence in early 1917. Many British vessels had been sunk by U-boats but increased shipbuilding and the use of captured German freighters saw the overall tonnage and carrying capacity of the massive British merchant fleet maintained at pre-war levels. With free access to global markets, literally thousands of ships carried food and much else to Britain from the United States, Canada, Argentina, Australia, New Zealand and elsewhere across the world. Thanks to the efforts of its merchant marine throughout the war, the British population was maintained on an adequate daily calorie intake.

> Before the war about 60 percent of the energy value of the British diet was derived from foodstuffs that were imported, and the Food (War) Committee of the Royal Society was able to ascertain that the supply of food to the UK population was sufficient to provide about 3,400 calories per person [adults] on average in the years immediately preceding the outbreak of War. In the first two years of the war, this figure increased to about 3,500 calories, before falling back to around 3,300 calories in 1917 and 1918.[1]

The situation was totally different in Germany, which prior to 1914 imported some 40 per cent of its food but was now surrounded by a 'ring of steel' and sealed off by the Royal Navy blockade that prevented imports from overseas. When war broke out over 600 German merchant ships sought refuge in neutral ports, and by early September 1914, Germany's merchant fleet had ceased to operate other than in the Black Sea and Baltic Sea.[2] Apart from the Battle of Jutland on 31 May – 1 June 1916, the German High Seas Fleet remained in harbour behind protective screens of mines. With virtually no German ships on the high seas, the British naval blockade was tasked with stopping and searching neutral vessels, and apprehending any carrying food bound for Germany. A double blow for

Germany was that home-grown food production seriously declined due to the conscription of farm workers and horses into the army, and also the severe shortage of imported fertilisers. Before the war, most of Germany's nitrates for fertiliser production were imported from Chile. German chemists developed methods of nitrate production through the fixation of atmospheric nitrogen, but virtually all of it was taken by the munitions industry.[3] With food imports halted, Germany faced significant shortages and hunger.

> With widespread malnutrition during the war, German children were on average three to five centimetres shorter than their pre-1914 peers. Average body weight in Germany declined from 60 kilograms in 1914 to 49 kilograms in 1917. Germany was facing a famine. Conscription withdrew about 40 per cent of the farm labour force. Women and children were drafted in but their productivity was much less due to inexperience, decreased calorific intake, and other factors. Prior to 1914, Germany was the world's biggest importer of agricultural products. About one-third of foodstuffs and one half of its animal feed were produced abroad.... The import of fertilizer, feed, and other intermediate products needed for agricultural production was virtually impossible.... Imported nitrogen crucial for both the armaments and agricultural sectors was greatly reduced, and what did come in was diverted mainly to armaments. In effect, agricultural production came to a near standstill. Milk supply collapsed. Meat consumption fell to the level of the first decade of the 19th century.... Official rations provided only 50-60 per cent of the nutritional needs of an average person. During 1916/17 the daily ration sank to around 1,000 calories, leading to an average of 20 per cent weight loss.[4]

With the German potato crop particularly poor in the winter of 1916-17, many families struggled to survive on turnips. The so-called 'Turnip Winter' led to a state of chronic starvation with greatly increased incidence of rickets, scurvy, anaemia and other debilitating disorders due to vitamin and mineral deficiencies. Neonatal and infant morbidity and mortality rates increased, with a leading German physician reporting that in 1916 alone, 80,000 German children had died of starvation.[5] Children and adults suffered increasingly from infectious diseases, especially tuberculosis.

With agricultural output decimated and food imports blocked, the German people were being starved, but how was it possible to feed the German army and keep it fighting fit for four long years? As in all coun-

tries involved in the war, in the first months of fighting millions of reserves were called up in Germany, and the army's strength quickly grew
to around 3.8 million men. By August 1916, almost 3 million German
soldiers were serving on the Western Front and another 1.7 million in the
east against Russia. Active soldiers required approximately 3,500 calories
per day in summer, and around 4,500 per day in cold winters.[6]

How did the German army compare to the British army in terms of nu-
trition? The food rations for British soldiers in the 1914-18 war, according
to the British National Army Museum, were basic but filling.

> Each soldier could expect around 4,000 calories a day, with tinned
> rations and hard biscuits staples. But their diet also included veg-
> etables, bread and jam, and boiled plum puddings. This was all
> washed down by copious amounts of tea[7]

German soldiers needed the same calorie intake. 'An army marches
on its stomach' goes the saying, and one of the great puzzles of the First
World War was how upwards of 4.5 million German soldiers were able
to be kept fed for four long years when Germany was being starved. To
those unaware of the machiavellian ways of the British ruling elite, the
answer is quite shocking. Their plan for crushing Germany economically, industrially, and in every other way, could not be achieved by a quick
military victory. It required a long war of attrition lasting years, and that
could only happen if they ensured that the German army was properly
fed. To that end, for most of the war the British ruling elite ensured that
food from overseas was allowed through to the German army to enable it
to keep fighting.

Before examining in detail how the above was achieved, we should
highlight the fact that much more than food was involved. War is always
good for business, and despite being on opposite sides in this war, the
Allies' trade with Germany continued in essential military materiel. By
way of example, following negotiations early in the war, Germany agreed
to supply Britain and her allies straightaway with 10,000 pairs of binoculars from the Zeiss factory in Jena, central Germany, and 5,000 pairs per
month thereafter. The German manufacturers announced they would be
happy to similarly supply 5,000 to 10,000 telescopic sights per month and
to provide as many range-finders as the British government required.[8]

> And what did Germany want in return for this astonishing bounty
> of tools that would better aim British rifles and howitzers at Ger-

man troops? One treasured commodity, vital for everything from telephone wires to factory machinery to the tyres and fan belts of motor vehicles ... a commodity abundant in the Allies' African and Asian colonies: rubber. Without rubber the Germans, among many other problems, faced the prospect of using steel tyres on their army trucks which rapidly chewed roads to bits. The rubber, it was agreed, would be delivered to Germany at the Swiss border. During August 1915, the first month of this top-secret devil's bargain, the Germans delivered to the British even more than first agreed to: some 32,000 pairs of binoculars, 20,000 of them higher quality types for officers. Records that would show how long the trade continued, or how much rubber the Germans received in return, have disappeared.[9]

The 'devil's bargain' as we shall see, extended to much more than just rubber, and included minerals and ores essential for explosives and weapons production being secretly sent into Germany to prolong the war. The British elite were starving the German civilian population while simultaneously feeding the German army and ensuring it had the munitions to keep fighting. The food was supplied through two major channels:

1) Food and other cargoes from the Americas were allowed to pass through the Royal Navy blockade of Germany to neutral Scandinavian countries. This was done in the full knowledge that much of the food was being unloaded at Scandinavian ports and put straight onto goods trains bound for Germany.

2) The provision of food through a 'charitable' organisation called 'Belgian Relief'. Ostensibly set up to help feed the Belgian civilian population, a significant quantity of the food supplied was transferred by canal barge and other transport to German troops on the Western Front.

THE ROYAL NAVY BLOCKADE OF GERMANY.

A blockade by one nation against another had been a strategy of war throughout history. In different epochs, different tactics have been employed to achieve similar ends, namely, defeat of the enemy by stopping its trade in necessary foodstuffs and resources, excluding it from the benefits of international exchange, and bringing about its ruin and defeat. The physical capacity of the Royal Navy to cut off the sea trade routes between Germany and her markets throughout the world was unquestioned.[10]

Two years before the war, the Committee of Imperial Defence (CID) in Britain decided that a close blockade of German ports – that is, British warships constantly patrolling the waters just outside the ports to prevent ships entering or leaving – would not be feasible. The blockading fleet would sustain severe losses until such times as the Germany navy was defeated or kept bottled up in harbour. Instead, it was decided that the blockading naval squadrons would operate on the outer edges of the North Sea.[11]

> Operating away from the enemy's defended coasts, British warships would be less vulnerable to attrition by floating mines, submarine torpedoes and mechanical wear and tear. Merchant ships coming across the Atlantic would have to pass through these cordons on their way to Germany or the neutral countries through which she traded. If ships did not call at British ports for inspection they would be stopped and searched, and if contraband was found or the final destination of the cargo was uncertain the ship would be embargoed.[12]

That was the official account of the means by which food and other cargoes would be prevented from reaching Germany. The reality would be very different. The blockade was set up as a gesture to placate the British public and convinced them that the government was doing all in its power to cripple Germany and end the war quickly.

Two British naval blockading squadrons were established. The Southern Squadron patrolled the English Channel, stopping and searching any vessels heading east through the Dover Straits towards Germany. It was a relatively straightforward task in that narrow channel compared to that of the Northern squadron which had to police a large area of the Atlantic from the tip of Scotland up to Iceland and across to Norway. The 10th Cruiser Squadron deployed to blockade the northern route initially comprised eight old coal-fired Royal Navy cruisers built in the early 1890s, each weighing around 7,000 tons.

> They crawled through mountainous seas putting duty first, risking life and limb to stop neutral vessels and send search parties in small open boats to check their cargoes for contraband. … To make matters even more difficult, the captains and crews became increasingly disheartened. Not by the state of their antiquated cruisers but by the ultimate fate of most of the neutral ships they boarded, caught with contraband, and sent to the contraband control base at Kirk-

wall [in the Orkney Islands]. The legal framework in which the navy believed they were working, assumed that any neutral vessel suspected of carrying contraband to Germany could be detained and taken before a judicial board with the powers to confiscate the cargo and the vessel. This was fine in theory but rarely happened in practice.... Time and again the crews put their lives at risk in wild seas only to receive orders from London to release the captive ships and let them proceed. This despite the fact that they knew the cargo was destined for Germany.[13]

The officers and men of the 10th Cruiser Squadron were determined to make the blockade effective and stop supplies getting through to Germany. They toiled in atrocious conditions in the north Atlantic with the ever-present danger of U-boat attacks. That danger was highlighted in early October 1914 when HMS *Hawke* of the squadron was torpedoed and went down with the loss of 525 men. In the first three years of the war they intercepted 8,905 ships, sent 1,816 into Kirkwall under armed guard, and boarded 4,520 fishing craft.[14]

But those British sailors could not know that their valiant efforts were being negated. Ships bound directly for German ports were stopped, while many, if not most, that were heading to the neutral Scandinavian countries were allowed to continue their passage. On docking in those neutral ports, the goods were loaded straight onto trains and taken over the border into Germany. From central depots there, the food was then transported to the front lines, east and west, to feed the German troops. Historians toeing the Establishment line would later suggest that Britain could do little or nothing to stop food going to Germany.

> Fearful of embittering neutral opinion and driving neutrals, especially the United States, into Germany's arms, they often released neutral ships containing meat, wheat, wool etcetera that the Navy had, sometimes at considerable risk, sent into port for examination.[15]

How disappointing that an American historian, Arthur J. Marder, should pen the nonsense that the United States might have allied with Germany in the First World War if Britain had properly implemented the naval blockade. Marder was a Bostonian and Harvard graduate who would later become a professor at Oxford University and fellow of Milner's old stronghold, Balliol College. Fake history was not confined to British historians.

Honest accounts were written by Rear-Admiral Montague Consett, the British Naval Attaché in Scandinavia from 1912 to 1918. and by the British jurist, George Bowles. Consett visited various Scandinavian docks every week and personally witnessed vast amounts of food being unloaded and then sent straight on to Germany by train. He wrote that Germany was neither prepared nor equipped for a long struggle, and the food being allowed through to her by the British via neutral ports meant that the war "was *prolonged* far beyond the limits of necessity."[16] George Bowles noted that if a proper blockade had been in place, war on continental Europe would have been over within six to eight months.[17] In other words, the horrendous slaughter could have been ended in March 1915 by a properly applied blockade. Neither Consett nor Bowles was aware, of course, that the good work of the Royal Navy in implementing the blockade was being deliberately sabotaged by the Milner Group in order to prolong the war, as will be discussed below.

Whenever the Northern Cruiser Squadron stopped a cargo vessel, armed British sailors were put on board to take it into Kirkwall for inspection by a Prize Court. An internationally agreed legal entity in wartime, the Prize Court had the jurisdiction to sit in judgement on all questions relating to the validity of the seizure of a ship and the goods it carried. The process should have been straightforward. If the cargo was deemed to be ultimately bound for Germany via a neutral country, the Court would prevent the ship from continuing its journey and confiscate the goods.

> On paper this system was flawless and fair. Given the acknowledged zeal and professionalism of the Royal Navy's blockading fleet, very little contraband should have reached Germany from August 1914 onwards. That is what the public, Press and Parliament in general believed. Winston Churchill had promised the blockade would bring Germany to her knees. ... Yet powers greater than government ensured that the Prize Courts were neutered. Behind the backs of the British people, in blatant defiance of the will of the British Parliament and widely accepted international law, the Prize Courts were sidelined and a more sinister authority created to exercise the real power over the blockade. ... The process was completely undermined by influences inside the British Foreign Office through an invention called the Contraband Committee.[18]

The Contraband Committee was set up by Maurice Hankey and Admiral Sir Edmond Slade, men who were deeply involved in the Milner Group's anti-German conspiracy. Hankey had a background in naval intelligence and was secretary of the Committee of Imperial Defence. Slade had served as Director of Naval Intelligence. Interestingly, his father was a Fellow of All Souls. Their Contraband Committee stymied and sabotaged the due lawful process. The entire blockade effort was prevented from working by "a deliberate and considered removal of the whole essential conduct of the war at sea from the Fleets and Prize Courts to the Foreign Office."[19]

A small committee of shadowy men thus acted as a hidden barrier to the excellent work of the Royal Navy out on the high seas. This committee, not the Prize Court, was making the final decision on every vessel intercepted by the 10th Cruiser Squadron. The vast majority of ships brought into Kirkwall for inspection were quickly sent on their way on orders from this committee in London under the pretext of "freeing neutral shipping from all avoidable delay." Thanks to the Contraband Committee, shipments from the Americas and Canada, to Scandinavia flourished as never before. Millions of tons of food and other vital supplies like cotton were shipped to the Nordic countries, and all appeared above board, but most of those supplies were then transported on to Germany. The men of the blockading force protested loudly but could do little or nothing to stop it. Cotton was used for clothing and military uniforms, but when treated with acid, the cellulose in the cotton formed the basic component of propellants and explosives. Vast amounts were passing through the blockade to Scandinavia then on to Germany for munitions production. Commander E. K. Chatterton of the Royal Navy stated:

> It was pathetic to know that Germany had obtained practically all she wanted of the last American cotton crop via neutral countries, though we could have stopped almost the whole lot.... So long as the Blockading Fleet was left alone to do its persistent duties, Germany was doomed.... She had gambled on a short, quick victory and lost. Nothing could now save her from eventual collapse except some further folly that might issue from Whitehall.[20]

3,353,638 bales of cotton – each weighing over 45 kgs – were shipped from the United States during the first five months of 1915 and allowed to proceed through the blockade to Scandinavia. Pre-war shipments for the same period for Scandinavian domestic needs were only 200,000 bales. The vast bulk of the excess was forwarded to Germany. Even British cotton dealers joined in the cotton bonanza of the war by importing large quantities from America then re-exporting a portion of it at considerable profit to neutral countries around Germany. Huge amounts of cotton were being imported for the British munitions industry but between January and May 1915, over half a million bales were re-exported. This was approximately fifteen times higher than a comparative period before the war. Most, if not all of it, ended up in Germany for explosives production.

Over 4 weeks in April/May 1915, Sweden imported 17,331 tons of cotton, of which 1,500 tons came directly from Britain. Pre-war Swedish imports for the same time period averaged 3,900 tons. All of the excess was going to Germany. Likewise, neutral Holland virtually doubled her cotton imports during the month of April that year to 16,217 tons, of which 5,352 tons were exported from Britain. Tellingly, re-exports of cotton to neutral countries which did not border Germany were considerably reduced.[21]

The war profiteering cotton merchants were well aware that the sudden vast increases in cotton orders from the neutral nations was due to the fact that they were then selling it on – at considerable profit – to Germany for munitions production.

> German shells rained death on Allied troops on the front line, that were dependent on cotton purchased from Britain. Sweden's total importation of cotton in 1913 was 24,800 tons, of which 1,940 tons came from Britain and the Empire. In 1915 there was a fivefold increase to 123,200 tons with 10,300 tons exported from Britain. Sweden's export of cotton to Germany increased from 236 tons in 1913 to 76,000 tons in 1915. Before any finger is pointed at others who profiteered from the war, the first and most disgusting culprits came from Britain herself.... From the very first days of war, merchants and importers in Stockholm, Oslo, Copenhagen, Helsingborg and Malmo found themselves inundated with orders from Germany to supply thousands of tons of animal feed, foodstuffs, ores, cotton and coal. Purchased from the Americas, North and South, from Britain and the British Empire, from other neutral countries world-wide these imports literally bounced from the quay-sides and dockyards to the goods trains and canal boats that ferried them to their final destination. Germany.[22]

In addition to cotton, coal from Britain helped keep Germany in the war. With its high energy content, English and Welsh coal was among the world's best for powering ships and railway locomotives. Rear-Admiral Consett records that in Denmark alone, State railways, gas works, electrical light and power stations, even breweries were dependent almost entirely on British coal.[23] Britain was supplying the Danes with coal that was fuelling their industries, and the trains carrying food and other Danish imports to Germany. Consett wrote:

> Special fast trains packed with fish, the staple diet of many of the Danes, carried it to Germany, when fish was unprocurable in Denmark; incidentally, be it mentioned, the trains were run on British coal, and the fishing tackle was supplied by Great Britain.[24]

The outraged Admiral noted that in the first two years of the war, large numbers of German railway trucks were to be seen in all the Scandinavian countries hauling goods to Germany by trains fuelled by British coal. He also wrote of British coal being used to transport high grade ore from Sweden to Germany for weapons and U-boat production:

> The haulage of ore from the mines to the coast was carried out to a large extent by the Swedish railways with British coal; its further transport by steamer across the Baltic was also (certainly for the first two years) effected by British coal.[25]

Danish ships served as a replacement for the tightly shackled German merchant fleet, and carried much of the Swedish ore to Germany. Not a single vessel belonging to the Danish owned East Asiatic line was sunk by German submarines during the war. Fuelled by British coal they shipped between four and five million tons of Swedish ore into Germany per year. Admiral Consett added:

> Nothing would have hastened the end of the war more effectively than the sinking of ships trading in ore between Sweden and Germany, or by economic pressure brought to bear on the Swedish ore industry.[26]

Sweden was also sending copper and nickel across the Baltic to Germany. Crucial for weapons and naval construction, British exports of copper to Sweden doubled from 517 tons in 1913 to 1,085 tons in 1915. During that same period, Sweden's export of copper to Germany rapidly increased. German reserves of nickel (essential for strengthening steel) were very low in 1914. In 1915, of Sweden's total imports of 504 tons of nickel, 65 per cent came from Britain or the empire. Much of this was sent straight to Germany. The furious Admiral Consett reported that Britain sent Sweden twelve times the amount of nickel in 1915 that it did in 1913 and that a great deal of it was going to the enemy.[27] Norway was likewise sending large amounts of nickel to Germany when it could readily have been stopped. In 1917, Norwegian civilians disgusted by the inaction of the British, eventually did stop it by taking it upon themselves to plant explosives in the nickel factory.

Consett revealed that two years into the war, supplies of ore and copper were still pouring across the Baltic into Germany.[28] The British Naval Attaché was tearing his hair out trying to get the British government to stop cotton, coal, and copper exports to Scandinavia, in the knowledge that the war could be ended within months. Leading players within the British Establishment not only knew all this was happening, they were actively facilitating it.

Britain also sent significant quantities of oil cake, vegetable oil and animal fats to Germany via Scandinavia. The glycerine was extracted for making explosives. Consett reported that in 1913 Britain exported 370 tons of tea to Denmark, but they had risen to 4,528 tons by 1915. By 1916 he found the wharves in Copenhagen choked with cases of tea, "a large part of which was from our colonies en route to Germany." Coffee was also re-exported from Britain to Germany via neutral ports. In 1913 Britain sent 1,493 tons of coffee to Sweden, Norway and Denmark. This fully met their demands, yet by 1915 the British coffee exports to those same countries had risen dramatically to 7,315 tons.[29] As ever, the excess was going straight to Germany. German troops enjoying tea and coffee were doubtless most grateful for this British largesse.

The provisioning of Germany by Britain and America in order to deliberately prolong the First World War is one of the greatest scandals of all time. Consett's book, *The Triumph of Unarmed Forces*, is essential reading for all who are interested in understanding exactly how it was done. He reveals how, in the period January – July 1916, Danish agricultural exports to Germany amounted to 117,000 tons, including 62,561 tons of meat. Consett explains how over that six-month period, Denmark provided one million meat rations per day for the Imperial German army. 'Fair enough,' one might say, Danish farmers had to survive, but Britain was supplying Denmark with animal feedstuffs, fertilisers, and coal that allowed her agricultural industry to operate. Those British exports to Denmark increased markedly from pre-war levels, yet Danish meat and dairy produce exports to Britain dropped by 25 per cent. Britain was providing the basic fodder and fertilisers to boost Denmark's agricultural output to feed the German army.

Danish and Swedish fish exports to Germany also continued on an enormous scale, rising from 55,819 tons in 1913 to 157,000 tons in

1916. Over the same period their fish exports to Britain fell from 8,677 tons to 1,902 tons. Despite this, in addition to supplying all of the petrol for their fishing fleets, Britain was selling these countries practically all of their fishing nets, yarn and rope. Special fish trains were running so frequently to Germany that at times the railways could scarcely meet the demands of the fish traffic. As we have seen, the trains were running on British coal. Germany was also supplied with a large tonnage of fish from Norway. Prior to the war (1913) annual Norwegian fish exports to Germany were around 78,771 tons. This rose to 194,167 tons in 1916. Consett pointed out that "during 1916 the fish rations to the German Army had been gradually increased." During the first two years of the war, not only was the fish feeding the German army, but providing much needed glycerine for explosives production. Like the Danish and Swedish, the Norwegian fishing industry depended not merely upon petrol supplies from Britain, but many other vital imports including fishing gear. Montagu Consett exposed how the Norwegian fishing industry, by far the largest and most important in Northern Europe, depended upon British or British-controlled supplies. He believed that "the moment and circumstances immediately following the outbreak of war could not have been more favourable for Britain purchasing the entire Norwegian catch in return for a guaranteed supply of all fishing accessories." The opportunity was ignored by the Government.[30]

After the war, Winston Churchill discussed the naval blockade of Germany in his book *The World Crisis, 1915*. He relates how he informed the British Cabinet in March 1915:

> The blockading lines are in every sense effective: no instance is known to the British Admiralty of any vessel, the stopping of which had been authorized by the Foreign Office, passing them unchallenged. It is not a case of a paper blockade, but of a blockade as real and as efficient as any that has ever been established.[31]

The great wordsmith Churchill was entirely correct in stating that the Cruiser Squadron allowed no merchant vessel crossing the Atlantic to pass unchallenged. Indeed, it was an immense achievement by the British sailors. What Churchill failed to mention, of course, was the Contraband Committee (of which he was possibly a member) was thereafter immediately allowing the vast majority of those ships to continue their journeys knowing the goods were ultimately bound for Germany.

In addition to the blockade scandal and ore from Sweden pouring into Germany, German armaments manufactures were supplied with vast quantities of French iron ore from the Briey basin.

BRIEY

Before the war, the mines and smelters around the Briey basin – the region that straddled the Franco-German border south of Luxemburg – provided the vast majority of both France and Germany's iron ore, and were therefore of great military significance. In 1913, of the 36,000,000 tons of iron ore produced in Germany, 29,000,000 tons (80 per cent of her entire production) came from Briey. The French iron ore supply of almost 20,000,000 tons (92 per cent of her supplies) came from the same source. After they had won the war of 1870-71 "which was really fought for the control of the valuable Lorraine iron basin," Germany annexed Lorraine, but left Briey to France.[32]

Inexplicably, when the war started in August 1914, the French simply walked away from Briey leaving the mines and smelters intact. German forces just walked in and took control of this crucially important industrial centre and its entire output with no resistance whatsoever. Although well within the capabilities of the Allied forces, never at any time did they attempt to drive the Germans from Briey, or bomb the area to interrupt production. It was producing millions of tons of raw materials turned into the weapons of death to be used against French and British troops, yet was immune from destruction throughout the war. "The loss of Briey to Germany would have brought the war to a rapid end as she would not have had sufficient minerals for armaments production."[33] A secret memo to Chancellor Bethmann-Hollweg from the Association of the six largest German industrial and agricultural manufacturers on 20 March 1915 included a warning that if the iron ore production from Lorraine was interrupted, the war would virtually be lost.[34]

Just weeks after the war ended, a member of the Chamber of Deputies, Eduoard Barthe, told the French parliament:

> I affirm that either by the fact of the international solidarity of the great metallurgy companies, or in order to safeguard private business interests our military chiefs were ordered not to bombard the establishments of the Briey basin which were being exploited by the enemy during the war. I affirm that our aviation service received instructions to respect the blast furnaces in which the enemy steel

was being made, and that a general who had wished to bombard them was reprimanded.[35]

With regard to the 'international solidarity' of 'private business interests,' General Smedley Butler of the U.S. Marine Corps would later famously write:

> War is a racket. It always has been. It is possibly the oldest, easily the most profitable, surely the most vicious. It is the only one international in scope. It is the only one in which the profits are reckoned in dollars and the losses in lives. A racket is best described, I believe, as something that is not what it seems to the majority of the people. Only a small "inside" group knows what it is about. It is conducted for the benefit of the very few, at the expense of the very many. Out of war a few people make huge fortunes. In the World War a mere handful garnered the profits of the conflict. At least 21,000 new millionaires and billionaires were made in the United States during the World War. They mainly admitted their huge blood gains in their income tax returns. How many other millionaires falsified their tax returns, no one knows.[36]

It was clear to many that the war could and should have ended in 1915 had Germany not been so freely, so deliberately, provided with food for her armies and the wherewithal to arm them. The sham British blockade and the 'protected' iron mines of Briey were important factors in deliberately prolonging the war, but there was more, much more. Vast amounts of food were sent in from America to feed the German troops through another sham enterprise: 'Belgian Relief'.

The Commission for Relief in Belgium

Mainstream history relates that the Belgian people were facing starvation under German occupation in the First World War, and an American relief organisation was created in October 1914 to feed them. We are told that throughout the war the Commission for Relief in Belgium (the CRB) fed millions of hungry Belgians with funding to the tune of one billion dollars (worth around $30 billion in 2023) from governments and charitable donations.

Led by Herbert Hoover, a man touted as 'a great American humanitarian,' the CRB had a fleet of several dozen ships conveying food from the United States to the neutral Dutch port of Rotterdam. From there it was taken by canal and river barges to cities, towns and villages throughout Belgium. A group of leading Belgian businessmen formed a committee, the Comité National de Secours et d'Alimentation, that handled the distribution to 'destitute' Belgians.[37]

Ostensibly this was a massive humanitarian effort to prevent Belgian civilians starving, but behind the façade of big-hearted benevolence the CRB was feeding some two million German soldiers on the Western Front. Establishment historians tell us that the CRB was providing food to between nine and ten million Belgian and French civilians, but such numbers never existed after war commenced in 1914.

The Belgian population prior to the outbreak of war was approximately 7.5 million,[38] but over 1.5 million refugees had fled the war-torn country.

> A source at the Belgian Ministry of Federal Foreign Affairs says that between August and October 1914, more than 1.5 million Belgians left their country, driven out by a fear of German atrocities and the violent conflict that was about to engulf their homeland. These refugees were initially welcomed with a surge of generosity, whether they arrived in France, England or the Netherlands.[39]

With some 1.5 million Belgian refugees fleeing Belgium, and the Belgian army of around 300,000 retreating to the Yser river close to the French border, the remaining Belgian population was not nine million as reported, but under six million. The figure of nine million is only accurate if three million German troops serving in Belgium and the Western front are added. And that, indeed, was the reality.

Regarding French civilians reportedly being fed by the CRB, the north-eastern parts of France occupied by the German army originally had around two million inhabitants, but many had fled before the German invasion. By the end of August 1914, 150,000 French refugees had gone to the French interior, and by January the number exceeded 500,000. By the end of 1915 it was almost 1 million. Some 250,000 French citizens also moved east to get away from the fighting fronts.[40]

> A number of important assumptions still exist which have helped conceal the clever sleight of hand behind the organised system that supplied food to both the civilians in Belgium and the German army on the Western Front. The first and most concerning is the extent to which the illusion of starvation or impending starvation in Belgium was created. Belgium was highly industrialised but at

least 60 per cent of the country comprised rich agricultural land which was intensively cultivated. During the war years the general conditions of farming were sound, though modest.[41] When war broke out Belgium found herself in a very favourable position with regard to food stocks. The new cereal crop had been exceptionally good and, despite the presence of an invading army, there was at first no shortage of food and prices hardly rose.[42] ... Much of the CRB food was sold and the profits allegedly flowed back to the relief fund to purchase more. What this amounted to, we will never know. But this is the essential problem with Belgian relief in all of its guises; it has been successfully covered-up and rebranded, and what is recorded lends itself to myth.[43]

Herbert Hoover, the man placed in charge of the CRB, was the American-born Stanford University geology graduate who made a fortune in corrupt mining enterprises in Australia and China. He had close links to the Rothschilds, Sir Edward Grey, Lord Percy, Lord Crewe and, not least, Lord Milner, leader of the Rhodes-Milner secret society since 1902.

In previous chapters we saw how, in the early years of the century, Milner was in South Africa, having successfully concluded the Boer War to steal the Transvaal's gold mines from the Boers. With the extremely dangerous conditions and slave wages, there was an acute shortage of African men willing to work in the now British-controlled mines. Herbert Hoover, who was in China at the time swindling millions of pounds from the Chinese government, helped Milner by recruiting thousands of Chinese men to sign up for the work in South African mines with promises of a wonderful, well-paid future in South Africa, in which their families would be raised in beautiful garden cities. In South Africa under Milner's jurisdiction, the Chinese 'coolies' were forced to work the mines in indentured servitude, with many fatalities in mining accidents. Decent wages and beautiful 'garden cities' were a construct of Hoover's twisted imagination. With no means of getting back to China, few of those who survived the atrocious conditions ever saw their loved ones again.

On the outbreak of war in 1914, the now multi-millionaire Hoover was living in London and mixing with Milner and leading members of his secret society. He was rebranded as a 'great humanitarian, and selected by them to head the privately run Belgian 'relief' organisation that would secretly feed the German army.

Hoover was the perfect fit. Unscrupulous, greedy, a ruthless exploiter of men and opportunities, he was utterly devoid of humanitarian sympathies. Knowing as he did, that the scam would prolong the war and all of the misery that followed, Hoover had the complete confidence of the Secret Elite. He was supposed to be neutral but his whole history was that of a rampant anglophile who had built his success inside the British Empire and been richly rewarded. Hoover had lived so long in London "that he had fairly intimate relations with many men close to the British Government."[44] He knew the top men in Britain, and he knew how to railroad an organisation and turn it into his own. His life's work had been built on such bully-boy tactics, whether the victims were farmers in the mid-west of the United States, miners in Australia, Chinese officials in Kaiping, or Chinese 'coolies' sold into slavery in the gold mines of South Africa,[45] ... Chosen for this task by the London elites who deliberately caused the war, he visited Ambassador Page on 10 October to seek diplomatic support for providing food for Belgium.[46]

We have seen how few if any Belgians were suffering from hunger in 1914-15, yet shiploads of CRB food that began arriving in Rotterdam in October 1914, were transported into Belgium by roads, canals and railways that were still functioning. In early 1915, the CRB extended its food supplies "to French civilians caught behind the battle lines on the Western Front." That was the perfect cover for Hoover's men to convey food right up to the front lines for the German army without questions being asked by concerned Belgians.

Questions *were* asked in the British parliament, however, with assurances being sought – and given – that the food was not being diverted to German troops. Quite incredibly, the team of 25 men employed to ensure it did not go to the German forces were American students from Oxford University, Rhodes Scholars no less. As Professor Quigley told us, such 'promising' young scholars had been carefully selected to swell the future ranks of the Milner secret society, and "were but one of several instruments through which the society would work."[47] In other words, the Rhodes scholars were the perfect choice for 'policing' Belgian Relief. Warned to expect hardship in Belgium, they had "luxuries thrust upon them, chateaux in which to live, automobiles in which to ride, and appointed offices in which to work."[48]

Herbert Hoover brought an old Stanford University friend, Professor Vernon Kellogg, to Brussels in 1915 to oversee the CRB. Kellogg was also a close friend of David Starr Jordan president of Stanford and a fellow member of the Advisory Council of the Eugenics Committee of the United States. Kellogg, who regularly dined with officers of the German High Command in the Belgian capital, gave a gushing account of the Rhodes Scholars:

> Its members have crossed the channel in convoyed English despatch boats, passed through closed frontiers, scurried about in swift motors over all the occupied territory in which few other cars than German military one's ever moved, visited villages at the front under shell fire, lived at the very Great Headquarters of all the German armies of the West, been trusted on their honor to do a thousand and one things and be in a thousand and one places prohibited to all other civilians, and have lived up to the trust.[49]

The Rhodes Scholars from Oxford University were, like Kellogg, mixing with high-ranking German officers in Belgium. They "lived up to the trust," according to Herbert Hoover's friend, but whose trust was he referring to? They were, as Quigley stated, "carefully selected to swell the future ranks of the Milner secret society," and almost the perfect cover for the Milner Group to placate members of the Westminster Parliament who were rightly concerned about CRB food going to feed the German army. Those backbench parliamentarians were reassured by Edward Grey and others that there was nothing to be concerned about because bright, honest, American students from Oxford University were policing the food aid and nothing underhand could happen.

The German military authorities in occupied Belgium were well aware that the students' 'authority' was a joke, but it suited them. They treated the young Americans like royalty, drove them around Belgium in chauffeured staff cars with American pennants flying, and kept them well clear of CRB food distribution centres supplying the German trenches. "The Rhodes scholars served the Secret Elite purpose as a mere fop to the pretence that the food was destined for Belgian mouths only."[50]

Baron Oskar von der Lanken, head of the German political department in occupied Belgium, wrote in his report to Berlin in August 1916 that the whole question of Belgian Relief wheat imports *was critical to the survival of the German army.* He acknowledged that the continuation of CRB food supplies to Belgium and the North of France was of "major self-interest to the Reich."[51]

> As his official reports between 1915 and 1918 demonstrated, von der Lancken took pride in Germany's success in using the CRB to its

own benefit. He mocked the ineffective checks made by the Rhodes students writing: "In spite of this supervision, we have, once again, successfully routed an appreciable quantity of foodstuffs to the front or to Germany, and just as profitably, made use of local products for the occupying force – by means of the clauses which were kept voluntarily elastic or thanks to arrangements contracted secretly with the neutral committee or again with their unspoken tolerance."[52]

In his half-yearly report to Berlin for the first six months of 1917, von Lancken wrote:

"We have continued successfully to export to Germany, or distribute to our troops, appreciable quantities of food. Certain parts of the agreements have been voluntarily exploited. The advantages which Germany accrues through the relief work continues to grow and grow."[53]

This was a breathtaking admission which blows all other claims to the contrary out of the water. Von Lancken's reports indicated collusion and tacit understanding. He clearly admitted that the German authorities were secretly rerouting appreciable quantities of relief food ... [54]

Independent elements within the Admiralty, angered by the fact that the naval blockade was being grossly interfered with and allowing food through to Germany, were similarly concerned about the same happening with 'Belgian Relief'. Allegations were made that Herbert Hoover was "untrustworthy and had sinister business connections with German mining corporations," and they suspected that CRB food was passing into German hands.[55] The government commissioned a 'formal investigation' (read whitewash) of these charges headed by Sir Sidney Rowlatt, a barrister and, like Lord Mersey of the *Lusitania* inquiry, a safe Establishment man. Rowlatt 'investigated' and declared Hoover and the CRB above all suspicion. Any further questioning of Belgian Relief was officially quashed, and to this day the Establishment's 'safe' historians fail to ask how a starving Germany was able to feed its armies for four long years.

It was not only food and the raw materials necessary for weapons and munitions production that Anglo-American Big Business supplied Germany with, but oil.

OIL

Germany had no independent, secure supply of oil, and prior to the First World War, over 90 per cent of oil sales were firmly in the grip of J.D. Rockefeller's Standard Oil with its majority holding in Deutsche Petroleum-Verkaufs-Gesellschaft (DPV).[56]

Austria-Hungary had a surplus of oil production from wells in Galicia, then the largest and most populous province of the Austrian Empire, but a large percentage of that Galician oil was controlled by yet another Standard Oil subsidiary company, Vacuum Oil Company AG, Vienna.[57] Another major player in Galicia was the British-owned Premier Oil and Pipe Line Company. By the beginning of the war in 1914, Premier had become one of the largest foreign companies operating in the region, producing almost a quarter of all the Galician oil. By the war's end, this London-based company had twelve Austrian subsidiaries, 21,000 acres of land, 110 oil wells and four large refineries.[58] Initially it provided 60% of the oil needs of Austria-Hungary and Germany, and made huge profits for its British owners in supplying the enemy, but its supply was unable to keep up with demand and Germany had to find new sources. With rapidly diminishing Galician supplies, Romania became the major source of oil available to Germany in the First World War.[59]

Romanian oil came from the major oilfields at Ploesti and Campina, 50 miles north of Bucharest, with the bulk of it loaded onto barges and taken up the Danube to Germany. German capital controlled only one of the oilfields there, Steaua Romana, while the majority were owned by British, Dutch, and American interests. Rockefeller's Standard Oil owned the Romana-Americana field, and Royal Dutch Shell controlled Astra Romana, the second largest oil producer in Romania. Indeed, control of oil throughout the world was in the hands of relatively few very powerful oil companies: Standard Oil (American) Royal Dutch/Shell (Dutch/British), Mexican Eagle (British), and the nascent Anglo-Persian Oil Company (British). Most of the Romanian oil sent to Germany during the war came from companies intimately linked to Anglo-American High Finance, and could have been stopped. There was, however, never any concerted effort made to close down those oil supplies. To placate concerned Members of Parliament in the Westminster Parliament, however, an illusion had to be created that serious attempts were made to destroy the Romanian oil wells before they fell into German hands in 1916.

A story was put about in Britain that the Romanian oilfields had been utterly destroyed[60] and the country's wheat stores despoiled so that the Central Powers gained little from the capitulation of Romania. It was a fantastic story; the stuff of legends.[61] A British Lieutenant-Colonel and Member of Parliament Norton Griffiths MP, had, according to reports placed in newspapers, single-handedly sabotaged the Romanian oilfields, which were spread over several hundred square kilometres, minutes before the German troops marched in. He had, allegedly, destroyed the oil wells together with 70 refineries and 800,000 tons of crude oil.[62] The plumes of smoke over Bucharest some 60 kilometres away were reported to have blocked out the sky, such was the devastation Griffiths was reported to have caused. It was as though Indiana Jones had taken on the might of the German army and thwarted their designs on Romanian oil. Unfortunately, Norton Griffiths was a legend in his own mind, a maverick self-publicist with a history of 'incredible' adventures.

There was some damage and disruption to production, but before the end of the war over one million tons of oil had been transported from the Ploiesti fields to the Central Powers, mainly Germany. Had it been otherwise, the German war machine would have ground to a halt.... In a session led by the Reich Chancellor on 1 October 1918, the Minister of War explained that Germany could only carry on fighting for a month and a half if Romania was not at their disposal.[63]

Thousands of barges with Romanian oil bound for Germany constantly moved up and down the Danube with no attempt made to stop them. As a measure of that oil's importance to Germany, General Ludendorff, Deputy Chief of Staff, wrote in his memoirs:

> As Austria could not supply us with oil, and as all of our efforts to increase production were unavailing, Romanian oil was of decisive importance to us. But even with deliveries of Romanian oil, the question of oil supplies still remained very serious, and caused us great difficulty, not only for the conduct of the war, but for the life of the country."[64] ... German High Command acknowledged that without oil, the war could not have continued.[65]

As planned in London, the war of attrition carried on through 1916 -1918. While the German civilian population was starved, food and war materiel to keep the German army fighting poured in through the British naval blockade, Belgian relief, the Briey mines, and Romanian oil wells. Cutting off just one of those supply routes could have ended the war, let alone cutting off two, three, or all four. As General Butler very correctly stated, war is a racket. A few men – those who very deliberately caused the war and prolonged it – made fortunes, lived in luxury, and died peacefully in their beds in old age. It was a very different story for those who did the fighting and dying. Tens of millions of men fighting this totally unnecessary war suffered horrendous deaths or dreadful wounds. Duped as they were, those armies of brave and willing men were determined to give their all to defeat as quickly as possible what they were led to believe was an evil enemy, and get back home to their families. Those aspirations did not fit with the ruling elite's aims, but that elite never at any time cared a whit for the wishes or ambitions of ordinary working men. Those millions of men killed or maimed for life were expendable pawns in the ruling elite's great game for global control. Those men who fortuitously survived the carnage of the war went home not to 'a land fit for heroes,' but to the same old routine of their families' struggle to survive on the breadline if not, indeed, in poverty.

One thing is certain, had the British soldiers and their families been able to grasp even a fraction of the truth regarding who and what was behind this war and the provisioning of the German army, there would have been a bloody revolution in Britain overnight. Bullets would have been flying not on the western front in France, but in and around the British Foreign Office, the Admiralty, Buckingham Palace, and major banking houses in The City.

What happened to the expendable pawns of the British working class? The original highly-trained British Expeditionary Force of some 160,000 professional soldiers was all but wiped out following the battles of 1914 and early 1915. A huge new volunteer army of several million civilians and part-time territorial soldiers replaced them, thanks in large part to the Milner Group's grotesque lies about Germany, German 'atrocities' in Belgium, and the sinking of the *Lusitania*.

The British army in France was initially under the overall command of Field Marshal Sir John French, a 'national hero' from the Boer War, but following the disastrous outcome for the British at the Battle of Loos in August/September 1915, he was sacked from his post and replaced by General Sir Douglas Haig of the new army. Haig was the senior officer who oversaw the Loos disaster, but with friends in high places in London he deviously managed to shift the blame onto Field Marshal French. Loos – in north-east France, approximately 100 kilometres south-east of the coastal city of Calais – was the scene of the biggest British offensive (25 September – 8 October 1915) against German forces on the

Haig

Western Front that year. American historian and writer, Adam Hochschild, (Harvard) relates:

> Late on the morning of September 26, 1915, German officers at the front near Loos could not believe what they saw. On the second day of a major battle, roughly 10,000 British troops were walking towards them across more than half a mile of no man's land. There had been no previous bombardment. The German machine guns were in protected bunkers behind long intact rolls of barbed wire, in belts sometimes up to 30 feet thick. The British, according to a German account, moved forward in 10 columns "each about a thousand men, all advancing as if carrying out a parade-ground drill.... Never had machine guns such straightforward work to do ... with barrels becoming hot they traversed to and fro along the enemy's ranks.... Some British officers were mounted on horseback, and so made even more conspicuous targets. The result was devastating. The fast-diminishing ranks kept moving until they reached the first row of unbroken barbed wire."[66]

In his book, *The Donkeys*, published in 1961, British writer and politician, Alan Clark, pulled no punches. Ordinary British soldiers on the western front fought bravely and gave everything but it was akin to lions being led by donkeys. Clark holds 'donkey' leadership responsible for the huge losses among the British infantry at Loos:

> In the first two hours of the Battle of Loos more British soldiers died than the total number of casualties in all three services on both sides on D-Day 1944. And slowly, as the field of operations widened, their fate became apparent. Again and again they were called upon to attempt the impossible, and in the end they were all killed. It was as simple as that.[67]

The few British soldiers who made it to the impenetrable barbed wire could do nothing but turn around and make their way back towards their own trenches through the blood and gore of their dead and dying comrades. The Germans were nauseated by the sight of the massacre on what they called the *Leichenfeld* – field of corpses – and in a moment of mercy held their fire as the few surviving British soldiers retreated. Just the day before, Field-Marshal Lord Kitchener had reviewed the new volunteer recruits, congratulating them on 'the honour that had fallen to them'.[68]

> For Sir Douglas Haig commanding the British troops, it was a promising opportunity: if the attack succeeded he would win great glory;

if it failed, the person blamed would likely be the already precarious Sir John French. The two feuding generals did not even have a telephone line connecting their temporary command posts.[69]

On the morning of the attack, Haig ordered chlorine gas to be released from 5,000 six-foot long cylinders. With very little wind, however, the choking poison gas that burned the skin and eyes remained in no-man's land, affecting not the German troops but the thousands of British soldiers ordered to walk in line towards the endless rows of barbed wire and German machine guns.

> In a few spots, the breeze blew the gas back into the British trenches. All told, the British suffered more casualties from their own gas than the Germans. The surprise gas attack was supposed to substitute for a massive artillery bombardment ... but neither Haig nor French seems to have given much thought to one crucial fact: gas does not cut barbed wire.... Corpses and body parts littered the ground and the air was rank with the smell of death. On the second day of the attack Haig ordered the fateful advance by two inexperienced reserve divisions directly against hilltop German machine guns and uncut barbed wire. This was the sight, and the slaughter, that German officers observed with such amazement.... In this brief spasm of carnage, out of 10,000 British officers and men, more than 8,000 were killed, wounded, or missing. As with many episodes from this war, it is hard for us to see the attack on September 26, 1915 as anything other than a blatant, needless massacre initiated by generals with a near-criminal disregard for the conditions their men faced.[70]

The fighting at Loos continued for another two weeks with more than 61,000 British casualties. Riding his white steed, Sir John French visited the wounded to offer comforting words. Astonishingly, a memo from his headquarters to the Ministry of Munitions stated that the battle losses had not altered the views of British commanders that men with bayonets closing on the enemy were superior to machine guns. General Haig laid all blame for the failure on General French because he had kept reserve battalions too far back from the front. Incredibly, he stated: "My attack was a complete success, and reserves should have been at hand *then*."[71] That was later shown to be a lie, but Sir John French lost his post as Commander-in-Chief of the Forces in France with his accuser, Haig, succeeding him.

> Haig became Commander in Chief three months after the blunderings of Loos. His period of command, first of a corps, then of an army, had exposed grave professional weakness in a man whose rise had always owed more to intrigue and patronage than to any evidence of talent as a soldier.[72]

Former British army officer, and Reader in Psychology at University College London, Dr. Norman F. Dixon, wrote:

> Only the most blinkered would deny that the First World War exemplified every aspect of high-level military incompetence. For sheer lack of imaginative leadership, inept decisions, ignoring of military intelligence, underestimation of the enemy, delusional optimism and monumental wastage of human resources, it has surely never had its equal.[73]

Focusing on Haig, Dr. Dixon wrote:

> The acknowledged dunce of the family, Haig's military career seemed directed towards trying to prove otherwise. It is an astonishing tribute to powers of disturbed achievement-motivation that out of a nation of millions of people fighting for its life, there should have arisen a leader of such *apparently* limited capacity: a man of such *apparently* mediocre intellect that he had the greatest difficulty in passing even the Sandhurst entrance examination and actually failed the Staff College examination where 'he attracted unfavourable comment' from his examiner ... [Haig] had been so completely outmanoeuvred in the pre-war training exercises of 1912 that the manoeuvres had to be abandoned a day earlier than scheduled; a man whom Lloyd George was to call 'utterly stupid' and Briand '*tete du bois*'. How did it come about?[74]

How, indeed, did it come about that such a man would be placed in charge of the British army in France in the midst of the greatest war the world had ever witnessed? Dr Dixon adds that Haig was in fact probably *not* of low intelligence, but that his educational backwardness and other characteristics were products of a mind constrained and inhibited by the emotional consequences of early damage to his self-esteem. He states that no more might ever have been heard of Haig were it not for his elder sister Henrietta who knew the Duke of Cambridge. He, in turn, was able to arrange Haig's entry into the Staff College.[75]

Douglas Haig (1861-1928) was born in Edinburgh, the son of a member of the wealthy Haig whisky family. His father, allegedly an abusive alcoholic who was absent from home most of the time, died when Douglas was a boy. His mother (who would also die young) sent him off to a private boarding school at the age of eight. Haig acquired a place at Oxford University ostensibly to study Political Economy and Ancient History. He joined the posh, super-rich, all-male, Bullingdon Club which smashed up local Oxford pubs and restaurants for fun and to this day has a toxic reputation (two of Britain's recent Prime Ministers – David Cameron and Boris Johnson were members). Spending much of his three years at Oxford playing polo or loafing, he got the minimum pass degree.

In 1894, Haig's next move was to the Royal Military Academy at Sandhurst. He exhibited an angry and suspicious nature, was unsociable and abrasive in the mess, and notoriously inarticulate. Joining the Queens' own Hussars (Cavalry), he got a prestigious place at the Staff College, Camberley, thanks to royal patronage. Making a special trip to the Royal Small Arms Factory at Enfield, he studied the new water-cooled Maxim machine gun that could fire 600 rounds per minute.

In 1898, Haig joined Kitchener's army, serving in Egypt and Sudan. At the Battle of Omdurman on 2 September 1898, Haig and Winston Churchill saw first-hand the huge destructive power of the machine gun when tens of thousands of Mahdist warriors were slaughtered in a matter of hours. Crucially, he knew exactly what machine guns were capable of when, 17 years later at Loos in France, he ordered tens of thousands of lightly armed young British soldiers to walk slowly out over open ground to face them.

Haig returned to Britain for a short time in 1899, and was appointed Major in the 1st Cavalry Brigade under Sir John French. French had made several bad financial investments, and was facing bankruptcy that would have ruined his career had Haig not lent him £2,500 (worth around £400,000 today). Haig gained several quick promotions thereafter. That same final year of the 19th century, French was selected to command the cavalry and went to fight in the Boer War in South Africa. Haig's loan to Sir John proved a profitable investment when French chose him as Chief Staff Officer and Assistant Adjutant General. It was in South Africa that Haig first came into contact with leading members of the secret society, Cecil Rhodes and Alfred Milner. In January 1901, Haig was given his own column of 2,000 men and sent to Cape Colony to pursue Boer raiders.

> Haig was also responsible for burning farms, executions, rounding up women and children and similar measures which gave the war its grisly notoriety.... Questions of morality were immaterial. Suffering was, to Haig, simply proof that his measures were working.... Thus farm burnings and the forced movement of people [into Milner's concentration camps] cleared the way for a new tide of righteous English imperialism. Haig accepted that part of his role was to make South Africa safe for the English to exploit its vast riches. He in fact urged Henrietta [his sister] to invest her millions in the new South Africa.[76]

We saw in earlier chapters how some 25,000 women and children of Dutch descent died in the concentration camps Haig had filled. From that moment, Alfred Milner knew Haig was capable of doing a good job for the ruling elite in future ventures. He was appointed Companion of the Order of the Bath – a mark of the king's favour – and promoted to Lieutenant-Colonel.

In South Africa, Haig befriended John Buchan, private secretary to Alfred Milner, and a member of the secret society.[77] Buchan would later play a major role in the falsification of the history of the First World War by writing *Nelson's History of The War.* Unsurprisingly, it lavished praise on Douglas Haig. On Haig's return to Britain after victory over the Boers in 1902, he was appointed aide-de-camp to King Edward VII. He also befriended the king's son, the Prince of Wales – later King George V. Lord Esher, who became Haig's patron, was one of the architects of the Committee of Imperial Defence, which organised Britain's part in the war with Germany a decade before it began, and "one of the most influential power brokers of the Edwardian age."[78]

Haig was now mixing with the highest echelons of the Milner Group and being groomed for a major military role in their forthcoming war with Germany. They knew for sure he could be relied upon to do whatever was necessary and would never question why they were prolonging the war. Indeed, Haig was one of them and by 1904 he became the youngest

Major-General in the British Army. A man who had no time whatsoever for the common man or ordinary soldier, he would have no qualms in recklessly sacrificing millions for the cause of Empire. Military historian Denis Winter writes:

> With military dogmas cut and dried before 1914, Haig felt no need to study the details of his profession, and many competent judges were astounded by the gaps in Haig's knowledge relating to the most elementary aspects of soldiering. Monash [Australian General] was one of them. In a letter to his wife he wrote: "Haig was, technically speaking, quite out of his depth in regard to the minutiae of the immense resources that were placed in his hands" … "Haig knew nothing about infantry or engineers and could not understand artillery." Nor indeed did he make the slightest effort to find out. Desmond Morton, one of Haig's ADCs, commented on the latter's "utter dislike of new ideas" which might disturb the threadbare dogmas he took into war.[79]

THE SOMME.

Just nine months after his disastrous command at Loos, and replacing Sir John French as overall commander in France, Douglas Haig, a lackey of the ruling elite who was far 'out of his depth,' was in charge of the major British offensive at the Somme. Once again, he ordered the British troops out of their trenches to attack German positions heavily guarded with machine guns. On the very first *day* of the battle, 1 July 1916, the British army suffered over 57,000 casualties. On that one day, 19,240 men were killed by machine-gun fire and artillery – and twice as many badly wounded – when they were ordered to walk slowly across the open ground of no-mans-land towards the German trenches. A week-long artillery bombardment had failed to destroy the German defences. Unlike the British in their poorly constructed trenches opposite, the German troops facing them had built strong, deep, and relatively comfortable positions that could withstand bombardment. Immediately after the week-long bombardment ended, and whistles blew for the British infantry offensive to begin, German machine gunners poured from their safe trenches, set up their guns, and slaughtered the British troops as they walked towards them.

British historians have attempted to defend Haig's behaviour at the Somme, suggesting he could not be aware that the German defences had survived the week-long artillery barrage. That, in the first instance, may have been so, but within hours, if not minutes, it became clear to all that they *had* survived and that this would be a horrendous slaughter that would make Loos look tame in comparison. Week after week, month after month, Haig ordered the men out of the trenches to face the slaughter. British reserve divisions constantly being brought up from the rear to replace the dead and wounded could see exactly what was happening but knew they would be shot at dawn by British firing squads should they refuse to leave the trenches. Ironically, it would have been a more honourable death for those young men than meekly acquiescing to this madman's orders and being killed in any case. In 140 days under Haig's command, the British army suffered 419,654 casualties at the Somme.

British historians toeing the Establishment line, of course, have whitewashed the entire despicable affair. Denis Winter, one of the few British historians brave enough to relate the truth, writes scathingly of the official British war historian, Brigadier-General Sir James Edmonds:

> The quantity of deception and downright lying dealt out by the British official historian makes astonishing reading today.... The end product of Edmond's work was therefore an official History which presented a fraudulent account of the Western front, supported by documents mischievously selected and leaks maliciously planted in the path of writers pressing too hard on the truth.... Edmonds had been given very precise instructions on method and story when he began his work, and when the work was completed thirty years later that commission had been faithfully executed.[80]

Compliant historians such as Edmonds had been 'precisely instructed' on the narrative they were to relate. Little or nothing has changed today with the purveyors of falsehood at Oxford and elsewhere. In response to Denis Winter's truthful revelations, one of the most egregious of the recent crop of 'court historians,' Professor Gary Sheffield, (Douglas Haig Fellow in the year 2000) writes:

> Denis Winter's *Haig's Command* is a deeply flawed book centred on a bizarre conspiracy theory.[81]

The Establishments old canard 'conspiracy theory' is rolled out to denigrate a truth-teller. Sheffield makes the preposterous suggestion that there was no strategic alternative in 1916 to his hero Haig's sacrifice of half a million British soldiers. It paved the way, he says, for a British victory in 1918, and the war could not have been won without such enormous sacrifice. Such is the disgraceful nonsense that passes for academic history in Britain today. Sheffield, of course, makes no mention whatsoever of the fact that the war would have been won, done and dusted in the spring of 1915 if the German army had not been provisioned by British ruling elites. Perhaps he doesn't know this? Perhaps he has conducted no in-depth research into the war? We can think of no better promotion for Denis Winter's excellent book than Sheffield's ludicrous comments about it. Thankfully, such British 'historians' are more and more being seen for what they are: craven purveyors of the Establishment's fake history, as detailed by Carroll Quigley. In a review of Sheffield's book praising Douglas Haig, the historian and journalist Frank McLynn wrote in *The Independent* newspaper:

> Since Sheffield wants to rescue Haig from the justifiable charge that he was an incompetent butcher, and to argue for Haig as the architect of victory in 1918, he ties himself in knots trying to demonstrate that the alleged technological determinism somehow ceased to operate in 1918. But Sheffield is not strong on logic: among his eccentricities are refusal to accept that the word "disillusionment" has any meaning…. It is an insult to the memory of those who died on the Western Front that the butcher who sent them there should have his reputation laundered in this way. One takes consolation from the fact that Sheffield's defence of Haig is utterly unconvincing, as is the rest of his book.[82]

One year after the Somme disaster, 'Butcher Haig' came up with another plan for a major offensive and 'war-winning breakthrough': British troops would break out of the Ypres salient they had occupied since 1914 in Flanders some 40 kilometres to the south of the Belgian coastal town of Ostend. The Third Battle of Ypres – also known as Passchendaele – was fought between July and November 1917. With heavy rain turning the battlefield into a sea of waist deep mud, many soldiers were literally sucked in and drowned/suffocated as they attempted to cross it. Passchendaele, perhaps even more so than the Somme, is remembered for its utter futility. British forces gained a muddy terrain just several miles across at a cost of over quarter of a million men killed, wounded or missing. Yet another Haig offensive was an utter disaster. Adam Hochschild writes:

> In Belgium, the wind was cold and bitter indeed. The total of British dead and wounded at Passchendaele, officially the Third Battle of Ypres, is in dispute, but a low estimate puts the estimate at

260,000; most reckonings are far higher. Haig ceaselessly trumpeted Passchendaele as a triumph, but few agreed ... The capture of a muddy, ruined village or two in Flanders seemed little to brag about. "For the first time," the war correspondent and novelist Phillip Gibbs later wrote, "the British Army lost its spirit of optimism, and there was a sense of deadly depression among many officers and men with whom I came in touch. They saw no ending of the war, and nothing except continuous slaughter." Men joked bitterly about where the front line would be in 1950. One officer calculated that if the British continued to gain ground at the pace so far, they would reach the Rhine in 180 years. It was during the autumn of 1917 that the British army experienced the nearest thing to mutiny on the Western Front: six days of intermittent rioting by several thousand troops at the big supply and training base in Etaples, France, in which a military policeman killed one soldier. Amid protests the red flag briefly flew, and one rebel was later tried and executed ... "Reinforcements shambled up past the guns with dragging steps and expressions of men who knew they were going to certain death" wrote one veteran about the mood around Ypres in October. "No words of greeting passed as they slouched along: in sullen silence they filed past one by one to the sacrifice." Haig, as usual, tolerated no dissent. When a brave Colonel told him that further fruitless attacks would leave no resources for an offensive the next spring, Haig turned white with anger.[83]

Historian A.J.P. Taylor wrote: "Those British generals who prolonged the slaughter kept their posts and won promotion."[84] We should note Taylor's words well. Generals – like Haig – *prolonged the slaughter'* and were rewarded for doing so. Haig was certainly well rewarded when war *was* eventually brought to an end. The British elites created an earldom for him and granted him a payment of £100,000 in recognition of the 'great service he had rendered the nation'. It would be the equivalent of over £4 million today. The 'grateful nation' also bought the old Clan Haig family estate at Bemersyde, and presented it to him. The cost to the taxpayer of the large stately home and 1,400 acres of prime land in the Scottish borders has never been disclosed. Haig happily saw out his days playing golf, and he founded a welfare organisation that helped ex-servicemen by raising funds through the sale of artificial poppies. He toured Britain and the Commonwealth officially unveiling war memorials to the fallen with the grotesque lie that they died for 'freedom and civilisation'.

Haig himself died peacefully in his bed in January 1928. His body lay in state at Westminster Abbey and his funeral was proclaimed a "national day of mourning."

Summary: Chapter 11 – War is a Racket

- Throughout the war, thousands of merchant ships carried food to Britain from every corner of the world and her entire population received sufficient calories.

- Food imports for the German civilian population were cut off, resulting in widespread malnutrition, starvation, and increased infant mortality.

- The German army, however, was maintained on an adequate diet thanks to the effectiveness of the British naval blockade being sabotaged by what was effectively a Milner Group committee in London.

- Millions of bales of cotton essential for explosives production were also allowed through the blockade, together with minerals such as iron, copper, and zinc essential for weapons manufacture.

- Food was also sent by the Anglo-American elites to feed the German forces through Herbert Hoover's Commission for Relief of Belgium.

- The iron ore mines and smelters of Briey were left completely intact and virtually handed on a plate to Germany at the start of the war when they could have been destroyed and German armaments and U-boat construction greatly diminished.

- The major oil wells and refineries in Romania owned by British and American companies were subjected to a token show of destruction but then continued supplying Germany with her essential oil requirements throughout the remainder of the war.

- Supplying all of the above to Germany was done in order to deliberately prolong the war. A protracted war of attrition was required to crush Germany economically and industrially, and break the spirit of the German people.

- On the war front, incompetent generals from the British ruling class – such as Douglas Haig – were put in charge of the army, and needlessly sacrificed hundreds of thousands of British soldiers. Those generals were then well rewarded by the British elite for their part in prolonging the war.

CHAPTER 12

UNITED STATES GOES TO WAR "FOR DEMOCRACY"

On 2 April 1917, US President Woodrow Wilson called an extraordinary session of the United States Congress and asked it to declare war on Germany. Wall Street's man in the White House had narrowly gained a second term in the Presidential election of 1916 after campaigning on the slogans "He kept us out of war" and "America First." Wilson now peeled off his pacifist mask when addressing Congress:

> Gentlemen of the Congress, I have called the Congress into extraordinary session because there are serious, very serious, choices of policy to be made, and made immediately, which it was neither right nor constitutionally permissible that I should assume the responsibility of making.
>
> On the 3rd of February last, I officially laid before you the extraordinary announcement of the Imperial German government that on and after the 1st day of February it was its purpose to put aside all restraints of law or of humanity and use its submarines to sink every vessel that sought to approach either the ports of Great Britain and Ireland or the western coasts of Europe or any of the ports controlled by the enemies of Germany within the Mediterranean.
>
> ...There is one choice we cannot make; we are incapable of making: we will not choose the path of submission and suffer the most sacred rights of our nation and our people to be ignored or violated. The wrongs against which we now array ourselves are no common wrongs; they cut to the very roots of human life. With a profound sense of the solemn and even tragical character of the step I am taking and of the grave responsibilities which it involves, but in unhesitating obedience to what I deem my constitutional duty, I advise that the Congress declare the recent course of the Imperial German government to be in fact nothing less than war against

the government and people of the United States; that it formally accept the status of belligerent which has thus been thrust upon it; and that it take immediate steps, not only to put the country in a more thorough state of defense but also to exert all its power and employ all its resources to bring the government of the German Empire to terms and end the war...

We have no quarrel with the German people. We have no feeling towards them but one of sympathy and friendship. It was not upon their impulse that their government acted in entering this war. It was not with their previous knowledge or approval. It was a war determined upon as wars used to be determined upon in the old, unhappy days when peoples were nowhere consulted by their rulers and wars were provoked and waged in the interest of dynasties or of little groups of ambitious men who were accustomed to use their fellow men as pawns and tools.[1]

The lies and hypocrisy were astounding. Over the previous two-and-a-half years the United States had been stoking the flames of war by sending vast amounts of money, and millions of rifles, bullets, artillery shells and heavy weaponry into Europe to facilitate the slaughter. The U.S military-industrial complex and Wilson's masters on Wall Street – essentially one and the same – had been making billions in war profiteering. With Orwellian doublespeak, Wilson the hypocrite added:

The world must be made safe for democracy. Its peace must be planted upon the tested foundations of political liberty. We have no selfish ends to serve. We desire no conquest, no dominion. We seek no indemnities for ourselves, no material compensation for the sacrifices we shall freely make. We are but one of the champions of the rights of mankind. We shall be satisfied when those rights have been made as secure as the faith and the freedom of nations can make them...[2]

George W. Norris, Republican Senator from Nebraska, spoke passionately against American entry into the war. President Wilson had spoken of "ambitious men" in Germany who used their fellow men as "pawns and tools." Senator Norris also spoke of such 'ambitious men,' but they were centred on Wall Street. Norris spoke truth to power and his speech is worth considering:

There are many honest, patriotic citizens who think we ought to engage in this war and who are behind the President in his demand that we should declare war against Germany. I think such people err in judgment and to a great extent have been misled as to the real history and the true facts by the almost unanimous demand of the great combination of wealth that has a direct financial interest in our participation in the war.

We have loaned many hundreds of millions of dollars to the Allies in this controversy. While such action was legal and countenanced by international law, there is no doubt in my mind but the enormous amount of money loaned to the Allies in this country has been instrumental in bringing about a public sentiment in favor of our country taking a course that would make every bond worth a hundred cents on the dollar and making the payment of every debt certain and sure. Through this instrumentality and also through the instrumentality of others who have not only made millions out of the war in the manufacture of munitions, etc., and who would expect to make millions more if our country can be drawn into the catastrophe, a large number of the great newspapers and news agencies of the country have been controlled and enlisted in the greatest propaganda that the world has ever known to manufacture sentiment in favor of war.

It is now demanded that the American citizens shall be used as insurance policies to guarantee the safe delivery of munitions of war to belligerent nations. The enormous profits of munition manufacturers, stockbrokers, and bond dealers must be still further increased by our entrance into the war. This has brought us to the present moment, when Congress, urged by the President and backed by the artificial sentiment, is about to declare war and engulf our country in the greatest holocaust that the world has ever known.

To whom does war bring prosperity? Not to the soldier who for the munificent compensation of $16 per month shoulders his musket and goes into the trench, there to shed his blood and to die if necessary; not to the broken-hearted widow who waits for the return of the mangled body of her husband; not to the mother who weeps at the death of her brave boy; not to the little children who shiver with cold; not to the babe who suffers from hunger; nor to the millions of mothers and daughters who carry broken hearts to their graves. War brings no prosperity to the great mass of common and patriotic citizens. It increases the cost of living of those who toil and those who already must strain every effort to keep soul and body together. War brings prosperity to the stock gambler on Wall Street – to those who are already in possession of more wealth than can be realized or enjoyed.

...Their object in having war and in preparing for war is to make money. Human suffering and the sacrifice of human life are necessary, but Wall Street considers only the dollars and the cents. The men who do the fighting, the people who make the sacrifices are the ones who will not be counted in the measure of this great prosperity ... The stockbrokers would not, of course, go to war because the very object they have in bringing on the war is profit, and therefore they must remain in their Wall Street offices in order to share in that great prosperity which they say war will bring. The volunteer officer, even the drafting officer, will not find them. They will be concealed in their palatial offices on Wall Street, sitting behind mahogany desks, covered up with clipped coupons – coupons soiled with the sweat of honest toil, coupons stained with mothers' tears, coupons dyed in the lifeblood of their fellowmen.

We are taking a step today that is fraught with untold danger. We are going into war upon the command of gold. We are going to run the risk of sacrificing millions of our countrymen's lives in order that other countrymen may coin their lifeblood into money.[3]

Another opponent of the United States going to war was Wisconsin Senator Robert La Follette (Progressive Republican). He stated that the war had no popular support and argued that the United States had been far from even-handed between Britain and Germany. La Follette called on Congress to stand firm against the war as "collective homicide could not establish human rights." The United States entering the war would be "treason to humanity." La Follette stated:

Mr. President, I had supposed until recently that it was the duty of senators and representatives in Congress to vote and act according to their convictions on all public matters that came before them for consideration and decision. Quite another doctrine has recently been promulgated by certain newspapers, which unfortunately seems to have found considerable support elsewhere, and that is the doctrine of "standing back of the President" without inquiring whether the President is right or wrong. For myself, I have never subscribed to that doctrine and never shall. I shall support the President in the measures he proposes when I believe them to be right. I shall oppose measures proposed by the President when I believe them to be wrong. The fact that the matter which the President submits for consideration is of the greatest importance is only an additional reason why we should be sure that we are right and not to be swerved from that conviction or intimidating in its expression by any influence of its power whatsoever.

If it is important for us to speak and vote our convictions in matters of internal policy, though we may unfortunately be in disagreement with the President, it is infinitely more important for us to speak and vote our convictions when the question is one of peace or war, certain to involve the lives and fortunes of many of our people and, it may be, the destiny of all of them and of the civilized world as well.

...You cannot distinguish between the principles which allowed England to mine a large area of the Atlantic Ocean and the North Sea in order to shut in Germany, and the principle on which Germany by her submarines seeks to destroy all shipping which enters the war zone which she has laid out around the British Isles. The English mines are intended to destroy without warning every ship that enters the war zone she has proscribed, killing or drowning every passenger that cannot find some means of escape. It is neither more nor less than that which Germany tries to do with her submarines in her war zone. We acquiesced in England's action without protest. It is proposed that we now go to war with Germany for identically the same action upon her part.... The failure to treat the belligerent nations of Europe alike, the failure to reject the unlawful "war zones" of both Germany and Great Britain is wholly accountable for our present dilemma. We should not seek to hide our blunder behind the smoke of battle to inflame the mind of our people by half-truths into the frenzy of war in order that they may never appreciate the real cause of it until it is too late. I do not believe that our national honor is served by such a course. The right way is the honorable way.[4]

It was a powerful assessment, but La Follette's critics scathingly suggested that he was "of more help to the Kaiser than a quarter of a million troops," and the controlled Press declared him to be a pro-German traitor to America. The Senate and House voted overwhelmingly in favour of entering the war, and on 6 April 1917, the United States declared war on Germany. In truth, it would have done so much earlier if the masters of finance had deemed it necessary and anti-war public opinion had sufficiently been turned. Wilson had gained a second term in 1916 by having kept America out of the war, indicating that the majority of voters approved of that stance, but minds were being poisoned with anti-German propaganda and lies across the US, including the Bryce Report fabrication about

German 'atrocities' in Belgium, the *Lusitania* sinking, and the Black Tom island explosion. Many churchmen also played a part in swinging public opinion in favour of war with sermons similar to the despicable anti-German lies spouted by the Bishop of London, who encouraged Christians to think that all Germans had to be killed. The famous American evangelist and former baseball star, Billy Sunday, spoke the following prayer at the opening session of Congress in early 1918:

> Thou knowest, O Lord, that we are in a life-and-death struggle with one of the most infamous, vile, greedy, avaricious, bloodthirsty, sensual, and vicious nations that has ever disgraced the pages of history. Thou knowest that Germany has drawn from the eyes of mankind enough tears to make another sea; that she has drawn blood enough to redden every wave upon that sea; that she has drawn enough groans and shrieks from the hearts of men, women, and children to make another mountain. We pray Thee that Thou wilt by Thy mighty arm beat back that great pack of hungry, wolfish Huns, whose fangs drip with blood and gore. We pray Thee that the stars in their courses and the winds and waves may fight against them.... We pray Thee that Thou will bless our beloved President and give him strength of mind and body and courage of heart for his arduous duties in these sorrow-laden, staggering days.... And Lord, may every man, woman, and child, from Maine to California and from Minnesota to Louisiana, stand up to the last ditch and be glad and willing to suffer and endure until final victory shall come. Bless our allies, and may victory be ours...[5]

In his evangelical tours of the U.S., Billy Sunday not only preached hatred against Germany and Germans, he sold war bonds at President Wilson's behest.[6] The warmongering preacher was a friend of President Wilson, J.D. Rockefeller Jr., Theodore Roosevelt, and Herbert Hoover. Like the 'good' Bishop of London, he operated at the heart of the Anglo-American Establishment. Like most who encouraged young men to fight and die, his end came with a peaceful death in his bed in old age.

With America now in the war, the mountain of British government debt for food and munitions supplied by the U.S. over the previous two years and more was transferred to the general debt of the U.S. Treasury. On 24 April 1917, Woodrow Wilson signed a war finance bill which opened the Federal Reserve System's floodgates and removed any possible liability from the J.P. Morgan bank which had until then provided the funds. Congress passed major amendments to the Federal Reserve

Act to enable monetary expansion that would cover the expected costs of the war. The currency in circulation more than doubled from $465m to $1247m by December 1917. The reform, it was argued, was necessary to finance the expected $2 billion dollar cost of participating in the war for a year. The debt burden was now placed on the U.S. taxpayer, not Wall Street, and at war's end, John Foster Dulles calculated that Britain and her allies owed the United States – more accurately, the Wall Street bankers – $12,500,000,000 at 5 per cent interest.[7] In today's money it represents an almost unimaginable sum.

All of the belligerent European countries had been bankrupted by the war, which was fought on a vast mountain of debt that would have to be made good by the ordinary taxpayer. As detailed in an earlier chapter, while the U.S. central bank – the Federal Reserve System – appeared to be a government institution, it was in fact controlled by the big players on Wall Street who used it to create money from thin air. They likewise used it to promote communism in Russia.

THE BOLSHEVIK REVOLUTION

November 1917 (October in the old Russian calendar) marked a major turning point in the war when the Bolsheviks seized power in Russia and deposed the czar. Understanding how the revolution was supported and partially funded by leading men in international finance is crucial to an understanding of twentieth century history, but a detailed study is beyond the scope of this book. Leon Trotsky, the supposedly impoverished 'exiled Russian revolutionist,' and leader of the revolution with Vladimir Len-nin, sailed from Spain to New York in late 1916. On arrival in the city, the supposedly near penniless Trotsky and his family initially stayed in the Hotel Astor near Times Square. Professor Richard B. Spence, (University of Idaho) writes in *Wall Street and the Russian Revolution*:

> Not only was this one of the most expensive hostelries in the city, it had a reputation as a gathering place for the Wall Street elite – a curious place for a revolutionary socialist to take his rest.[8]

From the Hotel Astor, Trotsky moved with his wife and two children to an apartment in the Bronx, complete with concierge, lift, telephone, and refrigerator. He relates in his memoirs, *My Life,* how he and his family were driven around New York in a chauffeur-driven car.[9] His stylish living standards were completely at odds with his alleged lack of money. Professor Spence indicates that William Wiseman, head of British intelligence, was actively monitoring Trotsky in New York and on 22 March, Wiseman sent a coded telegram to London stating that Trotsky was being backed by Jewish funds. Trotsky went to the British consulate at 44 Whitehall Street (the headquarters of British intelligence operating in New York under Wiseman) on 25 March and was issued with a visa that would allow him to pass through the British naval blockade.[10]

Professor Antony Sutton wrote that when Trotsky left New York for St. Petersburg to organise the Bolshevik phase of the Russian revolution, he was carrying $10,000 (worth approximately $235,000 today).[11] Mainstream historians suggest that the money came from German sources including, possibly, Max Warburg at the M.M. Warburg bank in Hamburg. Although no documentary evidence has been uncovered, others suggest that funds for Trotsky came from the Wall Street banker Jacob Schiff of the Kuhn, Loeb & Co. Bank.[12] Professor Sutton believed that Schiff was *not* involved in funding Trotsky or Bolshevism. Sutton wrote:

> It is significant that documents in the State Department files confirm that the investment banker Jacob Schiff, often cited as a source of funds for the Bolshevik Revolution, was in fact *against* support of the Bolshevik regime. This position was ... in direct contrast to the Morgan-Rockefeller promotion of the Bolsheviks. The persistence with which the Jewish conspiracy myth has been pushed suggests that it may well be a deliberate device to divert attention from the real issues and the real causes. The evidence suggests that the New York bankers who were also Jewish had relatively minor roles in supporting the Bolsheviks, while the New York bankers who were also Gentiles (Morgan, Rockefeller, Thomson) had major roles. What better way to divert attention from the real operators than by the medieval bogeyman of anti-Semitism?[13]

When Trotsky boarded the S.S *Kristianiafjord* at South Brooklyn pier on 27 March 1917 to sail for Russia, he was travelling under a passport issued by President Woodrow Wilson. Sutton writes:

President Woodrow Wilson was the fairy godmother who provided Trotsky with a passport to return to Russia to "carry forward" the revolution. This American passport was accompanied by a Russian entry permit and a British transit visa ... Jennings C. Wise makes the pertinent comment, "Historians must never forget that Woodrow Wilson, despite the efforts of the British police, made it possible for Leon Trotsky to enter Russia with an American passport." President Wilson facilitated Trotsky's passage to Russia at the same time careful State Department bureaucrats, concerned about such revolutionaries entering Russia, were unilaterally attempting to tighten up passport procedures.[14]

While Trotsky's journey from New York to Russia was being facilitated by banking elites, so too was Vladimir Lennin's journey from his exile in Switzerland. On hearing of Czar Nicholas II's abdication on 2 March 1917, Lenin and fellow Marxist revolutionaries were put on a German train at Zurich which was then 'sealed from the outside world' and given safe passage through Germany to the port of Sassnitz in northeast Germany. They boarded a Swedish ferry for Trelleborg, and from there went on to Russia. Lenin was aided on his journey by Jacob Furstenberg and Olof Aschberg. Furstenberg  was the son of a wealthy Jewish family who owned factories in Sweden. Olof Aschberg was head of the Nya Banken in Stockholm.

Sweden had dominated the market in illicit trade between the Allies and Germany (goods coming in through the sham naval blockade) since the early months of the war, and at the heart of much of that business sat a Swedish banker and Businessman, Olof Aschberg and his bank, Nya Banken. Furstenberg was an associate of Aschberg's and much of the money sent from both the United States and Germany for the Bolsheviks, passed through Nya Banken. Aschberg's London agent was the British Bank of Commerce, whose chairman, Earl Grey, was linked to the inner core of the Milner Group in London. Another important Nya Banken connection was Max May, vice-president of J.P. Morgan's Guaranty Trust of New York, also an associate of Olof Aschberg. Much of the "German" money transferred through Nya Banken to the Bolsheviks came via the Disconto-Gesellschaft bank. When one realizes that Disconto-Gesellschaft was part of the Rothschild Group and J.P. Morgan was a front for the Rothschilds on Wall Street, the hidden hand of Rothschild becomes apparent, yet again.

> Max Warburg, one of the most powerful bankers in Germany, was the older brother of Paul Warburg, the major force in establishing America's Federal Reserve System, which helped Wall Street fund the war in Europe. It is worth repeating that Max, himself a Rothschild agent and reputedly head of the German espionage system during the war, was involved with Arthur Zimmerman in ensuring Lenin's safe passage across Germany. Max Warburg was likewise involved in the safe passage of Trotsky to Russia. A U.S. State Department file, "Bolshevism and Judaism," dated 13 November 1918, asserted that there could be no doubt that the "Jewish Firm," Kuhn, Loeb & Company and its partners "started and engineered" the revolution in Russia. The report added that Max Warburg had also financed Trotsky, and that Aschberg and Nya Banken were involved. This tangled web makes little sense unless one understands how all of these named bankers and banks were closely linked to each other, and to their common goal of international control.[15]

Lenin and Trotsky seized power through an armed insurrection in St. Petersburg on 6-7 November 1917 (New Style). Rusia became a communist state and civil war broke out. On 3 March 1918, in the city of Brest-Litovsk (now Brest in Belarus), the new communist Russian rulers signed a treaty with Germany that ended Russian participation in the war. Russia had suffered millions of casualties in a conflict which the czar had been lured into with the false promise of gaining Constantinople and the Straits. For Britain and her Allies, that outcome was now conveniently voided. The old Ottoman Empire would still be carved up at war's end, but not by Russia. On the night of 16-17 July 1918, Czar Nicholas, his wife and their five children were slaughtered by the Bolsheviks in the basement of a house in Yekaterinburg

Some 40 German divisions were freed from Russia thanks to the Brest-Litovsk treaty and were transferred to the Western Front. With these extra troops, the German army then made one final desperate attempt to defeat the Allies in the spring offensive of 1918. Between March and July, they made significant advances in northern France and west Flanders in Belgium, with the casualties on both sides amounting to over one and-a-half million men. American troops poured in to support the British and French, however, and by August the German army was driven back from the territory it had gained. The British naval blockade was now being properly implemented, and food that had been made available to the German forces through Hoover's Belgian Relief scam was now turned off. As the starvation noose was tightened round the German army's neck, in late September the Kaiser was advised by German military leaders of the necessity for a ceasefire. Wilhelm would later (1922) write in his memoirs:

> General Groener who had gone to Berlin to study the situation, reported on his return that he had received very bad impressions regarding the Government and the sentiment prevailing in the country; that things were approaching revolution; that the Government was merely tearing down without setting up anything positive; that the people wanted peace at last, at any cost, no matter what kind of peace; that the authority of the Government was equal to zero, the agitation against the Emperor in full swing, my abdication hardly to be avoided any longer. Groener added that the troops at home were unreliable and disagreeable surprises might come in case of a revolt; that the courier chests of the Russian Bolshevist ambassador, seized by the criminal police, had disclosed some very damaging evidence that the Russian Embassy, in conjunction with the Spartacus group, had long since thoroughly prepared, without being disturbed, a Bolshevist revolution on the Russian model. The men back from leave, Groener went on, were infected by propaganda and had already carried the poison to the army. As soon as it had been made free by an armistice, the army would refuse to fight against the rebels upon its return home. Therefore, General Groener declared, it was necessary to accept, immediately and unconditionally, any sort of armistice, no matter how hard its conditions might be; the army was no longer to be trusted and revolution was imminent behind the front.[16]

In late October 1918, with Germany seeking an armistice, it was clear to most that the end of the war was imminent. The Admiralty chief of staff, Reinhardt Scheer, and Admiral Franz von Hipper, however, ordered the High Seas Fleet out from Kiel and into battle with the Royal Navy in the English Channel. Germany's major warships had been sitting idle in harbour since the naval battle of Jutland in 1916, and this was to be 'an honourable' last stand to preserve the prestige of the navy. Secret sailors' councils formed on German warships at Kiel and Wilhelmshaven had other ideas. They balked at a useless battle of prestige – a suicide mission – and refused to put to sea. Around 1,000 mutineers were arrested and the fleet immobilised. Within 48 hours, anti-government demonstrations grew around the town of Kiel with some 40,000 soldiers, sailors and workers taking part. That, in turn, triggered the formation of workers' and soldiers' councils across north Germany, and by 7 November revolution had reached Munich. The German Bundestag Research Section relates:

> The revolution of November 1918 was a consequence of the military defeat of the German Empire in the First World War and was triggered by the naval mutiny at the beginning of November 1918. Within only a few days this insurgency spread throughout the Empire with no appreciable resistance from the old order. It developed into a mass movement against the monarchical system as the working classes joined forces with the troops. Throughout the Empire, Workers' and Soldiers' Councils were formed and assumed political and military powers.... On 9 November 1918, the Imperial Chancellor, Prince Max of Baden, announced the abdication of the Emperor, and handed over the office of Chancellor of the Reich to Friedrich Ebert, chairman of the MSPD [Majority Social Democratic Party]. On the same day, Philipp Scheidemann (MSPD), proclaimed the republic from a window of the Reichstag building. A few hours later, Karl Liebknecht (USPD) [the recently formed Independent Social Democratic Party] proclaimed the 'Free Socialist Republic'.[17]

Prince Max of Baden had informed Kaiser Wilhelm that the overwhelming majority in the Reichstag demanded his abdication, and implored him to abdicate immediately. Wilhelm later wrote in his Memoirs:

> I went through a fearful internal struggle. On the one hand, I, as a soldier, was outraged at the idea of abandoning my still faithful, brave troops. On the other hand, there was the declaration of our foes that they were unwilling to conclude with me any peace endurable to Germany, as well as the statement of my own Government that only by my departure for foreign parts was civil war to be prevented.
>
> In this struggle I set aside all that was personal. I consciously sacrificed myself and my throne in the belief that, by so doing, I was best serving the interests of my beloved fatherland. The sacrifice was in vain. My departure brought us neither better armistice conditions nor better peace terms; nor did it prevent civil war – on the contrary, it hastened and intensified, in the most pernicious manner, the disintegration in the army and the nation.[18]

In reality, Wilhelm was given no choice but to abdicate and was accepted by the Netherlands into permanent exile. While arguably the most naïve among European royalty, he was the most honourable, especially when compared to his German relatives on the throne of England. Despite the despicable British propaganda, lies, and opprobrium heaped on him by British politicians and historians, Kaiser Wilhelm II was the only monarch in 1914 who had striven to prevent a major European war.

With the German people exhausted and starving, and revolution breaking out across the nation, Prince Max von Baden asked the Allies for talks to end the fighting. For the first time in the entire war, and after numerous German requests for peace over the years had been summarily rejected, the Allies agreed to an armistice. The German authorities mistakenly considered President Woodrow Wilson a man of honour and believed he would guarantee an honourable end to war for all concerned. Back in January 1918, Wilson had told Congress:

> It is our wish and purpose that the processes of peace, when they are begun, shall be absolutely open and they shall involve and permit henceforth no secret understandings of any kind. The day of conquest and aggrandisement is gone by.... What we demand in this war ... is that the world be made fit and safe ... for every peace-loving nation which, like our own, wishes to live its own life, determine its own institutions, be assured of justice and fair dealing by the other peoples of the world as against force and selfish aggression.[19]

Wilson certainly had good speech writers but he went on to insist that peace talks could only take place if the Kaiser abdicated. So much for each country 'determining its own institutions'. His 'Fourteen Points' address to Congress on 8 January 1918 proposed the principles which should be used in peace negotiations to end the war. They included:

1. Open diplomacy without secret treaties

2. Economic free trade on the seas during war and peace

3. Equal trade conditions

4. Decrease armaments among all nations[20]

In early November 1918, the new, interim German government naively based its hopes on Wilson's apparent altruism: with an armistice and 'freedom of the seas,' the blockade would be lifted and the German people properly fed for the first time in four years.

With the Kaiser under tremendous pressure to depart, a German delegation travelled by car and rail on the night of November 7-8 to a railway siding in the Forest of Compiègne, 80 kilometres north of Paris. Talks were held in the personal rail carriage of the French commander, Marshal Ferdinand Foch, who made it clear at the outset that he was not there to haggle over the conditions of an armistice, but rather, to dictate them. Within the 35 articles which comprised the proposed armistice, one in particular drew gasps of astonishment from the German delegation. Article 26 originally stated: "The existing blockade conditions set up by the Allied and Associated Powers are to remain unchanged. German merchant ships found at sea remaining liable to capture."[21]

At that first meeting on 8 November, the German representatives – including Matthias Erzberger, State Secretary and president of the German delegation – were stunned. None had anticipated such a monstrous condition. U-Boats were returning to their bases, and the Allied fleets reigned supreme on the high seas, yet the British naval blockade was to continue after the armistice. Interference with the blockade had played an important role in enabling the war to continue beyond 1915 by secretly supplying the German army, but its proper strict application over the last months of the war changed everything. Cutting off that supply route, together with stopping food getting to the German forces via Hoover's 'Belgian Relief,' effectively meant the end for Germany. Matters would be made worse by the imposition of Article 7 of the Armistice Treaty that Germany surrender 5,000 railway locomotives and 150,000 wagons in good working order.[22] With domestic food production decimated by the war, and the means by which to transport what they could still produce around the country taken away, the German population was effectively doomed. With Germany prepared to throw down her arms, continuation of the enhanced food blockade following the armistice was akin to deliberate genocide. The malnutrition, disintegration of public health, and deaths by starvation already badly affecting the civilian population, were bound to intensify dramatically with the continuation of the blockade.

The Treaty Articles also required all German troops to evacuate the Western Front within 14 days, and to hand over to the Allies 5,000 artillery pieces, 25,000 machine guns, and 1,700 aircraft. The U-boat fleet was to be confiscated and all major German warships taken to Scapa Flow in Scotland for internment.[23] Allied forces would occupy the left bank of the Rhine, with a neutral zone established on the right bank. Germany had to cede the territory of Alsace-Lorraine to France.

Mathias Erzberger refused to sign the document and sent an urgent telegram to his superiors in Berlin urging them to seek President Wilson's intervention. The soon-to-be new Chancellor, Friedrich Ebert, responded with Field Marshal von Hindenburg's approval, instructing Erzberger to sign immediately. When the meeting in Foch's railway carriage reconvened in the early hours of 11 November, however, Erzberger continued his protest. How, he asked, could he be expected to sign the death warrant of millions of German civilians by starvation? Continuation of the food blockade was an act of war, not an armistice. His persistence *appeared* to pay off when a change to the Article was made. It read:

> The Allies are of the opinion that once the armistice has been concluded the continuation of the blockade will not hinder the provisioning of Germany as shall be found necessary.[24]

It appeared to be a significant concession regarding the food blockade, and Erzberger took it in good faith. Food would be supplied to Germany as was found to be "necessary." It did not stipulate, however, what 'necessary' was or *who* would decide it. Erzberger did not know, could not know, that the revision to the article was simply a clever play with words, dissembling to conceal its true nature.

The Allies had won the war – a war they could have won four years earlier had they not secretly provisioned the German army – so why would a continuing blockade of any sort still be required? The stark reality is that the victorious Allies found it "necessary" to further *tighten* the blockade into 1919, not ease it. The armistice was merely the beginning of the end, for there was unfinished business. The completion of that business – getting Germany to accept the entire blame for the war – would require the starving to death of hundreds of thousands of German women, children and frail elderly. Moral blackmail was used to get the German authorities to sign the onerous Armistice conditions, and it would be used again seven months later with the Treaty of Versailles to get them to sign a false confession.

In Foch's railway carriage just before dawn on 11 November, with a heavy heart Matthias Erzberger put his name to the Armistice agreement. It would come into force at 11:00 A.M. (Central European Time) that same day. The unfortunate Erzberger would be vilified in Germany for signing the agreement, and was brutally killed just two years later by right-wing paramilitaries.

The silencing of the guns of the 'Great War for Civilization' at 11 A.M. on 11 November 1918 was only the end of phase one of that war. 1919 would see it segue into phase two: creating the conditions in Germany for a reactionary movement that would spawn a dictatorship.

Within two weeks of the signing of the armistice, millions of German soldiers were wearily trudging home. They found their families starving, their country in despair and on the brink of revolution. Karl Liebknecht, who had prematurely and hopefully proclaimed Germany a Free Socialist Republic on 9 November, was a member of the Spartacus League with Rosa Luxemburg, Clara Zetkin, and other international socialists. Having taken the name from Spartacus, the leader of the slave revolt in the Roman Republic in 73 BC, they would join forces with the Communist Party of Germany (KPD) with the stated goal of creating a soviet republic of Germany.

> ...the pang of dissent of November 1918 was genuine: it appeared to have been unmarred by sooty conspiracies and Bolshevik agitation, whose exponents, by then grouped in the so-called Spartakus league, formed but a trifling minority of the movement. And yet the insurgents, most of them Socialists drawn from the proletariat, middle-class intelligentsia, and non-commissioned officers, were now at a loss to make good of this exhilarating respite from the Junkers' *corvée*.. Like his *confrère* in the Soviet of St Petersburg in 1905, the Common Man of Germany's *Räterepublik* (Councils' Republic) of 1918 was meekly requesting benevolent stewardship from the top.[25]

'The top' had no intention of offering benevolent stewardship, and acted swiftly and brutally in dealing with a potential Soviet Republic. Friedrich 'Fritz' Ebert, now de facto head of government, moved quickly to crush the Spartacists, allying himself with the Deputy Chief of the General Staff, General Groener, and other senior ranking army officers. Collaborating with conservatives and loosely affiliated right-wing paramilitary groups of mercenaries known as Freikorps, these powerful reactionary forces were determined that Soldiers-Workers Councils, and other representatives of the lower classes would never get hold of the reins of power in Germany. They knew Spartacist leaders such as Karl Liebknecht and Rosa Luxemburg were not political lightweights who would quietly stand aside in the face of establishment pressure; they would have to be killed.

Dr Karl Liebknecht (1871-1919) studied law and political economy at Leipzig University, gaining his doctorate at the University of Wurzburg in 1897. He opened a lawyer's office in Berlin, and joined the Social Democratic Party (SDP). Anti-war and anti-militarist, Liebknecht wrote:

> Modern militarism wants neither more nor less than the squaring of the circle; it arms the people against the people itself; it is insolent enough to force the workers ... to become oppressors, enemies

and murderers of their own class comrades and friends, of their parents, brothers, sisters and children, murderers of their own past and future. It wants to be at the same time democratic and despotic, enlightened and machine-like, at the same time to serve the nation and to be its enemy.[26]

Rosa Luxemburg (1871–1919) was a Polish Jew who studied history, politics and economics at the University of Zurich. She gained a doctorate in 1897 before moving to Germany.

Rosa Luxemburg described by one of her colleagues as the "most brilliant intellect of all the scientific heirs of Marx and Engels," is one of the most original and influential thinkers in the history of Marxism. Her life and works stand out for the unique combination of intellectual rigour and political integrity, a rare ability to merge deep theoretical insight with sharp political vision, the development of knowledge which is at the same time militant activism. Luxemburg is best known for her contributions to some of the most important economic and political debates that have shaped the development of socialist thought: the critique of capitalism and the dynamics of capital accumulation, the development of globalisation and its relation to colonialism and imperialism, the limits of national self-determination, the relationship of revolution to democracy, the challenges of parliamentary reform, the role of strikes and trade unions in political organisation, political parties, the critique of liberal feminism, the analysis of racism in connection to capitalist exploitation. She defended freedom, understood as a form of individual and collective self-rule, which could only be fully realised in a democratic socialist society, and gave her life for the cause ...[27]

On 15 January 1919, far-right paramilitary Freikorps brutally murdered Liebknecht, Luxemburg, and other socialist activists – doubtless with Ebert and Groener's blessing. The petite Dr. Luxemburg's shattered body was dumped in the Landwehr Canal by the Freikorps thugs. Four days later, elections to the National Assembly were held.

The elections turned the path of the revolution decisively towards parliamentary democracy, even though the following months saw further bitter confrontations with the radical Left, including local uprisings and wildcat strikes. The MSPD [Majority Social Democratic Party] emerged from the elections of 19 January 1919 as the strongest party. On 6 February, the National Assembly constituted itself

in Weimar [city in central Germany] and on 11 February elected
Friedrich Ebert President of the Reich. The first government of the
Reich to be accountable to Parliament ... under the premiership of
Philipp Scheidemann (MSPD), took office on 12 February 1919.[28]

Thus, the Weimar Republic was born. Its constitution provided for a
popularly elected president with power over foreign policy and the military. The president was empowered to nominate the Chancellor, while the
parliament (Reichstag) would be elected by universal suffrage. It may have
been promising for Germany's future, but the Anglo-American financial
elites had other plans for the beleaguered country. In the first instance it was
suffering starvation. With the blockade tightened as the Allies 'found necessary,' food shortages were now worse than before the armistice. German
fishing boats were prohibited from operating, and death rates rose significantly. Children were already seriously malnourished, and child mortality
increased by 30 per cent. In adults over 70, the death rate increased by 33
per cent. Thousands were dying every day directly from starvation or diseases associated with starvation. With massive unemployment, ex-service
men were plundering farms trying to feed their starving children.

Throughout the first six months of 1919, the victorious allies held
meetings in Paris to decide the final terms to be imposed on Germany.
The so-called 'Peace Conference' was completely dominated by members
of the Milner Group and representatives of the leading Anglo-American
financiers. The very war criminals who had long planned and instigated
the war were now deciding Germany's fate. Germany, Austria, Hungary,
Turkey and Soviet Russia were allowed no input whatsoever. Detailing
the talks and delegates is beyond the scope of this book, but we gain some
useful insights into British attitudes from a House of Lords debate in the
UK Parliament on 6 March 1919. A concerned Viscount Wimborne rose
to ask the government what steps were being taken to relieve starvation in
Germany. The Marquess of Lansdowne, Leader of the Opposition, then
spoke in support of Wimborne's appeal for information, stating:

> I confess that I look with the utmost dismay upon the condition of
> things which prevail in Central Europe at this moment. It seems to
> me that we are approaching – I am afraid rapidly approaching – a
> catastrophe which may prove to be one of the most disastrous that
> has ever occurred in the history of the world. ... Now, my Lords,
> we may ask ourselves, how long is this process of turning the screw,
> of using the weapon of starvation, likely to last? It is apparently in-

tended to use it until Germany has accepted the terms which we desire to impose. … If we are to go on with the starving policy until all that welter of difficult international questions has been cleared up, I am afraid we shall find, as Mr. Winston Churchill feared, that there will be nobody left with whom to come to terms at all.

Lord Parmoor spoke in support of Lansdowne:

Has not every observer said that unless this blockade is relaxed we are bringing the horrors of actual famine home to millions of people on the Continent? It would be the most fearful crime in history.

For the government, The Earl of Crawford responded:

Lord Lansdowne asked when the blockade was going to be raised. I am afraid I cannot possibly answer a question like that except by consulting the supreme authority in Paris, and clearly I could not even then reply without obtaining from them a most carefully written and considered Note to communicate to Parliament.

The "supreme authority" in Paris comprised leading members of the Anglo-American Establishment who were deliberately starving Germany in order to render her completely impotent. With her population dying from starvation in significant numbers, the German authorities would be in no position to argue over whatever draconian peace terms the victorious Allies were going to impose.

In the debate in Parliament that day in March 1919, Lord Harris (Eton and Oxford) responded:

My Lords, I cannot help rising to express my surprise at one suggestion made by my noble and learned friend on the other side in his final remarks.… Not one word of sympathy came from the noble Lord as regards the state of affairs in Belgium and France.

What has Germany suffered? Her factories have not been destroyed. Her capacity for turning out munitions has not been destroyed by any enemy … She ought to be in full capacity for turning out material. But what of Belgium?

The Marquess of Salisbury – James Gascoyne-Cecil (Eton and Oxford) then stood to address the House of Lords. He was the son of Robert Gascoyne-Cecil, the 3rd Marquess of Salisbury who, as we have seen, was at the very core of the secret society:

My Lords, I agree entirely with Lord Harris, that our first duty is to our despoiled and maltreated Allies before we think of the communities of Central Europe, and I hope and believe that this is the view of the great authorities in Paris.

...Although our enemies have behaved wickedly to us, and although we have deep reason to complain, yet we cannot but be deeply sorry for the women and children and the poor who may be reduced to these awful straits. In anything that the Government can do to relieve this misery, let me assure them they will have the sympathy of the great mass of our people. We are not vindictive as a people, and speaking as an Englishman to Englishmen – and may I say as a Christian to Christians? – we must do what we can, consistently with the other great obligations upon us, to relieve the misery even of our enemies. I am greatly gratified that this is also the view of His Majesty's Government.[29]

Christians? These psychopaths were responsible for the deaths of many millions – including 800,000 of their fellow countrymen – in a war they deliberately started for nothing other than greater wealth and power. When that war ended, they were now literally murdering tens of thousands of children in Germany with their ongoing food blockade yet calling themselves 'Christians'. Macgregor and Docherty write:

The food blockade would continue until Germany had been suitably punished. The chosen instrument of "correction" was starvation. That would crush Germany. Starvation. Having conjured the monster they called 'the Hun,' falsely blamed its leaders for causing the war, sacrificed an entire generation for an absurd lie, accrued vast debts to enrich themselves and continued to embellish their own propaganda into received history, sympathy for a starving people was not part of the Secret Elite agenda. Old friends played their part. Arthur Winnington-Ingram, the war-mongering Bishop of London, reminded his congregation at Westminster Abbey on December 1, 1918 that it was essential that the Germans be punished. He invoked the propaganda surrounding Edith Cavell's execution, the tragic memory of the 10,000 gallant men of the merchant marine lost at sea, of hospital ships sunk, of women and children drowned and prisoners of war who had survived in half-starving conditions. His message was far from subtle. Punishment, he ranted, was warranted 'for the greatest crime committed for a 1,000 years'. Indeed. His bitter logic warned that should the German culprits be let off, the moral standard of the world would sink. In triumphant conclusion the good Bishop pronounced, 'God expects us to exact punishment'.[30] His blatant, vulgar lies were unchristian, but at least consistent with the bitter sermons he had preached since the war began. And the poisonous propaganda of the war years hardened hearts and made the final act of malice much easier for the Secret Elite. After the *Daily News* carried a report from a Swedish correspondent which showed that as many as 95 per cent of the population in some parts of Germany had been living in approximate starvation for at least two years, the cry of "Hun trickery" found popular voice.[31]

The Paris "Peace Conference," the starvation blockade, and punishment of the German people went on through the early months of 1919. The British Press was relentless in its denial of the true situation in Germany. On 3 January 1919, a leading article in *The Times* dismissed the "German Hunger Bogy" as spurious. "You don't see so many people with rolls of fat on them as you did five years ago, but you also see a healthier, harder and generally more fit population." *The Times*, Britain's foremost quality newspaper controlled by members of the Milner Group, was telling its readership that thanks to the food blockade, dear old England was actually making the German people healthier and fitter.

British troops in occupied Germany could see through the astonishing lies being generated by the British Press. General Herbert Plumer, Commander of the British Army of Occupation in Germany, stated that British soldiers were genuinely distressed by the sight of starving children scrabbling through the waste bins in British military camps in search of any discarded food scraps. Plumer admitted that the troubled soldiers were handing over some of their own rations to the starving children.[32] *The Times* did not report *that*.

SUMMARY: CHAPTER 12 – UNITED STATES GOES TO WAR "FOR DEMOCRACY"

- United States declared war on Germany 6 April 1917.

- The Federal Reserve System (the taxpayer) was handed responsibility for all war debt, while Wall Street bankers enjoyed massive war profits.

- Lenin and Trotsky, financed and facilitated by the international banking fraternity, went to Russia and seized control in October 1917.

- An armistice was declared between the new Soviet Russia and Germany and a peace treaty agreed between the two at Brest-Litovsk in March 1918.

• German troops facing Russia were moved west to join a large German offensive, but were finally driven back.

• With revolution spreading among German forces and civilians, the Kaiser was forced to abdicate and peace terms sought.

• The armistice came into force on 11 November 1918, with Germany subjected to punishing conditions and an ongoing blockade that led to hundreds of thousands of further German civilian deaths from starvation.

• 'Peace' talks were held in Paris during the first six months of 1919, but Germany was allowed no representation whatsoever.

• German officials called to Versailles in June 1919 were forced to accept the entire blame for the war, or the food blockade would continue with Germany starved and effectively dismantled.

CHAPTER 13

THE HALL OF SMOKE AND MIRRORS

No German delegates or legal representatives were allowed to attend the Paris peace talks, but on 7 May 1919, German officials were summoned to the Palace of Versailles near Paris and in the Hall of Mirrors there, were handed the Peace Treaty, which included the following Article 231:

> The Allied and Associated Governments affirm and Germany accepts the responsibility of Germany and her allies for causing all the loss and damage to which the Allied and Associated Governments and their nationals have been subjected as a consequence of the war imposed upon them by the aggression of Germany and her allies.

The German delegation was given an ultimatum to take back to the authorities in Berlin: acknowledge German guilt for starting the war or the food blockade would continue indefinitely and the bulk of the German population would starve to death.

It was stated as 'fact' that Kaiser Wilhelm II had used the occasion of Archduke Franz Ferdinand's assassination in June 1914 as an excuse to start the war, and Article 227 stated that he would be put on trial:

> The Allied Powers publicly arraign William II of Hohenzollern, formerly German Emperor, for a supreme offence against international morality and the sanctity of treaties. A special tribunal will be constituted to try the accused, thereby assuring him the guarantees essential to the right of defence. It will be composed of five judges, one appointed by each of the following Powers: namely, the United States of America, Great Britain, France, Italy and Japan. In its decision the tribunal will be guided by the highest motives of international policy, with a view to vindicating the solemn obligations of international undertakings and the validity of international morality. It will be its duty to fix the punishment which it considers should be imposed. The Allied and Associated Powers will address a request to the Government of the Netherlands for the surrender to them of the ex-Emperor in order that he may be put on trial.[1]

Wilhelm was 'guaranteed' the right to defend himself, but the chances of him getting a fair trial were non-existent. He had been turned into an international pariah, and his cousin, King George V, had declared him "the greatest criminal in history." In the British general election held soon after the armistice, prime minister David Lloyd George successfully campaigned under the banner "Hang the Kaiser." In the United States, cinemas screened *The Kaiser: Beast of Berlin,* which portrayed Wilhelm gloating over slaughtered Belgian civilians and the torpedoed *Lusitania.* Cinemagoers were encouraged "to hiss" every time his face appeared on the screen and were aroused to such rage that they would go outside thereafter to burn his effigy.[2]

The government of the Netherlands refused to extradite the former kaiser for trial, but that suited the Allies and was an arrangement likely to have been agreed in advance. Had Wilhelm been extradited, put in the dock, and allowed to call defence witnesses as 'guaranteed,' in order to challenge the utterly false prosecution evidence, it might well have opened a huge can of worms for the Anglo-American elites who were the real culprits. The 'refusal' to extradite neatly sidestepped that possibility.

The Versailles findings were based on an orchestrated litany of lies stating that Kaiser Wilhelm "desired" war, "prepared it maliciously," and "began it wantonly" by issuing a "blank cheque" for war at a meeting at Potsdam on 5 July 1914 with his army chiefs and leading bankers and industrialists.

Morgenthau

The 'truly damning evidence' regarding this 'infamous' meeting came from a leading American delegate to Versailles, Henry Morgenthau Sr. (1856-1946). A German-born American businessman and a friend and financial backer of President Woodrow Wilson, Morgenthau was a member of The Pilgrims society which, as previously detailed, was closely associated with Anglo-American Establishment elites.

Morgenthau had been the US ambassador at Constantinople (now Istanbul), from December 1913 until February 1916, and the evidence he presented at the Paris Peace Conference in 1919 had a decisive impact on the Treaty of Versailles. American historian, Thomas James Fleming – who served as president of the Society of American Historians – wrote:

> The war guilt clause curtly [Article 231] demanded that Germany acknowledge its responsibility "for causing all the loss and damage to which the Allied and Associated governments have been sub-

jected as a consequence of the war imposed on them by the aggression of Germany and its allies." Compounding the irony, this statement was written by a former [Woodrow] Wilson pupil, John Foster Dulles. The source of the assertion was a memoir by Henry Morgenthau, Wilson's ambassador to Turkey from 1913 to 1916 ... In a filed report on March 29, 1919, it [the Morgenthau memoir] has been cited as perhaps the primary piece of evidence by the Commission on the Responsibility for the Authors of the War and on Enforcement of Penalties.

Historians examining the evidence in the next decade concluded that Morgenthau was lying.[3]

* * *

Historian Thomas James Fleming was somewhat wide of the mark in suggesting that John Foster Dulles wrote Article 231. Dulles may well have had some input on the various Versailles Articles, including 231, but the German war guilt article was drafted by Philip Kerr (later the 11th Marquess of Lothian) together with Alfred Milner. Kerr, a member of the inner circle of the Rhodes-Milner secret society,[4] was one of Milner's key lieutenants in his Round Table Group, and prime minister Lloyd George's private secretary 1916-1919. At the Peace Conference, U.S. president Woodrow Wilson and French prime minister Georges Clemenceau treated Kerr not merely as Lloyd George's secretary, but as a very important emissary at the Conference in his own right. Indeed, Kerr was the first of the architects in Paris to lay the foundations of a peace plan based on co-operation between the two 'Anglo-Saxon' powers. The idea of Germany's guilt – as stated in Article 231- was drafted by Kerr himself. It represented the ideological justification not only for an extension of reparations, but for a treaty of a strongly negative and punitive nature.[5]

Philip Kerr stated that the peace treaty marked the end of a moral conflict to defeat "the greatest crime against humanity and the freedom of peoples that any nation, calling itself civilized, has ever consciously committed." That assessment was certainly accurate, but it pertained to Britain's actions, not Germany's. Germany, according to Kerr, "had to acknowledge sole guilt for the war and the savage and inhuman manner in which it was conducted." Kerr added that the Allied terms were a sincere and deliberate attempt to establish "that reign of law, based upon the consent of the governed, and sustained by the organized opinion of mankind, which was the agreed basis of the peace."[6] Kerr and Milner, with or without Dulles's input, may have been responsible for the actual wording of Article 231, but it was wholly based on the great Potsdam lie conjured by Henry Morgenthau.

Henry Morgenthau's memoir related how, during his time in Constantinople, the German ambassador there, Baron Hans von Wangenheim, revealed top-secret information to him about a 'Crown Council' meeting at Potsdam on 5 July 1914, which was held before Kaiser Wilhelm departed for his summer cruise (as previously discussed in chapter 7). Morgenthau gives no precise date for his supposed discussion with Wangenheim about this matter, but it was allegedly in August 1914 before the first battle of the Marne (which began on 5 September). Morgenthau later wrote:

> I shall always keep in mind the figure of this German diplomat, in those exciting days before the Marne.... The good fortune of the German armies so excited him that he was sometimes led into indiscretions, and his exuberance one day caused him to tell me certain facts which, I think, will always be of great historical value....
>
> The Kaiser, he told me, had summoned him to Berlin for an imperial conference. This meeting took place at Potsdam on July 5th. The Kaiser presided and nearly all the important ambassadors attended. Wangenheim himself was summoned to give assurance about Turkey and enlighten his associates generally on the situation in Constantinople which was then regarded as almost the pivotal point in the impending war. In telling me who attended this conference Wangenheim used no names, though he specifically said that among them were – the facts are so important that I quote his exact words in the German which he used – "*die Häupter des Generalstabs und der Marine*" – (the heads of the general staff and of the navy) by which I have assumed that he meant Von Moltke and Von Tirpitz. The great bankers, railroad directors, and the captains of German industry, all of whom were as necessary to German war preparations as the army itself, also attended.
>
> Wangenheim now told me that the Kaiser solemnly put the question to each man in turn: "Are you ready for war?" All replied "yes" except the financiers. They said that they must have two weeks to sell their foreign securities and to make loans. At that time few people had looked upon the Sarajevo tragedy as something that would inevitably lead to war. This conference, Wangenheim told me, took all precautions that no such suspicion should be aroused. It decided to give the bankers time to readjust their finances for the coming war, and then the members went quietly back to their work or started on their vacations. The Kaiser went

to Norway on his yacht, Von Bethmann-Hollweg left for a rest, and Wangenheim returned to Constantinople. In telling me about this conference Wangenheim, of course, admitted that Germany had precipitated the war. I think that he was rather proud of the whole performance, proud that Germany had gone about the matter in so methodical and far-seeing a way, and especially proud that he himself had been invited to participate in so epoch making a gathering. I have often wondered why he revealed to me so momentous a secret, and I think that perhaps the real reason was his excessive vanity – his desire to show me how close he stood to the inner counsels of his emperor and the part that he played in bringing on this conflict. Whatever the motive, this indiscretion certainly had the effect of showing me who were really the guilty parties in this monstrous crime.... The conspiracy that has caused this greatest of human tragedies was hatched by the Kaiser and his imperial crew at this Potsdam conference of July 5, 1914. One of the chief participants, flushed with his triumph at the apparent success of the plot, told me the details with his own mouth. Whenever I hear people arguing about the responsibility for this war or read the clumsy and lying excuses put forth by Germany, I simply recall the burly figure of Wangenheim as he appeared that August afternoon, puffing away at a huge black cigar, and giving me his account of this historic meeting. Why waste time discussing the matter after that?[7]

Morgenthau's fabrication that Kaiser Wilhelm called together a great council of the military and economic leaders of Germany at Potsdam on 5 July 1914, and told them that he had decided to plunge Europe into war, was presented as the primary piece of evidence against the kaiser and Germany. At the Paris Peace Conference, with no Germans allowed there to refute it, Morgenthau's great Potsdam lie was unquestioningly accepted as the truth, and formed the basis of Article 231 which declared Germany responsible for the war.

Morgenthau stated that his evidence was so damning that no further time "need be wasted" on the matter, but American historian, Professor Sidney B. Fay, was deeply suspicious and meticulously considered it further. Fay found "hardly a word of truth" in the entire Morgenthau narrative and demonstrated that Baron Wangenheim was *not* at Potsdam in July 1914.[8] Neither was the head of the General Staff, General von Moltke. He was some 300 miles to the south in Karlsbad 'taking the waters'. Moltke left his Karlsbad hotel on 14 May, but on the advice of his physician returned there on 28 June before the news from Sarajevo broke. He remained at Karlsbad until 25 July and was most certainly not at Potsdam on 5 July – nor at any other time – plotting a major European war together with the kaiser. The head of the German Navy, Admiral von Tirpitz, was likewise on vacation. He was in Tarasp in Switzerland from 2 July to 27 July and was not at any Potsdam meeting.[9]

Professor Fay examined the whereabouts of every individual who, according to Morgenthau's narrative, was at a war council meeting at Potsdam on 5 July 1914. None were. It simply never took place. The official narrative of the origins of the First World War is saturated with lies that blame Germany, and Henry Morgenthau's was the biggest lie of all. Professor Fay stated:

> Baron Wangenheim, according to the story, represents the Kaiser and the Council as deciding to delay action for two weeks in order to give the bankers time to sell their foreign securities. This is the opposite of the truth. There is much contemporary evidence in the Kautsky Documents that the Kaiser wished that, whatever action Austria took against Serbia, she should not delay. She should act as quickly as possible, while the sentiment in Europe, shocked by the horrible crime at Sarajevo, was still in sympathy with the Hapsburgs and indignant at regicide Serbs. When he read that the German Ambassador at Vienna, [Heinrich von Tschirschky] two days after Sarajevo, had "used every opportunity to warn Austria calmly but very energetically and earnestly against overhasty steps," the Kaiser made the marginal note: "Now or never! Who authorized him to do this? It is very stupid! It's none of his business, for it is purely Austria's affair to consider what to do in this matter, for it will be said afterwards, if things go wrong, that Germany was not willing! Tschirschky will please drop this nonsense! Matters must be cleared up with the Serbs, and that soon. That's all self-evident and the plain truth."... No, instead of urging delay, according to the Wangenheim story, the Kaiser, with his natural impetuosity, wanted Austria's action, whatever it might be, to be taken as quickly as possible.... The real reasons for the delay came wholly from Vienna and not at all from Berlin. Berchtold, the Austro-Hungarian Minister of Foreign Affairs, could not act against Serbia until he had secured the consent of Tisza, the premier of Hungary. It took two weeks to win Tisza over from his opposition to violent action against Serbia.[10]

British historians who buttress the Establishment lies on the First World War either fail to mention Morgenthau's Potsdam story or vainly attempt to support it. The majority of academic historians agree, however, that far from planning to plunge Europe into war, Kaiser Wilhelm attempted to keep the Austria-Serbia affair localised in order *to prevent* a European war. Professor Barnes wrote:

> There is no competent and informed historian in any country who has studied the problems of the genesis of the World War in a thorough fashion who does not regard the theory of war guilt held in Articles 227 and 231 of the Versailles Treaty to be wholly false, misleading and unjust.[11]

Did the German ambassador at Constantinople in 1914, Hans von Wangenheim, really pass false information to the U.S. ambassador, or was it made up in its entirety by Morgenthau as Professor Fay clearly stated? Morgenthau apparently never spoke of it to anyone until 1917, and Ambassador Wangenheim could not refute it for the straightforward reason that he died very suddenly in Constantinople on 26 October 1915, at the age of 56. Interestingly, the following day the *New York Times* questioned if he had been poisoned.[12]

It is likely that the great Potsdam lie was conjured in its entirety after Morgenthau returned to the United States in 1916, with Wangenheim playing no part in it whatsoever. He had no reason to damage Germany where he was considered an honest, respectable and loyal diplomat. A confidant of the kaiser's, he may well have become Chancellor of Germany at some stage in his career. Unlike the British and French ambassadors in Constantinople, Wangenheim took the job seriously.[13] Professor Fay wrote:

> Is it not extraordinary that Baron Wangenheim should have given to Mr Morgenthau so many picturesque details which are in flat contradiction with the facts? How could he have dared to make such an important revelation so prejudicial to the interests of his own Government? Germany at this time, in the early weeks of the War, was trying hard to win the good-will of the United States.... A statement such as Wangenheim's would have done Germany infinite damage.
>
> And is it not difficult to understand why the American Ambassador did not report to Washington what was perhaps the most important thing he had ever heard at Constantinople? Yet a careful search through the files of the State Department at Washington shows that there is no despatch or telegram recounting this inter-

esting conversation with Baron Wangenheim: nor does Mr. Morgenthau in his book say anything about having made report on the subject to Washington.[14]

Henry Morgenthau warrants closer attention. He was born in Mannheim, in the Grand Duchy of Baden, Germany, in 1856. The family moved to New York in 1866, and Henry graduated in law from Columbia University. He rapidly became a large-scale and exceedingly wealthy New York real-estate operator, and president of the Central Realty, Bond and Trust Company that bought and sold substantial properties in Manhattan and elsewhere. He worked closely with the big insurance companies controlled by J.P. Morgan.

> My position as president of this company involved me in a series of financial encounters with the biggest men in Wall Street, encounters that are worth describing because they illustrate the methods by which the great fortunes of the greatest period of expansion in American finance were made. I have not heard of any man who had intimate business relations with the financial giants of that period, who has described, from his own experience, the intrigues and passions, the personalities and methods, of those men who dominated the financial structure of America.[15]

Now extremely wealthy, Morgenthau mixed with a group of elite families in the New York area, including the Kuhns and Loebs of the Kuhn, Loeb & Co bank on Wall Street, and Jacob Schiff and Paul Warburg, the bank's directors.

> All these families trace their origins to Germany (a surprising number to Bavaria). They have referred to themselves as "the One Hundred," as opposed to the "Four Hundred." [America's richest families] They have been called the "Jewish Grand Dukes." But most often they have simply called themselves "our crowd." The men of our crowd made their fortunes as merchants or bankers ... For a long time you either belonged to "our crowd" or you didn't. For several generations the crowd was strikingly intramural when it came to marriage, making the crowd – to the larger crowd outside it – seem so cohesive and tight knit as to be impenetrable.[16]

The rich and powerful 'Our Crowd' to which Morgenthau belonged was clearly different from the White Anglo-Saxon Protestant (WASP) or Boston Brahmin elites of English forebears, (as discussed in chapter 3) but they became an integral part of the 'Eastern Establishment' – the financial and industrial elite that ruled the United States and linked close-ly with the British Establishment. Through his presidency of the Central Realty, Bond and Trust Company, Henry Morgenthau was close to all of the big players on Wall Street. He worked and socialised with Elihu Root, Paul Warburg, Jacob Schiff and other leading Money Power players. His son, Henry Jr., was one of Franklin Delano Roosevelt's closest friends.

Morgenthau Sr. joined Schiff and Warburg in donating large sums to Wilson's campaign fund for the 1912 presidential election. As previous-ly discussed, the rigged election saw Wilson gain the White House and sign off the corrupt Federal Reserve System Bill. Morgenthau had hoped for a cabinet-level position in Wilson's government thereafter, but in De-cember 1913 Wilson appointed him U.S. Ambassador to the Ottoman Empire. He was allegedly reluctant to accept the post until Wilson told him: 'Constantinople is the point at which the interest of the American Jews in the welfare of the Jews of Palestine is focussed, and it is almost indispensable that I have a Jew at that post ... I am sincerely anxious to have you accept Turkey.'[17] The significance of Wilson's comment became evident four years later when the Balfour Declaration of 1917 announced Britain's support for the establishment of a national home for the Jewish people in the then Ottoman region of Palestine.

Regarding the Morgenthau Potsdam lie, in 1990, Heath W. Lowry, Professor emeritus of Ottoman and Modern Turkish Studies, at Prince-ton University, published a book, *The Story Behind Ambassador Morgen-thau's Story*. Professor Lowry relates that in November 1917, Morgenthau sent a letter to his 'friend and confidant,' President Wilson. asking for his permission to begin the book project which included the Potsdam story. Professor Lowry writes:

> It is in this previously unpublished letter that Morgenthau set forth both his idea of writing a book, and his aims and objectives in de-siring to do so. He combined his concept with an appeal for the President's 'blessing' as it were for his proposal. Given the fact that his sole aim was fostering public support for the United States war effort by writing a work of anti-German, anti-Turkish propaganda which would "win a victory for the war policy of the government," he not surprisingly received it.
>
> ...Wilson had blessed the proposal and written: "I think your plan for a full exposition of some of the lines of German intrigue is an excellent one and I hope you will undertake to write and publish the book you speak of."[18]

Thus, the plan for spreading a great lie about 'German intrigue' at Potsdam on July 5, 1914, began taking shape with the U.S. President's support. A writer friend of President Wilson's, Burton J. Hendrick – 'an extreme Anglophile'- immediately contacted Morgenthau and the project began to materialize. Professor Lowry discusses the intrigues:

> As envisaged by Morgenthau, his 'story' was intended as wartime propaganda, i.e., as a contribution to the Entente war effort. It is against this background that we must attempt to examine how and by whom the book was actually written, as well as the larger questions concerning the accuracy or lack thereof of the 'story' it purports to tell.... Not only did Ambassador Morgenthau need the approval of President Woodrow Wilson to proceed with the plan for the book which bears his name, more importantly he needed the skilled hand of Burton J. Hendrick to actually write the work in question.... It appears that the actual concept of the book originated in the mind of Hendrick, who first suggested it to Morgenthau *in April of 1916*. It is through an examination of several thousand letters and documents ... that eventually the rather murky origins of the work in question emerge. For in point of fact, Ambassador Morgenthau's story emerged from the pen of Burton .J Hendrick.[19]

Morgenthau was the named author of *Ambassador Morgenthau's Story* – the book that carried the Potsdam lie – but it was written by one of the East Coast Establishment's favourite biographers, Burton J. Hendrick. Hendrick wrote for a number of different newspapers before joining the monthly magazine, *The World's Work*, a pro-big business magazine published by Doubleday, Page and Company. Hendrick was a friend of the publisher's co-owner and extreme Anglophile, Walter Hines Page, the U.S. Ambassador to Britain 1913 – 1918. A member of Pilgrims, Page was very close to the Milner Group and part of Quigley's 'Anglo-American Establishment'. As ever, it was a case of circles within circles.

Burton J. Hendrick was an important player in the Establishment's control of the writing of history and for his troubles was well remunerated and awarded at least three Pulitzer Prizes. The Morgenthau book – which would generate the greatest lie about the cause of the First World War and prove crucial to the outcome of the Versailles Treaty – had the fingerprints of the Anglo-American elite all over it.

Delving a little deeper into this particular rabbit hole, we find that in ghost-writing the Morgenthau book, Hendrick was aided by a rather mysterious character, Hagop S. Andonian. A dedicated anti-Turkish Armenian, he had been Henry Morgenthau's secretary and interpreter at the U.S. embassy in Constantinople. Andonian went over to the United States with Morgenthau in 1916 and played an important role in Morgenthau's book alleging that Muslim Turks committed genocide by murdering 1.5 million Armenian Christians during WW1. On the book's grim revelations, Turkish-Cypriot Professor, Ata Atun, writes:

> It is absolutely clear that he [Morgenthau] fabricated this book to serve the needs of Great Britain and create a base for the British to strengthen their excuse to step into the Middle East.[20]

The murky origins of the Morgenthau Potsdam lie get ever murkier, for the fingerprints of yet another very important member of the Anglo-American Establishment were all over it; none other than the U.S. Secretary of State, Robert Lansing. Lansing proofread and commented on every single chapter of the work in progress, making copious marginal notes suggesting alterations or omissions in the text. When the book was nearing completion, Morgenthau requested Lansing's permission to acknowledge his input, and thank him in the Preface. Lansing responded, "On the whole it would be advisable not to mention my name in connection with the book."[21]

Professor Lowry concludes:

> When one recollects the fact that prior to beginning his project, Morgenthau received the written blessings of the President of the United States, Woodrow Wilson, and that as the work progressed, each chapter received the personal stamp of approval of the U.S. Secretary of State Robert Lansing, it is clear that Morgenthau's book may be said to bear the imprimatur of the United States Government.[22]

Thus, the government of the United States of America gave authoritative approval to a book containing one of the greatest lies in history: that Kaiser Wilhelm deliberately plunged Europe into war in 1914 as part of a long-standing German plan for world domination.

Secretary of State Lansing played a dual role in taking the United States into the First World War in 1917 and creating the fake history of the war. His sister-in-law, Edith Dulles, was the mother of John Foster Dulles and Allen Welsh Dulles who would play major roles for the transatlantic elite in the genesis of the Second World War. Each and every one of the men involved in the Potsdam lie was an important member of the Anglo-American Establishment as defined by Carroll Quigley. And so too was Morgenthau's son, Henry Morgenthau Jr. (1891-1967). Just as Morgenthau senior had helped fund Woodrow Wilson's entry to the White House in the rigged election of 1912, Morgenthau junior was a major funder of Franklin Delano Roosevelt for the presidency 20 years later. Morgenthau Jr. was appointed U.S. Secretary of the Treasury (1934-45) and in 1944 would present his 'Morgenthau Plan' for postwar Germany:

> Morgenthau demanded that Germany be utterly destroyed as a nation, that its industry be dismantled, and it be reduced to a purely rural country.... Draper [Brigadier General Henry William Draper, chief of the American Economics Division] "protected" Germany from the Morgenthau Plan – but at a price. Draper and his colleagues demanded that Germany and the world accept the collective guilt of the German people as the explanation for the rise of Hitler's New Order, and the Nazi war crimes.[23]

Henry Morgenthau Sr's granddaughter, Barbara Tuchman, also played a role for the Establishment in creating fake history. Her book, *The Guns of August,* on the opening months of the First World War was published in 1962 to great praise from *The Times* and other organs of the controlled British press, and won the 1963 Pulitzer Prize for general non-fiction. The book assassinates Kaiser Wilhelm's character, and in terms of overall honesty, integrity, and un-biased recording of history, it adheres to the 'finest' traditions of the Morgenthau clan. Interestingly, she makes no mention whatsoever of the Potsdam lie or her grandfather's role in it. The least said about that the better, it seems.

When the Morgenthau lies, and the multiple layers of falsehood and propaganda added since by British historians are stripped away, it becomes patently clear that a European war was the last thing Kaiser Wilhelm desired. Canadian author John S Ewart:

> It is perfectly clear that, so far from wishing to precipitate a world – or even a European – war, Germany's principal anxiety was that the quarrel she wished to localize might take on larger proportions. Rapidity of action had for its purpose the localization of the war. On very many pages of the diplomatic documents may evidence of the fact be found.... At all events, a local and not a world war, was what Germany and Austria-Hungary desired. Indeed, in the Kaiser's view, the quarrel was of such an essentially local character that no Power, not even Germany had a right to interfere.[24]

THE HALL OF MIRRORS

In the Hall of Mirrors at the Palace of Versailles on 28 June 1919, exactly five years after the assassination of Franz Ferdinand, German delegates signed Article 231 accepting the entire blame for the war. Professor Preparata writes:

> By this Article Germany was coerced to accept the responsibility, and thus sign a 'blank check,' 'for causing all the loss and damage to which the Allied ... and their nationals have been subjected as a consequence of the war imposed on them by the aggression of Germany.' The apportionment of the prospective German spoils was thus tentatively arranged by the victors: 50 per cent to France, 30 per cent to Britain, and the remaining 20 per cent divided up amongst the lesser allies.[25]

Article 231 was headline news in newspapers across the world. Germany accepted the guilt for causing the First World War. The Allies had it in writing, so it had be true. The text of the Treaty ran to 240 pages with 440 highly punitive articles. Part VIII of the Treaty – later set by the 'Reparations Commission' – decreed that Germany must pay the general costs of the war to the Allies to the tune of $33 billion - the equivalent of 20 billion gold marks – worth around $600 billion in 2024.

Woodrow Wilson's Fourteen Points for peace had assured all countries that there would be 'no annexations' or 'punitive damages,' but Germany was forced to forfeit around 13 per cent of its territory and 10 per cent of its population – between 6.5 and 7 million people. France took Alsace-Lorraine, Belgium took Eupen and Malmedy, Denmark took Northern Schleswig, and in the East, newly independent Poland took large parts of Prussia and Silesia. Czechoslovakia got the Hultschin district. All German overseas colonies were seized. As a consequence of the lost territories, Germany lost almost 50 per cent of her iron ore production. Preparata writes;

> Having served its purpose, the decoy of the Fourteen Points was torn up and tossed in the trashcan.[26]

Articles 45-50 forced Germany to turn over its coal mines in the Saar Basin to France. In addition, Annex V stated that Germany had to deliver seven million tons of coal to France annually for the next ten years and was required to give to France the coal that would have been produced in the Nord and Pas de Calais region had the coal mines there not been destroyed in the war. That would amount to upwards of another 20 million tons per year. Germany would have to pay for the repair and restoration of all French coal mines damaged in the war. Additionally, eight million tons of German coal had to be delivered to Belgium annually, and eight-and-a-half million tons to Italy.

> Articles 233-4 stated that Germany must deliver livestock to the French government in monthly instalments: 500 stallions; 30,000 fillies and mares; 2,000 bulls; 90,000 milch cows; 1,000 rams, 00,000 sheep; and 10,000 goats. It must supply the Belgian government with livestock amounting to 200 stallions, 5,000 mares, 5,000 fillies, 2,000 bulls, 50,000 milch cows, 40,000 heifers, 20,000 sheep, and 15,000 sows.[27] In addition to farm animals, large quantities of agricultural machinery had to be handed over to France and Belgium.
>
> Articles 159-163 limited the size of the German army to 100,000 men, "devoted exclusively to the maintenance of order within the territory and to the control of the frontiers." Conscription to the army was proscribed. The existing German navy was confiscated and a future naval force was restricted to vessels under 10,000 tons. Building submarines or an air force was banned. In addition to the warships seized by the Allies, all German merchant ships over 1,600 tons and half of all ships between 1,000 and 1,600 tons were taken, together with one

quarter of all German fishing boats.[28] As detailed previously, the Allies also demanded that Germany surrender 5,000 railway locomotives and 150,000 wagons in good working order. Any reader who seriously doubted the assertion that this war was about crushing Germany may now wish to reconsider.

The diplomat and historian George F. Kennan wrote that the Versailles peace treaty "had the tragedies of the future written into it as if by the devil's own hand."[29] The British author Henry Wood Nevinson wrote that Article 231 laying the blame on Germany was "a lie of such grossness" that he wondered that the hand that wrote it "did not wither."[30] Professor Sidney B. Fay, widely recognised as one of the world's leading First World War historians, concluded that Article 231 was extorted by Britain from Germany "under the influence of the blindness, ignorance, hatred and the propagandist misconceptions to which the war had given rise."[31]

If there is truth in the adage 'history is written by the victors,' the history of the First World War and the Versailles Treaty represents its ultimate expression. Professor Fay clearly demonstrated in 1936 that the crucial evidence presented by Henry Morgenthau at Versailles about the kaiser supposedly announcing at the Potsdam meeting of 5 July that Germany was about to launch a war of European conquest, was nothing but a grotesque lie. Professor Harry Elmer Barnes wrote:

> Inasmuch as the post-War settlement was based upon the wartime assumption and the Versailles charge of the unique guilt of Germany in causing the World War, it is no more defensible than the cornerstone upon which it erected. As we now know for all time that there is not an iota of truth in Article 231 of the Treaty of Versailles.... A dawning consciousness of how badly we were deceived about the actual European situation from 1914 to 1918 may serve to make us rather more cautious and hesitant about capitulating to propaganda in the event of another European cataclysm.... We have to consider the manner in which Great Britain, France, Italy and Russia deceived us as to the facts relating to the outbreak of the World War...[32]

To this day, pro-Establishment British historians still attempt to deceive us with their accounts that in 1914 Germany was hell-bent on global domination and to that end deliberately started the world war. A telegram from Walter Hines Page – the U.S. ambassador to Britain – to President Wilson just four weeks into the war paints a different picture. Page was a staunch Anglophile, a member of the Pilgrims Society, and a friend of Sir Edward Grey and other leading players in the Milner Group. In other words, he was close to some of those in the cabal who had planned the war. His telegram of 3 September 1914, to President Wilson stated:

> Everybody in this city [London] confidently believes that the Germans, if they capture Paris, will make a proposal for peace, and that the German Emperor will send you a message declaring that he is unwilling to shed another drop of blood...[33]

The power brokers in London were fully aware that the official narrative that claimed Kaiser Wilhelm had deliberately set out on a war to conquer Europe was a lie. They knew because they were the very people who had planned the war and had concocted the lies about the kaiser. If Germany *had* succeeded in capturing Paris within six to eight weeks after being forced into war, it was deemed likely in London that Wilhelm would immediately sue for peace. Strange indeed that someone intent on conquering the world would call for peace after their first astonishing victory six or so weeks into the war. Peace was the very last thing the Milner Group wanted, and Page's telegram was a warning to the U.S. president that he must not react positively in any way should the kaiser send him peace feelers. Ambassador Page's telegram went on:

> The prevailing English judgment is that, if Germany be permitted to stop hostilities, the war will have accomplished nothing. There is a determination here to destroy utterly the German bureaucracy, and Englishmen are prepared to sacrifice themselves to any extent in men and money. The preparations that are being made here are for a long war; as I read the disposition and the character of Englishmen they will not stop until they have accomplished their purpose. There is a general expression of hope in this country that neither the American Government nor the public opinion of our country will look upon any suggestion for peace as a serious one which does not aim, first of all, at the absolute destruction of the German bureaucracy.[34]

That in a nutshell summed up why, during the war, repeated calls for peace negotiations were rejected by Britain. It would scupper everything the Anglo-American elites had long planned and aimed to accomplish through this war. Years of planning and preparation would be in vain if the war ended without Germany being crushed.

It is important to note that repeated German calls for peace were never mentioned at the Versailles stitch-up, and to this day most British historians have completely whitewashed them from their histories. We should look back and consider what peace overtures were actually made during the war. Apart from the widespread feeling in London that Germany would immediately sue for peace if she captured Paris in the early weeks of the war, the Walter Hines Page biography reveals that by May 1915 Germany actually had made numerous attempts to end the fighting:

> Between the Battle of the Marne [September 1914] and the sinking of the *Lusitania* [May 1915] four attempts were made to end the war; *all four were set afoot by Germany.* President Wilson was the man to whom the Germans appealed to rescue them from their dilemma. It is no longer a secret that the Germans at this time regarded their situation as a tragic one.[35]

Of course the situation was 'tragic' because never at any time did Germany desire a European or world war. The repeated German moves for peace through 1914 and 1915 were never revealed at Versailles, nor have they been to this day by British historians, because their narratives need to portray Germany as the aggressor. Britain also rejected all neutral attempts at mediation during the first two years of the war. Sir Edward Grey was "far from desiring to encourage an opening of any kind which offered the prospect of concluding a satisfactory peace."[36]

During the war. the voices in Britain calling for an end to the conflict were drowned out by a cacophony of deafening jingoism. In November 1916, Lord Lansdowne, a bitter critic of the war in the House of Lords, publicly called for peace negotiations "in order to save civilisation." He was roundly condemned as 'a traitor' by those in power in London including H.H. Asquith who was about to be replaced by David Lloyd George as prime minister. On entering 10 Downing Street on 6 December, Lloyd George immediately confirmed the demand that peace could *only* come after the defeat and crushing of Germany.

That same day, 6 December 1916, Pope Benedict XV repeated his July 1915 appeal to all belligerents to come to an understanding and make peace. It was "absolutely necessary," he said, that all sides made concessions with good grace, even at the cost of some sacrifice.

Chancellor von Bethmann-Hollweg immediately announced Germany's willingness to follow the Pope's appeal and discuss peace terms, but was rejected outright by the British, French and Russians. Bethmann-Hollweg made it clear to the Pope that the Central Powers *had not* willed war nor been responsible for starting it. When Bethmann approached the Allies and President Wilson with a peace note, the Allied governments condemned it as an "illusory" peace proposal, stating:

> The Allies cannot admit a claim which is untrue in each particular and is sufficient alone to render sterile all attempts at negotiations. The Allied nations have for thirty months been engaged in a war which they had done everything to avoid. They have shown by their actions their devotion to peace. This devotion is as strong to-day as it was in 1914; and after the violation by Germany of her solemn engagements, Germany's promise is no sufficient foundation on which to re-establish the peace which she broke. A mere suggestion, without statement of terms, that negotiations should be opened, is not an offer of peace. The putting forward by the Imperial Government of a sham proposal, lacking all substance and precision, would appear to be less an offer of peace than a war manoeuvre. It is founded on a calculated misrepresentation of the character of the struggle in the past, the present, and the future. As for the past, the German note takes no account of the facts, dates, and figures which establish that the war was desired, provoked, and declared by Germany and Austria-Hungary.... Fully conscious of the gravity of this moment, but equally conscious of its requirements, the Allied Governments, closely united to one another and in perfect sympathy with their peoples, refuse to consider a proposal which is empty and insincere.[37]

Once again, it was unadulterated 'black is white' Orwellian Doublespeak. The Allied governments were fully cognisant of the fact that Germany was *not* responsible for the war, but how dare she relate that truth to the Pope, the U.S. president, or anyone else. Since the German authorities had dared to state that fundamental truth, there would be no peace talks. In the British elite echo chamber, Germany was responsible for the war and her attempts to end it were for ulterior motives and totally insincere. Such reasoning to justify declining calls for peace negotiations voiced by Lord Lansdowne, the Pope, and Bethmann-Hollweg was a classic demonstration of Perfidious Albion at her most devious. The German Chancellor's overtures, the British government stated, were nothing more than a calculated attempt to influence the future course of the war, and to end it by imposing a German peace.

On 11 January 1917, the German government forwarded its 'Note to Neutrals' to governments across the world. It stated:

Our enemies describe the peace offer as a war manoeuvre. Germany and her Allies most emphatically protest against such a falsification of their motives which they openly stated. Their conviction was that a just peace acceptable to all belligerents was possible, that it could be brought about, and that further bloodshed could not be justified. Their readiness to make known their peace conditions without reservations at the opening of negotiations disproves any doubt of their sincerity.... Germany and her Allies made an honest attempt to terminate the war and pave the way for an understanding among the belligerents. The Imperial Government declares that it solely depends on the decision of our enemies whether the road to peace should be taken or not. The enemy Governments have refused to take this road. On them falls the full responsibility for the continuation of the bloodshed...[38]

The outrageous lies about Bethmann-Hollweg's genuine peace attempts in 1916 are reiterated to this day by British historians. The Australian historian, Professor Douglas Newton, however, presents a very different view:

The moderate conservative chancellor, Bethmann Hollweg, issued a note to the major belligerents. It recognised the 'catastrophe' of a war that threatened to ruin Europe. Germany proposed 'to enter even now into peace negotiations.' The conference could begin anywhere, with no preconditions.... As the diplomatic historian Zeman wrote: 'No one in London, Paris, Rome or Petrograd took Bethmann's offer for what it was: an action genuinely designed to put an end to the war.... Lest we imagine that the Entente Powers were determined to fight on nobly for the sake of democracy, we should remember that by this time their diplomats had entered into the Straits Agreement, the Treaty of London, the Sykes-Picot Agreements, the Bucharest Convention, and a string of colonial agreements, all specifying territorial aggrandisement and economic boycotts.... 'Bitter-enders' everywhere mobilised to stifle the movement for peace. Using emergency powers, they succeeded: critics were silenced, meetings banned, and moderates smeared as traitors. The British press in particular indulged in a fabulously inconsistent campaign: the Germans were so weak that they were 'squealing' for peace; the Germans were so strong that they would never negotiate. The reality – that Germany was a house divided, with strong socialist parties and emerging liberal elements pushing for peace and democratisation – could not be admitted....

Was peace possible? The Americans certainly believed so. Colonel House negotiated with Bernstorff, the German Ambassador, across those six weeks. House reported to Wilson on 15 January 1917, that the Germans' terms 'are very moderate and they did not intend to take any part of Belgium.' This gave 'a real basis for negotiations and for peace.' The next day he told Wilson that the USA could 'bring about peace much more quickly that I thought possible.' The Germans, wrote House, 'consent to almost everything that liberal opinion in democratic countries have demanded'.

But for moderate Germans to prevail they needed firm ground to stand upon – unambiguously moderate responses from the Entente. They never came. Of course, hawkish historians pretend to *know* what would have happened if negotiations had commenced. They argue, citing German obstinacy, that failure was certain. We know no such thing. The only thing we know is that face-to-face negotiations in the public view were evaded. It is significant that, *on the British side, advisers often urged the avoidance of any armistice because negotiations that followed would be bound to succeed.* Indeed, had negotiations begun, no negotiator would have dared rise from the table without striking a bargain, so powerful would have been the demand for peace among the suffering people of Europe.[39]

It would be a mistake to suggest that no voices of protest against the war had been raised in Britain. Many such protestors were locked in British prisons over the course of the war. The Scottish school teacher and anti-war socialist, John Maclean, for example, was imprisoned, brutally treated, and force-fed when he went on hunger strike. The Establishment broke him physically, but not his spirit. In a House of Commons debate on the war in February 1917, numerous members of parliament protested against continuation of the war and Britain's rejection of German peace proposals. Philip Snowden MP stated:

The people have always been warned about the dangers of a premature peace. They have been told that unless the war is fought to a decisive victory, they will have to fight it over again in the future. We must continue the War to save our children and our children's children from having to endure such sufferings. We are told that peace cannot be made with the enemy, because the enemy is too unscrupulous to observe his engagements. We are told that we must continue the War for the sake of those who have perished. These are the catch phrases and the subterfuges by which the people are blinded as to the real purpose of the War.[40]

After the Allied Powers' outright rejection of German peace proposals, Pope Benedict XV persisted in his attempts to bring the conflict to an end. The Catholic Textbook project relates:

> Since Germany had been the first to seek peace, Benedict told his nuncio to Bavaria, Archbishop Eugenio Pacelli, to inquire after the German government's desire for peace. In June 1917, Archbishop Pacelli met with German Chancellor Bethmann-Hollweg. In discussing Germany's war aims, Bethmann-Hollweg said he could agree to four points for peace:
> 1. that all nations limit their armaments;
> 2. that international courts be established to judge grievances between the warring sides;
> 3. that Belgium be restored to independence; and that
> 4. Germany and France come to a peaceful settlement over Alsace-Lorraine.

Kaiser Wilhelm had himself approved the four perfectly reasonable points outlined by Bethmann-Hollweg's plan and permitted him to submit a peace resolution to the German *Reichstag*. The military, however, in the form of Generals Hindenburg and Ludendorff, was not pleased with either Bethmann-Hollweg or his peace proposal, and their influence was used to force the chancellor to resign. Reluctantly, Wilhelm accepted Bethmann-Hollweg's resignation and appointed Georg Michaelis, a favourite of the generals, as chancellor.

Despite the fact he was a friend of the generals, Chancellor Michaelis told nuncio Pacelli that he too accepted the four points as a basis for peace talks. At Michaelis's urging, in July the *Reichstag* approved a resolution based on the points. In early August, Pope Benedict sent sealed envelopes to all of the warring governments. It was a proposal he had long been preparing for an end to the war and a permanent peace in Europe. Like his earlier calls for peace, it was based on his conviction that the warring powers should seek "peace without victory" through seven points:

> 1. Relations between nations should be governed by justice rather than the "material force of arms" – warfare.
>
> 2. Nations must reduce their armaments.
>
> 3. Instead of relying on armies and war to settle disputes, nations should establish an international institution with the ability to settle international disagreements and the power to enforce its decrees.

4. All nations should enjoy "true liberty and common rights over the sea."

5. The warring nations should seek no payments ("indemnities") from each other for the damages and costs of the war. To continue "such carnage" only "for economic reasons would be inconceivable."

6. Each side should evacuate foreign territories occupied during the war. Germany should evacuate Belgium and France, and, in return, the Allies should restore to Germany her foreign colonies.

7. Where different nations claim the same territory (for instance, Austria and Italy, Germany and France), they should discuss the future of the disputed territory in the light of justice. They especially should consider what the people of the territory desire as well as the "general welfare" of all nations.

The British ambassador told the Pope that as long as the Central Powers did not promise to withdraw from Belgium and guarantee that they would not cause another war, the British could not enter into peace talks with them. It was another feeble excuse, for point 3 in Bethmann's proposal had clearly stated that Belgium's independence would be restored.

France did not reply to the pope; neither did Italy – and, indeed, this was not surprising; for in the secret Treaty of London, they and Great Britain had agreed to exclude the pope from peace negotiations.

The United States Secretary of State, Robert Lansing, (member of the Anglo-American cabal) replied in a letter dated 27 August 1917. The object of the war "was to deliver the free peoples of the world from an irresponsible government which secretly planned to dominate the world." After lecturing the pope on the ideals of the American people, the letter added that the United States would not take the word of the present rulers of Germany as a guarantee of anything, and President Wilson doubted that the pope's peace plan could actually work.

The response of the Central Powers was more satisfactory with even the Ottoman sultan writing that he was "deeply touched by the lofty thoughts of His Holiness." Kaiser Wilhelm accepted the peace proposals, but Chancellor Michaelis' reply failed to mention Belgium. Archbishop Pacelli reminded him that without a discussion of the future of Belgium there would be no peace. Two days later, Michaelis advised Pacelli that the German government supported the pope's peace efforts and that Belgium should be the first item discussed in peace negotiations.[41]

On 29 November 1917, the *Daily Telegraph* published a letter from that persistent critic of the war, Lord Lansdowne:

Sir,

We are now in the fourth year of the most dreadful war the world has ever known; a war in which, as Sir W. Robertson has lately informed us, "the killed alone can be counted by the million, while the total number of men engaged amounts to nearly 24 million." Ministers continue to tell us that they scan the horizon in vain for the prospect of a lasting peace. And without a lasting peace we all feel that the task we have set ourselves will remain unaccomplished. But those who look forward with horror to the prolongation of the war, who believe that its wanton prolongation would be a crime, differing only in degree from that of the criminals who provoked it, may be excused if they too scan the horizon anxiously in the hope of discovering there indications that the outlook may not after all be so hopeless as is supposed. ... In my belief, if the war is to be brought to a close in time to avert a world-wide catastrophe it will be brought to a close because on both sides the peoples of the countries involved realize that it has already lasted too long. There can be no question that this feeling prevails extensively in Germany, Austria and Turkey. We know beyond doubt that the economic pressure in those countries far exceeds any to which we are subject here. Ministers inform us in their speeches of constant efforts "on the part of the Central Powers" to initiate peace talks."[42]

For writing about the genuine desire in Germany, Austria-Hungary and Turkey for peace, and the 'constant efforts' on the part of Germany to initiate peace talks, Lord Lansdowne was treated as a pariah by the British Establishment. In the post-war years these repeated German peace initiatives were either ignored by British historians or dismissed as devious German trickery. The Anglo-American Establishment's man charged with presenting Germany's peace proposals in a bad light was Burton J. Hendrick, an American writer, publicist, and associate of President Theodore Roosevelt and President Woodrow Wilson. As discussed above, Hendrick was in the pay of the east Coast elites and on their behalf had already ghost-written Henry Morgenthau's book containing the great Potsdam lie. In 1922, Hendrick also wrote the official biography of Walter Hines Page, the US ambassador to Britain during the war. A wordsmith and master of doublespeak who reversed the truth, with regard to the German peace initiatives, Hendrick wrote:

Peace now became the underground Germanic programme. Yet the Germans did not have that inexorable respect for facts which would have persuaded them to accept terms to which the Allies could consent. The military oligarchy were thinking not so much of saving the Fatherland as of saving themselves; a settlement which would have been satisfactory to their enemies would have demanded concessions which the German people, trained for forty years to expect an unparalleled victory, would have regarded as a defeat. The collapse of the militarists and of Hohenzollernism would have ensued. What the German oligarchy desired was a peace which they could picture to their deluded people as a triumph, one that would enable them to extricate themselves at the smallest possible cost from what seemed a desperate position, to escape the penalties of their crimes, to emerge from their failure with a Germany still powerful, both in economic resources and in arms, and to set to work again industriously preparing for a renewal of the struggle at a more favourable time.[43]

There we have the Anglo-American establishment spin. The dastardly, devious Kaiser Wilhelm and German 'oligarchs' had not been after peace at all, but were simply trying to delude the German people and attempting to postpone their plans for global conquest until more favourable circumstances arose.

Summary: Chapter 13 – The Hall of Smoke and Mirrors

- On 7 May 1919, in the Hall of Mirrors, Versailles, German officials were shown Article 231 of the Peace Treaty declaring Germany guilty of causing the war.

- The main piece of evidence of German guilt came from Henry Morgenthau, former US ambassador to Turkey.

- Morgenthau's evidence indicated that the German ambassador to Turkey had told him that Kaiser Wilhelm had called a meeting at Potsdam on 5 July 1914, and declared to Germany's military, banking and industrial leaders that he had decided to plunge Europe into war using Franz Ferdinand's assassination as an excuse.

- In the postwar years, American historians researched Morgenthau's Potsdam story and found it to be an utter fabrication. No such meeting had taken place.

- Further research indicated that the US President and Secretary of State were implicated in the genesis of Morgenthau's Potsdam lie.

- Although never mentioned at Versailles, it later became evident that both Germany and the pope had made numerous peace moves through 1914-18 but all were rejected outright by the Allies.

CHAPTER 14

TRUTH – THE FIRST CASUALTY OF WAR

The 1914-18 war was the greatest crime in the history of mankind, and the narrative of German guilt the biggest lie. British elites had long planned the war, deviously started it, and ended it by blaming Germany for having caused it. At Versailles, reality was comprehensively turned inside out by the perpetrators to make them appear the victims, and by controlling the writing of the history of the war they now did everything possible to ensure that the truth never emerged.

We have seen how immediately the war started in 1914, historians at Oxford University began churning out books and pamphlets that falsely blamed Germany and completely whitewashed the real culprits in the Milner Group that was closely linked to Oxford, and its associated financial elites. That fake Oxford history has been recounted and entrenched by generation after generation of Oxford and other British academics to the present day. When the war ended, the Milner Group and American associates employed another important method of control that shackled the efforts of non-Oxford academics in Britain and across the world who genuinely sought to uncover the truth about its origins. This involved the collection and concealment or destruction of all documentary evidence that clearly pointed to Britain's guilt and Germany's innocence.

In 1919 Europe was in effect a massive crime scene with some 20 million killed and as many badly wounded. The perpetrators now went about forensically cleaning the crime scene by removing their metaphorical fingerprints and other evidence in order to pin the blame on an innocent party. Germany was proclaimed guilty without a trial or defence lawyers being allowed to present any evidence or witnesses. A great deal of evidence of Germany's innocence existed, but the Milner Group set about ensuring that it never saw the light of day. U.S. Senator Hiram Warren Johnson wrote: "When war is declared the first casualty is always truth." No matter who is responsible for starting a war, at its end whoever wins holds all the aces while the losers are made to shoulder the burden of blame and guilt. *Spolia optima* – to the victor go the spoils and history is part of the booty. The abuses, manipulations, and distortions of truth are always greatest during war and in subsequent historical accounts of it. German historian Andreas Bracher writes:

> One of the common wisdoms everyone knows is that "history is written by the victors." It is fantastic how this truth has not been applied to the history of the world wars, and how much people are inclined to believe the official or dominating narratives. So much paper has been produced within the framework of these manufactured narratives meant to conceal the truth and serve the victors and the powerful. It has produced some kind of thick spiritual cloud surrounding people (especially in the West) that instinctively leads them to believe the lies and to reject or belittle truth. Since the truth seems so strange and bizarre compared to the lies they have always heard, they call it "conspiracy theory." Modern history writing is almost like a self-referential rhetorical practice, a fog that surrounds the truth and is meant to obscure the access to it. Every idea or fact that threatens to penetrate this rhetorical cloud and break through the fog towards reality will get people upset, will make a scandal, because it threatens to shake the equilibrium of inertia in which people have come to feel comfortable.[1]

Such control of the historical record is not merely of significance for a true understanding of past wars, but for the future peace of mankind. In 1949, George Orwell wrote in his chilling dystopia, *1984*: "Who controls the past controls the future: who controls the present controls the past." Orwell writes of a governmental department, "The Ministry of Truth," deliberately falsifying history in order to conceal the truth from the people. If the people do not know the truth about the past they cannot learn lessons from it, and are thus more easily controlled and lead into future wars. In Orwell's *1984*, a totalitarian political party led by "Big Brother" brainwashes the population into unthinking obedience, and maintains control through "Thought Police" and continual surveillance. Free thought is taboo. All information comes to the people via controlled media propaganda called "Newspeak" and the Party's slogans comprise "Doublespeak" – language that deliberately reverses the meaning of words: "War is Peace, Freedom is Slavery, Ignorance is Strength."

Just as Orwell's totalitarian entity controlled the future by controlling the past, so too does the group of powerful individuals who are detailed in this book. They have to control and corrupt academic history in order to whitewash their responsibility for much of the war and strife that has taken place across the world in the past 130 years and more. A considerable portion of the truth about the war of 1914-18 is still out there, yet academic pro-Establishment history is designed to conceal it, not to record it. *What* can we know about something; *how* can we know it, is a branch of philosophy called epistemology. It is particularly problematic for historical knowledge which must rely on potentially flawed, biased or mistaken witness or doctored documentary evidence. These are the historical 'sources,' and it is the reliance on compromised 'sources' to the exclusion of many other forms of evidence that has rendered the official historical record of the First World War utterly unreliable. When 'sources' have been destroyed or concealed, how reliable or otherwise are those documents that are allowed to remain in the public domain? Who wrote them? For what purpose were they written? Is the record complete? What is omitted? Has it in any way been fabricated or doctored to suit the ends of the author or his paymasters?

Problems concerning the nature of historical knowledge are well recognised, particularly by those who seek to place the discipline within a philosophical framework. German philosopher Max Weber concluded that historians themselves are either unwilling or unable to apply a philosophical analysis to their own subject. Indeed, there are some who believe that a philosophical enquiry into the nature of historical knowledge simply cannot be accomplished, least of all by historians themselves. In his book, *Historians' Fallacies*, (published 1970) David Hackett Fischer wrote:

> If there is a field-related logic of historical thought, then working historians must help to find it. But they have contributed little of consequence in the past forty years. Their articles and books on the nature of history tend to degenerate into mere exhortations, or manuals on the mechanics of citation, or metahistorical mumbo-jumbo. Many academic historians regard methodological and logical problems with suspicion and even hostility.[2]

Fischer says that history and its research methods remain a field in which self-reflection is apparently taboo with many in the academic history profession. Given the uses to which 'history' has long been put in the interests of the powerful, this observation is unsurprising.

In writing this book, and in making enquiries of living, working academic historians, we have often been struck, and regularly dumbfounded, by their apparent lack of intellectual curiosity concerning their own subject and its methods. Perhaps they know they have nothing to gain, and everything to lose, or perhaps the process by which some leading 'scholars' are chosen and inducted into their profession has ensured that intellectually curious candidates are filtered out and excluded. Professor Quigley describes in some detail how financial elites created and funded departments of Modern History, and the History of War at the University of Oxford prior to the global conflict that began in 1914. They carefully selected professors and senior lecturers who were subjected to the power of indoctrination and subsequently beholden to them for their exalted positions, long-term careers and incomes. To reiterate Carroll Quigley's words, the Milner Group was "able to monopolize so completely the writing and the teaching of the history of their own period."[3]

Young historians at Oxford are taught that their methodology and approach is the one and only true academic gold standard. Even if they had the intellectual wherewithal to challenge the paradigm and develop a new one, they have been socialised in a community of scholars from which they would be ostracised and would lose all intellectual and academic credibility if they became apostate. If they take 'alternative' historians such as Professors Sutton, Quigley, or Preparata seriously, they find themselves seeking a different career. History by its nature attracts natural conservatives – keen on tradition and enthralled to recognition by their 'betters'. All of these things work to explain the hold that the Oxford method has on practitioners of that profession, and most simply cannot break out of it.

Having been promoted and accepted as holding the 'gold standard,' this Oxford 'school' of history set the standards in the discipline and controlled entry to, and progression in, the profession. In science the objective truth persists and is amenable to investigation, but history is quite literally in the past, and if you define the way and means of how it is permitted to be investigated then you control the past – and hence the present and future. We have seen how Oxford academics became closely involved in the 'war effort' by publishing a series of Oxford pamphlets 'explaining' the war to the public and justifying it. Effectively, the great and the good of Oxford – historians and theologians alike – became successful recruiting sergeants for the British army.

David Hackett Fischer writes of the clear need to provide a means for applying logic and the scientific method to the study of history, and allowing for the sceptical, questioning view of history that challenges accepted wisdom and posits alternative explanations of historical events.

How, for example, do we judge the trustworthiness of the memoirs or autobiographies of those who have wielded power or global influence and may have had much to hide – men such as Lord Milner, Sir Edward Grey, or Sir Winston Churchill? Numerous such individuals are known to have left orders for the destruction of personal files, letters and other material on their death.

> Official memoirs covering the origins of the First World War were carefully scrutinised and censored before being released. Sir Edward Grey's *Twenty-Five Years* is an appalling excuse for a record of fact, and the convenience of his failing memory rings hollow ... Ambassador Sir George Buchanan's memoirs, *My Mission to Russia and other Diplomatic Memories,* contained information too revealing for publication. His daughter Meriel stated that he was obliged to omit passages from his book on pain of losing his pension. Utterly unacceptable as this is, in the light of the lies that have been purveyed as history, it is surely of even greater concern that Carroll Quigley pointed an accusing finger at those who monopolised "so completely the writing and teaching of history of their own period." There is no ambivalence in his accusation. ... Almost every member of the Milner Group was a fellow of one of three [Oxford] colleges – Balliol, New College or All Souls. The Milner Group largely dominated these colleges, and they, in turn, largely dominated the intellectual life of Oxford in the field of history.... They also created their own official history of key members for public consumption, striking out any incriminating evidence and portraying the best public-spirited image that could safely be manufactured. The immediate advantage lay with the victors, and they ensured that their voluminous histories carried the message that the 'Great War' had been Germany's responsibility.[4]

REMOVING THE INCRIMINATING DOCUMENTS

To oversee the forensic clean-up and the great heist of European war documents, the Anglo-American elites chose none other than their loyal servant Herbert Hoover. As detailed previously, Hoover had swindled the Chinese government out of coal mines in Kaiping, and made a great deal of money tricking thousands of Chinese 'coolies' to go to South Africa to provide Alfred Milner with virtual slave labour for the gold mines. Thereafter, Hoover was the 'great humanitarian' of Belgian Relief who had, in reality, helped feed the German army in order to prolong the war. He was a man perfectly fitted to oversee the clean-up of the European crime scene.

Hoover faced a massive undertaking with the clean-up, not only of the European war documents but also those relating to the Belgian Relief (CRB) scam. With registered offices in New York, London, Brussels, Rotterdam, Antwerp, Paris, Lille and Buenos Aires, documentation for purchasing agents, shipping agents, insurance brokers, bankers and auditors, statisticians and clothing buyers, the CRB had left in its wake a multiple tonnage of bank transactions, ledger entries, accounts, deposits and records of international exchange.

> The list was potentially endless, at least, theoretically, because no independent records ever saw the light of day. They were systematically taken after the war by Hoover's agents and shipped to the west coast of America. Ponder long and hard on this fact; the evidence was physically removed from its point of origin. It was to be as if the illegal importations to Germany and the malpractices of Belgian bankers and speculators had never happened.
>
> …Bad as Hoover's manipulation and removal of the CRB's records was, it is of relatively minor importance compared to the outrageous theft of the historical record from all across Europe. In 1919 he was given this important task as the Secret Elite set about removing documentary evidence pertaining to the origins of the war. Once more he had to be re-invented. The "great humanitarian" became a "lover of books and of history" who wished to collect manuscripts and reports relating to the causes of the war because they would otherwise "easily deteriorate and disappear." Hoover certainly made sure that anything incriminating 'disappeared'.[5]

From the beginning, Hoover drafted Ephraim Adams, professor of history at Stanford University, into the project. An old friend, Professor Adams' involvement gave the heist a cloak of academic respectability. For any outsider poking their nose in it was to be presented as a philanthropic act of preserving history, since the documents would "easily deteriorate and disappear" otherwise. Adams had intended to keep a diary covering the events, but Hoover advised against it because everything must be kept "entirely confidential."[6]

The clean-up had to begin immediately. Professor Adams, accompanied by his wife, arrived in Paris two weeks before the Versailles verdict of 28 June 1919. He and Hoover discussed how best to go about procuring the documentation, and how it would be shipped to Stanford University near San Francisco and concealed there until catalogued. It would be a massive undertaking requiring upwards of a thousand men working full-time.

With powerful friends, Hoover asked General John Pershing, commander of the American Expeditionary Force in Europe, to provide suitable men for the project. Among them, fifteen historians from various U.S. army regiments were identified and released to Hoover. They would remain in uniform and oversee the collection in different countries.

> With food in one hand and reassurance in the other, these agents faced little resistance in their quest. They were primarily interested in material relating to the war's origins and the workings of the Commission for Relief of Belgium. They made the right contacts, 'snooped' around for archives and found so many that Hoover "was soon shipping them back to the US as ballast in the empty food boats."[8] He recruited an additional 1,000 agents [most likely former American soldiers] whose first haul amounted to 375,000 volumes of the 'Secret War Documents' of European governments.[7] Hoover donated a $50,000 'gift' for the task. That would only have paid for around seventy of these agents for a year.[9]

How this vastly expensive project involving over one thousand men was funded has never officially been revealed. For answers we must go back to 1917 when President Woodrow Wilson had called on Herbert Hoover to serve as the nation's wartime food administrator. With the relaxation of the British naval blockade, and the U.S. government's withdrawal from European food relief in the summer of 1919, Hoover set up a quasi-private organisation, the "American Relief Administration." When he publicly requested Americans to contribute funds to this new 'charitable' organisation, ordinary working people across America responded as best they could. Tellingly, substantial sums came from various leading bankers on Wall Street.

Many German-Americans and others who had been sending relief to Germany were suspicious of Hoover's motives. How could this staunch Anglophile who had spouted vile anti-German propaganda during the war suddenly turn his attention to feeding those he clearly loathed? Strangely, for a man who was apparently now so keen to see starving German children fed, he publicly discouraged German-Americans from sending food and rendering aid to Germany through their own channels. This great 'humanitarian task,' he insisted, should be done through his Relief Administration and all donations sent there. Genuinely concerned, American citizens, however, created a separate charity, the "Society To Relieve Distress in Germany and Austria." They insisted that all monies donated to aid the hungry in Germany should be sent via the German Red Cross as opposed to Hoover's set-up. Concern over Hoover's activities grew, and he was accused of giving $8,000,000 (worth around $123,000,000 in purchasing power today) that was specifically donated to feed German women and children, to Poland, Serbia and other countries instead.[10]

What was going on? What was Hoover really up to with all this money? No definite proof emerged, but suspicion later arose that significant amounts of the charity money was being spent not to aid starving Germans as publicised – or indeed any other Europeans – but to cover the huge cost of gathering up the European war documents and shipping them to America. Cissie Dore Hill, the exhibits coordinator of the Hoover Institution Archives, wrote:

> Hoover told Adams that he was interested not in the war's military aspect but in its socioeconomic causes and effects as well as the issue of food administration. He put the structure of his post-war food relief organization, the American Relief Administration (ARA), at Adams's disposal.[11]

Hoover put 'the structure' of his food relief organisation at the 'disposal' of Ephraim Adams, but Adams had nothing whatsoever to do with food relief. Was this a deliberately obscure way of saying that the relief 'charity' was meeting the costs of the document heist? Cissie Dore Hill adds:

> In addition, he [Hoover] enabled two of Adams's former students to be released from their army duty. Private Robert C. Binkley and Lieutenant Ralph Lutz, the latter a professor at the University of Washington, became officially attached to the ARA; *actually both were out collecting documents.*
>
> Adams stayed in Paris to collect the propaganda produced by delegates to the Paris Peace Conference, while Lutz travelled throughout Eastern and Central Europe, setting up a network of contacts, including book dealers, libraries, and government personnel. A successful ploy when asking German government bureaucrats for materials was to pull out a large list of promised French materials, motivating the Germans to exceed the French in all departments.
>
> Stanford professor Frank Golder joined Lutz, and together they laid the foundations for the Eastern European and Russian collections, which are among Hoover's most distinguished collections. One of Golder's important contacts was Anatoly Lunacharsky, the

Soviet commissar for education, from whom Golder received copies of government directives. After the first $50,000 ran out, Hoover
continued to finance the collecting with large grants. He felt that
there would be "a thousand years to catalogue this library, but only
ten years in which to acquire the most valuable of material." Lutz,
now director, accelerated his collecting to a frenzied pace.[12]

Numerous American historians such as Lutz and Binkley were released to the ARA food agency and were being paid by it, but were in fact
overseeing the document heist. That it would take "a thousand years to
catalogue" provided the perfect excuse if independent researchers came
to examine documents at Stanford: "Sorry, they haven't been catalogued
yet. Come back another year – another century."

In 1920 Ralph Lutz was appointed Co-director of the Collections at
Stanford. Frank Golder (Ph.D. Harvard) was appointed curator of its War
History Collection, and in charge of gathering war documents from Soviet Russia. Anatoly Lunacharsky – mentioned above by Cisse Dore Hill
as an important contact of Golder's – was also a friend of Bolshevik leader Leon Trotsky. As we have seen, Trotsky had spent time in New York
in early 1917, being indulged and pampered by Wall Street bankers before being sent on a ship to Europe with a passport signed by Woodrow
Wilson and substantial amounts of cash provided by those bankers. As
ever, it was circles within circles. Hoover was an important member of
the Anglo-American elite circles that financed Trotsky and the Bolsheviks. Lunacharsky, the contact in Soviet Russia for Hoover's man Golder,
was the first Soviet People's Commissar and Trotsky's friend. With such
connections, gaining access to Russian documents and removing them
was relatively straightforward.

> The Russian documents undoubtedly contained hugely damaging
> information on how the assassination of Franz Ferdinand in Sa-
> rajevo on 28 June 1914 had been orchestrated through Petrograd
> [formerly St Petersburg] and how Russia's general mobilisation
> on Germany's eastern border had been the real reason for the war
> starting. It might appear strange that the Bolsheviks cooperated so
> willingly by allowing Hoover's agents to remove twenty-five car-
> loads of material from Petrograd.[13]
>
> However, when one realises that the international bankers in the
> secret society had financed and facilitated Lenin and Trotsky's
> return to Russia, as well as the Bolshevik Revolution itself, it be-
> comes clear: the Americans could have what they wanted. This as-

tonishing event was reported in the *New York Times* which claimed that Hoover's team "bought the documents" from a "doorkeeper" for $200 cash.[14]

And some people think that fake news is a twenty-first century concept.[15]

In addition, Hoover and Golders were informed of the whereabouts of an important collection of czarist archives concerning the war's origins concealed in Finland. Hoover later stated: "Getting them was no trouble at all. We were feeding Finland at the time."[16]

Collecting the pertinent British and French war documents posed no problems whatsoever. From Germany, it is known that fifteen carloads were taken. They included "the complete secret minutes of the German Supreme War Council," allegedly a 'gift' from Fritz Ebert, president of the post-war German Republic from February 1919 to February 1925. Hoover later explained away this extraordinary 'gift' by suggesting that Ebert had "no interest" in the work of his predecessors.[17]

According to the *New York Times*, Hoover's team also removed 6,000 volumes of German documents covering the complete official proceedings of the Kaiser's pre-war activities and his wartime conduct of the German empire.[18]

Macgregor and Docherty write:

> If Germany had been guilty of planning and starting the war – as decreed by Court Historians ever since – these documents would have proved it. Strange that none have ever been released. Had there been incriminating documents, it is certain that copies would have been sent out immediately to every press and news agency throughout the world proving Germany was to blame. The removal and concealment of the German archives by the Secret Elite was crucial because they would have proved the opposite: Germany *had not* started the war.[19]

Massive quantities of documents, acquired by fair means or foul, were used as ballast in empty merchant ships returning to the west coast of America. From the docks around San Francisco, they were taken to Hoover's alma mater, Stanford University, at nearby Palo Alto. The vast collection was kept under lock and key in the university library and other buildings until a dedicated repository – the Hoover Institution – could be built.

The website of the present-day Hoover Institution proudly boasts that Herbert Hoover advised the university president Ray Lyman Wilbur:

> "There will be a thousand years to catalogue this library but only ten years in which to acquire the most valuable of material." ... Herbert Hoover began his collection of rare historical artifacts decades before public and university libraries became interested in such material. Through his personal initiative and this talent for entrusting responsibility to the right people, Hoover assembled one of the world's largest and most comprehensive private libraries and archives on twentieth-century history.
>
> ... The Hoover War Collection, as it was initially called, rapidly expanded its collecting scope to include not just the causes and course of the First World War but its tumultuous aftermath. Within a few years, the collection became a library dedicated to documenting war, revolution, and peace in the modern era. The search for peace – that is, for a way to prevent a recurrence of war and the revolutions that inevitably spring from it – was at the heart of Herbert Hoover's project.[20]

Just as Belgian 'relief' is presented by the official Hoover website today in Orwellian doublethink that deliberately disguises or reverses the truth, so too is the great heist of European documents. Black is white, war is peace. Hoover, we are told, was a saintly figure whose heart lay in a mission to collect documents as a means of preserving peace in the world. It would be 22 years before *selected* documents were first made available to the public. What was concealed or incinerated will never be known.

The Hoover Tower opened on the Stanford University campus in 1941. An 87 metre structure built specifically to house the First World War documents, it has 15 floors of shelving extending in total to some 10.3 miles. An additional 25 miles of shelving is provided in the basement of the Herbert Hoover Memorial building and offsite storage. The fact that the tower has very few windows is perhaps a subliminal message that documents revealing the truth about the war and Belgian Relief will never see the light of day.

The Hoover complex at Palo Alto is not the only repository for documents pertaining to the origins of the First World War, for another such storage facility exists at Hanslope Park in England.

HANSLOPE PARK

For Western academic historians at the present day, memoirs and official documents are considered virtually the only 'legitimate' source

Security is tight at Hanslope Park

of information used to record history. Yet the reliability of British 'primary source documents' relating to the period before, during, and after the 1914-18 war is extremely dubious. We know from investigative journalist Ian Cobain's book, *The History Thieves: Secrets and Lies and the Shaping of a Modern Nation,* that in order to obscure the crimes of the British Empire, the authorities deliberately concealed documents "that might embarrass Her Majesty's Government or its police, military and public servants; or that might compromise its sources of intelligence or be used 'unethically' by any successor government."[21] The order went out from London: 'No such documents should be allowed to exist.' Accordingly, they were 'weeded' and subjected to either mass incineration, dumping at sea, or concealment in a repository 60 miles north of London at Hanslope Park, Buckinghamshire.

Purpose-built for the Foreign Office, millions of documents are held to this day at Hanslope Park in breach of the Public Record Acts. Three-story buildings cover a huge area encircled by two wire fences: one 3 metres high and topped with razor wire. The entire complex is covered by floodlights, intruder alarms and CCTV cameras positioned every few metres. Guards patrol the complex day and night. This not a British equivalent of Fort Knox for gold, but the high security establishment in which the British government conceals an enormous cache of documents under the title "Special Collections." The concealed documents cover fifteen miles of floor-to-ceiling shelving, including documents pertaining to the 'First' and 'Second' World Wars. There are so many documents that their catalogue entries alone occupy hundreds of metres of shelf space. Incinerators are fitted in buildings throughout the complex.

Hanslope Park is not only a highly secure facility, it is also a place that appears to be accustomed to handling – and destroying – large amounts of paperwork. This, possibly, explains why the special collections have been held there.[22]

Following Ian Cobain's revelations about the concealment of documents, 27 Fellows of the British Academy wrote collectively to the *Guardian* newspaper calling on the government to state its plans for releasing them:

> British scholars are concerned about reports (19 October 2013; 14 January 2014) that contrary to the 1958 Public Records Act the government has retained 1.2 million Foreign and Commonwealth Office files, going back to the Crimean War. They are evidently held at the ironically named HMG Communications Centre at Hanslope Park. Efforts to oblige the government to be clear on what files it holds and on plans to release them have not been successful.
>
> While GCHQ [Government Communications Headquarters] tells us that the government has wholly unexpected capacities to unearth information about its own citizens, the right of citizens to investigate UK foreign and colonial policy over the last 150 years and more is clearly being denied. Those of us who work on the history of some other countries are used to government obstruction when it comes to researching official papers, but the UK is supposed to be a free society. The writing of full and impartial accounts of the cold war, Britain's colonial past, and other key subjects depends on access to all the available records.
>
> As fellows of the British Academy, we call upon the foreign secretary to issue a statement about the government's plans to release these documents to the National Archives, and for a mechanism to be established to include professional historians and archivists in the process of declassification. We have today written to him, offering to meet and discuss this further.[23]

Gaby Weiner, Visiting Professor at Sussex University, added: "Why the culture of secrecy in British officialdom? Who is being protected? Surely we, as British citizens, have a right to know."[24]

The Foreign Office responded that the archive had accumulated over time and that "resources have not been available to review and prepare" them for release. The Foreign and Commonwealth Office minister told MPs that documents considered to be of the greatest public interest would be transferred to the National Archives in London over a six-year period.

Richard Drayton, Rhodes Professor of Imperial History at King's College London, was deeply sceptical. The size of the hidden archive was "staggering' and scandalous." It was *a manipulation of history* more associated with iron curtain regimes during the cold war – "regimes that managed and controlled the past." *The Guardian* newspaper reported:

> Mandy Banton, senior research fellow at the Institute of Commonwealth Studies, said it was "extremely likely" that the *archive had been culled to remove material that would most damage the reputation of the UK and the Foreign Office.* Banton, a Colonial Office records expert who worked at National Archives at Kew, south-west London, for 25 years, said she had been "very angry" when she discovered that the migrated archives had been withheld. "I would have been incandescent had I learned while still working there. In lying to me, the Foreign Office forced me to mislead my readers."[25]

Professor Margaret MacMillan, a British war historian and warden of St Antony's College, Oxford, stated:

> I am one of many historians who has benefitted from using the British archives and who had confidence that the documents had not been weeded to suit particular interests. Now I am wondering whether I will have to go back and *rethink my work on such matters as the outbreak of the First World War* or the peace conference at the end.[26]

Journalist Ian Cobain also revealed that the Ministry of Defence [MoD] was unlawfully holding tens of thousands of files at a separate facility in Derbyshire. "One MoD archivist describes it as looking like 'the final scene from *Raiders of the Lost Ark*,' in which box after box can be seen stretching into the distance." The MoD admitted it was also withholding tens of thousands of other files on the grounds that "they had been stored in a building in London where asbestos had been discovered." Unknown quantities of documents had also "been destroyed as a result of water damage."[27]

Cobain's research indicates that over the past century and more, successive British governments have been implicated in the mass destruction or concealment of important records and archives, and what we are left with are false memories. And with incineration of the European primary source documents pertaining to the true origins of the war – or their concealment at Palo Alto and Hanslope Park – came a carefully considered academic subterfuge. Academics at Oxford, Harvard, Stanford, and other leading universities who were beholden to the financial elites, insisted that primary source documents were absolutely essential for uncovering the truth about the First World War. It was a straightforward cover-up; remove the incriminating documents then apply the academic stricture of 'no documents, no proof.'

There was more.

> Together with the omission of crucial documents, control of the narrative itself is another mechanism for creating fake history. This, ironically, is achieved by applying the academic principles of historical research which are meant to prevent junk history; the peer review process. Peer review involves a manuscript or research proposal being read and evaluated anonymously by scholars who are themselves part and parcel of the system. They may have considerable expertise in the period, subject matter, languages, and documents with which the author deals, but they have a list of criteria to which the aspiring historical author must bend the knee. And herein lies the finesse of the overall system which prevents true history emerging. Work which fails to display knowledge of existing work or fails to provide what they deem as valid evidence, will not be approved. It will be damned as weak, and appropriate revisions and resubmissions will be demanded.
>
> In other words, the fake history of the approved 'eminent' Court Historian has to be included. Where valid documentary evidence has been destroyed, corrupted, removed, culled and so forth, then the author is limited to the scraps which have survived. Thus, at a stroke, the permanent withdrawal of primary source documents achieves its aim. Researchers cannot move beyond the parameters created by those who actually determine what can or cannot be accepted as history. They have to play the peer review game to advance their careers. They are required to stay on the mainline train and regurgitate that which the elites want us to believe is true history. Those who deviate or question the process are not tolerated. The only route is the mainline track, laid down by the great universities from chairs of history funded and controlled by the corrupted system.[28]

In the early 1970s, Canadian historian, Nicholas D'Ombrain, had an interesting experience of the 'corrupted system' when researching War Office records in London. He noted that files had been 'weeded' and over the period he was actually conducting his research some 80 per cent of the 'sensitive' files he was interested in were removed. He was unable to ascertain by whom, or why.[29]

It is patently evident that the historical record of the First World War was seriously compromised by concealment or destruction of documents and whitewashing of memoirs, yet the academic history Establishment insists to this day that such documents are the 'gold standard' upon which to build a 'history'. What kind of 'knowledge' can possibly emerge from the documents allowed to survive the cull? What 'truth' can possibly be told based on such an approach? The Milner Group and financial elite ensured that many primary source documents were destroyed or concealed then insisted that primary source documents must be used as the gold standard in academic history. It is a clever, simple, method of control. As they say in computer science: 'garbage in, garbage out'.

Thanks to Ian Cobain's revelations there is little doubt that the public are being misinformed, if not deliberately lied to, by the official war histories created for public consumption. Like dead men, burned and buried documents tell no tales. Or rather, those documents that are permitted to remain tell the tale that the powerful wish to be told. Few areas are more important to their purposes than control over the national myths and narratives upon which their political structures are built. Chief among these is the history that is taught about a nation's story, for upon that is built political 'legitimacy'. As an academic pursuit in western universities, it has been over-ridden by a mission to support power. The principle means by which this has been achieved has been to limit and narrow its sources of information and 'knowledge' to archival sources that are controlled by those who operate the levers of power.

The historical method is the totality of techniques and guidelines that its practitioners use to research and write about the past. The value of secondary and tertiary sources is entirely dependent on the existence and quality of primary sources. Primary sources are key, and thus were the main target of Herbert Hoover and those who control, distort and utilise 'history' in their own interests. Any 'history' that is based on such contaminated, distorted or absent primary sources, cannot within the very parameters of the paradigm of history, be relied upon to produce historical truth. Without the documents, the academic historian sees nothing, and hence knows nothing. Who benefits from such wilful blindness? How is such an approach meant to record the truth, or, it has to be asked, is failing to do so the method's true purpose? We should recall: *"When war is declared the first casualty is always truth."*

It should be clearly stated that most practitioners of history are decent, honest people who have been taught in the current paradigm, and like anyone schooled in such a paradigm they will accept it as the 'gold standard'. Others, however, who are steeped in the mores of power politics are not historians but propagandists.

It is clear that academic history of the First World War is in dire need of a revolution, but that is a matter that only those in the field are capable of accomplishing. Regrettably, there seems to be little enthusiasm among them for this urgent task, and they continue to rely on 'sources' which have been utterly compromised by the perpetrators of the war. Carroll Quigley explained that *there are* other ways of approaching the truth when documents are concealed or destroyed:

> I have devoted long years of study and much original research, even where adequate documentation is not available, but it should be equally evident that whatever value this present work has rests on its broad perspective. I have tried to remedy deficiencies of evidence by perspective, not only by projecting the patterns of past history into the present and the future but also by trying to place the events of the present in their total context by examining all the varied aspects of these events, not merely the political and economic, as is so frequently done, but by my efforts to bring into the picture the military, technological, social, and intellectual elements as well.[30]

Quigley's approach has much to recommend it, and it certainly informed our own. We set out to write this book understanding that we could not rely on official historical records to tell this tale. We have already stated that it is not a history book, but is a book about history – and more specifically – about the abject failure of mainstream British historian propagandists to relate honest accounts of the First World War and the disasters that followed on from the corrupt Versailles Treaty. The book is an investigation into the crimes of powerful Anglo-American elites and their collaborators and enablers. We have to look elsewhere than the history paradigm in order to address the research questions that confront us in understanding the events surrounding the wars to crush Germany.

When the authorities in the West want to jail you or even execute you, they will give you a 'fair' trial in which the standard of evidence sufficient to convict is 'beyond reasonable doubt'. In a civil trial the evidential base is even less restrictive: the 'balance of probability'. Judicial standards of evidence are much closer to those of the scientific method than those of the highly restricted historical one. Judicial systems accept the fact that human beings are capable of inferring the truth from the weight and volume of evidence presented.

We have taken both a scientific and a juridical approach to examining the events in question. We have looked at multiple strands of evidence, and multiple sources of evidence, including both official histories and the work of revisionist historians. We ask questions as to the probability of any given explanation being true based on a shared human understanding of how human beings behave in given circumstances.

Our approach has been to follow the example of the criminal law, and where appropriate, the civil law, which allows the consideration of circumstantial evidence. In fact, legal and state authorities often posit that circumstantial evidence can be just as compelling, or even more compelling, than traditional proof such as documents, forensic evidence, photographic evidence and so on. Circumstantial evidence allows for more than one explanation. It may or may not prove something, but at the very least it opens up intriguing avenues of further investigation. And when different strands of such evidence are drawn together and each corroborates the conclusions drawn from the others, there is every reason to take serious notice.

For hundreds of years lawyers and judges have talked about this 'cable' of circumstantial evidence. A cable is made up of many strands which individually are not particularly strong, but the more strands which are added to the cable the stronger it becomes. In many, if not indeed the majority of legal cases, it is this cable of circumstantial evidence and not direct evidence which solidly links an accused to the crime. Juries in the United States and elsewhere are entitled to reach a verdict on such evidence, and judges are able to condemn an individual to death on the strength of that verdict. The U.S. Supreme Court has stated that "circumstantial evidence is intrinsically no different from testimonial [direct] evidence," yet academic war historians deride its use.

Importantly, the law also allows that in some circumstances an *absence* of evidence that *ought* to be there should be treated as a type of proof. For example, if an alleged criminal were to destroy documents or other types of physical evidence, or to hide it, or to silence key witnesses by whatever means, that would allow a judge or jury to draw conclusions from such behaviour and to convict, provided other key tests were met. Given that most of those writing about history and political events choose to eschew such a forensic approach when dealing with controversial subjects in areas where evidence is either missing or withheld, one is left asking the question: "why?"

Why is the Hanslope Park material kept under high security? Why has so much material been incinerated? Why do mainstream historians neither strenuously object to these stark facts nor discuss them in their books? Why do mainstream historians in general never mention or consider the accounts presented by revisionists, even if only to disprove them?

Fortunately, some historians have provided many clues to this and why the powers-that-be wish it to be so. In writing this book, we have taken our lead from the brave and true academic historians willing to be informed by multiple and diverse sources – not just official archives. We have looked at the available documentary evidence – and much can be gleaned from that alone – that seems to have evaded the attention of other authors. But we also look at the monumental volume of circumstantial evidence, the gaps in evidence, the 'coincidences,' the links of friends and families, and indeed the quite literally unbelievable accounts of these momentous times and, not least, see what has been hidden in plain sight. Historian Andreas Bracher writes:

> History in former times had been written by people who were, on the one hand, close to the events, but, in the best case, also, when they wrote their records, removed enough to look back at these events from a point of view which was not coloured by any personal interests, but which would look at things from a wider perspective. History writing was not the métier of a "profession," but the self-imposed "mission" of loners, who wanted to understand the world. It was written by people who, by the shape of their biography, had come into a state where they would be able and willing to converse with truth. That history writing could become a profession, as in modern academia, in institutions financed by the government or powerful elites, and nevertheless be "truthful" and dispassionate, – nobody should have believed that. *"Wer Brot ich eß, des Lied ich sing'* (Who gives me the bread is the one whose song I will sing), is a German saying. That means modern academic historians will be, more or less, the spokespeople of those, who finance them, they will present the history as these people will want it to be presented. History writing is not (or should not be) about "facts," about revealing "the facts," but about uncovering the real forces behind the events. The right facts can reveal these "real forces" if put into the right context as facts can hide these real forces if put into the wrong context. "Lying with true facts" maybe one of the most common stratagems in modern journalism as in modern history writing. It means, putting certain facts together in such a way that a completely distorted picture emerges about what these facts mean, about what brought them forth, about what were the

forces that really shaped events and history. Where can the effective, event-shaping, powerful intentions be found, and where do the intentions just trickle away and are powerless masturbations? In the end the method of "telling lies with true facts" completely corrupts and confuses people's sense of truth, it distorts their intuition, because it teaches them a completely false idea of how "the mark of truth" can be recognized.[31]

The truth about the 1914-18 war has been corrupted in numerous different ways, but none match the emotional power of the engravings in stone on war memorials across every city, town, and village in Britain. They relate that the million or so young British men slaughtered in that war were 'The Glorious Dead' who bravely and willingly laid down their lives for civilisation so that we today 'might be free'. Each year on the anniversary of the 11 November 1918, armistice, memorial services across the entire country are held in remembrance of those killed. At the Cenotaph in London – just yards from 10 Downing Street and the British Foreign Office where the disastrous war was decided upon in 1904 and carefully planned – descendants of one of the master schemers, King Edward VII, stand to attention in their grand military uniforms and lay wreaths in great solemnity. At the same time a mile or so to the east at St Paul's Cathedral, the Bishop of London preaches that the British (not the German) war dead are safely in God's House. Today's Bishop of London makes no mention of the important part that one of her predecessors – the warmongering Bishop Winnington-Ingram – played in recruiting soldiers to that war on the basis of a great lie, and preaching that all Germans, good or bad, young or old, must be killed.

At the remembrance gatherings, banners proclaim, 'Lest we forget,' but the British people were hoodwinked then (as they are hoodwinked now) and most of them never grasped the truth in the first place let alone forgot it. Vast swathes of the British people have been conned into believing the great lies to this day. Those young men had indeed bravely and sincerely gone off to fight, but the sad stark fact is they had no inkling whatsoever that it was all lies and they had been totally duped. They were not fighting and dying for 'freedom and civilisation,' but for the further enrichment and greater power of bankers and other British ruling elites. What the war dead deserve is not religious cant or the posturing of the 'great and good' of the British ruling class (adorned with the now de rigueur poppies) on armistice day, but the TRUTH. In death, the soldiers of Germany, Austria-Hungary, Britain, France, Russia and elsewhere in the 1914-18 war share one common eulogy:

'Victims all of Power-Crazed Avarice, Rapacious Greed, and Abysmal Mendacity.'

Summary: Chapter 14 – Truth – The First Casualty of War

- By 1919, Europe was devastated and a massive crime scene. Those responsible for the war created a fake history that blamed Germany, and went about removing all traces of their guilt in a massive clean-up of the crime scene.

- Official memoirs of those responsible were sanitised to conceal guilt, and such individuals left orders for the destruction of personal files, letters and other relevant material on their death.

- To control the writing and teaching of history, the Anglo-American elites funded departments of Modern History in universities – at Oxford in particular – and selected the professors to run them.

- A team of American historians was brought together in 1919 by the elite's instrument, Herbert Hoover. With some 1,000 agents under their command, they scoured capital cities across Europe for documents pertaining to the origins of the war, and Hoover's 'Belgian Relief' scam.

- Hundreds of thousands of documents were taken by them from Europe and sent to Stanford University. The individuals responsible for the war were then able to decide what would or would not be allowed into the public domain.

- Official documents relating to Britain's prime role in the genesis of the war and British atrocities across its empire, were either incinerated or placed under high security at a special repository at Hanslope Park in England.

- Compromised academic historians at leading elite universities laid down the parameters for historical research. They were weighted heavily in favour of using primary source documents – the very material which was concealed at Hanslope Park and Stanford University.

- War memorials throughout Britain relate the lie that almost a million young British and Commonwealth soldiers who were duped and killed in the unnecessary war to crush Germany, gave their lives for 'liberty and civilization'.

CHAPTER 15

SOWING THE SEEDS OF CHAOS

Preparata

Members of the Milner Group doubtless raised their champagne flutes to toast the successful accomplishment of the first stage of their plan for global control. The masses had been encouraged to view the carnage of 1914-18 as 'the war to end all wars,' but it was neither the end nor the beginning of the end for the so-called First and Second World Wars were not unconnected entities but a continuum. In his outstanding book, *Conjuring Hitler, How Britain and America made the Third Reich*, the Italian historian, Professor Guido G. Preparata, relates that the so-called 'First World War' had merely been Act One of what was essentially a Thirty Years War between 1914 and 1945 – what he called the great 'siege of Europe' by Britain and America.

> The main objective of this titanic siege was the prevention of an alliance between Germany and Russia: if these two powers could have fused in an 'embrace,' so reasoned the British stewards, they would have come to surround themselves with a fortress of resources, men, knowledge and military might such as to endanger the survival of the British empire in the new century. From this early realization, Britain embarked upon an extraordinary campaign to tear Eurasia asunder by hiring France and Russia, and subsequently America, to fight the Germans. The vicissitudes of the first half of the twentieth century made up the epic of the great siege of Europe. World War I completed the first act of the attack, which was crowned by the imperial ingress of the United States on the grand chessboard. Germany had lost the war, but she had not been defeated on her own territory... [1]

The second act began with the Anglo-American cabal performing an "astounding political maneuvre" to resurrect a reactionary regime in Germany that would be manipulated into further conflict.

The premeditated purpose was to ensnare the new, reactionary regime in a two-front war (World War II) and profit from the occasion to annihilate Germany once and for all. To carry out these deep and painstaking directives for world control, two conditions were necessary: (1) an imposing and anti-German regime secretly aligned with Britain had to be set up in Russia, and (2) the seeds of chaos had to be planted in Germany to predispose the institutional terrain for the growth of this reactionary movement of 'national liberation'. The first objective was realized by backstabbing the Czar in Russia in 1917 and installing the Bolsheviks into power.[2]

Following the first act, the Milner Group and closely linked Anglo-American financial supremos planted the "seeds of chaos" in Germany with the disgraceful Versailles Treaty falsely blaming Germany for the war; crippling reparations payments and encouragement of rampant inflation. They manipulated the economic and political situation in Germany to undermine emerging democratic movements, and supported their chosen reactionary regime – the nascent Nazi Party – led by the then unknown Adolf Hitler. In the following chapters we examine the astonishing facts concerning how, from 1922 onwards, having selected the oddball, vagabond, German army corporal Hitler, the British and American secret intelligence services positioned special agents directly at his side to groom and prepare him for power. We see how, in 1933, one of those Anglo-American agents played a major role in deliberately burning down the Reichstag – the German parliament – and fanning the terror that followed. The Reichstag fire proved the key event in enabling Hitler to eliminate political opposition, seize dictatorial power, and begin a reign of terror against Jews and socialists in Germany. All the while, he was shielded and funded by the very same Anglo-American elites and passed off in the West as a good leader for Germany and an essential dam to prevent a flood of Russian communism into western Europe.

Leading members of the British Establishment and the controlled Press appeased Hitler and lulled him into considering the possibility, if not indeed the likelihood, that Britain would back him when it came to war against the 'Red Menace' of Soviet Russia. Like Kaiser Wilhelm before him, Hitler appears to have had little initial understanding that appeasement was a charade or that he and Germany were being set up by Perfidious Albion for another disastrous fall.

ADOLF HITLER

Hitler was born on 20 April 1889 in Braunau am Inn, an Austrian town close to the Bavarian border 280 km west of Vienna, and was baptised two days later in the Roman Catholic church. His father, Alois Hitler, was then a boorish 52 year-old-customs officer. His mother, 29-year-old Klara, came from peasant stock and had no education. Some Hitler biographers and historians suggest Alois was a violent bully, heavy drinker, and tyrannical figure, while others paint him in a softer light. Alois was the son of Maria Anna Schicklgruber who came from a peasant background in Strones, a small agricultural village some 100 km to the north-west of Vienna. A spinster, Maria Anna was 42 years old when she gave birth to Adolf Hitler's father in 1837. His baptismal record has a blank space where the father's name should have been registered, and the identity of Hitler's paternal grandfather is disputed to this day.

Maria Anna lived with her elderly father who had fallen on hard times, and Alois was born into poverty.[3] Five years later, Maria Anna – now 47 years old – married Johann George Hiedler, an itinerant mill worker who by many accounts was a lazy good-for-nothing. Johann George's younger brother, Nepomuk Hiedler, a successful and relatively well-off farmer, rescued young Alois from destitution and effectively adopted him. Nepomuk's wife was a pleasant woman who cared well for their three young daughters, and successfully integrated the adopted boy into the family. Although Alois retained his mother's Schicklgruber name, it is unknown if he ever saw her again. She died in poverty in 1847 when he was 10 years old.

Hitler's father now lived in agreeable conditions with Nepomuk and his wife, and had a harmonious relationship with their daughters. After elementary school he apprenticed to a nearby shoemaker, but in his early teens moved away to pursue the trade in Vienna. At the age of 18 he gave up shoemaking and joined the Austrian frontier guards. He appears to have been a diligent young man who, within five years, became a non-commissioned officer. After a series of further promotions, in 1871 Alois was assigned to the town of Braunau as assistant inspector of customs. He would be promoted four years later to full inspector.

In 1876, at the age of 39, Alois changed his name from Schicklgruber to Alois Hiedler, apparently after being promised an inheritance by Nepomuk to do so. He used a transliteration, however, and now called himself Alois Hitler. For many years there has been speculation and controversy regarding his paternity. Suggestions that he may have had Jewish ancestry have been dismissed by mainstream historians. Although Nepomuk Hiedler was only 15 years older than the boy he adopted, historian Milan Hauner considers it likely that he, not his brother, was Alois's biological father.[4] Historian Volker Ullrich is less convinced:

Whatever the truth may be, the identity of Adolf Hitler's paternal grandfather remains uncertain. It is hard to overlook the irony that the man who would later demand that all Germans prove their 'Aryan origins' was himself incapable of demonstrating his own – no matter how much the Fuhrer's official genealogy tried to convey the contrary impression.[5]

Hitler biographer Ian Kershaw writes: "The answers to these questions are lost in the mist of time." Kershaw dismisses suggestions that Alois was the illegitimate son of a Jewish businessman from Graz called Frankenberger, and believes that the only serious contenders for his paternity are Johann George Hiedler or his brother, Nepomuk.[6] Years later, in the summer of 1876, the parish priest added Johann George Hiedler to the register as being Alois's father.

Alois married twice before marrying Hitler's mother, Klara Pölzl. His first marriage to Anna Glassl was unhappy and bore no children. Before

Anna died, Alois was romantically involved with a young hotel cook, Franziska Matzelsberger. She quickly bore him a son, Alois Jr, in 1882 (half-brother of Hitler) and a daughter, Angela, (half-sister) in 1883. The following year, however, Franziska died at the age of 23 from tuberculosis. Within months of her death, Alois – now 48 years old – married Hitler's mother, Klara Pölzl. She had been working and living with the family as a servant and looked after Alois Jr and Angela when their young mother was dying. Klara was 25 years old at the marriage, and five months pregnant by Alois, so had conceived around the time Franziska lay dying. Alois's two children adored their stepmother, who had been in and out of their home since their birth.[7]

It is here that Adolf Hitler's ancestry becomes even more complicated, for his mother, Klara Pölzl, was Nepomuk Hiedler's granddaughter. If Alois was indeed Nepomuk's biological son – as suggested by Professor Milan Hauner – he was the half-brother of his new wife's mother. There is no definite evidence, but William Shirer writes that Alois and Klara had to apply for dispensation to marry.[8]

Following their marriage, Alois and Klara had three children in quick succession, Gustav born 1885, Ida born 1886, and Otto born 1887. Otto died shortly after birth, and Gustav and Ida both died of diphtheria around Christmas 1887. Alois and Klara's fortune took a turn for the better the following year. Nepomuk Hiedler died and left Alois money in his will. On 16 March 1889, when his wife was eight months pregnant with Adolf, Alois had sufficient money to buy a small farm.[9]

Adolf Hitler was born on 20 April 1889, and Alois's two children from his time with Franziska, Alois Jr and Angela, lived with the family as Klara's stepchildren. She had already cared for them when their mother was dying, and they got on well with her. Hitler's mother loved him, but his father appears to have been indifferent at best. Much has been written about the domestic and social forces which impacted on Hitler throughout his childhood – especially his troubled relationship with his father – and produced the adult he became. American historian Bradley F. Smith writes:

> A great distance separated the little boy [Adolf] from his father. Alois was seldom home. After working extended day and night shifts at the customs station, he filled his scanty free time with his friends and his bees.... He did not enjoy going home: when he joined the rest of the family, it was to achieve some specific end and not to be bothered with children. When he arrived home in an irritable mood, the older children and his wife bore the brunt of his wrath. Klara was wise enough in the ways of her husband to move the infant out of harm's way whenever the danger flags were flying. An occasional nod, smile or rumble reached the child directly from his father...[10]

As Alois progressed through the customs officer pay grades, his income was equivalent to that of an elementary school headmaster. In 1892 he was transferred from his customs post in Braunau to Passau, which lay further east on the Bavarian border. He was now 55 years old, Klara was 32, Alois Jr. 10, Angela 9, and Adolf 3.

Two years later he was reassigned to Leonding which lay close to the charming city of Linz in Upper Austria. Two other children came along, Edmund in 1894 and Paula in 1896. Edmund died age 6 from measles, so that only Adolf and his sister Paula survived to adulthood. When Alois retired from his job in customs, he bought a nine-acre smallholding to the south of Linz, and moved the family there. He now indulged his pastimes of beekeeping and spending time in local taverns. Family life appears to have been troubled, however, with Alois being a pompous, strict and humourless man. As a customs officer he was used to giving orders and being obeyed. Historian Ian Kershaw writes:

> Both at work and at home, he had a bad temper which could flare up quite unpredictably. He smoked like a chimney, and enjoyed a few drinks after work and discussion around the beer table more than going back home. He took little interest in bringing up his family, and was happier outside rather than inside the family home … Alois was an authoritarian overbearing, domineering husband and a stern, distant, masterful, and often irritable father. For long after their marriage, Klara could not get out of the habit of calling him uncle. … What affection the young children missed in their father was more than recompensed by their mother.[11]

Adolf Hitler was a sickly child, and having already lost two sons and a daughter it is understandable that Klara mollycoddled and fretted over him. The love and attention she gave Adolf appears to have caused some jealously on the part of his half-brother. Life in the Hitler household was far from idyllic. German-Austrian Historian Professor Brigitte Hamann wrote:

> Family life was not peaceful: the father had fits of rage and battered his eldest son, Alois, who in turn was jealous of Adolf, pampered by his young mother. The half-brother remarked about Adolf, "he was spoiled from early in the morning until late at night, and the step-children had to listen to endless stories about how wonderful Adolf was." But Adolf too was beaten by his father. According to Alois Jr, once Alois was even afraid he had killed Adolf. Alois Jr eventually left the family home aged 14 after 'a fierce fight' with his father and was disinherited.[12]

Accounts of Hitler's childhood and youth are patchy at best and must be treated with caution. Allegedly, he had all printed accounts of his childhood confiscated in 1933 and later burned. Unlike Alois, his mother Klara, by a few surviving accounts, was a calm, kind, and loving parent. Schoolfriends of Hitler later suggested that Alois demanded absolute obedience and often berated Adolf who "suffered greatly from his father's harshness." Adolf, according to the schoolfriends, was an avid reader but his father was a spendthrift who never gave him money to buy books.[13] During his rise to power, and his years as German dictator from 1933, the vast majority of stories related by people who knew him in his formative years were gushing and full of praise. After his death as a global pariah, all such accounts became scornful and derisory.

Historian Volker Ullrich warns against biographers overstating the case for the violence Hitler suffered at his father's hand in childhood being responsible for the murderous policies he pursued in later years:

> Physical punishment was an accepted method of child-rearing in those days, and it was hardly uncommon for turn-of-the-century middle class families to feature an authoritarian, punitive father on the one hand and a loving mother on the other. From all we know, Hitler seems to have had a fairly normal childhood. In any case, there are no obvious indications of an abnormal personality development to which Hitler's later crimes can be attributed. If Hitler had a problem, it was an overabundance rather than a paucity of motherly love. That may have contributed to his exaggerated self-confidence, his tendency towards being a know-it-all and his disinclination to exert himself in areas he found unpleasant.[14]

Professor Stephen H. Roberts from the University of Sydney spent 17 months study leave in Nazi Germany between 1935-37. He met Hitler and other leading Nazis, and wrote in 1937 that it was Klara, not Alois, who was responsible for any psychological imbalance in Hitler:

> It is an interesting point to know how much of Hitler's mental narrowness is due to the habit of his Waldviertel ancestors of inbreeding for centuries. Certainly his upbringing was not normal. He was the neurotic child of a neurotic, repressed mother. She warped him by impressing upon him how different he was from other children, and it is to Klara Poelzl (sic) that we must attribute that supreme conception of his difference from other men. She greatly reinforced his resentment complex.[15]

As if responding to Professor Roberts' charge against Klara, Bradley F. Smith wrote:

Despite the shadows that blur her personality, this woman who was to bring Adolf Hitler into the world emerges as the most compelling and sympathetic figure in the annals of the family. She lived her life under inauspicious circumstances and saw her hopes and dreams steadily come to naught over a span of twenty years. Yet in spite of all the blows she had to bear, she quietly returned again and again to fulfil her obligations humanely and conscientiously.... Her home and the furthering of the family interest were all-important; by careful management she was able to increase the family possessions, much to her joy.... Everyone who knew her agreed that it was in her love and devotion for the children that Klara's life centred. The only serious charge ever raised against her is that because of this love and devotion she was over-indulgent and thus encouraged a sense of uniqueness in her son – a somewhat strange charge to be brought against a mother.[16]

With the family moving regularly over the years to accommodate Alois's different customs postings, Adolf received his elementary education in different schools. In his first year at Fischlham school near Lambach in upper Austria, he was considered an excellent pupil and received top marks.[17] The following year, 1896, Adolf was moved to a Benedictine Roman Catholic school at Lambach monastery. He ranked among the top of his class over the following three years and was an altar boy and choirboy. He admired the priests, and the priesthood was possibly an early ambition before his dream of becoming an artist.

In 1899 when the family moved to Linz, Adolf received good school reports in geography, history and drawing but failed French, German and mathematics. He was made to repeat the first form. Hitler relates in *Mein Kampf* that he began mixing with some of the roughest boys in school and became "a juvenile ring-leader" who was "rather difficult to manage." He offers the excuse that he had purposefully done badly in certain subjects at school to rebel against his father's insistence that he should enter the Civil Service. Appalled by such a prospect, his ambition was to become an artist.[18] Hitler relates that he rebelled after his father told him he would never allow him to become an artist:

Naturally the resulting situation was not pleasant. The old gentleman was bitterly annoyed; and indeed so was I, although I really loved him. My father forbade me to entertain any hopes of taking up the art of painting as a profession. I went a step further and declared that I would not study anything else. With such declarations the situation became still more strained, so that the old gentleman irrevocably decided to assert his paternal authority at all costs.[19]

Adolf had little or no time for his sister, Paula, who would later relate that he got a thrashing every night because he came home late.[20] If true, such beatings suddenly ceased on 3 January 1903 when Alois Hitler died unexpectedly at the age of 65. He had gone for his usual morning walk to the local tavern, taken a glass of wine, and collapsed and died almost immediately.

Adolf, who was then 13 years old, later related that his father's death left the entire family "deeply bereaved."[21] The truth may well have been different. Thereafter:

> He muddled along in the old way, pointlessly failing and dreaming, with no purpose and little hope … he spent the bulk of his time reading, drawing and playing… By this time he had shed most of his need for companionship, becoming as he later said, something of a "solitary," who did not require other people to interest him or amuse him.[22]

In May the following year, Hitler's Roman Catholic confirmation took place in Linz. In September he was moved to a different secondary school, possibly due to poor discipline. The young Hitler suffered chest problems and was a pale and sickly youth for a spell, but in September 1905 his final *Realschule* report stated he was 'excellent' at gymnastics. His overall behaviour was 'satisfactory'; diligence was 'adequate'; religion was 'fair,' chemistry and physics, 'fair; while freehand drawing was 'excellent'.[23]

Despite previously promising his mother he would continue his schooling at the *Oberrealschule* – the next step up – and gain the secondary school diploma, his poor grades rendered him ineligible to move on to any further school qualifications and he left at the age of 16 with none. With no interest in learning a trade, he loafed about with his mother funding him thanks to Alois's legacy. Klara paid for piano lessons, but after four months he gave up. Over the next two years, he and his sole friend, August Kubizek, whom he met in Linz in the fall of 1905, began attending Wagner operas in the Linz Municipal Theatre. *Rienzi* apparently left him dumbfounded.

In May 1906, 17-year-old Hitler visited Vienna for the first time. Klara gave him money to spend on sightseeing, visiting museums, and attending Wagner operas. On returning home five weeks later, and throughout the rest of the year, he avidly read books on German history, art, and military matters. He painted bridges and buildings, and by the years end had attended every Wagner opera. In January 1907, Klara underwent a mastectomy for breast cancer and although it was seemingly successful, he was agitated about the possibility of losing her.

> This is a critical period in Hitler's life since he has no fixed career and refuses to learn a trade or finish school. His behaviour oscillates between dangerous fits of depression and brief moments of ecstatic activities. Often he wanders alone aimlessly for days and nights in the fields and woods surrounding Linz. His mother allows him to withdraw his patrimony from the bank, approximately 650 Kronen and go to Vienna and prepare himself for the entrance examination at the Academy of Fine Arts.[24]

Hitler returned to Vienna in October 1907 and sat the entrance exam for the General School of Painting at the Vienna Academy. He passed the first round, but on the following day failed because the Test Drawing was 'Unsatisfactory.' He later wrote in *Mein Kampf*:

> I was here for the second time in this beautiful city, impatiently waiting to hear the result of the examination but profoundly confident that I had got through. I was so convinced of my success that when the news that I had failed to pass was brought to me it struck me like a bolt from the skies.[25]

Hitler was advised that he would do better concentrating on architecture. He later applied to the School of Architecture but was declined on the grounds that he had not completed his secondary school education. He was, however, enjoying his time in Vienna and decided to stay on in the city until his money ran out.

Despite a mastectomy, Klara's breast cancer had metastasised and she was now dying. In Vienna, Adolf received an urgent message that he should return home immediately as his mother's end was near. He reached Linz *after* his mother finally succumbed four days before Christmas 1907. He relates that he and his sister Paula were "thrown into a world of misery and poverty" that was a "very painful" time in his life.[26]

Klara had been under the care of a kind and attentive Jewish doctor, Dr. Bloch, and Adolf sent him a 'thank you' card expressing his gratitude for all he had done for his mother. However, according to his friend Kubizek from the Realschule, who "knew him intimately" in Linz, Adolf was "distinctly anti-Semitic" prior to his departure for Vienna.[27] Professor Bradley Smith commented:

Adolf probably retained during this period his prejudice against Jews and a sympathy for Pan-Germanism, but it is difficult to believe that he was a raging racist or that his prejudices were as intense as they had been in the *Realschule* years.[28]

The family's resources had been hit hard paying for Klara's treatment and the funeral, but there was enough money remaining to ensure that Adolf and Paula were not left penniless. Members of Klara's family suggested to Adolf that he should get an apprenticeship and forget going back to Vienna as planned.

But Adolf scornfully rejected such mundane activities. He was a student, an artist, a painter, or whatever else was convenient at the moment, and he was not going to become a mere tradesman or worker.... From all indications he had not told the rest of the family that he had failed the entrance examination at the Academy. They were under the impression that he was actually participating in an organized program of study in Vienna.[29]

In February 1908, Hitler moved back to Vienna, and for the first months in the city rented a room with his friend from Linz, August Kubizek. A talented pianist, Kubizek had been awarded a place at the Vienna Conservatory. In September that year Hitler once again applied for a place at the Academy of Fine Arts and submitted sample drawings. To his further distress, he was not invited to sit the entrance examination. For reasons unknown, Hitler then broke off all contact with Kubizek and they would not meet again for many years.

By August 1909, Hitlers money had run out but he refused to take a job and struggled to pay for accommodation. Over the next four months he slept either in cheap lodgings or park benches, and ate at charitable soup kitchens. Thinly clad in clothes that were now rags, and the temperature plummeting in December that year, "he was desperate enough to take his place openly in the ranks of the tramps" at *Obdachlosenheim*, a massive shelter in the Meidling district of Vienna built by a Viennese philanthropic society for the homeless. The huge building, then barely a year old, was able to provide lodging for thousands of desperately poor men, women and children.

Hitler's entry into the *Obdachlosenheim* was a declaration of utter defeat. Shortly before Christmas (the exact date is unknown) he took his place in the long line of beaten men and women which formed in front of the shelter every evening. The people stood quietly, broken and dejected, until the gates were thrown open. They were segregated by sex, children going with the mothers, and led into long halls where benches were provided. If the crowd was too large for the regular facilities and the weather was severe, other large barn-like buildings were also used on a temporary basis ... Showers were provided for all, and vermin-infested garments, such as Hitler's, were disinfected. After their showers, the new arrivals returned to the main hall, which was fitted out with tables at one end where they were served a portion of bread and soup before retiring to assigned dormitories.[30]

During his stay in the *Obdachlosenheim* over that winter, Hitler befriended a young unemployed servant and drifter, Reinhold Hanisch, from Bohemia. With no one allowed to stay in the shelter during the day, the pair trudged across the city to a soup kitchen then back again for the shelter re-opening in the evening. It was a five-hour round trip, and Hitler struggled because of his weak condition and thin tattered clothes which offered little protection. "Hitler and Hanisch made the daily trip through town during the heart of the winter of 1909-1910."[31]

After some months, Hanisch suggested to Hitler that he should make postcard drawings of well-known buildings in Vienna and he would sell them on a 50-50 basis. He encouraged Hitler to write to his sister asking for money to buy the necessary drawing material, but Hitler wrote instead to his aunt Johanna who immediately sent him around 50 kronen. Hitler spent 12 kronen buying a winter overcoat from a pawn shop and began his art work straight away, copying photographs or paintings of Vienna scenes. By early spring 1910 they were earning enough to move to a modern, well-equipped men's hostel on the other side of the city with far better conditions. It had a canteen that provided nourishing meals at low prices, reading rooms which residents could use during the day, clean cubicles, and laundry facilities. In the registration book Hitler declared himself a painter and writer.

Over the summer of 1910, Hitler earned enough for occasional visits to the opera, and began to enjoy his time in Vienna. He befriended a part-time Jewish art dealer called Neumann, who regularly visited the men's hostel to buy his art work. "Hitler and Neumann had a number of long discussions in which they even considered the possibility of immigrating to Germany together."[32]

Hitler and Hanisch had a chequered relationship, and in August 1910, the business partnership disintegrated when Hitler reported him to the police for taking money that was rightfully his. Hanisch was given a seven-day prison sentence and would later become a thorn in Hitler's side. He would die in a prison in Vienna in 1937, possibly on Hitler's orders.[33] Hitler continued to draw and paint over the next three years in Vienna and with Hanisch gone he was able to approximately double his income. He bought some decent clothes, leading to a marked improvement in his appearance. Every day he sat in the reading room in the men's hostel painting water colours which he sold to Neumann and other Jewish dealers for three or four kronen. Relationships with the men were reported as always being polite and amicable.

Hitler led a solitary existence and, unusually for a young man in his early twenties, apparently showed no interest whatsoever in sex. In the hostel reading room, he didn't start conversations with other residents about politics, but interjected when he considered the time right. "Within my small circle I talked to them until my throat ached and my voice grew hoarse."[34]

> His calm façade remained unruffled until a discussion of political or social questions began. Even then he usually kept on working for a time, listening and contributing an occasional remark. Inevitably though, some statement would be made that irritated him. Then, according to Karl Honisch, who was a member of the reading room group in 1913, he would be completely transformed. Jumping up from his place at the table, he would throw down his brush or pencil and start a long and violent harangue.... After raging and gesturing wildly for a few minutes, he would slow down and search the faces of the group for a sign of sympathetic understanding. Unable to discover anything but the stolid visages of his *Männerheim* [men's hostel] companions, he would abruptly stop, and with a resigned wave of the hand, sit down to resume his painting.[35]

Politics became something of an obsession with Hitler, and he now frequented cafes in the city to sit for hours on end reading newspapers made available to customers. A regular visitor to the Austrian parliament, he sat for hours in the public gallery observing parliamentary debates. His comments in *Mein Kampf* make clear his growing contempt for parliamentary democracy even at that early stage. He describes his first visit to the parliament:

> The intellectual level of the debate was quite low. Sometimes the debaters did not make themselves intelligible at all.... A turbulent

mass of people, all gesticulating and bawling against one another, with a pathetic old man shaking his bell and making frantic efforts to call the House to a sense of its dignity by friendly appeals, exhortations, and grave warnings. I could not refrain from laughing. Several weeks later I paid a second visit.... Only a few deputies were in their places, yawning in each other's faces.... Then I began to reflect seriously on the whole thing. I went to the Parliament whenever I had time to spare and watched the spectacle silently but attentively. I listened to the debates as far as they could be understood.... Gradually I formed my own ideas about what I saw.[36]

Hitler outlined those ideas in *Mein Kampf*, and it is immediately clear that he did not believe in democracy. It was, he suggested, "the fore runner of Marxism" and the "the breeding ground in which the bacilli of the Marxist world pest can grow and spread." Parliamentary democracy produced "an abortion of filth and fire," but the fire had died out. Nobody could be called to account or held responsible if an act was passed that proved to have devastating consequences. What should a political leader do if they failed to coax members of parliament to consent to their policy? What was a statesman to do when confronted with the "obstinate stupidity" of his fellow citizens? He later wrote in *Mein Kampf*:

> Must not every genuine leader renounce the idea of degrading himself to the level of a political jobber? And, on the other hand, does not every jobber feel the itch to 'play politics,' seeing that the final responsibility will never rest with him personally but with an anonymous mass which can never be called to account for their deeds? ... The whole spectacle of parliamentary life became more and more desolate the more one penetrated into its intimate structure and studied the persons and principles of the system in a spirit of ruthless objectivity.... There is no other principle which turns out to be quite so ill-conceived as the parliamentary principle if we examine it objectively.[37]

Hitler later stated that it was through his 'enforced' poverty during those years in Vienna that he found a "common bond with the poor and dispossessed workers." In his famous tome, *The Rise and Fall of the Third Reich*, William L Shirer scoffs at Hitler's portrayal of his Vienna days as being 'enforced poverty':

> ... by the time Hitler came to Vienna in 1909 there was opportunity for a penniless young man either to get a higher education or to

earn a fairly decent living and, as one of a million wage earners, to live under the civilizing spell which the capital cast over its inhabitants.... Nor was he interested in learning a trade or in taking any kind of regular employment. Instead he preferred to putter about in odd jobs: shovelling snow, beating carpets, carrying bags outside the West Railroad Station, occasionally for a few days working as a building labourer.... He was forced to abandon a furnished room in the Simon Denk Gasse, and for the next four years he lived in flophouses or in the almost equally miserable quarters of the men's hostel at 27 Meldemannstrasse ... staving off hunger by frequenting the charity soup kitchens of the city.[38]

Shirer remarks that while Hitler later informed the world how hungry he had always been in Vienna, it never drove him to finding a regular job. He had, according to Shirer, "the petty bourgeoisie's fear of sliding into the ranks of the proletariat as a manual labourer." While Hitler did earn some money drawing or painting little pictures of well-known city landmarks, Shirer denounces them as "pitiful pieces."[39]

Hitler's professed bond with the poor and disposed is discussed by the German historian, Brigitte Hamann. Hitler, she says, counted himself among the educated, not the workers. Although he lived in cockroach-infested abodes and frequently went hungry, he showed no signs of solidarity with the needy and never joined them on the hunger rally in 1908.

> Hitler did not even consider getting into personal contact with his fellow sufferers, contact with people simply was disgusting to him, even physically ... He became intoxicated with his own words when he said about the working people, *I stood with them at the construction site, I was hungry with them when we were unemployed. I lay in the trenches with them, I know them, that magnificent people!* And when he cried out during the NSDAP meeting in 1920, *I am a working man, made of workers' flesh and blood*, this was nothing but political propaganda.[40]

All the while in Vienna, Hitler apparently read avidly. He relates in *Mein Kampf* that having the 'blinkers of a narrow petit bourgeois education' torn from his eyes in Vienna, they were opened to perils of "terrible significance for the existence of the German people: Marxism and Judaism."[41]

Millions of words have been written, and thousands of different interpretations accorded to the impact that Hitler's Vienna years had on his anti-Semitism and later actions against Jews:

He would claim later that already in Vienna he was able to unmask the Jews as the incarnation of all evil, conspiring to rule the world, responsible for the confusion of races, which he considered not as a symptom but as a cause of social misery around him, and of his own failure to climb up the ladder of social advancement ... His hatred of working-class organizations and his refusal to join a trade union earned him the title 'reactionary swine' among his room-mates in the men's hostel. At the same time he developed a deep distaste for parliamentary democracy, which he based on his personal observation of the Austrian Parliament.[42]

Hitler's detested parliamentary democracy but during his early years in Vienna he does not appear to have been overtly anti-Semitic. He relates in *Mein Kampf* that on first going to Vienna he believed that the Jews were a people persecuted on account of their faith, and he "abhorred" to hear remarks against them. "Although Vienna then had about two hundred thousand Jews among its population of two millions, I did not notice them ... In the Jew I still saw only a man who was of a different religion, and therefore, on the grounds of human tolerance, I was against that he should be attacked because he had a different faith ... The anti-Semitic press in Vienna was unworthy of the cultural traditions of a great people."[43]

Hitler added that his opinion changed over the course of his five years in Vienna and caused him a "great internal conflict." But "calm reason" was the victor over "sentiment," and he relates that he "began to see Jews in a very different light" from his days in Linz:

Cleanliness, whether moral or of another kind, had its own peculiar meaning for these people. That they were water-shy was obvious on looking at them.... What soon gave me cause for very serious consideration were the activities of the Jews in certain branches of life, into the mystery of which I penetrated little by little. Was there any shady undertaking, any form of foulness, especially in cultural life, in which at least one Jew did not participate? On putting the probing knife carefully to that kind of abscess, one immediately discovered, like a maggot in a putrescent body, a little Jew who was often blinded by the sudden light. In my eyes the charge against Judaism became a grave one the moment I discovered the Jewish activities in the Press, in art, in literature and the theatre ... here was a pestilence, a moral pestilence, with which the public was being infected. It was worse than the Black Plague of long ago.... Nature may bring into existence ten thousand such despoilers who act as the worst kind of germ carriers in poisoning human souls. It was a terrible thought, and yet it could not be avoided, that the greater number of the Jews seemed especially destined by Nature to play this shameful part.[44]

Hitler also wrote in *Mein Kampf*:

Should the Jew, with the aid of his Marxist creed, triumph over the people of this world. His crown will be the funeral wreath of mankind.... And so, I believe today that my conduct is in accordance with the will of the Almighty Creator. In standing guard against the Jew, I am defending the handiwork of the Lord.[45]

Bradley F. Smith writes:

Racial anti-Semitism had many attractions for a bitter but ambitious young man. Above all, the doctrine supplied a simple, effective and ego-satisfying explanation of self and society. One could transfer all weakness and inadequacy to the Jewish stereotype; every failure could be explained as the work of the same malevolent chameleon. To the young Hitler, desperately needing self-justification, the discovery of a hidden Jewish conspiracy, working its influence on all economic, political and religious affairs, was a godsend. The path to self-confidence and security which had eluded him so long clearly lay in the direction of racial anti-Semitism.[46]

On his twenty-fourth birthday, 20 April 1913, Hitler received a long-awaited share of his father's inheritance. It totalled 819 Kronen, and he was no longer an Austrian drop-out living in poverty. He told the reading room group that he had decided to move to Munich and apply for admission to the Art Academy. What he did not tell them was that throughout his years in Vienna he had failed to report for service in the Austrian army as required under Austrian law. "He optimistically concluded that after his twenty-fourth birthday he would be able to leave Austria without danger of pursuit by the Austrian authorities. He was wrong..."[47]

When Hitler left Vienna for Munich with a small piece of hand luggage on 24 June 1913, he probably did so, according to William L. Shirer, to escape military service. "This was not because he was a coward but because he loathed the idea of serving in the ranks with Jews, Slavs and other minority races of the empire."[48] Hitler later presented a different reason for his decision to leave Vienna:

A feeling of discontent grew upon me and made me depressed the more I came to realize the inside hollowness of this State and the impossibility of saving it from collapse. At the same time I felt perfectly certain that it would bring all kinds of misfortune to the German people. I was convinced that the Habsburg State would baulk and hinder every German who might show signs of real greatness, while at the same time would aid and abet every non-German activity ... and always the bacillus which is the solvent of human society, the Jew, here and there and everywhere – the whole spectacle was repugnant to me. The gigantic city seemed to be the incarnation of mongrel depravity.... Because my heart was always with the German Empire and not with the Austrian Monarchy, the hour of Austria's dissolution as a State appeared to me only as the first step towards the emancipation of the German nation. All these considerations intensified my yearning to depart for that country for which my heart had been secretly longing since the days of my youth.[49]

On arrival in Munich, Hitler registered with the Munich police as a "painter and writer," and gave his address as Schleissheimer-strasse 34 – a rented room he had seen advertised in the private residence of a family named Popp. He immediately began painting and selling tourist scenes. Hitler's landlady, Frau Popp, would later recall that over the period from June 1913 until the start of war in August 1914, he never had a single visitor and never went out in the evenings. He stayed in his room every night. Professor Ian Kershaw writes:

> He lived simply and frugally, preparing his paintings during the day and reading at night. According to Hitler's own account, "the study of the political events of the day," especially foreign policy, preoccupied him during his time in Munich. He also claimed to have immersed himself again in the theoretical literature of Marxism and to have examined thoroughly once more the relation of Marxism to the Jews.... In all the millions of recorded words of Hitler, however, there is nothing to indicate that he ever pored over the theoretical writings of Marxism, that he had studied Marx, or Engels, or Lenin (who had been in Munich not long before him), or Trotsky (his contemporary in Vienna). Reading for Hitler, in Munich as in Vienna, was not for enlightenment or learning, but to confirm prejudice.[50]

Ironically, it was in Germany in January 1914 that the Austrian military authorities finally caught up with Hitler. Failing to register for military service involved a fine, but leaving Austria to deliberately avoid conscription was considered desertion and carried a prison sentence. In an agitated state, Hitler was taken into custody overnight by the Munich police, and ordered to appear before a tribunal in Salzburg on a charge of deserting from Austrian military service.

On 5 February when he travelled to Salzburg, it appears that the years of rough living and malnourishment in Vienna came to his rescue. The doctor at the Austrian army medical examination deemed him unsuitable for combat or support duties because he was "too weak and, incapable of firing weapons."[51]

Extremely fortunate not to be imprisoned, Hitler returned to Munich. With no close friends, he secluded himself "like a hermit" and refused all invitations to eat with others. His lack of social contact was "the external symptom of a deep inner uncertainty."[52] William Shirer writes:

> He was twenty-four and to everyone except himself he must have seemed a total failure. He had not become a painter, nor an architect. He had become nothing, so far as anyone could see, but a vagabond – an eccentric, bookish one, to be sure. He had no friends, no family, no job, no home. He had, however, one thing: an unquenchable confidence in himself and a deep, burning sense of mission ... His destiny in that land he loved so dearly was to be such as not even he, in his wildest dreams, could then have imagined.[53]

Five months later, 28 June 1914, Hitler enthusiastically greeted the news that Archduke Franz Ferdinand and his wife, Sophie, had been assassinated in Sarajevo. On the outbreak of war, Hitler willingly volunteered for service in a Bavarian regiment. Thanks to the German army's desperate need for men for the war effort, the twenty-four-year-old recently declined by the Austrian army as a weakling unfit to bear arms was enlisted as an infantryman with the Bavarian Reserve Infantry Regiment, (the 1st Company List Regiment – named after the commanding officer, Colonel List). Raw recruits were trained and drilled near Munich for several months before transfer to west Flanders in Belgium and a baptism of fire. On the Menin Road near the town of Ypres in late October, 1914, Hitler's regiment was reduced from 3,600 men to 611. Of the 250 men in Hitler's Company, 208 were killed or badly wounded. On 3 November he was assigned to duties in regimental headquarters as a dispatch runner

In September 1916 at the Somme, Hitler was wounded in the left thigh when a shell exploded in the dispatch runners' dug out, and he spent al-

most two months in a Red Cross hospital near Berlin. Returning to duty, he was
awarded the Iron Cross for bravery but
many frontline soldiers in his regiment
did not consider him brave in any way.

Corporal Hitler

> Because he served in regimental head-
> quarters (HQ), they cold-shouldered
> him and his HQ peers for supposedly
> leading a cushy life as *Etappenschweine*
> ('rear-echelon pigs') a few miles be-
> hind the front. They also believed that
> the medals such men as Hitler earned
> for their bravery were awarded for
> having kissed up to their superiors in
> regimental HQ.[54]

Although a conscientious and reliable soldier, Hitler was never promoted beyond lance corporal (one grade above private) "because of a
complete lack of authority and incapacity to command."[55] He kept his
political views to himself during the war, and apparently made only one
real friend in the army, a fellow dispatch runner, Private Ernst Schmidt.
Hitler was considered an oddball by most soldiers in his regiment, and
became the butt of many barbed comments due to his complete lack of
interest in women. He took no part in their crude amusements or coarse
jokes, and never drank, smoked, or joined them on visits to French brothels. He remained 'an outsider' among the ordinary soldiers, but "behaved
obediently, even subserviently towards his superior officers."[56] Professor
Thomas Weber writes:

> Objectively speaking, Hitler had been a conscientious and good
> soldier. Yet the story of a man despised by the frontline soldiers
> of his unit and with an as yet indeterminate political future, would
> not advance his political interests when Hitler was trying to use his
> wartime service to create a place for himself in politics in the 1920's.
> The same was true of the fact that his superiors, while appreciating
> him for his reliability, had not seen any leadership qualities in him;
> they viewed Hitler as a prototype of someone who follows rath-
> er than gives orders. Indeed, Hitler never held any command over
> a single other soldier throughout the war.... In the 1920s Hitler
> would invent a version of his experiences during the First World
> war that was mostly fictional in character but that allowed him to

set up a politically useful foundational myth of himself, the Nazi party, and the Third Reich. In the years to come, he would continue to rewrite that account whenever it was politically expedient. And he policed his story about his claimed war experiences so ruthlessly and so well that for decades after his passing, it was believed to have a true core.[57]

Historian Milan Hauner, on the other hand, relates that Hitler received a regimental citation for "outstanding bravery" and was awarded the Iron Cross First class "for personal cold-blooded bravery and continuous readiness to sacrifice himself."[58]

Whatever the truth, conveying orders along the front lines as a dispatch runner was a dangerous posting. Hitler was wounded with shrapnel in 1916, and many runners were killed. Temporarily blinded in a British mustard gas attack in October 1918, he was admitted to Pasewalk military hospital in Pomerania and was recuperating there when the armistice was agreed. He later wrote:

> On November 10th the local pastor visited the hospital for the purpose of delivering a short address and that is how we came to know the whole story ... A feeling of profound dismay fell on the people in that assembly, and I do not think there was a single eye that withheld its tears. As for myself, I broke down completely when the old gentleman tried to resume his story by informing us that we must now end this long war, because the war was lost, he said, and we were at the mercy of the victor. The Fatherland would have to bear heavy burdens in the future. We were to accept the terms of the armistice and trust to the magnanimity of our former enemies. It was impossible for me to stay and listen any longer. Darkness surrounded me as I staggered and stumbled back to my ward and buried my aching head between the blankets and the pillow. I had not cried since that day I stood beside my mother's grave.[59]

Hitler had an intense hatred for the "gang of despicable and depraved criminals" who had agreed to the armistice.

> The following days were terrible to bear, and the nights still worse. To depend on the mercy of the enemy was a precept which only fools or criminal liars could recommend. During those nights my hatred increased – hatred for the originators of this dastardly crime ... Emperor William II was the first German Emperor to offer the hand of friendship to the Marxist leaders, not suspecting that they

were scoundrels without any sense of honour. While they held the imperial hand in theirs, the other hand was already feeling for the dagger. There is no thing as coming to an understanding with Jews. It must be the hard-and-fast 'Either-Or.' For my part I then decided that I would take up political work.'[60]

SUMMARY: CHAPTER 15 – SOWING THE SEEDS OF CHAOS

• The First World War comprised Act 1 of a Thirty Years War.

• Act 2 began with the Milner Group and elite Anglo-American financial associates deliberately creating economic and political chaos in Germany in 1919 and through the early 1920s.

• The Milner Group's aim was to encourage the growth of a reactionary movement in Germany which they would back financially and encourage into war with Soviet Russia, thus preventing the formation of a power bloc that could thwart their global control ambitions.

• Hundreds of minor political agitators appeared on the streets of Germany demanding change, but one in particular caught the attention of the Anglo-Americans, an army corporal called Adolf Hitler.

• Hitler came from a troubled background, with an allegedly violent father. An aspiring artist, he failed to get a place at the Vienna art school. After living rough in Vienna, he moved to Munich in 1913, and enlisted with a German regiment on the outbreak of war.

• Serving most of the war as a dispatch runner, Hitler was awarded the Iron Cross for bravery. At the war's end, he was a patient in a military hospital suffering temporary blindness after a mustard gas attack.

CHAPTER 16

HANFSTAENGL, HARVARD'S HERO

Lance Corporal Hitler's vision returned and he was discharged from Pasewalk Hospital on 19 November 1918. Approaching 30 years-of-age, he had no prospects: the future looked bleak. A return to the lonely existence of the pre-war small-time painter held no appeal so he chose to stay in the army.

> He had returned from the war dirt poor. His savings amounted to 15.30 marks by the end of the war, approximately 1 percent of the annual earnings of a worker. If he had opted for demobilization, he would have faced the prospect of living on the streets unless he managed to find immediate employment, which was no easy feat in the aftermath of the war.... Staying in the army by contrast provided Hitler with free lodging, food, and monthly earnings of approximately 40 marks ... Hitler's ultimate motive in refusing demobilization may well have been opportunistic. Nevertheless, he demonstrated through his active and unusual decision to stay in the army that he did not mind serving the new Socialist regime if that choice allowed him to avoid poverty, homelessness, and solitude.[1]

Hitler spent a few days in Berlin then took the train to Munich, a city that was now in the "People's State of Bavaria." On reporting to his regimental base at Oberwiesenfeld in north Munich, he found it "repulsive" that it was now in the hands of "Soldiers Councils."[2] On 6 December Hitler joined a detachment of soldiers on guard duty at a camp holding Russian prisoners of war in Traunstein, south-east Bavaria. He returned to his Munich barracks seven weeks later where, ironically, his unit was tasked with defending the new political regime against anti-Semitic attacks. Such incidents had been proliferating due to the involvement of Jews, including Kurt Eisner and Felix Fechenbach, in the revolution and overthrow of the Bavarian monarchy of the Wittelsbachs. Eisner, 51-year-old Minister President of the recently declared People's State of Bavaria, was assassinated by a far-right nationalist on 21 February 1919, just six weeks after Rosa Luxemburg and Karl Liebknecht had been brutally murdered. Fechenbach would be executed when the Nazis took power in 1933.

For some reason, Hitler attended Eisner's funeral with a few others from his regiment. He wore a black armband on one arm and a red socialist band on the other as he walked behind Eisner's coffin in the mass funeral procession.[3] Was he really demonstrating socialist beliefs at this point in his life as some suggest, or was he simply ordered to attend by the army? In April 1919, Hitler was selected as battalion spokesman and much to his surprise at this time, he discovered that he could stand up and address a room full of people with some confidence. He began tentatively contemplating a career in politics as his way out of poverty. In *The Rise and Fall of the Third Reich*, William Shirer describes the situation Hitler then found himself in:

> The prospects for a political career in Germany for the now thirty-year old Austrian without friends or funds, without a job, with no trade or profession or any previous record of regular employment, with no experience whatsoever in politics, were less than promising, and at first, for a brief moment, Hitler realised it. "For days," he says, "I wondered what could be done, but the end of every meditation was the sober realization that I, nameless as I was, did not possess the least basis for any useful action."[4]

How then within a few years was this strange man who had drifted along in the fringes of society, shaking the world with the thunderous tramping of his invading armies' jackboots? American journalist Louis P. Lochner who lived in Berlin for many years, met Hitler regularly and observed him at close range. Lochner described the situation he witnessed in early 1920s Germany as "progressive political chaos" with "the entire country debilitated by hunger, poverty and internecine strife."

> Into this situation of confusion, hopelessness and despair burst the raucous voice of a rabble-rouser and demagogue with a remarkable facility for being all things unto all men: Adolf Hitler. His techniques seemed so uncouth, his logic so faulty, his platitudes so insufferable, his manners so boorish, his record of personal achievement so blatantly non-existent, his educational background so spotty, his misrepresentation of historical facts so preposterous, and the rituals he created for his movement so ludicrous, that the majority of dependable democrats, including the intellectual strata

in the trade unions and the Social Democratic party, failed to take him seriously until it was too late. By the time they awoke from their blissful dream that Hitler was more or less a Charlie Chaplin-like comic figure, he had built up the most powerful political movement in modern history.[5]

Like most Hitler biographers, Louis Lochner and William Shirer present interesting and useful details, but offer no credible explanation for his meteoric rise to power. German historian Volker Ullrich writes, "there will always be aspects of Hitler we cannot explain" and that people would "never stop pondering this mysterious, calamitous figure." Ullrich doubted whether there would ever be a definitive biography of the man with "deep seated psychological complexes, huge destructive energy and a homicidal bent."[6]

Professor Sir Ian Kershaw, a British pro-Establishment historian with a close interest in Nazi Germany, suggests that Hitler's ability as a mob orator – "which was just about all he had to offer at the time" – does not explain his rise to power. "We should" says Kershaw, "look in the first instance less to his own personality than to the motives and actions of those who came to be Hitler's supporters, admirers and devotees – and not least his powerful backers."[7] Examining Hitler's "powerful backers" is indeed the only way one can ever get close to solving the mystery of how this oddball came to power in Germany. Tellingly, few British historians have ever undertaken such an examination.

Hitler spent the winter of 1918/19 on various routine army duties and in May was assigned to the political department of the 2nd Infantry Regiment in Munich. His unit was tasked with combatting "dangerous ideas" among the ranks "such as pacifism and socialism."[8] Head of the regiment's political department, Captain Karl Mayr, wrote that when Hitler first joined the department in June 1919 he was "like a tired stray dog looking for a master" and "ready to throw in his lot with anyone who would show him kindness."[9] If Mayr is to be believed, Hitler told him that following his discharge from Pasewalk hospital he had applied to the postal service as a mail-carrier, but was refused "because he was unable to pass the intelligence test."[10]

Irrespective of the veracity of that tale, Captain Mayr was impressed with Hitler's ability to communicate, sent him to anti-Bolshevik lectures and courses on politics at Munich University, and asked him to give anti-Bolshevik talks at indoctrination courses for socialist sympathisers and agitators in the ranks. Hitler found he could evoke positive responses from the soldiers and arouse their passion. "Almost by chance he had stumbled across his greatest talent. As he himself put it, he could speak."[11]

Hitler's army unit was tasked with carrying out surveillance on around fifty small political parties and organisations from the extreme Right to the far Left which had sprouted in every corner of Munich immediately after the war.[12] On 12 September 1919, Captain Mayr sent Hitler to a meeting of the German Workers' Party – the *Deutsche Arbeiterpartei* (DAP) – that was to be held that night in the *Sterneckerbräu* inn in Munich. Recently founded by a locksmith and far-right political agitator, Anton Drexler, the DAP was a small right-wing, pan-German, anti-Semitic, party with only a few hundred members. Mayr had ordered Hitler merely to observe the meeting, keep his mouth shut, and make mental notes, but when the speaker, Professor Adalbert Bauman, suggested that Bavaria should separate from Germany and join a new state with Austria, Hitler could not contain himself. He started a heated argument with Baumann, which ended when the professor picked up his coat and angrily walked out. Anton Drexler, however, approved of Hitler's intervention and invited him to join the party.

Captain Mayr later claimed that *he* had ordered Hitler to accept Drexler's invitation to join the DAP in order to foster the party's growth. Whatever the truth, on 19 October 1919 Hitler joined the party and began to speak at its regular meetings in Munich beer halls. Mightily impressed, Drexler soon made him party leader and agreed, when in January 1920, Hitler suggested changing the party name to the *Nationalsozialisticsche Deutsche Arbeitepartei* (NSDAP). Thus was born what became known as the Nazi party. Hitler had no time for socialism, and the term 'national socialist' was, according to some, added to the name of the party purely to appeal to left-wing workers. Hitler, indeed, had criticised and betrayed fellow soldiers sympathetic to socialism to Captain Mayr.

> We have seen that Hitler did not come to politics, but that politics came to him – in the Munich barracks. Hitler's contribution, after making his mark through a readiness to denounce his comrades following the Räterepublik [the short-lived and unofficial socialist regime in Bavaria in early 1919], had been confined to an unusual talent for appealing to the gutter instincts of his listeners ... coupled with a sharp eye to exploiting the main chance of advancement.[13]

At a public meeting of the new NSDSAP on 20 February 1920 in Munich's *Hofbräuhaus*, some 2,000 people attended, and Hitler presented a 25-point programme that he and Drexler had drafted. It included demands for equality of rights for Germany in dealing with other nations, and overturning the Treaty of Versailles. Hitler declared: "As long as the earth has existed, no people have ever been forced to sign such a shameful treaty." He demanded land and colonies to settle and feed the population, and that only those of German blood should be citizens of the State. No Jews would be allowed, and all non-citizens would be deported from the Reich.[14] When talking in private, however, Hitler blamed not Jews but the Catholic Centre Party for agreeing to the Versailles Treaty.[15]

In March 1920, Hitler was introduced to Dietrich Eckart (1868-1923), a well-educated journalist and political activist from an upper-middle class background who had loose links to the far right-wing Thule Society which provided a platform for counter-revolutionary activities. A close symbiotic relationship developed between them with Eckart becoming Hitler's teacher and political mentor over the next three years. Twenty years older than Hitler, Eckart was a German völkisch poet, author of the German translation of Ibsen's *Peer Gynt*, and a rabid anti-Semite. Historian Milan Hauner describes him as "a boastful Bavarian writer, drug addict and violent anti-Semite" who exercised "considerable influence upon Hitler."[16] Whether or not Eckart was a 'boastful drug addict' as Hauner suggests, he certainly encouraged the anti-Semitic opinions Hitler was now voicing. It had not always been so.

Eckart

> In Vienna Hitler had got to know anti-Semitic cliches and prejudices *without identifying with them*. Imperial Germany's military defeat, which nationalist circles explained by scapegoating Jews in particular, no doubt also reinforced Private Hitler's anti-Semitic leanings. But it was the experience of left-wing revolution and right-wing counter-revolution in Munich in 1918 and 1919 which vehemently radicalised anti-Jewish resentment in the Bavarian capital and made Hitler into what he would remain for the rest of his life; a fanatic anti-Semite whose primary political mission was to expunge a 'dangerous foreign tribe'.[17]

In June 1920, Hitler proclaimed that Russia had been taken over by a Jewish conspiracy. The Russian people had been abandoned to starvation and misery, and no one was blame but the Jews. Bolshevism, he argued, brought about the opposite of what it promised. Those who were on the top were not the workers but, without exception, Hebrews. He spoke of a "Jewish dictatorship" and a "Moscow Jew government" sucking the life out of the Russian people, and the NSDAP must become a battering ram against the "dirty flood of Jewish Bolshevism."[18]

That same month, June 1920, with money earned from his *Peer Gynt* translation and a second mortgage on his house, Eckart purchased the small *Volkischer Beobachter* newspaper and, together with his new friend Hitler, turned it into a rabid anti-Semitic propaganda organ. Eckart, who would edit the weekly paper for several years, mapped out Hitler's direction in the early period 1920-1922. He died of a heart attack in 1923, and Hitler would later relate that his friendship with Eckart was "one of the best things he experienced in the 1920s" and that he never again had a friend with whom he felt such "a harmony of thinking and feeling."[19]

Hitler was at that point in time still a member of the *Reichswehr*, but on 31 March 1920, he resigned after five and a half years in the lowest ranks. With no trade, job, connections, or prospects, he joined the long queues of other unemployed men dependent on soup kitchens for sustenance. He lived "like a down-at-heel clerk" in a squalid rented room in Munich that was no more than nine feet wide with cheap, worn linoleum and a threadbare rug.

> He had books on the shelves of his shabby room ... but what, exactly, he read is impossible to know. His lifestyle scarcely lent itself to lengthy periods of systematic reading. ... As it had been since his Vienna days, much of his time was spent lounging around cafes in Munich.[20]

Hitler was one of hundreds of other impoverished minor political agitators on the streets of Munich vying for attention and support. As we have seen, the fledgling democracy of the Weimar Republic was in the throes of revolution with political assassinations, profound poverty, mass unemployment, and the real prospect of civil war between the extreme Right and extreme Left. Now speaking at twice-weekly Nazi party meetings in beer halls across the city, Hitler insisted that the German army was betrayed in November 1918 and had never actually been defeated. He repeatedly warned of the danger of Jewish Bolsheviks attempting a communist revolution as had taken place in Russia in November 1917. He insisted that the misery of the German people was due to the presence of Jews, and the division of the nation into antagonistic classes.[21] It is a mistake to dismiss Hitler as nothing more than a boorish racist and thoughtless moron. He was certainly no intellectual giant, but how many who enter politics are? Ian Kershaw, writes:

> How do we explain how someone with so few intellectual gifts and social attributes, someone no more than an empty vessel outside his political life, unapproachable and impenetrable even for those in his close company, incapable it seems of genuine friendship, without the background that bred high office, without even any experience of government before becoming Reich Chancellor, could nevertheless have such an immense historical impact, could make the entire world hold its breath? Perhaps the question is, in part, falsely posed. For one thing, Hitler was certainly not unintelligent and possessed a sharp mind which could draw on his formidable retentive memory.[22]

In late 1920 the Nazi party took over a small weekly newspaper, the *Münchener Beobachter* and renamed it the *Völkischer Beobachter* (People's Observer). It published Hitler's controversial speeches and articles, and party membership grew steadily throughout 1921 with crowds of over 5,000 now attending meetings. In 1921 Hitler founded a private paramilitary organisation of Nazi storm troopers, the *Sturmabteilung* (SA). Known as the Brownshirts due to the colour of their uniforms' shirts, they were equipped with weapons and ammunition illegally supplied by sympathisers in the German army. Hitler decreed that the SA would become the "battering ram at the disposal of the movement" and insisted they "must be strong not only in words, but in deeds against our enemy, the Jew." By the autumn of 1921 armed SA thugs were not only protecting Nazi party leaders at meetings, but disrupting the meetings of political opponents and beating up Jews on the streets.[23]

In February 1922, in the Bürgerbräukeller Hitler told an audience of 2,300 that the choice for Germany was either a "People's Republic or a Jewish State." On 17 March the Bavarian parliament discussed deporting Hitler to Austria but Social Democratic leader, Erhard Auer, opposed his expulsion on the grounds that Hitler was "not to be taken seriously."[24]

On 24 June 1922, the industrialist and German Foreign Minister, Walter Rathenau, (the first Jew to hold a cabinet post in Germany) was assassinated by the right-wing terrorist group Organisation Consul which was made up of students and former Freikorps members. The group had been responsible for the assassination of Matthias Erzberger in August 1921. Erzberger, as we recall, was the German official who reluctantly signed the Armistice treaty in Foch's railway carriage in November 1918. The Brownshirts were not responsible for killing Rathenau but they were spreading fear and encouraging terror throughout Munich, and the authorities were now forced to act. Hitler was arrested, charged with inciting public violence, and sentenced to three months in prison. He served four weeks in Munich's Stadelheim prison, but returned to the fray the day after his release with a deeply racist speech before a large crowd at the Bürgerbräukeller:

> How long can this continue? The Jew knows precisely that his system is no blessing, that he is no master race. That he is an exploiter, that the Jews are a people of robbers. The Jew has never yet founded a civilization, but he has destroyed hundreds. He can show nothing of his own creation. Everything that he has is stolen.[25]

Despite his short spell in prison, and the threat of deportation to his native Austria, Hitler had no intention of ending his anti-Semitic rants. On 17 August 1922, he addressed a meeting of 6,000 at the Circus Krone, railing against the rapidly escalating inflation while blaming Jews for Germany's dire problems. All the while his Brownshirt gangs menacingly roamed the streets of Munich with the slogan, "We'll beat our way to the top."[26]

Hitler appointed Kurt Lüdecke, a former soldier, swindler and conman, as the party's unofficial ambassador and, with General Erich Ludendorff's approval, sent him to Italy to speak to Mussolini, leader of the fascist movement in Italy.

> Hitler provided Lüdecke, with a letter appointing him as "official representative in the Kingdom of Italy." Mussolini was apparently persuaded to receive the messenger from the unknown little "fascist brother party."[27]

Mussolini was a few years ahead of Hitler in the political landscape and about to seize power in Italy at the head of a huge fascist "March on Rome." Hitler, to an extent, was parroting the politics and gangsterism of "Il Duce" (the leader) who had sent army veterans onto the streets to beat up peace protestors in Milan, and had created the blackshirt groups of fascist thugs. Germany and Italy, together with Japan, would go on to form the "Axis Powers" of the Second World War.

In recent years (2009) a Cambridge University historian, Dr. Peter Martland, unearthed British secret intelligence documents which clearly indicated that Benito Mussolini had been a richly rewarded asset of British secret intelligence (later named MI5). He was being paid £100 per week in 1917 (worth over £8,000/week in 2024) when the average weekly income was less than £4. Mussolini's handler, Sir Samuel Hoare, was a Conservative member of the British parliament, and MI5's man in Rome.

British historian Christopher Andrew writes:

> Hoare's counter-subversion operations included bribing pro-Allied journalists, among them the former socialist Benito Mussolini, who in 1919 was to found the Fascist movement. Hoare paid Mussolini the then considerable sum of £100 a week.[28]

The documents uncovered by Dr. Martland revealed that, in addition to Mussolini, Hoare ran 100 British intelligence agents in Italy towards the end of the First World War.[29] Prominent in the Conservative party, Sir Samuel Hoare would go on to become British foreign secretary and in 1935 signed the pact that gave Mussolini – by then a dictator with much blood on his hands – control over Abyssinia (Ethiopia).

It is well-recognised that in the inter-war years the closely collaborating Anglo-American intelligence services had agents operating clandestinely across Europe, and it would be extremely naïve for anyone to believe they had none operating in Germany. Dozens of Anglo-American secret intelligence agents did indeed move in and out of Germany during the 1920s and 30s, including the British agent we met in New York in chapter 10,

Mussolini

the occultist and black magic practitioner Aleister Crowley. Crowley, who was involved with British Naval Intelligence in the sinking of the Lusitania in 1915, operated as a British spy in Germany in 1930-32.[30] Many interesting stories can be told about Crowley's activities in Germany, but our attention focuses on two major players, Ernst Hanfstaengl and William de Ropp. De Ropp was a naturalised British citizen originally from Lithuania (then part of the Russian Empire) who fought for Britain throughout the First World War in the Royal Flying Corp (the embryonic RAF).

We consider his role as an agent in Germany in due course, and focus first on the most important Anglo-American intelligence agent operating in Germany, Ernst Hanfstaengl.

Ernst 'Putzi' Hanfstaengl (1887-1975)

A German-American Harvard graduate and friend of leading politicians in Washington and top financiers on Wall Street, Hanfstaengl was placed directly at Hitler's side for 14 years between 1923 and 1937. Later chapters in this book reveal how Hitler and the far-right totalitarian socio-political ideology of his Nazi Party were promoted and funded by the Milner Group in London and associated ruling elites in the United States. The part Putzi Hanfstaengl played for them in grooming and preparing the former army corporal and shoddily dressed minor political agitator for power cannot be overstated. His role at Hitler's side for many years was absolutely crucial for his rise to power, yet mainstream establishment historians generally dismiss him in a few sentences as being no more than the Führer's "piano player" or "court jester." That so few today have even heard of Hanfstaengl is testimony to the success of the Anglo-American Establishment's fake history in whitewashing him and his true role from the record. That can only be corrected if we study him and his illustrious ancestry in some detail, for it is in his wealthy family background and extensive political and immensely rich and powerful friends that we find the key to this truly astonishing story.

Born in Munich on 2 February 1887 and baptised Ernst Franz Sedgwick Hanfstaengl, he came from a family that mixed with royalty and the world's top artists, writers, and musicians. The Hanfstaengl family was close to the Saxe-Coburg-Gotha dynasty that spawned the royal families of Britain and Germany. Putzi's German grandfather, Franz Hanfstaengl, born in 1804, was a gifted artist who studied at the Munich Academy of Fine Arts and became a leading pioneer in lithographic art reproduction. Over a 25-year period, Franz was commissioned to produce lithographic copies of the entire art collection of the Dresden Gallery, and grew very rich. Around 1833 he opened a fine art printing business and photographic studio in Munich.

Hanfstaengl stood in the forefront of the democratisation of art and images. For the first time in history, walls of domestic quarters, studies, and even bathrooms were decorated with reproductions of 'Old Masters.'[31]

One of the most famous photographers in Europe, Franz was appointed the official photographer to royalty and the nobility. His subjects included Queen Victoria, Kaiser Wilhelm I, Maximillian II, the king of Bavaria, Empress Elizabeth of Austria, German Chancellor Otto von Bismarck, Richard Wagner, Franz Liszt and famous writers such as Hans Christian Andersen. With his charm and warm, friendly, personality, virtually all of his famous clients became good friends.

In 1868, Franz's sons, Erwin and Edgar, took over the business and drove it on to even greater success. Erwin married the famous German opera singer, Marie Schroder, while Putzi's father, Edgar, married Katharine Heine, the daughter of an American, Colonel William Heine. Putzi's grandmother, Catherine Sedgwick, was a member of the famous Sedgwick clan of New England. Putzi wrote:

> I am in fact half American. My mother was born a Sedgwick-Heine. My maternal grandmother came from a well-known New England family and was a cousin of the General John Sedgwick who fell at Spotsylvania Court House in the Civil War and whose statue stands at West Point. My grandfather was another Civil War general, William Heine.… The Hanfstaengl's were substantial folk. For three generations they were privy councillors to the Dukes of Saxe-Coburg-Gotha and well known as connoisseurs and patrons of the arts. The family enterprise my grandfather founded was, and remains to this day, one of the pioneers of the art reproduction field.[32]

The Hanfstaengls became firmly established in European high society. Duke Ernst of Saxe-Coburg-Gotha (Putzi's godfather, and the man he was named after) was the brother of Prince Albert who married Queen Victoria in 1840. He was the uncle of Kaiser Wilhelm II and great uncle of King Edward VII of England. Putzi would write in 1957:

> My Hanfstaengl grandfather's photographs of three German Kaisers, Moltke and Roon, Ibsen, Liszt, Wagner and Clara Schuman set the standards of their time. My father kept an open house at the villa he built in the Liebgstrasse, at that time on the outskirts of Munich. Few names in the artistic world failed to grace the guest book over the years … My parents were friends of Fridtjof Nansen

and Mark Twain. The atmosphere was almost ostentatiously international. My mother had decorated part of the house in shades of green because it was the favourite colour of Queen Victoria, whose signed portrait, dedicated to my father on some occasion, looked at us from its heavy silver frame.[33]

In the 1890s, Putzi's father took the Hanfstaengl business to an international level by opening extremely profitable fine art galleries in fashionable parts of London and New York. Fabulously wealthy, they lived in luxury with Putzi and his four sibs cared for by servants and tutored by three English governesses. Putzi was taught to play piano by the cream of European musicians and by his teenage years had become a highly accomplished classical pianist.

The nickname 'Putzi' was first given to him in infancy. As a two-year-old he contracted diphtheria, a contagious bacterial infection that was frequently fatal in the days before vaccines and antibiotics. With Putzi close to death, his father had given up hope but the stricken child was saved thanks to the unfailing attention of a family servant. The old peasant woman, who had doubtless nursed many a sick child, sat by his bed day and night encouraging him to take sips of water and a little soft food while constantly crooning: "Putzi, eat this now Putzi."[34] To his dismay, the name – a Bavarian term of endearment for 'little fellow' – stuck despite him growing to become a six-foot-four towering hulk of a man.

Putzi was immensely proud of the American blue blood that flowed in his veins. Illustrious as his father's German ancestors were, they were a mere shadow in comparison to his mother's side. His American forebears were English Puritans who had left the mother country in the Great Migration of 1620-40. Generation after generation of his ancestors played major roles in the development of America from the earliest days of English colonial rule, through the Revolutionary War of 1775-83, the U.S. Constitution signed in 1787, and the American Civil War of 1861-65. Many of his forebears were considered American heroes, and we shall see how, collectively, they became an integral part of the rich and powerful 'Eastern Establishment' that has controlled America for many years.

Putzi's mother came from the New England, high society, Sedgwick clan, one of America's oldest and most notable families. Typical of their class and origins, the Sedgwicks intermarried with other equally rich and famous families through the centuries and mixed with some of the greatest figures in American history. The *Chicago Tribune* newspaper reported:

Dig deeply into any family history and you're bound to unearth a mosaic of tragedies and farces, but few families have given rise to as many prominent figures as the Sedgwick clan has, few have created such archival treasures, and few can trace their American lineage back to 1635.[35]

The Puritans left England to build a life of religious freedom in the new world and Putzi's ancestors would help establish a new financial and political aristocracy that after the War of Independence went on to rule the United States. When Putzi moved to America in 1905, he matriculated as a seemingly anonymous eighteen-year-old German student at Harvard University. It was his distinguished American family connections going back almost 300 years that immediately opened doors and afforded him a warm welcome in the homes of the immensely rich and powerful individuals who ruled the United States. Undoubtedly, it was these connections that also opened doors for his entry into secret intelligence work.

PUTZI'S PURITAN ANCESTORS.

20,000 Puritan Protestant dissenters who sailed to America in the early seventeenth century came largely from the eastern counties of England. Within that number, a small group of educated land-owners had the rights to a trading company – the Massachusetts Bay Joint-Stock Company – which had been granted jurisdiction over a large expanse of land in New England. Among them were many of Putzi's ancestors, including Samuel Stone, a Puritan minister from Hertford in England who sailed to the Massachusetts Bay colony on the *Griffin* in 1633. Reverend Samuel Stone was the co-founder of Hartford, now the capital of Connecticut, and a statue in his honour stands in his original hometown of Hertford in England.

American writer and Presbyterian minister, Chris Hedges, wrote:

> The Puritans, who hoped to create a theocratic state, believed that Satan ruled the wilderness surrounding their settlements, they believed that God had called them to cast Satan out of the wilderness of this promised land. That divine command sanctioned the removal or slaughter of Native Americans this hubris fed the deadly doctrine of manifest destiny. Similar apocalyptic visions of the world cleansed through violence and extermination nourished the Nazis.[36]

John Hopkins (b. circa 1607) was another six-times-great grandfather of Putzi's. An educated Puritan of good standing, he sailed to the Bay colony in 1634 and was made a Freeman (an individual admitted to the

Puritan church after they had undergone a detailed interrogation of their religious views and experiences by Puritan ministers). Hopkins initially settled in Cambridge near Boston, but in 1636 moved to Hartford. Together with his close friend, Reverend Thomas Hooker, he is considered the Founder of Connecticut.

Edward Colver (aka Culver), a six-times-great grandfather of Putzi, was a Puritan dissenter born in Dedham in Essex, England. Sailed with John Winthrop Jr. to Massachusetts Bay Colony in 1635. Colver was the founder of Dedham, Massachusetts.

Robert Sedgwick (b. 1611) was Putzi's six-times-great grandfather in the direct Sedgwick line, and the first of the Sedgwicks to go to America. Having had military training, he was appointed the military commander for Charlestown and built the early defences and fortresses of Boston, including Castle William. He was promoted to the rank of Major General of the Ancient and Honourable Artillery Company of Massachusetts, and commander of all Massachusetts militia. Also a successful businessman, Robert opened the first brewery in the colony, and in partnership with John Winthrop's son, John Jr., (later to become the governor of Connecticut) he opened the first iron works in America with smelting, forging, and casting. Reconstructed in modern times, the Sedgwick/Winthrop iron works (situated to the northeast of Boston) is now a National Historic Site.

Robert's sister, Sarah Sedgwick, (Putzi's six-times great aunt,) who had joined him in New England, married John Leverett, Governor of Massachusetts Bay Colony. Their grandson would later become president of Harvard for sixteen years. Leverett, like numerous other Puritans in the colony, would temporarily return to England to fight for Oliver Cromwell's parliamentary forces in the English Civil War. Robert Sedgwick corresponded regularly with Cromwell and was commissioned by him to raise a force to drive the Dutch from New York. After a settlement with the Dutch was reached, with brother-in-law John Leverett, Robert turned against the French colony in Acadia in the north-east territories. He captured forts at the mouth of the St. John River and at Port Royal, established a garrison, and added Nova Scotia to the British Dominion.

In early 1654, Cromwell asked Robert Sedgwick to return to England to prepare a military force to bolster England's conquest of Jamaica. English soldiers already on the recently captured island were in dire straits and reinforcements were urgently required. Robert sailed back to England with his wife and their five children and on arrival asked Cromwell to personally ensure that his family would be cared for should he die in Jamaica.

In England in July 1654, General Sedgwick and his troops boarded a fleet of 23 British warships and sailed for the West Indies. On arrival in Jamaica, they encountered a scene from hell. Townships and farms had been destroyed, leaving nothing but ruin across the entire island. Thousands had been killed by the English troops and large numbers of the troops themselves had died due to tropical diseases. Sedgwick's reports back to Cromwell make for grim reading. Soldiers lay on the ground begging the newly arrived troops for bread yet they had killed some 20,000 cattle and destroyed all sorts of fruit-bearing trees and provisions across the island.

Sedgwick had the dead buried and gradually restored some sort of order. With a heavy heart – and foreseeing his own death in that living hell – he wrote to Cromwell:

> ... I left behind me a dear and religious wife, who through grace hath much of the fear and knowledge of God in her. I also have five children, to me dear and precious. I would only beg this, that whatever hazard or hardship I may go through, my relations may not be forgotten. I only request what your highness was pleased to promise me, that they may not be troubled in obtaining it in such seasons, as may tend to her comfort.[37]

In early May 1656, General Sedgwick received a letter from Oliver Cromwell declaring him Governor General of Jamaica. He died just days later. On 24 May 1656, his second in command, Colonel D'Oyley, wrote to Cromwell with the news. True to his word, Cromwell provided his widow, Joana – Putzi's six-times-great grandmother – with an annual pension that would allow her to live in relative comfort for the rest of her days. She stayed on in England and of their five children, only William returned to America.

Several generations later, General John Sedgwick (b. 1742) Putzi's two-times-great grandfather, was an American Revolutionary War General, member of the Connecticut legislature and 'Son of the American Revolution'. He fought the British at Ticonderoga – one of the first engagements of the American War of Independence – and captured the fort there. He spent the winter of 1777-78 with George Washington at Valley Forge where some 2,500 revolutionary soldiers died from disease, hunger and severe cold. John's wife, Abigail, was related to Reverend Samuel Andrew, a founder of Yale University.

Theodore Sedgwick (b. 1746), Putzi's two-times-great uncle, served as a major alongside George Washington at the Battle of White Plains in the Continental War. He became one of the most important politicians in New England as Speaker of the House of Representatives, U.S. Senator from Massachusetts, Justice Massachusetts Supreme Court, and Delegate to the Continental Congress.

Theodore's wife, Pamela Dwight, was the daughter of Brigadier General Joseph Dwight of the equally illustrious New England Dwight clan. Theodore and Pamela's daughter, Catharine Maria Sedgwick, was a pre-eminent American writer and one of the driving forces behind the foundation of American literature. Their son, Theodore Jr., was a successful lawyer, politician, and Lieutenant Governor of Massachusetts. Pamela's cousin, Timothy Dwight Jr., was the president of Yale (1795-1817) and a fellow of the American Academy of Arts and Sciences. Pamela was also the great-aunt of Charles William Eliot who would become the long-term president of Harvard University from 1869 to 1909.

Theodore Sedgwick was a close friend of John Adams, leader of the Revolution and a Founding Father, who helped draft the Declaration of Independence. Adams served twice as vice-president under George Washington. Theodore worked for Adams's election to the presidency thereafter and was present at his swearing in as second President of the United States in 1797.

Another of Sedgwick's close friends was Founding Father Alexander Hamilton, chief aide to George Washington during the Revolutionary War and the first United States Secretary of the Treasury in Washington's government

Not all of Putzi's ancestors in America originated from English Puritan stock. His four-times-great grandfather, Adam Todd, came from Scotland and continued to wear the kilt and plaid proudly on moving to New England. Adam's eldest child Margaret (Putzi's three-times-great grandmother) aided starving revolutionary soldiers captured by the British and was thanked personally by George Washington at a lunch he held in her honour.[38] Margaret was officially named a "Woman Hero of the Revolution." Her younger brother, Adam Todd Jr. married a member of the Vanderbilts, one of the richest families in America. Her younger sister, Sarah Cox Todd, (times-three-great aunt of Putzi) married into the similarly astronomically wealthy Astor family. She was the grandmother of John Jacob Astor III who moved to England and purchased the magnificent Cliveden House. John Jacob's grandson, William Waldorf Astor Jr, and his wife Nancy became integral members of the British establishment, frequently entertaining leading members of the English ruling class and of

Milner Group at lavish house parties. Known as 'The Cliveden Set,' they exercised considerable power in England. Putzi Hanfstaengl remained close to the Astors, and in later chapters we examine their role and that of the 'Cliveden set' in appeasing Hitler.

Stewart Dean (b. 1748), two-times-great grandfather of Putzi, was a famous navigator and yet another American hero. In 1784, he personally built a small sloop, the *Experiment*, and sailed into maritime history with a return voyage to China, travelling 14,000 miles in 16 months with a crew of just seven men and two boys. Dean's daughter, Margaret, married Putzi's great grandfather, Roderick Sedgwick, a Wall Street broker.

General John Sedgwick, (b. 1813) Putzi's times-two-great uncle, was the highest-ranking Union soldier killed in the American Civil War. A large memorial in his honour stands at West Point and another magnificent statue of him mounted on his horse, Handsome Joe, is sited at Gettysburg.

> Confederate sharpshooters had been peppering the area all morning on May 9, wounding, among others, General William Morris. Staff officers cautioned Sedgwick not to approach the road, but he forgot their warnings a few minutes later when he walked over to untangle a snarl in his line. When his men warned him to take cover, Sedgwick responded by joking, "They couldn't hit an elephant at that distance." Just then, a sharpshooter's bullet crashed into his skull below the left eye, killing him instantly. When Grant [Union army general and U.S President 1869-1877] heard the news, he could hardly believe it. "Is he really dead?" he asked, later remarking that Sedgwick's death was "greater than the loss of a whole division of troops."[39]

William Heine (b. 1827), Putzi's maternal grandfather was an accomplished artist who trained at the Royal Academy of Art in Dresden under the famed Julius Hübner. Thereafter, he spent three years as a young artist in Paris before returning to Dresden. The composer, Richard Wagner, was his close friend. When revolution swept across Germany in 1848, Liberals such as Heine who took part later faced persecution when the revolt was suppressed. They fled for their lives with many sailing for America where they took U.S. citizenship and became known as the 'Forty-Eighters'.

William set up an artist studio at 515 Broadway in New York City. In early 1853 he was invited to join the U.S. consul to Central America on a short tour there as the official artist. His paintings created a hugely favourable impression in Washington, and U.S. President, Millard Fillmore personally commissioned him as official artist on the forthcoming U.S. naval expedition to Japan, which was to have huge implications for opening Japan to future trade and western expansionism. In New York in 1858, William married Catherine Sedgwick. They moved to Berlin where Putzi's mother, Katharine Heine, was born in 1859. At the outbreak of the American Civil War in April 1861, William returned to the U.S. and volunteered for the Union army. He served as Colonel of the 103rd New York Infantry and rose to Brevet Brigadier General. At the funeral of Abraham Lincoln, William was one of the generals who carried the coffin.[40]

Putzi was exceedingly proud of that fact that he was the product of a remarkable family packed with American heroes,' generation after generation for over two centuries. His Puritan ancestors believed they had established New England as the spiritual capital of Christendom and the headquarters of the Protestant revolution. Religious conviction and affiliations changed, and the Puritan brethren scattered into a whole galaxy of different sects, but family loyalties and societal connections among the elite, privileged, and powerful families of New England – such as the Sedgwicks – grew stronger down the centuries. Putzi's ancestors were part of a socially exclusive American aristocracy that employed key strategies such as intermarriage, family solidarity, kinship and business networks to promote their power and wealth. Everyone who was anyone knew their family history inside out and the intricate marital relationships between their ancestors and those of other famous families. Family histories were studiously recorded generation after generation in the family bible going back to the Great Puritan Migration. An article in the October 1935 issue of *The Atlantic* regarding the New England elites, commented: "Genealogy was a very popular hobby; and at every social gathering were many who could announce the precise degree of relationship between any two persons there."

Proud to be known as the 'Boston Brahmin,' they funded cultural and educational institutions and were invariably associated with Harvard University. Putzi's American mother – a snob who had rooms in her house painted green to please Queen Victoria – regaled him with stories of his illustrious Boston Brahmin ancestry, and of the many other famous American families who were the Sedgwicks' relations through marriage. Educated in a small cluster of private schools and then Harvard – the exclusive university created by their forebears – these white Anglo-Saxon Protestants (WASPs) had long believed they were set apart by God and destined to rule. Proud Americans as they were, the ruling elites of English Puritan descent remained staunch Anglophiles.

> In their first century and a half, they had customarily called England 'home'; then, after having started the war for independence, they had become violently pro-English again during the War of 1812; and now again, after their horror at England's attitude during the Civil War, they had reverted to their original love. They believed, and said repeatedly, that they were of purer English stock than the English themselves.... Only the English were their social equals.[41]

The Anglophile New England Brahmin elites were an integral component of the Eastern Establishment that rules the United States. Supporters and funders of racist eugenics, they had an almost megalomaniacal sense of their own destiny and that of the English-speaking peoples to civilise the world. This staunch Anglophilia of America's ruling elite was the basis of the longstanding 'Special Relationship' between Britain and the United States.

PUTZI GOES TO HARVARD.

Until the age of ten, Hanfstaengl was schooled at home by successive British governesses and spoke perfect English. From 1897, his education continued at one of Germany's most prestigious schools, the Royal Bavarian Wilhelm Gymnasium in Munich, which attracted the sons of the nobility and wealthy elites. All pupils were educated in English and the Classics – Latin and Ancient Greek. Eager to continue his education in the United States and discover more about his American heritage, in

Harvard

September 1905, Putzi, the now eighteen-year-old accomplished pianist sailed to New York. Influential family ties ensured him a rare and coveted place at Harvard University to study literature, history and philosophy. His plan was to stay at Harvard for four years, gain an Arts degree, then go on to run the prestigious Hanfstaengl art gallery his father had set up on Fifth Avenue. It would all go according to plan, but while running the gallery during the years of the First World War, Putzi's entire life would change after being introduced to numerous British secret intelligence agents operating in the city.

Taking up such a position himself, Putzi would return to Munich in 1921 and on behalf of Anglo-American elites (whose secret intelligence services operated in harmony) would spend 15 years alongside that "tired stray dog looking for a master," Adolf Hitler, grooming him for the role of German dictator. It is entirely possible that without Putzi Hanfstaengl's input, the world would never have heard of the name Hitler. To grasp the truth of this we must leave Hitler and Germany behind for several chapters and follow Putzi across the Atlantic to the United States.

Harvard University in Cambridge Massachusetts (some five miles from the centre of Boston) is considered the most prestigious university in America.

> Harvard was at the heart of the American establishment: it was here that the country's future political, intellectual, and business elites were formed and networked with one another.[42]

Harvard was founded in 1636 by the General Court of the Massachusetts Bay Colony as a college for training ministers for the Puritan church. As Captain of Charlestown, Boston, Putzi's ancestor, Robert Sedgwick, served sixteen consecutive terms on the General Court of the Bay Colony and played a significant role in establishing Harvard. They named it in memory of a young English Puritan minister, John Harvard, who died in the Colony at the age of 31, though he played no part in founding it.

The undergraduate Harvard College evolved and changed markedly over the centuries since co-founder Robert Sedgwick's day. Students came increasingly from the rich and privileged blue-blooded Anglophile families in Boston, Philadelphia and New York. Students with a family connection to the university were admitted at dramatically higher rates than other applicants, and Putzi had *many* such important connections. The famous linguist, writer and activist Noam Chomsky, a researcher at Harvard in the 1950s later wrote:

I remember there was a lot of Anglophilia at Harvard at the time – you were supposed to wear British clothes, and pretend you spoke with a British accent, that sort of stuff. In fact there were actually guys there who I thought were British, who had never been outside the United States.... And what I discovered is that a large part of the education at the really elite institutions is simply refinement, teaching the social graces: what kind of clothes you should wear, how to drink port the right way, how to have polite conversation without talking about serious topics.... Its extremely easy to be sucked into the dominant culture, it can be very appealing. There are a lot of rewards.... You begin to conform, you begin to adapt, you begin to smooth off the harsher edges – and pretty soon it's just happened, it kind of seeps in. And education at a place like Harvard is largely geared to that, to a remarkable extent in fact.[43]

In addition to expensive fees and appropriate family connections, it was difficult for young men to gain a place at Harvard unless they came from a select group of private 'feeder' schools. Merit rarely entered the equation. The 'best' people, the blue bloods, sent their sons to the 'best' schools in New England such as the famous Groton School, which was founded and run by Endicott Peabody. His daughter, Helen, was married to a relative of Putzi's, Robert Sedgwick. Education at these elite private prep schools (or private home tutelage) followed by Harvard, fuelled the self-serving ambition of the power elite of New England. Students from schools like Groton were most likely to get membership of exclusive clubs at the university, and those clubs helped members launch lucrative careers, irrespective of the fact that many had mediocre academic success. Educated at huge expense, they would go on to dominant positions in banking, politics, industry, the military and education. This repetitive cycle of expensive education and the assurance of high-paying jobs, allowed rich families to pass privilege down through their generations. To the present day, wealthy people are overrepresented at Harvard by a factor of six on the campus.[44]

When Putzi matriculated in the freshman class of 1905, getting a good degree was of secondary importance to making the 'right' connections. Sons of the *very* wealthy tended to mix only in their own exclusive social circle. Before leaving Munich, Putzi had been advised by a wealthy American friend and Harvard alumnus that being on the right side of the social chasm and mixing with rich peers was all-important. He joined the Harvard rowing club and was out on the Charles River training with the crew one early spring morning in 1906 when he dived into the icy cold water to save a young divinity student who was in serious difficulties after his canoe capsized. The following morning's *Boston Herald* declared him "Hanfstaengl, Harvard's Hero." With the publicity, and his illustrious Boston Brahmin ancestry and his reputation as an accomplished pianist, he became famous across the campus and popular with the elite 'in-crowd.'

> His larger-than-life character and the determination with which he threw himself into extracurricular activities soon made him one of Harvard's most popular and best-known students. His size and bulk won him a position on the Harvard crew; his voice made him cheer-leader for the football team and his general exuberance gained him many friends during the four years he was there. He was remembered by his contemporaries, according to *The New York Times,* "chiefly for his thunderous renditions of Wagnerian music and the apprehension felt by his hearers for any piano which he attacked at the university and later at the Harvard Club in New York City."[45]

Putzi was elected to membership of the prestigious Hasty Pudding Club, which dates back to 1795 and proudly boasts of being the oldest social club in the United States, with five U.S. Presidents having been members. Its offshoot, Hasty Pudding Theatricals, dates to 1844 and has regularly performed shows ever since. With musical and acting talent, Putzi became a leading member and was popular and much in demand with audiences. He wrote songs for the football team, and in later chapters we see how his musical, acting, and football cheerleader talents would be employed to good effect while grooming Hitler for power.

One of the most important friends Putzi had in the United States was Charles William Eliot, the long-standing president of Harvard.

> Just as he was gaining the affection of his classmates, Putzi was making inroads into the American establishment, becoming a frequent guest at the home of Charles William Eliot, the president of Harvard.'[46]

CHARLES WILLIAM ELIOT (1834-1926)

In 1869 at the age of 35, Charles William Eliot was elected the youngest-ever president of Harvard University. He served in that esteemed position for forty years, befriending international leaders in the political, business and banking world. A Boston Brahmin and Harvard trained scientist, his father had been mayor of Boston and treasurer of Harvard. Eliot's four-times-great grandfather, the Puritan Thomas Dudley, sailed from England with Putzi's Puritan ancestors and founded Cambridge, Massachusetts. Dudley was the co-founder of Harvard with Putzi's ancestor, General Robert Sedgwick. Over the following centuries, Putzi's family and Charles William Eliot's family intermarried, making them not merely friends but kin. It is likely that Eliot was responsible for Putzi gaining a place at Harvard, and virtually from the day of his arrival at the university as an 18-year-old freshman, Eliot and his wife took him under their wing. Putzi was greatly honoured to be a frequent guest at their home, for the Harvard supremo seldom indulged undergraduates, and none dared approach the great man uninvited on campus. Mrs. Eliot, née Ellen Derby Peabody, hailed from the famous Boston Brahmin Peabody clan, which also had links to Putzi's family. She was related to George Peabody who, as we have seen in an earlier chapter, opened the Peabody bank in London which soon morphed into the J.P. Morgan bank.

Charles William Eliot was a trustee of the Rockefeller Foundation, and a friend of both John D. Rockefeller and J.P. Morgan whose donations helped fund the building of the Harvard Medical School. Eliot was also a close friend of that other major Wall Street banker, Jacob Schiff. They enjoyed holidays together and were frequent hiking companions in the hills around Bar Harbor.[47]

Charles Eliot, then, was remarkably close to the leading bankers on Wall Street who were intricately linked to the London Rothschilds and at the very pinnacle of the Anglo-American High Finance. In yet another instance of wheels within wheels, Putzi was remarkably close to Eliot.

In their books, Professors Antony Sutton (*Wall Street and the Rise of Hitler*) and Guido Preparata (*Conjuring Hitler, How Britain and America made the Third Reich*] demonstrate how these banking friends of Eliot's were deeply involved in financing and promoting Hitler and the Nazi party through the 1920s and 30s. This, as we shall see, was occurring at the very time they had placed Putzi directly at Hitler's side. Eliot and Harvard had something in common with Hitler and Nazis: a strong interest in eugenics and in cleansing society of people they viewed as biological threats to the nation's health:

> In August 1912, Harvard president emeritus Charles William Eliot addressed the Harvard Club of San Francisco on a subject close to his heart: racial purity. It was being threatened, he declared, by immigration. Eliot was not opposed to admitting new Americans, but he saw

the mixture of racial groups it could bring about as a grave danger. "Each nation should keep its stock pure," Eliot told his San Francisco audience. "There should be no blending of races." Eliot's warning against mixing races – which for him included Irish Catholics marrying white Anglo-Saxon Protestants, Jews marrying Gentiles, and blacks marrying whites – was a central tenet of eugenics. The eugenics movement, which had begun in England and was rapidly spreading in the United States, insisted that human progress depended on promoting reproduction by the best people in the best combinations, and preventing the unworthy from having children. The former Harvard president was an outspoken supporter of another major eugenic cause of his time: forced sterilization of people declared to be "feeble-minded," physically disabled, "criminalistic," or otherwise flawed.... He also lent his considerable prestige to the campaign to build a global eugenics movement. He was a vice-president of the First International Eugenics Congress, which met in London in 1912 to hear papers on "racial suicide" among Northern Europeans and similar topics. Two years later, Eliot helped organize the First National Conference on Race Betterment in Battle Creek, Michigan.... Harvard administrators, faculty members, and alumni were at the forefront of American eugenics – founding eugenics organizations, writing academic and popular eugenics articles, and lobbying government to enact eugenics laws. And for many years, scarcely any significant Harvard voices, if any at all, were raised against it.[48]

Some view eugenics as a product of Nazi Germany, but extensive work in the field was conducted in Britain and the U.S. long before Hitler appeared on the scene. Driven by their prejudiced thinking about racial purity, together with social control imperatives and the vision of an Anglo-Saxon master race, tens of thousands of unmarried mothers, the poor and mentally and physically disabled people across America were rendered sterile against their will. In California alone, more than 20,000 men and women were subjected to this shameful undertaking. Many analysts believe these grotesque events in the United States inspired Hitler and the Nazis' eugenic atrocities.

> The concept of a white, blond haired, blue-eyed master Nordic race did not originate with Hitler. The idea was created in the United States ... Germany's budding eugenicists became desirable allies for the Americans. In this relationship America was far away the senior partner. In Eugenics, the United States led and Germany followed. This relationship continued during the Third Reich....

The Rockefeller Foundation played a major role in establishing and sponsoring major eugenics institutions in Germany. And during the Hitler years it funded Nazi controlled institutions in both Germany and Austria until 1939.[49]

Charles William Eliot may have been a close friend of the cultured and ultra-rich Jacob Schiff, and other leading Jewish bankers on Wall Street, but ordinary poor immigrant Jews and refugees from the pogroms in Russia were not welcome to mix with the race and blood of white Anglo-Saxons.

Certainly not everyone in America supported eugenics. In 1905, when Jane Stanford, the Christian co-founder of Stanford University, discovered that the university president, David Starr Jordan, was promoting anti-Jew, anti-black, and anti-Chinese eugenics policies on campus, she planned to have him removed. Shortly thereafter, Mrs. Stanford suffered a horrific death in a Honolulu hotel after being poisoned with strychnine. Through powerful connections, Jordan ensured that the death certificate pronounced her death as being due to heart disease. In 2003, Robert Cutler, Professor emeritus of Neurology at Stanford, published a book, *The Mysterious Death of Jane Stanford*, which presented compelling evidence that David Starr Jordan had been behind the murder in order to save his position as university president. Jordan of Stanford and Eliot of Harvard were leaders in the American eugenics movement.

Charles William Eliot was but one of Putzi's famous friends/relatives in the United States. Family connections meant everything to the Boston Brahmin, and everywhere one looks in Putzi's American ancestry, one finds important connections. Charles William Eliot's first cousin, fellow Brahmin and good friend, Charles Eliot Norton, was a Harvard graduate (1846) and member of Hasty Pudding. He was married to Putzi's second cousin, Susan Ridley Sedgwick. Susan's brother-in-law, William Darwin was the son of Charles Darwin, whose work on 'Social Darwinism' nourished the roots of eugenics. Charles Eliot Norton spent many years in Europe studying art, and became a close friend of John Ruskin at Oxford. Ruskin, as we have seen, was the inspiration for Cecil Rhodes, Alfred Milner, and English ruling class imperative to control the world.

Charles Eliot Norton was also a good friend of Rudyard Kipling, poet, journalist and propagandist for the British elites. Kipling made trips to visit Norton in the United States and regularly visited South Africa where his friends included Cecil Rhodes and Sir Alfred Milner, founder members of the secret 'Society of the Elect'. A fervent Freemason, Kipling moved in high Establishment circles and provided influential propaganda in support of the Establishment's war to wrench control of the gold fields from the Boers. From 1914 onwards, he also did much to promote and disseminate the British Establishment's lies and propaganda regarding the world war. Carroll Quigley names him as a member of the Cecil Bloc of the secret society.[50] Through Charles William Eliot, Putzi Hanfstaengl was directly or indirectly linked to these individuals. The reader will by now recognise the many and varied wheels within wheels of the Anglo-American elite circles.

Charles Eliot took Putzi under his wing at Harvard where, as a frequent guest at Eliot's house, he met some of the wealthiest and most famous people in America, who were also regular guests there – individuals such as John D. Rockefeller, J.P. Morgan and Jacob Schiff. Eliot was a trustee of the Rockefeller Foundation created in 1913, and Rockefeller was a generous benefactor of Harvard university. Schiff, the senior partner in Kuhn, Loeb & Co, spent holidays with Charles Eliot, and every second weekend the pair went hill walking together.

As a student at Harvard, Putzi was a friend of another student there, President Theodore Roosevelt's son, Theodore Jr. He took Putzi to meet his father and Putzi and the president became friends. With regular invitations to the White House thereafter, Putzi played the magnificent Steinway Grand to entertain the president's guests. On one occasion he broke seven of its bass strings with his exuberant style, but the president laughed it off. President Roosevelt enjoyed wide-ranging discussions with Putzi, and when he left the White House, they would see each other 'frequently' over the following  years at Roosevelt's magnificent summer home, Sagamore Hill, in Oyster Bay, where Putzi was always 'a welcome guest'.[51]

In his memoirs, Putzi names other students he grew close to at Harvard, who included the famous Walter Lippmann.[52]

WALTER LIPPMANN

Lippmann mixed in the same rarefied, wealthy and influential circles as Putzi and, like him, would become an important agent of the transatlantic elite. Born in New York City in 1889, he is officially remembered as an American writer, reporter and political commentator.

> The most influential journalist in America. Lippmann aimed to influence, not just report on events, so he spent more time working behind the scenes shaping events than reporting on them. He was a confidant of presidents, prime ministers, senators, generals, and above all, the elite that made and executed American foreign policy.[53]

Lippmann was a master at creating propaganda and directing the thrust of fake history. He is credited with being a founding father of Public Relations and its use as a propaganda system to misinform, control, and manipulate populations in the so-called Liberal Democracies. He wrote in 1916:

> We have reached a point where we are emerging from our isolation. Foreign trade is drawing us into the outer world; we are lending capital abroad, planning a merchant marine and a naval program. Wherever we go, we cannot help meeting that organization of one quarter of the human race which is known as the British Empire. We cannot ignore it – no world power can. And we have got to choose, and choose soon between antagonism and friendship. Germany made the choice about twenty years ago. She chose to challenge the mistress of the seas and brought down upon the world an unthinkable calamity. We have to make the same choice. Surely if there is any wisdom and humanity in us, we shall seek a self-respecting friendship with the British Commonwealth. I do not need to remind you of Canada, touching us at the noblest and longest frontier in the world, or of Australia and New Zealand, so like ourselves in democratic hope, subject to the same fears about the Orient. It seems to me that if two states so parallel in interest as America and England cannot find the way of cooperation, then there is little hope in the world.[54]

Lippmann kept up the 'Germany bad, England good' propaganda in 1917. Germany, he reported, was an enemy of the international order and preferred war to peace. He reiterated the Bryce Report lies about German atrocities in Belgium.

When Germany declared that Europe could not be consulted, that Austria must be allowed to crush Serbia without reference to the concert of Europe, Germany proclaimed herself an enemy of international order. She preferred a war which involved all of Europe to any admission of the fact that a cooperative Europe existed. It was an assertion of unlimited national sovereignty which Europe could not tolerate. This brought Russia and France into the field. Instantly Germany acted on the same doctrine of unlimited national sovereignty by striking at France through Belgium. Had Belgium been merely a small neutral nation the crime would still have been one of the worst in the history of the modern world. The fact that Belgium was an internationalized state has made the invasion the master tragedy of the war. For Belgium represented what progress the world had made towards cooperation. If it could not survive then no internationalism was possible. That is why through these years of horror upon horror, the Belgian horror is the fiercest of all. The burning, the shooting, the starving, and the robbing of small and inoffensive nations is tragic enough. But the German crime in Belgium is greater than the sum of Belgium's misery. It is a crime against the bases of faith at which the world must build or perish. The invasion of Belgium instantly brought the five British democracies into the war. I think this is the accurate way to state the fact.[55]

Lippmann gave the impression that he was on the progressive Left, but it was sham. Professor Quigley writes:

The Morgan firm decided to infiltrate the Left-wing political movements in the United States. This was relatively easy to do for these groups were starved of funds and eager for a voice to reach the people. Wall Street supplied both. The purpose was not to destroy, dominate, or take over but really threefold: (1) to keep informed about the thinking of Left-wing or liberal groups; (2) to provide them with a mouthpiece so they could "blow off steam," and (3) to have a final veto on their publicity and possibly on their actions, if they ever went "radical."... The best example of this alliance of Wall Street and left-wing publications was *The New Republic*, founded in 1914 by Willard Straight [a J. P. Morgan agent] ... The original purpose for establishing the paper was to provide an outlet for the progressive Left and to guide it quietly in an Anglophile direction. This latter task was entrusted to a young man only four years out of Harvard, but already a member of the Round Table group which has played a major part in directing England's foreign policy since its formal establishment in 1909. This new recruit, Walter Lippmann, has been, from 1914 to the present, the authentic spokesman in American journalism for the Establishments on both sides of the Atlantic in international affairs.[56]

Putzi's friend Lippman was deeply involved with the transatlantic elite and a member of the Milner Group's Round Table. He was also a friend of Woodrow Wilson and his alter ego, Col. Edward M. House, and would work for the American delegation on the disgrace and travesty of truth that became the Versailles Treaty in 1919.

Yet another student friend of Putzi's at Harvard who became deeply involved in the secret intelligence services and played a significant role for the U.S. elite was John Reed.

John "Jack" Reed

Jack Reed was born into one of the leading families in Portland on the Pacific northwest. He was educated at a private school before going on to Harvard. A member of Hasty Pudding Theatricals with Putzi and their mutual friend, Lippmann, Reed apparently backed socialism.

On graduating, he travelled around Europe for several years before be-coming a writer and a journalist for a New York City periodical, *Metropolitan Magazine* which was owned by J.P. Morgan interests.[57] In 1913, Reed covered the Mexican Revolution for the journal and in late 1914 the new editor sent him to Europe as a war correspondent. That new editor was none other than Putzi's friend, former U.S. President, Theodore Roosevelt. On retiring

from politics, Roosevelt edited the magazine from 1914 until his death in 1919, and wrote many articles arguing against U.S. neutrality in the war.

On 14 August 1917, Jack Reed received a new U.S passport and travelled to Russia on 'magazine work'. It was just weeks before the Bolshevik Revolution played out. The timing was immaculate. According to Professor Richard B. Spence, Reed had been tipped off about the exact day of Lenin's anticipated seizure of power.[58] Presenting himself as a socialist and a Bolshevik supporter, Reed befriended Trotsky and Lenin. He was a strange revolutionary.

The son of a wealthy family, Harvard man and bon vivant, he had nothing in common with the down-trodden proletarians whose cause he championed. As Antony Sutton noted, Reed was an "Establishment Revolutionary" who never lacked for rich influential friends to come to his defense, and who never lost the privileges of his class even while attacking it.[59]

Reed offered Lenin and Trotsky his support and wrote pro-Bolshevik propaganda for his American readership, but all was not as it seemed. Professor Antony Sutton writes:

> John Reed was not only financed from Wall Street, but had consistent support for his activities, even to the extent of intervention with the State Department from William Franklin Sands, executive secretary of the American International Corporation.[60]

The American International Corporation was set up in 1915 as an American investment trust by Frank Vanderlip, president of the National City Bank. The bank was controlled jointly by Rockefeller, Jacob Schiff, and Paul Warburg. In suggesting that Reed was in effect an agent of the Morgan interests, Antony Sutton adds:

> His [Reed's] anti-capitalist writing maintained the valuable myth that all capitalists are in perpetual warfare with all socialist revolutionaries. Carroll Quigley reported that the Morgan interests financially supported domestic revolutionary organizations and anti-capitalist writings. And we have presented in this chapter irrefutable documentary evidence that the Morgan interests were also effecting control of a Soviet agent, interceding on his behalf and, more important, generally intervening in behalf of Soviet interests with the U.S. government. These activities centred at a single address: 120 Broadway, New York City.[61]

120 Broadway just happened to be the headquarters of the Federal Reserve Bank of New York. 'The vehicle for pro-Bolshevik activity was the American International Corporation, also at 120 Broadway.'[62]

The American elite had placed Reed at the heart of Soviet Russia, just as they would place his good Harvard friend, Putzi Hanfstaengl, at the heart of the Third Reich. Three years after the revolution, however, Reed died, aged 33, from typhus and was given a hero's funeral. His body lay in state with a military catafalque guard before burial at the Kremlin Wall necropolis. Richard B. Spence, professor of history at the University of Idaho, gives a powerful account of Reed and his Wall Street connections in his excellent book, *Wall Street and the Russian Revolution, 1905-1925.*

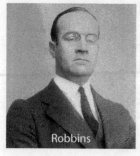
Robbins

Another close friend of Putzi's at Harvard was Warren Delano Robbins. They acted together in the Hasty Pudding club shows. Warren was the cousin of future U.S. President Franklin Delano Roosevelt (FDR) and via Warren, Putzi would become a good friend of FDR. Robbins would go on from Harvard to serve in various ambassadorial posts and in 1922 was second-in-command at the American embassy in Berlin. In the next chapter we shall see how it was Robbins who brought Putzi and Hitler together that year.

While at Harvard Putzi enjoyed the friendship of William Randolph Hearst, the famous newspaper baron, who was a close friend of Putzi's mother and had known Putzi since he was a young child.

WILLIAM RANDOLPH HEARST

With family wealth, Hearst developed the largest newspaper chain and media company in the U.S. He ran unsuccessfully for the U.S. Presidency in 1904.

Hearst had attended Harvard twenty years before Putzi and was a member of the Hasty Pudding theatricals. It is entirely likely that Hearst, as well as Charles William Eliot, was responsible for introducing his young family friend, Putzi, to many notables in New York.

Years later, when Hearst visited him in Berlin, Putzi was able to get Hearst direct access to Hitler and other leading Nazis, and acted as his interpreter. After this, Hearst gave Hitler considerable support in his newspapers. By then, Hearst owned the biggest media conglomerate in the world and was buying up radio stations to complement his newspapers. Putzi was well aware that his friend's support for Hitler was part of the Anglo-American elite's appeasement charade that is discussed in a later chapter. *The Times of Israel* recently published an article on media moguls in Britain and the United States who supported the Nazis and whose newspapers and magazines had a combined readership of 65 million:

> They regularly paid handsome fees to fascist leaders looking to promote their ideas to a global audience. William Randolph Hearst, for example, paid Hitler and other top Nazis an average of $1,500 per article – or $20,000 in today's money. "By giving fascist dictators access to the American public and allowing them to present

themselves as peace-loving champions of order, Hearst helped to normalize fascism for his 30 million readers," says [historian Kathryn S.] Olmsted. "These press barons did not just sell the news, they constructed it and lied as they reported events so they could make a lot of money and gain political influence, too."[63]

Putzi spent much of his time at Harvard enjoying life with his friends and barely scraped a degree. He graduated in 1909 and returned to Germany for one year's military service in the Royal Bavarian Foot Guards. He then went to Vienna for several months to study lithography, and afterwards returned to Munich for six months to gain some experience in the family art publishing business. He was preparing himself for running the Hanfstaengl art gallery in New York.

SUMMARY: CHAPTER 16 – "HANFSTAENGL, HARVARD'S HERO"

- Adolf Hitler remained in the army after the war and was posted to an intelligence unit in Munich that countered socialist and pacifist tendencies among serving soldiers.

- Tasked with carrying out surveillance at political meetings, Hitler developed an interest in politics and joined the small German Workers Party. He soon became its leader, and changed its name to the National Socialist German Workers Party (what became known by its detractors as the Nazi party – a term of abuse).

- Hitler decided to attempt a career in politics and left the army in 1920. He was soon drawing large crowds to his meetings, and formed a paramilitary group, the SA, which spread fear and terror on the streets of Munich.

- In 1922, Hitler made contact with Benito Mussolini, the fascist leader in Italy who would soon become prime minister. Almost 90 years later, it was revealed that Mussolini had been a very highly paid agent of British intelligence.

- Hitler and his Nazi party were selected by Anglo-American elites to conduct their planned war with Russia. Anglo-American intelligence agents, Putzi Hanfstaengl and William de Ropp, were placed directly at Hitler's side to prepare him for power and guide him on the road to war – and his and Germany's destruction.

- Born into a very rich and well-connected family in Germany, Putzi Hanfstaengl's mother was American with many famous American ancestors going back to the Puritans in the Boston area in the 17th century.

- Putzi spent four years at the elite Harvard University and had many important friends in the highest echelons of banking, politics, and the Press. A gifted pianist, he was a regular visitor at the White House, where he would entertain the president and his guests on the Steinway grand piano.

- Putzi graduated in 1909 and returned to Germany for one year of voluntary service in a guards regiment. His plan was to return to the United States permanently to run the family's exclusive art gallery in New York.

CHAPTER 17

AGENT HANFSTAENGL "BEFRIENDS" HITLER

Putzi Hanfstaengl returned to America in the autumn of 1911 to run the family art gallery on Fifth Avenue at Forty-fifth Street, one of the most expensive corners in New York. He lived in New York for the next ten years, enjoyed socialising with many famous and wealthy Americans and became closely involved with the Anglo-American intelligence services. Putzi later recounted in his memoirs:

> I took most of my meals at the Harvard Club, where I made friends with young Franklin D. Roosevelt, at that time a rising New York State Senator, and received several invitations to visit his cousin Teddy, the former President, who had retired to his estate at Sagamore Hill. He gave me a boisterous welcome ... and came out with a phrase which has stuck with me ever since: "Hanfstaengl, your business is to pick out the best picture, but remember that in politics the choice is that of the lesser evil."... The Hanfstaengl representation was a delightful combination of business and pleasure. The famous names who visited me were legion: Pierpont Morgan, Toscanini, Henry Ford, Caruso, Santos Dumont, Charlie Chaplin, Paderewski, and the daughter of President Wilson.[1]

Putzi was 24 years-old with no business experience but he knew some of the most important people in the United States and brimmed with the self-confidence of a Harvard man. He remained a close friend of Theodore Roosevelt, Charles William Eliot, and old student networks, and made many new friends at the gallery and nearby Harvard Club. He created an oasis of culture and tranquillity in the hurly-burly of Manhattan, quietly playing his grand piano or engaging an accomplished string quartet to play in the background as mega-wealthy customers viewed his regular exhibitions. Putzi relates that one of President Wilson's attractive daughters called in regularly, but gives no hint of a romantic link. Romance blossomed when an attractive young writer and illustrator, Djuna

Barnes, visited the gallery to demonstrate her port-
folio of drawings. Djuna, who became one of the
most prominent writers of her generation, was bi-
sexual and eventually decided on a female partner,
leaving Putzi heartbroken.

Djuna

The gallery opened from 7 A.M. to 8 P.M., but with a cultured and knowl-
edgeable assistant, Friedrich Denks, attending to the clientele in his absence, Putzi was able to enjoy extended breaks. He dined most days at the
exclusive Harvard Club on nearby West 44th street where, with his friendly nature and mastery of the spoken word, he became a popular member.
Putzi entertained other members and their guests with scintillating conversation and his repertoire of Bach, Beethoven, Brahms, and Wagner on
the club's grand piano.[2] His popularity during his university years never
waned, and old Harvard friends such as Walter Lippmann, John Reed,
and Warren Delano Robbins regularly joined him for dinner. Other well-
known individuals who socialised with Putzi at the Harvard Club included the young New York State Senator, Franklin Delano Roosevelt (FDR),
a Harvard graduate and distant cousin of President Theodore Roosevelt.
FDR would himself become US President (1933 to 1945) and take Putzi
to the White House in 1941 as an adviser on Nazi Germany.

Harvard Club

When the First World War began in August 1914, as a reservist with
military obligations following his year in the Lifeguards, Putzi should
have gone back to fight for Germany. A number of other German Americans successfully made their way across the Atlantic to enlist, but Putzi

was not among them. He made the excuse of being 'marooned' in America and later applied liberal coats of whitewash

> I was never able to suppress a yearning and an inferiority complex at the thought of the service I had missed, which decimated my generation and killed two of my brothers .... There was little doubt where American sympathies would fall in the long run, but I tried to keep the German flag flying as best I could.[3]

Putzi's eldest brother, Edgar, survived the war and never forgave him for failing to return to fight for Germany. In truth, it was neither cowardice nor being 'marooned' in the United States that stopped him. By 1914, Putzi was steeped in the American way of life and evidently now considered himself to be more American than German. Through many friends and relatives in high places in the Eastern Establishment, he undoubtedly knew that the 'neutral' United States was 100 per cent committed to Britain and supplying her with weapons and ammunition. Doubtless his good friend Theodore Roosevelt made the position clear to him, when regaling him with tales of his close links to the late King Edward VII and the "special relationship."

Putzi describes his years in New York as "a delightful combination of business and pleasure," and those years were also intriguing and exciting thanks to his involvement in the cloak-and-dagger world of secret intelligence. We have seen how Putzi's close friend at Harvard, John (Jack) Reed, went on to a stellar career as a US intelligence agent in Soviet Russia – cut short by his death from typhus in 1920. If we are to understand Putzi's involvement in this sphere of work, we must consider the closely associated Anglo-American intelligence services operating in New York in a little detail and consider the many contacts he had within it.

For centuries, Britain had relied on secret agents to gather intelligence about foreign powers and keep tabs on dissidents at home, and by the early 20th century was far more advanced in the field than the United States. As discussed in chapter 3, the US had no Federal intelligence service beyond its diplomats and a few military and naval attaches. It had no codebreaking agency such as Room 40 in the Admiralty in London and had only rudimentary communications security. With the "special relationship" leading agents from London were posted to New York to help the US develop its intelligence services, and at that time they operated virtually as one. Consequently, we describe Putzi operating not as an 'American' agent but an 'Anglo-American' agent.

One of Britain's leading intelligence officers, Sir Claude Dansey – codenamed 'Colonel Z' – had served in the British army in the Boer War and befriended Winston Churchill. Recruited to intelligence work he was promoted to lieutenant-colonel and was almost single handedly responsible for

Dansey

helping the Americans develop their secret service and, crucially, "for setting up the special relationship between the intelligence services of Britain and America which still exists to this day."[4]

Interestingly, it was Dansey who ordered the Naval Control officer at Halifax, Nova Scotia to release Trotsky after he had been removed from his ship and arrested while on his way from New York in 1917 to instigate the Bolshevik Revolution. Dansey was told by the MI6 station chief in New York, William Wiseman, that the information against Trotsky had come from a Russian agent.

However, Dansey reported: "I then asked him a few questions about the man, and from what I gathered, there is a strong possibility that he was an agent provocateur, used by the old Russian Secret Police. I told Wiseman he had better be discharged at once, and he said that he was going to do so."[5]

Thus, within weeks of his arrest in Halifax, Trotsky and his fellow revolutionaries were put on another ship heading for Russia.

With Dansey's input in the United States its intelligence service grew rapidly from two officers and three clerks to 300 officers and 1,000 clerks by the time the war ended seventeen months later.

> Essentially his objective was to make sure the United States created
> a first-rate service and that it would then co-operate and collabo
> rate with British Intelligence for their mutual benefit.[6]

To overcome the US intelligence service deficiencies, in 1916 Secretary of State Robert Lansing set up an inter-agency Bureau of Secret Intelligence – the secret service of the State Department (which would eventually become known as the Diplomatic Security Service – the DSS). Prior to that, the State Department had no secret service and "even the security of the department's communications with its embassies and consulates abroad was something of a joke."[7]

Like the vast majority of individuals selected for senior posts in the administration, Robert Lansing was a committed Anglophile and Germanophobe. He was a close friend of the British ambassador, Cecil Spring-Rice who, in turn, was a close friend of Theodore Roosevelt and served as best man at his second wedding. In his whitewash biography of Lansing, Lester H. Woolsey, Solicitor of the Department of State, wrote:

> Mr. Lansing early in July, 1915, came to the conclusion that the German ambition for world domination was the real menace of the war, particularly to democratic institutions. In order to block this German ambition, he believed that the progress of the war would eventually disclose to the American people the purposes of the German Government; that German activities in the United States and in Latin America should be carefully investigated and frustrated … the United States should enter the war if it should appear that Germany would become the victor; and that American public opinion must be awakened in preparation for this contingency. This outline of Mr. Lansing's views explains why the *Lusitania* dispute was not brought to the point of a break.[8]

"American public opinion must be awakened" in preparation for war. Lansing knew, of course, that "German ambition for world domination" was the fake narrative used by the Milner Group to justify the war. Public opinion in the US was against getting involved in the European war and had to be turned 180 degrees. Therein lay the importance of the *Lusitania* sinking and the Bryce Report lies about German atrocities in Belgium.

Under British intelligence guidance, Lansing recruited a small group of men as 'special agents,' including an individual named Leland Harrison who would "take charge of the collection and examination of all information of a secret nature."[9] Harrison, who came from a wealthy American family, was educated at the elite Eton College in England and Harvard thereafter. He served as 2nd Secretary at the U.S. embassy in London 1910-1912, and "was thus fully au fait with the London scene" and "a man of the greatest discretion."[10]

Leland Harrison worked closely with British intelligence operating out of the British consul offices on Whitehall Street, Lower Manhattan. The man initially in charge there was forty-four-year-old Captain Guy Gaunt of British Naval Intelligence. Officially based in the British embassy in Washington as 'naval attaché,' Gaunt spent most of his time in New York and was directly answerable to 'Blinker' Hall, Director of Naval Intelligence in Room 40 at the Admiralty in London. It is known that Gaunt and Hall communicated frequently, but no records have ever been made available to researchers despite repeated requests under freedom of information legislation.[11] Such documents were most likely destroyed or concealed at Hanslope Park.

Guy Gaunt was "an outgoing likeable man" who "soon had a host of American friends including Teddy Roosevelt and Franklin Roosevelt."[12] Both Roosevelts just happened to be friends of Putzi Hanfstaengl.

> Franklin Roosevelt's first encounter with the official world of intelligence came as Assistant Secretary of the Navy [1913-1920] where he found himself responsible for overseeing the Office of Naval Intelligence. It had been a small and sleepy outfit until the First World War catapulted it into the wider and rougher world of international intrigue. Roosevelt's enthusiastic embrace of its work marked an important moment in American intelligence. He spent much of 1916 organising the Naval Reserve Force, where he cast aside the pretence that Americans were innocents and recruited like-minded Ivy League friends for secret work. Like him, they regarded it as both glamorous and legitimate.[13]

Roosevelt

Vincent Astor

Guy Gaunt

As Assistant Secretary of the Navy, Franklin Roosevelt set up a "super-secret" intelligence operation in New York that would report directly to him, and work in close cooperation with British Military Intelligence. He recruited his cousin, Vincent Astor, who was serving at the time in the U.S. Naval Reserve.[14]

Vincent Astor was the hugely wealthy half-brother of the equally wealthy John Jacob Astor, who was yet another close friend of Putzi's. In later years (1934), Putzi would be 'guest of honour' at John Jacob's wedding breakfast. No evidence has been uncovered that Putzi was recruited to Roosevelt's 'super-secret' intelligence unit, but he was certainly close to most who were involved.

Guy Gaunt of British intelligence socialised with Putzi's friend Franklin Roosevelt, and other 'big hitters' in New York including Edward Mandell House who 'ran' Woodrow Wilson in the White House on behalf of Wall Street. Another of Gaunt's friends, Edward Stettinius, was a partner in the J.P. Morgan firm and deeply involved in the purchase of all Allied war supplies in the US Working closely with Bernard Baruch, Stettinius bought, shipped, and insured supplies on an unprecedented scale. He had thousands of factories built, stimulated methods of mass production, and was involved in illegally shipping explosives to Britain on the *Lusitania* and other passenger liners. The 'special relationship' was working well. Stettinius would later become the US Assistant Secretary of War.

In 1915, Guy Gaunt was recalled to London and replaced as head of British intelligence in New York by a banker/businessman, Sir William Wiseman. For his services, Gaunt was promoted to Admiral and received a knighthood. Sir William Wiseman arrived in the autumn of that year under the cover of being a merchant who headed the British Purchasing Commission, and went straight to work at Whitehall Street. A former British army officer and banker,  he had worked in New York before the war and knew his way about.

> Wiseman had many important contacts in business and banking from his days on Wall Street, and became a close friend of Colonel House, the President's personal adviser.... Wiseman's connection with House and Wilson proved to be of immense diplomatic value, and the special relationship which Dansey had established between the intelligence services was now so strong that all they needed was a liaison officer to act more or less as a postman.[15]

Wiseman stayed at the luxury Gotham hotel on Fifth Avenue, several blocks away from Putzi's gallery. Edward Mandell House also had rooms at the Gotham when he wasn't staying in the apartment he had been allocated in the White House. Partly educated in England, Mandell House was a 'British trained political operative.'[16]

> House and Wiseman worked closely together as a conduit of informal diplomacy between Britain and America, and controlling the spy and intelligence gathering network in the U.S.[17]

Professor Richard Spence relates that before departing New York in 1915, Guy Gaunt advised his replacement William Wiseman that one his most fruitful sources of intelligence in the US was the Morgan bank on Wall Street from where J P. Morgan ran a private intelligence service.

The Morganites employed a small army of private detectives who guarded ships docks and warehouses, but they used more sophisticated agents as well. High up in this clandestine array, and in contact with Gaunt, was a shadowy "Mr Green." Almost certainly the name was Greene, and she was no mister.[18]

Like the Rothschild dynasty in Europe, the J.P. Morgan outfit had developed its own highly efficient private network of detectives, spies and informants. The 'shadowy Mr Green' who worked for this Morgan network was in fact Belle Greene, the talented curator of the J.P. Morgan library and museum. Born in 1883, Belle was a twenty-two-year-old junior librarian at Princeton University in 1905 when she caught the eye of J.P. Morgan and was offered the dream job. Over a period of 40 years in charge, Belle would build the library and museum into one of the largest collections of rare works in the world. An attractive woman, she wore expensive Renaissance gowns, enjoyed the company of men, and daringly posed nude for artists. She was forty-six years younger than Pierpont Morgan and a question remains over their personal relationship. He was certainly infatuated with her, considered her a 'soul-mate' and left her $50,000 in his will when he died in March 1913. (worth around $1.5 million in purchasing power in 2023) On Pierpont's death, J.P. Morgan Jr. (Jack) took control of the Morgan empire but, unlike his father, was happily married and his relationship with Belle was cordial and platonic over many years. He too would eventually leave her a substantial sum of money in his will.

Belle Greene

Belle's father had been the first African American student to graduate from Harvard University, but she denied her black heritage and crossed the colour line to avoid the suffocating bigotry. With beautiful green eyes and olive coloured skin, throughout her adult life she claimed to be of Portuguese origin. Belle became one of the most important people in the art world, enjoying frequent trips to Europe as a VIP on ocean liners and staying in luxury hotels. With virtually unlimited Morgan funds and her own Morgan cheque book, she bought Leonardo da Vinci's notebooks, paintings by Michelangelo, Raphael and Rembrandt, and priceless historical artifacts for the museum. She is important to our narrative because just a short walk from her office was Putzi's gallery on Fifth Avenue and she visited him regularly.[19] Belle Greene was yet another important route through which Putzi became embroiled in the Anglo-American intelligence network.

According to J.P. Morgan's official biographer, Ron Chernow, Belle Greene performed intelligence work for the British,[20] and Professor Spence adds that under cover of her leading role in the Morgan library and art collection, she was ideally placed to offer her services to the Allied cause.[21] The Morgan set-up was exempted from mail censorship in and out of Britain and retained an in-house code developed by Edward Stettinius and his British contacts.[22] Belle worked in close collaboration with all British intelligence agents in the city, including Guy Gaunt and thereafter with his replacement, Sir William Wiseman. She was linked with Aleister Crowley who operated on behalf of Blinker Hall in British Naval Intelligence Room 40 and, as noted by Crowley himself, he and Belle Greene were lovers for a time.[23] Whether it was Belle Greene who introduced Crowley to Putzi, or vice versa, is unknown. The important point to keep in mind is that Putzi Hanfstaengl was closely involved with numerous members of the Anglo-American intelligence organisation.

In the *Lusitania* chapter we saw how British agent provocateur Crowley posed as an Irish nationalist who hated England despite having no connections whatsoever with Ireland. It provided suitable cover for infiltrating anti-British groups of Irish and Germans in New York. An English patriot, Crowley would later endure years of public vilification in England for his efforts but he knew – as did all secret intelligence agents – that it was a price that had to be paid. Vilification in the controlled press in one's home country was an integral part of their cover. Putzi would face the same vilification a few years later in the American press after he went to Germany as an Anglo-American agent and groomed the little-known Hitler for power.

As we saw in an earlier chapter, the occultist Crowley was in the pay of British secret intelligence on an undercover mission in New York. He had been recruited by his long-time friend, the Right Honourable Everard Feilding who, for years, was the secretary of London's Society for Psychical Research (SPR). Feilding worked for British Naval Intelligence in which Blinker Hall and Winston Churchill had leading roles at that time. Crowley also had a friend and supporter in the Kuhn, Loeb Bank on Wall Street – the "wholeheartedly pro-British" investment banker Otto Kahn.[24]

German-born Kahn was an important player for the Anglo-American financial elite and also served as an undercover British intelligence asset in New York.[25]

Crowley successfully infiltrated a German spy ring in New York and from this vantage point span a web of influence among German diplomats and spies who believed him to be the genuine article; he was thus able to garner much valuable information for Anglo-American Intelligence. As detailed previously, thanks in part to Crowley's encouragement of the German authorities, the *Lusitania* was torpedoed. Crowley later admitted to encouraging U-Boat attacks against other neutral ships as a means of encouraging the United States into the war. He also revealed that Guy Gaunt had been his accomplice and immediate chief in that endeavour.[26]

Professor Richard Spence writes:

> Hall [head of British Naval Intelligence in Room 40] was anxious about the mounting German threat in America and convinced that neutralizing it would require more than just counterpropaganda. He argued that the best way to combat German intrigues in the States was to expose them to the American public and government, who would abhor the destruction of property and fomenting of rebellion on their soil. Following Hall's logic, preventing German outrages was not necessary or even desirable. Far better to let them happen and then expose them. In fact, it might even be necessary to give the enemy a little help. The beastlier the Germans, the better. Hall communicated these ideas to Gaunt who was more than willing to carry them out.[27]

In addition to his role in the *Lusitania* sinking in May 1915, Crowley was likely involved in a major act of sabotage in the United States on 30 July 1916. Thousands of tons of munitions awaiting shipment to England exploded at the Black Tom Island munitions depot in New York harbour. The explosion, heard a hundred miles away, killed four men. Millions of dollars' worth of military equipment bound for England was destroyed, and tens of thousands of windows shattered, when the equivalent of a 5.5 magnitude earthquake rocked New Jersey and New York and damaged the Statue of Liberty. As detailed above, it was the J.P. Morgan private intelligence network that provided security for dock facilities.

At the time, the massive explosion was blamed on sabotage by German agents determined not to let ammunition reach the Allies. However, investigations in the 1930s – with a view to damages claims against the German government – found evidence that Putzi Hanfstaengl had been involved and provided the saboteurs with the dynamite to destroy the depot.[28]

If Putzi was involved in the Black Tom explosion, it was on behalf of Anglo-American Intelligence, not German. A false flag attack in which Germany was blamed, it helped turn American public opinion in favour of war with Germany. Did fellow agent Aleister Crowley assist Putzi in the Black Tom sabotage? They certainly knew each other and both were closely linked to Belle Greene. According to Putzi biographer, Peter Conradi, it was not Belle who introduced Putzi to Aleister Crowley, but a man named Frank Harris.[29]

Frank Harris is another individual worthy of some attention. Born in Ireland, his father was a British naval officer. Frank was sent to boarding school but ran away aged 13 and made his way to America. He spent time as a cowboy before attending Kansas University and gaining a law degree. On returning to Britain he became a journalist and dramatist expert on Shakespeare and befriended Oscar Wilde and George Bernard Shaw. Harris also edited the *London Evening News* which was owned by Lord Northcliffe, the virulent Germanophobe newspaper magnate who was a major source of British propaganda and anti-German lies during the First World War (Northcliffe also purchased *The Times*, which was effectively the mouthpiece of the Milner Group.) From 1894 to 1898 Frank Harris also edited a weekly magazine, *The Saturday Review of Politics, Literature, Science, and Art*, which amongst other things carried a series of articles in 1895-97 stating that *Germania est delenda* (Germany must be destroyed). Interestingly, Frank Harris was a guest at Winston Churchill's wedding in 1908.[30]

Harris

Frank Harris was a friend of Churchill's, and in another example of wheels within wheels, so too was Putzi. His biographer, Peter Conradi, tells us so[31] but gives no information whatsoever as to how or when that friendship arose. Strange indeed given that Churchill became one of the most famous names in history. Their friendship possibly arose through a family connection. Churchill's mother, Jennie Jerome, was a Boston Brahmin like Putzi's Sedgwick forebears. Putzi often travelled to Britain[32] where his brother ran the gallery on Pall Mall, and may have befriended Churchill at that time.

Irrespective of the Putzi-Churchill-Harris link, in New York during the First World War, Frank Harris professed anti-English and pro-German sympathies. Like Aleister Crowley, it was a ruse.to win the confidence of the Germans, and it succeeded with Harris helping Crowley penetrate the German spy circles in the city.[33]

Crowley researcher Steve Jackson relates that Crowley received sponsorship for his intelligence work from the J.P. Morgan Company, and that another agent of British Intelligence was a man named John Quinn.[34]

John , yet another friend and confidant of Belle Greene,[35] had a law degree and a degree in international relations from Harvard. He was

an extremely wealthy second generation Irish-American lawyer in New York, and an avid art collector. He had one of the largest private collections of modern art in the world and it is possible that he befriended Putzi either through the art scene or via their mutual friend Belle Greene. Quinn sponsored the work of Putzi's good friend from Harvard days, the famous poet T.S. Eliot, and was the very first man Aleister Crowley went to see when he stepped ashore in New York in October 1914. Like Crowley and Harris, Quinn professed to have Irish republican sympathies, but acted as a British agent and Crowley's temporary case officer.[36]

Quinn

Putzi Hanfstaengl was not simply an outsider who just happened to be passively connected to all of these individuals involved in the murky world of Anglo-American secret intelligence, spying, and false flag outrages, he was one of them. Crowley, Harris, and Quinn managed to persuade German Intelligence linked to their consulate in New York that they were Irish republicans who detested England and supported Germany. Putzi, despite his failure to return and fight for Germany, successfully convinced them he was a loyal German doing what he could to support the Fatherland. Maintaining that deception was especially important for Putzi throughout his years in New York. Anglo-American Intelligence leaders in New York were aware that any verbal support for Germany that he uttered was a ruse to hoodwink German Intelligence. Ordinary New Yorkers, however, saw only a huge, wealthy, 'German' strutting his stuff around his gallery and the posh Harvard Club when 'Germans' were killing Americans.

In October 1915 in a speech in New York, Theodore Roosevelt, pro-claimed: "There is not room in this country for hyphenated Americanism. Our allegiance must be purely to the United States. We must unsparingly condemn any man who holds any other allegiance." Roosevelt knew, of course, that his friend Putzi's allegiance lay with the United States and that any pro-German utterances were part of the charade. Others weren't so fortunate. In Illinois a German-American coalminer, Robert Pager, was lynched by a mob of some 300 men when he voiced pro-German senti-ments. No one was ever charged with his murder.[37]

James W. Gerard, Justice of the New York Supreme Court, declared:

> If there are any German Americans here who are so ungrateful for all the benefits they have received that they are still for the Kai-ser, there is only one thing to do with them. And that is to hog-tie them, give them back the wooden shoes and the rags they landed in, and ship them back to the Fatherland.'[38]

AMERICA GOES TO WAR

On 4 April 1917 when the United States declared war on Germany, German nationals in the country were classified as "aliens." Two large and two small internment camps were set up across the country, with several thousand German-Americans incarcerated for the duration of the war. They included 29 musicians from the Boston Symphony Or-chestra and its famous musical director, Karl Muck. Muck was interned on the basis of a false allegation that he had refused the orchestra permis-sion to play the Star-Spangled Banner when the US entered the war.

What chance then did Putzi stand of retaining his freedom when a letter was sent to the authorities by a member of the Roosevelt clan stating that he posed a dangerous threat to the United States? Nicholas Roosevelt, a Har-vard alumnus and first cousin once removed of Theodore Roosevelt, wrote:

> I have known Mr Hanfstaengl for many years and while I have not seen him since May of last year, I know him to be violently anti-American; to have been in close touch with the German em-bassy before it left; to be highly intelligent and an almost fanatical supporter of his fatherland. In consequence, I consider him a most dangerous man to have about, and in fact believe he would be best off on Ellis Island.[39]

Despite the strongly worded letter from a member of one of America's leading families, Putzi was not arrested, questioned, or taken into detention as an undesirable alien. In reality, the condemnatory letter was not a betrayal by his Roosevelt friends, but part of the official intrigues to build Putzi's cover for the day he was sent on his mission to Germany. The Roosevelt letter was ultimately for German eyes. Such accusations played a vital role in validating an undercover agent's story, and Putzi could have no better evidence of his 'love for Germany' when he returned there than the extreme denunciation by the mighty Roosevelts: he was 'violently anti-American' and 'fanatically supported' Germany.

The official narrative around this hugely serious Roosevelt charge relates that it was only thanks to Putzi's lawyer friend, Elihu Root, that he retained his freedom following the letter. Root was at very top of the legal profession, the most expensive attorney in the United States, and a major player for the Wall Street banking elite. Among his clients were some of the richest men in the world, including Andrew Carnegie and J.P. Morgan. Yet here in the midst of a war between the United States and Germany, Root was representing a 'dangerous' German who was 'violently anti-American,' and supposedly saving him from internment.

Like Putzi, Elihu Root was a close friend of Theodore Roosevelt's and undoubtedly knew Putzi from the president's regular parties at the White House and later at Sagamore Hill. Root was a rabidly anti-German war hawk and leading proponent of the US entering the war who would gladly have seen Putzi locked up in an internment camp had he not known his real standing as a loyal American intelligence agent. Root publicly declared that the war must continue until final victory no matter the peace proposals emanating from Germany. Professor Quigley considered Root to be an important player for Wall Street and part of the "system of influence" centred on the J.P. Morgan offices at 23 Wall Street.[40]

The Roosevelt letter was but a small part of the great machiavellian game that was being played. Putzi would have a copy of the letter as cover for his return to Germany and for getting closely involved with Hitler. He would, of course, need a feasible excuse if Hitler or his brownshirt thugs asked why he was not interned because of the damning letter. Hitler by then would most assuredly have known that the US authorities had interned many members of the Boston Symphony Orchestra simply for being German, so why not Putzi?

The official narrative around the Roosevelt letter relates that Putzi was allowed to retain his liberty after promising not to indulge in anti-American activities. As anti-German sentiment mounted in the US along with the Doughboy casualties, however, the authorities had to be seen to be taking *some* action against him. He relates that the Alien Property Custodian seized his Fifth Avenue gallery and would later sell off his artwork stock for a fraction of its worth. Putzi estimated its value at $500,000 (over $12 million at today's worth) but was sold for only $8,000.[41]

Putzi's whitewash memoir states that when the war ended, he was allowed to open another gallery – 'The Academy Art Shop' – on West Fifty-seventh Street opposite the Carnegie Hall. Professor Richard Spence gives a different account, stating that although the Hanfstaengl gallery on Fifth Avenue was taken over by the U.S. Alien Property Custodian in 1917, "Putzi continued to run it without apparent interference."[42]

Helene

In January 1920 Putzi met Helene Niemeyer, the daughter of a German businessman who had emigrated from Bremen in the 19th century. Just weeks later they married. Like Putzi, Helene was of mixed German-American origin, though she was born and raised in the US. One year after the marriage their son, Egon, was born and they moved shortly thereafter to Germany. According to Putzi, "I really felt it was time to return home."[43]

Putzi spent the best part of fourteen very happy and comfortable years in the United States, ten of them in New York City which was now enjoying something of a post-war boom. He had many important friends in high places and the future looked bright, yet he moved his new family to the broken, humiliated, and financially ruined Germany and we are asked to accept that it was due to nostalgia. His brother Edgar, who survived the war, had taken over the business in Germany and made it clear to Putzi that there would be no job for him if he returned to Germany.[44]

In reality, Putzi was not interested in a position with Edgar in the family business, or with anyone else. He was going to Munich on a mission for the Anglo-American intelligence services and, as we shall see, was clearly very well remunerated. At Hoboken on 5 July 1921, Putzi, Helene, and baby Egon boarded the liner *Amerika* bound for Bremerhaven.

The mood and state of the country they stepped into was grim. Broken and riven by destitution and political factions, and with stable government non-existent, post-war Germany sank into an orgy of political violence with some 400 political assassinations, most of which went unsolved and unpunished. Hundreds of thousands of women, children and elderly had starved to death, and those who survived were sick, bewildered and apathetic. Soup kitchens struggled to feed even the once well-off middle classes, and poverty stalked the demoralised masses.

> People watched helplessly as their life savings disappeared and their loved ones starved. Germany's finances descended into chaos, with severe social unrest in its wake.[45]

Putzi and Helene found a marked scarcity of staple foods. Milk for their hungry child was almost impossible to come by. Putzi later wrote that he felt a stranger in an even stranger land where the overwhelming characteristic of the people was "apathy and lack of self-respect." Politics had hopelessly split into a confusing number of parties vying for power, and Putzi considered "Germany a tame bear, sick, bewildered, being led about by scheming tricksters."[46] The situation for the masses was bad when they arrived, and was soon to get a lot worse with the disastrous hyperinflation that was taking off. Barely six weeks after their arrived, the financial meltdown started in earnest when the victorious Allies began sucking gold out of the country.

> On 31 August 1921, Germany paid her *first* billion gold marks of reparations. The transfer was a veritable ordeal: the money was raised by pawning with the international banking network thousands of tons of silver and gold, which were conveyed by caravans of railroad boxcars to Switzerland, Denmark and Holland, and by a fleet of steamers to the United States. The first remittance caused an immediate drop of the mark vis-à-vis the dollar, from 60 to 100 (marks per dollar).... The hyperinflation was approaching.[47]

Exactly as planned, the reparations led to worsening hunger, deep discontent, and increasing political chaos. The ensuing hyperinflation tearing the German economy apart gave rise to numerous radical and nationalist political factions, including that from which Hitler emerged. (The economic crisis generated by the Allies and how they manipulated Germany through it, is discussed in detail in chapter 19.)

Putzi and Helene were allowed time to settle in Munich and made no move to return from the stricken Germany to the now booming United States. Undoubtedly, their many influential friends and extended American families would have welcomed them back on the next ship, but Putzi was on an important mission and he intended to fulfil it. There was to be no reconciliation with his surviving brother, Edgar, but he saw his widowed mother regularly. Putzi made regular visits to the US embassy in Berlin, where his close friend from Harvard and Hasty Pudding Club days, Warren Delano Robbins – cousin to his other close friend, Franklin Delano Roosevelt, was second in command. Robbins was privy to the true reason for Putzi's return to Germany, as was his boss, Alanson B. Houghton, the U.S. Ambassador to Germany. Houghton was yet another Harvard graduate, wealthy industrialist, and member of the exclusive Jekyll Island club with J.P. Morgan and Rockefeller.

In November 1922, Warren Delano Robbins telephoned to tell Putzi that the assistant military attaché at the embassy, Captain Truman Smith, was on his way to Munich for a week to meet some people. After that, Truman Smith would like to discuss matters with Putzi. Like most if not all military attachés based at embassies, Truman Smith was an intelligence agent. A Yale graduate and member of the American patrician class, he had Puritan ancestors in Massachusetts dating back to the 17th century. They had founded the town of Groton where Endicott Peabody later opened his feeder school for Harvard. One of Truman Smith's grandfathers  was a U.S. senator from Connecticut, another was a wealthy stockbroker on Wall Street. Smith's father-in-law was similarly successful on Wall Street. Smith's friend was married to Allen Dulles, a very important player in the stitch-up of Germany at Versailles in 1919 and the man who would later become head of the CIA. Wheels within wheels as ever, and Truman Smith was a committed member of the Anglo-American conspiracy. He would later give a whitewash account of his visit to Munich in November 1922:

> Ambassador Houghton had been observing with interest and some trepidation the rise of a new German political group in Munich which called itself the National Socialist Party. Mr. Houghton thought that I was the appropriate member of staff to go to Munich, interview the party's leader, Adolf Hitler, and evaluate the present and future importance of National Socialism and its leader.[48]

As Professor Guido Preparata explained, in the immediate post-war years, the all-conquering Anglo-American cabal was seeking a reactionary party and leader in Germany that they could manipulate into power in preparation for another war on Russia.[49] The rabble-rousing corporal

Hitler and his tiny Nazi party had appeared on their radar as possible contenders for the role, hence Truman Smith's visit to assess him.

> The principal purpose of the visit was to assess the reported developing strength of the National Socialist movement. Although foreign diplomats in Berlin generally regarded this movement as being without significance and its leader, Adolf Hitler, as an uneducated madman, Mr. Houghton seems to have had, even at this early date, a premonition that the movement and its leader might play an important role in the disturbed Germany of the early twenties. The ambassador and Colonel Davis suggested to Captain Smith, before his departure from Berlin, that he try to make personal contact with Hitler himself and form an estimate of his character, personality, abilities and weaknesses. He was also instructed to obtain estimates of Hitler's ability and his party's strength and potentialities from representative Bavarian politicians, newspapermen, and army officers. The Bavaria of November 1922, and especially its capital, Munich, was a cockpit of political intrigue.... For a brief period in 1919, control of the city and the Bavarian government had been seized by the Communists. This revolt had been put down by the German military forces, but only after considerable bloodshed. By November 1922, Bavaria had turned politically far to the right. Munich was by this time the operating centre for a number of societies, all proclaiming nationalist and ultrapatriotic objectives. Hitler's National Socialist Party was by all means the most active and dynamic of these societies.[50]

Doubtless the Anglo-American elites were assessing other reactionary organisations and their leaders, but Ambassador Houghton's supposed 'premonition' about Hitler sealed Germany's fate. Arriving in Munich by train on 15 November, Truman Smith sought the views of the US consul, Robert Murphy, who would later move on to a senior position in US intelligence. Smith also had lengthy discussions with Crown Prince Ruprecht, General Ludendorff, Count Lerchenfeld (the Bavarian prime minister), and Adolf Hitler himself. Historian Milan Hauner writes:

> 20 November 1922: The U.S. Assistant Military Attaché, Captain Truman Smith, meets Hitler in Munich. The latter skilfully underlines his anti-Marxism and plays down his anti-Semitism. Hitler tells Smith that his movement is "a union of manual and brain workers to oppose Marxism." As for reparations, these must be paid, since it is a question of German honour, but they must first

be reduced to "a realistic sum."... "Parliament and parliamentarian-
ism must go ... only a dictatorship can bring Germany to its feet."
The USA and England should realize that it is much better that "the
decisive struggle between our civilization and Marxism be fought
on German soil. The USA must therefore help Nationalist Germany against Bolshevism." Finally, Hitler denounces the institution of
monarchy in Germany as an absurdity and declares that he wants
an understanding with France and not a war of revenge.[51]

The Milner Group and Wall Street banking associates could hardly
have asked for better. Here was the very man, the reactionary they were
looking for, to lead a dictatorship and Germany into another disastrous
war with Russia. Once they selected Hitler, their every effort would be
focussed on promoting him and the Nazis for power. Putzi Hanfstaengl
was about to be called into action and would play a leading role in that.
The Hoover Institution at Stanford later published Truman Smith's memoirs and reports in a book titled *Berlin Alert.* Following his meeting with
Hitler, Smith had written a few notes that same night.

Outside of the notes, only two memories of this meeting with Hitler
on November 20, 1922, have come down to Captain Smith over the years.
He remembers that the room in the house where Hitler received him
[Georgen Strasse 42] was drab and dreary beyond belief, akin to a back
bedroom in a decaying New York tenement. He also remembers distinctly that each time he asked a question of Hitler, it was as if he had pressed
a gramophone switch which set off a full-length speech. In consequence,
the interview lasted hours and covered many topics. No memory remains
with the author as to the identity of Hitler's aide present at the interview.
However, Mr. Ernst [Putzi] Hanfstaengl, in whose company Captain
Smith spent most of the following day, was rather certain that Smith had
told him at the time that the aide was Alfred Rosenberg. It is felt rather
surely that this was the first interview of any American diplomat with the
future führer. It is also thought that it was the second talk of any Western
diplomat with Hitler, Smith's interview following closely on the heels of
a British Control Commission officer, Colonel Stewart Roddie, who had
seen and talked with Hitler just a few weeks earlier.[52]

Prior to Truman Smith being sent by the American embassy to assess
Hitler, a leading British intelligence officer had been despatched to do
likewise. Perhaps the British also had an astonishing 'premonition'? Inso-
far as we are aware, no record of Colonel Roddie's report on his meeting
with Hitler has ever seen the light of day. Doubtless other candidates were

assessed but Hitler's oratory skills were unmatched, and he fitted the Milner Group's requirements almost to a tee. Putzi wrote:

> The Nazis were only one of numerous Right Wing radical organizations flourishing in Bavaria at the time, In fact, apart from the trump card they held in Hitler, they were by no means the most numerous or important. Bavaria had become the refuge of a whole rat-bag collection of militant nationals ... [53]

The Anglo-American intelligence services operated in close harmony in post-war Germany just as they did in the United States of America. With constant feedback between the two from agents such as Truman Smith and Stewart Roddie, Smith's formal report on Hitler was forwarded to the Military Intelligence Division of the General Staff in Washington on 25 November 1922.[54] Almost certainly the heads of Intelligence in London and Washington compared Stewart Roddie's and Truman Smith's reports on Hitler and came to an agreement that he fitted the bill. Their joint assessment would, of course, be passed further up the pecking order.

After his long meeting with Hitler, Truman Smith spent the following day with Putzi, telling him that Hitler was a "most remarkable fellow" who was "going to play a big part."[55] When Putzi accompanied Smith to the station to see him off on the Berlin train, leading Nazi party member, Alfred Rosenberg, was there to do likewise, and Smith introduced Putzi to him.

The next move was to get Putzi introduced to Hitler. He was scheduled to speak that same evening in the *Salvatorkeller*, and as if by magic, Truman Smith presented Putzi with a Nazi party Press pass to attend. He would be doing so as a representative of the American embassy (read US intelligence) and not in a private capacity.

At the beer-hall that night, Putzi sat at the Press table no more than 3 metres from where lance-corporal Hitler stood at the podium haranguing Jews, Communists, and Socialists as "enemies of the people" who would one day be *beseitigt* (removed or done away with).[56] When Hitler finished his

Poster announcing Hitler's meeting at Salvatorkeller where Putzi first met him

poisonous rant and the enthusiastic crowd made their way to the exits, Putzi approached the podium and introduced himself:

> Herr Hitler, my name is Hanfstaengl, Captain Truman Smith asked me to give you his best wishes. "Ah, yes, the big American" he answered. He begged me to come here and listen to you, and I can only say I have been most impressed. I agree with 95 per cent of what you said and would very much like to talk to you about the rest sometime. "Why, yes, of course," Hitler said, "I am sure we shall not have to quarrel about the odd five per cent." He made a very pleasant impression, modest and friendly. So we shook hands again and I went home.[57]

Several nights later, Putzi took Helene and some friends to hear Hitler speak at a Nazi party meeting in the Zircus Krone. Putzi had been impressed the first time he heard Hitler speak, but much less so now when he sat further back in the large crowd.

> The distance reduced the strength and magnetic appeal of Hitler's voice and made the whole thing more impersonal, more like reading a newspaper.[58]

Putzi later wrote that at the time his only thought, day in, day out, was where he could find material, models, suggestions and ideas for Hitler – ideas that would help him widen his emotional appeal. Hitler was a good speaker, but Putzi knew he could help him become a "great speaker." He wrote:

> Afterwards we went up and I introduced the ladies to Hitler. He was delighted with my wife, who was blond and beautiful and American. He accepted very readily when she said how pleased we would be if he would come to coffee or dinner at the flat. Soon he was visiting us frequently, pleasant and unassuming in his little blue serge suit.[59]

Hitler may have considered himself street-wise, but he swallowed the bait hook, line and sinker. He did not know it, but from that point in time he and his Nazi thugs would have the backing of some of the wealthiest and most powerful people on the planet. Regarding the funding of Hitler and the Nazis, in his memoirs Putzi innocently makes out that he had "no ideas where the Party revenues came from."[60]

The sophisticated and charming Putzi Hanfstaengl, friend of royalty, US presidents, and some of the richest men in the world, had nothing whatsoever in common with the socially awkward, friendless misfit who walked the streets of Munich in a dirty old trench coat, with a German Shepherd dog called 'Wolf' on a lead. Hitler lived alone in a tiny, grubby, rented room on the Thiersch Strasse in Munich where the floor was covered in cheap, worn linoleum and a couple of threadbare rugs. A makeshift shelf was screwed to the wall and an old chair and rough table were the only furnishings. His landlady found him a "nice man" but a "sulking" individual who for weeks would not say a word and never, ever spoke about his younger days.

> The Hanfstaengl household was the first to try to make Hitler socially acceptable ... and in these early years theirs was almost the only private circle in which he found himself at ease.[61]

Hitler quickly latched onto the Hanfstaengls as his surrogate family, frequently dining and socialising at their nice apartment in Munich. He enjoyed playing on the floor with young Egon and became the boy's godfather. Putzi relates that Hitler was infatuated with Helene. With an adoring look in his eyes he would bring her flowers, kiss her hands, and when she lounged on the sofa he sat on the floor at her feet with his head resting against her legs. Teased about this by Putzi, Helene laughed it off, insisting that Hitler was 'a neuter' with no sex life.

Hitler greatly enjoyed Putzi playing the piano, especially Wagner's *Meistersinger,* and *Lohengrin.* "I must have played them hundreds of times for him and he never grew tired of them." Hitler knew every nuance of the music from his young days in Vienna and, utterly enthralled, would march up and down the room waving his arms as though conducting an orchestra. Putzi also played popular modern football marches that he had either picked up at Harvard or composed himself.

I explained to Hitler all the business about cheer leaders and marches, counter marches and deliberate whipping up of hysterical enthusiasm. I told him about the thousands of spectators being made to roar 'Harvard, Harvard, Harvard, rah, rah, rah!' in unison and of the hypnotic effect of this sort of thing. I played him some of the Sousa marches and then my own Falarah, to show how it could be done by adapting German tunes and gave them all the buoyant beat so characteristic of American brass-band music. I had Hitler fairly shouting with enthusiasm. "That is it, Hanfstaengl, that is what we need for the movement, marvellous," and he pranced up and down the room like a drum majorette. After that he had the S.A. band practicing the same thing. I even wrote a dozen marches or so myself over the course of the years, including the one that was played by the brownshirt columns as they marched through the Brandenburg Tor on the day he took over power. Rah, rah, rah! Became Sieg Heil, Sieg Heil! But that is the origin of it and I suppose I must take my share of the blame.[62]

Putzi did much more than entertain the lonely Hitler. The little corporal undoubtedly had innate oratory skills that only became apparent after the war, but Putzi coached him on breathing techniques, emphasis and pace of speech, and how to address an audience with clarity, confidence, and impact.

> The man was open to influence and I felt encouraged to continue exerting all I could … I told him of the effective use in American political life of telling catch-phrases and explained how this was buttressed by snappy headlines in the newspapers, putting ideas over with a phonetic, alliterative impact.[63]

Putzi's mission was to polish this rough diamond, this gruff political agitator with no social graces and a 'really quite pathetic appearance'. Putzi was ideal for the job – a man who was never short of ideas and suggestions that would help Hitler widen his emotional appeal to the middle classes, and appear closer to a statesman than his present drab vagabond-like self. In his acting days in Hasty Pudding Theatricals at Harvard, Putzi had learned how important a strong stance and descriptive hand gestures were to the impact of

a performance. He advised Hitler on the importance of voice projection and proper hand movement to draw attention to what he was saying and to emphasise important parts of his speeches. Putzi assured Hitler that an active speaker left a better impression on an audience than someone who was awkward or inactive with his hands.

With Putzi's guidance, Hitler practised the public speaking techniques, and the simultaneous wildly exaggerated arm gestures he became famous for. To an extent, it was thanks to Putzi that he was now on the road to becoming the persuasive orator and firebrand able to whip massive audiences into a frenzy.

Putzi claimed later that the chant 'Sieg Heil' – and the accompanying arm movement – that became a feature of Nazi rallies was a copy of the technique used by football cheerleaders. Putzi would also have known the straight-arm salute from the United States. In his time there some schoolchildren were taught to use the gesture to salute the American flag and pledge allegiance.[64] It was also on Putzi's initiative that the Nazis began to use American college-style music at political rallies to excite the crowds.[65]

As Hitler's wild-eyed gesturing 'performances' improved, attendances at meetings grew ever larger. Putzi could do no wrong in Hitler's eyes, but it wasn't simply down to teaching him stage presence or playing his favourite music, for the 'big American' was providing hard cash. But where did the money Putzi was 'donating' to the Nazis come from? Putzi says in his 'autobiography' that he was forced to sell the art work in New York at a fraction of its true worth, leaving him and Helene in difficult financial circumstances. He officially had no job or salary, and his brother Edgar who now owned the German gallery had disowned him. Yet Putzi was somehow able to provide important funding to the Nazi party's newspaper, the *Völkischer Beobachter* (People's Observer), turning it from a modest four-page once or twice week-ly newspaper into an influential full-size dai-ly. Even *The Times* of London reported:

> At a time when many newspapers in Germany have been forced to cease publication, and others, owing to the enormous cost of production, [hyperinflation in Germany] are only able to continue with difficulty, Herr Hitler's paper, the *Völkischer Beobachter*, has been doubled in size, and with one exception is now the largest daily paper published in Bavaria.[66]

And how was Putzi able to purchase outright a magnificent house in Herzogpark, the most fashionable part of Munich? He relates that he bought the house with money received as the last payment of his liqui-dated Hanfstaengl interests in America. Perhaps, but he relates elsewhere that those assets had been sold off for a pittance. One might reasonably ask if the money actually came from his Anglo-American friends in the financial elite.

Putzi bought the house with its large and beautifully manicured gar-dens from Duchess Vallombrosa who had been married to the affluent American artist Walter Goldbeck. The sale came complete with a house full of fine antique furniture, important paintings, drawings and thou-sands of books. Most of the treasures in the house were in the library, a huge room that had been Goldbeck's studio where he painted the walls with figures of the Madonna and saints and angels. There was a Stein-way grand piano on which sat a terracotta bust of Benjamin Franklin by Jean-Antoine Houdon, preeminent neoclassical sculptor of the French Enlightenment.

Together with a country house in Uffing, south of Munich, Putzi now owned two homes in Germany. In addition, he would later acquire a mag-nificent town house close to the Reichstag building in Berlin. Helene had another child, a daughter, who did not survive infancy. Hitler was a frequent visitor at the grand Herzogpark house, and it was there that Putzi brought him into contact with people of some standing. They included William Bayard Hale, a classmate and friend of President Wilson at Princeton. Hale was now the chief European correspondent of Hearst newspapers, which were owned by Putzi's friend William Randolph Hearst. Putzi organised regular meetings between Hitler and Hale at the Hotel Bayerischer Hof in central Munich, and Hale (and Hearst) churned out propaganda on Hitler's behalf. Throughout 1923, with Putzi almost constantly by his side, Hitler addressed meetings across Munich and beyond, repeatedly singling out Jews as the chief enemies of the German nation. The party newspaper also went into overdrive.

> 8 February 1923: *Völkischer Beobachter* begins to appear daily instead of twice a week thanks to Hanfstaengl's $1,000 contribution [worth a great deal more today], which enables Hitler to buy two American rotary presses. During this period, Hanfstaengl becomes Hitler's most constant companion and introduces him to the wealthy industrialists in Munich. Hitler also feels drawn to Hanfstaengl's beautiful wife, Helene, and their children. His own private life remains spartan: he continues to live in a small, shabby sublet at 41 Thierschstrasse, which he shares with an Alsatian dog named Wolf.[67]

By the summer of 1923, Hitler was drawing crowds of 8,000 and more to his weekly meetings, and had 4,000 brownshirts marching around the streets under swastika banners and behind a Nazi band. He told the many gatherings that he embraced Eugenics (as was being promoted in Britain and the USA) and would forbid mixed marriages of the races. There would be no room in the German state for the alien, the criminal, the physically tainted, the diseased, the wastrel, the usurer, or anyone incapable of productive work. He now openly talked of a revolutionary march on Berlin to seize power – like Mussolini's successful march on Rome in October the previous year.

Through October and early November 1923, Putzi, Hitler, and other leading Nazis discussed an armed uprising to seize power in Germany. On the bitterly cold evening of 8 November 1923, Hitler and Putzi stuffed pistols into their coat pockets and went along to a public meeting organised by the Bavarian political authorities in the massive Bürgerbräukeller in Munich. They walked in and stood drinking beer to the side of the crowd of 3,000 while the Bavarian State Commissioner, Gustav von Kahr addressed the crowd. 20 minutes into Kahr's boring speech, the audience

was startled to hear the deep rumbling of heavy trucks and the clatter of hundreds of steel studded boots on the streets outside. Dozens of Nazi brownshirts suddenly burst in through the doors waving pistols and machine-guns, while hundreds more sealed off the streets outside. Handing Putzi his beer stein and, with his bodyguard at his back, Hitler strutted towards von Kahr, jumped up on a chair and silenced the crowd by firing his pistol into the ceiling. He roared:

> The national revolution has broken out. The *Reichswehr* [army] is with us. Our flag is flying on their barracks.[68]

Hitler was either misinformed or lying, for the majority of *Reichswehr* units refused to join the putschists. When Hitler and his armed gang advanced down the road through flurries of snow to the Feldhernhalle on Odeonsplatz the following morning, the police and army who remained loyal to the government had set up roadblocks, and gunfire was exchanged. Several police officers and 16 putschists were killed and many wounded. Hitler was pulled to the ground, injuring his shoulder. Extricated from the bloody scene by bodyguards, he was driven to Putzi's country house at Uffing, an hour's drive south of Munich. As prearranged, Helene was waiting there. She tended to Hitler and hid him in an attic bedroom. Putzi gives a strangely vague account of the events, saying he was separated from Hitler before the march on the Feldhernhalle and when the shooting began he escaped over the border to Kufstein in Austria. It might reasonably be speculated that he had quietly informed the authorities of the march on the Feldhernhalle and had then cleared out before the bullets started flying.

The following day, when police were tipped off (by persons unknown) about Hitler's whereabouts, several truckloads of police officers duly arrived at Putzi's house to arrest him. Putzi later stated that when he heard them coming, Hitler drew his pistol intending to commit suicide, but he (Putzi) had taught Helene ju-jitsu and she managed to wrench the gun from his hand. Hitler was arrested and charged with high treason. Virtually unknown outside Munich, Hitler now made the headlines in newspapers across the world. Putzi turned up in Munich several weeks later but neither he nor Helene were ever arrested or charged with aiding Hitler.

The trial began on 26 February 1924, before the People's Court in Munich. One month later, in his closing speech at the trial Hitler rejected the claim that he was led by ambition when he staged the *putsch*:

How petty are the thoughts of small men! My aim, from the very first day, was a thousand times more than becoming a minister. What I wanted to become was the destroyer of Marxism. This is my task, and I know when I settle this question – which I will – then the title of minister will become ridiculous ... I believe the time will come when the masses which today stand with our swastika flag on the streets will join forces with those who fired on us on 9 November ... that the hour will come when the Reichswehr soldiers will stand on our side ... It is not you esteemed gentlemen who will pass the ultimate verdict on us ... but the eternal court of history.[69]

On 1 April the Court passed sentence on Hitler and his co-defendants. The state prosecutor demanded an eight year term of imprisonment, but he got a five-year custodial sentence in Landsberg prison 40 miles south of Munich and would serve less than a year. The National-Socialist Party was dissolved by decree after the putsch. The treatment Hitler and other Nazi leaders received in Landsberg was akin to that of a five-star hotel, with flowers and huge food parcels arriving daily. It was described as being more like an exclusive delicatessen than a prison, with meats, fine cheeses, chocolates and expensive wines everywhere. When the jailers approached Hitler's room, they announced their arrival with a cheery cry of 'Heil Hitler.'[70] Higher powers were clearly looking after the chosen one.

Enjoying life in Landsberg Prison

According to official accounts, Hitler wrote the first volume of *Mein Kampf* (My Struggle) in Landsberg prison. It told of the need for Germans to seek *Lebensraum* (living space) in the East at the expense of the Slavs and the hated Bolsheviks, and identified Aryans as the "genius" race and Jews as the "parasites":

> People who can sneak their way, like parasites, into the human body politic and make others work for them under various pretences can form a State without possessing any definite delimited territory. This is chiefly applicable to that parasitic nation which particularly at the present time, preys upon the honest portion of mankind. I mean the Jew.[71]

Putzi visited Hitler regularly in prison over the 11 months he served of the five-year sentence, and he apparently played a significant part in the proof reading, if not indeed the writing, of *Mein Kampf*. Putzi himself relates that Hitler had given him parts of the manuscript and asked him to 'correct them'. He "readily agreed."

> It was really frightful stuff. I suppose I did not see more than the first seventy pages or so, but already his impossible political premises were evident and, quite apart from that, the style filled me with horror ... I set to work ...[72]

If Putzi did indeed "set to work" on *Mein Kampf*, it is possible, indeed likely, that he in turn would have been fed instructions regarding its contents and tone from Anglo-American financial hierarchy. It is not such an outlandish suggestion, for Hitler was being funded, groomed, and guided by them in many other ways.

Hitler trusted Putzi implicitly and they remained firm friends throughout his imprisonment. On his release from Landsberg on 20 December 1924, Hitler immediately made his way to Putzi's house in the brand-new Mercedes he had ordered while in prison. Money was now clearly no object. The once penniless vagabond was still very much in the foreign elite's plan and was being given a taste for the good life. Arriving at Putzi's door that day, little Egon greeted 'Uncle Dolf' with glee.

Hitler spent Christmas Day 1924 with the Hanfstaengls. Putzi played Christmas carols, but Hitler did not join in the singing and appeared depressed and genuinely at a loss as to what he should do next. "What now?" he asked Putzi. "You will go on," Putzi replied, "Your party still lives." He played the last part of the third act of Tristan und Isolde and the gloomy Hitler was instantly buoyed.[73]

Summary: Chapter 17 – Agent Hanfstaengl "Befriends" Hitler

- Putzi Hanfstaengl moved to New York in 1911 to run the family art gallery on Fifth Avenue and many famous individuals called in to see him.

- When war broke out in 1914, Hanfstaengl made no effort to fight for Germany. His brothers back home enlisted in the German army and two of them were killed.

- Many of Putzi's friends and associates in New York were secret agents of the closely cooperating Anglo-American intelligence services. His friend Franklin Delano Roosevelt, Assistant Secretary of the Navy, had his own 'super-secret' intelligence network.

- J.P. Morgan had his own private intelligence organisation headed by Belle Greene who regularly visited Putzi. Other agents, Aleister Crowley, Frank Harris, John Reed, and John Quinn were also linked to Putzi.

- As an agent of Anglo-American intelligence, Putzi returned to Munich in 1921. The American embassy brought him into contact with Adolf Hitler, and the Hanfstaengls acted as a surrogate family to the friendless loner.

- Hitler's attempt to seize power in Germany in 1923 in the 'Beer Hall Putsch' in Munich failed, and he was sent to prison. Putzi visited Hitler regularly in Landsberg and assisted him in writing part 1 of his autobiography, *Mein Kampf*.

- On his release from prison in December 1924, Hitler's first port of call was Putzi's house.

CHAPTER 18

FIRE AND BRIMSTONE

When Hitler was released from Landsberg Prison, Putzi advised him he should inform the government that he had moderated his views or the party might be banned indefinitely.[1] On 4 January 1925, Hitler went to see the new Bavarian prime minister, Heinrich Held, to tell him that he considered the putsch to have been a serious mistake. If Held released the other Nazi party members still held in Landsberg, they would do what they could to help him consolidate his power. Held naively took Hitler at his word, telling the Justice Minister, Franz Gürtner: "The wild beast is checked, we can afford to loosen the chain."[2] Weeks later, the emergency legislation banning the Nazi party and the *Völkischer Beobachter* was lifted.

On 27 Febr3uary, Hitler held a meeting at the Bürgerbräukeller – the scene of the putsch 15 months earlier. In this first speech after his release he declared the Nazi Party to be reconstituted, and yet again ranted about the dangers of Jews 'poisoning' pure Aryan blood. He ended by throwing down a challenge to the government:

> If anyone comes and wants to impose conditions on me, I shall say to him: "Just wait my little friend, and see what conditions I impose on you" ... I alone lead the Movement and no one can impose conditions on me.[3]

The authorities responded by banning Hitler from making public speeches. He complied, but continued to address closed party meetings. President Friedrich Ebert died of septicaemia at the age of 54 on 28 February 1925, and the national election to elect a new President was held on 30 March. The Nazi party candidate, General Erich Ludendorff, received only 1 per cent of the popular vote. No candidate gained an absolute majority, and a second round of voting was held in April. Paul von Hindenburg (Chief of the Great General Staff during the war) who was opposed to Hitler and the Nazi party, won the Presidency.

Now 36 years old, Hitler addressed party meetings in several cities across Germany, but spent most of the summer at his cottage at Berchtesgaden in the Bavarian Alps writing the second part of *Mein Kampf*. Once again, Putzi was involved in editing it. Hitler relaxed by touring Bavaria in his chauffeur-driven Mercedes. The American Dawes Plan (discussed in the next chapter) poured massive bank loans into Germany and with inflation now under control and living standards for the masses now improving, the NSDAP was losing its appeal. After the attempt to seize power by force had failed miserably, Hitler told members that the party would now operate within the democratic process:

> "If outvoting them takes longer than outshooting them, at least the results will be guaranteed by their own Constitution! Any lawful process is slow. But sooner or later we shall have a majority – and after that Germany."[4]

Hitler continued speaking at party meetings across Germany, but entered what became known as his 'quiet years'. He later described it as one of the happiest times of his life. Putzi Hanfstaengl wrote:

> These of course were the years of his political eclipse. He was not allowed to speak [in public] anywhere and although he was slowly reorganizing the Party it was a very gradual process and he was making little real impact. Economic conditions were improving out of recognition with the flood of American capital which was streaming into the country and the apparent stabilizing of the Central Government.[5]

Putzi relates that he and Helene continued seeing Hitler and never lost their conviction that he would fight his way to the top in German politics.[6] While Hitler was relaxing in the back of his luxurious Mercedes, Putzi gained a PhD from Munich University with his thesis on eighteenth century Bavaria. He claims to have been 'really very short of money'[7] yet was able to continue living in the grand Herzogpark house full of expensive antiques and paintings. For now, Hitler decided to live in beautiful Berchtesgaden rather than his dingy room in Munich, with his widowed half-sister, Angela Raubal, and her two daughters coming to live with him as housekeepers. Hitler became totally infatuated with his 17 year-old niece, Geli.

On the political front, Hitler was convinced these more prosperous years wouldn't last and decided to quietly bide his time. Party membership stood at around 17,000 at this time, but he would build on that when the right time came along – "as it was sure to." It came in late October

1929 when, thanks to deliberate manipulation by the banking elites, the Wall Street stock market crashed with a worldwide economic collapse followed by the Great Depression. The improved living conditions seen in Germany over the last few years evaporated: companies went bankrupt and unemployment soared. Once again hunger haunted the masses, and Hitler judged that the time was ripe for a comeback. He would make no further attempts to seize power by force, for without the support of the army, another putsch was bound to fail. Despite detesting the democratic system, he would play it to broaden his appeal to the masses and build the party's electoral base.

In 1930, when the coalition governing Germany collapsed, parliament was dissolved, and elections were set for mid-September. Hitler and Putzi sprang into action with speeches virtually every day across the entire country. The September election gave the Nazi party 6.5 million votes (18.3 per cent of the vote) and 107 seats out of 577 in the Reichstag. (They had won only 12 seats in the 1928 election). Following the electoral successes, Hitler and Rudolf Hess called on Putzi at his home. He was 'flattered' to accept their invitation to take control of the foreign press department of the Party. Hitler strode up and down Putzi's library, assuring him that he would be "part of his closest entourage." Thereafter, Putzi arranged all foreign press interviews with Hitler and other leading Nazis, and some days he was receiving more than a hundred calls from journalists. Edgar Mowrer, Berlin correspondent of the *Chicago Daily News* wondered what the affable Putzi, "who spoke perfect English with an American accent and was blessed with a cultured New England mother," was doing mixing with Hitler. "He should have been Nazi-proof."[8] Had Mowrer learned the truth about Putzi being an American intelligence agent, he would have had one of the biggest Press scoops of the twentieth century.

Gaining 18.3 per cent of the vote in the election was a considerable success, and the Nazis were now the second largest party in the Reichstag after the Social Democratic Party (SPD). Hitler's ultimate aim, however, was not simply to achieve a majority in the Reichstag but to hold supreme power in a dictatorship. At a meeting in Munich just two days after the election he expressed his contempt for parliamentary democracy:

> For us Parliament is not an end in itself, but merely a means to an end.... We are not in principle a parliamentary party – that would be a contradiction of our whole outlook – we are a parliamentary party by compulsion.[9]

In Britain, the *Daily Mail* published an interview with Hitler in which he argued that the Treaty of Versailles would have to be "obliterated" if Europe was to be saved from communism. "If Europe decides to make Germany serve a life sentence, then it must face the danger of having an embittered nation.… The English and Germans cannot remain enemies forever … To have a strong party in Germany which will form a bulwark against Bolshevism is in the interests not only of England but also of all nations."[10]

With the recession deepening, Germany was in economic freefall, but the money fairies stepped in with their support for Hitler, and he was able to buy a luxury nine-roomed house at Prinzregentenplatz 16, one of the most expensive streets in Munich. The Party was also able to purchase a magnificent building, the former Barlow Palace, on Brienner

Strasse in central Munich. With no expense spared it was totally refurbished to form Party headquarters and named 'the Brown House' after the Nazi colours.

Hitler's sister Angela remained in Berchtesgaden with her daughter, Elfriede, looking after his house there, while his niece Geli moved in with him to the new abode on Prinzregentenplatz. On 18 September the following year (1931), Geli was found dead in the house with a bullet wound to the head. Rumours circulated that the 23 year-old had a blazing row with Hitler that morning and suffered a broken nose and other injuries in addition to the gunshot wound. The distraught Hitler dismissed the

stories, and her death was registered as suicide. Putzi wrote:

> I am sure the death of Geli Raubal marked a turning-point in the development of Hitler's character. This relationship, whatever form it took in their intimacy, had provided him for the first and only time in his life with a release to his nervous energy which only too soon was to find expression in ruthlessness and savagery.… I had been around a long time and still played the piano for Hitler.… I became a mem-

ber of the inner circle again, largely on personal grounds. After the crisis of Geli Raubal's suicide, Hitler seemed to suffer a temporary fit of nostalgia for the old days. His infatuation for my wife, which had never been entirely stilled, brought him increasingly into our lives again.[11]

Now titled 'Dr. Hanfstacngl,' Putzi was firmly back at Hitler's side after the lull of the 'quiet years'. In his capacity as an Anglo-American agent, he was not alone. In the early 1920s, British Intelligence had planted an agent, Baron William (Bill) Sylvester de Ropp, in Germany; he posed as a journalist for *The Times*. Like Putzi, he quickly gained access to Hitler and his inner circle.

WILLIAM DE ROPP

De Ropp was naturalised British, having served with the British forces in the First World War. After the war he had offered his services to British intelligence, and was first seen on 30 April 1919, after which he was taken on as an agent. He worked as a journalist in Germany and the Baltic States, and during the 1920's, coded '821,' he reported regularly on German political matters.[12]

Bill de Ropp, described as one of the most 'mysterious and influential clandestine operators' of the era,[13] was, like Putzi, a fluent German speaker, and like Putzi, he quickly infiltrated the Nazi party and became a close confidant of Adolf Hitler. From a Baltic German family, de Ropp's Prussian father was a baron who owned a small estate in Lithuania, formerly part of the Russian empire. His mother was a Cossack from the Crimea. Born in Lithuania in 1886, Bill was educated in Dresden before moving to England in 1910. He is thought to have graduated from Birmingham University in electrical engineering, and in 1915 took the oath of allegiance to become a naturalised British citizen.

De Ropp's first wife, Ruth Fisher, undoubtedly played a role in his joining British Intelligence and serving the British Establishment. Ruth came from a wealthy line of members of the English ruling class. On her mother's side were the wealthy land-owning Denison family, educated at Eton and Oxford. Her great-uncle John Denison, Viscount Ossington, was speaker of the House of Commons from 1857 to 1872. On her paternal side, Ruth's uncle, Herbert Fisher, was a British historian and private secretary to the Prince of Wales – the future King Edward VII. Ruth's first cousin, H.A.L. Fisher, was the famous Oxford historian, close friend of Alfred Milner, and a member of the inner circle of the Rhodes-Milner secret society.[14] Together with his close friend Milner, Fisher was chief recruiter at Oxford for the Milner Group and played a major role in the appointment of the modern history professors at Oxford who would churn out the Establishment line on the world war.

Accordingly, when de Ropp operated as a British agent alongside Hitler, he was not simply some unknown Baltic baron's son, as mainstream historians would have us believe, but like Putzi, had direct links to the powerful segment of the Anglo-American Establishment that was actively promoting Hitler and the Nazis for war on Russia. It is important to recognise that Putzi Hanfstaengl and Bill de Ropp were not placed directly alongside Hitler to discourage him from war, but to continually encourage him into preparing for it while at the same time making him believe that Britain would not intervene. It was almost an exact re-run of the charade played out by Sir Edward Grey, King George V, and other leading British players in July 1914 to convince Kaiser Wilhelm II that Britain would not intervene.

Before De Ropp's moved to Germany to begin his mission, his wife Ruth died in the great influenza pandemic and he re-married. On arrival in Germany sometime around 1922, he made a connection with fellow Balt Alfred Rosenberg, who brought him into contact with Hitler. Interestingly, as we have seen, Rosenberg was also involved in linking Putzi with Hitler.

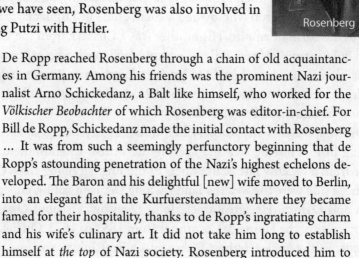

Rosenberg

De Ropp reached Rosenberg through a chain of old acquaintances in Germany. Among his friends was the prominent Nazi journalist Arno Schickedanz, a Balt like himself, who worked for the *Völkischer Beobachter* of which Rosenberg was editor-in-chief. For Bill de Ropp, Schickedanz made the initial contact with Rosenberg … It was from such a seemingly perfunctory beginning that de Ropp's astounding penetration of the Nazi's highest echelons developed. The Baron and his delightful [new] wife moved to Berlin, into an elegant flat in the Kurfuerstendamm where they became famed for their hospitality, thanks to de Ropp's ingratiating charm and his wife's culinary art. It did not take him long to establish himself at *the top* of Nazi society. Rosenberg introduced him to Adolf Hitler, who took an instant liking to the engaging, well-informed Balt from London. A close personal relationship developed between the Fuehrer and de Ropp. Hitler, using him as his confidential consultant about British affairs, outlined to him frankly his grandiose plans and even confided to him some of his intentions, a trust no other foreigner enjoyed to this extent [apart from Putzi]. Baron de Ropp reciprocated by becoming his chief agent of Anglo-German *raprochment*. He acted as Hitler's mouthpiece with influential Britishers the Fuhrer was anxious to reach and sway … Before long, Bill de Ropp was firmly established as Rosenberg's "English agent" with "a direct pipeline to Whitehall and Buckingham Palace at one end, and Hitler on the other.[15]

The Anglo-American elites now had two agents (at least) operating at the very heart of the Nazi Party. They were trusted implicitly by Hitler, who shared his intimate thoughts and future plans with them. It was a very dangerous business for them to be involved in, for had Hitler discovered that either of them was a double agent working for Britain and America, he would immediately have been tortured and killed. Incredibly, they succeeded in remaining close to Hitler until they eventually made their way across the border into neutral Switzerland and from there on to England – Putzi in 1937 and de Ropp in 1940. Putzi's intelligence contact, as we have seen, was Captain Truman Smith, who operated out of the US embassy in Berlin. De Ropp's intelligence contact in Germany was likely to have been Major Frank Foley who operated from the British Embassy under the guise of 'Passport Control Officer.'

FRANK FOLEY

Major Foley was a Sandhurst graduate and officer in the North Staffordshire Regiment during the First World War. Working from the 1920s onwards as 'Passport Control Officer' at the British embassy, Foley was head of the Berlin Station of the Secret Intelligence Service (SIS). Through numerous British agents he handled in Germany, Foley acquired key information on military research and development there. It later became known that he had aided thousands of Jews to escape Germany before 1939. It was seriously risky business, for

Hitler had his own intelligence services, the Abwehr and the Geheime Staatspolizei – the Secret State Police or 'Gestapo' – who 'took no prisoners'.

The 48-year-old Foley was hardly a novice at playing the intelligence game. On the contrary, this diminutive, bespectacled, and slightly overweight man had been in the shadows of this murky world since before the Armistice, when the War Office had noticed his courage, initiative, and leadership and headhunted him into the ranks of the Intelligence Service. Soon he was using his fluency in both French and German to recruit and manage a network of agents operating throughout northern Europe.[16]

De Ropp's handler in England was an RAF officer named Frederick Winterbotham. A leading player for British Intelligence, Winterbotham freely travelled back and forth to Germany during the 1930s and successfully conned Hitler into believing that he was his friend and wanted him to succeed.

FREDERICK WILLIAM WINTERBOTHAM

A pilot in the Royal Flying Corps during the First World War, Winterbotham's aircraft was shot down over enemy lines in July 1917. He spent the rest of the war in the German POW camp for British officers at Holzminden, where he learned to speak German. After the war, he studied for a law degree at Oxford University but then went into farming. When his farming ventures in various African countries failed, Winterbotham joined the Secret Intelligence Service which later became known as 'Military Intelligence Section 6' (MI6). Promoted to Group Captain, he was  tasked with building an Air Intelligence department, albeit on a much smaller scale to that of Blinker Hall's Naval Intelligence at Room 40. His first priority was to have an agent in Germany able to closely monitor developments in the Luftwaffe. Bill de Ropp, having been in the Flying Corps during the war and joined intelligence thereafter, was perfect for the job. Winterbotham wrote that de Ropp was:

A fully paid agent whose job would be to interpret the articles in *The Times* to Rosenberg; to try to influence Dawson, the editor of *The Times* in London, to be sympathetic towards the Nazis; and to do everything possible to make important British contacts for the Nazis in England.[17]

Winterbotham relates that around 1930 he received scanty intelligence that Germany had military pilots training secretly in Soviet Russia, and he needed further information:

> I therefore asked whether the agent who had been reporting on the Hitler antics could be brought to London so that I might have a talk with him.... He was a man of about forty years of age, a Baltic Baron who had been dispossessed of his lands by the Bolsheviks. He was now resident in Berlin, and was acting as a political correspondent of *The Times* newspaper as well as being one of our agents reporting on politics in Germany. But now came the more interesting part of his history: he had a British passport, he was married to a British wife, had served in the Wiltshire Regiment in World War 1 and during the war had transferred to the Royal Flying Corps. He had been found unfit to fly but operated in the balloon section, and was listed as being entirely pro-British. Apart from speaking perfect English he also spoke fluent German, Russian and French. I was elated, and felt that somehow here might be the man I had been looking for. His name was Baron William de Ropp. I arranged to meet Bill de Ropp at the end of 1931 in the lounge of an hotel not far from our office where we normally entertained agents from overseas, as it was undesirable to have them at head office. I must say I was a little surprised to find a perfectly normal Englishman about 5 foot 10, with fair hair, a slightly reddish moustache and blue eyes dressed in a good English suit. As he got up to shake hands he greeted me in perfect English without any trace of an accent. ... We went to a quiet corner table in the restaurant and conversation automatically turned to the old days in the Royal Flying Corps.[18]

De Ropp came to London for that first meeting between the two, but thereafter Winterbotham travelled to Germany, and de Ropp introduced him to Hitler and other leading Nazis. Although he was competent in German, Winterbotham pretended otherwise when meeting them:

> I still felt that my apparent inability to speak German was, at that moment, one of my best insurances against being thought to be a British agent or a professional intelligence officer.[19]

Winterbotham succeeded in concealing his role as head of the Air Intelligence Department of SIS, and passing himself off as nothing other than a genuinely friendly RAF officer who had been treated most kindly by Germans in the POW camp during the First World War. He "detested Bolshevism" and was "fully in tune" with Hitler's stated aim to destroy it. The spread of communism would be a disaster not merely for Germany, but also for his beloved England, and he personally believed that Germany and Britain should deal with the "scourge of communism" together. In other words, like Putzi and de Ropp, yet another British intelligence agent was encouraging Hitler to prepare for war against Russia. Winterbotham assured Hitler that he wanted nothing more than to ensure future cordial relations between the RAF and the Luftwaffe, and between England and Germany.

> Winterbotham went out of his way to sympathise with the aspirations of the Third Reich. He expressed himself in favour of its rearmament in the air as a balancing factor in European airpower...[20]

Winterbotham went to Germany regularly for meetings with Hitler, Goering, Rosenberg, and a number of generals, and, "as a friend," was allowed to visit military bases, observe manoeuvres, and assess the capabilities of the new German Air Force. He carried out his role superbly over the years, and Hitler swallowed the lie just as he did with Putzi and de Ropp. The closely collaborating Anglo-American intelligence services now had *three* agents close to Hitler.

In Berlin, Winterbotham obtained highly valuable top-secret information not only from his agents there, but from a disgruntled Luftwaffe colonel in return for significant amounts of money.[21] When Winterbotham was back in England, de Ropp communicated with him "through his contact in Berlin who normally forwarded his political reports to our head office."[22] Winterbotham does not name his 'contact' in Berlin, but it is likely to have been either the above-mentioned Frank Foley in the 'Passport Office' or Group Captain Malcolm Christie, air attaché in the British embassy.

MALCOLM CHRISTIE

Christie, like de Ropp and Winterbotham, had served in the Royal Flying Corps during the First World War and afterwards joined the secret intelligence service. Bilingual in English and German, he was posted to Germany as an intelligence agent from 1930 to 1939.

> Christie had excellent contacts everywhere in Europe, but most especially in Germany, which

he was able to pass on.... He was an extremely wealthy man, and had a house on the Dutch-German border, a perfect base for secret operations. He became president of Otto Coke Ovens, New York, a genuine position which gave him a bona fide reason to travel and to seek information about all manner of industrial concerns which might be potential customers.He was able to move easily in official and society circles in Berlin, especially those connected with flying, and was on the closest of terms with Goering and General Milch – who became Inspector General of the Luftwaffe.... In the early thirties, Milch was basically pro-British and was quite happy to provide Christie with a great deal of information.... The loose association of businessmen and other informants run by Claude Dansey (Colonel Z) and Christie was well established and operating smoothly, though on a very informal basis. The intelligence they provided supplemented that obtained by the official SIS, notably by the then Squadron-Leader F.W. Winterbotham, head of the Air Section, who was himself doing remarkable work in penetrating the higher echelons of the Third Reich. It gave clear warnings of German aims in Central Europe, and of the rate of rearmament, particularly in the air.[23]

Malcolm Christie would later report (1935) that some thirty German aircraft factories employing 40,000 men were operating round the clock in three-shift systems capable of producing 400 bombers per month. Christie reported that 9,800 aircraft had been built between 1933 and 1935, and some 300 airfields were being constructed for wartime use. Additionally, German munitions factories were producing large quantities of incendiary bombs.[24] Those aircraft would soon be taking off from those airfields to drop those incendiary bombs on cities across Britain killing tens of thousands of civilians. We shall see in due course how Anglo-American money paid for most of it.

Malcolm Christie was one of the first to reveal the rapidly increasing power of the Luftwaffe and predict Hitler's military and political objectives.[25] Christie reported not only to Winterbotham in Air Intelligence, but to Sir Robert Vansittart, Permanent Under-Secretary at the Foreign Office. Although it may sound somewhat insignificant, the post of Under-Secretary was in a fact a major government position with responsibility for advising the Foreign Secretary and ensuring continuity of foreign policy when governments changed. As such, the Milner Group always ensured the position was filled by one of their own.

Robert Vansittart

Of Dutch descent, Vansittart's ancestors had settled in England in 1670. He attended Eton College, joined the Foreign Office, and worked his way through the ranks to become a leading player in politics and intelligence. When his younger brother, Arnold, was killed at Ypres in 1915, he became an intense Germanophobe. Vansittart "had a wide variety of contacts across the world, which he made great use of to track the apparent resurgence of Germany."[26] With an exceedingly rich second wife, Vansittart had a large country mansion with its own ballroom, where many leading members of the Milner Group and the British ruling class were lavishly entertained, including his good friends King Edward VIII (later known as the Duke of Windsor), Wallace Simpson, and Winston Churchill. Like Franklin Delano Roosevelt in New York, Vansittart ran his own private intelligence gathering agency. It included Malcolm Christie, Klop Ustinov, and other British agents too numerous to mention, who were operating in a wide variety of commercial and industrial ventures across Germany.

> The most important connections, however, were probably the Germans who helped [Claude] Dansey and Vansittart. These included prominent men from industry, diplomacy and the armed service: Hans Ritter, a former German Air Force pilot and member of the General Staff, serving then as adviser to the Junkers aircraft company and in an honorary capacity as assistant to the air and military attachés in Paris; Carl Goerdeler, Chief Bürgermeister (Mayor) of Leipzig, who was later to be recognised as the leader of the German Resistance Movement.[27]

One of the most important Germans assisting British intelligence was the diplomat Wolfgang Gans zu Putlitz who came from an old and wealthy East Prussian Junker family.

Wolfgang Gans Zu Putlitz.

In the mid-1930s, Putlitz was sent as First Secretary to the German embassy in London, and was introduced to Vansittart by Klop Ustinov, the German Press Attaché at the embassy (and British double agent). Gans zu

Putlitz became one of the principal German sources of information in Vansittart's private intelligence
network. "It was also through Putlitz that Winston
Churchill, when outside the Government, obtained
his information about the true strength of the Luftwaffe."[28] Gans zu Putlitz wanted to draw Germany
away from the abyss Hitler was leading it into, and was
in contact with Putzi Hanfstaengl in Munich.[29] Professor Christopher Andrew writes:

> MI5's main source in the German embassy [London] was the aris-
> tocratic anti-Nazi diplomat Wolfgang Zu Putlitz ... (codenamed
> PADGHAM by the Security Service). He later recalled that at his
> fortnightly meetings with the MI5 agent Jona 'Klop' Ustinov, "I
> would unburden myself of all the dirty schemes and secrets which
> I encountered as part of my daily routine at the Embassy. By this
> means I was able to lighten my conscience by the feeling that I was
> really helping to damage the Nazi cause."... Putlitz insisted, and
> MI5's leaders believed, that the only way to deal with Hitler was to
> stand firm. Appeasement would make him even more aggressive.[30]

A significant number of other prominent Germans – such as Carl Goerdeler, the Mayor of Leipzig – were opposed to the Nazis and were feeding
information to Vansittart's intelligence agents within Germany. Some were
caught and executed while others formed the backbone of the German Resistance movement. In later pages we see how some of those exceedingly
brave Germans determined to stop Hitler were betrayed by the British authorities. The Anglo-American cabal was building Hitler up with one hand
while destroying the opposition to him in Germany with the other.

On the political front, a round of elections was scheduled in Germany
for 1932. Hitler and Putzi initially went on the election trail across different cities by car. Electioneering was an expensive business for the Nazis,
and the Welsh author, Gwynne Thomas, makes an interesting comment
on de Ropp as the source of some of its funding:

> The Nazi leader took an instant liking to him, particularly when he
> discovered that de Ropp had powerful connections among English
> society and was well informed about much of what was happening in
> London ... De Ropp not only enjoyed the Fuhrer's trust but became
> his spokesman in dealings with the many important British people
> Hitler wished to influence.... There is strong evidence that de Ropp

was instrumental in raising funds in the City of London to finance several of the Nazi election campaigns which ensured that by the end of 1933 the Nazi party was totally established and in control.[31]

Unfortunately Gwynne Thomas gives no source for the 'strong evidence' that de Ropp raised fund in The City for Hitler's electioneering.

With non-stop campaigning, in the presidential poll of 13 March 1932, Hitler got 30 per cent of the vote to Paul von Hindenburg's 49.6 per cent. The imposing Hindenburg had been the commander of the German army during the war and remained popular. The remainder of the vote went to the communist candidate, Ernst Thalmann. Although a distant second, Hitler had prevented Hindenburg getting the necessary absolute majority. A second runoff vote was scheduled for 10 April 1932. Hitler and Putzi now took campaigning literally to new heights by flying back and forth across Germany in a private aircraft. One evening when they landed back at the Ober-

wiesenfeld at Munich, Putzi found a telephone message waiting for him from Randolph Churchill, son of Winston, to say that his father and mother were visiting Munich and staying at the Hotel Continental. They would be delighted if Putzi and Hitler  would join them for dinner that evening. In his memoirs Putzi writes that he and young Randolph had "seen quite a lot" of each other and he had joined him several times on Hitler's electioneering flights.[32] Moreover, as previously detailed, Putzi biographer Stephen Conradi relates that Winston Churchill and Putzi were friends.[33]

Despite Putzi's cajoling, Hitler declined Winston Churchill's invitation to dinner. Putzi went along, made excuses for Hitler, and sat at the table between Winston and his wife, Clementine. In his memoirs, Putzi gushingly describes Mrs. Churchill as "serene, intelligent and enchanting." Joining them were other friends and travelling companions of the Churchills, Lord Camrose and Professor Frederick Lindemann. Camrose

(William Berry) had made his fortune from the First World War with his British propaganda magazine, *The War Illustrated*, which had a circulation of 750,000. He and his brother had later bought *The Telegraph* and many other British newspapers and had built a vast news empire. Lindemann was born in Germany, but became a naturalised British subject and professor of physics at Oxford University. Considered by many there to be an arrogant and sarcastic individual, he was strongly in favour of eugenics and forced sterilisation. He made no secret of his contempt for the working class and black people.[34]

After a hearty meal, political discussion, and much alcohol, Putzi played piano with Churchill accompanying him long into the night singing Scottish and Irish songs.

In the run-off presidential election held on 10 April, 84 year old Hindenburg's vote rose to 53 per cent, and he gained a second term as president. Hitler was happy to see his share of the vote increase by two million votes to 36.7 per cent. In addition to the presidential election, 1932 was Germany's year of elections with contests in various states and regions. They were held against a backdrop of deepening economic crisis and a growing unemployment rate of almost 30 per cent. The rise of the Nazis, and the continued reasonably strong showing of the Communists, combined with the inability of the centrist parties to set aside their differences, was making it impossible for anyone to form an enduring government.

On 31 July 1932, the first of the years two national elections for the Reichstag was held. Germany had been ruled at federal level since 1930 by a coalition headed by Chancellor Heinrich Brüning of the Catholic Centre Party, but he was unable to secure a parliamentary majority. In the July election the Nazis gained 123 seats to give them 230 out of 608 seats. This made them the stron-

gest party in the Reichstag. Leading Nazi Hermann Goering was appointed President of the Reichstag and moved into the Reichstag Palace, which was situated in the square at the back of the Reichstag. Even though Hitler did not achieve the absolute majority he had hoped for, he could still have expected to be named Chancellor. President Hindenburg, however, refused to call him. The result plunged the political system into a fresh crisis.

507

Franz von Papen, member of the ultra-right wing of the Catholic Centre Party was Chancellor, but yet another vote was decided on for November.

Meanwhile, there was further activity on the secret intelligence front. Frederick Winterbotham and Bill de Ropp exchanged confidential notes through the embassy bag with a view to bringing leading member of the Nazi Party, Alfred Rosenberg, to Britain.

Winterbotham writes:

> Bill's proposal was that he should bring Rosenberg to London on a visit, and that while in London he would introduce him to the editor of *The Times*, together with one or two members of Parliament or others in the public eye, and give me the opportunity of meeting him myself. Bill felt that if I was reasonably convincing, I might impress Rosenberg enough to be asked back to Berlin, which would then give me the opportunity to open up the contacts I needed to get the information required. He again stressed the fact that the Nazis were desperate to get British connections in high places and that if he could bring off this visit it would cement his job as Rosenberg's English agent.[35]

Winterbotham discussed the matter with Robert Vansittart who agreed to Rosenberg's visit. The invitation, however, should not come through the RAF but from Winterbotham himself in a private capacity. Winterbotham duly sent a handwritten invitation to Rosenberg, and a joint visit with him and de Ropp was scheduled for the autumn. Rosenberg, who had been close to Hitler for 10 years by this stage, was in a powerful position as editor of the *Völkischer Beobachter* and considered the Nazi party philosopher, who zealously promoted anti-Semitic policy.

Winterbotham greeted Rosenberg and de Ropp off the boat train at Liverpool Street Station in London and installed them in a hotel "noted for its excellence." The following day, Rosenberg was taken to a meeting with Geoffrey Dawson, editor of *The Times* and a member of the select inner core of the Milner Group. He had been Alfred Milner's private secretary in South Africa and had been as close to Milner as anyone. Dawson had been appointed the estate bursar of All Souls and rewarded with a directorship of Consolidated Gold Fields, as well as the editorship of *The Times* 1912-1941 (apart for 3 years).

> As editor of *The Times,* Dawson was one of the most influential figures in England. He used that influence in the directions decided by the Group.[36]

Winterbotham also took Rosenberg and de Ropp to the RAF officers' club in Piccadilly for dinner and glad handing with several Conservative Members of Parliament. The following day they had a lobster lunch at the luxury Savoy Hotel in the Strand where invited guests included Oliver Locker-Lampson, a Conservative MP and admirer of Hitler. Locker-Lampson had formed a quasi-military right-wing organisation named the Blueshirts, (as opposed to Hitler's Brownshirts and Mussolini's Blackshirts) and Rosenberg, the virulent hater of Jews and Bolsheviks, was well impressed.

Thereafter, Winterbotham took Rosenberg on a tour around the pleasant English countryside, with visits to country pubs, and "treated him as an important visiting dignitary."[37] When Rosenberg boarded the train at Liverpool Street Station on his homeward journey, he promised that as soon as the Nazis were in power, he would invite Winterbotham to Berlin to meet Hitler. In February 1934, he was true to his word and yet another British Intelligence agent had direct access to Hitler and the very highest levels of the Nazi Party. Winterbotham would regularly travel back and forth to Germany over the next five years offering the regime his support, consolidating British appeasement, and lulling Hitler into believing that Britain would approve when he attacked Bolshevik Russia. Winterbotham writes that his visits to Germany were closely connected with the rise of Nazi Germany and the rebirth of her mighty armed forces.[38] And lest there be any doubt that Winterbotham was meeting Hitler regularly, consider his observations:

> During the time in which I observed Hitler, I saw how each year took its toll of his health and sapped his joy in life: his features grew sallow and puffy and his expression increasingly troubled. I always found it impossible to assess his character, for his two personalities, a quiet, interesting talker and a staccato-voiced rabble rousing tub thumper, could seemingly be switched on and off at will. Not even his small sense of humour could account for his absurd quiff and moustache. How did it come about that this little Austrian corporal could achieve the authority and stature to lead a nation and finally the madness to alter the history of the world?[39]

How indeed?

On the political front in Germany, the November 1932 Reichstag election saw the National Socialists *lose* two million votes from their July success, with their share of the vote dropping from 37.3 per cent to 33 per cent. They lost 34 seats but remained the largest party in the Reichstag. The Communist Party went from 14.3 percent of the vote in July to 16.9

percent with a gain of 11 seats. The Communist Party now had 100 members in parliament. Political turmoil ensued, with civil war threatening to engulf Germany.

Kurt von Schleicher, a First World War army general-turned-politician, schemed against his personal friend Franz von Papen, who was forced to resign the Chancellorship on 17 November. Hitler was ready to step into von Papen's shoes as Chancellor, but President Hindenburg would not tolerate him taking power, and on 3 December 1932 it was the scheming von Schleicher who replaced von Papen. He would last only fifty-seven days in the post. William Shirer wrote:

> As the strife-ridden year of 1932 approached its end, Berlin was full of cabals, and cabals within cabals. Besides those of Papen and Schleicher, there was one at the President's Palace, where Hindenburg's son, Oskar, and his State Secretary, Meissner held sway behind the throne. There was one at the Kaiserhof hotel, where Hitler and the men around him were plotting not only for power but against each other. Soon the webs of intrigue became so enmeshed that by New Year's Day 1933, none of the cabalists was sure who was double crossing whom. But it would not take long for them to find out.[40]

Further significant losses in local elections in Thuringia led to much tension and many arguments within the Nazi Party which was now in danger of tearing itself apart. Gregor Strasser – one of the founders and leading members of the party – had a bitter disagreement with Hitler over strategy and resigned. (He would die at the hands of the Gestapo in the 'Night of the Long Knives' the following year – and so too would von Schleicher.)

In addition to the demoralising losses at the polls, Nazi Party finances were in a precarious state at the end of 1932. Joseph Goebbels complained

Thyssen

that "Scarcity of money has become a chronic illness with us." He added that "the financial situation of the Berlin organisation was hopeless with nothing but debts and obligations." The Nazis main German benefactor, Fritz Thyssen, warned at the time that there were simply no funds to meet the payroll of thousands of party functionaries or to maintain the SA, which alone cost two and a half million marks a week.[41]

On 4 January 1933, Hitler and von Papen met at the Cologne home of banker Kurt von Schroeder in an attempt to thrash out their differences and get rid of von Schleicher. Papen, who enjoyed the support of Hindenburg and felt confident about returning to the Reichstag as Chancellor, somewhat condescendingly told Hitler that he would be happy to share the top position with him. Hitler had other ideas, but how to overcome the hurdle of Hindenburg's strong disapproval? Kurt von Schroeder later wrote:

Kurt von Schroeder

> This meeting between Hitler and Papen on 4 January 1933 in my house in Cologne was arranged by me after Papen had asked me for it on about 10 December 1932. Before I took this step I talked to a number of businessmen and informed myself generally on how the business world viewed a collaboration between the two men. The general desire of businessmen was to see a strong man come to power in Germany who would form a government that would stay in power for a long time.[42]

Big business in Germany wanted Hitler in the Chancellery, and so too did the bankers. Their reasoning becomes clear in the next chapter.

> The Cologne banker [von Schroeder], a sympathizer and patron of the NSDAP, had acted as a particularly active mediator for his Nazi friends before. In the middle of November 1932, he and Hjalmar Schacht above all had initiated a submission to the Reich President which had been signed by fifteen industrialists. They had asked though without success, that following Papen's dismissal the new Cabinet should contain members of the Nazi movement in leading positions. Apart from [Hjalmar] Schacht, there were now a number of prominent representatives of heavy industry in the Ruhr, among them Fritz Thyssen, Paul Reusch and Albert Vogler, as well as some other influential bankers and businessmen which, like Schröder, belonged to a growing minority in big business. This minority advised that, in order to stabilize the presidential regime and to put the economy back on an even keel, the leadership in the Cabinet should be left to the Nazis. They had been driven to this position all the more strongly when the Communists emerged much strengthened from the November elections. Their fear was that a further crumbling of Nazi support would benefit the KPD. There was also the fact that Schleicher, in his radio address of 15

December in which he presented his government's programme, had, in contradistinction to Papen, presented himself as a "socially-minded general" and had advocated a broadening of the government base not just towards the Right. Rather he spoke of an inclusion of the Left reaching as far as the Christian and Social Democratic trade unions. This posture had been received with a sigh of relief among the forces of the democratic Left and Center. But it had been noted with considerable disquiet within the ranks of the conservative Right. This was therefore one of the reasons why Schleicher quickly lost the backing of heavy industry and agriculture which Papen had enjoyed during his chancellorship.[43]

The only real obstacle Hitler had to overcome now was Hindenburg's refusal to consider him becoming Chancellor. Some dirty tricks and a little blackmail were called for. On his eightieth birthday in 1927, the State and leading German industrialist made large cash donations to President Hindenburg which enabled him to regain his large family estate in East Prussia. It had been lost to the family due to overwhelming debts. To keep the estate in the family forthwith and avoid death duty, Hindenburg's son Oskar was registered as the legal owner. Other powerful Prussian landowners had also been given large financial 'gifts'.

Hindenburg

Various serious frauds had already come to light. The allegations included charges that the funds had been used to pay for gambling debts, the acquisition of race horses, for holiday trips to the Riviera and the keeping of mistresses. Members of the oldest noble families appeared to be involved in the scandal. There was even a rumour that "relatives of the Reich President had profited from the irregularities."[44]

It is unknown what pressure was applied to Hindenburg, but despite the NSDAP's reversals in the polls and waning popular support, on 28 January 1933 he gave his presidential assent to 44-year-old Adolf Hitler becoming Chancellor of Germany. The Nazis got into government not through the will of the people but through unworthy wrangling by half a dozen people. Once they got their foot in the door, however, in less than a month, they'd arranged the Reichstag Fire and then the Enabling Act, and then all was over for what was left of German democracy.

With Hitler installed as Chancellor, twenty-five thousand Nazi brown-shirts marched through the Brandenburg gate in a torchlight procession past the Chancellery. The Nazi band leading the marchers played stirring tunes, including *Young Heroes* composed by Putzi. Their straight arm salutes and Sieg Heil chants had also originated with the 'big American.' Newspapers in Mussolini's fascist Italy splashed photographs of the march across the front pages and reacted with joy. The Jews and many others in Germany trembled.

Hitler was now Chancellor but had no majority in parliament. He called on President Hindenburg to dissolve the Reichstag on 1 February and set another Reichstag election for 5 March in the hope that the NS-DAP might finally achieve the majority. It seemed a very risky strategy, for the communists had gained seats in the November election at the expense of the Nazis and they could gain even more at their expense in the re-run in March. Hitler was well aware of the risk but had a plan up his sleeve to decimate the communist vote.

Just after 9 P.M. on the evening of 27 February 1933, six days before the new election, the Reichstag – the German parliament building – went up in flames. A Dutch communist sympathiser, Marinus van der Lubbe, and three Bulgarian Bolshevists were quickly arrested and charged with the arson attack. Not all was what it appeared, however. Just before midnight a reporter from the *Wiener Allgemeine Zeitung* (Vienna) sent a telegram to his editor:

> There can be little doubt that the fire which is consuming the Reichstag was the work of hirelings of the Hitler government. It seems that the incendiaries have made their way to the Reichstag through an underground passage which connects the building with the palace of the Reichstag President.[45]

Hitler dismissed such reports and blamed the Communist Party in its entirety for destroying the home of German democracy. He warned the German people that the country was in imminent danger from a communist revolution and that President Hindenburg was about to declare a state of emergency with restriction of civil liberties.

> During the resulting public hysteria, whipped up by a barrage of Nazi propaganda, a Marxist revolution suddenly seemed imminent. Angry mobs took to the street with brownshirts to the fore, keen to vent their fury against their hated opponents. Protected by the police – now controlled by the Nazis – the storm troopers were freed of all restraints and the violence quickly escalated into a bloodbath. All over Germany, Communists, Jews and Social Democrats were attacked and beaten in their homes and in the streets, before being arrested and imprisoned. It was a time for settling old scores and anyone who had ever spoken out against Hitler was now a target. The election that followed took place in an atmosphere of manifest terror. While the parties of the left were more or less paralysed by state sponsored intimidation, the Nazis were able to blanket the nation with propaganda and mount huge rallies, thanks to the massive largesse bestowed on them by I.G. Farben and others. The result was only ever going to go the one way.[46]

Freedom of speech, of association, and of privacy of postal and telephone communication were all suspended. Immediately after the fire, Hitler made arson a capital offence, formed the *Geheime Staatspolizei* (Gestapo) secret state police, and opened the first of many concentration camps at Dachau near Munich. On 28 February 1933:

> Goring ordered the arrest of 4,000 communists and a ban on the entire communist and social democratic press. Citing the Reichstag fire, Hitler promulgated a decree signed by the president for the "Protection of the People and State" known as the 'Reichstag Fire Decree,' which suspended the basic guarantees of individual freedom under the Constitution. An orgy of violence and terror was unleashed by the SA throughout the country; opponents of Nazism were dragged off to improvised concentration camps.[47]

In the election just days later, the communist vote slumped while the National Socialists increased their share from 33 per cent to 44 percent. They were still 36 seats short of an overall majority, but with von Papen's Centre Party support, Hitler now had the necessary majority of 52 per cent in the

Reichstag. An "Enabling Act" was passed, giving Hitler power to bypass parliament and rule by decree. He quickly side-lined
von Papen, and Germany would now experience a
reign of terror. Within months, almost 30,000 people were interned in the concentration camps. Many
were tortured and murdered by Hitler's brownshirt
militia. Suppression of publications not considered
friendly to the Nazi cause further paved the way for
the establishment of a one-party state, and Joseph
Goebbels was appointed with an Orwellian title as
Reich Minister for "People's Enlightenment."

The fire that changed everything was caused not by communists but
by the Nazis themselves. Professor Guido Preparata describes the fire as
"an internally manufactured act of terror" on the strength of which subsequent emergency legislation annihilated the Leftist opposition.[48]

At the trial of putative arsonists, the case against the three Bulgarians
was quickly dropped and 'the patsy,' 24-year-old Marinus van der Lubbe,
stood alone in the dock. The prosecution maintained that
he had acted on behalf of a wider communist conspiracy.
Police reported finding him in the hall of the Reichstag on
the night of the fire in a "haggard condition." Observers at
the trial reported that van der Lubbe acted very strangely
throughout, drivelled, and made no sense when he spoke.
What they observed was "a human wreck, an unfortu-
nate doped up moron."[49] He was found guilty and would be guillotined in
Leipzig prison three days before his 25th birthday.

What really happened on the night of the fire? Hitler, Hermann Goering, and other top Nazis were in Berlin having dinner at Joseph Goebbels' house. Goering
was now President of the Reichstag, and his official residence, the Reichstag Palace, was adjacent to the parliament. The official story relates that Putzi was meant to
join the dinner party, but he felt unwell and stayed the
night in the palace. Putzi relates in his memoirs:

> I felt so shivery that I decided to go to bed in my room in the Go-
> ering's palace and sample the remedy [aquavit]. The Goebbels had
> invited me for later on, but I left a telephone message to excuse
> myself, put on a couple of old sweaters, piled the bed with blankets,

ordered relays of hot lemonade to alternate with the medicine and settled down to sweat. We were all due to leave again for Breslau the next day, and I had to do something dramatic.[50]

It seemed an incredible coincidence that Putzi was in the Reichstag Palace that very evening, for it was from there that the arsonists gained access to the Reichstag. The room Putzi allegedly 'slept in' at the palace that night was directly opposite the Reichstag. His whitewash biographer writes:

> As he lay drifting in and out of sleep, he suddenly became aware of a bright light. At first, he thought he must have forgotten to turn off the desk lamp in the adjoining room, but it was too bright and was flickering unlike any electric bulb. At that moment, Frau Wanda, the housekeeper burst in. "Herr Doktor," she cried, "the Reichstag is on fire."
>
> For a moment Putzi forgot about his fever. He jumped out of bed and ran to the window. He had always disliked the Reichstag building, which he likened to a giant gasworks. Now, as he looked across the square, he could see it was enveloped in flames. He rushed to the telephone and called the Goebbels's home, where dinner was in full swing. Trout was on the menu ... [51]

That is the official narrative, the laughable nonsense that we are expected to believe. Putzi was certainly in the Reichstag palace that evening, but not lying doped up in bed. Immediately after telephoning Goebbels, Putzi called Sefton "Tom" Delmer of the *Daily Express*, and Louis Lochner of the Associated Press, and they immediately made their way to the scene.

Biographer Peter Conradi does *not* explain to his readers that an underground service tunnel that ran between the boiler house and the Reichstag building went directly though the basement of the palace which sat between the two. The palace had ready access to the tunnel and it was from there that the arsonists gained entry to the Reichstag. The parliament building had huge solid oak doors, all of which were firmly locked at night. Just before 9 P.M. the watchmen made their final round inside the building and confirmed that all was well. No flammable liquids were discovered and nothing out of the ordinary was noticed in the Sessions Chamber. Watchmen outside who did regular circuits of the building reported that on the night of the fire they saw no one enter or leave the building between 9 P.M. and the start of the fire shortly thereafter.

Professor Antony Sutton wrote that the burning of the Reichstag was "one of the key events of modern times," and that Putzi Hanfstaengl played a "significant" role in it. At the time, it was blamed on the communists, "but there is little question in historical perspective that the fire was deliberately started by the Nazis to provide an excuse to seize political power."[52] Multiple small fires were set inside the huge building using a flammable liquid:

> There was only one way a group with flammable materials could have entered the Reichstag – through a tunnel that ran between the Reichstag and the Palace of the Reichstag President. Hermann Goering was president of the Reichstag and lived in the palace, and numerous S.A. and S.S. men were known to be in the Palace. In the words of one author, "The use of the underground passage, with all its complications, was possible only to National-Socialists, the advance and escape of the incendiary gang was feasible only with the connivance of highly placed employees of the Reichstag. Every clue, every possibility points damningly in one direction to the conclusion that the burning of the Reichstag was the work of the National-Socialists."
>
> Hanfstaengl directed operations within the Palace, the propaganda apparatus stood ready, and the leaders of the Storm Troopers were in their places. With the official bulletin planned in advance, the orders of arrest prepared, … the preparations were complete, the scheme almost perfect…. According to Nazi Kurt Ludecke, there once existed a document signed by S.A. leader Karl Ernst – who supposedly set the fire and was later murdered by fellow Nazis – which implicated Goering, Goebbels and Hanfstaengl in the conspiracy.[53]

American intelligence agent Putzi Hanfstaengl "directed operations" at the Reichstag fire, the false flag event, that enabled Hitler to seize power and led inexorably to the Second World War.

The first eyewitness reports of the fire started coming in to the fire service at 9:10 P.M. and it had firefighting appliances there by 9:18 P.M. It was clear to them that multiple small fires had deliberately been started in the building. Firefighters would readily have controlled them but at 9:27 P.M. a large explosion rocked the main debating chamber in the middle of the Reichstag, and a "sea of flames" gave the firefighters no chance to save it. The explosion was later explained away as a large build-up of explosive gases being generated by the small fires. It was a ludicrous explanation given that the small fires had not long started and the debating chamber was a massive space with a huge glass domed roof. It was, without doubt, due to incendiary explosives having been planted in the debating chamber. Hitler, Goring and Goebbels were on the scene by 9:45 P.M., and Hitler immediately spoke to British journalist Sefton "Tom" Delmer of the tabloid *Daily Express*, who had been summoned to the scene by Putzi. With no evidence whatsoever, Hitler told Delmer. "Without doubt this is the work of the communists."

When fire fighters eventually gained control, Hitler took Delmer on a tour of parts of the gutted Reichstag, telling him "You are now witnessing the beginning of a great new epoch in German history, Herr Delmer. This fire is just the beginning."[54] Hitler was well-acquainted with Delmer thanks to Putzi having arranged for him to join them on the aircraft they used for campaigning purposes. Delmer had flown numerous times with Hitler and had kept him up to date with opinion in England. Delmer had been born in Berlin to Australian parents but they had moved to England where the young Delmer studied modern languages at Oxford University. Following his time in Berlin reporting favourably on Hitler, he worked for a branch of British Intelligence – the Political Warfare Executive (PWE)[55] In other words, Delmer was a fellow agent of Putzi's in Anglo-American secret intelligence.

On the morning following the fire, the *Daily Express* (with a circulation of two million in Britain) carried Delmer's report of the incident on the front page with a photograph of the burning Reichstag and the headline: "Daily Express Correspondent accompanies Hitler into Blazing Building. Communist Arrested. Nothing shall stop us now says Hitler."[56]

In late March the deputy head of MI5, Guy Liddell, flew to Berlin where his host during his ten-day stay was none other than Putzi Hanfstaengl.[57] Liddell reported back to London that the Nazis were behind the Reichstag fire.[58] De Ropp's handler, Frederick Winterbotham, just happened to be in Berlin at the time and Alfred Rosenberg "took great delight" in showing him the blackened ruin of the Reichstag.[59]

Liddell

> Hitler appointed Rosenberg head of the NSDAP Foreign Policy Office, and on 1 April 1933, the first anti-Jewish boycott was organised throughout Germany. On 7 April Hitler told his ministers that war must be avoided until Germany became stronger militarily. That day, the *Völkischer Beobachter* published Hitler's speech in which he demanded the elimination of excessive numbers of Jewish intellectuals from cultural spheres. A law was passed with provisions for the purging of Jews, non-Aryans, and opponents of the regime. Jewish civil servants, professors and schoolteachers were to be sacked. Hitler declared Marxism the enemy of the people which would be 'rooted out and destroyed without mercy.' Books written by Jews and Marxists were burned in front of massive public rallies. In Germany there would be no further voting. The Fuhrer alone would decide.[60]

In June 1933, British pilots went to Germany on a goodwill visit and were personally greeted by Hitler. Luftwaffe pilots reciprocated by flying to Hendon Airport in West London. They enjoyed a cocktail party reception before dinner at the RAF Club in Piccadilly. Coach tours of London were laid on for the following day.[61]

In July, the Concordat between Nazi Germany and the Holy See was concluded, which stopped persecution of German Roman Catholics. Jews and Gypsies were deprived of German citizenship, however, and a law was passed which permitted the forced sterilisation of Gypsies, the mentally and physically disabled, and others considered 'inferior'. A great autobahn construction project got underway, with Hitler declaring it a milestone on the road towards building up the community of the German people.

Putzi Hanfstaengl, meanwhile, was having a romantic relationship with Martha Dodd, the glamorous blonde daughter of the American ambassador, William E. Dodd. According to later revelations by Putzi's son, Egon, Martha Dodd was but one of a number of women his father had an affair with.[62]

> Putzi was also making a name for himself abroad, especially in Britain, *to which he travelled often*. One British lady subject to his charms was Diana Mitford, the daughter of Lord Redesdale, and a renowned society beauty ... Diana was also close to Winston Churchill.[63]

Putzi invited Diana Mitford and her sister Unity to Germany for four days and introduced them to leading players in the Nazi party. Unity became infatuated with Hitler and got close to him, but it was considered to be a platonic friendship. The Mitfords would go on to play a major role in appeasement.

Among many others Putzi called on in London, was the wartime prime minister and now elder statesman (Father of the House) in the Commons, David Lloyd George. He gave Putzi a signed photograph to take back to Germany inscribed: "To Chancellor Hitler, in admiration of his courage, determination and leadership."[64]

In late February 1934, Freddy Winterbotham was in Berlin, and de Ropp assured Hitler that the nice RAF officer could be trusted as a "genuine friend of Germany." Winterbotham wrote:

> I first went to Germany to spy out the land in 1934. I was able to make close contact with Nazi leaders who at that time, were desperately anxious to get what they called "English connections with influence." These leaders were most anxious to impress upon me that Hitler did not want to involve Britain in war; he was personally obsessed with the notion that Britain should keep out of his future campaigns. Would I please explain this to my superiors? By pretending to show great enthusiasm for their regime and by exploiting their obsession for a neutral Britain, I was able to come and go in their country without any difficulty. The Germans knew only that I was a member of the Air Staff with evident connections in important places and that when I came to Germany I was on leave. They felt I was sympathetic to their cause and they hoped that I was putting that across to the Chiefs of Staff.... At times it was dangerous ... I was really playing a dangerous confidence trick, a game of double-bluff ... I had to praise the work of the Nazis to their faces in order to get them to talk with uninhibited enthusiasm about their plans for the future, which in fact they did, and yet at the same time to appear serious in my intentions to influence im-

portant people in London on the Nazis' behalf. This was the quid pro quo which allowed me to see and learn so much.[65]

Rosenberg took Winterbotham on a three-day tour of Germany, visiting various Luftwaffe airfields. On their return to Berlin, Rosenberg arranged an important lunch meeting with some senior officers at the famous Horcher restaurant. Winterbotham, de Ropp, and Rosenberg were joined by two Air Force Commodores, Wenninger and Kesselring, and one of Hitler's favourite generals, Walter von Reichenau. Winterbotham later wrote about the meeting:

> Rosenberg opened the proceedings by reminding me that I had asked the Fuhrer if I could learn more about the Russian plans, so the Fuhrer had then asked General Reichenau, who was the principal planner for the operation against Russia, to talk to me.... He was there to tell me all about it; it seemed incredible.... The General started talking in almost perfect English.[66]

Over the next few hour, Reichenau gave Winterbotham detailed information on the planned German invasion of Soviet Russia. Speed and surprise were to be two key elements of victory. Vast spearheads of panzer tanks would be driven into Russia, covering 200 miles per day. As they proceeded, motorised infantry and artillery would defend their flanks, while the Luftwaffe would help take care of all opposition from the air. Aerodrome landing strips would rapidly be established behind the advancing armies, complete with repair workshops, mechanics, armourers, refuellers and aerodrome guards. The aircraft would attack enemy positions, return immediately for fuel and weapons, then head out again. Cargo planes would continually ferry food rations and munitions to these advance airfields. If the tanks and armoured divisions proceeded at their scheduled speed, it would not take them long to reach their objectives of Leningrad, Moscow and the Black Sea. Von Reichenau was confident that with a spring start, it would all be over in the early summer.[67]

Seven years later, 22 June 1941, Germany invaded the Western Soviet Union across a 900-mile front with 3,500 panzer tanks, 3,000 armoured vehicles, 7,000 artillery pieces, 2,500 aircraft, 6,000 lorries, and over 3.5 million troops. "Surprise" was to be one of the two key elements necessary for the success of the attack, and one has to wonder if the information passed to two British agents (Winterbotham and de Ropp) that day in 1934 played any part in Germany's ultimate failure in Operation Barbarossa. It would cost Germany over 1 million casualties, and the Russians many more. The consequences of General Reichenau's astonishing revelations to Winterbotham that day in February 1934 are almost unfathomable.

In June 1934, Putzi received Hitler's permission to go to the United States for his Harvard class 25th year reunion. The chief Marshal of the celebration, Dr. Eliot Cutler (an eminent Harvard surgeon and soon to be Brigadier-General in the U.S. Army) had chosen his old friend Putzi as his

principal aide. Putzi sailed on the SS *Europa* with five large suitcases and three wooden crates (the contents of which have never been disclosed). The visit caused considerable controversy, but the State Department declared that it had no desire to intervene. Some 2,000 protestors greeted the *Europa* on arrival at Pier 86. Banners proclaimed, "Oust Nazi Hanfstaengl" and "Ship the Hitler agent back," but President Franklin Roosevelt sent a telegram to his old friend Putzi, wishing him a pleasant visit. NYPD officers smuggled him ashore.

At the reunion march-past in the Harvard football stadium where Putzi had once been cheerleader, former classmate Max Pinansky approached Putzi and ostentatiously shook his hand. It was controversial in the fact that Pinansky was Maine's first Jewish judge. Pictures of the handshake appeared on the front pages of the afternoon's newspapers, in which Putzi was hailed as a 'peacemaker'. That evening around the university campus, however, a large crowd of protesters denounced Hitler and the Nazis, and accused Harvard of disgracing itself by inviting Putzi. Police moved in and dispersed them.

The following week, Putzi attended the Rhode Island wedding of John Jacob Astor (arguably America's wealthiest bachelor) to the hugely wealthy Ellen Tuck French. Putzi was guest of honour at the prewedding lunch and sat in the Astor family pew at the church ceremony. Putzi had long known both the Astor and French families. The groom's father, Col. John Jacob Astor, had been one of Putzi's American family's closest friends. He drowned on the *Titanic* in 1912.

30 June 1934 was destined to go down in history as a date far more important than the Astor-French wedding. Back in Germany it was the "Night of the Long Knives," when Hitler ordered the murder of Nazis he considered might be plotting against him. Estimates ranging between 100 and 1,000 were slaughtered by the SS and Gestapo, including Ernst Röhm, leader of the SA.

Röhm

Putzi was shaken by the news, and relates that on his return from America he began to feel "insecure" and started smuggling out gold and platinum to London "to be ready for all eventualities." Regarding his safety, Putzi had spoken to an emissary who brought a message from his old friend President Roosevelt who was well aware of Putzi's true role and his dangerous situation in Germany. FDR's message was clear: "If things start getting awkward, please get in touch with our ambassador at once." Putzi relates: "The message heartened me enormously, and in due course I was to do just that."[68] The 'emissary' who brought FDR's message was John Franklin Carter, a 'journalist' working for Roosevelt's private intelligence agency. Carter's parents had been friends of Putzi's mother in the United States.[69] Like Roosevelt, Franklin Carter was well aware that Putzi was no fan of Hitler's, but was operating in Germany on behalf of the Anglo-American intelligence services.

In due course we consider Putzi's daring escape from Germany in 1937 with his mission accomplished. But first, we examine the massive financial and moral support Hitler received from British and American banking elites to build the new war machine needed for the onslaught on Russia.

SUMMARY: CHAPTER 18 – FIRE AND BRIMSTONE

- Hitler was banned from public speaking in 1925 and entered what became known as his "quiet years."

- When the Great Depression began in 1930, Hitler and Putzi campaigned heavily across Germany. The Nazi Party gained 18.3 per cent of the vote and 107 seats in the Reichstag, and was now the second-largest party.

- In addition to Putzi, numerous British intelligence agents were positioned in Germany. William de Ropp, like Putzi, managed to infiltrate the inner core of the Nazi Party and become a trusted confidant of Hitler's.

- In the presidential election of March 1932, Hitler gained 30 per cent of the vote to Paul von Hindenburg's 49.6 percent. Putzi's friend, Winston Churchill visited Munich that spring and invited Hitler for dinner, but he declined.

- In the July 1932 elections for the Reichstag, the Nazis increased their seats to 230 (out of 608), and the Nazi Hermann Goring was appointed the president of the Reichstag.

- In the second Reichstag election of November 1932, the Nazi vote dropped. It lost 34 seats in parliament, but after much political wheeling and dealing, on 28 January1933, Hitler became Chancellor of Germany. In a bid to get a majority, he insisted on another election which was called for 5 March.

- On the night of 27 February 27, 1933, a team of Nazi arsonists directed by Putzi Hanfstaengl, set fire to the Reichstag and destroyed it. Hitler blamed it on the communists, who suffered dramatic losses at the election held six days later.

- A State of Emergency was declared in Germany. Hitler opened concentration camps and began a reign of terror; communist members of the Reichstag were imprisoned or murdered. Germany was now under a dictatorship.

- Group Captain Frederick Winterbotham of British Intelligence gained the confidence of Hitler. He made frequent trips back and forth to Germany and was given highly confidential information about Hitler's plan to invade Soviet Russia.

- In 1934 Hitler ordered a bloody purge of his own party. Hundreds of Nazis who he considered might be disloyal to him were brutally slaughtered.

CHAPTER 19

A VAST TAPESTRY OF LIES

John Dalberg-Acton (1834-1902) philosopher, Regius Professor of Modern History at Cambridge University, and Liberal Member of Parliament, stated:

> Everything secret degenerates, even the administration of justice; nothing is safe that does not show how it can bear discussion and publicity.... The issue which has swept down the centuries and which will have to be fought sooner or later is the people versus the banks.[1]

British playwright and Nobel Prize winner, Harold Pinter agreed. When awarded the Nobel Prize in Literature in Stockholm in 2005, Pinter told the gathering:

> Truth in drama is forever elusive. You never quite find it but the search for it is compulsive. The search is clearly what drives the endeavour. The search is your task.... Political language, as used by politicians, does not venture into any of this territory since the majority of politicians, on the evidence available to us, are interested not in truth but in power and in the maintenance of that power. To maintain that power it is essential that people remain in ignorance, that they live in ignorance of the truth, even the truth of their own lives. What surrounds us therefore is a vast tapestry of lies...[2]

We have seen how a vast tapestry of lies was created to conceal Anglo-American guilt for the First World War and Germany's innocence. With the first phase of their plan successfully accomplished, The Milner Group and associated City and Wall Street bankers would go on to create another totally false narrative about their role in the rise of Hitler and fomenting the Second World War.

Pro-establishment historians describe the economic problems Germany faced after the First World War as deeply complex and difficult to understand, but when one strips away the tapestry of lies the situation becomes patently clear. In 1919 the victorious Anglo-American allies responsible for the war blamed the innocent Germans then looted the defeated Germany until the country was economically and politically wrecked. From 1924, American banks, J.P. Morgan – in particular – started pouring money into Germany to create a number of giant industrial cartels which would generate vast profits for Wall Street and help set Germany up for the second phase of the Thirty Years War.

To finance the 1914-18 war, Britain and France had taken huge loans from American banks – mostly J.P. Morgan – and from 1919 had to repay the loans plus interest. The difficulty, not least for the J.P. Morgan bank, was that Britain and France had been virtually bankrupted by the war and were struggling to pay their war debts to the United States. After the United States' formal entry into the First World War, the US provided Britain and France with loans amounting to $8.8 billion. The total sum of war debt owed to the U.S., including loans offered between 1919 and 1921, reached $11 billion. To solve their own financial problems Britain and France went after Germany, forcing it to pay enormous sums in reparations under extremely difficult conditions. The rigged Treaty of Versailles war reparations demands had effectively made Germany responsible for everyone's debts. She would be obliged to pay enormous sums of money to Britain and France who would then use it to pay their debt to Wall Street. The problem was, of course, how could the bankrupted Germany possibly meet the Versailles reparations demands?

In 1919 the German Finance Minister Mathias Erzberger, a conscientious and skilled politician, had begun to tax the wealthy, but the policy back-fired when wealthy Germans started sending their money abroad. The conversion of marks into foreign currency resulted in more depreciation, which in turn made imports even dearer and added to inflation. On 31 August 1921, Germany paid her first instalment of reparations. Thousands of tons of gold and silver were physically conveyed from the German banks by rail to Holland, Denmark and elsewhere then taken by ships to America. That caused an immediate devaluation of the mark against the dollar, diminishing Germany's ability both to recover economically and continue paying reparations.[3] The ensuing hyperinflation would tear Germany apart, gutting its financial sector and wiping out the savings of the middle classes. In his book, *When Money Dies, The Nightmare of the Weimar Hyperinflation*, Scottish historian and writer Adam Fergusson relates:

> On 27 April 1921, the Reparations Commission fixed Germany's total liability at 132,000 million gold marks, equivalent to £6,600

million [a vast sum at today's values]. The problem was how and over what period it must be paid. The Commission decided that Germany would pay 2,000 million gold marks – £100 million – a year and, in addition, a sum equal to 26 per cent of her exports. These terms were conveyed to Berlin accompanied by a threat of further sanctions – namely the occupation of the Ruhr which the French were pressing for – if compliance did not come within the week. This 'London Ultimatum' ... caused the Fehrenbach government to fall. It was supplanted by that of Dr. Wirth who ... accepted those terms knowing that heavy additional taxation would have to be imposed on the nation.[4]

With the theft of Germany's gold (which was now sitting in bank vaults in New York), Germany was like putty in the hands of the international bankers. When marks were mass-produced without the backing of gold, the currency collapsed and hyperinflation peaked in 1923 at over 500,000%. In the exchange rate, one U.S dollar was now worth millions of 'papiermarks,' with the papiermark  plummeting on the foreign exchange markets even faster than it fell in Germany. Weimar Germany was effectively reduced to a barter economy. It would be reconstructed according to the wishes of the bankers. British economist Lionel Robbins wrote:

> The depreciation of the mark of 1914-23 is one of the outstanding episodes in the history of the twentieth century. Not only by reason of its magnitude but also by reason of its effects, it looms large on our horizon. It was the most colossal thing of its kind in history: and, next probably to the Great War itself, it must bear responsibility for many of the political and economic difficulties of our generation. It destroyed the wealth of the more solid elements in German society: and it left behind a moral and economic disequilibrium, and breeding ground for the disasters which have followed. Hitler is the foster-child of the inflation.[5]

At the height of the German hyperinflation, some 18,000 printing machines were operating round the clock to put more and more virtually worthless money into circulation. By 1923 the inflation rate reached

578,512% and one dollar was worth 4.2 trillion papiermarks. The collapse meant that it was costing more to produce the banknotes than they were worth, and hungry Germans were using wheelbarrows to convey loads of paper money around trying to buy a loaf of bread. With the mind-boggling hyperinflation wreaking chaos, and domestic industrial production stagnating, Germany was failing to meet the punitive reparations payments or the deliveries of coal and timber to France and Belgium as imposed at Versailles. The Versailles Treaty had stripped Germany of 13 per cent of its territory, 15 per cent of its farmlands, a quarter of its coal mines and three-quarters of its iron production, and the German economy seemed beyond all hope of recovery. In 1923, when France and Belgium did not receive the coal and timber they demanded from Germany, they sent troops in to occupy the Ruhr valley and "take by force what could not be obtained voluntarily."[6]

The hyperinflation and distortions of the international system of borrowing and lending did not 'just happen'. They were carefully orchestrated by London and Wall Street bankers to create disastrous economic conditions in Germany and social chaos. Professor Sutton wrote:

> The final payments plan worked out at the "London Ultimatum" in May 1921 reflected the harsh and impossible terms and so provided a clear incentive to inflate to remove the burden of direct payments. What is extraordinary about the reparations program is the identity of the so-called experts engaged in making the reparations arrangements, incidentally creating the monetary and social chaos.... The Reparations Committee had as its U.S. members Brigadier General Charles G. Dawes and Owen D. Young of the General Electric Company.[7]

It is important to understand that the monetary and social chaos in Germany was not caused by the democratically elected governments of Britain and US per se, but by super-rich and powerful private citizens in the City and Wall Street who were accountable to no one. Senior members of the governments were certainly culpable in that – often for personal financial gain – they failed to control the bankers nefarious games concerning Germany. Having wrecked the German economy and political stability, from 1924 onwards those self-same bankers would now set about reconstructing Germany according to their own agenda. They would effectively control German politics, the German central bank, and much of industry.

The German economy was placed under the supervision of an American agent-general, which meant Germany was now effectively in foreign receivership.[8]

With their control of Germany, Wall Street bankers funded the creation of giant German industrial cartels (on the US model) that would create massive profits for them and eventually arm Nazi Germany to the teeth for war on Soviet Russia. That, in a nutshell, is what the so-called "Dawes Plan" and "Young Plan" were about. The vast 'Tapestry of Lies,' however, would present the plans as the work of decent men who genuinely cared about future peace and harmony in Europe – especially between France and Germany – and as bringing back decent living standards to the beleaguered people of Germany. As ever, it was Orwellian double-speak such as that exemplified by Frank Costigliola, professor of history at Connecticut University wrote:

> The foreign economic policy of the United States in the aftermath of World War I was not isolationist, but selectively interventionist. With a group of very able American businessmen-diplomats in the lead, the nation pressured the French to accept the Dawes Plan, which, it was hoped, would solve the reparations problem, encourage healthy economic recovery and growth (which would embrace large sales of American capital goods to Germany), and ensure peaceful contentment in two nations that were more bitter enemies than ever.[9]

The giant General Electric Company in the United States with which Charles Dawes was connected, was a J.P. Morgan entity formed in 1892. Morgan had financed the merger of several smaller companies, including that of the famous Thomas Edison, to form the General Electric cartel. The reality was, Dawes was not a "very-able" businessman seeking to ensure "peaceful contentment" between Germany and France, but a "very able" puppet of J.P. Morgan and acting on Morgan's behalf to screw Germany. It was Morgan and associated bankers who were controlling the reconstruction of Germany behind the scenes in order to set her up for another war with Russia.

529

The "Dawes" Plan (1924-1929)

When Germany could not afford to pay reparations to France, the French army was sent in to occupy the Ruhr. In response, almost the entire German workforce of the Rhine and Ruhr went on strike. With the situation spiralling out of control and endangering the carefully considered plans of the bankers, they had to act to resolve the dilemma with the so-called Dawes Plan. From that point in time, the real power that controlled reparations – the Reparations Committee – shifted to this new concept, the Dawes Plan. It would enable Germany to pay the outrageous reparations decreed at Versailles by borrowing vast amounts of money from Wall Street through the sale of German bonds. To encourage the bond issue, some financial manipulation was required.

Frank Costigliola wrote in *Business History Review*:

> Bankers in the United States were pessimistic about selling Dawes loan bonds to American investors. The problem was not a dearth of funds, but a lack of confidence in the European situation. To encourage Americans to buy high-interest foreign bonds and to combat the growing domestic recession, Governor Strong lowered the New York Reserve Bank's discount rate from 4.5 per cent to 3 per cent – the lowest rate in the world.... As for the Dawes loan, what the "market" would demand was in fact set by J. P. Morgan and Company, which was headed by J. Pierpont Morgan, Jr. Morgan, following the underwriting policy laid down by his father, insisted that his firm exercise primary control of the issue of the Dawes loan in the United States.... They [the bankers] were determined to wrest control over reparations (and with it the crucial power to decide if Germany were in default) away from the Allied governments and vest it in the Dawes Plan control machinery dominated by Americans [that is, the bankers].
>
> At 10 A.M. on October 14, [1924] a nation-wide syndicate of 400 banks and 800 bond houses led by J. P. Morgan and Company opened the German loan subscription books. By 10:15, the syndicate had received orders for the total American portion of the loan ($110,000,000) and had to turn away an additional $400-900,000,000. The new hunger for German bonds did not stop with the Dawes stabilization loan, for American investors began to buy large amounts of other German bonds. While bankers scrambled to find loan customers, German local governments and corporations rushed to get at the trough of American capital. In the years after 1924, American investors put up 80 per cent of the money borrowed by German public credit institutions, 75 per cent of that borrowed by local governments, *and 56 per cent of the loans to large corporations.*[10]

The American loans were a machiavellian economic manipulation that enabled Germany to pay war reparations to France and England, and for France and England to then pay their massive war debts to the Wall Street bankers. But of greater importance was the fact outlined above that more than half the money went to large corporations in Germany which, as we shall see in due course, would build up the Nazi military with American help.

On 11 March 1924, J.P. Morgan gave the Bank of France a six-month credit for $100,000,000. It committed the French to the success of the Dawes Plan. In other words, if the French wanted American loans they had better keep their noses, and everything else, out of Germany. That beleaguered country's future was for the Anglo-American banking elites to decide. The plan was named after the above- mentioned Brigadier General Charles G. Dawes, "a banker tied to the J.P. Morgan group whose prior career had been tainted with corruption and Republican Party payoff scandals in Illinois."[11]

Professor Guido Preparata writes:

> It bore Dawes' name, but it wasn't his plan – it actually 'made him sick,' out of modesty, to hear it said afterwards that he did it alone. No, in fact, the Dawes Plan was largely a J. P. Morgan production, directed by Montagu Norman [Governor of the Bank of England] who proceeded at this critical stage, by the proxy of his American colleagues, to blackmail the French. If the French wished to see their $100 million loan renewed, Morgan & Co. warned them, they had better adopt a 'peaceful foreign policy peremptorily.[12]

The Dawes Plan is presented by British Establishment-line historians as offering the destitute Germany a fair and equitable means of settling her war reparation debts while at the same time stabilising the mark and enabling her industrial growth. With Germany's gold now in American bank vaults, her gold-based marks were ultimately replaced by fiat marks based on dollar reserves loaned by the USA. It was now a debt-based currency which meant that the US (or rather Wall Street) literally owned the German economy and much of its productive capacity. Germany's gold ended up in Wall Street – as did much of Britain's and France's – since it was used to pay war debt to the US. Carroll Quigley wrote that the "Dawes" Plan was in fact "largely a J.P. Morgan production."[13] Quigley added:

> It is worthy of note that this system was set up by the international bankers and that the subsequent lending of other people's money to Germany was very profitable to the bankers. Using the American loans, German industry was largely re-equipped with the most advanced technical facilities, and almost every German municipality

was provided with a post office, a swimming pool, sports facilities, or other non-productive equipment. With these American loans Germany was able to rebuild her industrial system to make it the second best in the world by a wide margin. ... By these loans Germany's creditors were able to pay their war debts to England and to the United States .... Foreign exchange went to Germany as loans, back to Italy, Belgium, France and Britain as war reparations, and finally back to the United States as payments of war debts. It would collapse as soon as the United States ceased to lend, and in the meantime debts were being shifted from one account to another and no one was really getting any nearer to solvency. In the period 1924-1931, Germany paid 10.5 billion marks in reparations but borrowed abroad a total of 18.6 billion marks. Nothing was settled by all this, but the international bankers sat in heaven, under a rain of fees and commissions.[14]

Germany's sovereign national currency, hitherto backed by gold reserves, was replaced by U.S. bank-based debt currency. Quite a trick! The bankers got Germany's gold; Germany got the bankers' paper! And all the while the bankers took control of German industry and the German economy. Between 1924-1929, foreign investment in German industry totalled over 62 billion marks, with loans accounting for half of this. By 1929 German industry ranked second in the world, but by a considerable margin was in the hands of financial groups in the United States, in particular J.P. Morgan.

Germany was now an economic prisoner to the Anglo-American bankers, but the infernal beauty of the scam was that the 'loans' to Germany were really intended to restore Germany's military-industrial potential that would be used to wage the Anglo-American bankers' next war. The Dawes Plan stipulated that the Allies would select an agent-general to preside over Germany's economy, reparations transfers, and effective execution of the Plan. The man chosen for the position, Seymour Parker Gilbert, was serving as Under-Secretary of the U.S. Treasury. He was posted to Germany, effectively as economic czar, and when his mission was successfully accomplished, on his return home he was rewarded with a lucrative directorship of the Morgan Bank. The bankers now subjected Germany to the biggest financial con-trick the world had ever known, while at the same time preparing it for the next war. Ron Chernow writes:

> Aside from a stipulation that it would get back the Ruhr, what reconciled Germany to the Dawes Plan was the prospect of a giant loan floated in New York and Europe. Reparations would be largely paid with foreign money ... To give the loan international seasoning, half

the issue appeared in New York and the other half in London and other European capitals. The $110 million New York portion was enthusiastically received and oversubscribed. By seeming to settle the German question, the loan lifted a weight from the financial markets. For Weimar Germany it was a turning point. It became the decade's largest sovereign borrower. American capital and companies poured in: Ford, General Motors, E.I. Dupont, General Electric, Standard Oil of New Jersey, and Dow Chemicals. Unemployment plunged and Germany's economic slide was reversed into a five-year upturn. This revival would provide Adolf Hitler with a splendid industrial machine and money to finance massive rearmament.[15]

The Dawes Plan loans put much of German industry in American hands, and stipulated that the central bank must – like the British and US central banks – be removed from political control. The Anglo-American financial elite soon had their own man, Hjalmar Schacht, installed as president of the Reichsbank.

Hjalmar Horace Greely Schacht (1877-1970)

Schacht's ancestors on both his father's and mother's sides were proud Danes. When Danish resistance against Prussian and Austrian forces crumbled in a short war in 1864, the Schachts' homeland of Schleswig-Holstein was annexed into the Kingdom of Prussia by Bismarck (1867). Schacht's parents emigrated to the United States, took American citizenship and their first son, William, was born in the United States. Hjalmar would have been born there too had the family not returned to Europe in 1876 because his mother became ill while pregnant with Hjalmar. He was born in Tinglev, a small town which had long been Danish but had been annexed by the victorious Prussians in 1867. The Schacts and many other Danes remained deeply bitter about Prussia's annexation of parts of their homeland. One important Dane with such bitter feelings, as we have seen in chapter 3, was Princess Alexandra of Denmark, one of the Danish king's daughters, who married Prince Albert Edward, the eldest son of Queen Victoria. The Schachts were proud Danes, not Germans, and instilled that ethos in their children. Most of Schleswig-Holstein, including Tinglev, was returned to Denmark in 1920.

Hjalmar Schacht initially studied medicine but changed courses and graduated with a major in political economy. As a young banker, he worked for the Dresdner Bank in Berlin which was linked with J.P. Morgan on Wall Street. *Encyclopedia Americana* states:

> In 1905 Dresdner formed a close alliance with J.P. Morgan & Co. of New York, for joint action in international finance and issue operations, particularly the absorption of American securities by German investors.[16]

It was through the Dresdner Bank that J.P. Morgan floated American securities which would bring considerable investments to Wall Street,[17] and it was Schacht's involvement with this lucrative Morgan business that brought him to the attention of the Anglo-American elites. On a business trip to the United States in 1905 on behalf of the Dresdner Bank, the young Schacht was introduced to his brother freemason, President Theodore Roosevelt, and to J.P. Morgan himself.[18]

During the First World War, Schacht was assigned to Belgium to organize the finances for German food purchasing, and it is entirely likely that in that capacity he had regular contact with Herbert Hoover and the Belgian Relief scam that fed the German army and prolonged the war. Irrespective of how Schacht first became entangled with the American banking elites, his close association with them in the inter-war years to the overall detriment of Germany strongly indicates that his loyalty lay with them rather than with Germany. Professor Sutton wrote:

> In brief, Schacht was a member of the international financial elite that wields power behind the scenes through the political apparatus of a nation. He is a key link between Wall Street and Hitler's inner circle.[19]

Schacht's membership of the international financial elite first became apparent in late 1923, when substantial Dawes loans were first discussed with Germany. Money would only be made available to Germany if their central bank, the Reichsbank, was removed from political control and run by a banker who 'knew what he was talking about,' a man by the name of Hjalmar Schacht.

> Out of thin air and five days after Hitler's failed putsch on 13 November 1923, Schacht was catapulted on the public stage as Germany's new Commissioner for the National Currency.[20]

Almost immediately, Schacht requested a meeting with the Governor of the Bank of England, Montagu Norman, with whom he had been closely corresponding[21] "as he wished to consult him before commencing his duties as president of the Reichsbank."[22]

On 31 December, when Schacht arrived in London off the boat train, standing on Liverpool Street station's ice-cold platform to greet him personally was the mighty world banking guru, Montagu Norman. Thus began a long, close, and mysterious friendship. Professor Preparata comments that from that moment on Hjalmar Schacht and Montagu Norman were "like twins" rather than ordinary friends.[23]

Germany – a first-class Power before the war – was now economically wrecked, effectively placed in receivership, and under foreign control with a City/Wall Street puppet, Schacht, in charge of its central bank. He would be assisted in running the Reichsbank by a General Council of 14 members, half of them drawn from Allied countries.[24] Wall Street banker Gates White McGarrah II was appointed as the American director of the Reichsbank's general council. At the same time, McGarrah was a director of the Federal Reserve Bank of New York and the Bankers Trust Company which was controlled by J. P. Morgan.

With the German central bank removed from government control, it was now effectively being run by Wall Street through Schacht and McGarrah. Under their financial leadership, in November 1923 German hyperinflation was halted with the expedient of a temporary currency, the Rentenmark.

> The first notes were printed on November 15, 1923. One rentenmark could be exchanged for one trillion old marks (1,000,000,000,000). One U.S. dollar cost 4.2 rentenmarks, a return to the pre-WW1 exchange rate.... Taxes were raised, and four hundred thousand German public employees were sacked. But the rentenmark successfully stopped the German inflation so well that on December 22, 1923 Schacht was promoted to be president of the Reichsbank, while retaining his position as currency commissioner.... "Within a few weeks," notes John Weitz, Schacht's biographer, "he had virtually become Germany's economic dictator."[25]

Simultaneously, all subsidy payments to workers in the Ruhr were suspended, and a quarter of all government employees sacked. That, together with the huge Dawes loan, brought hyperinflation under control. The budget was quickly balanced and Schacht was feted in the press as "The Wizard" or the "Miracle Man."[26]

Historian Michael Burleigh writes:

> A loan of 800 million gold Marks promoted confidence in the new
> currency, and acted as a priming aid for a regularised schedule of
> payments on reparations. Since these stretched into the infinity of
> the late 1980s, and involved foreign control of Germany's railways
> and central bank, they did not allay nationalist resentment any
> more than currency stabilisation placated the struggling middle
> classes.[27]

As in many important events in Germany in the post-war years, it
was not Germans who decided but Anglo-Americans, with their man
Schacht playing a major role. In 1933 he was a central player in creating
the group of German industrialists and landowners that pushed Hindenburg to appoint the first Nazi government in 1933. Although Schacht
never joined the NSDAP, he would serve in Adolf Hitler's government
as President of the Reichsbank from 1933 to 1939 and as Nazi Germany's Minister of Economics from August 1934 to November 1937.
Schacht was tried at Nuremberg for "conspiracy" and "crimes against
peace" (planning and waging wars of aggression), but not war crimes or
crimes against humanity. He was acquitted of all charges at the behest
of the British judges, and although sentenced to eight years jail in post-
war Germany, he was released on appeal and opened a new bank, Deutsche Aussenhandelsbank
Schacht & Co. Schacht's
long and intimate rela-
tionship with the City
and Wall Street bankers
saved his skin. The Pow-
ers look after their own.
Interestingly, but not
surprisingly, in addition
to being close to Bank
of England Governor

Schacht   Putzi

Montagu Norman, Schacht was a "close friend" of Putzi Hanfstaengl.[28]
Hanfstaengl and Schacht played complementary roles in the heart of
Nazi Germany on behalf of the financial elite. They did so not to help
Germany, but to bring about its demise.

With the financial manipulations in 1924, the German people finally
experienced some respite. The tub-thumping Hitler lost his appeal to the

masses and, as we have seen, went into his quiet years at Berchtesgaden to bide his time.

William Shirer writes in *The Rise and Fall of the Third Reich*:

> Even many of his old comrades agreed with the general opinion that Hitler was finished, that now he would fade away into oblivion as had so many other provincial politicians who had enjoyed a brief moment on notoriety during the strife years when it seemed the Republic would totter. But the Republic had weathered the storms. It was beginning to thrive. While Hitler was in prison a financial wizard by the name of Dr. Hjalmar Horace Greely Schacht had been called in to stabilize the currency, and he had succeeded. The ruinous inflation was over. The burden of reparations was eased by the Dawes Plan. Capital began to flow in from America. The economy was rapidly recovering. Stresemann [Gustav Stresemann – chancellor and foreign minister of the coalition government] was succeeding in his policy of reconciliation with the Allies. The French were getting out of the Ruhr. A security pact was being discussed which would pave the way for a general European settlement (Locarno) and bring Germany into the League of Nations. For the first time since the defeat, after six years of tension, turmoil and depression, the German people were beginning to have a normal life.[29]

Germany's troubles may have appeared to be over thanks to the Dawes Plan loans and the "financial wizard" Schacht, but it was a mirage. William Shirer either did not understand what was going on in Germany at that time or, more likely, was playing a role in the tapestry of lies that obfuscated it. The stark reality was that Germany's international debt burden simply kept mounting *due to* the Dawes Plan, and she would be plunged into further turmoil at a time of the bankers choosing. This came with the Crash of 1929, the withdrawal of American investment from Germany and the country's consequent plunge into Depression. The Nazi Party's political fortunes suddenly revived dramatically. Hjalmar Schacht, who was clandestinely working for the international bankers, professed to be a genuine admirer of Hitler. In the 1930s, he drummed up support for Hitler and encouraged German bankers to give money to the Nazis. He told American journalist, Edgar Mowrer that "Germany will have no peace until we bring Hitler to power." Three weeks later, after Schacht had a meeting with Hitler around Christmas 1932, he had another meeting with Mowrer, telling him that he had Hitler "right in my pocket."[30]

Deeply involved in the deliberate economic manipulations that led to the re-emergence of Hitler was Schacht's "twin" and one of the greatest financial evil geniuses of all time: Montagu Norman, Governor of the Bank of England 1920-1944.

MONTAGU NORMAN (1871-1950)

From a wealthy English banking family, Montagu Norman served as Governor of the Bank of England for 24 years, the longest tenure of any Governor by a wide margin. Educated at Eton, both his father and grandfather had been Bank of England directors and were deeply entrenched in the British Establishment. Ron Chernow writes:

> For twenty-four years, Monty Norman reigned mysteriously in his mahogany office at the Bank of England. He came to the bank via the Anglo-American merchant bank of Brown Shipley and Company (Brown Brothers in New York). Many labels have been applied to Norman – madman, genius, hypochondriac, megalomaniac, conspirator, eccentric, visionary – all of which were true ... Despite – or perhaps to counter – rumours of Sephardic Jewish blood, he was viciously anti-Semitic.... A suppressed hysteric, he would erupt in tantrums that terrified bank employees and made his rule absolute. His thin smile rarely opened into laughter, as if that might shatter his mystique.... One of Norman's biographers described him as giving "the appearance of being engaged in a perpetual conspiracy." This conformed to his sense of central banking, which he approached as a priestly mystery, a rite best conducted in the deep shadows.[31]

Norman was a hugely influential figure; the *Wall Street Journal* referring to him as "the currency dictator of Europe." Carrol Quigley spoke of Norman's close ties to Wall Street, J.P. Morgan in particular:

> Norman rarely acted in a major world problem without consulting with J.P. Morgan's representative, and as a consequence was one of the most widely travelled men of his day.[32]

Montagu Norman, as we have seen, became a close friend – "the twin" – of Hjalmar Schacht who would serve Hitler as President of the Reichsbank and Minister of Economics. Professor Preparata writes that "Schacht was Montagu Norman's protégé."[33] Norman was also very close to J.P.

Morgan, with Ron Chernow describing him as "the most influential British ally in Morgan history."[34] Yet another 'very close friend' of Montagu Norman's was Benjamin Strong, Governor of the Federal Reserve Bank of New York from 1914 until his death at the age of 55 in 1928.

BENJAMIN STRONG (1872-1928)

Strong   Norman

An American banker and staunch Anglophile, Benjamin Strong's English Puritan ancestors sailed to Massachusetts in 1630. A leading J.P. Morgan player, he attended the Jekyll Island gathering in November 1910 with Paul Warburg and others to plan the corrupt US central bank. Strong was a devoted friend of Montagu Norman and spent so many intimate holidays with him that rumours arose of a homosexual relationship. Their get-togethers were so frequent and prolonged "and their collaborations so close that it is still impossible to determine accurately their relative roles in developing the ideas and projects that they shared."[35] Benjamin Strong, like so many, owed his career to the favour of the Morgan Bank, and in 1909 was made vice-president of the Bankers Trust which was dominated by Morgan interests. He was appointed Governor of the Federal Reserve Bank of New York in 1914 as the joint nominee of Morgan and of Kuhn, Loeb and Company.[36] Under the management of Strong, the New York Federal Reserve branch rapidly gained dominance over the entire Federal Reserve System.

> Strong was solidly in the Morgan mold [and] the House of Morgan benefitted incalculably from his patronage. In fact, the Morgan-Strong friendship would mock any notion of the new Federal Reserve System as a curb on private banking power. ... Ben Strong participated in postwar European reconstruction and currency stabilization with his British counterpart, Montagu Norman, Governor of the Bank of England after 1920. In Monty, he found a friend and alter ego. The divorced Strong and the bachelor Norman plunged into a relationship of such secret intimacy and convoluted intrigue as to arouse fears in both their governments. Taking long vacations together in Bar Harbor, Maine, and southern France, they fortified each other's distrust of politicians. They shared faith in the

gold standard and hoped to create autonomous central banks that could conduct global monetary policy free of political tampering.[37]

As Governor of the Federal Reserve Bank of New York, Benjamin Strong was closely linked not merely to J.P. Morgan on Wall Street, but to the Governors of the British and German central banks, Montagu Norman and Hjalmar Schact. When Strong died in October 1928 following surgery for an abdominal abscess, he was replaced as Governor of the Federal Reserve Bank of New York by George L. Harrison.

George L. Harrison

A member of the Skull and Bones secret society at Yale, and a graduate from Harvard Law School, Harrison served as general counsel to the Federal Reserve Board, and when Strong died in 1928 he took over as president of the Federal Reserve Bank of New York. When he departed his post as governor of the bank in 1940, his unstinting work for the bankers was rewarded with the highly lucrative presidency of the New York Life Insurance Company, then a J.P Morgan concern.

The central bank governors, Montagu Norman, Benjamin Strong, George L. Harrison and Hjalmar Schacht were extremely powerful financial operators in the 1920s and 30s, but by no means did they have the ultimate say in international banking. Carroll Quigley wrote:

> It must not be felt that these heads of the world's chief central banks were themselves substantive powers in world finance. They were not. Rather, they were the technicians and agents of the dominant investment bankers of their own countries, who had raised them up and were perfectly capable of throwing them down. The substantive financial powers of the world were in the hands of these investment bankers (also called "international" or "merchant" bankers) who remained largely behind the scenes in their own unincorporated private banks. These formed a system of international cooperation and national dominance which was more private, more powerful, and more secret than that of their agents in the central banks.... They could dominate governments by their control over current government loans and the play of the international exchanges.[38]

As intended, the Dawes Plan loans left the German government beholden to the international bankers who now controlled its central bank through their agent, Hjalmar Schacht. William Engdahl writes that in 1923 the overwhelming choice of the Reichsbank's board of governors for the president of the bank had been Karl Helfferich, former Deutsche Bank director and architect of the Baghdad railway project before the war. Helfferich, however, was killed in April 1924 "in a suspicious train accident." Engdahl added:

> The Dawes Plan was the Anglo-American community's reassertion of full fiscal and financial control over Germany.... On December 18, 1923 ... friend of the Anglo-American Morgan interests, Hjalmar Schacht was named president of the Reichsbank. The way was ready for the Dawes Plan to proceed ... Under the Dawes Plan, Germany paid reparations for five years until 1929. At the end of 1929, she owed more than at the beginning. It was a scheme of organized looting by the international banking community dominated by London and New York.... The London and New York banks began a vastly profitable lending to Germany, money which was recycled back to the banks of New York and London in the form of reparations with commission and interest. It was a vast international credit pyramid at the top of which sat London and ultimately, the New York banks. Between 1924 and 1931 Germany paid 10.5 billion marks in reparations, but borrowed 18.6 billion marks from abroad. Germany's recovery after 1923, under the guiding hand of Montagu Norman and his Reichsbank colleague, Hjalmar Schacht, was all controlled by the borrowings from the Anglo-Americans.[39]

In 1929 the Dawes Plan was superseded by the Young Plan. Named after Owen D. Young, lawyer, industrialist, and yet another senior player within the J.P. Morgan dynasty. Young was chairman of the board of the General Electric Company in New York, which, as we have seen, was a large combine created by Morgan in 1892. The new plan was a revision of the original Dawes bailout wherein Germany would now pay slightly reduced annual reparation instalments of 2 billion Reichsmarks until 1988. Including interest, the total was a staggering 112 billion Reichsmarks. The French benefitted financially from the plan when they agreed to vacate the Rhineland in 1930 – five years earlier than the original deadline imposed at Versailles.[40] The Young Plan came into effect in May 1930 but was suspended a year later in accordance with a moratorium from President Hoover because of the international financial crisis caused by the Great Depression. William Engdahl writes:

The pyramid collapsed in 1929, when the credit flowing from the New York and London banks to roll over the debt suddenly collapsed.... The unstable monetary order imposed after Versailles by London and New York bankers on a defeated central Europe came to an abrupt end. Montagu Norman, then the world's most influential banker as governor of the Bank of England, precipitated the crash of the Wall Street stock market in October 1929. Norman had asked the governor of the New York Federal Reserve Bank, George Harrison, to raise the U.S. interest rate levels. Harrison complied, and the most dramatic economic collapse in U.S history ensued in the following months ... Germany stood unique among major European industrial countries by the time of the 1929-30 New York stock market collapse. She owed international bank creditors an estimated 16 billion Reichsmarks in short term debts.[41]

Like the "den of robbers" cleansed from the temple by Christ, western bankers continued to bleed Germany dry, and after five years of improved living conditions for the German people, the bankers pulled the rug from under them. Hitler sat quietly through 1925-1929 preparing himself for big political moves, but as long as relative prosperity reigned, he and his National Socialist party remained on the periphery. The situation changed dramatically after the US Federal Reserve engineered the collapse of the stock market in the autumn of 1929. The dire economic circumstances of the early 1920s returned to Central Europe, and the Nazis were soon riding a wave of popular discontent. Basically, the bankers had looted Germany through reparations payments, but immediately when the country came under Hitler's dictatorship, they granted debt relief which freed funds for arming the Nazi state.

The Dawes and Young Plans provided the funds by which Germany could make the outrageous reparations payments, but we have seen how more than half of those funds enabled her to rebuild industrially and militarily through giant new cartels with one specific purpose – the next planned war. Professor Sutton wrote:

A practical example of international finance operating behind the scenes to build and manipulate the politico-economic systems is found in the German cartel system The three largest loans handled by Wall Street international bankers for German borrowers under the Dawes Plan were for the benefit of the three German cartels which a few years later aided Hitler and the Nazis to power. American financiers were directly represented on the boards of two of these three German cartels. The American assistance to German cartels has been described by James Martin as follows: "These loans for reconstruction became a vehicle for arrangements that did more to promote World War II than to establish peace after World War I.[42]

Guido Preparata writes;

> Up until 1930, some $28 billion flowed into Germany, 50 percent as short-term credits; The United States accounted for half that total. Only $10.3 billion was used for reparations, the rest went into many different and interesting directions.... Finally, when Germany resumed paying France the reparations, pacifying her, as it were, with an American-bred bone to gnaw at, the Franco-Belgian troops abandoned the Ruhr. This initiated Weimar's absurd cycle of the 'golden years' [and Hitler's 'quiet years]: the gold that Germany had paid as tribute after the war, sold, pawned, and lost during the inflation to the United States, was sent in the form of Dawes loans back to Germany, who then remitted it to France and Britain, who shipped it as payment for the war debts to the United States, who channelled it once again, burdened with an additional layer of interest to Germany, and so on.... The world, and even lenders at home, enquired of their politicians: "Why is Germany being boosted thus?" "She is our ally against Communism," they replied.... The money kept pouring in, and no one anywhere did anything to stop it. Germany was being turned into a veritable colony of Wall Street.... It was a house of cards: the moment Wall Street decided to recall its loans, Germany would plunge into complete, irremediable bankruptcy.... The fall was certain. It was just a matter of time.[43]

A significant amount of the money that poured into Germany was used in the creation of giant cartels that would eventually serve two purposes: (1) The funding of Hitler and the Nazis. (2) The means by which the mighty Nazi war machine could be constructed. Antony Sutton wrote:

> The three largest loans handled by Wall Street international bankers for German borrowers in the 1920's under the Dawes Plan were for the benefit of three German cartels which a few years later aided Hitler and the Nazis to power. American financiers were directly represented on the boards of two of the cartels. The amounts issued to the cartels by Wall Street syndicates were as follows;
> Allgemeine Elektrizitäts Gesellschaft (A.E.G.): $35,000,000.
> Vereinigte Stahlwerke (United Steelworks): $70,225,000.
> I.G. Farben: $30,000,000.[44] [massive amounts of money in today's worth.]

Allgemeine Elektrizitäts Gesellschaft (A.E.G.)

A.E.G., the 'General Electric' of Germany, was founded in 1883 by Emil Rathenau, a prominent Jewish businessman and industrial genius. It became one of the largest business concerns in Europe, building major power stations and carrying out the electrification of many major cities throughout the world. Emil Rathenau died in 1915 and his son, Walter, became chairman of the company. One of the founders of the German Democratic Party (DDP), after the First World War Walter Rathenau was appointed minister of reconstruction, and German Foreign Minister. He negotiated the Treaty of Rapallo (16 April 1922) with Soviet Russia whereby Germany would supply industrial technology to Russia in return for Russia abandoning any reparations claims. Germany would provide machinery and  equipment for Russia to expand her oilfields in Baku, and establish jointly owned oil and gasoline distribution centres in Germany to market the oil. It held great promise for future collaboration and allowed Germany "to get out from under the grip of British and American oil interests, which had a total monopoly on German petroleum sales since Versailles."[45]

Rathenau

> The horror of the English and French and their satellites, and the ill-concealed uneasiness of the Americans when the agreement became known, are the best proof of what promise the treaty held for Germany.[46]

Rathenau's Rapallo Treaty held great promise for Germany, indeed for the entire future peace of Europe, which was the very reason the Anglo-American elites were horrified. A Russo-German rapprochement was the stuff of their worst nightmares, and the possibility of Germans and Russians cooperating on oil supplies and much else undoubtedly sent cold shivers down spines in the City and Wall Street. Both the Treaty and Rathenau had to be killed off immediately. Fake news poured out of the controlled Press claiming that Rathenau was part of a Jewish Communist conspiracy, and he was assassinated in Berlin on 24 June 1922, allegedly by a small ultra-nationalist paramilitary group. Millions in Germany took to the streets in protest against the terrorist act, and monuments were built in Rathenau's memory. They would be destroyed immediately the Nazis took power.

Following Rathenau's assassination, US ambassador Alanson B. Houghton lamented that the United States had lost a friend who "meant to play the game much as I wanted." Houghton, however – who greatly assisted Charles Dawes with the German loans and was instrumental in linking Putzi with Hitler in 1922 – was quite willing to countenance a dictatorship of the Right.[47] Wall Street now began a steady infiltration of AEG through the multi-national giant General Electric Company (GE) in the United States. Created through mergers

Houghton

financed with J.P. Morgan and Vanderbilt money, General Electric was the most important industrial combination for installing electric power in towns and cities across the United States and elsewhere. Together with J.P. Morgan, the Roosevelt family was "one of the largest stockholders in the General Electric Company."[48]

The Morgan-Roosevelt General Electric infiltrated Germany's AEG through a General Electric subsidiary company called International General Electric Company (IGE).

> The foreign business of GE expanded to such a great degree during the war years of 1914 to 1918 that a new company, the International General Electric Company, was created to take over the foreign department of GE. IGE was incorporated under New York laws on January 13, 1919, and, incidentally, at the very moment the Paris Peace Conference was convening. IGE was in many respects a post-war plan of GE. Its operations were and are in the fields of foreign investment and as a manufacturing and selling organization of GE throughout the world.[49]

It was no coincidence that the head office of International General Electric was 120 Broadway. As we saw in chapter 16, it was also the headquarters of the Federal Reserve Bank of New York, *and* of the 'International Corporation' which conducted the pro-Bolshevik activity in the US.[50] Indeed, it was International General Electric that electrified the Soviet Union in the 1920s and 1930s. Professor Sutton revealed that "General Electric profited handsomely from Bolshevism," as well as "from national socialism in Hitler's Germany."[51]

With Walter Rathenau no longer in control of AEG, through the 1920s Wall Street money – the equivalent of around $1 billion in today's terms – poured into AEG, and four Americans were placed on its board of directors: Owen D. Young, Gerard Swope, Clark H. Minor, and E. Baldwin.

Owen D. Young, after whom the Young Plan was named, was a J.P. Morgan man and deputy chairman of the Federal Reserve Bank of New York at 120 Broadway. At that same address he was a director of International General Electric.

Gerard Swope, Chairman of International General Electric was, at the same time, president of its parent company, General Electric. He was also a director of the Morgan affiliated National City Bank on Wall Street which made billions from the First World War. Clark H. Minor was President of International General Electric. E. Baldwin was Vice-President of International General Electric. The entire affair was stitched up by Morgan men who were likewise linked with Putzi Hanfstaengl's close friend, Franklin D. Roosevelt.

On behalf of their Wall Street masters, Young Swope, Minor, and Baldwin moved into the German electrical industry through their directorships of AEG, "and gained, if not complete control as some have reported, then at least a substantial say in the internal affairs of both AEG and Osram."[52] The banking/industrial agreements between IGE and AEG date from the death of Walter Rathenau in 1922, and one must consider the possibility that his assassination was ordered from a much higher authority in the West.

Mainstream historians relate that Hitler and his war machine were financed by various German industries – such as AEG – but fail to relate how many of those German industries were under the control of western financial elites by the late 20s and 30s.

> International General Electric had four directors on the board of A.E.G. and another director on Osram, and significant influence in the internal domestic policies of these German companies. The significance of this General Electric ownership is that A.E.G. and Osram were prominent suppliers of funds for Hitler in his rise to power in Germany in 1933.[53]

Another American company deeply involved in collusion with German companies doing business with the Nazis was the International Telephone & Telegraph Company (ITT).

INTERNATIONAL TELEPHONE & TELEGRAPH COMPANY (ITT)

ITT was founded in 1920 by Sosthenes Behn, a US Colonel who served in the First World War.

Behn was born in the Danish Virgin Islands in 1884. He became an American citizen after the United States acquired the islands in 1917, and he earned a Distinguished Service Medal as a colonel in the signal corps in the Great War. The telephone was still a new gadget when he and his brother acquired small companies in Puerto Rico and Cuba. The Behn's named their small company International Telephone & Telegraph so that it sounded like the larger, established American Telephone and & Telegraph. ITT didn't stay small for long. *Backed by Morgan banking*, it expanded in the 1920s into a multinational conglomerate of telephone companies (including the telephone systems for whole nations), cable companies, and electronic manufacturers.[54]

Antony Sutton writes:

"In brief, I.T.T. was a Morgan-controlled company."[55] With the enormous financial power of J.P. Morgan behind him, Sosthenes Behn went to Berchtesgaden in August 1933 to meet Hitler. He also established close contact with Hermann Göring, who would become Chief of the Luftwaffe High Command, 1935-1945. In his book, *Trading with the Enemy, the Nazi-American Money Plot 1933-1949*, English-born journalist and biographer Charles Higham wrote of the close collusion between ITT, Standard Oil and the Gestapo:

During the early days of 1942 [i.e. after the US entered the war] Karl Lindemann, the Rockefeller Standard Oil representative in Berlin, held a series of urgent meetings with two directors of the International Telephone and Telegraph Corporation: Walter Schellenberg, head of the Gestapo counterintelligence service (SD), and Baron Kurt von Schröder of the Bank for International Settlements and the Stein Bank. The result of these meetings was that Gerhardt Westrick, the boss of ITT. in Nazi Germany, got aboard a Focke-Wulf bomber and flew to Madrid for a meeting in March with Sosthenes Behn, American ITT chief. In the sumptuous Royal Suite of Madrid's Ritz Hotel, the tall, sharp-faced Behn and the heavily limping Westrick sat down for lunch to discuss how best they could improve ITT's links with the Gestapo, and its improvement of the whole Nazi system of telephones, teleprinters, aircraft intercoms, submarine and ship phones, electric buoys, alarm systems, radio and radar parts, and fuses for artillery shells, as well as the Focke-Wulf bombers that were taking thousands of American lives.[56]

ITT quickly expanded its interests in Nazi Germany, and appointed Baron Kurt von Schröder of the Schröder banking family as guardian of its interests in Nazi Germany. Through von Schröder, ITT had access to the very heart of the Nazi power elite and was able to reinvest handsome profits in German armaments firms. Behn appointed Schröder to the boards of all ITT German companies, including Standard Elektrizitätswerke A.G. in Berlin, C. Lorenz A.G of Berlin, and Mix & Genest A.G. The Morgan bank and Behn were making vast amounts of money helping arm Hitler, and much of that profit was reinvested in the Nazis as the war progressed. Professor Sutton related that this reinvestment "clearly indicated" that Wall Street's claims that it was innocent of wrongdoing in German rearmament – and, indeed, that they did not even know Hitler's intentions, "are fraudulent."[57] Those investments included a major stake in the Focke-Wulf aircraft company that built fighters for the Luftwaffe during the war.

> Through the war, in addition to ITT's part ownership of Focke-Wulf, its subsidiaries supplied the German military with telecommunications, radar, electronic fuses for bombs, and electronics for V-2 rockets ... Colonel Behn was sheltered by powerful friends at the Pentagon and Wall Street who would see to it that he was protected throughout the war and after it. Incredibly, he was awarded the Medal of Merit, then the highest decoration given to American civilians.[58]

Lest there be doubt in any readers mind that J.P. Morgan/Wall Street held massive sway over Sosthenes Behn and the arming of the Nazis, Morgan official biographer Ron Chernow writes:

> During the 1920s the House of Morgan helped Sosthenes Behn to launch his worldwide empire of International Telephone and Telegraph.... With his taste for political intrigue, Behn and the House of Morgan were a natural match.... In the mid-1920s, J.P. Morgan and Company helped Behn take over telephone systems in Brazil, Argentina, Chile, and Uruguay, ousting the British from their former pre-eminence. The bank championed Behn's cause in numberless ways ... Lamont [Morgan partner] sometimes functioned

as Behn's secret plenipotentiary. In 1930, he had an audience with Mussolini solely to advance Behn's desire to build a factory in Italy. Deal-making in this era was always a discrete, behind-the-scenes operation...[59]

Of course the deal-making between ITT, Nazi Germany and fascist Italy, had to be discrete. ITT's Focke-Wulf aircraft were inflicting considerable death and destruction on the Allies.

ITT continued to supply Germany with advanced communication systems after Pearl Harbor, to the detriment of the Americans themselves, whose diplomatic code was broken by the Nazis with the help of such equipment. Until the very end of the war, ITT's production facilities in Germany as well as in neutral countries such as Sweden, Switzerland, and Spain provided the German armed forces with state-of-the-art martial toys. Charles Higham offers specifics:

After Pearl Harbor the German army, navy, and air force contracted with ITT for the manufacture of switchboards, telephones, alarm gongs, buoys, air raid warning devices, radar equipment, and thirty thousand fuses per month for artillery shells.... This was to increase to fifty thousand per month by 1944. In addition, ITT supplied ingredients for the rocket bombs that fell on London, selenium cells for dry rectifiers, high-frequency radio equipment, and fortification and field communication sets. Without this supply of crucial materials it would have been impossible for the German air force to kill American and British troops, for the German army to fight the Allies, England to have been bombed, or for Allied ships to have been attacked at sea.[60]

Had the people of Britain and America become aware of what was truly going on between Wall Street and Nazi Germany, Sosthenes Behn and the entire sordid gang in the J.P. Morgan organisation would very likely have been lynched.

I.G. FARBEN

Created in 1925 with the Wall Street money, *Internationale Gesellschaft Farbenindustrie A.G.* – or I.G. Farben for short – arose from the merger of six large German chemical companies.

Hermann Schmitz, the organizer of I.G. Farben in 1925, became a prominent early Nazi and supporter of Hitler, as well as chairman of the Swiss I.G. Chemie and president of American I.G. The Farben complex both in Germany and the United States then developed into an integral part of the formation and operation of the Nazi state machine, the Wehrmacht and the S.S. ... I.G. Farben directors materially helped Hitler and the Nazis to power in 1933. I.G. Farben contributed 400,000 Reichsmarks to Hitler's political "slush fund." It was this secret fund which financed the Nazi seizure of control in March 1933.[61]

Directors of the giant conglomerate included Max Warburg of the M.M. Warburg bank in Hamburg, and his brother, Paul Warburg of the Kuhn, Loeb & Co on Wall Street, one of the original planners of the Federal Reserve System at Jekyll Island. Paul Warburg's fellow directors on the American I.G. board were "not only prominent in Wall Street and American industry but more significantly were drawn from a few highly influential institutions."[62] They included Charles E. Mitchell, chairman of the National City Bank and the Federal Reserve Bank of New York; Edsel B. Ford, son of Henry Ford and president of the Ford Motor Company; and Walter Teagle, director of Standard Oil of New Jersey.[63]

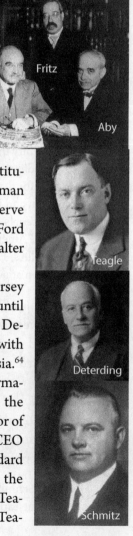

Teagle was president of Standard Oil of New Jersey from 1917 to 1937, then chairman of the board until 1942. He was a friend of the pro-Nazi Sir Henri Deterding, head of Royal Dutch-Shell, who agreed with his views about the ultimate need to destroy Russia.[64] Thanks to Teagle, Standard Oil supplied Nazi Germany with oil throughout the Second World War – the shipments going via Spain. Teagle was also a director of American I.G. and a good friend of I. G. Farben's CEO in Germany, Herman Schmitz. Under Teagle, Standard Oil of New Jersey developed intimate links with the German trust I.G. Farben, and through the 1930s, Teagle and Schmitz met regularly in New York or on Teagle's frequent trips to Germany where they went duck shooting together with Hermann Göring. Standard Oil invested heavily in I.G. Farben and I.G. Farben invested heavily in Standard.[65]

> In 1938 Teagle helped Schmitz get supplies of aviation fuel from a British subsidiary of Standard. The Luftwaffe planes that bombed London in 1940 were flying on this fuel. When the British government complained about American companies selling supplies to the people who were murdering its citizens, Standard switched all its tankers to Panamanian registry. They sailed to the island of Tenerife, where their fuel was offloaded into waiting German tankers. The planes that bombed Pearl Harbor in 1941 also flew on fuel sold to Japan by Standard Oil.... Senator Harry Truman told the press he believed Standard's activities amounted to treason.. Roosevelt stepped in and blocked antitrust actions against Standard.... Although there were other probes of its activities, Standard Oil continued doing business, through various circuitous routes, with both Germany and Japan throughout the war.[66]

Teagle, the man who arguably did more than anyone to keep the Nazi military and Luftwaffe on the move, was selected as one of 20th Century's Great American Business Leaders by Harvard Business School. In an Orwellian twist, in 1944 he established The Teagle Foundation "to advance the well-being and general good of mankind throughout the world."

Standard Oil also worked closely with I.G Farben in the production of synthetic oils:

> The I.G. Farben-Standard Oil cooperation for production of synthetic oil from coal gave the I.G. Farben cartel a monopoly of German gasoline production during World War II. Just under one half of German high octane gasoline in 1945 was produced by I. G. Farben and most of the balance by affiliated companies. In brief, in synthetic gasoline and explosives (two of the very basic elements of modern warfare), the control of German World War II output was in the hands of German combines created by Wall Street loans under the Dawes Plan. Moreover, American assistance to Nazi war efforts extended into other areas. The two largest tank producers in Hitler's Germany were Opel, a wholly owned subsidiary of General Motors (controlled by the J.P. Morgan firm), and the Ford A. G. subsidiary of the Ford Motor Company of Detroit. The Nazis granted tax-exempt status to Opel in 1936, to enable General Motors to expand its production facilities. General Motors obligingly

reinvested the resulting profits in German industry. Henry Ford was decorated by the Nazis for his services to Nazism. Alcoa [Aluminium Company of America] and Dow Chemical's [an American multinational corporation headquartered in Michigan] worked closely with Nazi industry with numerous transfers of their domestic U.S. technology. Bendix Aviation, in which the J.P. Morgan-controlled General Motors firm had a major stock interest, supplied Siemens & Halske A.G. in Germany with data on automatic pilots and aircraft instruments. As late as 1940, Bendix Aviation supplied complete technical data to Robert Bosch for aircraft and diesel engine starters and received royalty payments in return. In brief, American companies associated with the Morgan-Rockefeller international investment bankers – not, it should be noted, the vast bulk of independent American industrialists – were intimately related to the growth of Nazi industry. It is important to note that General Motors, Ford, General Electric, Du Pont and the handful of U.S. companies intimately involved with the development of Nazi Germany were – except for the Ford Motor Company – controlled by Wall Street elite – the J.P. Morgan firm, the Rockefeller Chase Bank and to a lesser extent the Warburg Manhattan bank.[67]

Professor Sutton and others confirm that American industrialists were heavily involved – making huge profits – in building the Nazi war machine. "At one point, General Motors and Ford together reportedly accounted for no less than half of Germany's entire production of tanks."[68]

A massive new corporate headquarters for I.G. Farben was built on Rothschild land in Frankfurt am Main, and with Wall Street funding it became the fourth largest company in the world. Professor Sutton relates that the rapid expansion of I.G. Farben was made possible by American bond issues and American technical assistance. Professor Preparata adds:

> Morgan & Co. and Rockefeller, via Chase National, promoted I.G. Farben on Wall Street and Germany was being gradually, but steadily rearmed. … The Anglo-Americans equipped what would become Hitler's war machine through well over 150 foreign long-term loans contracted in less than seven years: the more thorough and elaborate the fitting, the more devastating the German army, the bloodier the war, the more resounding the foregone victory of the Allies and the defeat of Germans, who were being set up, and the more sweeping and permanent the Anglo-American conquest. There was neither greed nor treason behind the Dawes bailout, but solely the long-term objective of fitting a prospective enemy with a

view to bringing him down in a fiery confrontation – a confrontation to be orchestrated at a later stage.[69]

The new I.G. Farben empire owned its own coal mines, iron and steel works, power plants, and had over 2,000 cartel agreements with foreign firms, including Standard Oil and DuPont in the United State. Without I.G. Farben's Wall Street loans, promotion on Wall Street by J.P. Morgan and Rockefeller, and its immense production facilities and vast international affiliations arming the Nazis, the Second World War would never have happened. Additionally, I.G. Farben directors materially helped Hitler and the Nazis to power in 1933 when they contributed 400,000 Reichsmarks to Hitler's political slush fund. "It was this secret fund which financed the Nazi seizure of control in March 1933."[70]

Created with Wall Street money, I.G. Farben would become the largest industry at Auschwitz during the Second World War. Hundreds of thousands of slave labourers imprisoned in the camps alongside the complex would produce 700,000 tons of oil per month, and 30,000 tons of rubber per year for the Nazi war effort. It was a hugely profitable war for I.G. Farben as it was getting workers for practically nothing. "Because of the need for slave labor hundreds of thousands of Jews from Poland, Russia, Germany, and western Europe were shipped to Auschwitz."[71]

> William Stamps Farish [chairman then president of the Standard Oil Company of New Jersey] was the principal manager of a worldwide cartel between Standard Oil Co. of New Jersey and the I.G. Farben concern. The merged enterprise had opened the Auschwitz slave labor camp on June 14, 1940 to produce artificial rubber and gasoline from coal. The Hitler government supplied political opponents and Jews as the slaves, who were worked to near death and then murdered.[72]

In March 1942, William Stamps Farish appeared in Newark, New Jersey, criminal court charged with criminally conspiring with the Nazi government in Germany. In plea bargaining, the charges were dropped and Farish, a multi-millionaire, was fined $1,000. Preparata writes:

Farish

> The full story of I.G. Farben and its world-wide activities before World War II can never be known, as key German records were destroyed in anticipation of Allied victory, but there are sufficient

testimonies to suggest that German-American technical and military collaboration shielded by complex corporate contracts, hosted in the "neutral" nodes (such as Holland and Switzerland), went on throughout the 1930s and well into the duration of the second world conflict.

During World War II, I.G. Farben would provision and supply the Nazi regime with the bulk, if not the entirety, of the following essential staples: synthetic rubber (100 percent), dyestuffs (100 percent, poison gas (95 percent), plastics (90 percent), explosives (84 percent), gunpowder (70 percent), aviation gasoline (46 percent), synthetic gasoline (33 percent), not to mention the manufacture of Zyklon B, the cyanide employed to annihilate the inmates of death camps...[73]

The financing of Hitler and Nazi Germany by the Anglo-American banking elites and leading industrialists is complex. It is a rabbit hole which runs very deep and much further research is needed if the whole truth is to emerge. Among many important books on this sordid matter are Diarmuid Jeffreys *Hell's Cartel, IG Farben and the Making of Hitler's War Machine*, and Edwin Black's *IBM and the Holocaust: The Strategic Alliance Between Nazi Germany and America's Most Powerful Corporation*.

From the mid-1920s the two major German combines of I.G. Farben and Vereinigte Stahlwerke (United Steelworks Co.) dominated the chemical and steel cartel system funded by Wall Street. I.G. Farben became the main producer of explosives and much more, while Vereinigte Stahlwerke had a steel-producing capacity greater than all other German iron and steel producers combined. These two combines would collaborate and by the eve of the Second World War produce 95 percent of German explosives.[74] Fritz Thyssen of the *Vereinigte Stahlwerke* is remembered as "the man who gave more money to Hitler than any other individual."[75]

VEREINIGTE STAHLWERKE A.G.

Formed in 1926 through the merger of smaller foundries and steel works, the Thyssen interests were the principal component in the merger of the *Vereinigte Stahlwerke* cartel.

Fritz Thyssen was chosen as chairman of the board of the new combine, a position he held until 1936. His job was not to be an easy one, for the German steel industry was in severe financial trouble after 1918.[76]

Thyssen's new *Vereinigte Stahlwerke* cartel was in serious financial difficulties until a Wall Street syndicate headed by Dillon, Read & Co, funded it to the tune of $70,000,000 (worth around $1,250,000,000 today).[77] Fritz Thyssen, according to pro-Establishment historians, was Hitler's largest benefactor, but those historians never reveal the true origins of the money he gave Hitler. Thyssen was associated with the Brown Brothers Harriman Bank on Wall Street, where the founding partner, W. Averell Harriman, was a Yale graduate and a member of the elite Skull & Bones secret society. A Democratic party politician, Harriman acted as an important channel for the vast amounts of money that flowed back and forth between Thyssen, I.G. Farben, ITT, and Wall Street in the 1920s and 30s. Other leading players in the bank were members of the Walker and Bush dynasties – the direct forebears of George H. W. Bush, 41st president of the United States, and his

Averell Harriman

Prescott Bush

son George W. Bush, 43rd president. The Harriman and Bush business interests would be seized in 1942 under the Trading With the Enemy Act:

> The 1942 U.S. government investigative report said that Bush's Nazi-front bank was an interlocking concern with *Vereinigte Stahlwerke* led by Fritz Thyssen and his two brothers. ... The investigation showed that *Vereinigte Stahlwerke* had produced 35 per cent of Nazi Germany's explosives ...[78]

The new Wall Street-funded cartels in Germany "not only helped Hitler to power in 1933; they produced the bulk of key German war materials used in World War II."[79] Thanks to armaments production for the forthcoming war, Wall Street made massive profits not merely from investments in Germany's United Steel, but through the U.S. steel cartel created by J.P. Morgan. Morgan had purchased U.S. Steel from Andrew Carnegie and merged it with a few other firms to create United States Steel in 1901.[80]

With vast amounts of money and gold flowing in and out of Germany during the 1930s and the Second World War, the international bankers needed a discrete means of conducting their financial intrigues that operated beyond the scrutiny of governments and the people.

It came in 1929 when the Bank for International Settlements opened in Basel, Switzerland.

Bank for International Settlements

Mainstream historians rarely discuss the Bank for International Settlements (BIS). Those who do, including Piet Clement, the present official BIS historian, portray it in a very innocent light:

> The creation of the Bank for International Settlements (BIS) in 1930 to deal with the settlement of First World War reparations payments was seen by central banks as an opportunity to put international cooperation on an institutional footing. Their initial vision of what the BIS might achieve in support of the gold exchange standard was ambitious. In the view of Montagu Norman and Hjalmar Schacht, the BIS needed to become a forum not merely for information exchange and for refining the techniques of managing the gold exchange standard, but a truly cooperative organisation capable of providing support to central banks in emergencies and for developing new financial arrangements.[81]

Officially then, the BIS was a straightforward organisation that simply provided a cooperative "forum for information exchange" and managed "the gold exchange standard." All very innocent: 'nothing to see here folks, move along'. As described in an earlier chapter, however, Carroll Quigley saw through the tapestry of lies:

> The powers of financial capitalism had another far-reaching aim, nothing less than to create a world system of financial control in private hands able to dominate the political system of each country and the economy of the world as a whole. This system was to be controlled in a feudalist fashion by the central banks of the world acting in concert, by *secret agreements* arrived at in frequent private meetings and conferences. The apex of the system was to be the Bank for International Settlements in Basel, Switzerland, a private bank owned and controlled by the world's central banks which were themselves private corporations.[82]

The new bank opened in Basel in 1930 was owned and controlled by the small group of astronomically wealthy and powerful men in the City, London, and Wall Street, New York, who were responsible for the First World War, and were now creating the right conditions for igniting the Second World War. Charles Higham writes in *Trading With the Enemy*:

> The BIS's ostensible purpose was to provide the Allies with reparations paid by Germany for World War 1. The Bank soon turned out

to be the instrument of an opposite function. It was to be a money funnel for American and British funds to flow into Hitler's coffers and to help Hitler build up his war machine.[83]

The BIS conducted this business in total secrecy, without political interference, and beyond democratic control. Montagu Norman and his "twin," Hjalmar Schacht – the bankers skilled "technicians" as Quigley called them – were heavily involved in setting up the BIS. They were the leading operatives in the BIS but it must be kept in mind that the real string pullers were elsewhere.

> For Hjalmar Schacht and Montague Norman, January 20, 1930, was a date to savour: they had created a bank beyond the reach of either national or international law. On that date the governments of the United Kingdom, France, Germany, Belgium, Italy, Japan, and Switzerland signed an extraordinary document. The Hague Convention guaranteed that the BIS would be the world's most privileged bank and legally protected bank. Its statutes, which remain in force to this day, essentially make the BIS untouchable.[84]

The "untouchable" BIS would facilitate the transfer of reparations money *out* of Germany, and the flow of high interest-earning Wall Street loans and bond sales *into* Germany that would fund Hitler and the Nazis. Money did not physically pass through the bank, which simply crunched and manipulated numbers.

To this day, the BIS operates beyond the eyes and ears of democratically elected governments and the people in its own 70 metres tall round tower building in the centre of Basel. In his investigative history, *Tower of Basel, The Shadowy History of the Secret Bank that Runs the World,* British journalist and author, Adam Lebor, says he found it strange that only a handful of the many well-informed people he knew had ever heard of the bank. It was the world's most secretive global financial institution. Lebor writes:

> The BIS is the most important bank in the world and predates

both the IMF and the World Bank. For decades it has stood at the centre of a global network of money, power, and covert global influence. The BIS was founded in 1930. It was ostensibly set up as part of the Young Plan to administer German reparations payments for the First World War. The bank's key architects were Montagu Norman, who was the governor of the Bank of England, and Hjalmar Schacht, the president of the Reichsbank who described the BIS as "my" bank. The BIS's founding members were the central banks of Britain, France, Germany, Italy, Belgium, and a consortium of Japanese banks. Shares were also offered to the Federal Reserve but it refused its allocation [it was against the constitution of the Federal Reserve to own shares] Instead, a consortium of commercial banks took up the shares: J.P. Morgan, the First National Bank of New York, and the First National Bank of Chicago. The real purpose of the BIS was detailed in its statutes: to "promote the cooperation of central banks and to provide additional facilities for international financial operations." It was the culmination of the central bankers' decades-old dream, to have their own bank – powerful, independent, and free from interfering politicians and nosy reporters. Most felicitous of all, the BIS was self-financing and would be in perpetuity. Its clients were its own shareholders – the central banks. During the 1930s, the BIS was the central meeting place for a cabal of central bankers, dominated by Norman and Schacht. This group helped rebuild Germany. The *New York Times* described Schacht, widely acknowledged as the genius behind the resurgent German economy, as "The Iron-Willed Pilot of Nazi Finance." During the war, the BIS became a de-facto arm of the Reichsbank, accepting looted Nazi gold and carrying out foreign exchange deals for Nazi Germany.[85]

The BIS was initially set up in an old hotel near Basel railway station. Its insignificant narrow doorway sat alongside a confectioner's shop, with the entrance barely noticeable. Not even a small bronze plaque marked the bank's existence.

> The bank's managers believed that those who needed to know where the BIS was would find it, and the rest of the world certainly did not need to know.[86]

The BIS played a highly significant role for the City and Wall Street banking cabals in the promotion of Nazism in the 1930s and the genesis of the Second World War. Since the immense yet occult and nefarious influence the BIS exerts on global events to the present day are beyond the scope of this book, we strongly encourage those who care about the future of our world to read Lebor's *Tower of Basel.*

The first president of the BIS, Gates W. McGarrah, was an American citizen and banker who had, since August 1924, been a director of Germa-

MvGarrah

ny's central bank, the Reichsbank, alongside Schacht. At the same time, McGarrah served as a director of the Federal Reserve Bank of New York and of the Astor Trust Company. A solid Eastern Establishment man, McGarrah was appointed the first president and chairman of the board of the BIS in April 1930. When his appointment was announced, *Time* magazine described him as a J.P. Morgan lookalike, and the bank itself as "the cash register of German reparations."[87] On taking up his appointment, McGarrah stated that the Bank was completely removed from any government or political control. Vice-president of the BIS was Carl Melchior, a partner in the MM Warburg bank. When the Nazis took power in 1933, Melchior – a Jew – was forced to resign from the BIS. None of his colleagues in the bank objected or challenged the Nazis regarding this. The position of Hjalmar Schacht as a director of the BIS was never questioned.

Kurt von Schröder, the German banker who, as we have seen earlier, hosted the Hitler-von Papen discussions at his Cologne home in January 1933, was another director of the BIS. A favourite of Hitler, von Schröder replaced Melchior as a director of the BIS when he was forced out.

> Kurt von Schröder was one of the most powerful and influential bankers in Nazi Germany, a scion of the dynasty whose empire included the J. Henry Schröder bank in London and Schrobanco in New York, whose board Allen Dulles joined in 1937. Sociable, cosmopolitan and well-travelled, von Schröder was known as a reliable, international financier, part of the new global elite who were equally at home in the gentlemen's clubs of London or the dining rooms of Wall Street. The German banker was especially close to Frank Tiarks, the director of the Bank of England, who was a partner in J. Henry Schröder bank in London … Hjalmar Schacht personally appointed von Schröder to the BIS board … Von Schröder enjoyed close personal links with the highest reaches of the Nazi party. He had helped to bring Hitler to power. In January 1933 von

Schröder had hosted the meeting at his villa in Cologne between Hitler and Franz von Papen.[88]

Another German, Hermann Schmitz, the CEO of I.G. Farben would join Schacht and von Schröder on the board of the BIS. The entire board was stitched up with British, American and German bankers who were working closely together for the same purpose: building Nazi Germany up for another great war against Russia.

When the US entered that war, the president of the BIS was an American lawyer, Thomas McKittrick. A Harvard graduate, McKittrick worked at one stage for the Morgan-affiliated National City Bank. He was a close family friend of Allen Dulles who played many important roles for the international banking cabal and would become Director of the CIA.

McKittrick

Author and investigator of the BIS, Adam Lebor, discussed McKittrick in an article published in the *Daily Telegraph* in 2013 following his examination of newly released Bank of England documents:

> Buried among the typewritten pages of the Bank of England's history is a name of whom few have ever heard, a man for whom, like Montagu Norman, the primacy of international finance reigned over mere national considerations. Thomas McKittrick, an American banker, was president of the BIS. When the United States entered the war in December 1941, McKittrick's position, the history notes, "became difficult." But McKittrick managed to keep the bank in business, thanks in part to his friend Allen Dulles, the US spymaster based in Berne. McKittrick was an asset of Dulles, known as Codename 644, and frequently passed him information that he had garnered from Emil Puhl, [vice president of the Reichsbank] who was a frequent visitor to Basel and often met McKittrick.

Allen Dulles

Declassified documents in the American intelligence archives reveal an even more disturbing story. Under an intelligence operation known as the "Harvard Plan," McKittrick was in contact with Nazi industrialists, working towards what the US documents, dated February 1945, describe as a "close cooperation between the Allied and German business world." Thus while Allied soldiers were fighting through Europe, McKittrick was cutting deals to keep the Germany economy strong. This was happening with what the US documents describe as "the full assistance" of the State Department.[89]

A fellow member of the BIS board with McKittrick was the British banker Sir Otto Ernst Niemeyer, a Balliol College graduate of Oxford, University. Together with his role at the BIS, Niemeyer served as a director of the Bank of England from 1938 to 1952. It is impossible to believe he had no knowledge of the fact that the BIS was, and long had been, funding the Nazi war machine. While researching the Bank of England documents,

Niemeyer

Adam Lebor discovered a quite astonishing story about the BIS transferring gold belonging to Czechoslovakia to Nazi Germany.

> The documents reveal a shocking story: just six months before Britain went to war with Nazi Germany, the Bank of England willingly handed over £5.6 million worth of gold to Hitler – and it belonged to another country. The official history of the bank, written in 1950 but posted online for the first time on Tuesday, reveals how we betrayed Czechoslovakia – not just with the infamous Munich agreement of September 1938, which allowed the Nazis to annex the Sudetenland, but also in London, where Montagu Norman, the eccentric but ruthless governor of the Bank of England, agreed to surrender gold owned by the National Bank of Czechoslovakia.
>
> The Czechoslovak gold was held in London in a sub-account in the name of the Bank for International Settlements, the Basel-based bank for central banks. When the Nazis marched into Prague in March 1939 they immediately sent armed soldiers to the offices of the National Bank. The Czech directors were ordered, on pain of death, to send two transfer requests. The first instructed the BIS to transfer 23.1 metric tons of gold from the Czechoslovak BIS account, held at the Bank of England, to the Reichsbank BIS account, also held at Threadneedle Street [London]. The second order instructed the Bank of England to transfer almost 27 metric tons of gold held in the National Bank of Czechoslovakia's own name to the BIS's gold account at the Bank of England.
>
> To outsiders, the distinction between the accounts seems obscure. Yet it proved crucial – and allowed Norman to ensure that the first order was carried out. The Czechoslovak bank officials be-

lieved that as the orders had obviously been carried out under duress neither would be allowed to go through. But they had not reckoned on the bureaucrats running the BIS and the determination of Montagu Norman to see that procedures were followed, even as his country prepared for war with Nazi Germany. His decision caused uproar, both in the press and in Parliament. George Strauss, a Labour MP, spoke for many when he thundered in Parliament: "The Bank for International Settlements is the bank which sanctions the most notorious outrage of this generation – the rape of Czechoslovakia." Winston Churchill demanded to know how the government could ask its citizens to enlist in the military when it was "so butter-fingered that £6 million worth of gold can be transferred to the Nazi government."

It was a good question. Thanks to Norman and the BIS, Nazi Germany had just looted 23.1 tons of gold without a shot being fired. The second transfer order, for the gold held in the National Bank of Czechoslovakia's own name, did not go through. Sir John Simon, the Chancellor of the Exchequer, had instructed banks to block all Czechoslovak assets.

The documents released by the Bank of England are revealing, both for what they show and what they omit. They are a window into a world of fearful deference to authority, the primacy of procedure over morality, a world where, for the bankers, the most important thing is to keep the channels of international finance open, no matter what the human cost. A world, in other words, not entirely different to today.[90]

At the beginning of this chapter, we quoted Lord Acton: "Nothing is safe that does not show how it can bear discussion and publicity. The issue which has swept down the centuries and which will have to be fought sooner or later is the people versus the banks."

Since Lord Acton departed this world in 1902, "the banks" have deliberately brought about two world wars, with 120 million slaughtered. The people remain in ignorance of this thanks to actions of contemptible 'court historians' continually adding to the tapestry of lies.

Summary: Chapter 19 – A Vast Tapestry of Lies

- In the years after the First World War, the innocent Germany was subjected to massive war reparations payments to the victorious Allies.

- Thousands of tons of gold were looted from the German central bank and shipped to the United States. Marks were mass produced without the backing of gold, and by 1923 the ensuing hyperinflation had utterly wrecked the German economy.

• The German central bank, the Reichsbank, was removed from German political control and Hjalmar Schacht, a banker with close ties to Wall Street and the Governors of the Federal Reserve Bank of New York and the Bank of England, was put in charge of it.

• The German economy and central bank were now effectively under the control of the elite Anglo-American bankers.

• Through the Dawes and Young Plans, American money poured into Germany. It brought hyperinflation under control and enabled the construction of giant cartels for the German military-industrial complex. The cartels would fund the rise of Hitler and construct the Nazi war machine.

• A secretive bank, the BIS, was set up just across the German border in Basel, Switzerland, that would enable the flow of cash and gold into and out of Nazi Germany. The BIS was owned and controlled by the international bankers in London and New York who were funding Hitler, and operated beyond all political control.

• Throughout the war, American oil was sent into Germany to fuel the Nazi military.

CHAPTER 20

EGGING HITLER ON

Adolf Hitler demonstrated his utter ruthlessness by burning the Reichstag, passing the Enabling Act that gave him dictatorial powers, and sending many socialist and communist members of parliament to concentration camps and their death. Jews were being systematically persecuted and made to live in constant fear while their shops, businesses, and livelihoods were destroyed. In 1934 potential rivals within his own party, the NSDAP, were brutally murdered on his orders, together with democratically elected past political opponents such as former Chancellor Kurt von Schleicher and former Minister-President Gustav Ritter von Kahr. It was plain for all to see – indeed the whole world knew what was happening – yet from 1934 until the beginning of the Second World War, Britain and the US poured money, weapons technology and much more into Nazi Germany. At the same time, a steady stream of British elites travelled back and forth to Germany to praise Hitler and encourage him in his plan to attack Soviet Russia. That, indeed, had been their prime motive throughout this entire vile affair while cleverly camouflaging their efforts to that end under the banner of "Appeasement."

APPEASEMENT

The original definition of the term appeasement was the attempt to bring about a state of peace, quiet, ease, or calm. Later, according to the Oxford English dictionary, the term broadened to mean "making someone calm or less hostile by agreeing to their demands."[1] In the context of the 1930s, establishment historian Ian Kershaw describes appeasement as "the attempt to seek an accommodation with Hitler" and make concessions to him in an attempt to prevent war.[2] Thus, the encouragement of Hitler is explained away in the great tapestry of lies as being conducted by well-intentioned people intent on avoiding war, but the intention was in fact quite the opposite. Could it really be merely a coincidence that the overwhelming majority of individuals who went to Germany to "appease" Hitler were linked to Oxford University, Fellows of All Souls, and members of the Milner Group? Of course it wasn't. They had selected him in the first instance, placed agents, Hanfstaengl and de Ropp directly alongside him to help groom him for power, and were pouring vast amounts of money into Nazi Germany to fund him and his mighty war machine for war on Russia.

One or two individuals did indeed visit Nazi Germany in an attempt to foster Anglo-German understanding in the hope of preventing another war, including Reginald Clifford Allen (Lord Allen of Hurtwood). A member of the Independent Labour Party, a pacifist and conscientious objector, Allen had almost died through maltreatment in an English prison in 1917 for refusing to fight in the First World War. Now, in 1935, he genuinely believed that Germany's legitimate grievances relating to the Versailles Treaty should be met. If she became belligerent in any way, however, Allen proposed that member countries of the League of Nations should step in and subdue her.[3] Lord Allen went to Germany and pleaded

Clifford Allen

with the Nazis to avoid conflict and end the brutality and harsh treatment of Jews. He was brushed off by Hitler, and ridiculed in the British mainstream newspapers as being a naïve nonentity, but a substantial majority of the British public agreed with Lord Allen's views. Carroll Quigley wrote:

> In Britain, persons who were on the Left tended to believe in the revision of the Treaty of Versailles in favor of Germany, collective security [through the League of Nations], general disarmament, and friendship with the Soviet Union. In the same period, the Right were impatient with policies based on humanitarianism, idealism, or friendship for the Soviet Union, and wanted to pursue a policy of "national interests" with strengthening of the empire, and conducting an aggressive commercial policy... The groups of the Left were in office in Britain for only about two years in the twenty years 1919-1939 and then only as a minority government. The Right were in power for eighteen of those twenty years, usually with an absolute majority. However, during those twenty years the people of Britain were generally sympathetic to the view of the Left in foreign policy, although they generally voted in elections on the basis of domestic rather than foreign policy. This means that the people were in favour of revision of Versailles, of collective security, of international cooperation, and of disarmament [Just as they had been in 1906 when they gave the Liberals standing on a

platform of peace and retrenchment a landslide victory, but were then duly betrayed by the secret warmongering of the Liberal Imperialists Asquith, Grey, Haldane, and Churchill.]

The British governments of the Right began to follow a double policy: a public policy in which they spoke loudly in support of what we have called the foreign policy of the Left, and a secret policy of the Right. Thus the *stated policy* of the government and the policy of the British people were based on support of the League of Nations, of international cooperation and of disarmament. Yet the *real policy* was quite different.... Britain rejected every effort of France and Czechoslovakia to strengthen the system of collective security ... Britain signed a secret agreement with France which blocked disarmament on land as well as on sea (July 1928) and signed an agreement with Germany which released her from her naval disarmament (1935). After 1935 the contrast between the public policy and the secret policy became so sharp ... and more insistent on revisionism (by that time called "appeasement") and opposition to the Soviet Union.[4]

In other words, as far as the Milner Group was concerned, and, Lord Curzon (Eton, Balliol, and Fellow of All Souls) admitted, the League of Nations was a "good joke."[5] Germany announced its withdrawal from the League in 1933, nine months after Hitler took power. The alleged reason being the refusal of Britain and France to agree to amend or cancel the Versailles diktats. Belligerents on the right in Britain such as the fascist Sir Oswald Mosley, denounced the League and were more than happy to see it effectively rendered powerless. Mosley and his friends – the high society Mitford sisters, Unity and Diana (daughters of Lord Redesdale), went to Berlin to meet Hitler. Starry-eyed in his presence, and greatly inspired by all he did and said, they returned singing his praises and attempted to spread fascism in Britain. Mosley on the Right and Allen on the Left visited Hitler for very different reasons. And so too the vast majority of British subjects who went

Unity

Diana

to Germany in the 1930s for discussions with the Nazis. Active members
of the Milner Group – as highlighted
throughout this book – were the very
people who had enabled Hitler's rise
in the first place and their motive for
visiting Germany was not to deter
him from war, but to encourage him

towards it. Lumping such individuals under the banner of "appeasement"
was a deception to conceal their true purpose. Professor Preparata writes:

> "Never forget" Ribbentrop was warned … by the military attaché of
> the Japanese embassy in London "that the British are the most cun-
> ning people on earth, and that they graduated to absolute masters in
> the art of negotiation as well as that of manipulating the press and
> public opinion." But neither Ribbentrop nor any other Nazi had the
> faintest idea of what sort of cunning they would be dealing with.[6]

From the time Hitler cleverly manoeuvred his way into power, British
elites shuttled back and forth to Germany to gladhand the former oddball vagabond who, along with American and German elitists, they had
helped groom and fund. A principle aim was to constantly reinforce the
belief that he would have Britain's support for war with Russia. It was a
war that the London elites well knew Hitler was planning for his own purposes. After all, while he had been planning a war against the USSR, the
London elites had been planning the destruction of Germany! In chapter
18 we saw how in 1934 at the famous Horsher's restaurant in Berlin, General Walter von Reichenau revealed to British intelligence agents Frederick Winterbotham and William de Ropp, Nazi Germany's plan to invade
Soviet Russia. It was not the only source of detailed information British
Intelligence had regarding this.

> In September 1936, Putlitz [the British double-agent operating in
> the German embassy in London] reported that the German am-
> bassador, Joachim von Ribbentrop and his staff regarded a German
> war with Russia as being "as certain as the Amen in church," and
> were confident that Britain would not lift a finger when Hitler be-
> gan his invasion … Putlitz's constant refrain during 1938 was that
> "Britain was letting the trump cards fall out of her hands. If she had
> adopted, or even now adopted, a firm attitude and threatened war
> Hitler would not succeed in this kind of bluff."[7]

Wolfgang zu Putlitz had no idea that far from calling Hitler's bluff and threatening war against him to put an end to his ambition, the ruling elites in Britain were constantly encouraging him. A Russo-German war was exactly what they wanted, and the very reason they had promoted Hitler in the first place.

In addition to a steady stream of "appeasers" travelling back and forth to Germany, the Anglo-American intelligence services had their agents, Putzi Hanfstaengl and Bill de Ropp, directly alongside Hitler constantly assuring him that British support was virtually guaranteed. Furthermore, Frederick Winterbotham, RAF officer and leading British intelligence agent, was regularly in Berlin talking to Hitler and other leading Nazis, assuring them of Anglo-German friendship and their shared enmity towards communist Russia. Virtually every message in Hitler's ear told him that Britain supported Germany's position as a bulwark against Bolshevism and would back him. This encouragement – deliberately mislabelled "appeasement" – was geared to ensuring that Hitler would be bold enough to move against Russia. Professor Carroll Quigley, one of the few academic historians who questioned the canonical Oxford view of appeasement, explained how the British ruling class encouraged Hitler while simultaneously hindering the French government's desire to stop him:

> Britain refused to allow France to take military action or to impose any sanctions [against Nazi Germany]. In a violent scene with Flandin [French Foreign Minister] on March 12th, Neville Chamberlain [British Chancellor of the Exchequer] rejected sanctions and refused to accept Flandin's argument that "if a firm front is maintained by France and England, Germany will yield without war."... Sir Austen Chamberlain [British statesman] had stated publicly that Britain would not use troops to enforce the Rhineland clauses and would use its veto power in the Council of the League to prevent this by others.
>
> ...The British attitude towards eastern Europe was made perfectly clear on many occasions. For example, on July 13, 1934, Foreign Secretary Sir John Simon denounced Barthou's [French prime minister] efforts to create an "eastern Locarno" and demanded arms equality for Germany. The other five items in the encirclement of France were: (1) the Anglo-German Naval Agreement of June 1935; (2) the alienation of Italy over sanctions: (3) the remilitarization of the Rhineland by Germany with British acquiescence and approval: (4) the Neutrality of Belgium: and (5) the alienation of Spain. Britain played a vital role in all of them except Belgium. Taken together, they changed the French military position so dras-

tically that France by 1938 found herself in a position where she could hardly expect to fulfil her military obligations to Czechoslovakia and the Soviet Union. *This was exactly the position in which the British government wished France to be, a fact made completely clear by recently published secret documents.* In May of 1935, France could have acted against Germany with all her forces, because the Rhineland was unfortified and there was no need to worry about the Italian, Spanish or Belgian frontiers or the Atlantic coastline. By the end of 1938 and even more by 1939, the Rhineland was protected by the new German fortified Siegfried Line.[8]

Perfidious Albion was playing not only Nazi Germany like a fiddle, but Republican France. In his book, *Conjuring Hitler,* Guido Preparata states categorically that appeasement was a "masquerade to entrap Germany."[9] He writes:

One wonders what the other powers were doing while Hitler was rearming. And the answer is that they – Britain, the USSR, and the United States – did all they could to facilitate his task. They provided the Nazis with resources, military know-how, patents, money, and weapons – in very large quantities. Why? To set the Nazis up, lead them on, and finally destroy them, and take Germany into the bargain at war's end. Throughout the 1930s the United States acted as a mere supplier to the Nazis in the shadow of Britain, who produced the entire show. This show had to end with Britain's participation in a worldwide conflict as the leader of the coalition of Allied forces against Nazi Germany. But the Hitlerites had to be duped into going to war against Russia with the guarantee that Britain, and thus America, would remain neutral. Hitler would not want to repeat the errors of World War I. Therefore Britain had to 'double' herself, so to speak, into a pro-Nazi and anti-Nazi faction – both of which, of course, were components of one and the same fakery. The complex and rather grotesque whole of Britain's foreign policy in the 1930s was indeed the result of these ghastly theatrical diversions with which the Hitlerites were made to believe that at any time the colorful Nazi-phile camp would overthrow the hawks of the War Party, led by Winston Churchill, and sign a separate peace with the Third Reich. The secret goal of this unbelievable mummery was to drive Hitler away from the Mediterranean in 1941, and into the Soviet marshes which the British would in fact allow him to 'cleanse' for three years, until the time would arrive to hem the Nazis in and finally crush them.

None of this would have been possible without the unreserved collaboration of Soviet Russia. The Soviets worked in unison with the anti-German directives of Britain as if they were her most faithful ally. They, like Britain, appeased the Fuhrer, and contributed abundantly to the Nazi war machine by shipping provisions to Germany throughout the entire length of the Nazi rearmament.[10]

Kathryn S. Olmsted, Professor of History at the University of California, is another historian who refused to be fettered to the British Establishment's controlled historiography. Her book: *The Newspaper Axis, Six Press Barons who Enabled Hitler,* (published 2022), comprehensively covers the important "appeasement" role played by the controlled Press.

> As World War II approached, the six most powerful media moguls in America and Britain tried to pressure their countries to ignore the fascist threat. The media empires of Robert McCormick, Joseph and Eleanor Patterson, and William Randolph Hearst spanned the United States, reaching tens of millions of Americans in print and over the airwaves with their isolationist views. Meanwhile in England, Lord Rothermere's *Daily Mail* extolled Hitler's leadership and Lord Beaverbrook's *Daily Express* insisted that Britain had no interest in defending Hitler's victims on the continent.
>
> These media titans worked in concert – including sharing editorial pieces and coordinating their responses to events – to influence public opinion in a right-wing populist direction, they echoed fascist and anti-Semitic propaganda, and they weakened and delayed both Britain's and America's response to Nazi aggression.[11]

Another historian/journalist who writes about the role of the British Press in "appeasement" is Richard Cockett. His useful contribution to the truth, *Twilight of Truth, Chamberlain, Appeasement & the Manipulation of the Press,* published in 1989, demonstrates how the British Government manipulated the "free" and "independent" British press between 1937 and 1940 by curbing its hostility to Fascist Italy and Nazi Germany. The newspapers were enlisted as active supporters of appeasement and to completely mislead the British people about the true state of European affairs. Journalist and author Will Wainewright adds:

> Almost the entire press poured forth news articles and twisted news stories designed to prove that Hitler meant little harm, and that warnings of danger were bad for business anyway.[12]

In the United States, the media likewise controlled "public opinion." One of the most dominant figures in American media history who went to sweet talk Hitler was William Randolph Hearst, a good friend of Putzi Hanfstaengl. Hearst owned twenty-eight newspapers and over a dozen popular magazines in the largest newspaper chain in the world. He reached one in four Americans, and had a news syndication service that distributed features and photographs around the entire world. He hired Mussolini, Hitler, and other top fascist officials to write self-serving articles for the Hearst press.[13] During the summer of 1934, Hearst was touring Europe and had dinner with Putzi Hanfstaengl in Munich. Days later the *Völkischer Beobachter* published an article by Putzi quoting Hearst congratulating Hitler and stating that the battles the Führer faced for Germany's advancement could only be viewed "as a struggle which all liberty-loving peoples are bound to follow with understanding and sympathy."[14] Putzi's lead article in the *Völkischer Beobachter* was thereafter widely reported in Hearst newspapers across the world, and Putzi arranged a meeting for Hearst with Hitler in Berlin. Hitler flew there the following day, with Putzi acting as translator. Hearst left the meeting singing Hitler's praises.

Another press baron visiting Hitler that year was Lord Rothermere (Harold Harmsworth), who owned Associated Newspapers in Britain – including the *Daily Mail* and *Daily Mirror* which had huge circulation figures. Rothermere's late brother and business partner, Viscount Northcliffe (Alfred Harmsworth), had also owned *The Times* – mouthpiece of the Milner Group. Except for a short interval from 1919-1923, it was edited by Geoffrey Dawson, Fellow of All Souls and a member of the inner circle of the Milner Group.[15] Under Dawson's editorship *The Times* in the  1930s was a strong advocate of "appeasement" along with Rothermere's newspapers.

On 19 December 1934, Lord Rothermere attended the Reich Chancellery as guest of honour at a dinner party given by Hitler to celebrate Anglo-German friendship.[16] Hermann Göring and Joachim von Ribbentrop were among the German guests. Ernest Tennant, a banker and close associate of the Milner Group, accompanied Rothermere to the dinner, together with George Ward Price, foreign correspondent of the *Daily Mail,* who spent much of his time in Germany. "Rothermere's subsequent article in the *Daily Mail* was violently enthusiastic about what Hitler had done for Germany."[17]

Ernest Tennant

Tennant, who accompanied Rothermere to the above mentioned dinner, with Hitler, was another who feigned support for the Nazis. Eton educated, he had served in the First World War as a captain in the British Intelligence Corps. Tennant was the cousin of Lord Glenconner, who had a significant interest in the massive munitions factory in Ardeer, Scotland, which made huge fortunes from the First World War. He was also a cousin of Margot Asquith, spouse of the Relugas conspirator and Liberal imperialist prime minister H.H. Asquith. A wealthy merchant banker and successful businessman with extensive business interests in Germany, Tennant funded and established the Anglo-German Fellowship (AGF) in 1935. It comprised leading businessmen, bankers and politicians including Montagu Norman of the Bank of England, and Geoffrey Dawson, editor of *The Times*. Tennant was a close friend of Joachim von Ribbentrop who became German ambassador to the United Kingdom in 1936, and Reich minister of Foreign Affairs in 1938.

> Tenant, whose business activities took him to Germany a great deal in the years 1932-36, had met Ribbentrop in 1932 and formed a close relationship with him. During 1933 Tennant was a considerable apologist for the Nazi movement … he had frequent meetings with Ribbentrop, often staying at his home in Dahlem.[18]

Tennant wrote in 1935:

> A smoke screen of anti-Hitler propaganda continues to obscure from the outside world the nature of the current developments in Germany, and it must be admitted that the Nazis themselves provide much of the inflammable material. … Yet, were the United States of America, France, Spain and several other countries daily to be examined under the same microscope and searched with the same careful scrutiny for subjects for abuse and mockery, the diagnosis in each case would be as bad as or worse than in the case of Germany.[19]

Ernest Tennant appeared to be a true Nazi sympathiser, but was operating on behalf of the British Establishment and its intelligence services. Together with other British agents, such as the mysterious Oxford and London School of Economics graduate Dr. Thomas Conwell-Evans, Tennant was focused on supplying "prompt and most accurate intelligence to the heart of the British government from credible German sources."[20]

George Ward Price

Price, who accompanied Rothermere and Tennant to Hitler's dinner on 19 December, was the *Daily Mail's* top European correspondent. Professor Olmsted writes:

> George Ward Price eagerly embraced the *Daily Mail's* policy on the Nazi regime. In a 1938 book, he described Hitler as a gentle soul who loved children and dogs and had a soldier's "aversion" to war. But his employer outdid even Price in his support for the Nazi regime ... Rothermere dismissed those who pointed to the Nazis' use of terror to maintain power.... The Nazis needed to act with determination to control the "alien elements" within Germany: "In the last days of the pre-Hitler regime there were twenty times as many Jewish government officials in Germany as had existed before the war. Israelites of international attachments were insinuating themselves into key positions in the German administrative machine." Hitler, he concluded, had "saved his country from the ineffectual leadership of hesitating, half-hearted politicians."
>
> ... Hitler himself believed Rothermere was "one of the very greatest of all Englishmen" and that the *Mail* was "doing an immense amount of good. I have the greatest admiration for him.".... After the Night of the Long Knives, when Hitler ordered the arrest and execution of dozens of Storm Troopers who he claimed were plotting against him, the *Daily Mail* praised him for heroic and speedy action against treachery. Rothermere came away impressed. Never before, he told his readers, had the chances for Anglo-German friendship been better. "Their interests, our own, and those of the entire civilised world will be best served by close and friendly co-operation between us."[21]

Over the next five years, George Ward Price was one of very few foreign journalists granted ready access to Hitler. His regular reports in the *Daily Mail* constantly praised the Nazi leader.

> In Nazi Germany, Price had the dubious honour of being the only foreign journalist trusted by Hitler ... Price was welcomed to interviews in the in the Reich Chancellery in a more privileged way that all other foreign journalists ... yet that access bore a heavy price in terms of

573

impartiality if you worked for the *Daily Mail*. Not only was Price beholden to Hitler for the interview right he was granted, he was actively encouraged to pursue a pro-Nazi line by his employer in London.[22]

Another influential British press baron who supported "appeasement" was the Canadian born Lord Beaverbrook (Max Aitken)

LORD BEAVERBROOK

Beaverbrook owned the *Daily Express,* one of the world's largest circulation newspapers. He was close to many leading British politicians, including Winston Churchill whom he regularly bankrolled.[23] Beaverbrook's *Daily Express* was inconsistent in its support for Hitler, but suggested that the Nazis presented little danger to Britain.

At times the *Daily Express* seemed sympathetic to the German regime. In 1936, for example, it published an embarrassingly positive op-ed about Hitler by David Lloyd George. The former prime minister described Hitler as the "George Washington of Germany" and praised him, as Rothermere had done for years, as the saviour of his country and responsible for "a marvellous transformation in the spirit of the people, in their attitude to each other, and in their social and economic outlook."[24]

Press barons Rothermere, Beaverbrook and Hearst played significant roles in encouraging Hitler and misleading the British and American public, but it was the Milner Group that played the leading role.

In *Tragedy & Hope*, Quigley outlines the bigger picture:

Lionel Curtis, Leopold Amery, Philip Kerr (Lord Lothian), Lord Brand, and Lord Astor [all members of the inner circle of the Rhodes-Milner secret society], sought to weaken the League of Nations and destroy all possibility of collective security in order to strengthen Germany in respect to both France and the Soviet Union, and above all to free Britain from Europe in order to build up an "Atlantic bloc" of Great Britain, the British Dominions, and the United States. They prepared the way for this "Union" through the Rhodes Scholarship organisation, through the Round Table groups (which had been set up in the United States, India, and the British Dominions in 1910-1917), through the Chatham House organization which set up Royal Institutes of International Affairs in all the Dominions and a Council on Foreign Relations in New York... This influential group sought to change the League of Nations from an instrument of collective security to an international conference centre for non-political matters, and to rebuild Germany as a buffer against the Soviet Union.[25]

Alfred Milner died in May 1925, and from then until his own death in 1940, Philip Henry Kerr was leader of the Group. We should remain cognizant of Quigley's comments about the Group under Kerr's direction. It retained, indeed increased, its power in the British government, especially in the field of foreign affairs, and played the major role in the policy of appeasement of Hitler. It controlled *The Times*, the Royal Institute of International Affairs (Chatham House) and, crucially, through Oxford University it retained control of the sources and the writing of history.[26]

PHILIP KERR, (LORD LOTHIAN)

As discussed on page 56, Born in 1882, Philip Kerr, a history graduate from New College Oxford, served in the South African government 1905-1910. He was a close acolyte friend of Alfred Milner and a leading member of Milner's Kindergarten. On his return to England he founded and edited the Milner Group's hugely influential *Round Table* journal. Kerr called for a "world state" with one political authority responsible for the entire world. That is, one world government. As prime minister Lloyd George's private secretary and

éminence grise in foreign affairs, Kerr played a major role in setting the harsh terms of the Versailles Treaty and reparations demands on Germany. On the death of his cousin in 1930, Kerr inherited the title 11th Marquess of Lothian, great wealth, and a huge country manor and 5,000 acre parkland estate, Blickling in Norfolk. As head of the Group, Lothian controlled the appeasement charade. He was in frequent contact with leading Nazi Joachim von Ribbentrop – a favourite of Hitler's – and the German ambassador in London October 1936 – February 1938. Lothian's positive comments about Hitler and Nazi Germany always received wide publicity in *The Times* and Rothermere and Beaverbrook papers.

In 1966, the Oxford-trained historian Martin Gilbert wrote the official whitewash on Lothian's important role in "appeasement":

In Lothian's view even Nazi anti-semitism was not necessarily a permanent feature of Hitler's Germany. He felt that 'in some degree the brutality of National Socialism is the reaction to the treatment given to Germany herself since the war,' and could be assuaged if Germany were now given 'her rightful place in Europe.' Lothian reiterated these views as frequently as he could. He had many opportunities. His House at Blickling was a centre of social gatherings with political undertones. He wrote frequently to *The Times*. He spoke often at the Royal Institute of International Affairs at Chatham House.... He spoke in the House of Lords, and corresponded continuously with a widening circle of supporters and sceptics.

Lothian was not alone after 1933 in ascribing German extremism to British action, in supporting German rearmament, and in advocating Treaty revision in Germany's favour.... Appeasement was a policy of hope. Anyone who felt that war with Germany could be avoided, naturally tried to work out the best way of doing so. The most obvious means were conciliation and understanding.[27]

There is no doubt whatsoever that Lothian was the motivating force behind the appeasement charade. He visited Hitler and ensured that a steady stream of his English ruling class friends did likewise between 1933-1939 to bolster Hitler's belief that he would have Britain's support if he attacked Russia. Thanks to the output of the Press barons and compliant Establishment historians, the vast majority of the British people – like the Nazis – had no inkling of the truth behind "appeasement." Guido Preparata writes:

> The perennially baffled public and many on the sidelines of political power were completely out of touch with political reality and could not comprehend the game that was being played. Britain was pushing Hitler to war against the Soviet Union.[28]

In truth, Lord Lothian and the British ruling elites looked down their noses at Hitler and considered him a poorly educated, uncivilised, thuggish bully. Those were the traits that had drawn them to him in the first place and made him almost the perfect individual for leading Germany into a disastrous war in which it would be smashed and reduced to a vassal state. Everything done now was to encourage him into the trap and then spring it.

Meanwhile, as part of the great game that was being played, Lothian repeatedly expressed the view publicly that reforming the Nazis and avoiding war would best come about if the Allies were willing to make big concessions to Germany. They should revise the territorial clauses of the Versailles

Treaty in Germany's favour and allow her to rearm. Establishment historian Timothy Pleydell-Bouverie, Christ Church, Oxford, writes:

> In January 1935 Lothian travelled to Berlin where he was sched-
> uled to attend a meeting of the Rhodes Scholarship Committee.…
> The Germans were excited by Lothian's visit. He was "without
> doubt the most important non-official Englishman who had so far
> asked to be received by the Chancellor," communicated Ambas-
> sador Leopold von Hoesch, adding that Lothian was "favourably
> inclined towards Germany and wishes to contribute to promoting
> better understanding between Germany and England." Lothian
> was accordingly granted an audience with Hitler, lasting over two
> hours, during which he was treated to a lecture on the dangers of
> Russia, the lack of French goodwill, and the importance of An-
> glo-German friendship. Lothian was impressed by Hitler's sincer-
> ity. He considered the Fuhrer "a prophet."… Two days later, in an
> article for *The Times,* he declared that the central fact in Europe
> today was "that Germany does not want war and is prepared to re-
> nounce it absolutely as a method of settling her disputes with her
> neighbours, provided she is given real equality.[29]

And so the leader of the Rhodes-Milner secret society that had selected Hitler for power went to meet him and thereafter announced that he
was a peace-loving prophet. Most of Lothian's Round Table cabal, together with British Establishment elites and Oxford court historians, would
adhere to this sham until such times as Hitler entered their trap. Guido
Preparata writes:

> How could the Nazis be most suitably bamboozled into stepping
> anew, into a pitfall on two fronts? The answer: by dancing with
> them. And dance the British would, twirling round the diplomatic
> ballroom of the 1930s, always leading, and drawing patterns as they
> spun that followed in fact a predictable trajectory.… The Milner-
> ite, anti-Bolshevik appeasers of Germany in the 1920s had posed
> as the anti-French party and had given their blessing to the secret
> rearmament of Germany with a view to revamping it as 'the bul-
> wark' against Communism. The true core of the imperial monolith
> was the Milner Group … and a heterogeneous collection of back-
> benchers such as Churchill and Lloyd George.[30]

Lord Lothian returned to Germany in early May 1937, for meetings
with Hitler, Göring and Hjalmar Schacht. On his return he announced
that Germany sought 'adjustments in eastern Europe,' including Austria,

Czechoslovakia and Poland. He suggested that these 'adjustments' *were not unreasonable*.[31] Armenian-Iranian historian Manuel Sarkisyanz wrote:

> During the Berlin Olympics of 1936 he [Lord Lothian] wrote to Anthony Eden, the British Foreign Minister, opposing assistance to nations in Eastern Europe against whom Germany had claims: "Europe will not come to terms peacefully with Germany … until it knows it cannot get us in on the anti-German side. Indeed, if it was sure that we could be dragged in, the anti-German group might precipitate a war in the next few months before Germany is fully re-armed." Yet this "friend of Germany" had in 1919 vigorously rejected any mitigation of the Peace Diktat forced on Germany at Versailles … Then, to satisfy Hitler's claims, this peer" advocated concessions to Nazi Germany, and most at the expense of other countries." Kerr presented Adolf Hitler as a "visionary, rather than a gangster," "a prophet," "one of the creative figures of this generation." After a personal interview with Hitler [he was] effectively proselytizing for the Nazis, declaring that Hitler "was a fabulous Führer, who was only strengthening the army in order to be able to protect the Reich from Communist attack…. The British exhortation to the German regime of 1937 was certainly not wasted. According to Dr. Hjalmar Schacht, it was told that "you cannot have colonies but Eastern Europe lies before you." As Schacht commented, "Germany was being advised from the English side to make war against the East."[32]

Through the 1930s, Lord Lothian kept up the pretence until being appointed British ambassador to the United States in April 1939. Over a six-year period, from Hitler seizing power in 1933, Lothian had enlisted many of his ruling class friends and fellow members of the Milner Group to reinforce the appeasement scam. Such individuals were regular weekend guests of Waldorf and Nancy Astor at their grand house in St James's Square in central London or at Cliveden, their even grander country house by the River Thames some 30 miles to the West. In 1919 Lady Astor had been the first female to take her seat in parliament. Viscount Astor owned *The Observer* newspaper. Both were members of the inner core of the secret society.[33]

In addition to Lord Lothian, the Astors' guests included influential people such as Geoffrey Dawson, Robert Brand, and Lionel Curtis:

Geoffrey Dawson, (Eton, Magdalene College, Oxford, member of Milner's Kindergarten, Fellow of All Souls, and long-time editor of the Milner Group-controlled newspaper, *The Times*.

Robert Henry Brand – Baron Brand, (New College, Oxford, Fellow of All Souls, Milner's Kindergarten, managing director of Lazard Brothers Bank.)

Lionel Curtis (New College, Oxford, Fellow of All Souls, Milner's Kindergarten, Milner's Secretary, lecturer in Colonial History, Oxford University, inspiration for The Royal Institute of International Affairs – Chatham House – and the Council on Foreign Relations in the US.)

Together with the Astors and Lord Lothian, Dawson, Brand and Curtis were members of the inner circle of the Rhodes-Milner secret society. Many other members of the Milner Group and Anglo-American high society visited Cliveden, including Tom Lamont, senior director of the J.P. Morgan bank and leading player in the City – Wall Street circle.

> The New-York partners [of J.P. Morgan and Co.] travelled in aristocratic British circles and were frequent visitors at the Astor Estate at Cliveden. No less than the House of Morgan itself, Nancy Astor represented a marriage of American capital and British aristocracy.... On the eve of World War II, Lamont's friendship with the Astors took on important political dimensions. Cliveden, the Astor estate on the Thames, had become a gathering place for politicians and intellectuals who favored appeasement of the Nazis.[34]

The elite cabal was assured of complete privacy and confidentiality at Cliveden when discussing Milner Group affairs, including promotion of Hitler, appeasement, the coming war, and their long-term plan for one-world government. Lady Astor took great exception to the title 'Cliveden Set' which was later given to the group, and denied its existence.

> In response to the onslaught of hostile publicity she persuaded her dear friend George Bernard Shaw to write an article that denied the existence of any such Group. On 5 May, 1938 she herself wrote a letter to the Daily Herald to deny the existence of the set, claiming that there was no "no group which week-ends at Cliveden, in the interests of Fascism..."[35]

Lady Astor could not, of course, declare that the powerful friends who frequented Cliveden were staunch British race patriots, Empire loyalists, and Germanophobes out to destroy Germany. Her denial in the Daily Herald was a clever piece of dissembling to disguise the reality. As she said, there were no meetings at Cliveden "in the interests of fascism." True, but the Milner Group certainly held meetings there regarding how best to encourage Hitler into the trap. Carroll Quigley writes:

> The whole inner core of the Milner Group, and their chief publications, such as *The Times* and the *Round Table*, approved the policy of appeasement completely and prodded it along with calculated indiscretions when it was felt necessary to do so.[36]

In reality, there was not the slightest sympathy or genuine support at Cliveden for the German or Italian fascists. They were simply being manipulated in the global interests of the Milner Group by encouraging them into war against the Soviets. The regular visits by Group members to parley with Hitler were about buoying him up for that war. Like their leader Lord Lothian, they were mostly Edwardian Teutophobes who disliked Germany, detested Hitler and the Nazis and were simply using them to their own geopolitical ends.

Others leading British Establishment players taking part in the appeasement game were Lord Londonderry, Lord Halifax, King Edward VIII, Sir Neville Henderson, Sir John Simon, David Lloyd George, Neville Chamberlain, Leopold Amery, Sir Samuel Hoare, Sir Arthur Salter, Sir Anthony Eden, Alfred Duff Cooper (Viscount Norwich).

LORD LONDONDERRY (1878 - 1949)

Charles Stewart Henry Vane-Tempest-Stewart, was educated at Eton and the Royal Military College, Sandhurst. From one of the wealthiest aristocratic families in Britain, Londonderry owned huge tracts of land in Northern Ireland and extensive lucrative coal-fields in County Durham in north-eastern England. He served as an officer in the Royal Horse Guards and a Unionist member of parliament. When his father died in 1915 he became the 7th Marquess of Londonderry, taking over the family seat of Mount Stewart in Northern Ireland.

Lord Londonderry was brought up to regard wealth, privilege and power as a birthright. And so, throughout his life he did.[37]

Londonderry's wife Edith (Marchioness of Londonderry) was the granddaughter of the third Duke of Sutherland and raised at Dunrobin Castle. Her Sutherland ancestors have long been held in contempt in Scotland for their role in the notorious Highland Clearances which began in 1750 and continued for over a century. Upwards of 100,000 rural highlanders were evicted from their small crofts on the orders of the wealthy landowning ruling class to free the ground for more profitable sheep farming. In their born-to-rule mentality, the Londonderry's were well-matched, and both would play important roles in "appeasement." Lady Londonderry was a close friend of Prime Minister Ramsay MacDonald and is considered to have used her influence with MacDonald in getting her husband a Cabinet position in 1931 as Secretary of State for Air. He held the position until 1935 when dismissed by prime minister Stanley Baldwin. Richard Griffiths writes:

> Lord Londonderry was Secretary of State for Air from 1931 to 1935. After his removal from office he was to become an outspoken spokesman for the German regime. No such views were in evidence up to that time, however. His attitudes to Germany as Minister were complex but in no way yielding.
>
> By early 1936, after a visit to Germany [lasting three weeks] on which he met Göring, Hitler and Ribbentrop, Londonderry showed himself, in a letter to Ribbentrop, to be very sympathetic to the Nazi regime. He expressed doubts about Nazi anti-Semitic policy, but in a tone which showed him to be seeing it as a tactical error rather than a crime: "As I told you, I have no great affection for the Jews. It is possible to trace their participation in most of those international disturbances which have created so much havoc in different countries, but on the other hand one can find many Jews strongly ranged on the other side." From now on, his letters to the press and his public statements were to mark him out as a leading pro-German.[38]

Lord Londonderry became a prominent member of the Anglo-German Fellowship, made six visits to leading Nazis in Germany over the next three years, and wrote letters to *The Times* expressing support for Hitler and his regime. Lady Londonderry regularly joined him on his German visits and with her aristocratic lady friends played her own important role in the appeasement game. Julie V. Gottlieb, Senior Lecturer in History at the University of Sheffield, UK, writes:

> The troupe of Guilty Women was made up of famous and notorious figures. Many were to be found among the Tory elite, such

as Lady Austen Chamberlain Lady Nancy Astor, Edith Lady Londonderry, the Rt. Hon. Unity Mitford, and London hostesses who entertained the Nazi dignitaries without compunction. Some were members of the European aristocracy (or had married into it), such as the London-based 'Nazi Princess' Stephanie Hohenlohe. The Princess was employed as Press Baron Lord Rothermere's European emissary. She was on intimate terms with Hitler and the lover of the Fuhrer's personal adjunct Fritz Wiedemann – despite the fact, apparently known to the Nazi elite, of her Jewish parentage. She had wormed her way into London society and spread Hitler's message through her networks that included the Cliveden Set, the circle around the Prince of Wales and Wallis Simpson, and the Londonderry's, while she was accompanied on her visits to the Nuremberg rallies by Ethel, Lady Snowden, the latter having moved quite a distance from her feminist and Christian Socialist roots to become an admirer of the Nazi regime.[39]

Historian Julie Gottlieb presents interesting and useful facts about aristocratic ladies and their "appeasement" of the Nazis, but appears to have swallowed the Oxford accounts from the vast tapestry of lies. Two of the Mitford sisters, Diana and Unity, were genuinely pro-Nazi and not playing an 'appeasement game,' but Gottlieb clearly has little or no inkling of the realities behind "appeasement" and the real motives of these rich and pampered female members of the British Establishment.

However understandable given their activities, the Londonderry's were wrongly labelled Nazi sympathisers. On his regular trips to Nazi Germany, Londonderry was operating there with full-knowledge and agreement of British intelligence. There is no record of him having interacted with British agent Frederick Winterbotham in Germany during any of Winterbotham's frequent trips there, but having worked together at the Air Ministry they certainly knew each other well. Winterbotham relates in his memoirs that he attended one of the famous parties thrown by the Londonderrys:

> Poor Lord Londonderry had been Baldwin's scapegoat. A most delightful man, I'd always felt that he was far too sensitive to be in the hurly-burly of politics in the thirties: he was much suited to his role of brilliant political host at Londonderry House. Here he and his wife gave glittering parties for diplomats, politicians, writers and artists; he performed to perfection the delicate job of intermingling the various sections of national life. When I was invited to one of

these sometime later, Lord Londonderry smilingly asked whether the new Secretary of State was giving me all the support I needed.[40]

Lord Londonderry and Group-Captain Winterbotham were players in the same team that was duping Hitler and encouraging him towards war. We have seen in earlier chapters how Winterbotham arranged visits for Nazi chief Alfred Rosenberg and Luftwaffe pilots to Britain, and afforded them five-star treatment. That was yet another component of "appeasement."

Despite British mainstream history recording otherwise, King Edward VIII was yet another who took part in the appeasement charade. Preparata writes:

> The masquerade's most picturesque visual effect was the dressing of the pro-Nazi party appeasers with a royal presence. Edward passed the audition.[41]

Charles Higham wrote:

> To cement the impression that they wished to create in Hitler's mind, the British Establishment cast the Prince of Wales and future (very briefly) King Edward VIII as an opinionated, zealous Nazi supporter.[42]

Edward did not have to act very hard to get into character, and he certainly gave an Oscar-winning performance as the Nazi King of England which had Hitler in raptures.

> To make him [Hitler] dream even more wildly, the British Services cast Edward VIII, the Prince of Wales and successor to the British throne, as an outspoken, fervent Nazi partisan. The Nazis are thenceforth made to believe that there truly is in England a wide and pervasive Nazi-phile underground headed by a royal scion, and fed by deep capillaries inside the political apparatus, the near totality of the corporate structure, and vast sections of the intelligentsia. It is all stupendous make make-believe; in truth, not one of such British "sympathizers," not even those few homegrown gangs of fascist copycats, appears to be wholly genuine
>
> ... There follows the heyday of *appeasement*, the biennium 1936-1937, feasts, diplomatic exchange, sharing of military intelligence (mostly on the part of the Nazis), and the celebration of the winter and summer Olympics, during which the Germans and the British seem to revel before public scrutiny in a newly found passionate idyll. In September 1936, no less a personage than the old Premier

Lloyd George – Britain's glorious WWI victor as well as one of Versailles's negotiators-in-chief – pays an official, and much publicized visit to Hitler in his retreat in Obersalzberg. The old Welsh fox, the enemy of yore, exudes such joyful enthusiasm while conversing with Hitler that the latter, already in heaven, feels himself propelled to even loftier spheres of empyrean bliss. After bad-mouthing the Czechs in the presence of the Fuhrer, Lloyd George confides to British reporters that Hitler is the "greatest German of the age."

Three months later, in December 1936: coup de theatre. Slated to succeed his father to the British throne, Edward VIII sensationally abdicates … Since 1935 the British Services have prepared Edward to play the role of the "Nazi candidate."… The abdicating Edward, who now assumes the title of Duke of Windsor, will play an important part during the first years of the War. … The Windsors – Edward and Wally [Simpson] – marry in June 1937, and in October, they are officially invited by the Third Reich on a grand tour of Germany. The event is an immense success. Edward is introduced to Himmler, Goebbels, and Rudolf Hess. This last is an encounter for which the duke has been coached two years previously by the British Services.[43]

LLOYD GEORGE

As described above by Guido Preparata, Lloyd George went to Berchtesgaden in September 1936 for talks with Hitler. Thereafter, he praised Hitler in the British press, played down Germany's aggressive intent and attacks against the Jewish community. In a phrase that would later haunt him, Lloyd George described Hitler as "the George Washington of Germany."

LORD HALIFAX

Edward Frederick Lindley Wood, educated at Eton and Oxford, Fellow of All Souls, member of the Milner Group, Viceroy of India 1926-1931, Secretary of State for Foreign Affairs February 1938 – December 1940, British Ambassador to the United States, December 1940 – May 1946.

In November 1937, Lord Halifax, on a mission on behalf of the British Foreign Office, rejoins Hitler in his alpine retreat. In the course of the exchanges, Halifax assures the Führer that England has nothing to object to Germany's seizure of Austria and Czecho-slovakia, and disingenuously, he adds that he trusts Germany will incorporate these areas without the use of force. Hitler, who has been sold arms by the British for the past four years, quite naturally disregards this last, insincere point, and readies the army immedi-ately thereafter to occupy Austria. In February, Neville Chamber-lain, the English Premier and chief promoter of appeasement, de-clares in an official speech that England is not willing to guarantee Austria's independence. This was the signal.[44]

Carroll Quigley wrote:

> Halifax opened the third and last stage of appeasement in Novem-ber 1937 by his visit to Hitler in Berchtesgaden ... Halifax had a long conversation with Hitler on 19 November 1937 in which, whatever may have been Halifax's intention, Hitler's government became con-vinced of three things: (a) that Britain regarded Germany as the chief bulwark against communism in Europe; (b) that Britain was prepared to join a Four Power agreement of France, Germany, Italy and her-self: and (c) that Britain was prepared to allow Germany to liquidate Austria, Czechoslovakia, and Poland.... the German rulers assumed that this willingness of the British government to accept the liquida-tion of Austria, Czechoslovakia, and Poland implied that the British government would never go to war to prevent this liquidation...[45]

It was also made clear that German colonial demands would be met by giving them the Belgian Congo and Angola. This, according to Carroll Quigley, "was an essential part of the appeasement programme." Alfred Duff Cooper, Secretary of State for War 1935-1937, and First Lord of the Admiralty thereafter, identified the "Big Four" responsible for the policy of appeasement as Neville Chamberlain, Samel Hoare, Sir John Simon and Lord Halifax.[46] Chamberlain's role is discussed in the next chapter.

SIR JOHN SIMON.

A leading "appeaser," Simon was educated at Fettes College, Edinburgh and Wadham Col-lege, Oxford. A Fellow of All Souls and member of the Milner Group,[47] he was a good friend of its lead-er, Lord Lothian. Simon entered Parliament in 1906

and went on to hold many senior Cabinet posts: Solicitor General (1910-1913), Attorney General (1913-1915), Home Secretary (1915-1916), Foreign Secretary (1931-1935), Home Secretary again (1935-1937), Chancellor of the Exchequer (1937-1940), Lord Chancellor (the most senior position in the British legal system 1940-1945). Simon had talks with Ribbentrop in London in December 1934. In March 1935 he went to Berlin for discussions with Hitler, Ribbentrop and German Foreign Minister Konstantin von Neurath.[48] Quigley wrote:

> Hitler was given ample assurance by the Milner Group, both within and without the government, that Britain would not oppose his efforts "to achieve arms equality." Four days before Germany officially denounced the disarmament clauses of the Treaty of Versailles, Leopold Amery [member of the inner circle of the Milner Group] made a slashing attack on collective security, comparing the League [of Nations] which exists, and the league of make-believe, a cloud cuckoo land.... Four days later Hitler announced Germany's rearmament, and ten days after that, Britain condoned the act by sending Sir John Simon on a state visit to Berlin. When France tried to counterbalance Germany's rearmament by bringing the Soviet Union into her eastern alliance system in May 1935, the British counteracted this by making the Anglo-German Naval Agreement of 18 June 1935. This agreement, concluded by Simon, allowed Germany to build up to 35 percent of the size of the British Navy (and up to 100 percent in submarines). This was a deadly stab in the back to France, for it gave Germany a navy considerably larger than the French in the important categories of ships (capital ships and aircraft carriers) in the North Sea, because France was bound by treaty in these categories to only 33 percent of Britain's.[49]

It was Perfidious Albion at its worst.

SIR ARTHUR SALTER

Educated at Oxford City High School and Brasenose College, Oxford. Fellow of All Souls College and member of the Milner Group.[50] After the First World War, Salter was a member of the Supreme Economic Council and general secretary to the Reparations Commission, and Director of the Economic and Finance Section of the League of Nations.

In 1934 he was appointed Gladstone Professor of Political Theory and Institutions at Oxford University, and member of parliament for Oxford University. Quigley wrote:

> Sir Arthur Salter, of the Milner Group and All Souls, offered his arguments to support appeasement. He quoted Smuts's speech of 1934 with approval and pointed out the great need for living space and raw materials for Japan, Italy, and Germany. The only solution, he felt, was for Britain to yield to these needs.[51]

SAMUEL HOARE (VISCOUNT TEMPLEWOOD)

Hoare was educated at Harrow School and New College, Oxford. A Fellow of New College, he was a member of the Milner Group.[52] Also a member of the Anti-Socialist Union, he was elected as member of Parliament for Chelsea in 1910. We have seen in an earlier chapter how Hoare, working for British Intelligence, was posted to Rome in 1917 and ran some 100 agents there including one Benito Mussolini, a journalist. The future fascist dictator was being paid the very substantial sum of £100 per week by British Intelligence at that time. Among much else,  it financed his first forays into Italian politics.[53] *Time* magazine wrote of Hoare:

> Back when the war was only a threat and appeasement was a strange new word, the name of Sir Samuel Hoare was a symbol of abasement before fascism. As Britain's Foreign Secretary in 1935, he joined Laval in a deal to throw Ethiopia to Mussolini. As First Lord of the Admiralty in 1937, he helped throttle Republican Spain, thus paving the way for Franco. He applauded Munich loudly. Just before the fall of France he presented his credentials to Francisco Franco, and became His Majesty's Ambassador to Spain. In Madrid he gave embryonic Falange salutes and watched the fruits of appeasement ripen and fall. [54]

During the 1920s, Hoare was Secretary of State for Air. In 1936 he was appointed First Lord of the Admiralty before serving as Home Secretary (1937-1939). From the time Hitler came to power, Hoare – as a member of the Milner Group – was one of leading "appeasers."

The evidence linking the Milner Group to so-called appeasement is overwhelming. From day one the charade was really about British ruling elites egging Hitler on to re-arm Germany and prepare for his war on Soviet Russia. Preparata summed it up:

> In November 1937, after all this profusion of geniality on the part of Britain, the time came to thrust the Führer forward on to war. *The mission of Lord Halifax on November 19 to the alpine residence of Hitler was the turning point in the dynamics leading to World War II.* ... The Nazis now stared at three different facets of a single front urging them to expand their European stronghold before aggressing the Soviets.
>
> In synthesis, Halifax told Hitler that: (1) Britain considered Germany the bastion against Communism; (2) Britain had no objection to the German acquisition of Austria, Czechoslovakia, and Danzig; and (3) Germany should not use force to achieve her aims in Europe.
>
> In the light of (1) the agenda set in *Mein Kampf,* which all British stewards had studied carefully, (2) the world's full-fledged rearmament, (3) the steady and intense supply of British and American weapons the Nazis had received during the past four years, and (4) the Reich's notorious preparations for Barbarossa, Hitler was justified in disregarding entirely the specious warning not to use force: in brief, Britain was urging him to go ahead. Ordinary Britons, and the rest of the world, were told nothing of this autumnal pact.[55]

Arguably, the 'vast tapestry' of Establishment lies about the rise of Hitler and the origins of the Second World War has never been more successful than in concealing what "appeasement" was really about.

Summary: Chapter 20 – Egging Hitler on

- Despite Adolf Hitler's thuggery and brutal behaviour being clear for all to see, the elites of the Milner Group encouraged him every step of the way.

- The official history recounts that the approaches to Hitler were honest attempts at dialogue and making concessions in order to avoid war. They termed it "appeasement."

- Professor Guido Preparata and several other truth-telling historians describe "appeasement" as a subtle deception to ensure that Hitler was sufficiently confident to attack Russia.

• Press Barons aided and abetted the Milner Group in keeping the truth hidden from the British and American public.

• Leading members of the British Establishment, including King Edward VIII, Lord Lothian, Lord Londonderry, Lord Halifax, and Lord Astor, personally visited Hitler over the years 1934-1939 to assure him of their support.

• Numerous members of the Cabinet likewise visited Hitler to assure him of the British government's support.

• The overwhelming majority of those who took part in the charade to egg Hitler on were graduates of Oxford, Fellows of All Souls, and members of the Milner Group.

CHAPTER 21

"PEACE FOR OUR TIME"

We have seen how the Milner Group and its close associates in international banking in the City and Wall Street were responsible for the First World War, for that travesty of justice the Treaty of Versailles blaming the innocent Germany, and for grooming Adolf Hitler for power thereafter. The Group controlled the British government of Liberal imperialists before and during the 1914-18 war, but how did they control it in the run up to war in 1939?

Prior to the First World War it had long been the case that those who held leading positions in British politics – whether Conservative or Liberal – did so thanks to their considerable wealth and connections. To create an illusion that the electorate was being offered a clear choice, the Conservatives and Liberals differed marginally in their domestic policies such as rates of income tax, spending on public services, education, etc. Foreign policy, however, was sacrosanct no matter which party was in government. Professor Carroll Quigley and other honest historians and philosophers have clearly revealed that the all-important matter of continuity in Britain's foreign relations was dictated not by elected politicians – Quigley described them as the technicians who merely implement policy – but by the Milner Group. As detailed in earlier chapters, it was an immensely powerful organisation that operated behind the curtain and was unknown to the British people.

One might have expected to see significant changes in foreign policy implemented by the 'socialist' Labour Party under prime minister Ramsay MacDonald (1929-1931), but it was a hung parliament, and MacDonald's power was effectively neutered, not least by the deflationary policy of the Bank of England. The central bank, as we have seen, was controlled by financial elites in the City. Quigley wrote:

MacDonald

In fact, the Bank of England's policy made it almost impossible for the Labour Party to govern. Without informing his Cabinet, Ramsay MacDonald entered upon negotiations with Baldwin [the previous Conservative prime minister] and King George as a result of which MacDonald became prime minister of a new government, supported by Conservative votes in Parliament. The obvious purpose of this intrigue was to split the Labour Party and place the administration back in Conservative hands. In this intrigue the Milner Group apparently played an important if secret role.[1]

Quigley relates that Ramsay MacDonald's son, Malcolm MacDonald, played an important role in the political intrigues of the early 1930s, and should "probably be considered a member of the Milner Group from 1932 onward." The Milner Group also placed a Balliol College graduate and Modern History lecturer at Oxford University, Godfrey Elton, within the Labour Party and close to Ramsay MacDonald. From within, he played a part in the Milner Group's intrigues to neuter the socialist Labour Party.[2] On the control of British politics, Quigley wrote:

Malcom MacDonald

> Until 1915 the two parties represented the same social class – the small group known as "society." In fact both parties Conservatives and Liberals – were controlled from at least 1866 by the same small clique of "society." This clique consisted of no more than half-a-dozen chief families, their relatives and allies, reinforced by an occasional recruit from outside. These recruits were generally obtained from the select educational system of "society," being found in Balliol or New College at Oxford or at Trinity College, Cambridge, where they first attracted attention, either by scholarship or in the debates of the Oxford or Cambridge Union. Having attracted attention in this fashion, the new recruits were given opportunities to prove their value to the inner clique of each party, and generally ended by marrying into one of the families which dominated these cliques.
>
> …The Conservative party represented a small clique of the very wealthy…. Of the 415 M.P.'s on the Conservative side in 1938, 44 percent (or 181) were corporate directors, and these held 775 directorships. As a result, almost every important corporation had a director who was a Conservative M.P. These M.P.'s did not hesitate to reward themselves, their companies, and their associates with political favors. In eight years (1931-1939) thirteen directors of the "Big Five banks" and two directors of the Bank of England were raised to the peerage by the Conservative government.[3]

Professor Quigley adds that *the Milner Group was at the peak of its power and control over politics in the period just before the Second World War.*[4] As we saw in chapter 19, the Group permeated virtually every facet of the British government just as it had before the 1914-18 war. Quigley wrote:

> Any effort to write an account of the influence exercised by the Milner Group in foreign affairs in the period between the two World Wars would require a complete re-writing of the history of that period.[5]

During that period the Conservative Party was largely controlled by Stanley Baldwin – Earl Baldwin of Bewdley (1867-1947). Educated at the exclusive Harrow School and Trinity College Cambridge, Baldwin came from a wealthy family who accrued even greater wealth thanks to the First World War (and yet again through the Second World War) with their large investments in the iron and coal industries. Baldwin dominated the Conservative party in the inter-war years, serving on three separate occasions as Prime Minister during that period (for the third and final time in 1935-1937) and was able to influence government policy in the financial interests of his own family. He was a member of the "The Club," an elite dining club in London, which had a

S. Baldwin

total of forty members, virtually all of whom were also members of the Milner Group. Baldwin was also a Rhodes Trustee.

If we look at the list of Rhodes Trustees, we see that the Milner Group always had complete control … In the 1930s the Board was stabilized for a long period as Amery, Baldwin, Dawson, Fisher, Holland and Peacock, with Lothian as secretary. Six of these seven were members of the Milner Group, four from the inner core.[6]

Stanley Baldwin was also intimately linked to the Milner Group through his membership of another exclusive dining club, "The Ark," set up by Lady Londonderry in her lavish London house in Park Lane. It was there that the rich and famous mixed for social interaction and political discussion.[7] British industrialist and author A.P. Young wrote:

> On June 7, 1935, Stanley Baldwin replaced Ramsay MacDonald as Prime Minister, and held the leading post for nearly two years – a most vital span, when Hitler was allowed to advance without

hindrance along a path seen to be leading to war by those with eyes and hearts willing to learn the truth ... He [Baldwin] could never have read *Mein Kampf*.[8]

Baldwin was in fact well-acquainted with Hitler's views in *Mein Kampf*, and knew from British Intelligence re-ports that he was planning to imple-ment them. As Prime Minister during the period June 1935 – May 1937, Baldwin supported the "appease-ment" charade. He had looked on be-nignly while Hitler trashed the terms of the Versailles Treaty by rearming Germany and sending troops into the Rhineland. As leader of the Con-servatives in July 1934, he defended Germany's rebuilding of her air force,

saying she had "every right to make herself secure."[9] Likewise feigning sympathy with Mussolini in Italy and the fascist Franco in Spain, Bald-win persuaded many countries to sign a non-intervention pact during the Spanish Civil War. It was another example of perfidious Albion and its habitual intrigues toward other nations, for while Baldwin publicly endorsed Mussolini and Hitler, they were "both lunatics" in his eyes.[10] The "ap-peasement" masquerade was acted out to en-courage those "lunatics" into war, and prime minister Baldwin was enthusiastically play-ing his part. When Ambassador Ribbentrop

Ribbentrop

arrived back in Germany from Britain in the spring of 1936, he reported directly to Hitler that Baldwin was "completely on the German side."[11]

As part of the absurd pretence, the Baldwin government pandered to Mussolini – the former British agent – and signed an agreement with Italy on 2 January 1937. It recognised the Italian conquest of Abyssinia (now Ethiopia) where Mussolini's forces reportedly slaughtered some 350,000 civilians. Baldwin also made friendly overtures to Mussolini after 75,000 Italian soldiers were sent to support the Spanish fascists. Squadrons of the Italian Legionary Air Force later joined Luftwaffe planes in bombing Span-ish towns, including Barcelona and Guernica, with high civilian losses.

Following the abdication of Edward VIII, and the coronation of King George VI on 28 May 1937, an ailing Stanley Baldwin tendered his resignation as prime minister due to "nervous exhaustion." Neville Chamberlain became prime minister of the National (coalition) government. Essentially, it was a matter of exchanging like for like.

George VI

Neville Chamberlain (1869-1940) was the son of successful Birmingham businessman, politician, and Cabinet Minister, Joseph Chamberlain. He was educated at the private and prestigious Rugby School and Mason Science College, Birmingham. In 1919, after years in the family business and involvement in civic duties in Birmingham, Chamberlain was first elected to parliament at the age of 49. From 1931 to 1937 he served as Chancellor of the Exchequer and became prime minister in 1937 when Baldwin went to the House of Lords. When Chamberlain

Chamberlain

took up residence in No. 10 Downing Street, appeasement moved into its the most critical phase and he is remembered as the individual most closely identified with it.

Neville Chamberlain was on intimate terms with Geoffrey Dawson, editor of *The Times* and member of the inner circle of the Milner Group.[12] Chamberlain was a regular guest at Astor parties at Cliveden[13] where he discussed the European situation and "appeasement" with Dawson and Lord Lothian, leader of the Milner Group. Chamberlain was instructed by Lothian on the moves he had to make regarding Hitler, and there is no doubt that the Milner Group was pulling the prime ministers strings. It had always been so. Professor George A. Lanyi wrote:

> It has been denied that Lothian and his Cliveden friends had any direct influence on Neville Chamberlain, who conducted a personal diplomacy. But Chamberlain was enough of a politician to know that his foreign policy needed the support of influential circles and of the important organs of public opinion with which they were connected. Such aid and comfort Lothian provided.[14]

Under the influence of the Group, in December 1937 Chamberlain removed Sir Robert Vansittart from his important post as Permanent Under-Secretary at the Foreign Office. With no connection to Oxford University, Vansittart had entered the Foreign Office as a clerk at the age of 21 and worked his way through the ranks. A firm Teutophobe, Francophile, and anti-appeaser who believed Britain needed to stand up to Hitler, Vansittart had been leaking information to the press, so he was "elevated" to the high-sounding position of Chief Diplomatic Adviser which was actually devoid of any influence or power. "Long considered by the Clivedenites as their bête noire, Vansittart's fall was greeted by them with cries of joy."[15] He was replaced as Under-Secretary by Sir Alexander Cadogan, educated at Eton and Balliol College, Oxford.

In the House of Lords on 17 February 1938, Milner Group leader, Lord Lothian, decried the League of Nations and spoke in support of "appeasement." Quigley writes:

> This extraordinary speech was delivered in defense of the retiring of Sir Robert Vansittart. Sir Robert, as Permanent Under Secretary in the Foreign Office from 1930 to 1938, was a constant thorn in the side of the appeasers. The opening of the third stage of appeasement at the end of 1937 made it necessary to get rid of him and his objections to their policy. Accordingly, he was "promoted" to the newly created post of Chief Diplomatic Adviser, and the Under Secretaryship was given to Sir Alexander Cadogan of the Cecil Bloc [of the Rhodes-Milner secret society]. This led to a debate in February 1938. Lord Lothian intervened to insist that Sir Robert's new role would not be parallel to that of the new Under-Secretary but was restricted to advising only on "matters specifically referred to him by the Secretary of State, and he is no longer responsible for the day-to-day work of the Office." From this point, Lothian launched into a long attack on the League of Nations, followed by a defense of Germany.[16]

Chamberlain – or more accurately, the Milner Group – was ruthless with another individual who challenged "appeasement," Foreign

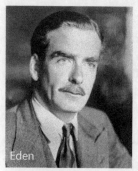

Secretary Sir Anthony Eden. Like Vansittart, Eden was *not* a member of the Milner Group. Chamberlain so undermined Eden's influence that in desperation he finally resigned in February 1938.[17] Free of the restraints of high office, Eden later stated: "How terrible had been the influence of the Cliveden Set ... A defeatist, pampered group that prevented us from taking a strong line which could have made for peace."[18] Eden discussed his resignation when addressing the House of Commons on 21 February:

Eden

596

I rise to ask the leave of the House to make a personal explanation. This is for me, both on personal and political grounds, a most
painful occasion. No man would willingly sever the links which
bind him with colleagues and friends, still less when, as in my case,
I am only too conscious to how great an extent those colleagues
have encouraged and sustained me during the two years that I have
held the responsible office from which I have just resigned. But, Sir,
there are occasions when strong political convictions must over-
ride all other considerations. Of such occasions only the individual himself can be the judge; no man can be the keeper of another
man's conscience. Therefore, I stand before the House to-day to
give the House in a few brief sentences an account of my reasons
for having resigned the office of Foreign Secretary.

...I do not believe that we can make progress in European appeasement, more particularly in the light of the events of the past
few days – and those events must surely be present in all our minds
– if we allow the impression to gain currency abroad that we yield
to constant pressure. I am certain in my own mind that progress
depends above all on the temper of the nation, and that temper
must find expression in a firm spirit. That spirit, I am confident, is
there. Not to give voice to it is, I believe, fair neither to this country
nor to the world.[19]

With Eden gone, prime minister Chamberlain was now surrounded
by ministers who would encourage and support every move to egg Hitler
on to war: Sir John Simon, Chancellor of the Exchequer, Oxford University, Fellow of All Souls and member of the Milner Group; Sir Samuel
Hoare, Secretary of State for Home Affairs, Oxford University, Fellow of
New College and member of the Milner Group; Lord Halifax, Secretary
of State for Foreign Affairs, Oxford University, Fellow of All Souls and
member of the Milner Group. William Ormsby-Gore (4th Baron Har-
lech), Eton, Oxford University, member of the Milner Group. Malcolm
MacDonald, Secretary of State for Dominion Affairs, Oxford University
and member of the Milner Group. Major "appeasers" Simon, Hoare and
Halifax "became Chamberlain's inner Cabinet."[20]

We have seen how Halifax, just three months before he became British
Foreign Secretary on 21 February 1938, had been at Berchtesgaden for
talks with Hitler. Professor Peter Hoffmann wrote:

When Halifax visited Hitler on 19 November 1937, instructed by
the foreign secretary, but taking positions at some variance with

Eden's views and anticipating his own term as foreign secretary, he had indicated that the British government would not attempt to block amicable revisions of the treaty of Versailles concerning Danzig, Austria, Czechoslovakia, armaments and colonies.[21]

Halifax departed Berchtesgaden leaving Hitler with the distinct impression that the British government considered Germany to be the bulwark against communism and was happy for him to move his forces east to face Russia by invading and liquidating Austria, Czechoslovakia, and Poland if it could be done without involving Britain in war. In addition to Halifax encouraging Hitler and his leading henchmen to take such action, others in Britain were involved, including the Duke of Windsor, influential British Press barons, the Anglican Church Archbishop, Cosmo Lang and, not least, Lord Lothian, the Milner Group supremo.

> In July 1938 Lord Lothian hosted a four-day gathering of German visitors, including a number of dedicated Nazis from the Deutsche Gruppe at his stately home, the magnificent and picturesque Jacobean Blickling Hall. During a lavish weekend of hospitality, his guests, who included a representative of the Reich Propaganda Ministry, discussed ways of furthering Anglo-German relations with a British group who were mostly very sympathetic to the new Germany. Those present included several who Princess Stephanie [von Hohenlohe] had befriended. Among them were Lord Astor, owner of the *Observer* newspaper; Sir Thomas Inskip; and Arnold Toynbee, who had just returned from a meeting with Hitler in Berlin. Another was the influential editor of *The Times*, Geoffery Dawson. The Blickling weekend resulted in a document entitled 'How to deal with Hitler,' which painted the Nazi leader as a reasonable statesman. The outcomes from the weekend debate were transmitted next day to the government.[22]

How else was Hitler supposed to respond with such overtures of British friendship and encouragement to expand East? It is worth repeating Carroll Quigley:

> The German rulers assumed that the willingness of the British Government to accept the liquidation of Austria, Czechoslovakia, and Poland implied that the British Government would never go to war to prevent this liquidation.[23]

After the Second World War, the usual British Establishment excuse for the "appeasers" was that they acted with the best of intentions. They were good men doing all they could to preserve peace but misjudged Hitler and failed to grasp just how much of a threat he actually posed. This was utter nonsense.

With one hand, the Milner Group in London was encouraging Hitler towards war while with the other it was discouraging, disheartening and demoralizing the resistance to him within Germany.

Suppressing the German Resistance

Understanding the German Resistance (later called the Widerstand) is fraught with difficulties. Not least because the tapestry of lies created by the Milner Group to conceal the true origins of the wars was extended to deliberately diminish the magnitude of the resistance's membership and activities. At every turn, Germany and Germans had to be castigated. They were "all the same," "all fascists," and nobody there "cared a damn" about Hitler trashing democracy and neighbouring countries. Historians beholden to, and well rewarded by, the Milner Group created the tapestry, but what of the majority of neutral British researchers who have singularly failed to dig deeper, ask questions, and look beyond the tapestry of lies for answers? There can be no excuses for their failures.

What does mainstream history tell us? William L. Shirer's *The Rise and Fall of the Third Reich* (published 1960) is reputedly the bestselling book on the history of Nazi Germany.

> The most widely read account in the English-speaking world is probably that of William Shirer in *The Rise and Fall of the Third Reich* which, while commendable for its scope, has undoubtedly reinforced anti-German prejudices. A more careful and scholarly summary of the previous interpretations has been provided up to 1957 by Professor Andrew Whiteside. Since then all scholars have become deeply indebted to Professor Karl Dietrich Bracher, formerly of Berlin, now of Bonn, for two notable and indispensable studies of the rise of Nazism, *Die Auflösung der Weimarer Republik* (Cologne, 1955), and its equally valuable sequel *Die Nationalsozialistische Machtergreifung* (Cologne, 1960). Historians have now been forced to re-examine their previously held theories in the light of the comprehensive accounts here provided of the processes by which Hitler was allowed to rise to supreme power in Germany.[24]

Sixty years on from the publication of that paper by John Seymour Conway, Professor of History at the University of British Columbia, British historians still commend *The Rise and Fall of the Third Reich* to students. Thus Shirer's book goes on 'reinforcing many prejudices" and none more so than about the anti-Nazi German resistance. Shirer wrote:

> Though much would later be written about the German "resistance" movement, it remained from the beginning to the end a small and feeble thing, led, to be sure, by a handful of courageous and decent men, but lacking followers. The very maintenance of its bare existence was, admittedly, difficult in a police state dominated by terror and spying. Moreover, how could a tiny group – or even a larger group, had there been one, rise up in revolt against the machine guns, the tanks, the flame throwers of the S.S.?[25]

According to the great wordsmith Shirer, resistance in Germany to Hitler was a "tiny, feeble thing" with only a handful of men that "barely existed," yet on other pages of the book he presents details that clearly contradict that statement. William Lawrence Shirer was a journalist and European correspondent of the *Chicago Tribune* 1925-1932. In 1934 he was hired by the Berlin bureau of the Universal News service owned by William Randolph Hearst. As indicated in chapter 20, Hearst, a close friend of Putzi Hanfstaengl, was an American press baron and one of the Anglo-American Establishment's leading "appeasers" whose newspapers sang Hitler's praises. In 1937, Shirer was hired by Columbia Broadcasting System (CBS) as

CBS war correspondent William L. Shirer in Compiegne, France, reporting on the signing of the armistice between Germany and France on June 22, 1940. The building in the background enshrines the railroad car in which Marshal Foch accepted the German request for an armistice ending WWI on November 11, 1918.

a broadcast journalist in Berlin to provide "news" on events in Nazi Germany.

In *All Hell Let Loose, the World at War 1939-1945* (published 2011), British Establishment journalist and military historian, Sir Max Hastings, (Oxford) discusses resistance groups and partisans in France, Soviet Russia, Albania, Italy and Yugoslavia, but makes no mention of the resistance in Germany.

Another British Establishment historian, Sir Ian Kershaw (DPhil Oxford University), writes in *Popular Opinion & Political Dissent in the Third Reich* that nonconformist, dissenting strands of opinion fell for the most part "well short of real opposition let alone resistance to Nazism."[26] Kershaw concludes:

Widespread though the discontent was in all sections of the population with the results of Nazi social and economic policies, it seldom became translated into political opposition. Dissent was overwhelmingly verbal. Frequently it amounted to no more than the traditional grumblings about prices, pay, labour shortages, work conditions, bureaucratic controls, and many other grievances which people in all societies find to preoccupy them.... observers agreed that criticism of the regime was at its most vehement among the peasantry and *Mittelstand*. Yet this produced few outward signs of opposition ... peasant opposition was minimal compared to, for instance, that offered by Soviet peasants during Stalin's forced collectivization in the early 1930s. Though disenchanted by Nazi policies, German farmers seldom felt their existence as a class threatened. From middle class social groups there was even less active opposition, whatever their undoubted grievances...[27]

No doubt then, according to yet another Oxford-linked historian, that while some in Bavaria were discontent under Nazi rule and grumbled over a few things, opposition to Hitler was virtually non-existent. The anti-German message was clear: just as in 1914 the vast majority of the German people had willingly followed the "monstrous" Kaiser Wilhelm II into a disastrous war against peace- loving nations, they now blindly followed Hitler into another war of Germany's making with barely less than a whimper of dissent. "What was wrong with the German people?"

Two disastrous world wars were generated by an immensely rich, powerful, and psychopathic Anglo-American cabal, but it was ordinary Germans who were painted as the outcasts of Europe and civilised society. They had, according to the Milner Group's lie factory at Wellington House, London, demonstrated that in 1914-18. Recall the great Potsdam lie at Versailles in 1919 that in July 1914 Kaiser Wilhelm had announced his plan for a war of European and global conquest and that all Germans gleefully followed him. Recall the great lie that all German soldiers were evil. They bayoneted babies, chopped the breasts off nuns, gang-raped pubescent girls in front of their mothers, and crucified captured Allied soldiers. It "was true" according to the official report of that great and noble British Lord, James Bryce (Oxford) and his friend, the Bishop of London (Oxford), Arthur Foley Winnington-Ingram. As we recall, the good

Winnington-Ingram

Bishop prayed for the killing not merely of German soldiers, but *all* Germans, young and old.

Mainstream history relates that tens of millions of British, French, Russian, Belgian, American and other nationalities had been prepared to give up their lives fighting against the "evil Hun" during 1914-18. Yet 20 years later out of a population of some 80 million Germans, none but a "tiny feeble handful" were prepared to make a stand against the latest manifestation of evil.

Like British accounts of the world wars in general, accounts relating to the Resistance in Germany before and during the Second World War are not to be trusted. No matter the honesty and integrity of individuals writing on the matter, their work is suspect if they have not grasped the fact that a tapestry of lies was created to conceal the reality. Despite such British attempts to conceal the truth about the Resistance among a morass of lies and disinformation, some excellent books on the matter are available. Constraints on space dictate that we can give no more than a brief account of the brave and principled position of the Germans who resisted Hitler. Students wishing to research the subject are well advised to read *Confront!: Resistance in Nazi Germany*, edited by Professor John Michalczyk of Boston. Released in 2004, the book is a compilation of 14 papers presented by leading academic researchers at an international conference on the German Resistance held in Massachusetts in 2002. Also recommended are books and articles by the late Peter Hoffmann, Professor of History at McGill University in Montreal, and fellow of the Royal Society of Canada.

British historians relate that German resistance to Hitler was exceedingly limited and came late in the war. That belated resistance, they scathingly suggest, arose only because senior German army officers realised that defeat was imminent and were merely trying to curry favour with the Allies and save their skin. The German people generally are painted as either Nazis or cowards, but it is worth recalling that in November 1932 the NSDAP gained only 32 per cent of the vote. It later increased thanks to the false flag destruction of the Reichstag and wrongly blaming the communists, but at no time did Hitler have a majority of the democratic vote in Germany.

The British narrative lie is nailed by the proven fact that, among others, numerous senior figures in the Wehrmacht were attempting to work out the best way to act against Hitler before the war even started. It is easy to level the charge that they clearly did not try hard enough, but it must be understood that terrible torture and death awaited members of the resistance and their families if the slightest whiff of their activities was discovered. A considerable number did indeed ultimately suffer such a gruesome end. The real warmongers were in London, but no one in Britain was resisting *them*.

Beck

Canaris

The German resisters included General Ludwig Beck, Chief of the General Staff of the Army, 1933-1938; Admiral William Canaris, head of the Abwehr (military intelligence, 1935-1944), and Canaris's chief assistant, Colonel Hans Oster. Other key military figures in the so-called Oster conspiracy to kill Hitler and avert war were General Erwin von Witzleben, General Count Erich von Brockdorff-Ahlefeldt, General Erich Hoepner and General Carl-Heinrich von Stülpnagel.

State Secretary in the Foreign Office, Ernst von Weizsäcker, was actively involved, together with Johannes Popitz, Prussian Minister of Finance and Minister of State 1933-1944. Carl Goerdeler, former Reich Price Commissioner, played an important part and his role will be considered in a little detail in due course.

In her important book, *The Good Germans*, published 2020, Catrina Clay, multi-award-winning director of television documentaries at the BBC, relates that in addition to a number of senior military, political, and diplomatic corps individuals, many ordinary citizens attempted to resist. They included women's and students' groups – comprising a broad spectrum of Christians, Jews, communists, and atheists – who lived in fear yet found the courage to resist, and in much greater numbers than ever recorded or suggested by British historians.

> The membership of the Nazi Party when they came to power through a fateful coalition of right-wing parties in 1933 was some two million. For them, Hitler was their Führer, the man who would lead them out of their desperate lives following Germany's humiliating defeat in the First World War and the chaos of the Weimar years which followed. But what of those two-thirds of Germans who did not vote for the Nazis and had to live through the Nazi terror regime, then the Second World War and then, once it was all over, suffer the opprobrium of the whole world as more and more of the atrocities perpetrated by the Nazis became public knowledge, extermination camps and all? Not to mention their own

feelings of guilt, because many of those Good Germans ended up believing it had all been their fault. What of them?[28]

When Hitler gained dictatorial power through the Enabling Act in 1933, substantial numbers of opponents were put in concentration camps and murdered. The killings continued and people were understandably afraid of the Gestapo and the "machine guns, tanks, and flame throwers of the S.S.," as William Shirer states in *The Rise and Fall of the Third Reich*. Yes, of course many people were afraid of the Nazis but it is a travesty of truth to suggest that none but a mere handful in Germany resisted.

Civilian resistance against a foreign invading force had long been viewed as a brave and noble act of patriotism – such as by the French and Norwegian Resistance during the Second World War. Resistance against one's own government during times of crisis or pending war, however, is deemed cowardly and traitorous, and never tolerated. In Britain during the First World War, many who resisted government orders to don a uniform and fight were locked up and severely punished with back-breaking hard labour. When the United States entered the war in 1917, deeply religious Hutterites and Mennonites were similarly imprisoned with a considerable number brutally beaten to death by the prison guards. With everyone expected to rally round their country's flag in times of strife or war, in Germany in the 1930s it was especially difficult and dangerous for individuals and groups to resist their own government.

It is all too easy for us to say that it would have been straightforward for the German Resistance to get rid of Hitler with a single bullet, but its great concern was that his tyrannical rule would then immediately be replaced by another if the Allies reinforced the conditions of the Versailles Treaty and worse. For that reason when seeking British help, they constantly sought assurances from the British power brokers that they would allow democracy and freedom to flourish in Germany if Hitler was assassinated. If, on the other hand, the Allies were simply going to impose further draconian measures on Germany post-Hitler, it was a somewhat futile exercise. We consider it likely that the latter is exactly what the Milner Group would have done had the Resistance killed Hitler. The point of the exercise – as per Halford Mackinder's geopolitical strategy – was to effectively smash

Mackinder

Germany and keep it under Anglo-American control. It could never be permitted to upset the balance of power through a well-established and permanent alliance with Russia.

After the war, Germany was reduced to subservient vassal status: its people were maliciously burdened with guilt and became extremely reluctant to ask questions or speak truth to power. Sadly, it remains that way today, if not worse. 80 years on from the end of the Second World War, with some 40 major US military and air force bases still spread throughout Germany, when the US tells successive cringing German governments to jump, they ask "how high?." Had Hitler been assassinated by the resistance in the late 1930s, that state of affairs would assuredly have been implemented six or seven years earlier, for the Milner Group *always* had a plan B. Some 80 million lives could have been spared, and much misery and horror averted, but in plan A there was nothing like war to generate massive profits for the banks and industrialists – while simultaneously killing off "useless eaters."

Interesting as counter-factual history is, as we all know, Hitler wasn't assassinated. American author Michael Thomsett writes about the Resistance in *The German Opposition to Hitler* (1997):

> Theirs was, by necessity, a hidden resistance. Its members were German citizens uniting against their own country's government with the intention of assassinating its leader, Adolf Hitler. Although Hitler was a charismatic leader who was able to consolidate his power to the extent of nullifying opposition, he was not entirely unopposed. If it seemed that no cry was raised against Hitler, it was because all the usual outlets – newspapers, radio, books – were closed to the voices of dissent.
>
> All forms of opposition to Hitler had to take place in secret. There was no political debate in Germany. The personal danger to anyone who disagreed with Hitler made joining the resistance extremely serious. Nevertheless, thousands of people did join. And eventually, it was not just a resistance of words; their intention was to remove their country's leader from power, by assassination if necessary.[29]

Leading players in the resistance repeatedly requested the British government's help in their efforts to put an end to Hitler and his madness, but were spurned on every occasion. The Paris-born British historian Basil Liddell Hart, son of a Methodist minister, noted in his book, *History of the Second World War* (1970):

Scant encouragement was given by the British Government to several secret approaches made by groups in Germany who wanted to overthrow Hitler and make peace if they could get satisfactory assurance as to the peace conditions that the Allies had in mind.[30]

Hart added:

Envoys of the widespread anti-Nazi movement in Germany made known to the Allied leaders their plans for overthrowing Hitler, and the names of many leading soldiers who were prepared to join such a revolt, provided that they were given some assurance about the allied peace terms. But then, and later, no indication or assurance was given them, so that it naturally became difficult for them to gain support for a "leap in the dark."[31]

Unusually for a British historian, Liddell Hart (he attended neither Eton nor Oxford, nor was in any way linked to the Milner Group) emphasizes that the anti-Nazi Resistance movement in Germany was "widespread" and could readily have accomplished its mission to take Hitler out before the Second World began had Britain given its support by standing firm against Hitler.

Professor Peter Hoffmann writes in *German Resistance to Hitler* (1988):

German Resistance to the Nazi government was a direct response to its fundamental injustice and destructiveness. Arbitrariness, criminality, dictatorial oppression, police excesses, persecution of religious leaders and political opponents, and the persecution of so-called non-Aryans (Jews and Gypsies) and the frivolous unleashing of another war – these were the principal causes of the Resistance. For many, the persecution of the Jews was the most important single factor.[32]

According to the vast tapestry of Oxford lies, however, virtually the entire German people fell blindly under the spell of Hitler and obeyed his every command. All Germans, the tapestry implies, were inherently wicked warmongers. They had been "responsible" for the horrors of the First World War and would now be made to share collective responsibility for the even greater disaster that was about to befall mankind. We recall how in 1915 the Bishop of London, Arthur Foley Winnington-Ingram, (educated at Oxford University) turned the war into a "Holy War." *All* Germans were "evil" and should be killed. Such vile lies, together with Lord Bryce's slanders against the German people and the false accusation that no-one in Germany opposed the evil Nazis, continued in similar ways in the 1930s. In 1948, Hans Rothfels, Professor of History at the University of Chicago explained:

> At the time it was an almost universally accepted view in this country [United States] that there was not and never had been a German opposition to Hitler worth speaking of; that the Germans, differently from other people and because of either inborn wickedness or an acquired habit of obedience or a specifically obnoxious political philosophy, voluntarily adhered or meekly submitted to a tyrannical regime of gangsters; that they deliberately closed their eyes to the horrible crimes committed by Germans, and so on. According to this view it was only when "Prussian generals" were faced with defeat that they started a movement to save their skins or to preserve the General Staff for World War III. This misconception can be explained, in part, by objective difficulties which barred access to truth. A movement opposing a terroristic and thoroughly totalitarian regime operates under conditions which are unimaginable to anybody who has never lived in such a "police state." To take a stand, to say nothing of a public stand, was not only a matter of personal heroism (which seems a comparatively rare phenomenon in any modern society), but also a matter of gravely endangering one's family and one's friends
>
> It has been aptly said that Germany, after 1933, was "an occupied country," though in a very different sense than other countries were to be. There was in Germany nothing of the glamour which deservedly surrounds a "Resistance" fighting a foreign conqueror and a tyrannical power from outside. There prevailed instead, and particularly so in later years, an atmosphere of deadly silence, which probably deceived a good many Germans no less than it deceived the public of Britain and the United States. Any mentioning of names in clandestine propaganda or in broadcasts abroad might have been dangerous. This danger, of course, increased with the outbreak of war, which exposed any opposition to the charge of high treason.
>
> ...There were many reasons, then, for a deceptive picture of "all quiet." And the German Intelligence and Counter Intelligence (*Abwehr*), which was staffed with some of the most active members of the opposition, saw to it that this deceptive veil was kept as closely knit as possible. In particular, a "zone of silence" was drawn around the leading men of the conspiracy.[33]

Klemens von Klemperer, Professor of History at Smiths College, Massachusetts, wrote in 1992:

As for the impact of the Widerstand [the name later given to the German resistance] upon the conduct of Allied diplomacy and the war, it must be stated at the outset that it was for all practical purposes minimal in spite of unceasing efforts on the part of the Germans to establish ties with the 'other side'. Actually, throughout the whole period of Nazi domination, especially from 1938 to 1945, a stream of emissaries kept going abroad, to London especially and also to Washington, and after the outbreak of war, to neutral capitals of occupied countries. They went in order to explore reactions to Nazi policies, to inform, to warn of impending war, to press for definition of peace terms, to negotiate with the 'enemy' on conditions for facilitating a coup and on territorial terms to be offered to a post-Nazi Germany, to help prisoners of war as well as deportees and Jews, to establish ties with Resistance movements abroad, and last but not least to say to the world: 'we are here'.[34]

If the impact of the German resistance was "minimal," it was not for the want of trying, but due to the fact that the British ruling elite decreed it would be so. The Milner Group was encouraging Hitler to start a major war, not trying to stop him, and the resistance was given short shrift. American academics specialising in the anti-Nazi German resistance comprehensively nail the British Establishment lie that the resistance was a small and insignificant movement. Their books detail many individuals within the resistance who held senior positions within the German armed forces, the political apparatus, and the diplomatic corps, or were simply ordinary concerned citizens. Irrespective of their standing or status, they were being undermined by Britain in their determination to stop Hitler

We have seen how on his visit to Germany in November 1937, Lord Halifax effectively gave Hitler the green light to annex Austria and makes moves against Czechoslovakia and Poland. He assured Hitler that the purpose of his visit and message had been cleared at the highest levels of the British government. It was a very important aspect of what was miscalled "appeasement" but, in reality, was encouragement for Hitler and his war plans. With countries to the east of Germany – Austria, Czechoslovakia, and Poland – under Hitler's control, his forces would be able to rapidly advance further east against Russia when the time was considered appropriate. Quigley wrote:

> The countries marked for liquidation included Austria, Czechoslovakia, and Poland, but did not include Greece and Turkey, since the Milner Group had no intention of allowing Germany to get down onto the Mediterranean "lifeline."[35]

Sir Neville Henderson, the British Ambassador in Berlin, and one of the Chamberlain group, played his part in the appeasement charade. The son of a director of the Bank of England, Henderson was educated at Eton and accepted for officer training at Sandhurst but joined the diplomatic corps instead. Carroll Quigley writes that as the ambassador in Berlin, Henderson reinforced Halifax's statement that changes in Europe were acceptable if accomplished without "the free play of forces" and that he [Henderson] personally expressed himself in favour of the German annexation of Austria – the Anschluss. With British support for the move, Hitler summoned the Austrian Chancellor, Kurt Schuschnigg, to Berchtesgaden. At the meeting on 12 February 1938, Schuschnigg made it clear to Hitler that he was strongly opposed to him absorbing Austria into the Third Reich.

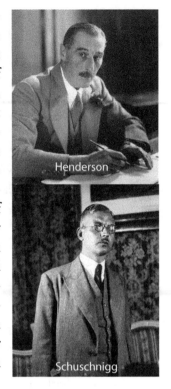

Henderson

Schuschnigg

> Hitler told the Austrian leader that Lord Halifax agreed "with everything he (Hitler) did with respect to Austria and the Sudeten Germans." Chamberlain and others made it perfectly clear, both in public and private, that Britain would not act to prevent German occupation of Austria or Czechoslovakia.[36]

Confident of British backing, Hitler was abusive and threatening to Chancellor Schuschnigg, presented him with far-reaching demands, and coerced him into signing the agreement.[37] In its lead article on 17 February 1938, the Milner Group-controlled newspaper *The Times* supported the Anschluss:

> Versailles had been wrong in its "ban on the incorporation of Austria in the German Reich, which was "one of the least rational, most brittle, and most provocative artificialities of the peace settlement." This had been followed by a stupid refusal to allow the Customs Union between the two countries. Germany should be allowed to extend her influence. In subsequent articles *The Times* had made it clear that it was aware of pro-German feeling in Austria.[38]

In the House of Commons the prime minister also gave the green light for the annexation of Austria. Guido Preparata writes:

> In February, the prime minister, Neville Chamberlain and the Secretary of the Treasury, Sir Eric Simon, [Milner Group] announced in the House of Commons that Great Britain could not be expected to support Austrian independence. This was the signal.[39]

On 12 March 1938, Hitler sent his troops across the Austrian border and the following day incorporated Austria into the German Reich. There was little reported active opposition from the Austrian people, and a plebiscite held thereafter by the Nazis indicated an apparently astonishing 99 per cent support of Austrians for the Anschluss.

Whatever the truth behind the plebiscite, Austria was now under Hitler's control. On 18 March, Russia sent Britain a proposal for an international conference to stop Hitler's aggression. "The suggestion was rejected at once."[40]

Professor Preparata writes:

> Hitler marched into Austria and asked the Austrians thereafter to sanction the deed with a referendum: 99.7 percent swung to his side in favour of *grossdeutsch* unity – the push to the east had begun, Czechoslovakia was next. On April 21, 1938, General Keitel [Chief of the Wehrmacht High Command] received orders from Hitler "to draft plans for invading Czechoslovakia."
>
> It is important to emphasise that at this point not a single manoeuvre on the path to war was the fruit of Hitler's strategy or imagination: the schemers of Versailles had prepared the route for him long ago, and the British stewards were now facilitating the progression. By sequestering the 3.4 million Sudeten Germans (22 percent of the population) into the artificial creation of Czechoslovakia in 1918-20, the old treaty furnished the Führer with the beautiful pretext of claiming these back into the Reich in the name of "ethnic self-determination" – and so Hitler did.
>
> The British press – again, the *Daily Mail* of the appeasing Rothermere – opened fire with a leader on May 6 denouncing Czechoslovakia as a hateful country, inhabited by rascals, whose treatment of the German-speaking Sudetens was an outrage that Britain could not tolerate. Once more France, the helpless Marianne forsaken by Britain, scurried around frantically to patch up some kind of belated common front against this Nazi juggernaut – whose 15-year incubation France's mischievous pride had ultimately favoured. In May she supplicated the Russians to intervene

on her side against Germany. She appeared to be utterly unaware that both Britain and Russia, who always seemed to be playing in tandem, had no intention whatever of stopping Hitler at this point. Russia replied that she would do so as long as Poland and Romania afforded her passage of Soviet troops in their territory. Which was a bluff, because the Soviet Union did nothing to dissipate the rancor and seething hostility that divided her from Poland on one hand and Romania on the other. France then implored both countries but they refused: they did not trust the Russians, least of all in their home – "Give up," said Poland to France, "Czechoslovakia is dead."

…The combined forces of Britain, Russia, Czechoslovakia and France would have literally pulverized the Wehrmacht in 1938: all the powers involved knew this. Especially Britain, who, within two weeks of Hitler's annexation of Austria, moved to emasculate Czechoslovakia and allow Hitler and herself to complete military preparations. Already on March 24, Neville Chamberlain, sending another smoke signal to the Nazis, announced that Britain would refuse to lend assistance to the Czechs if they were attacked or to France if she went to their rescue.[41]

Around this time – several months after the Anschluss – a well-respected member of the German Resistance, Carl Goerdeler – former Mayor of Leipzig and the politician chosen by the Resistance to become Chancellor of Germany if Hitler was ousted – went to London in a bid to garner British support for the planned putsch. Professor Hans Rothfels writes of Goerdeler:

Goerdeler

Unable to prevent an anti-Semitic demonstration of the Nazi party in Leipzig (the removal of the Mendelssohn monument) he resigned his office [as Mayor of Leipzig] in 1936. He was then employed in Stuttgart as an adviser to Robert Bosch, one of the most liberal and socially progressive German industrialists, who provided him with the financial means and, still more important, with the necessary cover for his far-flung anti-Nazi activities. They extended practically to all non-communist groups of the opposition, many of which found in him their rallying point. He was in contact with the military, of course, and with businessmen, with other retired civil servants and active members of the foreign office, but also with professors and churchmen (especially Archbishop Count von Preysing of Berlin and Protestant Bishop Wurm of Württemberg), with trade unionists and socialist leaders. In addition, he had many friends abroad, and he travelled incessantly; through England and France, through Sweden and Belgium, through the Balkans and the Near East, through the United States and Canada. There is no doubt that in the years before the war, he did all in his power to make the outside world aware of what was in store and of the true character of the Nazi regime.[42]

Goerdeler, a principal coordinator of the Resistance, had already visited Britain in 1937 and met a leading Scottish engineer and devout Christian, A.P. Young, a leading engineer in the aircraft magneto industry. Young later described his first meeting with Goerdeler over dinner with some trusted English friends in the National Liberal Club in London in June 1937:

> Goerdeler impressed all of us with his forceful, humorous and likeable personality; and his superb moral courage dominated the man. He left no doubts in our minds about the evil things that Hitler and his associates were doing and would continue to do with increasing speed if no check were applied. He felt that Britain could exert such a check by being much more forceful in her negotiations with Hitler and his associates. He pleaded most earnestly for a *firm* policy in dealing with Hitler as the only one that Hitler would understand aright: and the only policy likely to retard his evil purposes. We must in all our dealings be firm, and "call black black and white white," as he put it. Any equivocation or appeasement would be interpreted as weakness, would inflame Hitler's megalomaniac propensities; and would discourage the liberal forces inside Germany who had no illusions about the Hitler regime, and who, as Goerdeler contended, were anxious to co-operate with us to find a solution to the Hitler problem.
>
> I recall so well Deedes [Brigadier-General Sir Wyndham Deedes] saying to me as we walked out of the dining room when the party was breaking up: "I understand Goerdeler has decided with commendable courage to go forth and fearlessly condemn the Hitler regime regardless of what the personal consequences may be." Within a few days of this dinner meeting, Deedes introduced Goerdeler to Sir Robert Vansittart, Permanent Under-Secretary of State for Foreign Affairs. Goerdeler must have deeply impressed Vansittart when they met for the first time in early July. Soon afterwards, with Goerdeler's warnings ringing in his ears, he wrote a forceful memorandum advocating a clear and firm policy in our

dealings with Hitler. He intended to circulate it to the Cabinet, but Anthony Eden, the Foreign Secretary, would not agree. Eden made a wrong decision: one of many made by him as appeasement spread its sinister wings over the land.

If only Vansittart's views at that vital moment – more than a year before Munich – had been allowed to penetrate the mind of the cabinet, and especially the minds of its younger members, the resistance to the growing tide of appeasement might have been effective. But it was not to be. This important document was found by Vansittart's biographers among his papers at his home, Denham Place. Vansittart in disgust had scrawled across it: "Suppressed by Eden."[43]

Many good people in Britain were deeply concerned about Hitler, and attempted to help the many good people in the German Resistance, but they had no knowledge whatsoever of the Milner Group or the fact that it controlled the government and British foreign policy.

Consequently, the true reason certain British politicians and officials were "appeasing" Hitler was never apparent to them. Carol Quigley discussed Sir Robert Vansittart – who was not a member of the Milner Group and had no links to Oxford University:

> Sir Robert, as Permanent Under Secretary in the Foreign Office from 1930 to 1938, was a constant thorn in the side of the appeasers. The opening of the third stage of appeasement at the end of 1937 made it necessary to get rid of him and his objections to their [Milner Group] policy. Accordingly he was "promoted" to the newly created [toothless] post of Chief Diplomatic adviser, and the Under-Secretaryship was given to Sir Alexander Cadogan of the Cecil Bloc.[44]

Vansittart refused to play the Milner Group's "appeasement" games, and for trying to prevent another disastrous world war, was kicked out of his powerful position in the Foreign Office. His replacement, Sir Alexander Cadogan (Eton and Balliol College, Oxford, and son of Earl Cadogan), was a member of the Cecil Bloc of the Rhodes-Milner secret society and one of its trusted players. Despite the setback of Vansittart being 'kicked upstairs' to a newly created and utterly powerless post, A. P. Young continued his efforts to support Goerdeler and the wider German Resistance:

> I made many journeys to the Continent for the purpose of seeing Goerdeler secretly, and reporting his views on the Hitler menace

when, according to plan, it began to raise its brutal head just prior to Munich [Chamberlain's infamous meeting with Hitler at Munich]. Thereafter, it spat fire and brimstone on a startled, horrified and palpably bewildered world."[45]

The 'X' Documents, a book published in 1974 by A.P. Young, reveals in detail the unflinching efforts of Goerdeler and other Germans to get Britain's help in overthrowing Hitler. The book is essential reading for anyone who doubts the commitment or astonishing bravery of many Germans in the resistance, or is unaware of the disgraceful manner in which their efforts were constantly and very deliberately frustrated by Lord Halifax, Sir Neville Chamberlain, and others in the British Establishment.

Professor Rothfels writes that Goerdeler supported the plans of senior German military officers to remove Hitler. He went to London on numerous occasions in 1937 and 1938 to keep A.P. Young updated and drum up British government support for the coup. Messages from Goerdeler to that end were conveyed by Young to Chamberlain and Halifax, and reiterated by Baron Ernst von Weizsäcker, Secretary of State in the German Foreign Office and another member of the Resistance. Weizsäcker instructed Theodor Kordt, Chargé d'Affaires in the German embassy in London and member of the Resistance, to make unofficial contact with Downing Street and confirm that Goerdeler's information was accurate: powerful elements in the German army were ready and willing to attempt a coup d'état if Britain agreed to certain conditions.

> Having asked to be received in utmost secrecy, Theodor Kordt was invited to come to the backdoor of No. 10 Downing Street during the night of September 5 [1938]. In his conversation with Lord Halifax he emphasised the necessity for the British government to take an unqualified stand against Hitler's plan to use force. If such a firm stand was adopted by the statesmen of the Western Powers, the German army would refuse to fight against Czechoslovakia. This, at least by implication, meant a promise to overthrow the Hitler regime. The same communication was made to an influential conservative member in the House of Commons, Sir Horace Wilson and, as will be shown later, it reached Winston Churchill too.
>
> While awaiting British action, General Beck was prepared to press the button. A setback, of course, occurred when Chamberlain decided to fly to Berchtesgaden.[46]

In addition to Goerdeler and Kordt's approaches to Britain on behalf of the resistance, Ewald von Kleist-Schmenzin, a lawyer and secret emissary of Admiral Canaris, General Beck and Colonel Oster, went to London to discuss the situation with Sir Robert Vansittart. Although no longer  in a position of power in the Foreign Office, Vansittart kept members of the Cabinet fully informed of the planned coup, and supported it. Real power in the Cabinet lay, of course, with the Milner Group thanks to its members Lord Halifax, Samuel Hoare and Viscount Simon in senior positions.

William Shirer confirmed that numerous members of the German Resistance travelled back and forward to London from 1937 onwards to discuss the situation with British leaders and request coordinated action. The Resistance needed to know if they were correct in assuming that Britain and France would go to war against Germany if Hitler attacked Czechoslovakia.

> For this purpose they had decided to send trustworthy agents to London not only to find out what the British government intended to do but, if necessary, to try to influence its decision by informing it that Hitler had decided to attack the Czechs on a certain date in the fall, and that the General Staff, which knew this date, opposed it and was prepared to take the most decisive action to prevent it if Britain stood firm against Hitler to the last. The first such emissary of the plotters, selected by Colonel Oster of the Abwehr, was Ewald von Kleist, who arrived in London on August 18.
>
> ...Kleist repeated what he had been instructed to tell, stressing that Hitler had set a date for aggression against the Czechs and that the generals, most of whom opposed him, would act, but that further British appeasement of Hitler would cut the ground from under their feet. If Britain and France would declare publicly that that they would not stand idly by while Hitler threw his armies into Czechoslovakia and if some British statesman would issue a solemn warning to Germany of the consequences of Nazi aggression, then the German generals, for their part, would act to stop Hitler.
> ...On August 21, Colonel Oster sent an agent to inform the British military attaché in Berlin of Hitler's intention to invade Czechoslovakia at the end of September. "If by firm action abroad Hitler can be forced at the eleventh hour to renounce his present intentions, he will be unable to survive the blow," he told the British.

615

General Halder [Chief of Staff of the Army High Command who would later implement Operation Barbarossa against Russia] had a feeling that the conspirators were not getting their message through effectively enough to the British, and on September 2 he sent his own emissary, a retired Army officer, Lieutenant Colonel Hans Boehm-Tettelbach, to London to make contact with the British War Office and Military Intelligence. Though the colonel saw several important personages in London, he does not seem to have made much impression on them.[47]

Members of the Germany military planned to seize Hitler as soon as he had issued the final order to attack Czechoslovakia and haul him before one of his own People's Courts. He would be tried on the charge of recklessly endangering Germany by leading her into a European war, and that he was no longer competent to govern the country.

None of those individuals in the Resistance had any inkling that the very people to whom they were appealing for help in London had long been grooming and funding Hitler and encouraging him towards war. Resistance within Germany and Hitler's overthrow was the last thing they wanted. Fringe members of the Cabinet – the "weaker brethren" as Chamberlain privately named those who disagreed with him – "raised only tentative difficulties."[48] As with everything else relating to the Second World War, it is virtually impossible to understand the truth behind appeasement or the German resistance without grasping that stark fact.

From August 1938, German forces had been mobilising against Czechoslovakia, and Ribbentrop informed ambassador Sir Neville Henderson in Berlin that Germany was determined to act. Incredibly, the British government sent Lord Runciman to Czechoslovakia to browbeat the Czechs and urge them to be more accommodating.[49] 24 years earlier, Britain had allegedly gone to war against Germany to defend the sovereignty of a "neutral" nation. Now, she was encouraging Germany to invade one. Perfidious Albion indeed.

On 12 September, Hitler made a speech at Nuremberg announcing that the German army was mobilised on the Czech frontier and that he supported the Sudeten Germans in their demand for freedom. Had the British government at that point in time issued an unequivocal statement that it would not stand by and allow Germany to invade Czechoslovakia, leading officers in the German army would have made their move against Hitler. One unambiguous sentence to that effect from Chamberlain might well have prevented the horrors of the Second World War.

Preventing the war was the last thing the Milner Group wanted. A coup against Hitler that negated everything they had planned and intrigued for over the past 20 years was unacceptable. Countering the anti-Nazi calls – within Britain as well as Germany – and pending a visit by prime minister Chamberlain to Germany to see Hitler, the Milner Group's mouthpiece, *The Times*, carried the following letter:

> There are many elements in Nazi policy which we all deplore, but ... the internal constitution of Germany is not our business, and if the impression is created that Herr Hitler is regarded in this country with nothing but hatred and suspicion the negotiations will be wrecked before they begin.... Admittedly there are some who do not wish to reach an understanding with Germany, preferring to plunge the world into war rather than tolerate the continuance of a State [Germany] which constitutes a barrier to world revolution.... Let all who are not obsessed by ulterior motives unite to show that England has not forgotten its manners, and that we are prepared to deal with our neighbours in a spirit of reason and generosity. Thus and thus only can civilization be saved.[50]

Such weasel words in what was then considered to be Britain's leading quality newspaper. With its doublespeak and dissembling, those attempting to maintain peace were accused of being warmongers obsessed by ulterior motives who preferred to plunge the world into war rather than accommodate Hitler.

Peacemakers in Britain and those in Germany who were planning to take Hitler out had to be thwarted, not encouraged. To that end, on 13 September, 1938, Chamberlain sent a letter requesting a meeting with Hitler:

> In view of the increasingly critical situation I propose to come over at once to see you with a view to trying to find a peaceful solution. I propose to come across by air and am ready to start tomorrow. I should be grateful for a very early reply.[51]

Hitler agreed, and Chamberlain flew off to Germany on 15 September. He went not to threaten the Nazi leader with war if he attacked Czechoslovakia – as the Resistance had repeatedly requested – but to give Britain's agreement for him to invade the Sudetenland – that part of Czechoslovakia bordering Germany. The new Republic of Czechoslovakia had been carved out of the dismembered Austro-Hungarian empire following its defeat in 1918. The independence of the new state was recognised by the Treaty of Saint-Germain in 1919 and thereafter by the Treaty of

Trianon, signed at Versailles in June 1920. That defined Czechoslovakia's borders and formally ended Allied action against Austria-Hungary. The majority of 3 million-plus ethnic Germans (*Sudetendeutsche*) in Czechoslovakia, resided in the border regions of Bohemia and Moravia which were now included under the new name 'Sudetenland'. Professor R.A.C. Parker wrote:

> Czechoslovakia, a state imagined during the First World War and created in its aftermath, contained the largest group of ethnic Germans under foreign rule. Over 3 million, more than one-fifth of the total population of Czechoslovakia, were German, most in the frontier regions of Bohemia and Moravia, but with a colony in Prague, where a German university continued side by side with the Czech university as a remnant of the time, a century before, when Prague had been dominated by German language and culture. The Germans in the Sudeten areas of Czechoslovakia had not been part of Bismarck's Reich and they did not have the associations with the Reich possessed by Germans in western Poland. In the 1920s, therefore, German attitudes to Czechoslovakia were comparatively benign and most of the political representatives of the Germans in Czechoslovakia became ready to accept the new state ... In the 1930s things changed ... the depression hit the German-speaking areas of Czechoslovakia hard. Exporting industries endured high levels of unemployment and the return of Hitler's Germany to full employment caused the Sudeten German Party, led by Konrad Henlein ... to secure the votes of most Sudeten Germany.[52]

In 1938, Konrad Henlein – who supported German annexation of the Sudetenland and would join the Nazi party in 1939 – started street protests and an uprising against the Czech government. These troubles were helped along by British newspapers – as we have seen, Rothermere's *Daily Mail* in particular – promoting a campaign of propaganda and lies that Czechoslovakia was a "hateful country inhabited by rascals." Hitler simultaneously made radio broadcasts to the Sudeten Germans stating that the Czech authorities were jailing and torturing the German minority.

In London meantime:

> Chamberlain did not tell the assembled ministers [the "weaker brethren"] of his plan to see Hitler to settle the Czechoslovakian problem.... The Prime Minister went to Balmoral and informed King George VI who, according to Horace Wilson [senior civil servant], gave his "cordial concurrence" to his plan. Back in Lon-

don … he told Vansittart who "fought the idea tooth and nail" …
When the full cabinet next met on 12 September, Chamberlain
continued to keep his secret. Horace Wilson told him to be careful
not to mention it "either in or out of the Cabinet."[53]

With Germany scheduled to begin her attack on 25 September, Chamberlain had a meeting with Hitler at Berchtesgaden on 15 September.
Hitler informed him that the Sudeten Germans and their land must be
incorporated into Germany or it would be war. If the British government
agreed to the principle of self-determination for the Sudeten Germans, he
would be prepared to negotiate.

> Next day the British Minister flew home. The British Government
> decided, in consultation with the French, to force the Czech Government to agree to cede all territory with more than 50 per cent Sudeten German inhabitants to Germany. With difficulty, the Czechs were
> persuaded to agree to this plan. The bribe offered to them was that the
> British and French Governments undertook to guarantee the future
> boundaries of the now truncated Czechoslovakia against aggression.
> … Mr. Chamberlain sighed with satisfaction when this distasteful
> scheme had, by the united efforts of himself and the French Premier,
> been crammed down the reluctant gullet of the Czech rulers and eventually, with many a groan and retch, swallowed into their stomachs.[54]

France had a defence alliance with Czechoslovakia dating back to
1924, but the London elites overcame that potential difficulty by refusing
to pledge British support should France go to the aid of Czechoslovakia
and consequently become embroiled in a war with Germany. The message went out from the controlled Press in London: Hitler's forces were
invincible and France would be crazy to risk war against them for the sake
of the Czechs. Russia also indicated that she would not assist France in
the defence of Czechoslovakia against Germany. Preparata concludes:

> To defang the Czechs, England promoted an extraordinary campaign of dis-information. First, the British government refused to
> pledge its help to France if the latter made bold to come to the succour of Czechoslovakia in the case of a German attack. Then, the
> British stewards diffused the rumour that Hitler's war machine was
> invincible and that to resist him would be folly…[55]

The Milner Group would carefully manipulate the entire Sudetenland
situation not least because the region had formidable fortifications along

its border with Germany, together with a well-equipped Czech army of around a million men that could well stall a German attack on Russia to the east. In September 1938, the pawns on the chessboard were being positioned for the big moves yet to come in the game.

Following discussions with Cabinet members – in reality, the Milner Group – Chamberlain flew back to Germany on 22 September for another meeting with Hitler, this time at Bad Godesberg on the west bank of the Rhine in west central Germany.

> Hitler told him bluntly that although he perceived the British Government had advanced far beyond the point of agreeing to the principle of self-determination for the Sudeten Germans he had unfortunately changed his mind. The proposals which Mr. Chamberlain brought were no longer acceptable. The procedure suggested was too slow. Hitler demanded in fact that almost every part of Czechoslovakia where a German could be found should be handed over at once to the Reich. The whole affair was to be completed by October 1. There was to be no more delay or negotiation. Hitler also said that this was the last of his territorial ambitions in Europe, that he wanted to be friends with England, and that if the Sudeten question could be got out of the way, he would like to resume conversations with the British Premier.
>
> Mr. Chamberlain came home once more. He passed on Hitler's proposals to the Czechs who refused them, and completed full mobilisation of their army.[56]

Hitler had told Chamberlain it was non-negotiable. The Sudetenland must be handed over to Germany no later than 2 P.M. on 28 September or he would take it by force. In London, the Czechoslovak ambassador in Britain, Jan Masaryk, had a meeting with Lord Halifax, Secretary of State for Foreign Affairs, to discuss the crisis. In his excellent book, *The Bell of Treason, The 1938 Munich Agreement in Czechoslovakia,* historian Pierre Caquet writes that Halifax was prepared to browbeat Masaryk:

> The Czechoslovak ambassador, finally provoked beyond the niceties of diplomatic etiquette, did not hesitate to use the words to which he was sometimes accustomed in private: "Halifax insisted we should consider whether it is not better to give in to Hitler than be crushed. I responded negatively. He announced that the prime minister remains convinced that Hitler is *bona fide* and that, if he received the Sudetenland, he will forever leave Europe in peace. At my expression of astonishment at such criminal naiveness, he re-

peated what he had said. Chamberlain was but the messenger, he insisted. When I explained how amazed and appalled I was that the English premier should have become an errand-boy of gangsters, Halifax, deeply affected, repeated: Unfortunately, so it is.[57]

"An errand-boy of gangsters" indeed. Presumably Masaryk did not appreciate just how close he was to the truth about Chamberlain.

When the Czech government rejected Hitler's "memorandum," France began mobilising its army: it was evident that the Milner Group's planning could go badly awry. They had to call Hitler's bluff and keep control of the situation by mobilising the Royal Navy. That lent the appearance that Britain would join France in war against Germany should Hitler proceed. He agreed to Chamberlain's call to hold fire and further discuss the matter. Chamberlain flew out once more to Germany, accompanied by Frank Ashton-Gwatkin, an economic counsellor and significant player in the foreign office (educated at Eton and Balliol College, Oxford).

On 29 September, 1938, Chamberlain had a meeting with Hitler, Mussolini, and French Prime Minister Édouard Daladier in Munich. It appeared to all that Europe was on the very brink of another disastrous war, and Chamberlain's alleged "peace-keeping" mission was roundly applauded in Britain. He was, in fact, about to sell Czechoslovakia down the river.

> The Prime Minister at Munich in effect agreed with Hitler that his Godesberg demands should be granted. The Czechs were told that if they objected to the deal they would fight against Germany alone. They surrendered their objections.[58]

On Chamberlain's return to London, a huge cheering crowd greeted him at the airport. He waved a piece of paper in the air – the Munich Agreement, co-signed by Hitler – and announced: "My good friends... I believe it is peace for our time. We thank you from the bottom of our hearts. Go home and get a nice quiet sleep … Britain and Germany would consult on all points of difficulty and settle matters peacefully."

With his shuttle diplomacy the British prime minister, Sir Neville Chamberlain, had supposedly "saved the world from war."

Summary: Chapter 21 – "Peace For Our Time"

- The Milner Group controlled British politics in the first half of the 20th century, and ensured that foreign policy remained constant no matter which political party – Conservative, Liberal or Labour – formed the government.

- Cabinet members linked to the Milner Group travelled to Germany to encourage Hitler in the belief that Britain supported his ambition to control Austria, Czechoslovakia, Poland and, most importantly, Russia.

- Resistance within Germany to Hitler was falsely described by certain historians and writers as being virtually non-existent.

- In truth, many senior members of the German armed forces military and some individuals within German commerce wished to have Hitler arrested or assassinated before war began.

- Members of the German Resistance travelled back and forth to Britain for discussions with the British authorities. If Britain stopped appeasing Hitler and threatened him with war should he attack Czechoslovakia, it would be the signal for the Resistance to make their move.

- The signal never came, because the British government (Milner Group) had no wish to stop Hitler when his forces invaded the Sudetenland region of Czechoslovakia.

- Carl Goerdeler, a Resistance leader, constantly sought support in Britain and America but was spurned at every turn.

- British prime minister Neville Chamberlain visited Hitler on three occasions in 1938. On his return from Munich in September that year, Chamberlain waved a piece of paper co-signed by Hitler and stated that there would be no war in Europe.

CHAPTER 22

ONCE MORE INTO THE ABYSS

On 30 September, 1938, when Sir Neville Chamberlain returned from his meeting with Hitler in Munich, waved his piece of paper in the air and made his 'Peace for our time' announcement, the greatly relieved masses throughout Britain cheered. Germany was to be given a free hand to annex the Sudeten area of Czechoslovakia after Chamberlain and French prime minister Édouard Daladier accepted Hitler's word that he would have "no further territorial demands to make in Europe." On his return, Chamberlain told the crowd greeting him at Heston airfield, London, that any points of difference between Britain and Germany would be settled peacefully. Everyone could relax and go home for "a nice quiet sleep." Few if any in Czechoslovakia saw it that way, but the prime minister was lauded in the House of Commons as the great peacemaker of Europe:

> The British Parliament discussed the decision reached by the Premier at Munich. Throughout this debate the mood of hysterical approbation was prolonged. M.P.s vied with each other in their exertions to lick the hand of the Premier – or even touch the hem of his garment in debate. Mr. Victor Raikes, the Tory Member for South East Essex, gave expression to the sentiment of at least five out of six M.P.s of all parties at that moment when he exclaimed, "There should be full appreciation of the fact that our leader will go down in history as the greatest European statesman of this or any other time."[1]

The following week, as the thoroughly duped members of parliament swallowed the deception and cheered and lauded the new prince of peace and 'greatest ever European statesman,' German tanks and troops advanced unopposed across the Czechoslovakian frontier to take over the Sudetenland. It included, intact, all the fortifications and gun emplacements the Czechs had spent fortunes on over the previous years in an effort to prevent such a German invasion. The British ambassador to Prague, Sir Basil Newton, harboured serious recriminations about the role he played in the dastardly deed.

The most momentous though to him probably the least agreeable task of his career was to present to President Beneš of Czechoslovakia in September, 1938, the decision of the British and French Governments that he must hand over the Sudeten area to Germany or forfeit all hope of support from the two western powers.[2]

Via their glove-puppet Chamberlain, the Milner Group had given Hitler a free hand in the Sudetenland, handed him Czechoslovakia's formidable western defences on a plate, and managed to pass it off as a great peace-keeping venture. It all came about with King George VI's blessing, but with the bulk of the Cabinet, and certainly all backbench MP's, in complete ignorance of the Munich Agreement's true nature. It was virtually a re-run of events leading to the First World War when King George V gave his blessing to the Milner Group's intrigues for war while the majority of Cabinet members, Parliament, and the British people were kept completely in the dark. *Practice makes perfect.*

On 11 October, the despairing German resistance leader Carl Goerdeler wrote to a friend in the United States. He didn't name the recipient, but it was possibly Cordell Hull, U.S. Secretary of State:

Dear ....!

The developments of the last few weeks can only be described as very dangerous. An excellent opportunity has been missed. The German people wanted no war; the army would have done everything to avoid it. Only Hitler, Himmler and Ribbentrop were in favour of war. The growing internal difficulties worried them a lot. On the other hand, they made no secret vis-à-vis the army of their conviction that England and France were neither willing nor able, to protect Czechoslovakia. Nobody in Germany wanted to believe them. But they were proved correct. If England had shown a resolute attitude ... Hitler would never have used violence.

...You can hardly imagine the despair that prevails among the people and also in the army against the brutal and insane dictator of terror, Hitler and his satellites. Hitler and Göring bluffed the whole world. But the world was warned and informed in good time. If the people had heeded the warnings and then had acted, Germany would already today be free from a dictator and turn against Mussolini. In a few weeks' time, we could start to develop and create lasting world peace based on just and equitable reason and decency. A purified Germany with a government of decent men would have been prepared, together with England and France to immediately address the Spanish problem, to get rid of Mussolini, and create peace in the Far East, in co-operation with the United States. But now Mr. Chamberlain has given up all the positions without even the slightest concession of Hitler. Only a good friend of dictators or an inexperienced youth could act like that. I can only imagine that he and his clique of nobles themselves are fascists and imagine that the capitalist profit system can be saved with the help of National Socialism…[3]

The conspiracy in London was so complex and ran so deep that it was impossible for the decent and dedicated Goerdeler – or anyone else beyond Milner Group circles – to comprehend the awful reality of what was actually going on.

A week after selling Czechoslovakia down the river, with his accustomed doublespeak Chamberlain gave an account of his dealings with Hitler to the House of Commons.

> He justified his actions by saying that under the new system of guarantees the new Czechoslovakia would find a greater security than she had ever enjoyed in the past. In addition he announced that the British Government were going to make a present of £30,000,000 to the Czechs to help them overcome the economic difficulties they would be bound to meet on account of their loss of valuable territory.[4]

On 3 October 1938, the First Lord of the Admiralty, Duff Cooper (Viscount Norwich), denounced the Munich Agreement and resigned from the government. He stated that "War with honour or peace with dishonour" he might have accepted, but not "war with dishonour." Like many, Duff Cooper could see that "appeasement" followed by the disgraceful sell-out of Czechoslovakia were direct steps that would lead not to peace but to a European war. That day in the House of Commons, Chamberlain said he regretted Cooper's resignation but that

Duff Cooper.

Cooper was mistaken. Accomplished liar Chamberlain added in his usual weasel words:

> I say in the name of this House and of the people of this country that Czechoslovakia has earned our admiration and respect for her restraint, for her dignity, for her magnificent discipline in face of such a trial as few

nations have ever been called upon to meet.... It is my hope, and my belief, that under the new system of guarantees, the new Czechoslovakia will find a greater security than she has ever enjoyed in the past.

We must recognise that she has been put in a position where she has got to reconstruct her whole economy, and that in doing that she must encounter difficulties, which it would be practically impossible for her to solve alone. We have received from the Czechoslovak Government, through their Minister in London, an appeal to help them to raise a loan of £30,000,000 by a British Government guarantee. I believe that the House will feel with the Government that that is an appeal which should meet with a sympathetic and even a generous response.[5]

In a House of Commons debate two days later, Chancellor of the Exchequer and member of the Milner Group, Sir John Simon, requested that:

This House approves the policy of His Majesty's Government by which war was averted in the recent crisis and supports their efforts to secure a lasting peace. We now invite the House, by its vote, to declare that the action which has been taken in this emergency is approved.... And mark this, in Munich, in September, 1938, German men and women, after the signing of an agreement which put an end to a tense situation, flocked to cheer not the German Fuhrer who had won a victory, but the British Prime Minister, who, rightly or wrongly, in their minds symbolises peace.[6]

Next day, 6 October, Chamberlain stated in the House of Commons:

...When we were convinced, as we became convinced, that nothing any longer would keep the Sudetenland within the Czechoslovakian State, we urged the Czech Government as strongly as we could to agree to the cession of territory, and to agree promptly. The Czech Government, through the wisdom and courage of President Benes, accepted the advice of the French Government and ourselves. It was a hard decision for anyone who loved his country to take, but to accuse us of having by that advice betrayed the Czechoslovakian State is simply preposterous. What we did was to save her from annihilation and give her a chance of new life as a new State, which involves the loss of territory and fortifications, but may perhaps enable her to enjoy in the future and develop a national existence under a neutrality and security comparable to that which we see in Switzerland to-day. Therefore, I think the Government deserve the approval of this House for their conduct of affairs in this recent crisis which has saved Czechoslovakia from destruction and Europe from Armageddon.[7]

As ever throughout this entire saga, the biggest lies were the best lies. Had Chamberlain denounced Hitler's demand to annex the Sudetenland and told him such action would be met with a massive military response from Britain, France, Czechoslovakia and other allied states, the military coup against Hitler would have forged ahead in Germany and he would now be languishing in a prison cell with a death sentence hanging over him. Had there been any justice in the world, he would have been joined there by a considerable number of "distinguished" individuals from London.

Not everyone viewed the matter in this light, however. British Establishment historian A.J.P. Taylor considered the Munich Agreement "a triumph for British policy," a "triumph for all that was best and most enlightened in British life," and a victory for the right to self-determination.[8] It will doubtless come as no surprise to readers that Taylor had been both a student and lecturer at Oxford University.

Far from the invasion of Czechoslovakia being the end of Hitler's plans, it was merely the beginning. On the night of 9-10 November 1938, synagogues throughout Germany were desecrated and destroyed. The action was allegedly in response to the murder of Ernst vom Rath, a German diplomat in Paris by a 17-year-old Jew of Polish origin, Herschel Grynszpan. Grynszpan was upset because his parents had become stateless having been forced to leave Germany for Poland where they were also rejected.

KRISTALLNACHT

In the "Night of Broken Glass," Joseph Goebbels delivered an antisemitic speech in Munich, calling for an attack on Jewish communities across Germany and Austria. His instructions were communicated through the Nazi party apparatus to all districts, and the thugs went into action. Nazi paramilitaries, members of the Hitler youth and some civilians embarked on an orgy of violence and terror, setting synagogues on fire,

Kristallnacht – 1938

Kristallnacht – 1938

wrecking Jewish cemeteries and businesses. The shattered glass from the windows of many looted shops owned by Jews littered the streets. Jewish homes were broken into and furniture wrecked, with ordinary working men hauled away to concentration camps. Upwards of a 100 honest law-abiding Jews were brutally beaten to death. President Roosevelt wrote that he could scarcely believe such things could occur in a twentieth-century civilization. Was he really unaware that the Soviets had already murdered millions of Russian citizens 1917-1938; the Japanese had killed about 200,000 in Nanjing in 1937; the Italians had killed up to 350,000 Abyssinians; and both sides in the Spanish Civil War had committed countless atrocities?

Restrictions were now placed on the participation of Jews in cultural performances, and all Jewish children were expelled from state schools and prohibited from attending any but Jewish schools. Jewish doctors and lawyers were barred from practicing their professions, and their business-es 'aryanized,'[9]

Historian and Anglican priest, Richard Griffiths wrote;

> Many of the men were carried off to concentration camps. Fami-
> lies were driven from their homes. Gentiles were forbidden to give
> them shelter, or even to sell them the essentials of life. Even the

most foresighted of observers could not have expected anything on this scale. By 15 November *The Times* correspondent was reporting from Munich that "the condition of most Jews here is one of misery, terror and despair."... The many protests recorded in *The Times* in the first week tailed off, and one was left, as so often, with *The Times* correspondence column trivialising the issue.[10]

Despite the terror being inflicted on Jews, the Anglo-American banking elites – and it has to be said that some were themselves Jews – continued pouring money into Nazi Germany to strengthen Hitler's armed forces.

Just a few months after Chamberlain's betrayal of the Czechs and *Kristallnacht,* Hitler demanded more. The reluctant British ambassador in Prague, Basil Newton, once again played a part by arranging a meeting between the new Czech president, Emil Hácha, and Hitler in Berlin. Hácha was presented with the stark reality: either agree to the German occupation of Czechoslovakia in its entirety and cooperate fully with it, or resistance would be mercilessly crushed by the full force of the Wehrmacht. By 15 March 1939, Hitler was standing in Prague castle declaring it the greatest triumph of his life and that he would enter history as the greatest German ever.[11]

Chamberlain had spoken in the House of Commons in October about sending financial aid to Czechoslovakia, but quite the reverse happened. With the connivance of Montagu Norman and the Bank of England, large quantities of Czechoslovakia's gold held in London was sent to Germany. Carroll Quigley writes:

> The British government accepted the events of March 15th except for feeble protests. These were directed less against the deed itself than against the risk of agitating public opinion by the deed. On March 15th Chamberlain told the Commons that he accepted the seizure of Czechoslovakia and refused to accuse Hitler of bad faith. But two days later, when the howls of rage from the British public showed that he had misjudged the electorate, he went to his constituency in Birmingham on March 17th and denounced the seizure. However, nothing was done except recall Henderson [British ambassador] from Berlin "for consultations" and cancel a visit by the president of the Board of Trade planned for March 17-20. The seizure was declared illegal but was recognized in fact at once, and efforts were made to recognize it in law by establishing a British consulate general accredited to Germany in Prague. Moreover £6,000,000 in Czech gold reserves in London were turned over to

Germany with the puny, and untrue, excuse that the British government could not give orders to the Bank of England.

The German acquisition of the Czech gold in London was but one episode in an extensive, and largely secret, plan for economic concessions to Germany.[12]

In 2013, British investigative journalist Adam LeBor – author of the excellent *Tower of Basel: The Shadowy History of the Secret Bank That Runs the World*,' studied historical documents newly released by the Bank of England. In an article in the *Daily Telegraph*, LeBor wrote:

The documents reveal a shocking story: just six months before Britain went to war with Nazi Germany, the Bank of England willingly handed over £5.6 million worth of gold to Hitler – and it belonged to another country.

The official history of the bank, written in 1950 but posted online for the first time on Tuesday, reveals how we betrayed Czechoslovakia – not just with the infamous Munich agreement of September 1938, which allowed the Nazis to annex the Sudetenland, but also in London, where Montagu Norman, the eccentric but ruthless governor of the Bank of England agreed to surrender gold owned by the National Bank of Czechoslovakia.

The Czechoslovak gold was held in London in a sub-account in the name of the Bank for International Settlements, the Basel-based bank for central banks. When the Nazis marched into Prague in March 1939 they immediately sent armed soldiers to the offices of the National Bank. The Czech directors were ordered, on pain of death, to send two transfer requests.

The first instructed the BIS to transfer 23.1 metric tons of gold from the Czechoslovak BIS account, held at the Bank of England, to the Reichsbank BIS account, also held at Threadneedle Street.

The second order instructed the Bank of England to transfer almost 27 metric tons of gold held in the National Bank of Czechoslovakia's own name to the BIS's gold account at the Bank of England.

To outsiders, the distinction between the accounts seems obscure. Yet it proved crucial – and allowed Norman to ensure that the first order was carried out. The Czechoslovak bank officials believed that as the orders had obviously been carried out under duress neither would be allowed to go through. But they had not reckoned on the bureaucrats running of the BIS and the determination of Montagu Norman to see that procedures were followed, even as his country prepared for war with Nazi Germany.... Thanks to

Norman and the BIS, Nazi Germany had just looted 23.1 tons of gold without a shot being fired ... The BIS was so useful for the Nazis that Emil Puhl, the vice-president of the Reichsbank and BIS director, referred to the BIS as the Reichsbank's only "foreign branch" ... [13]

Czech gold was the least of the benefits Nazi Germany received courtesy of the Milner Group and Anglo-American banks. Preparata writes:

> The British plan, clearly, was to dismember Czechoslovakia which, with 34 sterling divisions, 1 million men, well trained, and with high morale, could very well stall Hitler in the middle of Europe. [14]

With the stage well and truly set for a European war, the appeasement charade was now dropped by all and sundry. According to the British government appeasement had been a "well intentioned effort to preserve peace," but the tune quickly changed and Britain now geared up for the war its elites had long been planning. The brand-new government line was that Hitler was "beyond redemption" and Britain must now rapidly escalate its military preparedness. *The Times* and Lord Lothian, leader of the Milner Group, began a campaign for conscription, which was duly delivered with the National Service Act of 26 April 1939.

> Although Prime Minister Chamberlain, on his return from the last visit to Germany, had waved his piece of paper in the air and told the listening world "This is Peace in our time," the main discussion in Parliament immediately switched to the issue of rearmament.
>
> On this point, the whole House was united. Mr. Churchill marched in step with Mr. Chamberlain. Mr. Attlee and Mr. Duff Cooper and the whole gang of them lined up with the Government. There was a now a unanimous and spontaneous viewpoint – expressed most vigorously by those who had said that "Peace in our Time" was a reality and not an old man's dream – that Britain must now rearm day and night, night and day.
>
> ... Mr. Chamberlain said in the Munich debate, "We must renew our determination to fill up the deficiencies that yet remain in our armaments." Sir Samuel Hoare declared, "We are perfectly prepared to have our record examined as to our defence preparations. We are determined to fill up the gaps which have shown themselves in our defensive armaments." Mr. Burgin remarked, "Because we believe it is a contribution to peace we will examine and make good gaps and deficiencies in our own system of active and passive defence." Sir

Thomas Inskip assured the House of Commons, "The essential war materials, including a number of rare metals, have been accumulated in stock sufficient to carry us through a long war." Sir John Simon told the House that the Government had seen shortcomings in their defensive arrangements and would hasten to put them right. In fact, over the question of rearmament absolute unanimity was achieved. Even the minority members who opposed the Munich settlement were soothed and silenced by the expressed resolve of the Government now to set about the rearmament of Britain with energy. Britain was not ready to fight. But she was going to get ready now. This propaganda had success. Everyone, even Mr. Chamberlain's bitter critics, believed that we were about to rearm on a scale which would amaze the world. So the nation was comforted.[15]

Thus was the sham of appeasement jettisoned and immediately replaced by a new charade that Britain's renewed vigour for massive spending on armaments was "a contribution to peace." Professor Preparata summed it up:

On October 21 [1938], Hitler issued orders to invade the rump of Czechoslovakia and turn it into a protectorate, which punctually came to pass on March 14, 1939 – the Czechs offered no resistance. And Montagu Norman, picking the pockets of the senseless victims, remitted to the Reichsbank, treacherously, £6 million of Czech gold held in custody at the Bank of England. That Norman was in close contact with the Chamberlain faction is certain (it couldn't have been otherwise), but the nature and content of their interaction have never been revealed.

Now, to finish off Versailles, only Poland remained – and after that Germany would be at the gates of the Soviets: Captain Winterbotham, the British spy, had recently returned from Eastern Prussia, where the district leader had confided to him that Barbarossa [the German attack on Russia] should be operational by May 1941. There was *nothing* that England did not know.

The stewards changed costumes once more. Appeasement, as a public stance, was finished: after the Czech invasion it could no longer be 'sold' to the masses. So a different configuration emerged: the pro-Nazi Peace Party took the back-seat to posture as an elitist den of frondeurs, while the Round Table and the anti-Bolsheviks fused in an informal 'diarchy,' whereby the visible front, led by Halifax, made a pretence of enforcing tough-dealing with the Nazis, while the secret front, staffed with the Chamberlain group, continued to bestow upon Hitler concessions and 'friendly' *assurances that Britain wouldn't fight.*

Hitler had gone as far as he had been allowed, and it was time for Britain to set him up on the Western Front and thus precipitate war ... Chamberlain informed the House of Commons that "in the event of any action that clearly threatened Polish independence, His Majesty's Government would feel themselves bound at once to lend the Polish Government all support in their power.[16]

One more British hypocrisy was at the forefront, for there was no way that Britain alone could stop Germany from invading Poland. Its guarantee to Poland was therefore empty. Unfortunately, the Polish regime was too naive to see this.

The British elites were deceiving Poland while simultaneously feeding Hitler conflicting information. One faction of the Milner Group was publicly talking tough regarding British military action against any German attack on Poland, while another faction of the same group was whispering in Hitler's ear that he mustn't worry because that threat was simply a bluff for public consumption. It was essential that Hitler did not get cold feet at this stage or he might abandon war on Poland and his ultimate aim of war on Russia. With reservations, Hitler accepted that Britain wanted the same outcome – destruction of communist Russia – and come the day it would not oppose him as he began that task by invading Poland and moving east. With Anglo-American money continually pouring into Germany via the BIS in Basel, Hitler was reassured and continued building his military for the big showdown with Russia.

Hitler attended the launch of the first German aircraft carrier, *Graf Zeppelin*, at Kiel and gave orders for the construction of four more. On 5 January 1939 he invited the Polish foreign minister to Germany in an unsuccessful attempt to win Poland over to an alliance against the Soviet Union. On 17 January he insisted to Admiral Erich Raeder that the building of six new battleships must be rapidly completed. On 1 February he reorganised the Luftwaffe into three efficient air fleets. On 14 February he attended the launch of Germany's greatest battleship, *Bismarck,* in Hamburg.

On 23 March, Hitler arrived in Memel, East Prussia, on the battleship *Deutschland* and delivered a speech about the 'coming war'. He was informed that the Polish government would consider any attempt by Germany to change the status of the free city of Danzig as a cause for war. Danzig (now Gdańsk, Poland), situated on the Baltic coast, had long been a German city with its population of 400,000 comprising 95 per cent Germans. The Versailles Treaty had taken Danzig and a "corridor to the sea" through Prussia from the defeated Germany and given it to Poland. In the 1930s numerous countries considered it fair and reasonable that the city should be returned to Germany.

The noted French journalist and author, Raymond Cartier, wrote that it was a "monument to ignorance and error" that gave "chaotic and brutal Poland vast territories inhabited by Germans." "Creating the Danzig Corridor," said Cartier, "defied geography and politics."[17] Hitler was determined to return Danzig to Germany, but the Poles refused to negotiate. On 31 March he was informed that Britain, together with France, had made an unconditional offer of assistance to Poland if Germany threatened her. The cards were now being stacked for war but Hitler still believed certain assurances that Britain would quietly accept him invading Poland as they had Czechoslovakia.

On 1 April 1939, Hitler attended the launch of the battleship *Tirpitz* at Wilhelmshaven, and ordered plans to be drawn up for an attack on Poland by 1 September. On 11 April, he issued the directive for Operation *Fall Weiss* – the destruction of Polish armed forces and the annexation of Danzig. The attack, he said, was to begin without a formal declaration of war. On 28 April Hitler told the Reichstag that the enormous military booty taken from Czechoslovakia with annexation of the Sudetenland was enough to arm forty German divisions. On 22 May, he attended the signing of the pact between Germany and Italy, and kept up a busy schedule of meetings about war preparations through June and July.

> On 19 August 1939, Hitler told Carl J. Burckhardt [Swiss diplomat], the League of Nations High Commissioner for the Free City of Danzig, that his anti-communism remained as strong as ever: "Everything I undertake is aimed at the Soviet Union. If the West is too stupid and blind to see this, I shall be forced to come to an understanding with the Russians, defeat the West, and then marshal my forces against the Soviet Union. I need the Ukraine so that they cannot starve us out, as they did in the last war."[18]

Burckhardt immediately passed this message on to London where it was, without doubt, met with considerable enthusiasm. The situation was evolving almost exactly as the Milner Group wished and had long planned: Hitler appeared oblivious to the trap he was being encouraged to fall into. The German and Russian armies would effectively annihilate each other and Germany once and for all would be utterly smashed.

Burckhardt

The Soviets in the meantime would agree to a pact with Germany while its forces overran France. Thereafter, that pact would be pulled apart, and they would fight each other to the death. "Two birds killed with one stone" was music to the Milner Group's ears. Hitler would order commencement of Operation Barbarossa – which Britain and Russia had long known about – and his forces would then be sucked into the vast expanses of Russia and effectively destroyed there. Each side would suffer massive losses in the deadliest military operation in history.

On 23 August 1939, Germany signed a non-aggression pact with the Soviet Union – the Molotov-Ribbentrop Pact – that partitioned Central and Eastern Europe between their spheres of influence. It promised co-operation in the invasion of Poland and its division between them, with Germany taking western Poland and Russia taking the east. That same day the British ambassador to Berlin, Sir Neville Henderson, presented Hitler with a letter from prime minister Chamberlain stating that Britain would stand by its guarantee to Poland.

> Hitler prepared a long reply which he concluded with his usual reassurance that "all my life I fought for Anglo-German friendship. The attitude adopted by British diplomacy – at any rate up to the present – has, however, convinced me of the futility of such an attempt. Should there be any change in this respect in the future, nobody could be happier than I." Handing his letter over to Henderson, however, Hitler added threateningly: "At the next Polish provocation I'll act. The question of Danzig and the Corridor must be settled one way or another."[19]

On 31 August 1939, Hitler issued the final order – Directive No.1 – to attack Poland. At 4.45 A.M. the following morning, troops began their assault on the country. The British and French ambassadors in Berlin

presented notes of protest that demanded the withdrawal of all German troops by 11 A.M. on 3 September. When the ultimatum expired unanswered, Britain and France declared war on Germany. It was to be a death sentence for some 70 million people across the world.

As in London in August 1914 when their Milner Group predecessors successfully manipulated the world into war, the current cabal and their banking elite associates once more raised their glasses to toast the success of years of meticulous planning for war. They would be further enriched by billions in war profiteering, Germany would be smashed, and a potential major obstacle to their New World Order plan – a Russo-German alliance – successfully removed.

The German-Soviet non-aggression pact signed by Molotov and Ribbentrop on 23 August agreed to split Poland between them, and on 17 September, Russian forces invaded eastern Poland as agreed. Polish forces suffered some 200,000 dead or wounded before their last units surrendered in early October. The British and French governments notably did not declare war on the Soviet Union for its part in destroying Poland's independence.

The French army mounted a limited attack into the Saar region of Germany on 7 September 1939, but withdrew after 6 weeks. Thereafter, French and British troops dug in facing the German border, but with few notable military operations and relatively little fighting on the ground, it became known as the "Phoney War." At sea, however, the German Kriegsmarine and the British Royal Navy were aggressively attacking each other and British and German merchant shipping. The aircraft carrier *Courageous* (UK) and the battleships *Royal Oak* (UK) and *Graf Spee* (Germany) were sunk as well as numerous German U-boats

On 9 April 1940, British plans to occupy Norway were pre-empted by Germany when its paratroopers invaded the country. Norway would be used as a base for naval operations against the Allies, and its supplies of iron ore and other minerals seized. Some 300,000 German troops would remain in Norway for the duration of the war. Denmark was also occupied by Germany on 9 April as a necessary prelude to the invasion of Norway. Fighting lasted only a few hours.

On 10 May, 1940, Hitler ordered a major offensive in the west with the invasion of France, the Netherlands, Belgium and Luxemburg. German control of those countries would, he believed, protect the industrial Ruhr from Allied air attacks, provide bases for sea and air attacks on Britain, and forestall French action against western Germany. That same day, 10 May,

Neville Chamberlain was replaced as British prime minister by Winston Churchill.

German forces advancing rapidly into France drove the British army, together with French and Belgian troops, back to the town of Dunkirk on the Channel coast. Between 26 May and 4 June, 1940, some 340,000 British and Allied soldiers were evacuated by ships and small boats from Dunkirk harbour and surrounding beaches to ports in southern England. An estimated 62,000 Allied soldiers were killed, wounded, or captured at Dunkirk. Hitler could readily have ordered tanks and infantry to advance and kill or capture many of those who escaped, and could have made greater use of the Luftwaffe to bomb the Allied troops on the beaches, but for reasons which are still debated to this day, he chose not to deprive the Allies of those 340,000 men.

On 10 June 1940, Italy joined Germany and declared war against France and Britain. On 13 June, the French garrison withdrew from Paris and in order to prevent its destruction, declared it a "Free City." German forces marched unopposed into the French capital 24 hours later. France signed an Armistice with Germany on 22 June, and Hitler flew to Paris early next morning to make a short propaganda tour of the city before returning to Germany. Interestingly, he visited Napoleon's tomb at Les Invalides, perhaps imagining himself resting for eternity in such a magnificent setting.

In the Reichstag on 19 July 1940, Hitler announced that he would "appeal to reason" with regard to England, saying that it had never been his intention to destroy the British Empire. Flushed with success, but utterly deluded and ignorant of the British elites long-term machiavellian planning, he warned against his appeal for peace with Britain being viewed as weakness. If rejected, he would unleash every force that Germany could muster against her. Churchill responded, making it clear that the war would continue until Germany was utterly crushed. He provocatively ordered the RAF to bomb Berlin on 25-26 August in response to 2 German bombers dropping bombs on East London the previous night. Both bombers, according to Germany, had been seeking only military targets but got lost and accidentally bombed the city. The RAF destroyed housing and railway yards in Berlin, killing and injuring some 40 civilians and rendering 900 homeless. In the following week, Churchill ordered further RAF bombing raids on three consecutive nights. Göring, having previously boasted that the British would never be able to bomb German cities, was enraged. On 7 September 1940, 350 German bombers flew over London dropping incendiary devices and high-explosive bombs. The "Blitz" had begun, and an estimated 40,000 British civilians would be killed over the next year. RAF bombers (together with US air force bombers after 1941) responded throughout the war with carpet bombing and destruction of German towns and cities, resulting in the death of an estimated 600,000 German civilians.

A German Luftwaffe Heinkel He 111 bomber flying over Wapping and the Isle of Dogs in the East End of London at the start of the Luftwaffe's evening raids of 7 September 1940.

In Berlin on 27 September 1940, Germany, Italy, and Japan signed a defensive alliance, the Tripartite Pact, which they naively believed might deter the United States from entering the war. These "Axis Powers" would later be joined by Hungary, Romania, Croatia, and Bulgaria. In December, Hitler set out directive No. 21: "Case Barbarossa," the plan for German forces to crush communist Russia in a quick campaign. We have seen previously how British, Russian, and American intelligence had known for years what was coming. Recall the naïve German general revealing the plan in almost exact detail to British Intelligence agent Frederick Winterbotham seven years earlier in Horsher's restaurant in Berlin.

On Sunday 22 June, 1941, Operation Barbarossa – the biggest land offensive in history – began. An estimated 3.5 million German troops with 600,000 motorised vehicles, 3,000 panzer tanks, 2,500 aircraft and 7,000 heavy artillery pieces invaded Russia in three parallel attacks across a 2,500 plus kilometre front. Germany (with Italy and her other alliance partners) was now at war on two fronts: against Britain in the west, and Russia in the east. On 12 July 1941, Britain signed an alliance with Russia. Stalin requested an immediate British invasion of Western Europe to relieve the pressure from Germany in the east. That being virtually impossible at the time, Churchill and Roosevelt sent a mission to Moscow to determine Russia's material needs. The mission in September was headed by Wall Street man, Averell Harriman, together with the British newspaper magnate, Lord Beaverbrook. An agreement would later be reached for sending material aid to the Soviets.[20]

Operation Barbarossa

The Anglo-American elites knew it would soon be time – as had long been planned – to bring the United States into the war. It would be achieved by provoking Japan into action against the US navy at Pearl Harbor.

Japan, like Britain and other European countries, had imperialist intent in East Asia. Since the 1870s, the Japanese elite believed that to join the western nations as a "modern state" and survive in the cutthroat imperialist world, they had to have a colonial empire. Like the British, French, Dutch and increasingly the Americans, they had to have subservient markets for Japanese goods and convenient sources of raw materials. Consequently, Japan engaged in wars against China (1894-5), Russia (1904-05), and China again (1937-1945) as well as taking control of Korea in 1910.

In China, the Japanese set up puppet governments, and controlled China's major eastern cities, railroads and harbours. In April 1941 Japan signed a non-aggression pact with Soviet Russia, and was keen to reach a similar agreement with the United States. Washington rejected all Japanese overtures of friendship and peace. The American ambassador to Tokyo, Joseph C. Grew, had worked relentlessly to maintain the peace between the two countries, but his reports and recommendation to the White House and State Department were rejected or ignored. On 18 August 18,1941, Ambassador Grew in Tokyo pleaded with Washington to accept an invitation from the Japanese prime minister, Fumimaro Konoe, to meet at a neutral venue for a last-ditch attempt to prevent war:

Grew

> The Ambassador reports as follows for Secretary Hull and Under Secretary Welles:
>
> He says that naturally he is not aware of the reaction President Roosevelt will have to the proposal made today orally by the Japanese Minister for Foreign Affairs. The Ambassador urges, however, with all the force at his command, for the sake of avoiding the obviously growing possibility of an utterly futile war between Japan and the United States, that this Japanese proposal not be turned aside without very prayerful consideration. Not only is the proposal unprecedented in Japanese history, but it is an indication that Japanese intransigence is not crystallized completely owing to the fact that the proposal has the approval of the Emperor and the highest authorities in the land. The good which may flow from a meeting between Prince Konoye and President Roosevelt is incalculable. The opportunity is here presented, the Ambassador ventures to believe, for an act of the highest statesmanship, such as the recent meeting of President Roosevelt with Prime Minister Churchill at sea, with the possible overcoming thereby of apparently insurmountable obstacles to peace hereafter in the Pacific.[21]

Roosevelt summarily rejected the meeting, and Prince Konoe resigned as prime minister. He was replaced by Hideki Tojo, a hardline General who was prepared to give the US a war if that was what it wanted.

It was indeed what Roosevelt, and the Anglo-American Establishment behind him, wanted. The objective was to provoke Japan and goad her into making the first move that would provide Roosevelt with the excuse for taking the US to war. A considerable majority of the American people were against getting involved in the war then raging in Europe, and a momentous event was needed to turn that opinion 180 degrees. It was achieved through a Japanese attack on the US Pacific fleet at Pearl Harbor which changed the entire course of the war, and guaranteed Germany's defeat. The Pearl Harbor attack was only successful thanks the complicity and connivance of the White House and Washinton elites, and warrants considerable scrutiny.

The Anglo-American elites knew in advance in 1915 that the *Lusitania* was about to be subjected to a German U-boat attack and facilitated it. Now, in 1941, they knew the US Pacific fleet at Pearl Harbor was going to be attacked by Japanese bomber planes and smoothed the way for it. In both instances, American lives were very deliberately sacrificed to provide the excuse for taking the United States to war. American author Robert B. Stinnett writes:

> Pearl Harbor was not an accident, a mere failure of American Intelligence, or a brilliant Japanese military coup. It was the result of a carefully orchestrated design, initiated at the highest levels of our government. According to a key memorandum, eight steps were taken to make sure we would enter the war by this means. Pearl Harbor was the *only* way, leading officials felt, to galvanize the reluctant American public into action.[22]

THE US PROVOKES JAPAN.

To provoke the Japanese government into the attack on Pearl Harbor, the US government imposed a total embargo on exports to Japan – including much-needed oil, metals, war materiel and credits – and froze all Japanese financial assets in the US. Establishment historians falsely portray these hostile actions against Japan as efforts to deter Japanese aggression. Revisionists historians and Pearl Harbor researchers disagree. Robert B. Stinnett wrote:

> Throughout 1941, it seems, provoking Japan into an overt act of war was the principal policy that guided FDR's actions toward Ja-

pan ... Roosevelt's cabinet members, most notably Secretary of War Henry Stimson, are on record favoring the policy ... Stimson's diary entries of 1941 place him with nine other Americans who knew or were associated with this policy of provocation during 1941.[23]

British historian A.J.P. Taylor wrote:

In August 1941 the United States government imposed a total embargo on supplies to Japan, particularly supplies of oil and of credits. *From that moment Japan was doomed either to surrender at discretion or to go to war.* The Japanese had six months' supply of oil. Actually as usual they overstated their distress. They could have lasted out for a year or two but the doctrine was 'We have only got six months – before that we must break through the ring.' In anything but a technical sense the United States had declared war on Japan by thus attempting to close the ring.[24]

"Surrender at discretion" meant Japan agreeing to unconditional surrender and being left entirely at the mercy of the US. Roosevelt, of course, knew that the Japanese would never contemplate such a surrender, embargo or not, and would choose war. Prime minister Tojo did indeed choose to come out fighting, and he and other hardliners in Tokyo began setting out plans for an attack on the US Pacific fleet based at Pearl Harbor on Hawaii. The fleet had been moved there from its original base in San

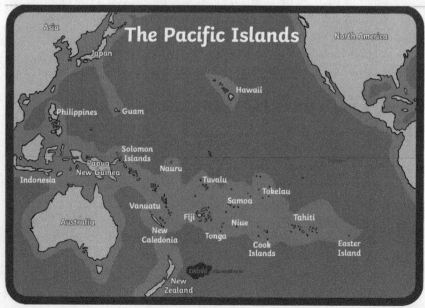

Diego in April 1940 to cut the voyage distance to the strategically important Pacific Islands, the Philippines, and elsewhere in the Pacific rim.

Mainstream history recounts that on 7 December 1941, the United States was taken "completely by surprise" when 353 fighters, bombers and torpedo planes took off from Japanese aircraft carriers in the Pacific Ocean north of Hawaii and attacked the U.S. fleet at Pearl Harbor in Oahu Island. They killed and wounded thousands of U.S. servicemen and destroyed many warships. The United States declared war on Japan the following day and from that precise moment Germany's fate was sealed. The US joined Britain in what became mythologised and sanitised in America as the "Good War." As in the First World War, a tapestry of lies and propaganda portrayed this new war as a conflict between good (Britain and the US) and evil (Germany and Japan). Young Americans were asked to enlist and stand up against the "warmongering tyrants," and American mothers were urged to give up their sons for a "just and noble crusade with God on their side."

On his return to the US from Japan following the declaration of war, Ambassador Joseph Grew submitted a frank report stating that the Washington administration had failed to do all that was possible to avert war and had disregarded all of his efforts to that end. 133 pages cut from Grew's lengthy report remain missing to this day. He was neither a member of the select Milner Group's London-Washington axis, nor privy to its deep intrigues and conspiracies.

In addition to the American naval base at Oahu (a small island approximately 60 km by 40 km in the Hawaiian archipelago), there was a directly adjacent air field (Hickam) with 140 US fighter planes. Several other American air fields were sited across the island with a variety of fighter and reconnaissance aircraft. The Pacific fleet was under the command of Admiral Husband E. Kimmel, while responsibility for guarding the military installations on Hawaii lay with Lieutenant-General Walter Short. Kimmel commanded hundreds of US navy aircraft on three carriers based at Pearl, while Short commanded 234 army aircraft including 152 fighters. He also had two infantry divisions and anti-aircraft guns to defend the island. To aid the defences, in early 1941 an air warning system with

Kimmel

Short

six separate radar units was installed at various sites on the mountains on Oahu, with a coordinating centre at Fort Shafter where radar contacts were supposed to be reported and evaluated. The system was operational 3 months before the Japanese attack but was unreliable.

Captain Joseph Taussig, senior deck officer on the battleship USS *Nevada* at Pearl Harbor and in charge of naval anti-aircraft batteries, later spoke of the failure of the radar warning system operational there at the time. Taussig was badly wounded in the attack but bravely continued his duties and was awarded the Navy Cross and Purple Heart. It might be expected that he more than most would be critical of the radar operatives for not raising the alarm about incoming Japanese planes, but he blamed the system, not the men. Taussig wrote in 1972:

> I do not think it strange that the so-called "radar warning" was ignored for as Sir Winston might have put it, it had much to be ignored about. On 7 December 1941, this experimental equipment was extremely unreliable, mostly because it was, so to speak, "false-return prone." A flight of gulls, for example, could snafu the entire system, and anyone purporting to see a "flight of bombers" on an "A-scope" circa December 1941 was indeed a seer of great perception. One aircraft made the same mess on the scope as a hundred – and any number of boats, ships, and seagulls could do the same thing.[25]

Another difficulty arose because American planes were flying in and out of Hawaii at all hours. Since the radar crews were not kept informed about those flights, it was impossible for them to distinguish the radar contact of a friendly aircraft from that of an enemy. As Taussig said, the system was extremely unreliable and only manned by a skeleton staff.

What actually happened that day, Sunday 7 December, 1941?

At 6.00 A.M. (Hawaiian time) the first sorties of 183 planes (fighters, dive bombers and torpedo bombers) took off from the decks of Japanese aircraft carriers some 240 miles to the north of Hawaii, and headed south in formation. At 6.30 A.M., as the US navy stores ship *Antares* approached the entrance to the harbour, lookouts onboard spotted the conning tower of a small submarine. (5 midget

2-man submarines had been strapped to the decks of larger Japanese submarines and released close to Oahu). The nearby destroyer, *USS Ward*, was alerted and within minutes with her 4-inch guns and depth charges, sank the submarine. Captain William Outerbridge on *Ward* immediately reported to the duty officer at Fleet headquarters: "We Have Attacked, Fired Upon and Dropped Depth Charges on a Submarine Operating in the Defensive Sea Area." For some reason the duty officer did not sound the general alarm as might have been expected

At 7:00 A.M. at the northernmost radar site on Oahu, two junior enlisted men saw a return echo on their oscilloscope. They reported it to the Air Information Centre at Fort Shafter as looking like a large flight of aircraft approaching from the north. Lt. Kermit Tyler at the Information Centre mistakenly assumed it to be 12 American bomber planes due to arrive at the Hickam airfield that very morning and took no action. No warning of the approaching planes was received by the navy, the ground defences, or the American interceptor fighter pilots.

It was a calm, quiet Sunday morning with many of the men having been given the weekend off. The anti-aircraft batteries were largely unmanned. The gunners had been well-trained, but their equipment was dated and lacked accuracy. No 'action stations' alerts had been sounded on the ships in harbour, and no pilots had been called to get their fighter planes off the ground. Suddenly, at 7:55 A.M., the skies above the naval facilities and airfields on the island were black with Japanese war planes roaring in to drop bombs and torpedoes. The attack lasted for 30 minutes and the planes departed.

A 15-minute lull was followed by the arrival of a second wave of 170 Japanese planes which resumed the attack. Within an hour, 3,435 American service men and women had been killed or badly wounded, with many suffering horrendous burns. Six US battleships, three cruisers, three destroyers and several other vessels were sunk or badly damaged in the harbour. 151 US aircraft on the apron at the adjacent Hickam air base and other airfields were destroyed. Many of the planes had been taken from their protective bunkers days earlier and parked wing-tip to wing-tip in the open, supposedly to prevent sabotage by Japanese citizens resident on Hawaii. This was despite the fact that there had never been any previous incidents with saboteurs, nor indication that they were about to happen.

The Japanese lost five midget submarines, 29 aircraft and 129 men. Officially, it was "only by luck" that the aircraft carriers based at Pearl Harbor and packed with planes were unharmed. They had been ordered to sail some days before the attack.

All appeared straightforward. The Japanese had sprung a "surprise attack" and the Pearl Harbor commanders, Admiral Husband Kimmel and General Walter Short, had failed miserably in their duty to protect the fleet and the men. Blame for the disaster was placed squarely on their shoulders. They were relieved of their duties, demoted, and eventually retired in disgrace. Both asked to be court-marshalled in order to present their version of events and defend themselves, but were denied the opportunity.

Admiral Kimmel's eldest son, Manning, a US submarine captain, attempted to investigate the affair and rescue his father's hitherto excellent reputation, but was killed in 1944 when his boat struck a mine. Years later, one of Kimmel's grandsons, Lieutenant Commander Thomas Kimmel, took up the baton and relentlessly pursued the truth. A naval officer who went on to have a stellar career with the FBI, Thomas Kimmel stated that at no time had the US government shown any real interest in uncovering and revealing the truth about Pearl Harbor. It was, he stated bluntly, "the largest cover-up in US history." He added that some historians had helped in his search for the truth while others had done "immeasurable harm." Unfortunately he did not name the latter. Such allegations by descendants of the old Admiral (he died in 1968 aged 86) might be dismissed as attempts to uphold the good family name, but many independent historians and researchers have also categorically stated that Kimmel and Short were scapegoated in order to protect the US president, Franklin D. Roosevelt. The truth about Pearl Harbor and America's entry into the Second World War, they say, was intended to be buried for all time.

646

In the 1940 presidential election, Roosevelt (standing for an unprecedented third term) had pledged that under his watch the US would not go to war. Like Woodrow Wilson, a previous Wall Street puppet in the White House who promised in the 1916 election to keep America out of the war in order to gain another term, Roosevelt simply repeated the exercise. Throughout his campaign for the presidency in the November 1940 election, Roosevelt insisted that, like the vast majority of the electorate, he was strongly in favour of non-intervention and against US entanglement in the European war. He repeatedly promised American parents that their sons would not be sent to fight in that war if he was re-elected. He would only ever contemplate going to war if the USA was directly attacked by a foreign power. Republican presidential candidate, Wendell Willkie, advised the electorate that Roosevelt was lying and secretly planning to take the country into the war. Saving Britain and defeating Germany, said Wilkie, was Roosevelt's first priority. So strong were Roosevelt's denials, however, that he won the presidential election with a comfortable majority.

Back in 1917, following his election victory, Wilson had then taken the American people to war on the basis of lies about the Lusitania sinking, about Belgian atrocities, and the Germans' lifting restrictions on U-boat activity. Now, Roosevelt would take them to war on the basis of a huge lie about Pearl Harbor. It later emerged that he had deliberately goaded Japan and was aware of their intended attack on Pearl Harbor weeks before it took place. He did nothing to prevent it or warn the commanding officers in Hawaii, and effectively sacrificed the lives of over 2,000 young Americans.

The day following the attack, Roosevelt declared to Congress that 7 December 1941 was a date which would "live in infamy." He stated that in addition to the attack on Pearl Harbor, over the past 24 hours Japan had undertaken a "surprise" offensive extending throughout the Pacific area, with attacks against Malaya, Hong Kong, the Philippine Islands, Guam, Wake Island and Midway Island. He added: "Always will our whole Nation remember the charac

ter of the onslaught against us." To instil fear in the American people, he said that they, their territory and their interests "were in grave danger" and asked that a state of war be declared between the United States and Japan. No matter how long it took:

> The American people in their righteous might will win through to absolute victory. With confidence in our armed forces, the unbounding determination of our people, we will gain the inevitable triumph so help us God. I ask that the Congress declare that since the unprovoked and dastardly attack by Japan on Sunday, December 7, 1941, a state of war has existed between the United States and the Japanese Empire.[26]

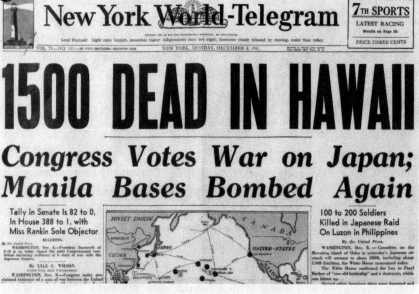

That day, 8 December 1941, the Senate voted 82-0 in favour of war, with the House voting 388-1 in favour. Thanks to Pearl Harbor, Roosevelt was able to jettison the promises that got him re-elected. Captain Russell Grenfell, a recognised authority in naval warfare with over thirty years' service in the Royal Navy and Navy Staff College, was blunt in his assessment of Roosevelt's role in the Pearl Harbor disaster. In his book *Main Fleet to Singapore,* (1952) he wrote:

> Japan was meant by the American President to attack the United States.... It is very questionable whether the word treachery is a legitimate one to use in these circumstances.

Grenfell believed that Roosevelt's behaviour was traitorous rather than treacherous. While American and British historians beholden to the Establishment continued bolstering the official account blaming Kimmel and Short, independent researchers and writers categorically stated otherwise. They present compelling evidence of a cover-up at the very top of the US administration. The president had been provided with intelligence intercepts that gave advance warning of a Japanese attack. It came as a "surprise attack" to Admiral Kimmel, General Short, and the navy at Pearl Harbor because Washington withheld that crucial information from them.

The servicemen and women at Pearl Harbor were sacrificed in order to give Roosevelt his excuse for war. It was absolutely essential that Japan struck the first blow or Congress and the American people would reject war. He and his loyal Establishment men in Washington did nothing to prevent it. Indeed, they facilitated it.

For some time, US and British Intelligence services were readily able to intercept and decrypt the Japanese diplomatic and military codes. Indeed, the system was so refined that they were reading the Japanese messages before the intended recipients. The first indication came eight weeks before the Pearl Harbor attack, that is, on 9 October, when a message from Tokyo to the Japanese agent in Honolulu was intercepted and decoded. It instructed the consul to provide a map dividing the waters of Pearl Harbor into five sub-areas, specifying what warships were in each area and whether they were tied up at wharves, buoys, or in the docks, et cetera. Michael Gannon, Distinguished Service Professor Emeritus of History at the University of Florida, wrote:

> The effect of these five designations was to place what had been called an "invisible grid" over Pearl Harbor. Consul General Kita's messages, which were sent in a low-grade consular cipher known as J-19 were intercepted by U.S. Navy operators in Station Hypo at Pearl Harbor … but Commander Rochefort, Chief of the Combat Intelligence Unit of the Fourteenth Naval District [Hawaii] was under orders to send all consular intercepts, unread, by Clipper pouch to Washington, for decryption and evaluation there. This meant that the Pacific Fleet, the principal instrument of our military power in the Pacific, was not equipped to monitor the enemy beyond its harbor wall.[27]

Unnamed senior navy officers in Washington proposed that the grid might be a plan for an air attack on Pearl Harbor, but the suggestion, like the intercepted message itself, were never acted upon nor passed to Admiral Kimmel. By November, the closely collaborating British and US naval intelligence services were aware that the Japanese navy was mobilising. On 25 November, Admiral Yamamoto sent several radio messages to the task force that would attack Pearl Harbor. (It consisted of six aircraft carriers carrying 450 planes, escorted by two battleships, two cruisers, eleven destroyers, oilers, and twenty full-size submarines with midget submarines strapped to them.) The messages were intercepted and decoded by British Intelligence at Bletchley Park in England and immediately shared with US Naval Intelligence. An official message sent to all Pacific commanders on 27 November, including Admiral Kimmel at Pearl Harbor, stated "This dispatch is to be considered a war warning." It advised that "an aggressive move by Japan is expected within the next few days." The "War message," however, was "weak and ambiguous" according to Pearl Harbor researcher, Captain James Johns (Army Aviation, retd.), and "didn't warn of a thing." The gist of the Washington message, probably as intended, led Admiral Kimmel and General Short to understand that any Japanese attack targets would be in the South Pacific, that is, thousands of miles from Pearl Harbor. Admiral Kimmel received only a few vague messages, enough to constitute "affirmative misrepresentation." He had asked for *all* vital information, and the few messages he did receive persuaded him that he was getting it. Kimmel and Short were in fact being kept in the dark as to all important intelligence intercepts going through Washington.

US Intelligence knew from the first days of December that the Japanese Embassy in Washington had been ordered to destroy all its codes and prepare members of staff for departure. That alone was a sure sign of war coming. Intercepts indicated that the large naval task force was assembling at Hitokappu Bay on the Kuril Islands off northern Japan.

Captain Johns states that in the early hours of the morning of 26 November – 12 days before Pearl Harbor – Winston Churchill made a scrambler telephone call to FDR at the White House, telling him "They are coming." According to Johns (though, as far as we are aware, it has never been confirmed), Churchill had just been informed by British Intelligence that the large Japanese task force had departed the Kuril Islands the day before, and was heading *not* south towards Malaya or Singapore, but east towards Hawaii. It would likely arrive there on Monday 8 December. With the time difference, that in fact was Sunday 7 December in Hawaii. Later in the morning of 26 November, Secretary of State Cordell Hull had a meeting with the Japanese ambassador and handed him a 10-point note. It included demands that Japan withdraw from all occupied areas, stop the war in China, and restore the original Chinese government and monetary system. The Japanese ambassador knew that the demands meant the end of any meaningful negotiations.

The official narrative relates that because the Japanese fleet maintained complete radio silence, Washington had no knowledge whatsoever that it was heading for Hawaii. It was quite incredible then, that the US authorities issued strict instructions to the 14th Naval District (Hawaii) and the 16th Naval District (San Francisco) to keep all sea lanes from Hawaii west to the Orient clear of commercial and military shipping. The "Clear Lanes" order specifically instructed that all transpacific traffic must divert south through the Solomon Islands to the Torres Strait, between Australia and New Guinea.[28] This added 7 days and thousands of miles to their journeys, but the Japanese fleet had to be given a route clear of any traffic that could forewarn Kimmel and Short at Pearl Harbor. It was essential that as Admiral Nagumo crossed the North Pacific to Hawaii, he could be confident that his fleet had not been discovered by the enemy or he might well turn back. Nagumo was doubtless painfully aware that had three or four hundred US bomber and torpedo planes suddenly appeared in the skies above him, he would have little or no time to get his own planes airborne to defend the fleet. Six fully laden Japanese aircraft carriers, two battleships, and a dozen other warships would be sitting ducks. Nagumo must have considered himself blessed on that voyage, but little did he know that Washington had gone to great lengths to afford him a clear route to Hawaii.

One of the most controversial pieces of evidence regarding whether or not the US authorities knew of the Pearl Harbor attack in advance, was a coded Japanese alert to its forces known as the "Winds execute" message. Four days before Pearl Harbor, Japanese news broadcasts came with a weather report at both the beginning and end of the normal news items: "*higashi no kaze, ame; nishi no kaze hare*" ("Easterly wind, rain, westerly wind, fine"). The message was picked up by the navy's east coast Japanese radio monitoring station at Cheltenham, Maryland, and passed to the cryptanalysis section in Washington.[29] It was aware that the "winds execute" message was timed for the eve of war with the United States. The message was later dismissed as a myth by Roosevelt's men, but a whistleblower and senior member of Naval Communications Intelligence, cryptologist Captain Laurance Safford, confirmed that it removed any remaining doubt that war with Japan was coming. Safford

Safford

wanted to immediately warn Pearl Harbor and other Pacific bases to place all defences on high alert, but was refused permission to do so by the Director of Naval Communications, Admiral Leigh Noyes.

Former U.S. Navy photographer turned journalist and Pearl Harbor investigator, Robert B. Stinnett spent 17 years digging into archives and uncovered official documents that were never meant to see the light of day. He wrote:

> In his postwar testimony to Congress, Admiral Husband Kimmel maintained that he would have been ready to defend Pearl Harbor "If I had anything which indicated to me the probability of an attack on Hawaii." The information that Kimmel needed was available ... Seven Japanese naval broadcasts intercepted between November 28 and December 6 confirmed that Japan intended to start the war and that it would begin at Pearl Harbor. The evidence that poured into American intelligence stations is overpowering. All the broadcasts have one common denominator: none ever reached Admiral Kimmel.[30]

No effort was spared by Washington to ensure that the Japanese attack on Pearl Harbor succeeded, but they first had to ensure the safety of the US aircraft carriers based there. According to Captain James Johns, a message was sent from Washington to Pearl Harbor to get the carriers out to sea and take the modern faster ships with them. They were to leave behind eight old and slow World War One-era battleships. At the time, the US Navy had seven aircraft carriers in service, each with a full complement of planes. Four carriers were stationed on the east coast, poised to deal with German navy raiders and U-boats in the Atlantic. Three others, *Saratoga, Enterprise,* and *Lexington* were based at Pearl Harbor.

Saratoga had been on prolonged refit from early January 1941 at the Bremerton naval yard near Seattle. At the time of the attack she was in San Diego to receive her air wing, which had been training in southern California. The other two carriers anchored at Pearl were ordered to sea. *Enterprise* departed with an escort of three heavy cruisers and nine destroyers. *Lexington* was suddenly dispatched to ferry dive bombers to the American base on Midway Island 1140 nautical miles distant in the mid-Pacific, with an escort of three heavy cruisers and five destroyers. She had eighteen planes of Scouting Squadron 231 aboard which could, indeed should, together with other spotter planes, have been conducting 360-degree patrols of the ocean around Hawaii. Thus, two aircraft carriers, six heavy cruisers, fourteen destroyers, and hundreds of aircraft were made safe from the attack that Washington knew was coming.

The U.S. and British Intelligence services were deciphering all Japanese diplomatic and military communications, which they collated under a single system given the code name "Magic."

> In August 1940 War Department cryptanalysts had created an electromechanical decryption device that penetrated the high-grade Japanese diplomatic cipher code-named "Purple." With this equipment the Army and Navy alternated daily in "breaking" intercepted Japanese diplomatic (DIP) radio traffic. Thus Hull [US Secretary of State, Cordell Hull], who was one of the few Washington officials to see machine's product, called "Magic," was privy to all of Nomura's instructions from Tokyo, as well as his reports home.[31]

"Magic" held substantial amounts of secret Japanese naval information from both the Japanese "Purple" code which was used by their diplomats, and their "J-19" code which served their agents and spies. Consequently, "Magic" contained information on the time and place of the coming attack on Pearl Harbor, and the Japanese deception to cover the attack. Through interception of the J series codes, US intelligence knew of Tokyo spy orders transmitted in the J-19 code system, which directed preparation of bomb plots for the Pacific Fleet anchorages in Pearl Harbor.

> Short's intercept operators, unable to decode the bomb plot messages, forwarded to Washington. They were decoded and, when translated, revealed the bomb plots – but Washington clammed up. Not a word of the bomb plots that targeted Pearl Harbor was sent to Short or to Kimmel.[32]

It was known in Washington when the Japanese fleet would sail, the route it would take, and how and when it would launch the attack. US and British Intelligence shared the "Magic" information with each other, but it was not made available to Pearl Harbor. Clearly the authorities had to carefully ensure that the Japanese did not discover that their codes and intelligence transmissions were compromised, but the intelligence should have been shared with the senior commanders at Pearl, Kimmel and Short. They had no idea that "Magic" even existed. Kimmel was entirely dependent on Washington for crucial information, but Washington was deliberately withholding it from him. As previously discussed, he had specifically asked to be forwarded *all* information that had a bearing on his command and had been assured he would get it. The sporadic intercepts he *did* get lulled him into a false sense of security. The completely innocent Admiral Kimmel at the doomed Pearl Harbor, like the completely innocent Captain Turner on the doomed *Lusitania* twenty-six years earlier, was to be thrown to the wolves and made to shoulder the blame.

At 9 P.M. on the evening before the attack, a Japanese Purple message was sent to Japan's ambassador in the US. It was instantly decrypted and sent to Roosevelt by Commander Shulz of US Intelligence. The president immediately declared "This means War." With such a declaration Roosevelt, as Commander-in-Chief of the armed forces, should have immediately informed the heads of the army and navy. America was going to war with Japan, but to swing public opinion in favour of that war they had to let the Japanese make the first move. The head of the army, General George Marshall, later testified on oath that he "couldn't remember" if the president had informed him. Admiral Harold Stark, head of the Navy, also later testified that he "could not remember."

In England, Winston Churchill knew from British intelligence intercepts of Japanese messages that the attack was coming. He had advised Roosevelt of this with his scrambler telephone call on 26 November. When Churchill received confirmation that the Japanese had attacked Pearl Harbor, he 'just happened' to be entertaining the US Ambassador, Gilbert Winant, and Presidential Envoy, Averell Harriman, at Chequers, the prime minister's official country residence in Buckinghamshire. Harriman, a member of Skull & Bones and the Anglo-American establishment, was a leading player in Brown Brothers Harriman & Co on Wall Street, one of the largest private investment banks in the world. He had led the Anglo-American aid mission to Stalin earlier in the year. As detailed in chapter 19, Harriman

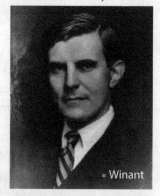

• Winant

was closely linked to Fritz Thyssen, the leading German industrialist and steel magnate. In the 1930s, Harriman had been deeply involved in funnelling vast amounts of money from Wall Street to Hitler via Thyssen. As ever, the bankers were funding both sides in the war. Harriman's business interests would be seized in 1942 under the US Trading With the Enemy Act.

As they enjoyed the pleasures of the great country house at Chequers that weekend, Churchill, Harriman and Ambassador Winant undoubtedly had foreknowledge of the world changing event that was about to take place on the other side of the planet. Churchill later recounted his feelings at the moment news broke of the Japanese attack:

> No American will think it wrong of me if I proclaim to have the United States at our side was to me the greatest joy. I could not foretell the course of events. I do not pretend to have measured accurately the martial might of Japan, but now at this very moment I knew that the United States was in the war, up to the neck and in to the death. England would live; Britain would live; the Commonwealth of Nations and the Empire would live. How long the war would last or in what fashion it would end no man could tell, nor did I at this moment care. Once again in our long island history we should emerge, however mauled or mutilated, safe and victorious...
>
> Hitler's fate was sealed. Mussolini's fate was sealed. As for the Japanese, they would be ground to powder. All the rest was merely the proper application of overwhelming force. The British Empire, the Soviet Union, and now the United States, bound together with every scrap of their life and strength, were, according to my lights, twice or even thrice the force of their antagonists.... United we could subdue everybody else in the world. Many disasters, immeasurable cost and tribulation lay ahead, but there was no more doubt about the end.... Being saturated and satiated with emotion and sensation, I went to bed and slept the sleep of the saved and thankful.[33]

As Sir Winston Churchill slept soundly that night in cold, dreary England, 7,300 miles away in the beautiful sunny Hawaiian islands, hundreds of badly burned and mutilated American sailors writhed in agony, expendable pawns in the Anglo-American elites' Great Game.

On 8 December, Roosevelt immediately dispatched the Secretary of the Navy, William Franklin Knox, to Pearl Harbor to report on the damage and responsibilities. One week later his report was an unequivocal exoneration of Kimmel and Short. They had never been given the vital information which was available in Washington about the impending Japanese attack, and had been denied the basic necessities for their defence. Knox's report was never published or made public. Buried away in the files, it was only discovered years later by Senator Homer Ferguson. Kimmel, the fifty-eight-year-old Kentuckian who had been in charge at Pearl Harbor for ten months, had, according to the Knox Report, "trained this powerful fleet to maximum readiness and proficiency with what ships, aircraft, and weapons he was supplied. His officers and men were at concert pitch. They were ready to sail."[34]

Such information had to be buried in order to blame Kimmel. A massive cover-up followed with the Chief of Staff ordering that a lid be put on the affair. He told senior officers; "This goes to the grave with us." After having buried the Knox report, Roosevelt commissioned Supreme Court Justice Owen Roberts to go to Hawaii to "investigate." No fingers must point at Washington being involved. Kimmel and Short had to carry the can no matter what. Their reputations and careers would have to be destroyed to protect Washington. Roosevelt considered Owen Roberts a safe pair of hands and a dependable ally who had been clamouring for war against Japan. Indeed, all members of the 'Roberts Commission' were Roosevelt yes-men. As members of the military they were under strict orders not to reveal any information whatsoever about "Magic" or the intercepted Japanese codes that warned of the attack.

The Roberts Commission (18 December 1941-25 January 1942) reported in the first instance to the president. He very much liked it, for it cast sole blame on Kimmel and Short for the success of the Japanese attack. They were "derelict in their duty." The report added a nice little commendation to please Roosevelt: all high officials and army and navy chiefs in Washington were praised for "performing their duties admirably and without fault." There was no need to bury *this* report. The Roberts Commission presented its findings to Congress on 28 January, 1942, and the report blaming Kimmel and Short was immediately published. Thereafter, four separate committees, all personally appointed by Roosevelt, whitewashed the Pearl Harbor disaster. Throughout the entire war the American public believed Kimmel and Short were to blame, and they became two of the most hated men in America.

All of the material gathered as evidence for the corrupt Roberts Report conveniently disappeared – in particular, the so-called "Winds execute" message received by Naval Communications on 4 December, giving notice in the Japanese "weather report" code of an attack upon the United States. After retiring from his post in the Supreme Court, Owen Roberts reportedly burned all of his legal and judicial papers, leaving no collection, as was the normal practice.

The disgraced Admiral Kimmel and General Short resigned and were denied court martials to try and prove their innocence.

> The public was demanding court-martials and execution of the Hawaiian commanders. One newspaper stated that if Kimmel and Short had any honor, they would commit suicide. Both would have

welcomed court-martials because within that legal process, they could have at least presented their sides of the story. But this would compromise national security, so they were denied.[35]

In the autumn of 1943, a concerned naval officer, Captain Laurance Safford, the leading cryptologist in US Naval Intelligence mentioned earlier, uncovered evidence that neither Kimmel nor Short had been provided with the critical intelligence necessary to perform their duties. Captain Safford was one of the men primarily responsible for breaking the Japanese codes and an expert on "Magic." Kimmel agreed to meet him in secret in New York. Safford asked the broken and despondent Admiral if he had had available to him in Hawaii the decoded Japanese diplomatic and spy communications that were available in Washington prior to the attack. Kimmel responded: "What in the world are you talking about"? With Safford's help, a long search for the truth began.

Three years after Pearl Harbor, the British Minister of Production, Oliver Lyttelton, gave a speech at the Savoy Hotel in London to the English branch of the American Chamber of Commerce. In a moment of unguarded frankness he stated:

Lyttelton

> Japan was provoked into attacking the Americans at Pearl Harbor. It is a travesty on history ever to say that America was forced into the war. Everyone knows where American sympathies were. It is incorrect to say that America was ever truly neutral even before America came into the war.[36]

Lyttleton's comments caused faux outrage in Washington, and in the House of Commons shortly afterwards he was forced to make a grovelling apology to the US administration.

A Naval Court of Inquiry later found no evidence whatsoever to support the charge of dereliction of duty against Admiral Kimmel. Rear Admiral Thomas A. Brooks, Director of Naval Intelligence 1988-1991, wrote: "Kimmel's superiors committed perjury, suborned perjury, destroyed evidence and intimidated witnesses. Testimony during nine separate investigations into Pearl Harbor presents a sordid picture of Washington officials covering themselves at the expense of the two Pearl Harbor commanders. Kimmel and Short's seniors in Washington shared culpability and acted in a disgraceful fashion in their attempt to deflect all the blame." The evidence that Roosevelt wanted America in the war alongside Britain, and allowed the Pearl Harbor attack to achieve that, is overwhelming. The Oxford 'court historians', however, made a valiant effort to conceal the truth behind the tapestry of lies. For example, Oxford-trained pro-Establishment military historian, John Keegan (Balliol College, Oxford) writes:

> American historians have disputed for years the issue of whether Roosevelt "knew"; those who believe he did imply that he had sought and found in foreknowledge of Japanese "infamy" the pre-text he needed to draw the United States into the war on the side of Britain. It is an extension of the charge that there was a secret understanding between Roosevelt and Churchill, perhaps con-cluded at their August meeting in Placentia Bay, Newfoundland, to use Japanese perfidy as a means of overcoming American domestic resistance to involvement. Both these charges defy logic."[37]

We suggest that it is Keegan's account of Pearl Harbor that defies not only logic, but all of the evidence that became available. That evidence clearly points to appalling lies being told throughout by the US government. Leading players in Washington, the president in particular; (1) deliberately provoked the attack; (2) failed to warn Kimmel and Short that it was going to happen; (3) scapegoated them of false charges of dereliction of duty and ruined their careers.

On being appointed to the post of Pacific Fleet commander, Kimmel had advised Admiral Harold A. Stark, Chief of Naval Operations in Washington, about the deficiencies in the defences of Oahu. He specifically pointed to the small number of obsolescent land based aircraft that were essential for constant medium and long range (500 miles) reconnaissance of the seas around Hawaii, and the inadequacy of anti-aircraft guns for the defence of Pearl Harbor. Rear-Admiral Claude Charles Bloch, overall commander of the Fourteenth Naval District at Pearl Harbor at the time of the attack, would later tell the Roberts Commission that the Navy Department *had* allocated long range reconnaissance aircraft to Hawaii for the protection of Pearl Harbor, but "their delivery was indefinite."[38] Kimmel was told just to get on with it. All US bases were short on defences, he was advised, and Pearl Harbor was better defended than most.

At the kangaroo court that was the Roberts Commission, Kimmel's one time friend Admiral Stark basically sold him down the river and he was charged with dereliction of duty. Before Kimmel died in 1968, Stark sent him a conciliatory letter, but Kimmel drafted a bitter response:

You betrayed the officers and men of the Fleet by not giving them a fighting chance for their lives and you betrayed the Navy in not taking responsibility for your actions; you betrayed me by not giving me information you knew I was entitled to and by your acquiescence in the action taken on the request for my retirement; and you betrayed yourself by misleading the Roberts Commission as to what information had been sent to me by your statements made under oath before the Court of Inquiry that you knew were false. I hope that you never communicate with me again and that I never see you or your name again that my memory may not be refreshed of one so despicable as you.[39]

The Americans and Japanese fought many bloody battles in the Pacific War, while the enormous slaughter continued in Europe, North Africa and elsewhere. In the West, the bloodiest conflict came in southern Russia with the Battle of Stalingrad (August 1942 – February 1943). Both sides suffered appalling losses with over a million casualties each. Stalingrad was the turning point of the war in Europe when the Axis forces were eventually driven back.

On 6 June 1944, with Operation Overlord came the massive Allied assault on the beaches of Normandy in France. As Russian forces moved in inexorably from the East, destroying most of the Wehrmacht, German forces in the West were gradually driven back across France and western Germany by the western Allies. Eventually, the Allied and the Soviet armies met in central Germany, and the Americans allowed the Soviets to take Berlin.

Some writers have suggested that Hitler escaped from his Berlin bunker to Argentina in 1945, but on this particular topic the received history appears to more reliable. According to it, in the early hours of 29 April 1945, Hitler married Eva Braun in a short civil ceremony in the Führerbunker near the Reich Chancellery in Berlin, as the Red Army closed in on the city. The following day, 30 April, Eva refused Hitler's demand that she should escape from the bunker, and bit into a cyanide capsule. Hitler shot himself. Their bodies were carried from the bunker to the Reich Chancellery garden, doused in petrol and burned. Hitler was 56 years old, Eva was 33. Hitler's death was announced on German radio the following day. On 8 May 1945, the Allies accepted the unconditional surrender of Germany's armed forces.

On 6 August and 9 August 1945, the Americans detonated two atomic bombs over the cities of Hiroshima and Nagasaki in Japan, killing an estimated 200,000 civilians. On 2 September 1945 on board the battleship USS *Missouri* in Tokyo Bay, the Japanese formally surrendered, and the Second World War ended.

Summary: Chapter 22 – Once More Into The Abyss

• Prime minister Neville Chamberlain had talks with Hitler in Berlin in late September 1938 and agreed to a German takeover of the Sudeten part of Czechoslovakia. German troops moved in within days.

• On 14 March, 1939, German forces then invaded the main body of Czechoslovakia. The Bank of England transferred £6 million worth of Czech gold to Germany. The "appeasers" in Britain now immediately swung 180 degrees in favour of rapidly increasing Britain's already massive armaments reserves for the imminent war against Germany.

• On 1 September 1939, the German army invaded Poland. 48 hours later Britain and France declared war on Germany. Thus began the Second World War.

• In June 1940, German forces entered Paris and France signed an Armistice with Germany.

• In June 1941, German forces began a massive offensive – Operation Barbarossa – against Russia.

• In August 1941, the United States imposed an embargo on all goods to Japan and froze her financial assets as a means of provoking her into war.

• On 7 December 1941, Japanese aircraft attacked the US fleet based at Pearl Harbor. Washington was aware of the coming attack but failed to warn the Pearl Harbor commanders. The United States declared war on Japan, and Germany declared war on the United States.

• On 6 June 1944 – "D-Day" – Allied forces landed on the beaches of Normandy in France and fought their way to Germany.

• Hitler committed suicide in his Berlin bunker on 30 April 1945. Germany surrendered unconditionally on 8 May.

• On 6 and 9 August 1945, the United States detonated atomic bombs over two Japanese cities. The Japanese formally surrendered on 2 September, ending the Second World War.

AFTERWORD

The thesis put forward in this book is that accounts of the First World War and Hitler's subsequent rise to power written by historians linked to Oxford University cannot be trusted. The early chapters of the book describe how a leading academic historian in the United States, Professor Carol Quigley, presented well sourced evidence about the existence of an all-powerful group of individuals which, from the earliest years of the twentieth century, operated behind the scenes in Britain and the United States. In his book, *The Anglo-American Establishment* published in 1981, Quigley revealed how this secret group led by Lord Alfred Milner was closely linked to Oxford University and completely monopolized the writing and teaching of the history of their own period. Crucially, the group also controlled politics and the Press.

Quigley gained a great deal of insider information on the 'Milner Group' from a whistleblower, Sir Alfred Zimmern. A member of the group who left it after major disagreements with Milner, the Oxford educated Zimmern was an English classical scholar, historian, political scientist, and Professor of International Relations at Oxford. He was also a founder of the League of Nations and the Royal Institute of International Affairs.

The two friends, Quigley and Zimmern, were highly regarded academics on the international stage, and because they could not be dismissed as 'conspiracy theory' cranks, their revelations have simply been airbrushed by the Milner Group, Oxford University, and the Anglo-American Establishment. One might expect academic rebuttals of Quigley's thesis by historians linked to Oxford University – but nothing. That Quigley's work has been completely blanked by British mainstream academics, politicians, and the Press, tells us just how powerful were the individuals he was exposing.

Milner and his loyal followers in the 'Kindergarten' have long since departed this world, but the immense power of the oligarchy and its globalist aspirations for one world government live on and thrive under the guidance of new blood. In response to accusations of this type against him, billionaire David Rockefeller wrote in his 2003 book, *Memoirs*:

For more than a century ideological extremists at either end of the political spectrum have seized upon well-publicized incidents such as my encounter with Castro to attack the Rockefeller family for the inordinate influence they claim we wield over American political and economic institutions. Some even believe we are part of a secret cabal working against the best interests of the United States, characterizing my family and me as 'internationalists' and of conspiring with others around the world to build a more integrated global political and economic structure--one world, if you will. If that's the charge, I stand guilty, and I am proud of it.

It has become increasingly evident that those elites who picked up the baton of the Milner Group in recent years have no fixed enemies or firm friends – only their interests – and these drive their alliances and determine their enemies at any given time. They do, of course, still falsely present their aim for one world government as being of great benefit to humanity. As Professor Quigley noted 60 years ago, their ultimate aim was control over every government on the planet. Did they actually achieve that? Russia? China? Evidence from the current state of the world suggests that their task is not yet complete. Many more millions are yet to die, just as many millions have died at their hands since 1945. The American writer William Blum (1933-2018), who devoted himself to making sense of state terrorism, stated: "In my lifetime, the United States has overthrown or attempted to overthrow more than 50 governments, most democracies. It has interfered in democratic elections in 30 countries. It has dropped bombs on the people of 30 countries, most of them poor and defenceless. It has fought to suppress liberation movements in 20 countries. It has attempted to murder countless leaders."

Since Blum wrote that in 2005, we have seen the US and its allies wage war on countries including, Iraq, Afghanistan, Syria, and Libya, among many others. At the time of writing this we are witnessing the US and its NATO puppets supporting genocide in Palestine and stirring mayhem in the oil-rich Middle East. The fall of communism in Russia in December 1991 did not end the war against Russia, just as the "War to end war" did not end in 1918. Meanwhile, they utter blood-curdling threats against Iran and China. It has been argued that in the light of all of this horror we are already in the early stages of the Third World War, a war that, should it go nuclear, would likely be the end of all of us.

On a relatively mundane note, readers may wonder what became of the British and American agents placed close to Hitler in the 1920s and 30s, and who played such important roles in helping him gain power. Ernst 'Putzi' Hanfstaengl, the piano-playing Harvard graduate who coached Hitler and played a major role in burning the Reichstag in 1933, later related that he made a daring escape from Germany in 1937 when Hitler had become suspicious of him and planned to have him killed. He travelled to England via Switzerland and settled in London with his son Egon, who was also Hitler's godson. When the war began in 1939, Putzi was arrested as an enemy alien and placed in an internment camp. He wrote to numerous leading figures in British Intelligence and the Foreign Office, including Sir Robert Vansittart and Sir Samuel Hoare (who handled British intelligence agents, including Mussolini, in Italy), asking for help in securing his release but they all turned their backs on him. Should the truth about Putzi ever come out it could open pandora's box. He was sent to an internment camp in Canada where, in 1942, his old friend President Franklin Roosevelt sent a private plane to bring him to Washington where Putzi would become a White House adviser on the Nazis. Roosevelt arranged a villa for Putzi to live in near Washington, complete with a cook, a housekeeper, and a Steinway grand piano for his entertainment. When Roosevelt died on 12 April 1945, the new President, Harry S Truman, wanted to send Putzi back to England, but his erstwhile friends – including Churchill – refused to accept him. He was eventually sent to Germany where his autobiography was ghost-written by a British writer with connections to the intelligence services. It completely whitewashed all of Putzi's links to the American and British Intelligence services. Putzi died in Germany in November 1975 age 88. A whitewash biography written years after his death by another British writer, Peter Conradi, once again concealed his role in grooming Hitler for power on behalf of the Anglo-American elites.

William Sylvester de Ropp also made his way across the border to Switzerland where he remained until the war began. He then went home to England to lead a quiet life and died there in 1973 aged 86.

Frederick Winterbotham continued in his active role in the RAF and British Intelligence until the end of the war. He died in England in 1990 at the age of 92.

Like intelligence agents Hanfstaengl, de Ropp and Winterbotham, the vast majority of those responsible for the wars died peacefully in their comfortable beds in old age surrounded by their families. The millions they tricked into doing the actual fighting were not so fortunate. While the overall human toll in the First World War was horrendous, it was largely overshadowed by that of the war which lasted from September 1939 until September 1945 in which an estimated 60 to 80 million were killed (the majority civilians) with at least as many again suffering life-changing wounds. On average, some 60,000 were killed or wounded each and every *day* of every week, month, and year of the six-year long war.

This is the point where we are supposed to ask what can be learned from that, and to say that we hope our revelations of the Establishment's lies about the First and Second World Wars will remind us of the importance of "learning from history": how in 1919-1939 we had failed to learn from 1914-1918, and the many lies about that disaster, and how that in turn led to the catastrophe of 1939-45. Certainly, in an ideal world the people should learn from the mistakes of the past through the study of history so as not to repeat them. As we have shown, however, reality is very different. If people are tutored in fake history, how can they learn anything from it? And even if they learn from it, if their 'democratic' politicians answer, not to the 'the people' but to a secretive higher authority, then 'the people' have little or no agency to "change" anything – even if they had a mind educated to do so.

As we have argued in this book, if you wanted to design a method that limits or denies the people's access to objective truth, it would be Western academic historiography. Indeed, we believe that historiography was specifically, and carefully designed for that very purpose – and that its high priests have lived and worked in Oxford colleges, with All Souls as its fountainhead. The purpose of their fake 'History' is not to reveal and teach the truth, but rather to obscure the underlying realities of war, and to propagandise a 'truth' that serves their oligarch masters.

If anyone can learn lessons from this book it is the German people. All of them without exception – individually and collectively – are constantly reminded that Germany was responsible for inflicting not one but two horrific wars on the world. This *Kriegsschuld* (war guilt) drummed into young Germans from their earliest schooldays is akin to a relentless psyops campaign wherein generation after generation of Germans have been made to accept the alleged guilt of their forefathers and internalise the burden of responsibility. Anxious and self-doubting as a consequence, they are unwilling (scared even) to pose serious questions about the wars. Any who do so, no matter how liberal, compassionate and caring, are immediately and ridiculously lumped together as being "Nazis" or Hitlerites and anti-Semitic racists. Thus ordinary Germans and successive German governments have been kept in a state of almost total subservience to the

Anglo-American elite's narrative. Germany became but one of their vassal states in 1945 and remains so to this day. US military bases and their proxy NATO bases, together with tens of thousands of military personnel, are spread throughout the country, financed of course through taxation of the German people.

Hopefully we have succeeded in showing Germans that Germany was *not* responsible for the First World War in any shape or form. Thereafter, Hitler and the Nazis (utter disasters for Germany and the world) were fomented and funded by the very same group of Anglo-American elites who *were* responsible for the 1914-18 war. *They* very deliberately created the terrible hunger, dreadful living conditions, and resentment in Germany in the immediate post First World War years that encouraged fascist reactionaries such as Hitler to come to the fore. *They* positioned British and American intelligence agents directly alongside the ragamuffin Hitler to coach him and groom him for power. *They* played a major role in burning the Reichstag that enabled Hitler to seize dictatorial power and destroy democracy. *They* funded Hitler and the building of his massive Nazi war machine. *They* encouraged Hitler to send his forces into Austria, Czechoslovakia, and Poland. *They* sent Hitler 26 tons of gold that belonged to Czechoslovakia. *They* very deliberately spurned all approaches by the German Resistance for help in removing Hitler. In short, *they* very deliberately created the Frankenstein monster that led Germany to disaster. *They* controlled production of the fake history that laid the blame on ordinary Germans that has kept them subservient ever since. We urge the German people of all ages today to think deeply about these matters and to fearlessly ask important questions. Remember the old saying: if you want to know who controls you, guess whom you are not allowed to criticise.

What our research has shown is that really the only people to learn lessons from the wars were the elite Anglo-American predators who caused them in the first place. They learned long ago that wars are always immensely profitable and increase their power over us, while getting rid of millions of those they regard as "useless eaters." They have learned well that, through their control of education and the media, the masses will swallow virtually any lie, the bigger the better, about the evil nature of their intended target. They have learned the lesson that generating fear in the masses is the answer. That the "great unwashed" (as they see the working man), will willingly queue up at recruiting stations to take up arms and kill strangers if they are repeatedly fed lies that their country and

665

their families are in grave danger from the designated "enemy." They tell us that 'our' freedom and 'our' liberties need to be protected, but what they really mean is that their profits and their power need to be protected. And that is dependent on creating fear at home and war and terror abroad. In reality, we are in thrall to state terrorism and the terrorists are our Western states. Spending on "defence" and ever more lethal new weapons is, we are told, essential to keep up with or ahead of "the enemy." Throw in some religious cant that "God is on our side" and we will happily slaughter and kill in His name. And all the while they mouth pious lies and platitudes about freedom and democracy, and use their controlled media and pliant 'journalists' and 'historians' to ram these lies down our throats – from cradle to grave.

As we have shown in this book, their overall aim has never changed, though their membership, stratagems, and targets have evolved since the earliest years of the twentieth century and will continue to evolve over time. The crushing of Germany and the prevention of an alliance between that country and Russia was the aim of the 1914-18 war. It was presented to the public as the 'war to end war'. The creation of mutual enmity and destruction between Germany and Russia was likewise the aim in 1939-45 and was presented as the "Good war" against "evil Fascism." That phase ended with the US gratuitously dropping atomic bombs on the defenceless citizens of Hiroshima and Nagasaki in Japan – an egregious act of state terrorism. But even here the real target was not just Japan, but according to some thinkers and military strategists, Russia. As that giant of truth, the late William Blum suggested: "It has been asserted that the dropping of the atomic bombs was not so much the last military act of the Second World War as the first act of the Cold War. Although Japan was targeted, the weapons were aimed straight to the red heart of the USSR. For more than 70 years, the determining element of US foreign policy, virtually its sine qua non, has been 'the communist factor.'" The Second World War and a battlefield alliance with the Soviet Union did not bring about an ideological change in the anti-communists who owned and ran America. It merely provided a partial breather in a struggle that had begun when the Milner Group and financial elites on Wall Street facilitated the Bolshevik takeover of Russia in October 1917. It is hardly surprising then, that 28 years later, as the Soviets were sustaining the highest casualties of any nation in the Second World War, the US systematically kept them in the dark about the atom bomb project, while sharing information with the British.

According to Manhattan Project scientist Leo Szilard, the US Secretary of State, James F. Byrnes, said that the bomb's biggest benefit was not its effect on Japan but its power to "make Russia more manageable in Europe." General Leslie Groves, Director of the Manhattan Project, testified in 1954: "There was never, from about two weeks from the time I took charge of this Project, any illusion on my part but that Russia was our enemy, and that the Project was conducted on that basis."

We are only too well aware that the testimony of US defence and security insiders needs to be treated with an appropriate degree of scepticism and circumspection. Nevertheless, the subsequent forty years saw a concerted, and ultimately successful, effort by the US and its allies to destroy the Soviet Union, despite the involvement of the Powers in setting it up in 1917. One has to assume that its purpose had by that time been served. There is also little doubt that the Cold War itself was hugely profitable, and provided cover for control and suppression of home populations. The destruction and atomisation of the Soviet Union, which became the aim in the years 1945-1980, was presented as the struggle against "Godless Communism." And yet, even after the defeat of "Godless Communism" and Russia's reversion to Orthodox Christianity, it remains a designated enemy. Clearly, the cessation of fighting in 1945 was not the end of the Anglo-American elites' wars, but merely the end of that phase of their war on the world.

The few who have cared to study geopolitics and history – real as opposed to fake – in the hope of coming to some understanding of what is really going on and changing things for the better, may feel that they are like ants trying to move mountains. They should keep in mind that most of the tyrants and dictators in history failed in the end. What happened to the Roman Empire, after all? The Mongol, the Spanish, the French, the British Empires? Meanwhile, what we can do is bear witness. This book is our witness statement to posterity – however long or short it might be.

NOTES

Introduction

1. Guido Preparata, *Conjuring Hitler*, p. xv.
2. David Hackett Fischer, *Historians' Fallacies – Towards a Logic of Historical Thought*, p. 302.
3. Ibid., p. 314.
4. John V. Denson, *A Century of War*, p. 10.
5. H. W. Wilson, *The Great War, The Standard History of the All-Europe Conflict*, pp. 3-5.
6. Ibid., p. 1.
7. Daniel Inman, 'Theologians, War, and the Universities,' in *Journal for the History of Modern Theology*, https://www.academia.edu/23490205/Theologians_War_and_the_Universities_Early_English_interpretations_of_the_Manifesto_of_the_Ninety_Three_1914_15
8. H.E. Barnes, *The Genesis of the World War*, p. 44.
9. Ibid., p. xi.
10. Ibid., p. 302.
11. Ibid., pp. 683-6.
12. Ibid., p. 707.
13. Ibid., pp. 34-35.
14. H.E. Barnes, *In Quest of Truth and Justice*, p. x.
15. Henry Wood Nevinson, *Saturday Review of Literature*, 20 November, 1926.
16. Sidney B. Fay, *The Origins of the World War*, vol. two, p. 210.
17. Ibid., pp. 548-9.
18. Emil Ludwig, July 1914, p. 11.
19. Knuth, *The Empire of "The City,"* p. 9.
20. Ibid., pp.76-77.
21. Ibid., p. 104.
22. E.S. Herman and N. Chomsky, *Manufacturing Consent, The Political Economy of the Mass Media.* https://www.monvoisin.xyz/wp-content/uploads/2020/11/Noam-Chomsky-Edward-Herman-Manufacturing-Consent-1988.pdf
23. Howard Zinn, *A People's History of the United States.* https://files.libcom.org/files/A%20People%27s%20History%20of%20the%20Unite%20-%20Howard%20Zinn.pdf

Chapter 1 – Carroll Quigley – Oracle or Oddball?

1. Carroll Quigley, *The Anglo-American Establishment*, pp. 3-5.
2. Ibid., p. *ix*.
3. Ibid, p.15.
4. Ibid, p.7.
5. Carroll Quigley, *Tragedy & Hope, A History of the World in Our Time*, p. 950.
6. Quigley, *The Anglo-American Establishment*, pp. x-xi.
7. Ibid, pp. 5-7.
8. John P. Cafferky, *Lord Milner's Second War, The Rhodes-Milner Secret Society*, pp. 2-4.
9. *Carroll Quigley Endowed Chair Brochure.* http://www.carrollquigley.net/endowed_chair_brochure.htm

10. Ibid.

11. William J. Clinton, Address Accepting the Presidential Nomination at the Democratic National Convention in New York, 16 July 1992.

12. Quigley, *The Anglo-American Establishment*, p. 197.

13. Kevin Cole, 'Professor Carroll Quigley and the Article that said Too Little: Reclaiming History from Omission and Partisan Straw Men,' https://www.academia.edu/9167996/Professor_Carroll_Quigley_and_the_Article_that_Said_Too_Little_Reclaiming_History_from_Omission_and_Partisan_Straw_Men

14. *Washington Post* Sunday Magazine, 23 March, 1975.

15. Sevak Gulbekian, 'Brothers of the Shadows: A Perspective on Conspiracies,' in *New Dawn* No. 86 (September-October 2004.

16. Carroll Quigley – Rudy Maxa interview. https://www.youtube.com/watch?v=3111UysDWr0

17. Quigley, *The Anglo-American Establishment*, p. 33.

18. Sarah Gertrude Millin, *Rhodes*, pp. 29-30.

19. J. A. Hobson, *John Ruskin, Social Reformer*, p. 20.

20. Ibid, pp. 13-14.

21. W.G. Collingwood, *The Life and Work of John Ruskin*, vol 1, p. 80.

22. Richard Ingrams, 'Typical Art Critic, in *Literary Review*, January 1988. https://literaryreview.co.uk/typical-art-critic

23. Jennifer M. Lloyd, 'Raising Lilies: Ruskin and Women,' *Journal of British Studies*, Vol. 34, No. 3, (Jul., 1995) https://www.jstor.org/stable/175983?read-now=1&seq=1#page_scan_tab_contents

24. Ibid.

25. Hobson, John Ruskin, *Social Reformer*, p. 31.

26. Ibid., p. 171.

27. Ibid., pp. 201- 202.

28. Lloyd, 'Raising Lilies: Ruskin and Women,' *Journal of British Studies*, Vol. 34, No. 3, (Jul., 1995)

29. Kate Millet, 'The Debate over Women: Ruskin versus Mill,' Victorian Studies, Vol. 14, No. 1, *The Victorian Woman* (Sep., 1970) https://www.jstor.org/stable/3826407?read-now=1&seq=1#page_scan_tab_contents

30. Collingwood, *The Life of John Ruskin*, vol. 11, pp. 72-73.

31. Hobson, John Ruskin, *Social Reformer*, p. 49.

32. Ibid., pp 340-341. 33 Ibid., p. 192. 34 Ibid., pp. 193-194.

35. John Ruskin, 'Imperial Duty,' https://www.gutenberg.org/files/19164/19164-h/19164-h.htm#LECTURE_I

36. Quigley, *Tragedy & Hope*, p. 130.

Chapter 2 – The Society of the Elect

1. Carroll Quigley, *The Anglo-American Establishment*, p. 311.

2. Cecil Rhodes, '*Confession of Faith*' 1877. https://pages.uoregon.edu/kimball/Rhodes-Confession.htm

3. Matthew Sweet, "A Bad Man in Africa," *London Independent*, 16 March 2002.

4. Quigley, *Anglo-American Establishment*, pp. 84-85.

5. Ibid, p. 49.

6. Thomas Pakenham, *The Boer War*, p. 517.

7. Emily Hobhouse, *The Brunt of War and Where it Fell*, https://archive.org/details/bruntwarandwher01hobhgoog/page/n114/mode/2up

8. W.T Stead, cited in Hennie Barnard, *The Concentration Camps 1899-1902*, www.boer.co.za/boerwar/hellkamp.htm

9. John Hamill, *The Strange Career of Mr Hoover Under Two Flags*, pp. 151-2.

10. G. Docherty and J. Macgregor, *Hidden History, The Secret Origins of the First World*

War, pp. 52-3.

11. Quigley, *Anglo-American Establishment*, p. 52.

12. A. M. Gollin, *Proconsul in Politics: A Study of Lord Milner in Opposition and in Power*, pp. 41–42.

13. Quigley, *Anglo-American Establishment*, p. 62.

14. Ibid., p. 134.

15. Ibid., p. 141.

16. Ibid., p. 33.

17. Ibid., p. 3.

18. Quigley, *Tragedy & Hope*, p. 137.

19. Quigley, *Anglo-American Establishment*, p. 15.

20. Ibid., p. 18.

21. Ibid., p. 20.

22. Ibid., pp. 18-19.

23. Ibid., p. 312.

24. Rothschild Archives, https://www.rothschildarchive.org/collections/rothschild_faqs/rothschild_and_gold

25. Knuth, *The Empire of 'The City,'* p. 70.

26. Quigley, *Anglo-American Establishment*, p. 311.

27. Quigley, *Tragedy & Hope*, pp. 51-53.

28. Rainer Liedtke, *Agents for the Rothschilds: A Nineteenth-Century Information Network*. file:///C:/Users/Owner/Downloads/10.1515_9783110415162-003.pdf

29. Niall Ferguson, *The House of Rothschild, The World's Bankers. 1849-1999*, pp. xxiii-xxv.

30. Docherty and Macgregor, *Hidden History*, p. 24.

31. Ferguson, *The House of Rothschild*, pp. xxii.

32. The Rothschild Archive https://www.rothschildarchive.org/business/rothschild_clients

33. Ferguson, *The House of Rothschild*, p. 332.

34. Ibid., p. 332.

35. Ibid., p. xxvii.

36. Rainer Liedtke, *Agents for the Rothschilds: A Nineteenth-Century Information Network*. file:///C:/Users/Owner/Downloads/10.1515_9783110415162-003.pdf

37. Ferguson, *The House of Rothschild*, p. xxvii.

38. Ibid., p. 295.

39. The Rothschild Archive, https://guide-to-the-archive.rothschildarchive.org/the-london-banking-house/depts/partners-room/nathaniel-mayer-1st-lord-rothschild-1840-1915

40. Quigley, *Anglo-American Establishment*, p. 33.

41. Ibid., p. 91.

42. H. J. Mackinder, 'The Geographical Pivot of History,' in *The Geographical Journal*, Vol. 23, No. 4 (April 1904) pp. 421-437. https://www.jstor.org/stable/1775498

43. Quigley, *Tragedy & Hope*, p. 950.

44.

Chapter 3 – The 'Special Relationship'

1. Robert K. Massie, *Dreadnought, Britain, Germany and the Coming of the Great War*, p. 27.

2. Keith Middlemas, *The Life and Times of Edward VII*, p. 31.

3. Stanley Weintraub, *Edward the Caresser*, p. 126.

4. *Daily Express*, 9 Oct 2015 – Dirty Bertie: How Royal playboy took Victorian Paris by storm with a THREE-WAY love seat. https://www.express.co.uk/news/royal/610974/Prince-Bertie-three-way-love-seat-Paris-lust-Royal-Prince-of-Wales-playboy

5. Peter Hof, *The Two Edwards, How King Edward VII and Foreign Secretary Sir Edward Grey Fomented the First World War*, pp. 68-9.

6. Niall Ferguson, *The House of Rothschild*, pp. 249-251.

7. Wilhelm II, *The Kaiser's Memoirs*, p. 103.

8. A.J.A. Morris, *The Scaremongers – The Advocacy of War and Rearmament 1896-1914*, pp. 17-18.

9. Gerry Docherty and Jim Macgregor, *Hidden History*, pp. 64 – 65.

10. Ferguson, *House of Rothschild*, p. 250.

11. Hof, *The Two Edwards*, p. 19.

12. Carroll Quigley, *Tragedy & Hope*, p. 133.

13. John Hamill, *The Craft – A History of English Freemasonry*, p. 170.

14. David Fromkin, *The King and the Cowboy*, pp. 172-174.

15. Quigley, *Tragedy & Hope*, p. 956.

16. Kai T. Erikson, *Wayward Puritans*, p. 139.

17. Anton Chaitkin, *Treason in America, From Aaron Burr to Averell Harriman*, pp. 106-107.

18. S. Foster Damion, 'The Genesis of Boston,' in *The Atlantic*, October 1935.

19. Webster Tarpley and Anton Chaitkin, *George Bush, The Unauthorized Biography*, pp. 138-139.

20. Docherty and Macgregor, *Hidden History*, pp. 211-12.

21. Anne Pimlott Baker, *The Pilgrims of the United States*, p.3.

22. Docherty and Macgregor, *Hidden History*, p. 158.

23. Carroll Quigley, *The Anglo-American Establishment*, pp. 120-121.

24. Quigley, *Tragedy & Hope*, p. 324.

25. Stephen Birmingham, *Our Crowd*, p. 26.

26. Ibid., p. 28.

27. "Belmont, August," *The National Cyclopaedia of American Biography* (New York, 1901), 2:499. https://hd.housedivided.dickinson.edu/node/17398

28. John E Morris, "August Belmont Jr, The Forgotten Financier of the Gilded Age," *Financial History*, Winter 2021. https://www.proquest.com/openview/346b7146fc33d-3c41e2c3b2edcf783ee/1?pq-origsite=gscholar&cbl=1946335

29. Ferguson, *The House of Rothschild*, p. 456.

30. Ibid., p. 117.

31. Ibid., p. xxvii.

32. George Wheeler, *Pierpont Morgan & Friends, the Anatomy of a Myth*, p. 18.

33. The Rothschild Archive. https://www.rothschildarchive.org/collections/rothschild_faqs/rothschild_and_gold

34. Ron Chernow, *The House of Morgan*, p. 417.

35. Ibid., p. 15-16.

36. Ibid

37. Ferguson, *House of Rothschild*, p. 348.

38. Wheeler, *Pierpont Morgan & Friends*, pp. 74-75.

39. Chernow, *House of Morgan*, p. 22.

40. Nomi Prins, *All the Presidents' Bankers*, p. 2.

41. Wheeler, *Pierpont Morgan & Friends*, p. 21.

42. Chernow, *House of Morgan*, p. 139.

43. Wheeler, *Pierpont Morgan and Friends*, pp. 6-7.

44. Ellen Hodgson Brown, *Web of Debt*, p. 15.

45. The Writings of Jefferson, vol. 7 (*Autobiography Correspondence and other Writings*) Committee of Congress: Washington, D.C., 1861) p. 685.

46. Antony C. Sutton, *The Federal Reserve Conspiracy*, p. 56.

47. Quigley, *Tragedy & Hope*, p. 937.

48. Brown, *Web of Debt*, p. 19.

49. Ron Chernow, *The House of Morgan*, p. 79.

50. Prins, *All the Presidents' Bankers*, p. 2.

51. Chernow, *House of Morgan*, p.101.

52. Ibid., pp. 152-153.

53. Prins, *All the Presidents' Bankers*, pp. 2-5.

54. Chernow, *House of Morgan*, pp. 106-8.

55. G. Edward Griffin, *The Creature From Jekyll Island*, pp. 418-49.

56. Brown, *The Web of Debt*, p. 121.

57. Gerard Helferich, *An Unlikely Trust, Theodore Roosevelt, J.P. Morgan and the Improbable Partnership That Remade American Business*, pp. 186-187.

58. Louis Brandeis, *Other People's Money and How the Bankers Use It*, pp. 32-33.

59. Brown, *The Web of Debt*, p. 7.

60. Chernow, *House of Morgan*, p.167.

61. Ibid., p. 171.

62. Ibid., pp. 191-195.

63. Brown, *Web of Debt*, p. 120.

64. George R. Conroy, *Truth* magazine, Boston, 16 December 1912.

65. Jacob Henry Schiff, Jewish Encyclopedia https://jewishencyclopedia.com/articles/13266-schiff

66. Naomi Cohen, *Jacob H Schiff, A Study in American Jewish Leadership*, p. 16.

67. Chernow, *The House of House of Morgan*, p. 90.

68. Ron Chernow, *The Warburgs*, p. 12.

69. Quigley, *Tragedy & Hope*, p. 311.

70. Ferguson, *The House of Rothschild, The World's Banker*, 1849-1999, p. 234.

71. Ibid., p. xxviii.

72. Brown, *The Web of Debt*, pp. 120-122.

73. Quigley, *Tragedy & Hope*, p. 324.

74. Griffin, *The Creature from Jekyll Island*, p. 5.

75. Ibid., p. 23.

76. Ibid., p. 19.

77. Docherty and Macgregor, *Hidden History*, pp. 220-21.

78. Antony Sutton, *The Federal Reserve Conspiracy*, p. 83.

79. Griffin, *The Creature from Jekyll Island*, pp. 451-452.

80. Sutton, *The Federal Reserve Conspiracy*, p. 83.

81. Ibid,, pp. 83-84.

82. Ibid., pp. 87- 89.

83. Ibid., p.99.

84. Ibid., p. 111.

85. Ibid., p. 114.

86. The Writings of Jefferson, vol. 7. (Committee of Congress: Washington, D.C. 1861) p. 685.

87. Docherty and Macgregor, *Hidden History*, p. 223.

88. Sutton, *The Federal Reserve Conspiracy*, pp. 102-103.

89. Quigley, *Tragedy & Hope*, pp. 326-327.

90. Guido Giacomo Preparata, *Conjuring Hitler*, p. xvi.

Chapter 4 – War by Royal Warrant

1. Quigley, *The Anglo-American Establishment*, p. 5.

2. Ibid., p. 14.

3. Ibid., p. 312.

4. Ibid.

5. Ibid., pp. 31-32.

6. Robert K Massie, *Dreadnought: Britain, Germany, and the Coming of the Great War*, p. 601.

7. Robert Gibson, *Best of Enemies: Anglo-French Relations Since the Norman Conquest*, p. 210.
8. Richard F. Hamilton and Holger H. Herwick, *Decisions for War, 1914-1917*, p. 35.
9. Gordon Martel, *The Origins of the First World War*, revised 3rd edition, p. 56.
10. John V Keiger, *France and the Origins of the First World War*, p. 103.
11. Edward E. McCullough, *How the First World War Began*, pp. 67-68.
12. George Monger, *The End of Isolation: British Foreign Policy 1900-1907*, p. 145.
13. Gerry Docherty & Jim Macgregor, *Hidden History*, p. 66.
14. Sidney Bradshaw Fay, *The Origins of the World War, Vol. 1*, p. 165.
15. Centenary of the Entente Cordiale, State Banquet, Paris, 5 April 2004. https://www.royal.uk/centenary-entente-cordiale-state-banquet-paris-5-april-2004
16. Michael Howard, *The Franco-Prussian War*, p. 40.
17. McCullough, *How the First World War Began*, pp. 328-9.
18. Peter Hof, *The Two Edwards*, pp. 3-4.
19. Quigley, *The Anglo-American Establishment*, p. 30.
20. Iain Sharpe, 'Campbell-Bannerman and Asquith – An uneasy political partnership,' in *Journal of Liberal History*, Issue 61, Winter 2008-09.
21. Frederick Maurice, *Haldane 1856-1915*, p. 146.
22. John Wilson, *CB: A Life of Sir Henry Campbell-Bannerman*, pp. 426-429.
23. Ibid., p. 430.
24. John P. Cafferky, *Lord Milner's Second War*, p. 91.
25. *The Times*, London, 7 November 1905.
26. T.P. O'Connor, *Sir Henry Campbell-Bannerman*, pp. 125-6.
27. Quoted by Dr Pat Walsh in, *Roger Casement on Sir Edward Grey*. https://drpatwalsh.com/2017/08/15/roger-casement-on-sir-edward-grey/
28. Quigley, *Tragedy & Hope*, p. 133.
29. Quigley, *Anglo-American Establishment*, p. 25.
30. Ibid.
31. Docherty & Macgregor, *Hidden History*, p. 72.
32. John P. Cafferky, *Lord Milner's Second War*, p. 104.
33. Richard Haldane, *Before the War*, pp. 45-46.
34. Adam Hochschild, *King Leopold's Ghost*, pp. 111-112.
35. Jerome L. Sternstein, *King Leopold II, Senator Nelson W. Aldrich and the Strange Beginnings of American Economic penetration of The Congo*, African Historical Studies, Vol 2, No 2, (1969) Boston University. https://www.jstor.org/stable/216355
36. G. Docherty & J. Macgregor, *Hidden History*, pp. 106-107.
37. Francis Neilson, *How Diplomats Make War*, pp. 179-180.
38. Docherty & Macgregor, *Hidden History*, p. 325.
39. Alexander Fuehr, *The Neutrality of Belgium*, chapter IV, https://net.lib.byu.edu/~rdh7/wwi/comment/belgneut/BelgTC.htm#TC
40. J.S. Ewart, *The Roots and Causes of the War (1914-1918), Vol.1*, p. 163.
41. Takahashi Korekiyo, *The Rothschilds and the Russo-Japanese War, 1904-06*, pp. 20-21.
42. Docherty & Macgregor, *Hidden History*, pp. 94-95.
43. G. P. Gooch, *Before the War, Studies in Diplomacy, vol I*, p. 291.
44. Ibid., p. 290.
45. Ibid., pp. 291-292.
46. J.A. Farrer, *England Under Edward VII*, p. 217.
47. Edgar Sanderson & Lewis Melville, *King Edward VII, His Life and Reign*, pp. 73-74.
48. Docherty and Macgregor, *Hidden History*, p. 95.
49. Rose Louise Greaves, *Some Aspects of the Anglo-Russian Convention and Its Working in Persia*, Bulletin of the School of Oriental and African Studies, University of London, Vol. 31, No. 1 (1968), pp. 69-91.

50. Hansard, House of Lords Debate, 06 February 1908 vol 183 cc999-1047.

51. J.A. Farrer, *England Under Edward VII*, p. 218.]

52. Niall Ferguson, *The Pity of War*, pp. 60-61.

53. Gooch, *Before The War*, p. 282.

54. Robert Zedlitz-Trützschler, *Twelve Years at the Imperial German Court*, p. 178.

55. Sanderson & Melville, *King Edward VII*, p. 74.

56. E.D. Morel, *Diplomacy Revealed*, pp. 73-74.

57. Ibid., pp. 75-76.

58. Hof, *The Two Edwards*, p. 51.

59. Sanderson & Melville, *King Edward VII*, p. 74.

60. Morel, *Diplomacy Revealed*, pp. 77-78.

61. Ibid., p. 77.

62. Ibid., pp. 79-80.

63. Hof, *The Two Edwards*, p. 75.

Chapter 5 – Britain – "Invaluable to the Cause of Human Liberty"

1. John Arbuthnot Fisher, *Memories and Records, vol. II*, pp. 134-5.

2. Gerry Docherty and Jim Macgregor, *Hidden History*, p. 258.

3. W. Morgan Shuster, *The Strangling of Persia*, https://dn790000.ca.archive.org/0/items/stranglingofper00shusuoft/stranglingofper00shusuoft.pdf

4. *Bathurst Times*, 28 December 1911, https://trove.nla.gov.au/newspaper/article/110019736?searchTerm=%E2%80%9Cmowed%20down%20every%20living%20creature%20in%20the%20streets

5. Geoff Simons, *Libya and the West. From Independence to Lockerbie*, p. 7.

6. Public Records Office, Grey Papers, FO 800/70, p. 198.

7. E. D Morel, *Diplomacy Revealed*, p. 185.

8. Francis Neilson, *The Makers of War*, p. 15.

9. A. J. A. Morris, *The Scaremongers: The Advocacy of War and Rearmament 1896-1914*, p. 286.

10. Docherty & Macgregor *Hidden History*, pp. 177-178.

11. J. S. Ewart, *The Roots and Causes of the Wars*, p. 841.

12. David Lloyd George, Mansion House Speech, 21 July 1911. https://net.lib.byu.edu/estu/wwi/1914m/llgeorge.html.bak

13. Joachim Remak, *The Origins of World War I*, p. 45.

14. Max Montgelas, *The Case for the Central Powers*, p. 44.

15. Geoffrey Barraclough, *From Agadir to Armageddon: Anatomy of a Crisis*: p. 68.

16. Sidney B. Fay, *The Origins of the World War, Vol I*, p. 289.

17. Meeting of the Committee of Imperial Defence 23 August,1911. http://www.dreadnoughtproject.org/tfs/index.php/114th_Meeting_of_the_Committee_of_Imperial_Defence.

18. Docherty and Macgregor, *Hidden History*, p. 181.

19. Wilfrid Scawen Blunt, *My Diaries, Vol II*, pp. 398-399.]

20. Blunt, *My Diaries:* https://archive.org/details/mydiaries0002unse/page/476/mode/2up

21. A. W. Dockter, 'The Influence of a Poet: Wilfrid S Blunt and the Churchills,' *Journal of Historical Biography* vol. 10 (Autumn 2011): 70-102.

22. Hansard, Volume 122, column 1155-1156 House of Lords Debate, 21 May, 1942.

23. Serge Sazonov, *Fateful Years, 1909-1916*, pp. 57-61.

24. Friedrich Stieve, *Isvolsky and the World War*, pp. 89-90.

25. John S. Ewart, *The Roots and Causes of the War (1914-18)*. Vol 2, p. 919.

26. Niall Ferguson, *The Pity of War*, p. 146.

27. Ewart, *The Roots and Causes of the Wars, vol II*, pp. 945-6.

28. Ferguson, *Pity of War*, p 61.

29. Docherty & Macgregor, *Hidden History*, pp. 226-7.
30. Sean McMeekin, *July 1914, Countdown to War*, p. 66.
31. Joseph Ward Swain, *Beginning the Twentieth Century*, p. 95.
32. Edward E. McCullough, *How the First World War Began*, p. 147.
33. Swain, *Beginning the Twentieth Century*, p. 95.
34. H. E. Barnes, *The Genesis of the World War*, pp. 387-8.
35. Friedrich Stieve, *Isvolsky and the World War*, p. 117.
36. Docherty & Macgregor, *Hidden History*, pp. 203-4.
37. Barnes, *The Genesis of the World War*, pp. 122-3.
38. Ibid., p. 117.
39. Docherty & Macgregor, *Hidden History*, pp. 206-7.
40. Troy R.E. Paddock, *Contesting the Origins of the First World War*, p. 115.
41. Fay, *The Origins of the World War*, vol I. pp. 329-331.
42. Dominic Lieven, *Towards the Flame, Empire, War and the End of Tsarist Russia*, pp. 238-9.
43. Laurence Lafore, *The Long Fuse, An Interpretation of the Origins of World War I*, pp. 174-5.
44. John F.V. Keiger, *France and the Origins of the First World War*, p. 67.
45. H. E. Barnes, *The Genesis of the World War*, pp. 124-5.
46. Keiger, *France and the Origins of the First World War*, p. 138.
47. Herbert Feis, *Europe: The World's Banker, 1870-1914*, p. 211.
48. Frederick Bausman, *Let France Explain*, p.161.
49. Morel, *Diplomacy Revealed*, p. 275.
50. Keiger, *France and the Origins*, p. 139.
51. Barnes, *The Genesis of the World War*, pp. 128-9.
52. L.C.F. Turner, *Origins of the First World War*, p. 29.
53. Friedrich Stieve, *Isvolsky and the World War*, p. 60.

Chapter 6 – An Avenue of Assassins
1. Christopher Clark, *The Sleepwalkers*, p.106.
2. Ibid., pp.106-7.
3. Ruth Henig, *The Origins of the First World War*, p. 23.
4. David Stevenson, *1914-1918*, p. 11.
5. S. B. Fay, *The Origins of the World War*, Vol II, p.21.
6. Ibid., p.22.
7. H. E. Barnes, *The Genesis of the World War*, p. 183.
8. Gerry Docherty and Jim Macgregor, *Hidden History*, p. 242.
9. Eugenii Nicolaevich Shelking, *The Game of Diplomacy*, p.192.
10. Barnes, *The Genesis of the World War*, p. 157.
11. Edith Durham, *Twenty Years of Balkan Tangle*, Chapter 19, https://www.gutenberg.org/cache/epub/19669/pg19669.txt
12. David James Smith, *One Morning in Sarajevo*, p. 84.
13. Barnes, *The Genesis of the World War*, pp. 156-7.
14. Durham, *Twenty Years of Balkan Tangle*, Chapter 16.
15. Vreme, No. 1381 22 July 2017, https://www-vreme-com.translate.goog/vreme/covek-od-koga-su-strepeli-vladari/?_x_tr_sl=sr&_x_tr_tl=en&_x_tr_hl=en&_x_tr_pto=sc
16. Smith, *One Morning in Sarajevo*, p. 87.
17. Durham, *Twenty Years of Balkan Tangle*, Chapter 16.
18. Max Montgelas, *The Case for the Central Powers*, p. 114.
19. Fay, *Origins of the World War*, vol II, p. 45.
20. Barnes, *Genesis of the World War*, p. 210.
21. Ibid., p. 169.

22. Ibid., p. 170.

23. Fay, *Genesis of the World war, vol. II*, pp. 95-6.

24. Smith, *One Morning in Sarajevo*, p. 50.

25. James Lyon, *Serbia and the Balkan Front, 1914, The Outbreak of the Great War*, pp. 57-58.

26. Fay, *Genesis of the World War, vol II*. p. 10.

27. Ibid., p. 56.

28. John S. Ewart, *The Roots and Causes of the Wars*, Vol. II, p. 1013.

29. A statement from the Serbian group Narodna Odbrana (1911) https://alphahistory.com/worldwarI/Narodna-odbrana-1911/

30. Fay, *Genesis of the World War, vol. II*, footnote, p. 66.

31. Ibid., p. 101.

32. Hew Strachan, *The First World War*, p. 9.

33. R.W. Seton-Watson, *Sarajevo*, p. 78.

34. Lyon, *Serbia and the Balkan Front*, p. 63.

35. Luigi Albertini, *Origins of the War of 1914, vol. II*, pp. 282-3.

36. Fay, *Origins of the World War*, pp. 61-2.

37. Ibid., pp. 63.

38. Smith, *One Morning in Sarajevo*, pp. 166-7.

39. Fay, *The Origins of the World War, Vol II*, p. 45.

40. Smith, *One Morning in Sarajevo*, p. 214.

41. Barnes, *The Genesis of the World War*, pp. 169-70.

42. Fay, *Origins of the World War, vol. II*, p. 65.

43. Ibid., p. 65-6.

44. Ibid., p. 66.

45. Barnes, *The Genesis of the World War*, p. 222.

46. Laurence Lafore, *The Long Fuse*, p. 209.

47. Max Montgelas, *The Case for the Central Powers*, p. 115.

48. Barnes, *The Genesis of the World War*, p. 222.

49. Hansard, House of Commons Debate, 30 June 1914, vol. 64, cc214-6.

50. Douglas Newton, *The Darkest Days, The Truth Behind Britain's Rush to War, 1914*, pp. 16-17.

51. Ewart, *The Roots and Causes of the Wars*, vol. II, p. 1018.

52. Ibid.

53. Docherty & Macgregor, *Hidden History*, p. 257.

54. Ewart, *The Roots and Causes of the Wars, vol. II*, p. 1022.

55. Ibid., pp. 1020-1.

56. Fay, *The Origins of the World War, vol II*, p. 332.

57. Irene Cooper Willis, *England's Holy War*, p. 59.

58. Barnes, *In Quest of Truth and Justice*, p. 47.

Chapter 7 – The July Crisis

1. Franz Joseph to Kaiser Wilhelm II, 2 July 1914, cited by Christopher Clark, *The Sleepwalkers*, p. 401.

2. Christopher Clark, *The Sleepwalkers*, p. 401.

3. Sidney B Fay, *The Origins of the World War, Vol. II*, pp. 208-209.

4. David E. Kaiser, *Germany and the Origins of the First World War*, The Journal of Modern History, Vol. 55 No. 3 (September 1983) p. 466.

5. Max Montgelas, *The Case for the Central Powers*, p. 118.

6. Ibid.

7. A.J P. Taylor, *How Wars Begin*, p. 106.

8. Montgelas, *Case for the Central Powers*, pp. 118-9.

9. Sean McMeekin, *July 1914*, p. 105.

10. Fay, *The Origins of the World War, Vol. II.* p. 198.

11. Samuel R Williamson, 'The Origins of World War I' in the *Journal of Interdisciplinary History,* Vol. 18, No. 4, The Origin and Prevention of Major Wars (Spring, 1988), pp. 795-818.]

12. Sean McMeekin, *The Russian Origins of the First World War,* p. 44.

13. Pierre Renouvin, *La Crise Européenne et la Grande Guerre,* p. 113.

14. Gerry Docherty and Jim Macgregor, *Hidden History,* p. 287.

15. John S. Ewart, *The Roots and Cause of the Wars, Vol I.* p. 569.

16. Peter Hof, *The Two Edwards,* p. 110.

17. Edward E. McCullough, *How the First World War Began,* p. 277.

18. G. Lowes Dickinson, *The International Anarchy,* p. 477.

19. Annika Mombauer, *The Origins of the First World War,* p. 13.

20. Barnes, *The Genesis of the World War,* p. 222.

21. Hansard, House of Commons Debate, 30 June 1914, vol.64, cc214-6.

22. Douglas Newton, *The Darkest Days, The Truth Behind Britain's Rush to War, 1914,* pp. 16-17.

23. Laurence Lafore, *The Long Fuse,* p. 216.

24. McMeekin, *The Russian Origins of the First World War,* p. 46.

25. Barnes, *The Genesis of the World War,* pp. 179-180.

26. Ewart, *The Roots and Causes of the Wars, vol. II.* p. 1064.

27. Christopher Clark, *The Sleepwalkers,* pp. 425-6.

28. Edward Mandell House, *The Intimate Papers of Colonel House,* p. 272.

29. Barnes, *The Genesis of the World War,* p. 150.

30. F. von Wiesner Report, *Red Book,* Vol. I, pp. 653-4.

31. C. Oman, *The Outbreak of the War of 1914-1918,* p. 9.

32. R.W. Seton-Watson, *Sarajevo,* p. 289.

33. Ibid., pp. 217-8.

34. Carroll Quigley, *The Anglo-American Establishment,* p. 312.

35. McMeekin, *The Russian Origins of the War,* p. 44.

36. Niall Ferguson, *The Pity of War,* pp. 28-30.

37. Max Hastings, *Catastrophe,* p. 49.

38. J. F. V. Keiger, *Raymond Poincaré,* p. 132.

39. Fay, *The Origins of the World War, Vol. II,* pp. 277-8.

40. Max Hastings, *Catastrophe,* pp. 49-50.

41. Docherty and Macgregor, *Hidden History,* pp. 265-266.

42. McMeekin, *The Russian Origins of the First World War,* p. 53.

43. Hew Strachan, *The First World War,* p. 16.

44. Keiger, *Raymond Poincaré,* p. 163.

45. Ibid., p.165.

46. Marc Trachtenberg, *French Foreign Policy in the July Crisis, 1914.* https://issforum.org/ISSF/PDF/3-Trachtenberg.pdf

47. Ibid.

48. McMeekin, *The Russian Origins of the First World War,* p. 45.

49. Ibid., p. 52.

50. Ibid., p. 44.

51. Douglas Newton, *The Darkest Days, The Truth Behind Britain's Rush to War, 1914.* p. xxi.

52. Robert L. Owen, *The Russian Imperial Conspiracy 1892-1914,* pp. 24-25.

53. Ibid., pp. 1-3.

54. Ibid.

55. Ibid., p. 69.

56. Fay, *The Origins of the World War, Vol. II,* p. 282.

57. Ibid., p. 283.

58. Emil Ludwig, *July 1914*, p. 77.

59. Barbara Tuchman, *The Guns of August*, p.73.

60. Ibid.

61. Troy R. E. Paddock, *Contesting the Origins of the First World War*, p. 31.

62. Stefan Schmidt, *Frankreichs Aussenpolitik in der Julikrise 1914*, p. 95.

63. Douglas Newton, *The Darkest Days*, p. 29.

64. J. F. V. Keiger, *Raymond Poincaré*, p. 167.

65. Ibid., pp. 170-171.

66. William Jannen Jr., *The Lions of July*, p. 68.

67. La Grande Guerre: French Prints of World War One, https://www.fitzmuseum. cam.ac.uk/index.php/research/online-resources/la-grande-guerre-french-prints-of-world-war-one

68. McMeekin, *The Russian Origins of the First World War*, p. 44.

69. Barnes, *The Genesis of the World War*, p. 328.

70. Buchanan to Grey, 24 July, British Documents 101, in Geiss, *July 1914*, p. 196.

71. David Stevenson, 1914-1918, *The History of the First World War*, p. 29.

72. Niall Ferguson, *The Pity of War*, p. 147.

73. Max Hastings, *Catastrophe*, pp. 51-53.

74. Fay, *The Origins of the World War*, Vol II. p. 286.

75. Ibid., pp. 338-9.

76. Ibid.

77. Ibid., p. 340.

78. Barnes, *The Genesis of the World War*, pp. 201-202.

79. Docherty & Macgregor, *Hidden History*, p. 272.

80. Ewart, *The Roots and Causes of the Wars*, Vol. II, p. 1037.

81. Stone, *World War One, A Short History*, pp. 20-21.

82. David Stevenson, *1914-1918*, p. 16.

83. McMeekin, *The Russian Origins of the First World War*, p. 44.

84. Quoted in, Francis J. Reynolds, Allen L. Churchill & Francis T. Miller, *The Story of the Great War, Vol. I.*

85. Docherty & Macgregor, *Hidden History*, p. 277.

86. Ferguson, *The Pity of War*, p. 156.

87. Docherty & Macgregor, *Hidden History*, p. 274.

88. McCullough, *How the First World War Began*, p. 279.

89. Marc Trachtenberg, *The Meaning of Mobilization in 1914*, International Security, Vol. 15, No. 3, pp. 120-22.

Chapter 8 – Mobilisation, "the most decisive act of war"

1. Imanuel Geiss, *July 1914: The Outbreak of the First World War, p. 190.*

2. Ibid., p. 186.

3. H. E. Barnes, *The Genesis of The War*, p. 324.

4. Docherty & Macgregor, *Hidden History*, pp. 280-1.

5. Stephen J. Cimbala, *Military Persuasion; Deterrence and Provocation in Crisis and War*, p. 58.

6. Gerry Docherty & Jim Macgregor, *Hidden History*, p. 282.

7. Sean McMeekin, *The Russian Origins of the First World War*, p. 62.

8. Sidney B Fay, *The Origins of the World War*, p. 439f.

9. Sean McMeekin, *The Russian Origins of the First World War*, pp. 60-61.

10. Francis Neilson, *How Diplomats Make War*, p. 258.

11. Max Hastings, *Catastrophe*, p. 70.

12. Wilson, H.W. & Hammerton, J.A. (eds) *Illustrated History of the Great War, vol. 1*, p. 29.

13. Douglas Newton, *The Darkest Days, Britain's Rush to War, 1914*, pp. 50-53.

14. Peter Hof, *The Two Edwards*, p. 131.

15. Patrick J. Buchanan, *Churchill, Hitler and the Unnecessary War*, p. 43.

16. Fay, *The Origins of the World War, vol II*, p. 424.

17. Helmuth von Moltke, cited by Thomas Meyer, *Light for the new Millennium*, pp. 80-82.

18. Op cit. p.83.

19. Fay, *The Origins of the World War, Vol, 2*, pp. 425-6.

20. Wolfgang Effenberger, *Europas Verhängnis 14/18: Die Herren des Geldes greifen zur Weltmacht*, p. 237.

21. Docherty and Macgregor, *Hidden History*, p. 278.

22. H. E. Barnes, *The Genesis of the World War*, pp. 354-356.

23. George F. Kennan, *The Fateful Alliance*, p. 161.

24. Ibid., p. 250.

25. Ibid., p. 251.

26. Ibid.

27. Ibid., p. 149.

28. Ibid., pp. 153-154.

29. Fay, *The Origins of the World War*, vol. II, pp. 524-525.

30. Douglas Newton, *The Darkest Days, The Truth Behind Britain's Rush to War*, p. 107.

31. Cited in Neilson, *How Diplomats Make War*, p. 256.

32. Ibid.

33. Lichnowsky to Jagow, London, 29 July 1914, DD349, cited in Geiss, *July 1914*, p. 256.

34. Docherty and Macgregor, *Hidden History*, p. 291.

35. Christopher Clark, *The Sleepwalkers*, pp. 509-510.

36. Effenberger, *Europas Verhängnis 14/18: Die Herren des Geldes greifen zur Weltmacht*, p. 195.

37. Docherty and Macgregor, *Hidden History*, p. 297.

38. Hermann Lutz, *Lord Grey and the World War*, p. 241.

39. *Manchester Guardian*, 30 July 1914.

40. *Daily News*, 1 August 1914.

41. Fay, *The Origins of the World War*, vol. II, pp. 374-375.

42. Docherty and Macgregor, *Hidden History*, p. 285.

43. Barnes, *The Genesis of the World War*, p. 260.

44. *The Times*, July 30, 1914.

45. J. S. Ewart, *The Roots and Causes of the Wars, vol II*, p. 1082.

46. Wilhelm II to Pourtalès. Cited in Barnes, *The Genesis of the World War*, pp. 267-269.

47. J.M.K. Vyvyan, New Cambridge Modern History, XII, *The Era of Violence 1898-1945* (Cambridge, 1960), 354.

48. Docherty and Macgregor, *Hidden History*, p. 296.

49. Vyvyan, New Cambridge Modern History, XII, *The Era of Violence 1898-1945* (Cambridge, 1960), 354.

50. Fay, *The Origins of the World War*, p. 523.

51. John Hance, *Chaos, Confusion, and Political Ignorance*, p. 274.

52. Isvolsky to Sazonov, cited in Fay, *The Origins*, p. 531.

53. Fay, *The Origins of the World War*, vol. 11, p. 533.

54. Ibid., pp. 527-528.

55. Docherty and Macgregor, *Hidden History*, p. 321.

56. Ibid., p 320.

57. Douglas Newton, *The Darkest Days, The Truth Behind Britain's Rush to War, 1914*, dust jacket. 58 K.M. Wilson, 'The British Cabinet's Decision for War, 2 August 1914,'

British Journal of International Studies, Vol. I, No. 2 (Jul., 1975), pp. 148-159.

59. Newton, *Darkest Days*, pp. 286-287.

60. Richard M. Hamilton and Holger F. Herwig, *Decisions for War*, p. 140.

61. Ibid., pp. 140-141.]

62. Wilson, 'The British Cabinet's Decision for War, 2 August 1914,' *British Journal of International Studies, Vol. I, No. 2* (Jul., 1975), pp. 148-159.

63. Hamilton & Herwig, *Decisions for War*, p. 141.

64. E. D. Morel, *Truth and the War*, p. 297.

65. Douglas Newton, *The Darkest Days*, p. 180.

66. Wilson, 'The British Cabinet's Decision for War, 2 August 1914,' British *Journal of International Studies, Vol. 1, No. 2* (Jul., 1975), pp. 148-159.

67. Newton, *Darkest Days*, pp. 200-201.

68. Richard Haldane, *Before the War*, pp. 45-46.

69. Sir Edward Grey's speech, 3 August 1914, Hansard, https://api.parliament.uk/historic-hansard/commons/1914/aug/03/statement-by-sir-edward-grey

70. Ibid.

71. Ibid.

72. Ibid.

73. Hansard, 3 August 1914. https://hansard.parliament.uk/Commons/1914-08-03/debates/25b671de-0c0a-47ff-9508-e5bf08879d98/WarInEurope

74. Docherty and Macgregor, *Hidden History*, p. 342.

75. Newton, *The Darkest Days*, p. 271.

76. *The Guardian*, 5 August 1914, 'Britain Declares War on Germany.'

Chapter 9 – The 'Schlieffen Plan'

1. Niall Ferguson, *The Pity of War*, pp. 92-93.

2. Sun Tzu, *The Art of War*.

3. George Malcolm Thomson, *The 12 Days, 24 July to 4 August 1914*, p. 192.

4. E. McCullough, *How the First World War Began*, p. 252.

5. L.C.F. Turner, *The Origins of the World War*, p. 29.

6. Christopher Clark, *The Sleepwalkers*, p. 331.

7. Ibid., p. 332.

8. Thomas Meyer, *Light for the New Millenium*, p. 89.

9. J.M. Winter, *The Experience of World War I*, pp. 74-75.

10. Thomson, *The 12 Days*, p. 195.

11. A.J.P. Taylor, *War by Timetable*, p. 121.

12. Annika Mombauer, *The Origins of the First World War*, pp. 199-200.

13. Holger H. Herwig, *The Marne 1914*, p. 30.

14. Gary Sheffield, *Forgotten Victory*, p. 32.

15. Ibid., p. 33.

16. Terence Zuber, *The Schlieffen Plan Debate 1999-2014*, https://terencezuber.com/schlieffendebate.php

17. Ibid.

18. Terence Zuber articles: https://terencezuber.com/

19. Inventing the Schlieffen Plan, https://global.oup.com/academic/product/inventing-the-schlieffen-plan-9780198718055?cc=gb&lang=en&#

20. Troy R.E. Paddock, *Contesting the Origins of the First World War, An Historiographical Argument*, pp. 70-71.

21. Thomas Fleming, *The Illusion of Victory, America in World War I*, pp. 51-52.

22. H. W. Wilson, and J. A. Hammerton, *The Great War, The Standard History of the All-Europe Conflict, Vol. I.* p. 148.

23. Fleming, *The Illusion of Victory*, p. 52.

24. Ibid.

25. Carroll Quigley, *The Anglo-American Establishment*, p. 313.

26. Ibid.

27. Ibid., p. 312.

28. Ibid., p. 24.

29. Ibid., pp. 68-69.

30. Bryce Report. http://www.gwpda.org/wwiwww/BryceReport/bryce_r.html

31. Trevor Wilson, *The Myriad Faces of War*.

32. Fleming, *The Illusion of Victory*, p. 53-54.

33. Ferguson, *The Pity of War*, p. 232.

34. Jim Macgregor and Gerry Docherty, *Prolonging the Agony*, p. 48.

35. H. E, Barnes, *In Quest of Truth and Justice, De-Bunking the War Guilt Myth*, pp. 94-95.

36. Joseph Ward Swain, *Beginning the Twentieth Century*, pp. 446-447.

37. Ferguson, *The Pity of War*, p. 232.

38. Trevor Wilson, *Lord Bryce's Investigation into Alleged German Atrocities in Belgium, 1914-15,* Journal of Contemporary History, Vol. 14 (1979), 369-383.

39. Ibid.

40. Ibid.

41. Quigley, *The Anglo-American Establishment*, p. 313.

42. Carroll Quigley, *Tragedy & Hope*, pp. 263-264.

43. Arthur Ponsonby, *Falsehood in Wartime, Propaganda Lies of the First World War*, Foreword.

44. Trevor Wilson, *Lord Bryce's Investigation into Alleged German Atrocities in Belgium, 1914-15,* Journal of Contemporary History, Vol. 14 (1979), 369-383.

45. *Daily Mail*, September 22, 1914.

46. Albert Shaw Clifton, *The Salvation Army's Actions and Attitudes in Wartime: 1899-1945*, pp. 299- 231.

47. *The Times*, 12 October 1914.

48. Quigley, *The Anglo-American Establishment*, p. 25.

49. *The Times*, 10 February 1915

50. Arthur Winnington-Ingram, *The Potter and the Clay*, Chapter IV (42) https://www.gutenberg.org/files/44291/44291-h/44291-h.htm]

Chapter 10 – Some Disturbing Truths

1. Adam Hochschild, *To End All Wars*, p. 246.

2. Denis Winter, *Death's Men, The Soldiers of the Great War*, p. 132.

3. Hochschild, *To End All Wars,* p. 137.

4. John Moody, *The Masters of Capital: A Chronicle of Wall Street*, pp. 164-165.

5. Ibid., pp. 166-167.

6. Daniel M. Smith, *Lansing and the Formation of American neutrality Policies 1914-1915*, Historical Review, vol.43 No 1, p. 69.

7. Willian Engdahl, *A Century of War*, p. 52.

8. Walter Millis, *Road to War, America 1914-1917*, p. 98.

9. J. Kenworthy and G. Young, *Freedom of the Seas*, p. 72.

10. Colin Simpson, *Lusitania*, p. 36.

11. John V. Denson, *A Century of War, Lincoln, Wilson, and Roosevelt*, p.135.

12. Eugene Davidson, *The Making of Adolf Hitler*, p. 89.

13. Eugene G. Windchy, *Twelve American Wars, Nine of Them Avoidable*, p. 339.

14. Ibid., pp. 339-340.

15. Mitch Peeke, *The Lusitania Story – A Struggle for the Truth*. https://firstworldwar-hiddenhistory.wordpress.com/2015/05/02/guest-blog-mitch-peeke-the-lusitania-story-a-struggle-for-the-truth/

16. Ibid.

17. Richard B Spence, *Secret Agent 666, Aleister Crowley, British Intelligence and the Occult*, p. 18.

18. Carroll Quigley, *The Anglo-American Establishment*, p. 16 et passim.

19. Tobias Churton, *Aleister Crowley in America*, p. 83.

20. Ibid., p. 176.

21. Joseph Kenworthy and George Young, *Freedom of the Seas*, pp. 79-80. https://archive.org/details/freedomofscas00strauoft/page/80/mode/2up

22. Spence, *Secret Agent 666*, p. 13.

23. Ibid., p. 83.

24. Ibid.

25. Ibid., p. 8.

26. Churton, *Crowley in America*, p. 279.

27. Library of Congress, https://blogs.loc.gov/law/2015/05/the-sinking-of-the-lusitania/

28. *The Washington Times*, 1 May 1915.

29. Peeke, Jones & Walsh-Johnson, *The Lusitania Story*, p. 45.

30. Burton J. Hendrick, *The Life and Letters of Walter Page*, vol. 1. p. 436.

31. Edward Mandell House and Charles Seymour, *The Intimate Papers of Colonel House*, vol.1. p. 432.

32. The *Lusitania* Resource, Mr. William Thomas Turner, Captain, Royal Naval Reserve, https://www.rmslusitania.info/people/deck/william-turner/

33. Windchy, *Twelve American Wars*, p. 341.

34. Peeke, *The Lusitania Story*, Centenary Edition, p. 57.

35. Ibid., p. 63.

36. Patrick Beesly, *Room 40*, pp. 120-122.

37. Ibid., p. 118.

38. Ibid., pp. 120-122.

39. Ibid., p. 102.

40. Peeke, *The Lusitania Story*, p 180.

41. Simpson, *Lusitania*, (Merseyside Edition) p. 139.

42. Ibid., p. 146.

43. Mitch Peeke, *Disaster, Rescue, and Recovery*. www.lusitania.net/disaster.htm

44. Simpson, *Lusitania*, p. 149.

45. Peeke, *The Lusitania Story*, pp. 73-74.

46. Beesly, *Room 40*, p. 119.

47. Ibid., pp. 108-109.

48. Peeke et al, *The Lusitania Story*, p. 84.

49. Colin Simpson, *Lusitania*, p. 180.

50. Ibid., p. 182.

51. Ibid., pp.198-199.

52. Beesly, *Room 40*, p. 117.

53. Peeke, *Lusitania Centenary edition*, p. 86.

54. Beesly, *Room 40*, p. 114.

55. The *Lusitania* Resource, https://www.rmslusitania.info/primary-docs/mersey-report/the-ship/#cargo

56. Ibid, https://www.rmslusitania.info/primary-docs/mersey-report/torpedoing/

57. Titanic Inquiry Project, https://www.titanicinquiry.org/Lusitania/Report/Repnav.

58. Winston Churchill, *The World Crisis, 1915*, pp. 334-335.

59. Ibid.

60. The *Lusitania* Resource, https://www.rmslusitania.info/people/deck/william-turner/#shadow

Chapter 11 – War is a Racket

1. Ian Gazeley and Andrew Newell, *The First World War and working-class food consumption in Britain*, European Review of economic history, Volume 17, Issue 1.

2. C. P. Vincent, *The Politics of Hunger*.

3. G. J. Meyer, *A World Undone, The Story of the Great War*.

4. Matthias Blum. 'War, food rationing, and socioeconomic inequality in Germany during the First World War,' in Economic History Review, 66, 4 (2013), pp. 1063 -1083.

5. G. J. Meyer, *A World Undone, The Story of the Great War*, p. 415.

6. National Institute of Health, *Military Recommended Dietary Allowances*, https://www.ncbi.nlm.nih.gov/books/NBK209042/

7. National Army Museum, *An Army Marches on its Stomach*, https://www.nam.ac.uk/explore/army-marches-its-stomach#:~:text=By%20the%20First%20World%20War,-by%20copious%20amounts%20of%20tea.

8. Adam Hochschild, *To End All Wars*, p. 161.

9. Ibid.

10. J. Macgregor and G. Docherty, British Naval Blockade, https://firstworldwarhiddenhistory.wordpress.com//?s=Blockade&search=Go

11. A.C. Bell, *A History of the Blockade of Germany*, p. 31.

12. William Philpott, *Attrition, Fighting the First World War*, p. 54.

13. Macgregor & Docherty, *Prolonging the Agony*, p. 79.

14. G. F. Bowles, *The Strength of England*, p. 173.

15. Arthur J. Marder, *From Dreadnought to Scapa Flow*, Vol. II, pp. 374-375.

16. Montague Consett, *The Triumph of Unarmed Forces*, p. vii.

17. Bowles, *The Strength of England*, p. 173.

18. Macgregor and Docherty, British Naval Blockade https://firstworldwarhiddenhistory.wordpress.com//?s=Blockade&search=Go

19. Bowles, *The Strength of England*, p. 173.

20. E. Keble Chatterton, *The Big Blockade*, pp. 166-167.

21. Archibald Bell, *A History of the Blockade*. http://www.wintersonnenwende.com/scriptorium/english/archives/blockade/bgy15.html

22. Macgregor and Docherty, British Naval Blockade, https://firstworldwarhiddenhistory.wordpress.com//?s=Blockade&search=Go]

23. M.W.P. Consett, *The Triumph of Unarmed Forces*, p. 118.

24. Ibid., p. xiii.

25. Ibid., p. 80.

26. Ibid.

27. Ibid., p. 201.

28. Ibid., p. 141.

29. Ibid., p. 98.

30. Macgregor and Docherty, https://firstworldwarhiddenhistory.wordpress.com//?s=Blockade&search=Go

31. Winston Churchill, *The World Crisis, 1915*, p, 295.

32. Clarence K.J. Streit, *Where Iron is, there is the Fatherland*, p. 2.

33. Fernand Engerand, *La Bataille de la Frontiere, Briey*, p. 7.

34. Ibid., pp. 1-2.

35. Streit, *Where Iron is, there is the Fatherland*, p. 46.

36. Smedley Darlington Butler, *War is a Racket*, page 1.

37. George H. Nash, *An American Epic, Herbert Hoover and Belgian Relief in World War I*, Prologue Magazine, Spring 1989, Vol. 21, No. 1.

38. Belgium – The National Archives, https://www.nationalarchives.gov.uk/first-world-war/a-global-view/europe/belgium/#:~:text=Overview,population%20of%20about%207.5%20million.

39. *The Brussels Times*, December 17, 2018. 'How Belgians became refugees during the

First World War'. https://www.brusselstimes.com/52562/how-belgians-became-refu-gees-during-the-first-world-war

40. International Encylopedia of the First World War, https://encyclope-dia.1914-1918-online.net/article/refugees_france#:~:text=During%20World%20War%20I%2C%20about,partially%20or%20wholly%20invaded%20departments.

41. Louis Delvaux, *Annals of the American Academy of Political and Social Science, vol. 247, Belgium in Transition (September 1946)* p. 144.

42. *Rapport sur l'activite du Bureau Federal des Co-operatives Intercommunales de Ravitail-lement*, in General Report on the functioning and operations of the Comité National de Secours et Alimentation – Quatrième Parte, p. 267.

43. Macgregor and Docherty, The Commission for Relief in Belgium, https://first-worldwarhiddenhistory.wordpress.com/2015/08/26/the-commission-for-relief-in-belgium-4-a-very-belgian-solution/

44. Walter W. Ligget, *The Rise of Herbert Hoover*, p. 223.

45. John Hamill, *The Strange Case of Mr Hoover Under Two Flags*, pp. 150-160.

46. Macgregor and Docherty, The Commission for Relief in Belgium, https://first-worldwarhiddenhistory.wordpress.com//?s=Belgian+relief&search=Go

47. Carroll Quigley, *The Anglo-American Establishment*, p. 35.

48. Tracy Barrett Kittredge, *The History of the Commission for Relief in Belgium 1914-1917*, Primary Source Edition, p. 90.

49. Cited by Edwin Morse, *The Vanguard of American Volunteers in the Fighting Lines and In Humanitarian Service, Part V.*

50. http://www.gwpda.org/wwiwww/AmerVolunteers/Morse5.htm

51. Macgregor & Docherty, https://firstworldwarhiddenhistory.wordpress.com/2015/09/18/commission-for-relief-in-belgium-10-circulating-lies-deny-ing-truth/

52. Michael Amara et Hubert Roland, *Gouverner En Belgique Occupée*, p. 214.

53. Ibid., p. 344.

54. Ibid., p. 298.

55. Macgregor and Docherty, https://firstworldwarhiddenhistory.wordpress.com/2015/09/18/commission-for-relief-in-belgium-10-circulating-lies-deny-ing-truth/

56. George H. Nash, *Herbert Hoover*, p. 176.

57. William Engdahl, *A Century of War, Anglo-American Oil Politics and the New World Order*, p. 25.

58. Alison Frank, 'The Petroleum War of 1910: Standard Oil, Austria, and the Limits of the Multinational Corporation,' in *The American Historical Review*, 114 (1) p. 41.

59. Alison Frank, *Oil Empire, Visions of Prosperity in Austrian Galicia*, pp. 171-173.

60. Daniel Yergin, *The Prize*, p. 163.

61. *The Times*, 11 December, 1916.

62. Daniel Yergin, *The Prize*, pp. 164-5.

63. David Stevenson, *With Our Backs to the Wall: Victory and Defeat in 1918*, p. 225.

64. Macgregor and Docherty, Hidden History, The Oil Story, https://firstworldwarhid-denhistory.wordpress.com//?s=romanian+oil&search=Go

65. Pierre de la Tramerye, *The World Struggle for Oil*, p. 103.

66. Macgregor and Docherty, Hidden History, The Oil Story, https://firstworldwarhid-denhistory.wordpress.com//?s=romanian+oil&search=Go

67. Adam Hochschild, *To End All Wars*, p. 162.

68. Alan Clark, *The Donkeys*, p. 11.

69. Hochschild, *To End All Wars*, p. 162.

70. Ibid., pp. 162-3.

71. Ibid., pp. 163-5.

72. Ibid., p. 167.
73. Denis Winter, *Haig's Command, A Reassessment*, p. 41.
74. Norman F. Dixon, *On the Psychology of Military Incompetence*, chapter six. https://www.jstor.org/stable/45346045
75. Ibid., pp. 249-250.
76. Ibid.
77. Gerard J, De Groot, *Douglas Haig, 1861-1928*, pp. 87-88.
78. Quigley, *The Anglo-American Establishment*, p. 313.
79. Winter, *Haig's Command, A Reassessment*, p. 32.
80. Ibid., p. 163.
81. Ibid., pp. 254-255.
82. Gary Sheffield, *Forgotten Victory*, p. 254.
83. *The Independent*, 29 June 2001. https://www.johndclare.net/wwi3_SheffieldandMosier_Review.htm
84. Hochschild, *To End All Wars*, pp. 291-292.
85. A. J. P. Taylor, *The First World War*, p. 84.

Chapter 12 – United States goes to war "for democracy"

1. U.S. National Archives, https://www.archives.gov/milestone-documents/address-to-congress-declaration-of-war-against-germany#:~:text=On%20April%202%2C%201917%2C%20President,States%20into%20World%20War%20I.
2. Ibid.
3. 1917 speech by Senator George Norris in opposition to American entry to the European War. https://www.khanacademy.org/humanities/world-history/euro-hist/american-entry-world-war-i/a/1917-speech-by-senator-george-norris-in-opposition-to-american-entry
4. La Follette speech on American entry. Wisconsin Historical Society, https://content.wisconsinhistory.org/digital/collection/tp/id/26837
5. Proceedings and Debates of the second session of the 65th Congress of the United States, http://www.christoph-heger.de/US-Kongre%DF-Gebet_1918.pdf
6. Lyle W. Dorset, *Billy Sunday*, p. 93.
7. William Engdahl, *A Century of War*, pp. 55-56.
8. Richard B. Spence, *Wall Street and the Russian Revolution*, p. 136.
9. Leon Trotsky, *My Life*, p. 271.
10. Richard B. Spence, *Wall Street and the Russian Revolution*, p.148.
11. Antony Sutton, *Wall Street and the Bolshevik Revolution*, p. 23.
12. Spence, *Wall Street and the Russian Revolution*, pp. 138-130.
13. Sutton, *Wall Street and the Bolshevik Revolution*, p. 189.
14. Ibid., p. 25.
15. Macgregor and Docherty, *Prolonging the Agony*, pp. 459-460.
16. Wilhelm II, *The Kaiser's Memoirs*, pp. 284-285. https://www.gutenberg.org/files/43522/43522-h/43522-h.htm
17. The November Revolution, 1918/1919, Historical Exhibition Presented by the German Bundestag,
18. https://www.bundestag.de/resource/blob/189772/8b9e17bd8d64e64c8e3a95fc2305e132/november_revolution-data.pdf
19. Wilhelm II, *Kaiser's Memoirs*, p. 289.
20. US National Archives, President Wilson's 14 Points (1918). National WW1 Museum and Memorial, Fourteen Points
21. Ibid.
22. UK National Archives, ADM 1/88542/290.
23. John Maynard Keynes, *The Economic Consequences of the Peace*, p. 50.
24. David Lloyd George, *War Memoirs Vol. 2*, Appendix, pp. 2045.

25. Suda Lorena Bane and Ralph Haswell Lutz, *Blockade of Germany*, p. 4.
26. Guido Preparata, *Conjuring Hitler*, p. 49.
27. Karl Liebknecht, *Militarism and Anti-Militarism*, https://www.marxists.org/archive/liebknecht-k/works/1907/militarism-antimilitarism/index.htm
28. Rosa Luxemburg, Stanford Encyclopaedia of Philosophy, 13 April 2022. https://plato.stanford.edu/entries/luxemburg/
29. Globalsecurity.Org, November Revolution, 1918/1919 https://www.globalsecurity.org/military/world/europe/de-revolution.htm
30. Food Situation in Central Europe, debated Thursday 6 March 1919. https://hansard.parliament.uk/lords/1919-03-06/debates/9e25c18c-5c73-49ea-b5cf-0ae8ae8a4138/FoodSituationInCentralEurope
31. *The Times*, 2 December 1918, p. 5.
32. Macgregor and Docherty, *Prolonging the Agony*, p. 485.
33. Herbert Hoover, *American Epic* 2, pp. 337-8.
   Chapter 13 – The Hall of Smoke and Mirrors
1. UK National Archives, https://www.nationalarchives.gov.uk/pathways/firstworldwar/aftermath/p_versailles.ht
2. Thomas Fleming, *The Illusion of Victory*, p. 248.
3. Ibid., pp. 173-4.
4. Quigley, *The Anglo-American Establishment*, p. 312.
5. Andrea Bosco and Alex May, 'The Round Table, the Empire/Commonwealth and British Foreign Policy,' London 1997.
6. David P. Billington, *Lothian. Philip Kerr and the Quest for World Order.* p. 62.
7. Henry Morgenthau, *Ambassador Morgenthau's Story*. Full text at http://www.gwpda.org/wwi-www/morgenthau/Morgen06.htm
8. S. B. Fay, *The Origins of the World War, Vol. II*, p. 169.
9. Ibid., pp. 172-3.
10. Fay, *The Origins of the World War, Vol. II*, pp. 175-6.
11. H.E. Barnes, *The Genesis of the World War*, p. 683.
12. *New York Times*, 27 October, 1915.
13. Sean McMeekin, *The Russian Origins of the First World War*, p. 100.
14. Fay, *The Origins of the World War*, p. 182.
15. Henry Morgenthau, *All in a Life-Time*, Chapter V. https://www.gutenberg.org/files/63538/63538-h/63538-h.htm#CHAPTER_IX
16. Stephen Birmingham, *Our Crowd*, pp. 8-9.
17. Henry Morgenthau, *All in a Life-Time*, Chapter IX.
18. Heath W Lowry, *The Story Behind Ambassador Morgenthau's Story*, https://www.tallarmeniantale.com/morgenthau-story.htm
19. Ibid.
20. Ata Atun, *Misleads in the Book Titled Ambassador Morgenthau's Story*, International Journal of Academic Research in Business and Social Sciences, June 2013, Vol. 3, No. 6.
21. Heath W. Lowry, *The Story Behind Ambassador Morgenthau's Story*.
22. Ibid.
23. Webster Griffin Tarpley & Anton Chaitkin, *George Bush, The Unauthorized Biography*, p. 55.
24. J. S. Ewart, *The Roots and Causes of the Wars, Vol. II.*, p. 1071.
25. Guido Preparata, *Conjuring Hitler*, p. 75.
26. Ibid.
27. The Versailles Treaty June 28, 1919 : Part VIII https://avalon.law.yale.edu/imt/partviii.asp
28. Share of annexed merchant ships in the Treaty of Versailles https://www.statista.com/statistics/1086814/treaty-versailles-share-annexed-merchant-ships/

29. Cited by Adam Hochschild, *To End All Wars: A Story of Loyalty and Rebellion*, p. 357.

30. Henry Wood Nevinson, *Saturday Review of Literature*, 20 November 1926.

31. Fay, *The Origins of the World War, vol II*, pp. 548-549.

32. Harry Elmer Barnes, *In Quest of Truth and Justice*, pp. 2-3.

33. Burton J. Hendrick, *The Life and Letters of Walter H. Page, vol I*, p. 402.

34. Ibid.

35. Ibid p. 398.

36. W. B Fest, *British War Aims and German Peace feelers During the First World War*, The Historical Journal, xv, 2 (1972) p. 285-286.

37. J. A. Hammerton, *A Popular History of the Great War, Vol IV, A Year of Attrition, 1917*, pp. 256-260.

38. D. G. Lowes Dickinson, *Documents and statements relating to peace proposals & war aims*, pp. 16-18.

39. Douglas Newton, *The forgotten and ignored German peace initiative of 1916*, https://johnmenadue.com/douglas-newton-the-forgotten-and-ignored-german-peace-initiative-of-1916/

40. Hansard, House of Commons Debate on War Policy, 20 February 1917 vol 90 cc1177-289. https://api.parliament.uk/historic-hansard/commons/1917/feb/20/war-policy

41. *Pope Benedict Issues a Peace Plan*: August 1, 1917. Light to the Nations II: The Making of the Modern World. https://www.catholictextbookproject.com/post/pope-benedict-issues-a-peace-plan-august-1-1917

42. J.A. Hammerton, *A Popular History of the War*, pp. 272-276.

43. Burton J. Hendrick, *The Life and Letters of Walter H. Page, vol I*, p. 400.

Chapter 14 – Truth – The First Casualty of War

1. Andreas Bracher, personal communication to Jim Macgregor.

2. David Hackett Fischer, *Historians' Fallacies*, p. 4.

3. Carroll Quigley, *The Anglo-American Establishment*, p. 197.

4. Docherty and Macgregor, *Hidden History*, p. 353.

5. Macgregor and Docherty, *Fake History*, https://firstworldwarhiddenhistory.wordpress.com//?s=hoover+Institution&search=Go

6. Ephraim Adams, *The Hoover War Collection at Stanford University, California; a report and an Analysis*, (1921), p. 7.

7. Whittaker Chambers, Hoover Library. http://whittakerchambers.org/articles/time-a/hoover-library/

8. *New York Times*, 5 February 1921.

9. Macgregor and Docherty, *Clearing up Before Clearing Out*, https://firstworldwarhiddenhistory.wordpress.com//?s=herbert+hoover&search=Go

10. Charles E Strickland, 'American Aid to Germany, 1919'. In *The Wisconsin Magazine of History*, Vol. 45, No 4 (1962), p. 263.

11. Cissie Dore Hill, *Collecting the Twentieth Century*, https://www.hoover.org/research/collecting-twentieth-century

12. Ibid.

13. Whittaker Chambers, Hoover Library, http://whittakerchambers.org/articles/time-a/hoover-library/

14. *New York Times*, 5 February 1921.

15. Macgregor and Docherty, *Burning Correspondence to Permanently Removing the Evidence*. https://firstworldwarhiddenhistory.wordpress.com/

16. Whittaker Chambers, Hoover Library.

17. Ibid.

18. *New York Times*, 5 February 1921.

19. Macgregor and Docherty, *From Burning Correspondence to Permanently Removing the*

Evidence. https://firstworldwarhiddenhistory.wordpress.com/

20. The Hoover Institution, https://histories.hoover.org/hoover-today/

21. Ian Cobain, *The History Thieves*, Location 2114 Kindle Edition.

22. 22 Ian Cobain, *The Guardian*, 18 October 2013.

23. *https://www.theguardian.com/politics/2013/oct/18/foreign-office-historic-files-secret-archive*

24. 23 Open letter copied to *the Guardian* newspaper published 22 January 2014.

25. https://www.theguardian.com/uk-news/2014/jan/22/vital-access-records-britains-colonial-past

26. Ibid.

27. 25 *The Guardian*, 18 October 2013.

28. https://www.theguardian.com/politics/2013/oct/18/foreign-office-historic-files-secret-archive

29. *The Guardian*, 13 January 2014. https://www.theguardian.com/politics/2014/jan/13/foreign-office-secret-files-national-archive-historians-legal-action

30. Ian Cobain, *The Guardian*, 6 October 2013. https://www.theguardian.com/uk-news/2013/oct/06/ministry-of-defence-files-archive

31. Macgregor and Docherty, *The Peer Review Process.* https://firstworldwarhiddenhistory.wordpress.com/

32. Nicholas D'Ombrain, *War Machinery and High Policy*, p. xiii.

33. Carroll Quigley. *Tragedy and Hope*, (Kindle Locations 52-56.

34. Andreas Bracher, personal communication to authors.

Chapter 15 – Sowing the Seeds of Chaos

1. Guido Preparata, *Conjuring Hitler*, pp. xvii-xviii.

2. Ibid.

3. Bradley F. Smith, *Adolf Hitler, His Family, Childhood & Youth*, p.18.

4. Milan Hauner, *Hitler, A Chronology of his Life and Times*, p. 1.

5. Volker Ullrich, *Hitler, A Biography, Vol. 1*, p15.

6. Ian Kershaw *Hitler, Hubris*, pp. 8-9.

7. Smith, *Adolf Hitler*, p. 35.

8. William L. Shirer, *The Rise and Fall of the Third Reich*, pp. 9-10.

9. Smith, *Adolf Hitler*, p. 31.

10. Ibid., pp. 51-52.

11. Kershaw, *Hitler, 1889-1936 Hubris*, pp. 11-12.

12. Brigitte Hamann, *Hitler's Vienna Years*, pp. 7-8.

13. Ibid., p. 10.

14. Ullrich, *Hitler, A Biography*, Vol. 1, p. 19.

15. Stephen H Roberts, *The House that Hitler Built*, p. 3.

16. Smith, *Adolf Hitler*, pp. 41-42.

17. Hauner, *Hitler, A Chronology of his Life and Times*, p. 2.

18. Adolf Hitler, *Mein Kampf* (72nd Jaico Impression 2016), pp.18-19.

19. Ibid., p. 22.

20. Hamann, *Hitler's Vienna Years*, p. 11.

21. Hitler, *Mein Kampf*, p. 28.

22. Smith, *Hitler*, pp. 92-93.]

23. Hauner, *Hitler, A Chronology of his Life*, p. 4.

24. Ibid., p. 5.

25. Hitler, *Mein Kampf*, p. 30.

26. Ibid., p. 29.

27. Hauner, *Hitler*, p. 88.

28. Smith, *Hitler*, p.107.

29. Ibid., p. 113.

30. Ibid., pp. 128-129.
31. Ibid., p. 130.
32. Ibid., p.138.
33. Joachim C. Fest, *Hitler*, p. 13.
34. Hitler, *Mein Kampf*, p. 67.
35. Smith, *Hitler*, p. 145.
36. Hitler, *Mein Kampf*, pp. 80-81.
37. Ibid., pp. 83-87.
38. Shirer, *The Rise and Fall of the Third Reich*, p. 18.
39. Ibid., p. 19.
40. Hamann, *Hitler's Vienna*, pp. 183-184.
41. Hitler, *Mein Kampf*, pp. 31-33.
42. Hauner, *Hitler, A Chronology*, p. 9.
43. Hitler, *Mein Kampf*, p. 59.
44. Ibid., pp. 58-63.
45. Ibid., p. 69.
46. Smith, *Hitler*, p. 149.
47. Ibid., p. 150.
48. Shirer, *Rise and Fall*, p. 27.
49. Hitler, *Mein Kampf*, pp. 122-3.
50. Kershaw, *Hitler, Hubris*, p.84.
51. Ullrich, *Hitler, A Biography*, vol 1, p. 49.
52. Ibid.
53. Shirer, *The Rise and Fall of the Third Reich*, pp. 27-28.
54. Thomas Weber, *Becoming Hitler*, p. xvii.
55. Hauner, *Hitler, A Chronology*, p. viii.
56. Ulrich, *Hitler, Ascent 1889-1939*, pp. 61-62.
57. Weber, *Becoming Hitler*, pp. xvii-xviii.
58. Hauner, *Hitler, A Chronology*, pp. 14-15.
59. Hitler, *Mein Kampf*, p. 189.
60. Ibid., p. 191.
  Chapter 16 – "Hanfstaengl, Harvard's Hero"
1. Thomas Weber, *Becoming Hitler*, pp. 10-11.
2. Adolf Hitler, *Mein Kampf*, p. 192.
3. Thomas Weber, *Hitler's First War*, p. 251.
4. William Shirer, *The Rise and Fall of the Third Reich*, p. 33.
5. Louis P. Lochner, *Tycoons and Tyrant*, p. 8.
6. Volker Ullrich, *Hitler, Vol. 1: Ascent*, p. 11.
7. Ian Kershaw, *Hitler 1889-1936, Hubris*, pp. 131-2.
8. Shirer, *The Rise and Fall*, p. 35.
9. Kershaw, *Hitler, 1889-1936*, p. 122.
10. Milan Hauner, *Hitler, A Chronology of his Life and Times*, p. 17.
11. Kershaw, *Hitler, 1889-1936*, p. 124.
12. Ibid., p. 126.
13. Kershaw, *Hitler, 1889-1936*, p. 128.
14. Ullrich, *Hitler, A Biography Volume 1*, pp. 88-89.
15. Thomas Weber, *Becoming Hitler*, p. 65.
16. Hauner, *Hitler, A Chronology*, p. 21.
17. Ullrich, *Hitler, Volume 1. Ascent*, p. 105.
18. Ibid., pp. 107-108.
19. Ibid.
20. Kershaw, *Hitler, 1889-1936*, p. 158.

21. Hauner, *Hitler, A Chronology,* p. 25.
22. Kershaw, *Hitler, 1889-1936,* p. xxiv.
23. Ullrich, *Hitler, Volume 1. Ascent,* p. 114.
24. Hauner, *Hitler, A Chronology,* p. 34.
25. Ibid., p. 35.
26. Ullrich, *Hitler, Volume 1. Ascent,* p. 115.
27. Arthur L. Smith, Jr. 'Kurt Lüdecke: The Man Who Knew Hitler,' *German Studies Review, Vol. 26, No. 3 (Oct., 2003),* pp. 597-606.
28. Christoper Andrew, *The Defence of the Realm, The Authorized History of MI5,* pp.105-105.
29. *The Guardian,* 13 October 2009.
30. *Tobias Churton, The Beast in Berlin,* p. 2.
31. *New York Almanack,* April 2020, House of Hanfstaengl: Munich and Manhattan. https://www.newyorkalmanack.com/2020/04/house-of-hanfstaengl-munich-and-manhattan/
32. Ernst ('Putzi') Hanfstaengl, *Hitler -The Missing Years,* pp. 23-24.
33. Ibid.
34. Ibid., p. 25.
35. *Chicago Tribune,* February 4, 2007.
36. Chris Hedges, *American Fascists: The Christian Right and the War on America.*
37. Sedgwick library. http://www.sedgwick.org/na/library/books/sed1896/sed1896.html
38. Richard Henry Greene, *The Todd Genealogy,* p. 21.
39. The Death of John Sedgwick. Battle of Spotsylvania Court House – May 9, 1864. https://www.battlefields.org/learn/articles/death-john-sedgwick
40. Hanfstaengl, *Hitler, The Missing Years,* p. 24.
41. S. Foster Damion, *The Genesis of Boston, The Atlantic,* October 1935 issue.
42. Peter Conradi, *Hitler's Piano Player,* p. 18.
43. Noam Chomsky, *Understanding Power,* p. 238.
44. *The Guardian,* 23 January 2019.
45. Conradi, *Hitler's Piano Player,* p. 19.
46. Ibid., p. 20.
47. Naomi W. Cohen, *Jacob H. Schiff, A Study in American Jewish Leadership,* p. 78.
48. Adam S. Cohen, *Harvard's Eugenics Era,* Harvard magazine, March-April, 2016. https://www.harvardmagazine.com/2016/03/harvards-eugenics-era
49. David Turner, 'Foundations of Holocaust: American eugenics and the nazi connection' in *The Jerusalem Post,* 30 December 2012.
50. Carroll Quigley, *The Anglo-American Establishment,* p. 31.
51. Hanfstaengl, *Hitler – The Missing Years,* p. 27.
52. Ibid., p. 26.
53. Steven T. Usdin, *Bureau of Spies,* p. 207.
54. Walter Lippmann, *What Program Shall the United States Stand for in International Relations?,* Annals of the American Academy of Political and Social Science, Vol. 66, July 1916, pp. 60–70.
55. Lippmann, *The World Conflict in its Relation to American Democracy,* Annals of the American Academy of Political and Social Science, Vol. 72, July 1917, pp. 1–10.
56. Carroll Quigley, *Tragedy & Hope,* pp. 938-9.
57. Antony Sutton, *Wall Street and the Bolshevik Revolution,* p. 44.
58. Richard B. Spence, *Wall Street and the Russian Revolution,* p. 105.
59. Ibid., p. 178.
60. Sutton, *Wall Street and the Bolshevik Revolution,* p. 171.
61. Ibid., pp. 143-144.

62. Ibid., p. 171.

63. J.P. O'Malley, *The Times of Israel,* 12 August 2022.

Chapter 17 – Agent Hanfstaengl "befriends" Hitler

1. Ernst 'Putzi' Hanfstaengl, *Hitler – The Missing Years,* pp. 27-28.

2. Peter Conradi, *Hitler's Piano Player,* p. 24.

3. Hanfstaengl, *Hitler – The Missing Years,* pp. 26-28.

4. Anthony Read and David Fisher, *Colonel Z, The Secret Life of a Master of Spies,* p. 119.

5. Richard Norton-Taylor, *The Guardian,* 5 July 2001.

6. Read and Fisher, *Colonel Z,* p. 120.

7. James Srodes, *Allen Dulles – Master of Spies,* p. 45.

8. Lester H. Woolsey, 'Robert Lansing's Record as Secretary of State' in *Current History* 29.3 (1928): 386-387.

9. Srodes, *Allen Dulles – Master of Spies,* pp 82-83.

10. Patrick Beesly, *Room 40,* p. 233.

11. Ibid.

12. Ibid., p. 228.

13. David Stafford, *Roosevelt and Churchill, Men of Secrets,* https://archive.nytimes.com/www.nytimes.com/books/first/s/stafford-roosevelt.html

14. Richard B. Spence, *Secret Agent 666,* pp. 170-171.

15. Read and Fisher, *Colonel Z,* p. 121.

16. Edward Mandell House and Charles Seymour, *The Intimate Papers of Colonel House,* p. 5.

17. H. Keith Melton & Robert Wallace, *Spy Sites of New York City, A Guide to the Region's Secret History,* p. 61.

18. Spence, *Secret Agent 666,* pp. 58-59.

19. Ibid., p. 98.

20. Ron Chernow, *The House of Morgan,* p. 189.

21. Spence, *Secret Agent 666,* p. 9.

22. Chernow, *House of Morgan,* pp.188-189.

23. Spence, *Secret Agent 666,* p. 59.

24. Tobias Churton, *Aleister Crowley in America,* p. 176.

25. Spence, *Secret Agent 666,* p. 53.

26. Ibid., p. 82.

27. Ibid., p. 66.

28. Steven T. Usdin, *Bureau of Spies,* p. 77.

29. Conradi, *Hitler's Piano Player,* p. 29.

30. Spence, *Secret Agent 666,* p. 68.

31. Conradi, *Hitler's Piano Player,* pp. vii-viii.

32. Ibid., p. 123.

33. Spence, *Secret Agent 666,* p. 68.

34. Belle da Costa Greene, A Biographical Sketch https://www.toutfait.com/belle-da-costa-greene-a-biographical-sketch-of-a-friend-acquaintance-of-aleister-crowley/

35. Spence, *Secret Agent 666,* p. 60.

36. Ibid., p. 54.

37. Mary J. Manning, *Being German, Being American.* https://www.archives.gov/files/publications/prologue/2014/summer/germans.pdf

38. James W. Gerard, *Speeches on German-American Loyalty.* https://history.hanover.edu/courses/excerpts/227gerard.html

39. Nicholas Roosevelt letter quoted by Peter Conradi, *Hitler's Piano Player,* pp. 31-32.

40. Carroll Quigley, *Tragedy & Hope,* p. 53.

41. Hanfstaengl, *Hitler – The Missing Years,* p. 28.

42. Spence, personal communication to authors.

43. Hanfstaengl, *Hitler -The Missing Years*, p. 29.

44. Conradi, *Hitler's Piano Player*, p. 34.

45. Adam Ferguson, *When Money Dies*, p. 29.

46. Conradi, *Hitler's Piano Player*, p. 38.

47. Guido Preparata, *Conjuring Hitler*, p. 115.

48. Robert Hessen, ed. *Berlin Alert, The Memoirs and Reports of Truman Smith*, p. 17.

49. Preparata, *Conjuring Hitler*, p. xviii.

50. Hessen, *Berlin Alert*, pp. 43-44.

51. Milan Hauner, *Hitler, His Life and Times*, p. 37.

52. Hessen, *Berlin Alert*, p. 46.

53. Hanfstaengl, *Hitler – The Missing Years*, p. 75.

54. Hessen, *Berlin Alert*, p. 46.

55. Hanfstaengl, *Hitler – The Missing Years*, p. 32.

56. Hanfstaengl, *Hitler – The Missing Years*, pp. 35-36.

57. Ibid., pp. 36-37.

58. Ibid., p. 38.

59. Ibid., pp. 38-39.

60. Ibid., p. 55.

61. Conradi, *Hitler – The Missing Years*, p. 14.

62. Hanfstaengl, *Hitler – The Missing Years*, p. 51.

63. Ibid., pp. 52-53.

64. School children pledging allegiance to the flag, https://www.visitthecapitol.gov/artifact/school-children-pledging-their-allegiance-flag-southington-connecticut-photograph-fenno

65. Conradi, *Hitler's Piano Player*, p. 45.

66. *The Times*, 27 September 1923.

67. Hauner, *Hitler, A Chronology of his Life and Time*, p. 39.

68. Hanfstaengl, *Hitler – The Missing Years*, p. 97.

69. Hauner, *Hitler, A Chronology of his Life and Time*, p. 47.

70. Conradi, *Hitler's Piano Player*, p. 68.

71. Hitler, *Mein Kampf*, p. 146.

72. Hanfstaengl, *Hitler – The Missing Years*, pp. 127-128.

73. Conradi, *Hitler's Piano Player*, p. 70.

Chapter 18 – Fire and Brimstone

1. Ernst Hanfstaengl, *Hitler – The Missing Years*, p. 126.

2. Otto Strasser, *Hitler and I*, p. 59.

3. Konrad Heiden, *Der Fuehrer, Hitler's Rise to Power*, p. 205.

4. Douglas O. Linder, *Hitler's Remarks In and About Prison*, https://famous-trials.com/hitler/2534-hitler-s-remarks-in-and-about-prison

5. Hanfstaengl, *Hitler – The Missing Years*, p. 140.

6. Ibid., pp. 128-130.

7. Ibid.

8. Peter Conradi, *Hitler's Piano Player*, p. 84.

9. Milan Hauner, *Hitler: A Chronology of His Life and Time*, p. 68.

10. *Daily Mail*, 27 September 1930.

11. Hanfstaengl, *Hitler – The Missing Years*, pp. 168-171.

12. Keith Jeffery, *The History of the Secret Intelligence Service, 1909-1949*, p. 295.

13. Ladislas Farago, *Game of Foxes*, p. 78.

14. Carroll Quigley, *The Anglo-American Establishment*, p. 312.

15. Farago, *Game of Foxes*, pp. 77-78.

16. R.T. Howard, *Spying on the Reich*, pp. 71-72.

17. F. W. Winterbotham, *The Nazi Connection*, p. 24.

18. Ibid., pp. 21-22.
19. Ibid., p. 64.
20. Farago, *Game of Foxes*, p. 80.
21. Howard, *Spying on the Reich*, p. 147.
22. Winterbotham, *The Nazi Connection*, p. 23.
23. Anthony Read and David Fisher, *Colonel Z*, pp. 168-169.
24. Ibid.
25. Peter Day, *The Bedbug, Klop Ustinov: Britain's Most Ingenious Spy*, pp. 55-56.
26. Howard, *Spying on The Reich*, p. 46.
27. Read and Fisher, *Colonel Z*, p. 174.
28. John Pomeroy, *The Fifth Man, Labour History*, No. 110 (May 2016), pp. 173-178.
29. Day, *The Bedbug*, pp.101-102.
30. Christopher Andrew, *The Secret World, A History of Intelligence*, p. 612.
31. Gwynne Thomas, *King Pawn or Black Knight*, p. 26.
32. Hanfstaengl, *Hitler – The Missing Years*, p. 184.
33. Conradi, *Hitler's Piano Player*, pp vii-viii.
34. Madhusee Mukerjee, *The Most Powerful Scientist Ever*, Scientific American, https://www.scientificamerican.com/article/the-most-powerful-scientist-ever/
35. Winterbotham, *The Nazi Connection*, p. 24.
36. Quigley, *The Anglo-American Establishment*, pp. 61-62.
37. Winterbotham, *The Nazi Connection*, p. 34.
38. Ibid., p. 44.
39. Ibid., p. 60.
40. William Shirer, *The Rise and Fall of the Third Reich*, p.175.
41. Ibid., p. 176.
42. Kurt von Schroeder, *German History in Documents and Images*, https://ghdi.ghidc.org/sub_document.cfm?document_id=3941
43. The Nazi "Seizure" of Power, https://www.johndclare.net/Rempel_Nazi28.htm
44. Ibid.
45. Matt Robinson, *Who Was Really Responsible For The Reichstag Fire?* https://www.berlinexperiences.com/who-was-really-responsible-for-the-reichstag-fire-mythbusting-berlin/
46. Diarmuid Jeffreys, *Hell's Cartel, IG Farben and the Making of Hitler's War Machine*, p.143.
47. Hauner, *Hitler*, p. 90.
48. Preparata, *Conjuring Hitler*, p. 203.
49. Ibid., p. 208.
50. Hanfstaengl, *Hitler – The Missing Years*, pp. 200 -201.
51. Conradi, *Hitler's Piano Player*, p. 109.
52. Sutton, *Wall Street and the Rise of Hitler*, p. 118.
53. Ibid., pp. 119- 120.
54. Benjamin Carter Hett, *Burning The Reichstag*, p. 15.
55. Richard Deacon, *A History of the British Secret Service*, p. 354.
56. *Daily Express*, 28 February, 1933.
57. Andrew, *The Defence of the Realm, The Authorized History of MI5*, p.189.
58. Day, *Klop Ustinov, Britain's Most Ingenious Spy*, p. 75.
59. Winterbotham, *The Nazi Connection*, pp. 40-41.
60. Hauner, *Hitler*, pp. 92-93.
61. Winterbotham, *The Nazi Connection*, p. 102.
62. Conradi, *Hitler's Piano Player*, p. 122.
63. Ibid., p. 123.
64. Hanfstaengl, *Hitler – The Missing Years*, p. 212.

65. Winterbotham, *The Nazi Connection*, pp. 4 – 5.

66. Ibid., p. 82.

67. Ibid., pp. 83-88.

68. Hanfstaengl, *Hitler – The Missing Years*, p. 188.

69. Steve Usdin, 'John Franklin Carter's Career as FDR's Private Intelligence Operative,' *Studies in Intelligence Vol. 65*, No. 2 (Extracts, June 2021)

Chapter 19 – A Vast Tapestry of Lies

1. John Dalberg-Acton (1834-1902) philosopher, Liberal politician, Regius Professor of Modern History, Cambridge University.

2. Harold Pinter, Nobel Lecture, 2005, Art, Truth and Politics. https://www.nobel-prize.org/prizes/literature/2005/pinter/lecture/

3. Guido Preparata, Conjuring Hitler, p 115.

4. Adam Fergusson, When Money Dies, The Nightmare of the Weimar Hyperinflation, p. 36.

5. Lionel Robbins, Foreword in, Constantino Bresciani-Turroni, The Economics of Inflation: A Study of Currency Depreciation in Post War Germany, p. 5. https://cdn.mises.org/The%20Economics%20of%20Inflation%20A%20Study%20of%20Curren-cy%20Depreciation%20in%20Post-War%20Germany_2.pdf

6. Antony Sutton, Wall Street and the Rise of Hitler, p. 23.

7. Antony Sutton, Wall Street and FDR, The True Story of how Franklin D. Roosevelt Colluded with Corporate America, p. 38.

8. Scott Stockdale, History's Greatest Fraud, p. 158.

9. Frank Costigliola, 'The United States and the Reconstruction of Germany in the 1920s,' The Business History Review, Vol. 50, No. 4 (Winter, 1976), pp. 477-502.

10. Ibid.

11. William Engdahl, A Century of War, p. 73.

12. Preparata, Conjuring Hitler, p. 163.

13. Carroll Quigley, Tragedy & Hope, p. 308.

14. Ibid., pp. 308-309.

15. Ron Chernow, The House of Morgan, pp. 249-250.

16. Encyclopedia Americana (1920) The Dresdner Bank, https://en.wikisource.org/wiki/The_Encyclopedia_Americana_(1920)/Dresdner_Bank,_The

17. New York Times, 4 November 1905. https://www.nytimes.com/1905/11/04/archives/jp-morgan-co-form-new-foreign-al-liance-dresdner-bank-is-to-float.html.

18. Liaquat Ahamed, Lords of Finance, p. 40.

19. Sutton, Wall Street and the Rise of Hitler, pp. 17-18.

20. Preparata, Conjuring Hitler, p. 161.

21. Engdahl, A Century of War, p. 73.

22. Hjalmar Schact visit to London https://history-commons.net/artifacts/2580699/desire-of-herr-schacht-to-visit-london/3603294/

23. Preparata, Conjuring Hitler, p. 162.

24. Ibid., p. 163.

25. Adam Lebor, Tower of Basel, pp. 7-8.

26. Liaquat Ahamed, Lords of Finance, The Bankers who Broke the World, p. 190.

27. Michael Burleigh, The Third Reich, A New History, p. 60.

28. Peter Conradi, Hitler's Piano Player, p. 135.

29. William Shirer, The Rise and Fall of the Third Reich, p. 112.

30. Andrew Nagorski, Hitlerland, p. 92.

31. Chernow, The House of Morgan, p. 245.

32. Quigley, Tragedy & Hope, p. 62.

33. Preparata, Conjuring Hitler, p. xviii

34. Chernow, The House of Morgan, p. 202.

35. Lester V. Chandler, Benjamin Strong, Central Banker, p. 259.

36. Quigley, Tragedy & Hope, p. 326.

37. Chernow, The House of Morgan, p. 244.

38. Quigley, Tragedy & Hope, pp. 326 -327.

39. Engdahl, A Century of War, pp. 73-74.

40. Preparata, Conjuring Hitler, p. 191.

41. Engdahl, A Century of War, pp. 75-78.

42. Sutton, Wall Street and the Rise of Hitler, p. 28.

43. Preparata, Conjuring Hitler, pp. 166-177.

44. Sutton, Wall Street and the Rise of Hitler, pp. 28-29.

45. Engdahl, A Century of War, pp. 69-70.

46. John Ryan, 'Walter Rathenau Studies': An Irish Quarterly Review, Vol. 11, No. 43 (Sep., 1922), pp. 379-399.

47. Frank Costigliola, 'The United States and the Reconstruction of Germany in the 1920s'. The Business History Review, Vol. 50, No. 4 (Winter, 1976), pp. 477-502.

48. Sutton, Wall Street and the Rise of Hitler, p. 49.

49. M. L. Flaningam, 'International Co-operation and Control in the Electrical Industry: The General Electric Company and Germany, 1919-1944,' The American Journal of Economics and Sociology, Vol. 5, No. 1 (Oct., 1945), pp. 7-25.

50. Sutton, Wall Street and the Bolshevik Revolution, p. 171.

51. Ibid., p. 50.

52. Ibid., p. 52.

53. Ibid., p. 55.

54. John Strausbaugh, Victory City, p. 352.

55. Sutton, Wall Street and the Rise of Hitler, p. 78.

56. Charles Higham, Trading with the Enemy, the Nazi-American Money Plot 1933-1949, p. 93.

57. Sutton, Wall Street and the Rise of Hitler, p. 79.

58. Strausbaugh, Victory City, p. 353.

59. Chernow, The House of Morgan, p. 308.

60. Jacques R. Pauwels, 'Profits "Über Alles!" American Corporations and Hitler'. Labour / Le Travail, Vol. 51 (Spring, 2003), pp. 223-249 (27 pages) Canadian Committee on Labour History https://www.jstor.org/stable/25149339

61. Sutton, Wall Street and the Rise of Hitler, p. 34.

62. Ibid., p. 47.

63. Ibid., Sutton, p. 48.

64. Higham, Trading with the Enemy, p. 33.

65. Strausbaugh, Victory City, pp. 349-350.

66. Ibid., pp. 350-351.

67. Sutton, Wall Street and the Rise of Hitler, p.31.

68. Pauwels, Profits "Über Alles!"

69. Preparata, Conjuring Hitler, pp. 170-171.

70. Sutton, Wall Street and the Rise of Hitler, p. 34.

71. James Pool, Hitler and his Secret Partners, pp. 324-325.

72. Webster Tarpley and Anton Chaitkin, George Bush, The Unauthorized Biography, p. 46.

73. Preparata, Conjuring Hitler, pp. 169-171.

74. Sutton, Wall Street and the Rise of Hitler, p. 31.

75. James and Suzanne Pool, Who Financed Hitler, The Secret Funding of Hitler's Rise to Power 1919-1933, p. 158.

76. Ibid.

77. Sutton, Wall Street and the Rise of Hitler, p. 29.
78. Tarpley and Chaitkin, George Bush, The Unauthorized Biography, pp. 29-35.
79. Sutton, Wall Street and the Rise of Hitler, p. 24.
80. Library of Congress, 'This Month in Business History, Banker J. P. Morgan Born,' https://guides.loc.gov/this-month-in-business-history/april/jp-morgan-born
81. Piet Clement, The Norman–Schacht Vision and Early Experience of the Bank for International Settlements, 1929–1933. https://www.cambridge.org/core/books/abs/spread-of-the-modern-central-bank-and-global-cooperation/institutionalizing-central-bank-cooperation/EAB57D5948DF8257CC9B72127EFA844B
82. Quigley, Tragedy & Hope, p. 324.
83. Higham, Trading With the Enemy, p. 2.
84. Adam Lebor, Tower of Basel: The Shadowy History of the Secret Bank that Runs the World, pp. 19-20.
85. Ibid., pp. xviii-xix.
86. Ibid., pp. xix-xx.
87. Time, 3 February 1930.
88. Lebor, Tower of Basel, pp. 34-35.
89. Adam Lebor, The Telegraph, 31 July 2013. https://www.telegraph.co.uk/finance/bank-of-england/10213988/Never-mind-the-Czech-gold-the-Nazis-stole....html
90 Ibid.

Chapter 20 – Egging Hitler On

1. Pocket Oxford English Dictionary, Tenth Edition, 2005.
2. Ian Kershaw, Making Friends with Hitler, pp. xiv-xv.
3. Richard Griffiths, Fellow Travellers of the Right, p. 150.
4. Carroll Quigley, Tragedy & Hope, pp. 286-287.
5. Ibid.
6. Guido Preparata, Conjuring Hitler, p. 234.
7. Christopher Andrew, The Secret World, pp. 612-613.
8. Quigley, Tragedy & Hope, pp. 578-579.
9. Preparata, Conjuring Hitler, p. 228.
10. Ibid., p. 204.
11. Kathryn S. Olmsted, The Newspaper Axis, Six Press Barons Who Enabled Hitler, jacket.
12. Will Wainewright, Reporting on Hitler, p. 199.
13. Olmsted, The Newspaper Axis, p. 5.
14. Peter Conradi, Hitler's Piano Player, p. 173.
15. Carroll Quigley, The Anglo-American Establishment, p. 312.
16. Milan Hauner, Hitler, A Chronology, p. 106.
17. Griffiths, Fellow Travellers of the Right, p. 164.
18. Ibid., pp. 116 -117.
19. E.W.D. Tennant, 'Herr Hitler's Constructive Policy,' The English Review, 1908-1937; London, (Jan 1935): 36-48.
20. Charles Spicer, Coffee with Hitler, pp. 251-252.
21. Olmsted, The Newspaper Axis, pp. 29-31.
22. Wainewright, Reporting on Hitler, p. 140.
23. Olmsted, The Newspaper Axis, p. 91.
24. Ibid., p. 95.
25. Quigley, Tragedy & Hope, p. 582.
26. Quigley, Anglo-American Establishment, p. 5.
27. Martin Gilbert, The Roots of Appeasement, pp. 146-147.
28. Preparata, Conjuring Hitler, p. 78.
29. Tim Bouverie, Appeasing Hitler, pp. 49-50.
30. Preparata, Conjuring Hitler, pp. 229-231.

31. Bouverie, *Appeasing Hitler*, p.133.
32. Manuel Sarkisyanz, *Hitler's English Inspirers*, p. 210.
33. Quigley, *Anglo-American Establishment*, p. 312.
34. Ron Chernow, *The House of Morgan*, p.p. 436-437.
35. Julie V. Gottlieb, *Guilty Women, Foreign Policy and Appeasement in Inter-War Britain*, p. 75.
36. Quigley, *Anglo-American Establishment*, p. 271.
37. Ian Kershaw, *Making Friends with Hitler, Lord Londonderry and Britain's Road to War*, p. 8.
38. Richard Griffiths, *Fellow Travellers of the Right*, pp. 140-141.
39. Gottlieb, '*Guilty Women,' Foreign Policy, and Appeasement* p. 65.
40. F.W. Winterbotham, *The Nazi Connection*, p. 132.
41. Preparata, *Conjuring Hitler*, p. 233.
42. Charles Higham, *The Duchess of Windsor: The Secret Life*, p. 109.
43. Guido Preparata, *The Incubation of Nazism*, p. 99-102.
44. Ibid.
45. Quigley, *The Anglo-American Establishment*, p. 275.
46. Gottlieb, *Guilty Women*, p. 65.
47. Quigley, *Anglo-American Establishment*, p. 313.
48. Hauner, *Hitler*, p. 108.
49. Quigley, *Anglo-American Establishment*, pp. 269-270.
50. Ibid., p. 313.
51. Ibid., p. 272.
52. Ibid., p. 313.
53. *The Guardian*, 13 October 2009.
54. *Time*, 30 August 1943, 'Appeasement's End?'
55. Preparata, *Conjuring Hitler*, p. 238.

Chapter 21 – "Peace For Our Time"
1. Quigley, *The Anglo-American Establishment*, p. 228.
2. Ibid., p. 229.
3. Carroll Quigley, *Tragedy & Hope*, pp. 471-474.
4. Quigley, *Anglo-American Establishment*, p. 159.
5. Ibid., p. 227.
6. Ibid., p. 87.
7. Ian Kershaw, *Making Friends with Hitler*, p.p. 22-23.
8. A.P. Young, *The 'X' Documents*, pp. 18-19.
9. Guido Preparata, *Conjuring Hitler*, p. 232.
10. Kershaw, *Making Friends with Hitler*, p. 120.
11. Ibid., p. 165.
12. Norman Rose, *The Cliveden Set*, p. 79.
13. Ibid., p. 149.
14. George A Lanyi, 'The Problem of Appeasement,' *World Politics*, Vol. 15, No. 2 (Jan., 1963), pp. 316-328.
15. Rose, *The Cliveden Set*, p. 175.
16. Carroll Quigley, *The Anglo-American Establishment*, p. 279.
17. Arthur H. Furnia, *The Diplomacy of Appeasement: Anglo-French Relations and the Prelude to World War II*, p. 253.
18. Rose, *The Cliveden Set*, p. 194.
19. Hansard, HC Debate 21 February 1938 vol 332 cc45-5245
20. Furnia, *The Diplomacy of Appeasement* p .254.
21. Peter Hoffmann "The Question of Western Allied Co-Operation with the German Anti-Nazi Conspiracy, 1938-1944," *The Historical Journal*, Vol. 34, No. 2 (Jun., 1991), pp.

437-464.

22. Jim Wilson, *Nazi Princess, Hitler, Lord Rothermere and Princess Stephanie von Hohenlohe*, p. 86.

23. Quigley, *The Anglo-American Establishment*, p. 275.

24. J. S. Conway, *Machtergreifung or 'Due Process of History': The Historiography of Hitler's Rise to Power*, The Historical Journal, Vol. 8, No. 3 (1965)

25. William L Shirer, *The Rise and Fall of the Third Reich*, p. 372.

26. Ian Kershaw, *Popular Opinion & Political Dissent in the Third Reich*, p. vii.

27. Ibid., pp. 374-375.

28. Catrine Clay, *The Good Germans*, p. 1.

29. Michael Thomsett, *The German Opposition to Hitler*, p.1.

30. Basil Liddell Hart, *History of the Second World War*, p. 35.

31. Ibid., p. 713.

32. Hoffmann, *German Resistance to Hitler*, p. 52.

33. Hans Rothfels, *The German Opposition to Hitler, an Appraisal*, pp. 15-17.

34. Klemens von Klemperer, *German Resistance Against Hitler, The Search for Allies Abroad 1938-1945*, p. 5.

35. Quigley, *Anglo-American Establishment*, p. 273.

36. Ibid., p. 277.

37. Ibid.

38. Richard Griffiths, *Fellow Travellers of the Right*, p. 293.

39. Preparata, *Conjuring Hitler*, p. 238.

40. Quigley, *Anglo-American Establishment*, pp. 276-277.

41. Preparata, *Conjuring Hitler*, pp. 238-240.

42. Rothfels and Wilson, *German Opposition to Hitler*, pp. 85-86.

43. Young, *The 'X' Documents*, pp. 24-25.

44. Quigley, *Anglo-American Establishment*, p. 279.

45. Young, *The 'X' Documents*, p. 25.

46. Rothfels and Wilson, *German Opposition to Hitler*, pp. 58-59.

47. Shirer, *The Rise and Fall of the Third Reich*, pp. 379-381.

48. R.A.C Parker, *Chamberlain and Appeasement*, p.157.

49. "Cato," *Guilty Men*, p. 49.

50. Cited in Griffiths, *Fellow Travellers of the Right*, p. 305.

51. Documents on German Foreign Policy 1918-45, Series D., 1937-45, U.S. Department of State, Washington.

52. Parker, *Chamberlain and Appeasement*, p. 157.

53. Ibid., pp.158-159.

54. "Cato," *Guilty Men*, pp 50-51.

55. Preparata, *The Incubation of Nazism*, p. 104.

56. "Cato," *Guilty Men*, p. 51.

57. P.E. Caquet, *The Bell of Treason, The 1938 Munich Agreement in Czechoslovakia*, p, 158.

58. "Cato," *Guilty Men*, p. 53.

Chapter 22 – Once More into the Abyss

1. "Cato," *Guilty Men*, p. 54.

2. *The Times*, 17 May 1965, Sir Basil Newton obituary.

3. Carl Goerdeler, Letter to an American Politician, 11 October 1938. In *Goerdeler's "Politisches Testament," Dokumente des anderen Deutschland*. 1945 Verlag Friedrich Krause.

4. "Cato," *Guilty Men*, p. 55.

5. Hansard, 3 October 1938. Prime Minister's Statement, Volume 339.

6. Hansard, Policy of His Majesty's Government, Volume 339: debated on Wednesday 5 October 1938.

7. Hansard, Commons Chamber, Volume 339: debated on Thursday 6 October 1938.

8. A.J.P. Taylor, *The Origins of the Second World War*, p.189.

9. Milan Hauner, *Hitler*, pp. 138-139.]

10. Richard Griffiths, *Fellow Travellers of the Right*, pp. 338-339.

11. Richard J. Evans, *The Third Reich in Power, 1933–1939*, p. 683.

12. Carroll Quigley, *Tragedy & Hope*, p. 644.

13. Adam LeBor, *The Telegraph*, July 31, 2013.

14. Guido Preparata, *Conjuring Hitler*, p. 241.

15. "Cato," *Guilty Men*, pp. 56-57.

16. Preparata, *Conjuring Hitler*, p. 242.

17. Raymond Cartier, *Le Monde Entre Deux Guerres (1919-1939)* p. 22.

18. Hauner, *Hitler*, p. 145.

19. Ibid., p. 146.

20. Quigley, *Tragedy & Hope*, p. 727.

21. US Department of State, Office of the Historian, Papers relating to the foreign relations of the United States, Japan, 1931–1941, Volume II, "The Ambassador in Japan (Grew) to the Secretary of State." https://history.state.gov/historicaldocuments/frus1931-41v02/d310

22. Robert B. Stinnett, *Day of Deceit, The Truth About FDR and Pearl Harbor*, jacket.

23. Ibid., p. 9.

24. A.J.P. Taylor, *How Wars Begin*, p. 55.

25. Joseph K. Taussig, Jr., "I Remember Pearl Harbor," Naval Institute of Proceedings, December 1972. https://ww1.prweb.com/prfiles/2014/06/03/11910704/HEK-Reasons%20to%20Support.pdf

26. Library of Congress, Speech by Franklin D. Roosevelt, 8 November, 1941. https://www.loc.gov/resource/afc1986022.afc1986022_ms2201/?st=text

27. Michael Gannon, *Pearl Harbor Betrayed*, pp 191-192.

28. Ibid., p. 188.

29. James Johns, *Reassessing Pearl Harbor*, p. 137.

30. Stinnett, *Day of Deceit*, pp. 203-4.

31. Gannon, *Pearl Harbor Betrayed*, p. 89.

32. Stinnett, *Day of Deceit*, p. 66.

33. Winston Churchill, International Churchill Society, Pearl Harbor, https://winstonchurchill.org/publications/churchill-bulletin/bullertin-162-dec-2021/pearl-harbor/

34. Gannon, *Pearl Harbor Betrayed*, p. 11.

35. James Johns, *Reassessing Pearl Harbor, Scapegoats, a False Hero and the Myth of the Surprise Attack*, p. 166.

36. *Time*, 3 July 1944, 'U.S. At War: L'Affaire Lyttelton,' https://time.com/archive/6789516/u-s-at-war-laffaire-lyttelton/

37. John Keegan, *The Second World War*, p. 254.

38. Gordon W. Prange, *Pearl Harbor, The Verdict of History*, p. 404.

39. Michael Gannon, *Pearl Harbor Betrayed*, p. 282.

SOURCES CONSULTED

Abrahams, Ray H., *Preachers Present Arms*, Pennsylvania, Herald Press, 1933

Ahamed, Liaquat, *Lords of Finance, The Bankers Who Broke the World*, US, Penguin Press, 2009

Aikin, K.W.W., *The Last Years of Liberal England, 1900-1914*, London, Collins, 1972

Albertini, Luigi, *Origins of the War of 1914*, Oxford University Press, 1952

Allen, Gary, None Dare Call it Conspiracy, New York, Amereon Ltd, 1972

Allen, Marin, *Hidden Agenda, How the Duke of Windsor Betrayed the Allies,* New York, , M. Evans and Company, Inc, 2000

Allen, Martin, *The Hitler/Hess Deception, British Intelligence's Best Kept Secret of the Second World War*, London, Haper Collins, 2003

Amery, Leo, *Times History of the War in South Africa*, London, Low Marston and Co. Ltd, 1900

Andrew, Christopher, *Secret Service, The Making of the British Intelligence Community*, London, Heinemann, 1985

Andrew, Christopher, *The Defence of the Realm: The Authorised History of MI5*, London, Penguin Books, 2009

Andrew, Christopher, *The Secret World, A History of Intelligence*, London, Penguin Random House, 2018

Aronson, Shlomo, *Hitler, the Allies, and the Jews*, Cambridge University Press, 2004

Arrighi, Giovanni, *The Long Twentieth Century*, London, Verso, 1994

Arthur, Max, *Forgotten Voices of the Great War*, London, Ebury Press, 2002

Ascher, Abraham, *Was Hitler a Riddle*? Stanford University Press, 2012

Baaijen, Mees, The Global Mafia & Their World Domination Project, 2024, awaiting publication.

Baker, Anne Pimlott, *The Pilgrims of Great Britain: A Centennial History, London,* Profile Books, 2002

Baker, Anne Pimlott, *The Pilgrims of the United States: A Centennial History*, London, Profile Books, 2003

Ballard, Robert, *Lusitania*, New Jersey, Madison Press Books, 1995

Barnes, Harry Elmer, *In Quest of Truth and Justice: De-Bunking the War-Guilt Myth*, Colorado Springs, Ralph Myles Publisher, 1972

Barnes, Harry Elmer, *Who Started the First World War*, California, Institute for Historical Review, 1984

Barnes, Harry Elmer, *The Genesis of the World War*, Alfred A. Knopf, 1927

Bausman, Frederick, *Let France Explain*, London, George Allen & Unwin Ltd, 1922

Beesly, Patrick, *Room 40, British Naval Intelligence 1914-1918,* Oxford University Press 1982

Beevor, Antony, *The Second World War,* London, Weidenfeld & Nicolson, 2012

Bennet, Gill, *Churchill's Man of Mystery,* London, Routledge, 2009

Birmingham, Stephen, *Our Crowd,* London, Macdonald & Co., 1967

Black, Edwin, *IBM and the Holocaust, The Strategic Alliance*
Between Nazi Germany and America's most Powerful Corporation, London, Little Brown and Company, 2001

Black, Edwin, *War Against the Weak, Eugenics and America's Campaign to Create a Master Race,* New York, Four Walls Eight Windows Publishing, 2003

Bloch, Michael, *Operation Willi, The Plot to Capture the Duke of Windsor July 1940,* London, Weidenfeld and Nicolson, 1984

Bourne, John, Liddle, Peter and Whitehead, Ian, *The Great World War 1914-45,* vol. 2, London, Harper Collins, 2001

Bouverie, Tim, *Appeasing Hitler, Chaberlain, Churchill and the Road to War,* London, Vintage, 2019

Broszat, Martin, *The Hitler State, the Foundations and development of the internal structure of the Third Reich,* Essex, Longman group, English translation 1981

Brown, Ellen Hodgson, *The Web of Debt, The Shocking truth About Our Money System,* Louisiana, Third \Millenium Press, 2007

Buchan, John, *A History of the First World War,* Moffat, Lochar Publishing, 1991

Buchanan, George, *My Mission to Russia and Other Diplomatic Memories,* vols 1 and 2, London, Cassell, 1923

Buchanan, Patrick J., *Churchill, Hitler and the Unnecessary War,* New York, Three Rivers Press, 2008

Burleigh, Michael, *The Third Reich, A New History,* London, Macmillan, 2000

Cafferky, John P., *Lord Milner's Second War, The Rhodes-Milner Secret Society, The Origin of WWI, and the Start of the New World Order,* Self-published, 2013

Caquet, P.E., *The Bell of Treason, The 1938 Munich Agreement in Czechoslovakia,* London, Profile Books,2018

Carlyon, L.A., *Gallipoli,* London, Bantam Books, 2002

Carnegie, Andrew, *Problems of Today,* London, George Allen & Sons, 1908

Carr, E.H., *What is History?,* London, Macmillan, 1961

Carr, W.G., *Pawns in the Game,* Ontario, Federation of Christian Laymen, 1958

Chaitkin, Anton, *Treason in America, From Aaron Burr to Averell Harriman,* New York, New Benjamin Franklin House, 1984

Chapman, Stanley, *The Rise of Merchant Banking,* London, George Allen and Unwin, 1984

Charnley, John, *Chamberlain and the Lost Peace,* Chicago, Ivan R. Dee Publisher, 1989

Cato, *Guilty Men,* London, Victor Gollancz, 1944

Chatterton, Kebble, *The Big Blockade,* London, Hutchinson and Co, 1932

Chernow, Ron, The House of Morgan, New York, Grove Press, 2001

Chernow, Ron, *The Warburgs,* New York, Random House, 1993

Chernow, Ron, *Titan, The Life of John D. Rockefeller, Sr.,* New York,

Chevalier, Gabriel, *Fear*, English translation of *La Peur* (1930), London, Profile Books, 2008

Childers, Erskine, *Lord Roberts, War and the Arme Blanche*, London, E. Arnold, 1910

Childers, Thomas, editor, *The Formation of the Nazi Constituency 1919-1933*, New Jersey, Barnes & Noble Books, 1986

Chomsky, Noam, *Understanding Power*, London, Vintage, 2003

Churchill, Randolph S., *Winston S. Churchill*, Vol. II, Boston, Houghton Mifflin, 1967

Churchill, Winston S., *My Early Life*, London, Butterworth, 1930

Churchill, Winston S., *The World Crisis, 1915*, London, Thornton Butterworth Limited, 1923

Churton, Tobias, *Aleister Crowley in America, Art, Espionage and Sex Magick in the New World*, Rochester, Inner Traditions, 2017

Cimbala, Stephen, J., *Military Persuasion: Deterrence and Provocation in Crisis and War*, Pennsylvania University Press, 1994

Clark, Christopher, *Kaiser Wilhelm II: Profiles in Power*, London, Longman, 2000

Clark, Christopher, *The Sleepwalkers: How Europe Went to War in 1914*, London, Penguin, 2013

Clark, R.T., *The German Resistance, Carl Goerdeler's Struggle Against Tyranny*, New York, Frederick A Prager Inc. 1958

Clarke, Ignatius, *Voices Prophesying War*, Oxford University Press, 1966

Clay, Catarine, *The Good Germans, Resisting the Nazis, 1933-1945*, London, Weidenfeld & Nicolson, 2020

Cobain, Ian, *The History Thieves, Secrets, Lies and the Shaping of a Modern Nation*, London, Portobello Books, 2016

Cochran, M.H., *Germany Not Guilty in 1914*, Colorado Springs, Ralph Myles Publisher, 1972

Cockett, Richard, *Twilight of Truth, Chamberlain, Appeasement & Manipulation of the Press*, London, Weidenfeld and Nicolson, 1989

Cole, Margaret, *Beatrice Webb*, London, Longmans Green and Co., 1945

Collingwood, W.G., *The Life and Work of John Ruskin*, vols I and II, London, Methven & Co., 1893

Conradi, Peter, *Hitler's Piano Player*, New York, Carroll & Graf Publishers, 2004

Consett, M.W.W.P., *The Triumph of Unarmed Forces (1914-1918)*, London, Williams and Norgate, 1923

Cowles, Virginia, *The Kaiser*, New York, Harper and Row, 1963

Cowles, Virginia, *The Rothschilds: A Family of Fortune*, London, Futural publications Ltd, 1973

Cowles, Virginia, *Winston Churchill, The Era and the Man*, London, Hamish Hamiliton Ltd, 1953

Crozier, Brian, *Free Agent, The Unseen War, 1941-1991*, London, Harper Collins, 1993

Cruttwell, C.R.M.F., *A History of the Great War*, London, Granada Books, 1982

Davidson, Eugene, *The Making of Adolf Hitler, The Birth and Rise of Nazism*, London, Macdonald and Jane's, 1977

Day, Peter, *The Bedbug, Klop Ustinov, Britain's Most Ingenious Spy*, London, Biteback publishing, 2015

Deacon, Richard, *A History of British Secret Service*, London, Panther Books,1980

Dedijer, Vladimir, *The Road to Sarajevo*, London, Macgibbon & Kee, 1967

Delattre, Lucas, *A Spy at the Heart of the Third Reich*, New York, Grove Press, 2003

Dobrorolski , Sergei, *The Mobilisation of the Russian Army, 1914*, Berlin, Deutsche Verlagsgesellschact fur Politik und and Geschichte, 1922

Docherty, Gerry and Macgregor, Jim., *Hidden History: The Secret Origins of the First World War*, Edinburgh, Mainstream Publishing, 2013

D'Ombrain, Nicholas, War Machinery and High Policy Defence Administration in Peacetime Britain, 1902-1914, Oxford University Press, 1974

Dunlop, Ian, *Edward VII and the Entente Cordiale*, London, Constable, 2004

Durham, Edith, *The Sarajevo Crime*, London, Allen & Unwin, 1920

Durham, Edith, *Twenty Years of Balkan Tangle*, London, Allen & Unwin

Edward, David, *Inside Asquith's Cabinet*, London, John Murray, 1977

Elton, G.R., *The Practice of History*, Sidney University Press, 1967

Engdahl, F. William, *A Century of War, Anglo-American Oil Politics and the New World Order*, London, Pluto Press, 1992

Engdahl, F. William, *Manifest Destiny, Democracy and Cognitive Dissonance*, Wiesbaden, Mine Books, 2018

Engelbrecht, H.C. and Hanighen, F.C., *Merchants of Death*, New York, Dodd, Mead and Co, 1934

Erikson, Kai T., *Wayward Puritans, A Study in the Sociology of Deviance*, Pearson Education Inc, 2005

Ewart, J.S., *The Roots and Causes of the Wars*, vols I and II, New York, George H. Doran Company, 1925

Farago, Ladislas, *The Game of Foxes, British and German Intelligence Operations*, London, Hodder and Stoughton, 1971.

Farrer, David, *The Warburgs*, London, Michael Joseph, 1974

Farrer, J.A., *England Under Edward VII*, London, Allen & Unwin, 1922

Fay, Sidney B., *The Origins of the World War*, New York, The Macmillan Company, 1936

Feis, Herbert, *Europe: The World's Banker, 1870-1914*, New York, Norton and Company, 1965

Ferguson, Niall, *The House of Rothschild: The World's Banker, 1849-1999*, London, Penguin Books, 1998

Ferguson, Niall, *1914: Why the World Went to War*, London, Penguin Books, 2003

Ferguson, Niall, *The Pity of War*, London, Penguin Books, 1998

Fergusson, Adam, *When Money Dies, The Nightmare of the Weimar Hyper-Inflation*, London, Old Street publishing, 2015

Ferris, Paul, *The House of Northcliffe: A Biography of an Empire*, New York, World Publishing, 1972

Fest, Joachim C., *Hitler*, London, Penguin Books, 1973

Fischer, Fritz, *Germany's Aims in the First World War*, London, Chatto and Windus, 1967

Fischer, David Hackett, *Historian's Fallacies, Towards a Logic of Historical Thought*, New York, Harper Colophon Books, 1970

Fisher, H.A.L., *A History of Europe*, London, Edward Arnold and Co., 1936

Fisher, Irving, *The Money Illusion*, New York, Adelphi Company, (1928) reprinted 2011,

Fisher, Baron John Arbuthnot, *Memories and Records*, vols 1 & 2, New York, Geoge H. Doran Co., 1920

Fitzpatrick, J. Percy, *The Transvaal Within*, Charlestown, Bibliobazzar, 2009

Fleming, Thomas, *The Illusion of Victory; America in World War 1*, New York, Perseus Book Group, 2003

Friedrich, Otto, *Blood & Iron, From Bismarck to Hitler, the Von Moltke Family's Impact on German History*, New York, harper Collins, 1995

Fromkin, David, *A Peace to End All Peace, The Fall of the Ottoman Empire and the Creation of the Modern Middle East*, New York, Avon Books, 1989

Fromkin, David, *The King and the Cowboy, Theodore Roosevelt and Edward the Seventh, Secret Partners*, New York, Penguin Press, 2008

Fromm, Erich, *The Anatomy of Human Destructiveness*, London, Pimlico, 1973

Fuehr, Alexander, *The Neutrality of Belgium*, New York and London, Funk and Wagnall, 1915

Gannon, Michael, *Pearl Harbor Betrayed*, New York, Henry Holt and Company, 2001

Gardiner, A., *The War Lords*, Toronto, J.M. Dent & Co., 1915

Geiss, Immanuel, *July 1914: The Outbreak of the First World War: Selected Documents*, London, B.T. Batsford Ltd, 1965

Gerard, James W., *My Four years in Germany*, Londo, Hodder and Stoughton, 1917

Gerard, James W., *Face to Face with Kaiserism*, London, Hodder and Stoughton, 1928

Gilbert, Martin, *The Roots of Appeasement*, London, Weidenfeld and Nicolson, 1966

Gilbert, Martin, *Winston S. Churchill: The Challenge of War 1914-1916*, Michigan, Hillside College Press, 1971

Gill, Anton, *An Honourable Defeat, A History of German Resistance to Hitler 1933-45*, UK, Sharpe Books, 2018, (first published 1994)

Gollin, A.M., *Proconsul in Politics: A Study of Lord Milner*, London, Anthony Blond Ltd, 1964

Gooch G.P. & Temperley, Harold, *British Documents on the Origins of the War, 1898-1914*, London, H.M.S.O., 1927.

Goodrick-Clarke, Nicolas, *The Occult Roots of Nazism*, London, Bloomsbury publishing, 2004

Goodson, Stephen Mitford, *A History of Central Banking and the Enslavement of Mankind*, London, Black House Publishing, 2014

Gottlieb, Julie V., *'Guilty Women' Foreign Policy and Appeasement in Inter-War Britain*, London, Palgrave Macmillan, 2015

Gottlieb, W.W., *Studies in Secret Diplomacy*, London, Allen & Unwin, 1957

Grady, Tim, *A Deadly Legacy, German Jews and the Great War*, Yale University Press, 2017

Grant and Temperley, *Europe in the Nineteenth and Twentieth Centuries*, London, Longmans, Green and Co, 1934

Green, S.J.D. and Horden, peregrine, All Souls and the Wider World, Oxford Uni9versity Press, 2011

Grenfell, Captain Russell, *Unconditional Hatred*, New York, The Devin-Adair Company, 1953

Grey, Edward and Dorothy, *Cottage Book, Ichen Abbas, 1894-1905*, London, Gollancz, 1999

Grey of Fallodon, Edward, *Twenty-five Years:1892-1916*, London, Hodder and Stoughton, 1928

Griffin, G. Edward, *The Creature from Jekyll Island; A Second Look at the Federal Reserve*, California, American Media, 1994

Griffiths, Richard, *Fellow Travellers of the Right, British Enthusiasts for Nazi Germany, 1933-1939*, London, Faber and Faber, 1983

Grigg, John, *Lloyd George, The People's Champion (1902-1911)*, Berkely, University of California Press, 1978

Haldane, Richard Burdon, *An Autobiography*, London, Hodder and Stoughton, 1924

Halperin, Vladimir, *Lord Milner and the Empire*, London, Oldham Press Ltd, 1952

Hamann, Brigitte, *Hitler's Vienna, A Portrait of the Tyrant as a Young Man*, London, Tauris Parke, 2010

Hamilton, John Maxwell, Manipulating the Masses, *Woodrow Wilson and the Birth of American Propaganda*, Louisiana State University Press, 2020

Hamilton, Richard F., and Herwig, Holger H., *Decisions for War, 1914-1917*, Cambridge, Cambridge University Press, 2004

Hamill, John, The Strange Career of Mr Hoover Under Two Flags, New York, William Faro, Inc., 1931

Hanfstaengl, Ernst, *Unheard Witness*, New York, J.B. Lippincott Company, 1957

Hanser, Richard, *Putsch, How Hitler Made a Revolution*, New York, Pyramid Books, 1971

Hansl, Proctor W., *Years of Plunder*, New York, H. Smith and R. Haas, 1935

Harand, Irene, *Hitler's Lies, An Answer to Hitler's Mein Kampf*, Mumbai, Jaico publishing, 2013

Hardach, Gerd, *The First World War, 1914-1918*, London, Pelican Books, 1977

Hart, B.H. Liddell, *History of the First World War*, London, Pan Books, 1930

Hart, B.H. Liddell, *History of the Second World War*, London, Cassell & Company Ltd, 1970

Harvey, A.D., *Collision of Empires: Britain in Three World Wars*, London, Hambledon Press, 1992

Hauner, Milan, Hitler: A Chronology of his Life and Time, Basingstoke, Palgrave Macmillan, 1983

Havinghurst, Alfred F., *Britain in Transaction, The Twentieth Century*, University of Chicago Press, 1979

Helferich, Gerard, *An Unlikely Trust, Theodore Roosevelt and J.P. Morgan*, Connecticut, Lyon Press, 2018

Henig, Ruth, *The Origins of the First World War*, London, Routledge, 1989

Hett, Benjamin Carter, *The Death of Democracy, Hitler's Rise to Power*, London, William Heinemann, 2018

Hett, Benjamin Carter, *The Nazi Menace, Hitler, Churchill, Roosevelt, Stalin and the Road to War*, New York, henry Holt and Company, 2020

Hill, Cissie Dore, *Collecting the Twentieth Century*, Hoover Digest, Hoover Institute on War, Revolution and Peace, 2000

Higham, Charles, *Trading with the Enemy, The Nazi-American Money Plot 1933-1949*, Authors Guild 'Bankinprint.Com' Edition, 2007

Hitchins, Keith, *Romania 1866-1947*, Oxford University Press, 1994

Hitler, Adolf, *Mein Kampf*, Mumbai, Jaico Publishing, 1988

Hobson, J.A., *John Ruskin: Social Reformer*, London, James Nisbet & Co Ltd, 1898

Hoffman, Peter, *German Resistance to Hitler*, Harvard University Press, 1988

Holdsworth, John Thom, *Money and Banking*, New York, D. Appleton and Co., 1917

Hough, Richard, *Winston and Clemetine: The Triumphs and Tragedies, of the Churchills*, London, Bantam Books, 1989

House, Edward Mandell and Seymour, Charles, *The Intimate papers of Colonel House*, Boston, Houghton Mifflin, 1926

Howard, Michael, *The First World War*, Oxford University Press, 2002

Howard, R.T., *Spying on the Reich, The Cold War Against Hitler*, Oxford University Press, 2023

Immerman, Richard H., *John Foster Dulles, Piety, Pragmatism, and Power in U.S. Foreign Policy*, Wilmington, Scholarly Resources Inc., 1999

Jeffery, Keith, *Field Marshall Sir Henry Wilson: A Political Soldier*, Oxford University Press, 2008

Jeffery, Keith, *The Secret History of MI6, 1909-1949*, New York, Penguin Press, 2010

Jeffreys, Diarmuid, *Hell's Cartel, IG Farben and the Making of Hitler's War Machine*, London, Bloomsbury Publishing, 2008

Jenkins, Roy, *Churchill*, London, Pan Books, 2001

Joll, James and Martel, Gordon, *The Origins of the First World War*, London, Pearson, 1984

Jones, Nigel, *The Birth of the Nazis*, London, Constable & Robinson Ltd, 1987

Johns, James, *Reassessing Pearl Harbor, Scapegoats, A False Hero and the Myth of a Surprise Attack*, North Carolins, McFarland & Company Inc. 2017

Katz, Irving, *August Belmont, A Political Biography*, Columbia University Press, 1968

Kaufman, Richard F., *The War Profiteers*, New York, Anchor Books, 1972

Keegan, John, *The Penguin Book of War*, London, Penguin Books, 2000

Keegan, John, *The First World War*, London, Hutchinson, 2001

Keegan, John, *The Second World War*, London, Hutchinson, 1989

Keiger, John F.V., *France and the Origins of the First World War*, New York, St Martin's Press, 1983

Keiger, John F.V., *Raymond Poincaré*, Cambridge University Press, 1997

Kelen, Emery, *Peace in Their Time*, London, Victor Gollancz, 1964

Kennan, George F., *The Fateful Alliance: France, Russia, and the Coming of the First World War*, New York, Pantheon Books, 1984

Kennedy, A.L., *Old Diplomacy and New: From Salisbury to Lloyd George, 1866-1922*, London, John Murray, 1922

Kershaw. Ian, *Hitler, 1889-1936 Hubris,* London, penguin Books, 1998

Kershaw, Ian, *Hitler, 1936-1945 Nemesis,* London, Penguin Books, 2001

Kershaw, Ian, *Making Friends with Hitler, Lord Londonderry and Britain's Road to War,* London, penguin Books, 2005

Kershaw, Ian, *Popular Opinion & Political Dissent in the Third Reich: Bavaria 1933-1945,* Oxford, Clarendon Press, 1983

Kitson, Sir Arthur, *The Banker's Conspiracy,* UK, Three Martyrs Publishing Ltd, 2012 (first published 1933)

Klemperer, Klemens von, *A Noble Combat, The letters of Shiela Grant Duff and Adam von Trott zu Solz 1932-1939,* Oxford, Clarendon Press, 1988

Klemperer, Klemens von, *German Resistance Against Hitler, The Search For Allies Abroad 1938-45,* Oxford, Clarendon Press, 1994

Knock, Albert J., *The Myth of a Guilty Nation,* Alabama, Ludwig von Mises Institute, 2011

Knuth, E.C., *The Empire of 'the City* California, The Book Tree, 1944

Kotkin, Stephen, *Stalin, Waiting for Hitler 1929-1941,* Penguin Random House UK, 2018

Kühl, Stefan, *The Nazi Connection, Eugenics, American Racism, and German National Socialism,* Oxford University Press, 1994

Laffin, John, *British Butchers & Bunglers of World War One,* Stroud, Sutton Publishing, 1988

Lafore, Laurence, *The Long Fuse: An Interpretation of the Origins of World War I,* Illinois, Wavelength Press, 1977

Landes, Davis S., *The Unbound Prometheus,* Cambridge University Press, 1969

Lane, Barbara Miller and Rupp, J. Leila, Nazi ideology before 1933, A Documentation, Manchester university Press, 2014?

Langewiesche, Dieter, *Liberalism in Germany,* New jersey, Princeton University Press, 1988

Lapping, Brian, *End of Empire,* London, Paladin Grafton Books, 1985

Larson, Erik, *In the Garden of Beasts,* London, Doubleday, 2011

Lebor, Adam, *Tower of Basel, The Shadowy History of the Secret Bank that Runs the World,* New York, Public Affairs (member of the Perseus Group, 2013

Lee, Dwight E., *The Outbreak of the First World War,* Boston, D.C. Heath and Co., 1958

Lee, Sidney, *King Edward VII: A Biography,* London, Macmillan and Co., 1925

Lees-Milne, James, *The Enigmatic Edwardian: The Life of Reginald, Second Viscount Esher,* London, Sidgwick and Jackson, 1986

Legge, Edward, *King Edward in his True Colours,* Charleston, Nabu Press, 2011

Legge, Edward, *More about King Edward,* London, Eveleigh Nash, 1913

Levy, James P., *Appeasement & Rearmament, Britain 1936-1939,* Rowman & Littlefield publishing, 2006

Lewinsohn, Richard, *Sir Basil Zaharoff,* London, Victor Gollancz, 1929

Ligget, Walter W., *The Rise of Herbert Hoover,* New York, The H.K. Fly Company, 1932

Lincoln, Ignatius T., *Revelations of an International Spy,* New York, Robert M. McBride and Co., 1916

Lindqvist, Sven, *Exterminate All the Brutes,* London, Granta Books, 1997

Lloyd George, David, *War Memoirs,* vols 1 & 2, London, Oldham Press, 1938

Lochner, Louis P., *Tycoons and Tyrant, German Industry from Hitler to Adenauer,* Chicago, Henry Regnery Company, 1954

Lockhart, R.H. Bruce, *Memoirs of a British Agent,* London, Putnam, 1932

Ludwig, Emil, *July 1914,* London, G.P. Putnam' sons, 1929

Lundberg, Ferdinand, *America's 60 Families,* New York, Vanguard Press, 1937

Lutz, Hermann, *Lord Grey and the World War,* New York, Alfred A. Knopf, 1928

Lynch, E.P.F., *Somme Mud,* London, Bantam Books, 2008

McArthur, Brian, *For King and Country,* London, Abacus, 2008

McCormick, Donald, *The Mask of Merlin: A Critical Biography of David Lloyd George,* New York, Holt, Rinehart and Wilson, 1963

Mackay, R.F., *Fisher of Kilverstone,* Oxford University Press, 1973

Mackenzie, David, *Apis: The Congenial Conspirator: The Life of Colonel Dragutin T. Dimitrijevic,* New York, Boulder press, 1989.

Macgregor, Jim, and Docherty, Gerry, *Prolonging the Agony,* Oregon, Trineday, 2017

McCullough, Edward E., *How the First World War Began,* New York, Black Rose Books, 1999

McMahon, Paul, *British Spies and Irish Rebels,* Suffolk, The Boydell Press, 2008

Manchester, William, *The Arms of Krupp (1587-1968),* London, Michael Joseph Ltd, 1964

Martel, Gordon, *The Origins of the First World War,* London, Pearson Longman, 1987

Marr, Andrew, *The Making of Modern Britain,* London, Macmillan, 2009

Marwick, Arthur, *The Deluge, British Society and the First World War,* Middlesex, Pelican Books, 1965

Massie, Robert K., *Dreadnought: Britain, Germany and the Coming of the Great War,* New York, Random House, 1991

McDonough, Frank, *The Hitler Years, Triumph 1933-1939,* London, Apollo Books, 2019

McMeekin, Sean, *History's Greatest Heist, The Looting of Russia by the Bolsheviks,* Yale University Press, 2009

McMeekin, Sean, *The Russian Origins of the First World War,* Harvard University Press, 2011

Meyer, T.H. (editor), *Light For the New Millenium, Rudolf Steiner, Helmuth von Moltke, Eliza von Moltke Letters,* London, Rudolf Steiner Press, 2014 edition

Middlemas, Keith, *The Life and Times of Edward VII,* London, Weidenfeld & Nicolson, 1972

Middlemas, Keith, *Pursuit of Pleasure, High Society in the 1900s,* London, Book Club Associates, 1977

Millis, Walter, *Road to War: America, 1914-1917,* Massachusetts, Riverside Press, 1935

Milner, Viscount, *Constructive Imperialism: Unionists and Social Reform,* Slough, Dodo Press, 2009

Mock, James R. and Larson, Cedric, *Words that Won the War,* Connecticut, Cobden Press, 1984

Mombauer, Annika, *The Origins of the First World War,* London, Longman, 2002

Montgelas, Max, *British Foreign Policy under Sir Edward Grey*, New York, Alfred A. Knopf, 1928

Montgelas, Max, *The Case for the Central Powers*, London, Allen & Unwin Ltd, 1925

Morel, E.D., *Diplomacy Revealed*, London, National Labour Press, 1921

Morel, E.D., *Pre-War Diplomacy: Fresh Revelations*, London, Independent Labour Party, 1919

Morel, E.D., *The Secret History of a Great Betrayal*, London, Caledonian Press, 1923

Morel, E.D., *Ten Years of Secret Diplomacy*, London, National Labour Press, 1915

Morel, E.D., *Truth and the War*, London, National Labour Press, 1918

Moore, R.K., *Escaping the Matrix*, Wexford, Cyberjournal, 2005

Morton, Andrew, *17 Carnations, The Windsors, The Nazis, and the Cover-Up*, London, Michael O'Mara Books, 2015

Muir, Ramsay, *Britain's Case Against Germany*, Manchester University Press, 1914

Murray, H. Robertson, *Krupps and the International Armaments Ring*, London, Holden and Hardingham, 1915.

Nagorski, Andrew, *Hitlerland, American Eyewitnesses to the Nazi Rise to Power*, New York, Simon & Schuster, 2012

Nash, George H., *The Life of Herbert Hoover, The Humanitarian 1914-1917*, New York, W.W. Norton and Co., 1988

Neilson, Francis, *How Diplomats Make War*, New York, Bibliolife, 1923

Neumann, Robert, *Zaharoff, the Armaments King*, London, Allen & Unwin Ltd, 1936

Newbold, J.T. Walton, *How Asquith Helped the Armaments Ring*, Manchester, National Labour Press, 1916

Newbold, J.T. Walton, *How Europe Armed for War, 1871-1914*, London, Blackfriars Press Ltd, 1916

Newbold, J.T. Walton, *The War Trust Exposed*, Manchester, the National labour Press, 1913

Newton, Douglas, *The Darkest Days, The Truth Behind Britain's Rush to War, 1914*, London, Verso, 2014

Nimocks, Walter, *Milner's Young Men*, London, Hodder and Stoughton, 1968

Nock, Albert Jay, *The Myth of a Guilty Nation*, New York, B.W. Huebsch Inc., 1922

Norman, C.H., *A Searchlight on the European War*, London, Labour Publishing Company, 1924

Norwood, Stephen H., *The Third Reich in the Ivory Tower, Complicity and Conflict on American Campuses*, Cambridge University Press, 2009

O'Brien, James, *Hoover's Millions and How he Made Them*, Carlisle, Western Australia, Hesperian Press, 2015

O'Brien, Terence H., *Milner*, London, Constable and Co., 1979

O'Connor, Thomas Power, *Sir Henry Campbell-Bannerman*, London, Hodder and Stoughton, 1908

Olmsted, Kathryn S., *The Newspaper Axis, Six Press Barons Who Enabled Hitler*, Yale University Press, 2022

Orlow, Dietrich, *The History of the Nazi party 1933-1945*, University of Pittsburgh Press, 1973

Owings, W.A. Dolph, and Pribic, Elizabeth and Nikola, *The Sarajevo Trial, Part 1*, Chapel Hill, Documentary Publications, 1984

Paddock, Troy R.E., *Contesting the Origins of the First World War, An Historiographical Argument*, Oxfordshire, Routledge, 2020

Pakenham, Thomas, *The Boer War*, London, Abacus, 1979

Parker, R.A.C., *Chamberlain and Appeasement, British Policy and the Coming of the Second World War*, London, The Macmillan Press, 1993

Pearson, Michael, *The Sealed Train, Journey to Revolution, Lenin 1917*, UK, Readers Union, 1975

Perris, George Herbert, *The War Traders: An Exposure*, London, National Peace Council, 1913

Peterson, H.C., and Fite, Gilbert C., *Opponents of War, 1917-1918*, Connecticut, Greenwood Press, 1957

Petropoulos, Jonathon, *Royals and the Reich*, Oxford University Press, 2006

Podmore, Will, *British Foreign Policy Since 1870*, London, self-published, 2008

Ponsonby, Arthur, *Falsehood in Wartime, Propaganda Lies of the First World War*, London, Allen and Unwin, 1928

Pool, James, *Hitler and his Secret Partners, Contributions, Loot and Rewards, 1933-1945*, New York, Pocket Books, 1997

Pool, James, *Who Financed Hitler, The Secret Funding of Hitler's Rise to Power, 1919-1933*, New York, Pocket Books, 1997

Powell, Jim, *Bully Boy, The Truth About Theodore Roosevelt's Legacy*, New York, Crown Forum, 2006

Prange, Gordon W., *Pearl Harbor, The Verdict of History*, New York, McGraw-Hill Book Company, 1986

Preparata, Guido Giacomo, *Conjuring Hitler, How Britain and America Made the Third Reich*, London, Pluto Press, 2005

Preparata, Guido Giacomo, *The Incubation of Nazis, A Tale of Extreme Measures Undertaken by Britain to Safeguard Imperial Primacy 1900-1944*, Perugia, Italy, Ad Triarios Press, 2023

Preston, Diana, *Wilful Murder: The Sinking of the Lusitania*, London, Corgi Books, 2002.

Prins, Nomi, *All The Presidents' Bankers, The Hidden Alliances that Drive American Power*, New York, Nation Books, 2014

Pugh, Martin, *Hurrah for the Blackshirts, Fascists and Fascism in Britain Between the Wars*, London, Pimlico Publishing, 2006

Quigley, Carroll, The *Anglo-American Establishment*, California, GSC & Associates, 1981

Quigley, Carroll, *Tragedy & Hope, A History of the World in Our Time*, California, GSC & Associates. First printing New York, The Macmillan Company, 1966

Rankin, Raymond, *The Inner History of the Balkan War*, London, Constable & Co., 1914

Read, Anthony, and Fisher, David, *Colonel Z, The Secret Life of Master of Spies*, New York, Viking Penguin Inc., 1985

Reeves, John, *The Rothschilds: The Financial Rulers of Nations*, London, Sampson Low, 1887

Remak, Joachim, *Sarajevo: The Story of a Political Murder*, New York, Criterion Books Inc., 1959

Renouvin, Pierre, *The Immediate Origins of the War (28 June-4 August, 1914)*, Yale University Press.

Renouvin, Pierre, *La Crise Europeene et la Grande Guerre*, Paris, Alcan, 1934

Repington, Charles, *The First World War*, New York, Houghton Mifflin, 1920

Roberts, Stephen H., *The House that Hitler Built*, London, Methuen Publishers, 1937

Rohl, John C.G., *Wilhelm II: The Kaiser's Personal Monarchy*, Cambridge University Press, 2004

Roland, Paul, *Nazis and the Occult*, London, Arcturus Publishing Ltd, 2012

Rose, Norman, *The Cliveden Set, Portrait of an Exclusive Fraternity*, London, Pimlico, 2001

Roth, Cecil, *The Magnificent Rothschilds*, London, R. Hale, 1939

Rothbard, Murray N. *Wall Street, Banks and American Foreign Policy*, New York, Center for Libertarian Studies, 1995

Rothfells, Hans and Wilson, Lawrence, The German Opposition to Hitler: An Appraisal, Illinois, Henry Regnery Company, 1948

Rowse, A.L., *All Souls and Appeasement*, London, Macmillan & Co Ltd, 1961

Royle, Trevor, *The Kitchener Enigma*, London Michael Joseph, 1985

Royle, Trevor, War Report, Edinburgh, Mainstream Publishing, 1987

Sampson, Anthony, *The Seven Sisters: The Great Oil Companies and the World They shaped*, London, PFD, 2009

Sanders, Liman von, *Five Years in Turkey*, Sussex, The Naval & Military Press Ltd. originally published 1927

Sarkisyanz, Manuel, *Hitler's English Inspirers*, Belfast, Athol Books, 2003

Sazonov, Sergei, *Fateful Years, 1909-1916*, New York, Ishi Press, first printing 1928

Schweitzer, Arthur, *Big Business in the Third Reich*, Indiana University Press, 1964

Seldes, George, *Facts and Fascism*, New York, In Fact Publishing, original 1947

Seton-Watson, R.W., *Europe in the Melting-Pot*, London, Macmillan and Co., Ltd, 1919. Reprint, Forgotten Books, 2018

Seymour, Charles, *The Intimate Papers of Colonel House*, Boston, Houghton Mifflin Company, 1926

Sheehan, James, *The Monopoly of Violence*, London, Faber and Faber, 2007

Shelking, Eugenii Nikolaevich and Makvoski, L.W., *The Game of Diplomacy*, London, Hutchison and CO., 1918

Shelking, Eugenii Nikolaevich and Makvoski, L.W., *Recollections of a Russian Diplomat: The Suicide of Monarchies*, New York, Macmillan., 1918

Shirer, William L., *Berlin Diary, The Journal of a Foreign Correspondent 1934-1941*, New York, Ishi Press International, 2010 (first published 1941)

Shirer, William L., *The Rise and fall of the Third Reich*, London, Arrow Books reprint, 1998

Simpson, Colin, *Lusitania*, Updated Merseyside edition, Wirral, UK, Avid publications, 1988

Sladen, Douglas, *The Real Truth About Germany*, New York, Knickerbocker Press, 1914

Smith, Bradley F., *Adolf Hitler, His family, Childhood & Youth*, Hoover Institution Publications,1967

Smith, David James, *One Morning in Sarajevo: 28 June 1914*, London, Phoenix, 2008

713

Solzhenitsyn, Alexander, *August 1914,* London, penguin Books, 1992

Spence, Richard B., *Wall Street and the Russian Revolution, 1905-1925,* Oregon, Trineday, 2017

Spender, J.A., *The Life of the Right Honourable Sir Henry Campbell-Bannerman,* London, Hodder and Stoughton, 1923

Spicer, Charles, *Coffee With Hitler: The British Amateurs Who Tried to Civilize the Nazis,* London, One World Publications, 2022

Srodes, James, *Allen Dulles, Master of Spies,* Washington, Regnery Publishing, 1999

Stedman, Andrew David, *Alternatives to Appeasement, Neville Chamberlain and Hitler's Germany,* London, Bloomsbury Academic, 2011

Stevenson, David, *1914-1918: The History of the First World War,* London, Penguin Books, 2004

Stinnett, Robert B., *Day of Deceit, The truth about FDR and Pearl Harbor,* New York, The Free Press, 2000

Stone, Norman, *World War One: A Short History,* London, Allen Lane, 2007

Strachan, Hew, *The First World War,* London, Simon & Schuster, 2006

Stead, Wiilliam T., *The Last Will and Testament of Cecil John Rhodes,* London, 1902

Stieve, Friedrich, *Isvolsky and the World War,* New York, Alfred A. Knopf, 1926

Strasser, Otto, *Hitler and I,* 1940, Publisher unknown

Strausbaugh, John, *Victory City, A History of New York and New Yorkers During World War II,* New York, Twelve, Hatchette Book Group, 2018

Sutton, Antony C., *The Best Enemy Money Can Buy,* Montana, Liberty House Press, 1986

Sutton, Antony C., *The Federal Reserve Conspiracy,* Oregon, CPA Book Publishers, 1995

Sutton, Antony C., *Wall Street and FDR, The True Story of How Franklin D. Roosevelt Colluded with Corporate America,* Sussex, Clairview Books, 2013

Sutton, Antony, *Wall Street and the Bolshevik Revolution: The Remarkable True Story of the American Capitalists Who Financed the Russian Communists,* Sussex, Clairview Books,

Sutton, Antony C., *Wall Street and the Rise of Hitler, ; The American Financiers who Bankrolled the Nazis,* Sussex, Clairview Books, 2010

Swain, Joseph Ward, *Beginning the Twentieth Century,* New York, W.W. Norton & Company, Inc., 1933

Tarpley, Webster G., and Chaitkin, Anton, *George Bush: The Unauthorized Biography,* Washington DC, Executive Intelligence Review, 1992

Taylor, A.J.P., *The First World War, An Illustrated History,* London, Penguin, 1966

Taylor, A.J.P., *English History 1914-1945,* London, Penguin, 1965

Taylor, Edmond, *The Fall of the Dynasties: The Collapse of the Old Order, 1905-1922,* New York, Doubleday Inc., 1922

Thomas, Gordon, and Lewis, Greg, *Defying Hitler, The Germans Who Resisted Nazi Rule,* London, Caliber Publishing 2020

Thomas, Gwynne, *King Pawn or Black Knight,* Edinburgh, Mainstream Publishing, 1995

Thomas, Rosamund M., *Espionage and Secrecy: The Official Secrets Act 1911-1989,* London, Taylor and Francis, 1991

Thompson. J. Lee, *Forgotten Patriot,* New jersey, Rosemount Publishing, 2007

Thompson, J. Lee, *A Wider patriotism: Alfred Milner and the British Empire*, London, Pickering & Chatto, 2007

Thompson, J. Lee, *Northcliffe: Press Baron in Politics 1865-1922*, London, John Murray, 2000

Thomsett, Michael, *The German Opposition to Hitler*, UK, Crux Publishing, 2016

Thomson, David, *England in the Nineteenth Century*, Londo, Penguin Books, 1950

Thomson, George Malcolm, *The Twelve Days*, London, The History Book Club, 1966

Tooze, Adam, *The Wages of Destruction, The Making and Breaking of the Nazi Economy*, London, Penguin Books, 2006

Toye, Richard, *Lloyd George and Churchill, Rivals for Greatness*, London, Pan Books, 2007

Toynbee, Arnold J., *Survey of International Affairs 1935*, vol 1, Oxford University Press, 1936

Trevelyan, G.M., *Grey Of Fallodon*, London, Longmans Green and Company, 1937

Trotsky, Leon, *My Life*, New York, Charles Schribner, 1930

Trotsky, Leon, *The Balkan Wars 1912-13*, New York, Pathfinder Press, 1921

Tuchman, Barbara W., *The Guns of August*, New York, Ballantine books, 1962

Tulloch, Hugh, *Acton, Historians on Historians*, London, Weidenfeld and Nicolson, 1988

Tumulty, Joseph Patrick, *Woodrow Wilson as I Know Him*, Garden City, New York, Doubleday Publishing Company, 1927

Turner, Henry Ashby, Jr., *German Big Business and the Rise of Hitler*, Oxford University Press, 1985

Turner, L.F.C., *Origins of the First World War*, New York, W.W. Norton, 1970

Turner, John, *Lloyd George's Secretariat*, Cambridge University Press, 1980

Twigge, Stephen, Hampshire, Edward, and Macklin Graham, *British Intelligence, Secrets, Spies and Sources*, London, The National Archives, 2009

Ulrich, Volker, *Hitler, A Biography, Volume 1, Ascent*, London, Vintage, 2017

Union of Democratic Control, *The Secret International, Armaments Firms at Work*, London, 1932

Vidal, Gore, *Perpetual War for Perpetual Peace*, UK, Clairview Books, 2002

Viereck, George Sylvester, *The Strangest Friendship in History: Woodrow Wilson and Colonel House*, Connecticut, Greenwood Press, 1976

Wainewright, Will, *Reporting on Hitler, Rothay Reynolds and the British Press Spy in Nazi Germany*, London, Biteback publishing, 2017

Waller, W., *War in the Twentieth Century*, New Yorks, Revisionist Press, 1974

Ward, A.W. and Gooch, G.P., *Cambridge History of British Foreign Policy*, vol. 3, Cambridge University Press, 1924

Wark, Wesley K., *The Ultimate Enemy, British Intelligence and Nazi Germany, 1933-1939*, Cornell University Press, 1985

Weber, Thomas, *Becoming Hitler, The Making of a Nazi*, Oxford University Press, 2017

Wegerer, Alfred von, *A Refutation of the Versailles War Guilt Thesis*, New York, Alfred A, Knopf, 1930

Weinberg, Gerhard L., *A World At Arms, A Global History of World War II*, Cambridge University Press, 1994

Weintraub, Stanley, *Edward the Caresser, the Playboy Prince who became Edward VII*, New York, The Free Press, 2001

Westwell, Ian, *World War 1*, London, Hermes House, 2008

Wheeler, George, *Pierpont Morgan and Friends, The Anatomy of a Myth*, New Jersey, Prentice-Hall, Inc., 1973

White, J.A., *Transition to Global Rivalry: Alliance Diplomacy and the Quadruple Entente, 1895-1907*, Cambridge University Press, 2002

Wile, Frederic William, *Men Around the Kaiser*, Danvers, General Books, 2008

Wilhelm II, Kaiser, *My Memoirs (1878-1918)*, London, Cassell and Co, 1922

Willis, Irene Cooper, *England's Holy War*, New York, Alfred A, Knopf, 1928

Wilson, Derek A., *Rothschild: The Wealth and Power of a Dynasty*, London, Simon & Schuster, 1988

Wilson, H.W., and Hammerton, J.A., *The Great War: An Illustrated History*, vol 1, London, The Amalgamated Press Limited, 1914

Wilson, Jim, *Nazi Princess, Hitler, Lord Rothermere and Princess Stephanie von Hohenlohe*, Stroud, UK, 2011

Wilson, John, C.B.: *A Life of Sir Henry Campbell-Bannerman*, London, Constable, 1973

Wilson, Keith M., *The Policy of the Entente*, Cambridge university Press, 1985

Wilson, Trevor, *The Myriad Faces of War*, Cambridge, Polity Press, 1986

Winter, Denis, *Haig's Command: A Reassessment*, London, Viking Books, 1991

Winterbotham, F.W., *The Nazi Connection*, New York, Harper & Row Publishers, 1978

Winterbotham, F.W., *Secret and Personal*, London, William Kimber Publishing, 1969

Yeadon, Glen, & Hawkins, John, *The Nazi Hydra in America*, California, Progressive Press, 1999

Yergin, Daniel, *The Prize: The Epic Quest for Oil, Money and Power*, New York, Simon & Schuster Ltd, 1991

Young, A.P., *The 'X' Documents, The Secret History of Foreign Office contacts with the German Resistance 1837-1939*, London, Andre Deutsch Limited 1974

Index

Symbols

717